ΣΤ

MW01058216

RICHARD
WAGNER

RICHARD WAGNER

A Life in Music

MARTIN GECK

Translated by
STEWART SPENCER

THE UNIVERSITY OF CHICAGO PRESS
CHICAGO AND LONDON

Martin Geck is professor of musicology at the Technical University of Dortmund, Germany. His other books include *Johann Sebastian Bach: Life and Work* and *Robert Schumann: The Life and Work of a Romantic Composer*.
Stewart Spencer is is an independent scholar and the translator of more than three dozen books.

The University of Chicago Press, Chicago 60637
The University of Chicago Press, Ltd., London
© 2013 by The University of Chicago
All rights reserved. Published 2013.
Printed in the United States of America

22 21 20 19 18 17 16 15 14 13   1 2 3 4 5

ISBN-13: 978-0-226-92461-8 (cloth)
ISBN-13: 978-0-226-92462-5 (e-book)
DOI: 10.7208/chicago/9780226924625.001.0001

Originally published as *Wagner: Biografie.* © 2012 by Siedler Verlag, a division of Verlagsgruppe Random House GmbH, Munich, Germany.

The translation of this work was funded by Geisteswissenschaften International, translation funding for humanities and social sciences from Germany, a joint initiative of the Fritz Thyssen Foundation, the German Federal Foreign Office, the collecting society VG WORT, and the Börsenverein des Deutschen Buchhandels (German Publishers and Booksellers Association).

Frontispiece: Bronze medallion by Anton Scharff (1845–1903) of Vienna. Wagner sat for him at Schloss Fantaisie near Bayreuth in June 1872 in the wake of the official ceremony accompanying the laying of the foundation stone of the Bayreuth Festspielhaus on May 22, 1872. (Photograph courtesy of the author.)

Library of Congress Cataloging-in-Publication Data

Geck, Martin.
  [Wagner. English]
  Richard Wagner : a life in music / Martin Geck ; translated by Stewart Spencer.
    pages cm
  Translation of: Geck, Martin. Wagner. München : Siedler, 2012.
  Includes bibliographical references and index.
  ISBN 978-0-226-92461-8 (cloth : alk. paper) — ISBN 978-0-226-92462-5 (e-book)   1. Wagner, Richard, 1813–1883. 2. Composers—Germany—Biography.   I. Spencer, Stewart, translator. II. Title.
  ML410.W1G2913 2013
  782.1092—dc23
  [B]

                                                                              2013014426

Additional figure credits: Portrait of Felix Mendelssohn Bartholdy, p. 18, photograph courtesy AKG-Images. Portrait of Giacomo Meyerbeer, p. 43, photograph courtesy of AKG-Images. Portrait of Heinrich Heine, p. 65, photograph copyright Süddeutsche Zeitung Photo / Rue des Archives. Portrait of Josef Rubinstein from a woodcut engraving, *An Evening at Richard Wagner's*, p. 92, photograph courtesy Ullstein Bild / Roger Viollet. Portrait of Arnold Schoenberg, 1922, p. 123, photograph courtesy Interfoto—Imagno. Paul Bekker, 1920 (detail, reversed), p. 143, from a photograph with Oskar Kokoschka et al., photograph courtesy of AKG-Images. Portrait of Angelo Neumann, 1881, p. 169, photograph courtesy of AKG-Images. George Steiner, p. 196, photograph by Jürgen Bauer, courtesy of Ullstein Bild. Portrait of Sergei Eisenstein, 1929, p. 225, photograph courtesy of Ullstein Bild. Ernst Bloch, p. 259, photograph courtesy of Interfoto—Sammlung Karl. Berthold Auerbach, ca. 1865, p. 288, photograph by Franz Hanfstaengl, courtesy of Ullstein Bild—adoc photos. Theodor Adorno, ca. 1968, p. 315, photograph courtesy of AKG-Images. Gustav Mahler, 1907, p. 352, photograph courtesy AKG-Images.

♾ This paper meets the requirements of ANSI/NISO Z39.48-1992 (Permanence of Paper).

CONTENTS

INTRODUCTION: FIGURING OUT WAGNER?

ix

CHAPTER ONE

The Archetypal Theatrical Scene: From *Leubald* to *Die Feen*

I

A WORD ABOUT FELIX MENDELSSOHN

18

CHAPTER TWO

The Blandishments of Grand Opera: *Das Liebesverbot* and *Rienzi*

23

A WORD ABOUT GIACOMO MEYERBEER

43

CHAPTER THREE

"Deep shock" and "a violent change of direction": *Der fliegende Holländer*

47

A WORD ABOUT HEINRICH HEINE

65

CHAPTER FOUR

Rituals to Combat Fear and Loneliness: *Tannhäuser und der Sängerkrieg auf Wartburg*

69

A WORD ABOUT JOSEF RUBINSTEIN

92

CHAPTER FIVE

A Bedtime Story with Dire Consequences: *Lohengrin*

97

A WORD ABOUT ARNOLD SCHOENBERG

123

CHAPTER SIX

The Revolutionary Drafts: *Achilles, Jesus of Nazareth,*
Siegfried's Death, and *Wieland the Smith*

127

A WORD ABOUT PAUL BEKKER

143

CHAPTER SEVEN

"*We have art* so as not to be destroyed by the truth": The *Ring*
as a Nineteenth-Century Myth

147

A WORD ABOUT ANGELO NEUMANN

169

CHAPTER EIGHT

"My music making is in fact magic making, for I just cannot
produce music coolly and mechanically": The Art of the
Ring—Seen from the Beginning

173

A WORD ABOUT GEORGE STEINER

196

CHAPTER NINE

"He resembles *us* to a tee; he is the sum total of present-day
intelligence": The Art of the *Ring*—Wotan's Music

199

A WORD ABOUT SERGEI EISENSTEIN

225

CHAPTER TEN

"A mystical pit, giving pleasure to individuals":
Tristan und Isolde

229

A WORD ABOUT ERNST BLOCH

259

CHAPTER ELEVEN

"A magnificent, overcharged, heavy, late art":
Die Meistersinger von Nürnberg

263

A WORD ABOUT BERTHOLD AUERBACH

288

CHAPTER TWELVE

"They're hurrying on toward their end, though
they think they will last for ever": The Art of the
Ring—Seen from the End

291

A WORD ABOUT THEODOR W. ADORNO

315

CHAPTER THIRTEEN

"You will see—diminished sevenths were just not
possible!": *Parsifal*

319

A WORD ABOUT GUSTAV MAHLER

352

CHAPTER FOURTEEN

Wagner as the Sleuth of Modernism

357

NOTES

367

BIBLIOGRAPHY

405

GENERAL INDEX

425

INDEX OF WAGNER'S WORKS

439

INTRODUCTION

FIGURING OUT WAGNER?

Cosima Wagner's diaries run to nearly one million words—over 2,500 pages in the two-volume German edition and only slightly less in Geoffrey Skelton's English-language translation. The first entry is dated January 1, 1869, the last one February 12, 1883. Barely a day is omitted. Moreover, Wagner himself—and it is around him that these entries revolve—kept a close eye on his wife's record of their lives together, a point confirmed by entries in his own hand. At first sight, then, the final fifth of Wagner's life seems to be seamlessly documented, so much so, indeed, that it appears to require little effort to figure out who Wagner was.

But what does the term "document" mean in such a context? Of course, these diaries include many undisputed facts. And yet how many of the incidents related here are given a tendentious gloss? And how many are simply suppressed? The main problem is that Cosima dedicated her diaries to her children: "You shall know every hour of my life, so that one day you will come to see me as I am."[1] But she was writing these lines at the very time that she and her two illegitimate daughters by Wagner (Isolde and Eva), were fleeing from a loveless marriage with Hans von Bülow and moving to Tribschen on Lake Lucerne in order for her to live with him in what was pilloried at the time as "sin."

Her daughters were too young to be able to make any sense of this information. But her diary was in any case never designed to leave any trace of the intimate affair between its author, Cosima von Bülow, and its subject, Richard Wagner. As a result, their eldest daughter Isolde, affectionately known as "Loldi," is passed off as the daughter of Hans von Bülow. Even as late as 1914, when Isolde—prompted by her husband, who was anxious to advance his claim to his Wagnerian inheritance—took her mother to court in an attempt to prove who her father was, Cosima won the case on a technicality but was forced to admit under oath that she had slept with Wagner at the time of the child's conception. In the wake of this public revelation, Isolde's name could never again be mentioned in Cosima's presence. Yet how can we square even this one tiny detail with the line from Cosima's diary, "You shall know every hour of my life"?

But are not the many thousands of comments that Wagner himself made between 1869 and 1883 about his life and works, about art, politics, and religion, about the "Jewish question" and about vivisection—everything, in short, about God and the world—a veritable mine of information? Not only are they a mine, they are also a minefield. After all, these remarks—at least to the extent that they were made within the family circle—are known to us almost entirely through Cosima's record of them. It appears that she made these entries in her diary at irregular intervals, often days apart, relying on the notes that she jotted down in the meantime. But how reliable was this method? And which remarks did she record without any explanation? Which did she suppress? And which did she alter in keeping with her own interpretation of them?

As we have seen, Richard Wagner read her jottings, at least from time to time, but not once did he make any attempt to correct them. And yet this does not mean that he never felt that Cosima had misunderstood him throughout these final fourteen years of his life—to assume otherwise would fly in the face of reason. Rather, he evidently had no desire to meddle in his wife's affairs but preferred on this point at least to leave her to her own devices. We do not need to interpret this, as many of Cosima's biographers have done, as an instance of her iron rule: marital relations can rarely be reduced to such simplistic terms. But we would certainly not be wrong to speak of Cosima and her husband inhabiting parallel worlds. And these two worlds cannot be aligned simply by our arguing that Cosima regarded herself as Wagner's mouthpiece.

Can we expect a greater degree of authenticity from the new critical edition of Wagner's nine thousand or so surviving letters, an edition that now runs to twenty-two volumes and has reached the year 1870? And what about the "truth" of Wagner's autobiography, *My Life*, in which the composer devotes some eight hundred pages to an account of the first four-fifths of his life, leaving a gap of only four years before Cosima's diaries take over? The mere fact that Wagner dictated his memoirs to Cosima and intended them to be read above all by King Ludwig II suggests that his interpretation of the "truth" was occasionally fast and loose. This does not mean that we must necessarily accuse Wagner of wanting to present an unduly flattering picture of himself. If we ignore simple gaps and genuine lapses of memory, then his conscious or unconscious desire to surround himself and the creative process with an aura of mystery will have played a greater role here.

Here, too, there are various traps lying in wait to catch the unwary biographer. Even such an intelligent writer as Martin Gregor-Dellin, whose contribution to Wagnerian literature cannot be dismissed out of hand, is repeatedly guilty of falling under the narcotic spell of Wagner's life and works and, like Isolde, sinking and drowning in this sea of self-mystification. While on the one hand claiming to maintain a certain skepticism toward Wagner's own account of his life, there are times when Gregor-Dellin identifies so intensely with his subject that he gives the impression that he actually witnessed the events he is describing. And where Wagner and Cosima remain monosyllabic, Gregor-Dellin becomes positively voyeuristic: "As for Wagner, he succumbed to the lure of her shapely breasts, drew her to him and smothered her with passionate kisses."[2] Thus Gregor-Dellin describes Wagner's late infatuation for Judith Gautier, a relationship that remains, at best, a matter for speculation.

By then in his sixties, Wagner used the Bayreuth factotum Bernhard Schnappauf as a go-between, and the latter dutifully delivered the composer's little love letters to his beautiful and cultured French admirer after she had visited him during the 1876 Bayreuth Festival. Even after Judith had returned to Paris, Wagner continued to place orders for silk fabrics, cosmetics, and perfumes with her, until Cosima discovered what was going on behind her back and, having made a scene, ensured that in future the correspondence was conducted through her. The historian may report this with a tolerably clear conscience even though he or she is bound to rely on Cosima's diaries in support of his or her account. But practically everything else about this "affair," if such it was, is speculation, albeit speculation that has long since become an integral part of the myth surrounding the composer. Does it make any sense to counter this version of events in an attempt to demythologize Wagner? Is it worth our while to do so in the case of Mathilde Wesendonck, toward whom Cosima harbored such ill feelings that she destroyed all her late husband's letters to his muse from the time when he had been working on *Tristan und Isolde*, even though the letters in question had already been published, albeit in censored form, so that we shall presumably never know the true facts of the matter? "Wahn, Wahn, überall Wahn!," one is tempted to echo Hans Sachs's despair at the universality of human folly.

I earned my spurs as a Wagner scholar while working on *Parsifal* as part of the Wagner Collected Edition. This was at a time when there was already a lively debate about Wagner's works and their influence and about the institution of "New Bayreuth," but as yet there was no serious Wagner scholarship that was worthy of that name. As a result, I was not a little proud when, together with my colleague Egon Voss, I was able to uncover an act of self-mystification on Wagner's part dating from the time of his work on *Parsifal*. In spite of his claims to the contrary in his autobiography, the first prose sketch of the work was produced not on a "sunny" Good Friday following Wagner's move into his new home—his "Asylum" or "Refuge" in the grounds of the Wesendoncks' villa in Zurich—but some weeks later. His autobiographical account is intended to invest the event with a symbolism that it did not have at the time. When our edition of *Parsifal* was published in 1970, it was not yet possible to consult Cosima Wagner's diaries, which were still locked away in the vaults of a bank. Had we been able to do so, we would have stumbled across an entry for April 22, 1879: "R. today recalled the impression which inspired his 'Good Friday Music'; he laughs, saying he had thought to himself, 'In fact it is all as far-fetched as my love affairs, for it was not a Good Friday at all—just a pleasant mood in Nature which made me think, "This is how a Good Friday ought to be."'"[3]

This does not need to be seen as an expression of cynicism on Wagner's part. Perhaps he was trying to say: "I know that I am guilty of mystifying certain incidents in my life." In that case the sentence might continue: "But I need to do so." Or take another example: Wagner was fond of stressing that he often wrote his music "in a sort of insane, somnambulistic state."[4] And in his autobiography he recalls very specifically how, after a lengthy search, the orchestral prelude to *Das Rheingold* suddenly "dawned" on him in September 1853, when, after a tiring walk, he sank into a "kind of somnambulistic state" and collapsed on a couch in the northern Italian resort of La Spezia, with "the feeling of being immersed in rapidly flowing water."[5]

As Wagnerians now know, this is a belated attempt to cast a veil of mystery over the true facts of the matter, for the first draft of the prelude to *Das Rheingold*, which was written two months after his visit to La Spezia, is less specific than Wagner's description of his déjà-vu experience would require it to be. But Wagner needed to mystify the compositional process[6] in order to dispel any possible self-doubts about his working method. After all, it required a certain courage to persuade future audiences to accept 136 bars of pure E-flat major as a meaningful opening for the four evenings that make up the *Ring*. But he may also have been prompted to surround the work's genesis with this aura of mystification by his reading of Schopenhauer's

"Essay on Spirit Seeing and Everything Concerned Therewith." Here the Sage of Frankfurt discusses somnambulism and "visions of all kinds" that take place beyond the laws of time and space and, regardless of physical causality, occur within a nonindividual space.[7]

Wagner saw himself as the champion of a new mythology and seized on such notions with palpable glee—not just in this particular case but with regard to his whole life and creative output. It would be naïve to accept all his comments at face value, just as it would be foolhardy to accuse him of systematic lying. And however much credit I am willing to give Wagner scholars for attempting to reach increasingly "sound" conclusions by continuously assessing the available material, I do not expect that this process will produce any significant results. There are two reasons for this, one of them general, the other specific.

In general, our memories are fallible. "The Veil of Memory" is the title of a book by the medievalist Johannes Fried that deals with the habitual unreliability of our powers of recollection. Fried draws attention not only to the vagueness of the surviving medieval sources but also to striking gaps in the memory of even our close contemporaries. To take a single example: the accounts put forward by the two nuclear physicists Niels Bohr and Werner Heisenberg of their conversations about the possible development of nuclear weapons in Germany and the United States differ in astonishing ways—within years of their meeting in the autumn of 1941 they were no longer able to agree on what they had discussed or even on where and when they had met. And yet there is no need to accuse either of them of malicious intent.[8]

In the specific case of Wagnerian research, this means that because the most important statements about Wagner's life and works are almost always based on individual recollections and personal opinions, it is impossible to use them to establish an objective and at the same time meaningful picture of Wagner. This aim is all the more futile in that Wagner himself was unwilling to distinguish between reality and dreams. Indeed, we should be guilty of seriously misjudging him if we were to adopt a superior tone and insist on drawing such a distinction.

This leads me on to a third point: Wagner refused consistently to distinguish between "life" and "art." For him, there was only one truth: the truth of his mission. It was against this background that he interpreted his life and works as a *Gesamtkunstwerk*, a synthesis of all the arts that did not preclude the depiction of embarrassing or even catastrophic events but which never called into question the higher meaning of that mission.

There is little point, therefore, in distinguishing—as Martin Gregor-Dellin does—between "the everyday world" and "art" and between "character" and "works."[9] The German political theorist Udo Bermbach argues that in writings such as *Art and Revolution* Wagner was drawing up "plans for an art—*his* art—that would be capable of governing our lives."[10] Christian Kaden likewise believes that myth, as expounded in the *Ring*, for example, does not abandon itself to otherworldly illusions but deals, rather, with "the threat to the world of appearances and the destabilization of illusion." As a result, it remains "true to life."[11]

In spite of interpretations such as these, there is no way of resolving the tension between Wagner's life and works. On the one hand the German medievalist Peter Wapnewski has argued in favor of the view that these works may be seen as "a monumental attempt to come to terms with feelings of guilt and deceit" and as a "great call for redemption," while at the same time warning—quite rightly—against the desire to impose the winding pathways of life and works on one another as if they were somehow congruent: "Wotan's guilty conscience is not that of a man like Wagner sinning against his Bavarian God or betraying Otto Wesendonck's magnanimity or Minna's or Mathilde's love."[12]

Wagner himself was aware of these ambivalences. On one occasion we find him insisting that it was not necessary to have suffered everything oneself in order to write about it. Goethe, for example, had had enough "wisdom" in his youth to write the first part of *Faust* in an emotional vacuum: "One sees how stupid it is to assume that poets must first live through what they write."[13] But while working on *Parsifal*, he was moved to say almost the exact opposite: "I have always been fated to carry out in prose (in life) what I have put into my poetry—that scene with the swan, people will think it came from my views on vivisection!"[14]

Musicologists can, of course, avoid the pitfalls that confront Wagner's biographers by concentrating on the music and examining the specifics of Wagner's harmonic writing, for example. But by limiting ourselves to a single moment in the history of modern composition, we cannot hope to do justice to the "Wagner phenomenon," since even the most fundamentalist music theorist must have realized by now that Wagner's music cannot be interpreted simply on the basis of the notes on the printed page—even when the music is examined on its own terms, many compositional decisions can be understood only when seen, as it were, from the stage. (Whereas Theodor Adorno struggled to come to terms with this phenomenon, Robert Schumann was more than happy to revise his initially

Mein Leben.

Erster Theil:

1813—1842.

The title page of the first, privately printed edition of Wagner's autobiography, *Mein Leben* (My Life), shows a vulture (in German: *Geyer* or *Geier*) as a heraldic bird. Published in 1870, this was the first of four volumes and covered the period from Wagner's birth in 1813 to his return to Germany from Paris in 1842. At the time of its publication, Wagner was living in Switzerland and so he used the services of the Basel printer G. A. Bonfantini, prevailing on Nietzsche to see the proofs through the press. Wagner dictated the text to Cosima and then revised her manuscript. The original print run was limited to fifteen copies intended for Wagner's patron, King Ludwig II of Bavaria, and for a small number of "trusted" friends. After Wagner's death, Cosima tried to round up all the surviving copies with the intention of destroying them, but Bonfantini had secretly run off an extra copy, and this was acquired by Wagner's early biographer, Mary Burrell. It was in order to quell speculation about its contents that Cosima authorized the first official publication in 1911. A few sentences that she had suppressed were made available in 1929–30. The first fully authentic edition appeared in 1963. (Photograph courtesy of the Nationalarchiv der Richard-Wagner-Stiftung, Bayreuth: A4295-I.)

unfavorable view of *Tannhäuser* once he had attended a performance of the work.)

There is little point in asking whether Bach or Mozart scholarship is confronted by similar problems, for whereas we know little about the biographical and contemporary context of *The Art of Fugue* and the *Jupiter* Symphony, our knowledge of Wagner fills many real and imaginary volumes. Or to put it in postmodern terms: even during his own lifetime Wagner was consciously "tweeting" his own life and works. In certain cases we may be able to get behind his imaginary web pages, but we shall never do so in a more generalized way. We can only attempt to make meaningful use of these pages.

This brings me to my book. For many years I toiled in the field of Wagner scholarship and helped to lay the foundations of the weighty Wagner *Werk-Verzeichnis*, the standard catalogue of Wagner's works and their musical sources. But then I no longer felt any great desire to make any more sense of the composer. To find meaningful access to the sources that continue to produce a veritable wealth of new information now means trying to forge a link between two different kinds of Wagnerian discourse separated by a period of over two decades. In my own view, the older discourse has now acquired a historical aspect and can no longer be adequately experienced and described except to the extent that it is reflected in its present-day counterpart. It is a truism that as ordinary mortals we cannot jump into the same river twice or see from its banks where the waves of the sea originate. We can only watch those waves breaking on the beach.

Any such discourse is a language game on a particular subject, guided by particular interests and necessarily incomplete. And the very term "language game" implies that there is no point in seeking to distinguish between truth and untruth, justice or injustice, right or wrong. Of course, the author has the right to applaud certain events or to shake his head at others. But essentially he will limit himself to observing the game's rules and practicalities and then reflect on what that game means to him personally. Nor will this discourse be confined to Wagner and his stage works. Creativity itself is a language game and, indeed, one of the most meaningful conceivable.

In order to prevent my interest in those language games that bear the label "Wagner" from degenerating into vagueness, I should like to end these remarks by stating my ethos as an author: it is not Wagner that I want to figure out but myself and my age. What is it that continues to fascinate us about *Tristan und Isolde* and the *Ring*? What ideas and ideologies are conveyed by the artist and his work? Does Wagner's anti-Semitism detract from his works? Are there central messages in Wagner to offset the postmodern arbitrariness of "anything goes"? Or, to put it another way, what is it that motivates us when we draw closer to Wagner or turn away from him? What values, good and bad, do we consciously assimilate through the medium of his operas and music dramas? Which values are subliminally brought home to us through his world of music theater?

As I say, we are dealing with values both good and bad. Walter Benjamin once wrote that "without exception the cultural treasures" that the historical materialist "surveys have an origin that he cannot contemplate without horror."[15] And Joachim Kaiser, the doyen of German-language music critics, begins his book on the composer with the sentence "Our love of Wagner is as infected as the wound that is suffered by Amfortas."[16] As for my own perception of Wagner's works, I feel both fascination and horror in equal measure. At the same time, I admit that my way of writing about Wagner is guided more by the kind of sympathetic interest felt by Thomas Mann than by the anger evinced by those two disappointed admirers Nietzsche and Adorno: I can write only about the art that ultimately fascinates me in all its contradictory complexity.

The present account draws on the theory and aesthetics of music as well as on philosophy, cultural history, and biography, but even though it seeks to combine these various disciplines, this does not make it a *Gesamtkunstwerk*. It does, however, illustrate my own misgivings about filtering complex processes to such an extent that they finally disappear down a black hole of blank abstraction. This would be an accurate reflection neither of Wagner's view of art nor of our own particular experience of it.

As for the factual information contained in the following pages, I can vouch for it with all the seriousness of a Wagner scholar. The rest is "poetry" in the sense understood by the American historian Hayden White in his book, *Tropics of Discourse*, in which Clio, the oft-neglected muse of history, is rehabilitated as a writer of poetry.[17] With the exception of the framework of facts within which he operates, the historian, in White's view, is no more than an interpreter. May Clio help me to ensure that my self-imposed task of interpreting Wagner for my readers turns out to be tolerably successful.

A silhouette of Wagner by an unknown artist dating from the late fall of 1835. The first known likeness of the composer, it was a gift to the actress Minna Planer, whose favors he was currently courting, while simultaneously working on his opera *Das Liebesverbot* (The Ban on Love). The couple married in November 1836. (Photograph courtesy of the Nationalarchiv der Richard-Wagner-Stiftung, Bayreuth: Bi 3228.)

CHAPTER ONE

The Archetypal Theatrical Scene

FROM *LEUBALD* TO *DIE FEEN*

"The wildest anarchy" — The paternity issue — Sense of
separation in early childhood — Early enthusiasm for the
theater — The "more intimate objects" in his sisters' wardrobe
and Proust's madeleine — The schoolboy drama *Leubald* — The
myth of Hero and Leander as Wagner's archetypal theatrical
scene — Composition exercises to set *Leubald* to music —
Beethoven's incidental music to *Egmont* as a model — Early
sonatas, overtures and a C-major symphony for the Leipzig
Gewandhaus — A "wedding" not to the liking of Wagner's sister
Rosalie — *Die Feen*: a respectable first opera for a twenty-year-
old composer — Wagner's discovery of the redemptive power
of music as the embodiment of love — An anticipatory glance
at Nietzsche's *Birth of Tragedy from the Spirit of Music* — A look
ahead to later chapters: "Redemption through Destruction" as
a leitmotif — Congruence between Wagner's life and works?

W agner's childhood memories revolve constantly around two key
ideas — chaos and the theater: "I grew up in the wildest of anarchy,"
he told his second wife, Cosima, in July 1871.[1] And in his autobiography he
speaks of a mother whose "anxious and trying relations with a large family"
were never conducive to a "comforting tone of motherly solicitude," still
less to feelings of tenderness: "I hardly remember ever being caressed by
her, just as outpourings of affection did not take place in our family; on
the contrary, quite naturally a certain impetuous, even loud and boisterous
manner characterized our behaviour."[2]

Friedrich Wagner died six months after Wagner's birth, and nine
months later his widow, Johanna Rosine, married a family friend, Ludwig
Geyer, and, together with the rest of her family, moved from Leipzig to
Dresden. Wagner was known as Richard Geyer until his fifteenth year and
in maturity he was never entirely certain if he was in fact Geyer's son. But

it may be significant that he chose a vulture (German *Geyer*, or *Geier*) as a heraldic beast on the first page of his privately published autobiography, the initial volume of which appeared in 1870. And in 1879, in a letter to King Ludwig II, he described a family celebration held to mark his sixty-sixth birthday in the following words: "In front of a new painting of my wife by Lenbach [. . .] stood my son Siegfried in black velvet, with blond curly hair (just like the portrait of the young Van Dyck): he was intended to represent my father Ludwig Geyer, reborn to significant effect."[3]

The real Geyer seems to have been a good replacement as a father figure, albeit extremely strict. In August 1873 Wagner spoke about his childhood over lunch and recalled (via Cosima) "how he was thrashed by his father Geyer with the whip he had bought with stolen money, and how his sisters cried outside the door."[4] Known to his sisters as "Master Moody" on account of his hypersensitivity,[5] Wagner was seven when he was sent to board with Pastor Christian Ephraim Wetzel in Possendorf near Dresden. When Geyer died a year later, the boy found board and lodging with Geyer's younger brother, Karl, in Eisleben, where he spent the next thirteen months. He then spent a brief period with his Uncle Adolf in Leipzig, but was obliged to sleep in a large, high-ceilinged room whose walls were hung with sinister-looking paintings of "aristocratic ladies in hooped petticoats, with youthful faces and white (powdered) hair." According to his—much later—reminiscences, not a night passed without his waking up "bathed in sweat at the fear caused by these frightful ghostly apparitions."[6]

Adolf Wagner was unwilling to undertake any real responsibility for his nephew's education, and so at the end of 1822 Wagner returned to live with his family in Dresden, where he attended the city's Kreuzschule. In 1826 his mother moved to Prague with four of his sisters, Rosalie, Clara, Ottilie, and Cäcilie, and the now thirteen-year-old youth was offered a room in the home of one Dr. Rudolf Böhme, whose family life was later described by Wagner as "somewhat disorderly."[7] At the end of 1827 he finally moved back to Leipzig, where his mother and sisters had settled following their Bohemian adventure. He attended St. Nicholas's School, and it was during this time as a fifteen- and sixteen-year-old schoolboy that he wrote his "great tragedy" *Leubald*.

A decade later we find Wagner writing to his fiancée, Minna Planer: "O God, my angel, on the whole I had a miserable youth."[8] His youth may not have been any harsher than that of many another adolescent from his social background, but there is no doubt that it was anarchically unsettled: "Who is my father?," "Does my mother love me?," "Where is my home?," and "Who are my models?"—these are questions that the young Wagner presumably asked himself more frequently than most other children of his age. And if he was dissatisfied with having to swim with the tide, then he himself would have to provide his existence with a sense of direction and open up new horizons.

Such views are never conjured out of thin air but are found within the subject's own immediate environment, and this brings us to the second of the key ideas that emerge so forcefully from Wagner's reminiscences of his youth: the theater. It would be wrong to lay undue emphasis on Friedrich Hölderlin's lines, "But where there is danger, rescue, too, is at hand," yet as far as Wagner is concerned, there is no doubt that the theater saved his life in the deepest sense, especially during his early years. From the very outset the anarchy of his environment was directly related to his tendency to indulge in theatrical, self-promotional behavior. More specifically, it was related to his love of the stage. Although his mother warned all her children against the godlessness of a life in the theater, she was so lacking in the courage of her own convictions that four of Wagner's six elder siblings embarked on such a career: Rosalie was to be the Gretchen in the first Leipzig production of Goethe's *Faust* in 1829; Clara was only sixteen when she sang the title role in Rossini's *La Cenerentola*; and Rosalie was seventeen when she took the main part in Weber's *Preciosa*. Wagner's elder brother Albert, finally, enjoyed a successful operatic career in Leipzig in a repertory that included Mozart's Tamino and Belmonte.

Although Friedrich Wagner was a police actuary by profession, he came from a family of artists and academics. He studied law and had an amateur's love of the theater. Among his circle of acquaintances were Goethe, Schiller, and E. T. A. Hoffmann. But in this regard he could not begin to compete with his eccentric brother Adolf, a well-known figure in Leipzig who held a doctorate in philosophy and was a distinguished translator of Sophocles and the proud possessor of a silver beaker presented to him by Goethe as a token of the poet's gratitude for the dedication of a collection of Italian verse. According to his autobiography, the young Wagner enjoyed listening to his uncle's effusions. In the course of their extended walks together, Adolf also declaimed Shakespeare's plays to him.

Wagner's surrogate father, Ludwig Geyer, was the quintessential bohemian. A successful playwright, actor, and portrait painter, he also helped to train Wagner's older brother and sisters for their careers in the theater. It seemed only natural that Wagner himself would follow in their footsteps. In adulthood he recalled "how at the age of 5, since he could not sing, he imitated Caspar's piccolo and flute trills with '*Perrbip*,' climbed on a chair to represent Samiel looking over an imaginary bush, and said, 'Perrbip, perr- bip.'"[9] In point of fact Wagner must have been seven when he first encoun- tered *Der Freischütz*, but there is no doubt that he came into contact with leading musicians such as Weber at a very early age. "If I had never had the experience of Weber's things," he told Cosima in October 1873, "I believe I should never have become a musician."[10]

Initially it was his love of the theater in general that proved the domi- nant factor:

> What attracted me so powerfully to the theatre, by which I include the stage itself, the backstage area and the dressing rooms, was not so much the addictive desire for entertainment and diversion that motivates today's theatregoers, but rather the tingling delight in my contact with an element that represented such a contrast to normal life in the form of a purely fan- tastical world whose attractiveness often bordered on horror. In this way a piece of scenery or even a flat—perhaps representing a bush—or a theatri- cal costume or even just a characteristic piece of a costume appeared to me to emanate from another world and in a certain way to be eerily interesting, and my contact with this world would serve as a lever that allowed me to rise above the calm reality of my daily routine and enter that demoniacal realm that I found so stimulating.[11]

Nor was it long before Wagner had had his first taste of the theater: "After being terrified by *The Orphan and the Murderer* and *The Two Galley Slaves* and similar plays that traded in gothic horror and that featured my father [Ludwig Geyer] in the role of the villains, I was obliged to appear in a num- ber of comedies. [. . .] I recall featuring in a tableau vivant as an angel, en- tirely sewn up in tights and with wings on my back. I had to adopt a graceful pose that I had found hard to learn."[12] When he was twelve, he recalled reading aloud from Schiller's *The Maid of Orleans* to the "well-educated" wife of his godfather, Adolf Träger.[13] That his godfather gave him not only a pike-gray dress coat with an impressive silk lining but also a red Turkish waistcoat may well have helped to blur the distinction between "art" and "life."

But what was all this when set beside the intimacies of his sisters' bou- doir! There, according to Wagner's later account,

> it was the more delicate costumes of my sisters, on which I often observed my family working, that stimulated my imagination in the most subtly excit-

ing ways. It was enough for me to touch these objects, and my heart would beat anxiously and wildly. Despite the fact that, as I have already said, there was little tenderness in our family, particularly as expressed in the form of hugging and kissing, my exclusively feminine surroundings were bound to exert a powerful influence on my emotional development.[14]

Readers so inclined may see in this passage a justification for Wagner's later fondness for choice silks and exquisite perfumes and may dismiss that predilection as feminine or even abnormal. In this they would be following a well-worn path. But it would be more helpful in this context to follow up a remark that the composer made to the music critic Karl Gaillard at the time he was working on *Tannhäuser*: "And so, even before I set about writing a single line of the text or drafting a scene, I am already thoroughly immersed in the musical aura of my new creation."[15] He was aware of his "foolish fondness for luxury,"[16] he admitted to his benefactress Julie Ritter in 1854, but he needed it to survive. Less than a week earlier he had told Liszt: "I cannot live like a dog, I cannot sleep on straw and drink common gin. Mine is an intensely irritable, acute, and hugely voracious, yet uncommonly tender and delicate sensuality which, one way or another, must be flattered."[17]

We are still concerned with the young Wagner's most basic question: what prospects did he have within his own anarchistic milieu? We are dealing here not with titillating biographical details but with the impulses that triggered Wagner's creativity. Here our principal witnesses are Marcel Proust and Baudelaire. In a famous passage in *À la recherche du temps perdu*, Proust recounts the way in which a madeleine dipped in tea could activate his "mémoire involontaire" and usher in an act of spontaneous memory. He goes on to explain how

> Above all in Baudelaire, where they are more numerous still, reminiscences of this kind are clearly less fortuitous and therefore, to my mind, unmistakable in their significance. Here the poet himself, with something of a slow and indolent choice, deliberately seeks, in the perfume of a woman, for instance, of her hair and her breast, the analogies which will inspire him and evoke for him
>
> > the azure of the sky immense and round
>
> and
>
> > a harbour full of masts and pennants.[18]

Proust's remarks about Baudelaire could equally well apply to Wagner, whom he idolized for a time. And when Wagner, writing in his autobiography, recalls the sensual stimuli that were triggered when he touched his sisters' "more delicate costumes," this is more than a mere reminiscence of his childhood and adolescence: it is also an aesthetic reflection on the part of the composer of *Tannhäuser, Lohengrin,* and *Tristan und Isolde* concerning the synesthetic potential of his works. According to Proust, Baudelaire's linguistic images were the result of a "slow and indolent choice," and it is in this spirit that we should read the above passage from *My Life,* a memoir by no means intended for a mass readership eager for gutter-press sensationalism. In writing this, Wagner was seeking reassurance and expressing his wish that "life" and "art" should be in harmony. If, in his adolescence, he had not known the stimulus of the items in his sisters' wardrobe, he would presumably have invented it or at least devised something similar to clarify his conviction that the oneness of life and art was no accident but was predetermined by fate: everything had to happen just as it did indeed happen.

The reader may find this hubristic, and yet we cannot fail to admire the consistency with which the young Wagner approached his life's work. While still at school, he not only developed a burning enthusiasm for the stage as the only thing that gave meaning to his life—after all, many other budding actors have felt the same—but he also wanted to write his own plays and in that way to create his own world of the theater both as an actor and in his own imagination. He was not content to declaim Hamlet's "To be or not to be" from the classroom lectern. Rather, he perfected his knowledge of Greek in order to be able to read Sophocles and translate passages from the *Odyssey.* And if his account in *My Life* is not an exaggeration, then he was still in his early teens when, an otherwise poor pupil, he wrote a vast epic poem on the Battle of Parnassus.

Whereas we know about such feats only from Wagner's own much later account of them, his five-act tragedy *Leubald* allows us to test its author's claims for ourselves. In maturity Wagner himself no longer had access to the manuscript, which he believed had been lost, and this may explain why he adopted such a mocking tone when referring to a youthful "misdemeanor" that he claimed represented an amalgam of Shakespeare's *Hamlet, Macbeth,* and *Lear* and Goethe's *Götz von Berlichingen.*[19] The rediscovery of the manuscript allows us to form an impression of what Wagner was capable of achieving between the ages of thirteen and fifteen. *Leubald* is no naïve schoolboy play, as it is usually described by writers on Wagner, but an example of its author's ability to maintain three stylistic registers over an extended period—the play would last around six hours in performance. For the lofty style deemed appropriate to the characters who inhabit the highest echelons of feudal society, Wagner prefers blank verse—iambic pentameters—in the tradition of Shakespeare's plays. The common people, by contrast, speak in coarse prose that is again modeled on Shakespeare. Between these two extremes is a third stylistic register that Wagner reserves for members of the spirit world, who converse with one another in rhyme and in song.

Leubald contains much that is hugely impressive alongside other passages that are inconsistent, long-winded or linguistically awkward. And—in spite of Wagner's own claim in his "Autobiographical Sketch"—it is not true that forty-two people die in the course of the play.[20] The actual figure is fourteen. And yet the piece teems with all manner of acts of violence and crudity. Nonetheless, questions of plagiarism and immaturity pale into insignificance beside the undoubted fact that Wagner has succeeded with breathtaking skill in introducing his archetypal scene into the piece and, as it were, fixing it once and for all. In brief, the plot revolves around Leubald's infatuation with Adelaide. At this stage he does not know that her father, Roderich, secretly poisoned Leubald's own father. But his father then appears to him as a ghost to demand revenge not only on Roderich but on his whole clan. It is not long before Leubald does as his father's ghost bids and murders Roderich and his family. Only Adelaide, who has been hopelessly in love with Leubald since their earlier brief encounter, is able to escape. Even though her father informs her with his dying breath that it is Leubald who has visited so terrible a punishment on her family, nothing will sway her in her love for him.

But Leubald himself grows increasingly unhinged as it becomes clear to him that Adelaide belongs to the very family that he has sworn to destroy. His father's ghost continues to urge him to acts of bloody revenge, driving him to the point of madness and persuading him to consult a witch in the hope of exorcising his father's spirit. But in the witch's mirror he sees himself lying lifeless in his dead lover's arms, whereupon he kills the witch. He is then pursued by a whole army of ghosts demanding his own blood in addition to that of Adelaide. In his deluded frenzy he fatally injures her and dies in her arms.[21]

On the basis of this outline scenario it is possible to reconstruct an archetypal scene grounded as much in the ancient Greek legend of Hero and Leander as in Shakespeare's tragedy *Romeo and Juliet*: love is invariably bound up with tragedy, and ultimate union is possible only in death. It is against this background that we should see Wagner's drama about Leubald and Adelaide: two lovers united by destiny are destroyed by the hostility between their two families. In the case of *Leubald*, Wagner took over this structural obstacle from *Romeo and Juliet*. Although it was to assume different forms in his later stage works, it remains ever present. Only the emphasis was to change, for alongside the tragedy that is found when the lovers' happiness is thwarted we increasingly find the sense of foreboding inherent in love itself. This is what Wagner was referring to in the case of the *Ring*, when he spoke of the way in which the "love which alone brings happiness" had emerged "in the course of the myth as something utterly and completely destructive."[22] In the 1865 prose draft of *Parsifal*, the hero similarly announces that "strong is the magic of him who desires, but stronger is that of him who renounces."[23]

It would be naïve to assume an unthinking connection between Wagner's archetypal scene and his childhood reminiscences concerning the "wildest anarchy" of his upbringing, to say nothing of his unsatisfactory bond with his mother, the lack of intimacy within the family circle, and his uncertain picture of his father. After all, there are enough imaginative people in the world who have a similar childhood but who do not feel impelled to write plays on the subject. At the same time, Wagner was not dependent on the circumstances of his own life in his quest for models for this scene: the motif of Hero and Leander is found not only in the writings of his favorite authors from Sophocles to Shakespeare and Schiller but also in the gothic novels and dramas about fate by many of his contemporaries. And yet it is difficult not to be impressed by the young Wagner's powers of self-portrayal and his ability to impose a sense of structure on his life and art. And our admiration increases when we note how consistent is his continuing commitment to his plan to turn his own private myth into one that is universal in its appeal.

What was still missing was the music. But even while he was working on *Leubald*, it was already becoming clear to Wagner that a spoken drama was not enough, for although such a work might exorcise the anarchy of an existence overshadowed by baleful ill fortune, it could not redeem such a life. Wagner was not joking when, years later, while he was working on *Götterdämmerung*, he noted with a sigh: "I am no composer, [. . .] I wanted only to learn enough to compose *Leubald und Adelaïde*."[24] Even at that early date he needed music to open up the drama to the world of myth, for in his eyes myth alone was capable of propelling it in the direction of "redemption."

Within days of this reminiscence of *Leubald*, Wagner was visited at Tribschen by Nietzsche, and the two men discussed Mozart's *Le nozze di Figaro*, prompting Wagner to comment: "One has only to compare Beaumarchais's (incidentally excellent) play with Mozart's operas to see that the former contains cunning, clever, and calculating people who deal and talk wittily with one another, while in Mozart they are transfigured, suffering, sorrowing human beings."[25] A year earlier, while working on a particularly somber passage in act 3 of *Siegfried*, he had told Cosima that "music transfigures everything, it never permits the hideousness of the bare word, however terrible the subject."[26]

Even as a fifteen-year-old boy whose technical abilities were nowhere near good enough for him to set *Leubald* to music, Wagner was already dimly aware that his future lay in the field of *music* drama. He was not simply a composer. Rather, his musical creativity would be fired by the stage — one is almost tempted to say that this was the *only* way in which it would be fired. In *Opera and Drama* he described music explicitly as a "woman" who may have needed the poet to "impregnate" her, but who ultimately "gives birth" to the musical drama on her own.[27]

It is against this background that we should see Wagner's encounter with Beethoven's music in 1827—the year of Beethoven's death. If Wagner had any clearer ideas about the music he planned to write for *Leubald*, then those ideas may have been inspired by Beethoven's incidental music to Goethe's *Egmont*, which would from an early date have encouraged him to believe that music and drama could be combined to create a unique new synthesis of the arts.

But he needed a practical basis on which to implement this idea. A gothic drama like *Leubald*, in which the lovers' ultimate death was preceded by a veritable spree of serial killings and by scenes of sexual violence, chuckle-headedness, and ghostly apparitions, was hardly suited to such a treatment. At the same time Wagner needed a knowledge of music. He was in fact already attempting to learn the fundamentals of composition, initially on his own and then, willingly or otherwise, through private lessons. It was on this basis that he wrote his first songs, sonatas, and overtures between 1829 and 1832. Although most of these early works have been lost, one of them has survived in the form of a Symphony in C Major (WWV 29). It was even performed at the Leipzig Gewandhaus in January 1833 and, according to a letter that Wagner wrote to his publisher in March 1878, continued to engage his "powerful interest" to such an extent that only weeks before his death in 1883 he conducted a performance of it at the Teatro La Fenice in Venice as a birthday present for his wife.[28]

Following the success of his symphony, the nineteen-year-old Wagner felt ready to face the challenges of his first opera, *Die Hochzeit* (The Wedding), the subject of which was inspired by *Ritterzeit und Ritterwesen* (The Age and Essence of Chivalry) by the German medievalist and folklorist Johann Gustav Gottlieb Büsching: Ada and Arindal are planning a conventional wedding, but on the eve of the ceremony she is almost raped by one of the wedding guests, Kadolt. She manages to force her attacker onto the balcony and catapults him over the parapet. But at his funeral service she sinks lifeless beside his body.

Wagner later destroyed the libretto of *Die Hochzeit*, but it seems clear from his incomplete account of its plot that in death Ada is united with the man with whom she had secretly been smitten—namely, Kadolt.[29] If so, the story bears striking similarities to Wagner's archetypal scene in which desire is associated with tragedy, and union is possible only in death. But Wagner's favorite sister, Rosalie, was so appalled by its antinuptial message that Wagner quickly abandoned the project: without the support of his sister, who was one of the stars of the Leipzig stage in addition to being the family's principal breadwinner and spokesperson, the work of the inexperienced twenty-year-old composer stood little chance of acceptance.

Astonishingly, Wagner not only took over the names of Ada and Arindal when drafting a libretto for his next opera, *Die Feen* (The Fairies), he also— and above all—remained true to his archetypal scenario: while trying to make amends to his sister and the rest of his family, he was evidently not prepared to do anything that would compromise his calling. On this occasion no rival seeks to interpose himself into a legitimate relationship. Rather, the plot revolves around the clash between the fairy realm and the world of human beings: the King of the Fairies looks askance at the fact that the fairy Ada is happily married to Arindal, the mortal king of Tramond. He agrees to release her into the world of human beings only on condition that Arindal pass a series of tests, but these are so cruelly demanding that Arindal fails, whereupon Ada is turned to stone. The spell is broken by music when Arindal's enchanted singing restores his bride to life and he can belong to her for all eternity as the immortal ruler of the fairy kingdom. The work ends with a chorus of celebration:

> Ein hohes Loos hat er errungen,
> Dem Erdenstaub ist er entrückt!

Drum sei's in Ewigkeit besungen,
Wie hoch die Liebe ihn beglückt!

[He's won a great reward indeed and shaken off this mortal coil. And so until the end of time we'll sing of love's most joyous boon!]

But is there really cause for celebration here? In ending the work on this note, Wagner departed radically from his source in Carlo Gozzi's *La donna serpente*. In Gozzi's tragicomic fairy tale, the female protagonist becomes human alongside her human husband, whereas Arindal, having led a relatively unhappy life in his earthly kingdom, is spirited away to fairyland and to a world that is evidently superior to the one he has left behind. The moral of the story is that for mortals true happiness in love can be found only in a world beyond our own.

This is a conciliatory variant of Wagner's archetypal scene, for although the characters are denied happiness in the human world, there is at least the prospect of a higher world by way of consolation. And it almost goes without saying that it is music that makes this conciliatory ending possible, for it is music that allows Arindal to gain access to the higher world.

In *Die Feen*, "redemption through music" is first and foremost dramaturgical in character: musically speaking, Wagner is less successful at depicting the redemptive function of music than he was to be in *Der fliegende Holländer* (The Flying Dutchman) and *Tristan und Isolde* or at the end of *Götterdämmerung* (Twilight of the Gods). At the same time we have no reason to be patronizing toward a work which, however much it may reflect the influence of Spohr, Weber, or Marschner, has been described by Carl Dahlhaus as one of "the typical products of a composing kapellmeister who made ready use of ideas from various quarters."[30] Other representatives of what was then the new medium of the German-language "grand romantic opera," as Wagner called *Die Feen*, were likewise struggling at this time to produce works capable of meeting the demands of the sentimental German singspiel in the tradition of *Die Zauberflöte* (The Magic Flute) and *Der Freischütz*, while not forfeiting the verve that audiences found so appealing in the operas of Bellini and Auber.

The twenty-year-old Wagner proved surprisingly adept at achieving this twofold aim, and in his depiction of mystic events using "'magic' combinations of chords,"[31] he stumbled upon "the foundations of his own genius."[32] The magic formula of the overture's opening bars recalls not only *Die Zauberflöte* but also the opening of Mendelssohn's inspired overture to *A Midsummer Night's Dream*, a piece that Wagner presumably already knew at this time. In later life Wagner sought to distance himself from *Die Feen*, while nonetheless stressing its importance as an example of the "sacred seriousness" of his "original feelings."[33]

Nor was it any accident that he felt it was music that had led to the conciliatory ending of *Die Feen*.[34] There is no doubt, then, that with this last-named work Wagner had taken a decisive step as far as his later output was concerned: the pessimistic idea that underpins his archetypal scene and that may be summed up as the belief that meaningful love is impossible in a meaningless world is now accompanied—contrapuntally, as it were—by the conviction that there is indeed something that extends beyond death: music. Although none of Wagner's later works features an Arindal opening the gates to another world by singing and playing the harp, it is enough to recall the number of works that end with the sounds of one or more harps to see the importance of such transcendence: *Der fliegende Holländer*, *Tannhäuser*, *Das Rheingold* (The Rhinegold), *Die Walküre* (The Valkyrie), *Siegfried*, *Götterdämmerung*, *Tristan und Isolde*, and *Parsifal*.

By writing *music* dramas, Wagner ensured that the corrupt and hostile world with which men and women have to deal in their everyday lives is transcended in the direction of redemption. In his first major work, *The Birth of Tragedy from the Spirit of Music*, Nietzsche—approaching the subject from the standpoint of Schopenhauer's pessimism—brought his own particular brand of personal enthusiasm to the idea, prompting a no less elated response in Wagner: "He is happy to have lived to read it," his wife noted in her diary in January 1872.[35] His reaction is hardly surprising, for his youthful admirer had provided welcome historical and philosophical backing for his own ideas about the classical synthesis of the arts from the spirit of music. Even more importantly, Nietzsche's book offered its readers a description of the world uncannily close in character to Wagner's archetypal scene and aptly summed up in Peter Sloterdijk's words: "The usual individual life is a hell made up of suffering, brutality, baseness, and entanglement. [. . .] This life is made bearable only by intoxication and by dreams, by this twofold path to ecstasy that is open to individuals for self-redemption."[36]

It was in this sense that Nietzsche was later to describe *Tristan und Isolde* as "the actual *opus metaphysicum* of all art"[37] and to suggest that love and the death of lovers can rise above the trivial world only by being borne aloft on a wave of music. Wagner's claim in *A Communication to My Friends* that "I can conceive of the spirit of music only in *love*"[38] can be effortlessly inverted: true love can be grasped only in the spirit of music. In turn this leads to an even more crucial point: since Wagner's understanding of love shifts constantly between pure and impure, lustful and renunciatory, narcissistic and sociable, tyrannical and meek, animalistic and sublime, it is impossible to pin it down or define its meaning, with the result that music alone provides the only definition of love that the composer—or any other artist—can make us feel. Although this sounds vague to the point of unhelpfulness, it does in fact make sense, for Wagner spent his entire life believing only in his art—and this is true even when he was committed to the bourgeois revolutions of 1848–49. He was enough of a realist to see that there was literally nothing on earth that he could do to counter the world's inherent baseness and evil. In this he followed Nietzsche's dictum: "*We have art* so that we are not destroyed by the truth."[39] And yet he interpreted it in a very specific way: even within the world of art, it is music alone that is capable of offering the listener not fruitless intellectual or rational explanations, but meanings that our senses can grasp at once. And although Wagner invests this ability with a metaphysical dimension that is grounded in art, he still sets out from a physical and psychological reality: in every culture music embodies first and foremost the principle of universal reconciliation that Wagner himself termed "love."

It hardly needs adding that our experience of music has changed with the passage of time and that our need for harmony is tested to its limits by the art music of the modern world—not least by Wagner himself. And yet there is no other art form that can compare to music in its ability to express not only our *desire* for an ideal world but also the *fulfillment* of that desire through the actual performance of the music. This means that in Wagner's stage works two realities converge: the action embodies the social reality of a world that is hopelessly evil, while the music encapsulates the psychological and anthropological reality of a "principle of hope" that can be grasped by our senses. This ambivalence may help to explain the fascination that Wagner continues to exert on us.

Against this background, Wagner's archetypal scenario may be seen to produce a leitmotif that permeates the whole of his output for the stage: "redemption through destruction."[40] Adriano and Irene, the Dutchman and Senta, Tannhäuser and Elisabeth, Lohengrin and Elsa, Tristan and Isolde, Siegfried and Brünnhilde, and Parsifal and Kundry are all "couples" who find a quietus in death or at the very least are transported into an alternative existence. It is the task and function of the music to ensure that the "lifeless" sinking away that is often mentioned in the stage directions is transformed into the state of "gentle reconciliation" in which Isolde dies her *Liebestod*, or love-death.

If I refer to "redemption through destruction" as a leitmotif, it is because it is not a fixed formula from which Wagner's thinking can be seamlessly derived, but a leading idea that assumes different forms and that explains much, but not everything. There appears to be a variant of the motif even in *Die Meistersinger von Nürnberg* (The mastersingers of Nuremberg), a work in which we might least expect it. When Hans Sachs proclaims at the end

> Zerging' in Dunst
> das heil'ge röm'sche Reich,
> uns bliebe gleich
> die heil'ge deutsche Kunst!

[Although the Holy Roman Empire may fade away, we shall still have holy German art!]

Wagner is imagining the end of a particular social reality to which only "holy art" can reconcile us—and there seems little doubt that he was ultimately thinking of his own specific art here.

Nonetheless, it must be admitted that *Die Meistersinger von Nürnberg* remains peripheral to this particular line of argument and that the motif acquires a note of deadly seriousness only in the other works, all of which end in death, ensuring that physical or figurative destruction is a central theme in all of them. Clearly all of their scenarios revolve around the notion of doom. The fact that doom also signifies redemption is a point that Nietzsche observed when he noted that "there is nothing about which Wagner has thought more deeply than redemption: his opera is the opera of redemption."[41] Only in *Tannhäuser*, of course, does such redemption rest on the intervention of a merciful God, whereas in every other case it is bought at the cost of "sweat, anguish, and want" and achieved only through "self-annihilation."[42]

These terms are taken from Wagner's essay "Jews in Music."[43] Here we are interested in one particular aspect of this text, according to which Wagner holds out the promise of "redemption" through "self-annihilation" and "destruction," offering it not only to Jews, as many writers have claimed on the strength of a—possibly consciously—cursory reading of the *corpus delicti*. True, the Jews are in particularly urgent need of "self-annihilation" because it is they who have "corroded" the "living organism" of modern society, but inasmuch as this organism can no longer be saved, all the members of this society are doomed to perish.

The *Ring* clearly demonstrates that this also applies to the tragic figure of Wotan: "Wodan [*sic*] rises to the tragic heights of *willing* his own destruction," Wagner informed August Röckel in January 1854:

> This is all that we need to learn from the history of humankind: *to will what is necessary* and to bring it about ourselves. [. . .] Observe him closely! he resembles *us* to a tee; he is the sum total of present-day intelligence, whereas Siegfried is the man of the future whom we desire and long for but who cannot be made by us, since he must create himself on the basis of *our own annihilation*.[44]

Writing about himself in 1851 in the earliest—handwritten—version of *A Communication to My Friends*, Wagner insisted that "I am not a republican or a democrat or a socialist or a communist but an artist, and as such I am a thoroughgoing revolutionary wherever my gaze, my wishes, and my will extends, destroying the old in creating the new!"[45] Shortly beforehand, he had repeatedly spoken of the need to "destroy capital"[46] and bring about the "destruction of the state,"[47] demands that he had made in his role as a Dresden revolutionary.

Here the motif of "redemption through destruction" dominates Wagner's theoretical statements, too. And if they strike a more somber note than the message of his music dramas, it is because the musical dimension is missing: music alone has the power that allows us to feel the element of redemption, adding a note of joy to the pessimism of self-annihilation.

Wagner's ideas about "destruction" and "self-annihilation" in his stage works are every bit as real as every other aspect of his music theater: death occurs not just metaphorically but in the spirit of a higher reality. As for his own life on earth, Wagner no doubt shared Martin Luther's conviction that the old Adam needed to be destroyed every day but that this did not mean laying violent hand to himself. In this sense it would be misguided to assume a straightforward link between life and works and to regard the two as congruent in every way. Even so, there can be little doubt that Wagner himself repeatedly equated the two. As Christian Kaden has emphasized, the myth that unfolds in the *Ring*, for example, is not concerned with unreal illusions but aims to "threaten the world of appearances and to question our illusions by destabilizing them." From this point of view, it remains "true to real life" as experienced by Wagner himself.[48]

It is in this sense that Wagner identifies with his own Flying Dutchman in *A Communication to My Friends*, claiming that the character "arose so

Die Feen: a scene from act 3 of Emilio Sagi's 2009 production at Paris's Théâtre du Châtelet, which treated the opera as a fairy-tale revue. (Photograph courtesy of Ullstein Bild—Roger Viollet/Colette Masson.)

often from the swamps and billows of my life, and drew me to him with such unresisting power." And he writes rhapsodically about Senta as "the as yet non-existent, longed-for, dreamt-of, and infinitely womanly woman" who alone was able to redeem the Dutchman in him.[49]

Before we attempt to interpret this is a purely figurative sense, we would do well to recall a letter that Wagner wrote to Liszt at the time of *Tristan und Isolde*:

> Since I have never in my life enjoyed the true happiness of love, I intend to erect a further monument to this most beautiful of dreams, a monument in which this love will be properly sated from beginning to end: I have planned in my head a *Tristan* and *Isolte* [*sic*], the simplest, but most full-blooded musical conception; with the "black flag" that flutters at the end, I shall then cover myself over in order to die.[50]

That nothing changed even during Wagner's years in Munich in the 1860s is clear from the many depressing and even desperate entries in his so-called *Brown Book*, a diary nominally concerned with the intensity of his feelings for Cosima. Even his comments during his final decade in Bayreuth are marked by a sense of decline and transience.

But how is it possible to reconcile Wagner's view of himself as the Dutchman and even as Ahasuerus, the Wandering Jew whose myth, in Dieter Borchmeyer's view, is "a myth about Wagner's life as an artist,"[51] with a man whose increasing artistic successes turned him into one of the leading figures of his age, living in Wilhelminian affluence in his villa, Wahnfried, and looking back on two marriages and numerous affairs? The answer is simple: archetypal scenarios and leitmotifs are emblematic of an inner reality that invariably keeps one step ahead of its outer counterpart. Although it is possible to live in both worlds simultaneously, it is the inner experience that will always enjoy the higher degree of significance.

Toward the end of his life Wagner expressed his thoughts on this theme in his essay "The Stage Consecration Festival Drama in Bayreuth":

> Which of us can spend his whole life gazing freely and openly at a world of murder and robbery that is organized and legitimized by lying, deceit, and hypocrisy without occasionally having to turn away with a feeling of shuddering disgust? Where then is our gaze directed? Often, no doubt, into the depths of death. But to those of us who are cut off from all this by their destiny and who have a different calling, the truest reflection of the world may indeed seem to be a message from its innermost soul, a message that

prophesies redemption. To be able to forget the actual world of deception in this prophetic reflection must surely be the reward for the painful truth of our recognition of all its wretchedness.[52]

It is very much in the tradition of Greek antiquity that Wagner invested the musical drama with a cathartic, purifying force: by seeing through the world's iniquities and by reflecting them in his art in the form of a "prophetic reflection," the artist enables his community of listeners to forget the world's wickedness. In doing so, he speaks for the "innermost soul" of the world, a soul that reminds us about "redemption" and prophesies its advent.

A Word about Felix Mendelssohn

When Wagner looked at Felix Mendelssohn, he saw himself—incredibly—as the underdog. To his inner eye, Mendelssohn seemed a Jewish child of fortune, a banker's son hailing from a good home, with exquisitely educated private tutors, and enjoying the blessing of the elderly Goethe, to say nothing of his distinguished artistic career: when he was eleven, his parents arranged a performance of his singspiel *Soldatenliebschaft* (Soldiers' Love) with members of the Royal Orchestra; by the time he was seventeen his inspired overture to Shakespeare's *A Midsummer Night's Dream* was on everyone's lips; and he had only just turned twenty when half of Berlin paid tribute to him for his epoch-making revival of Bach's *St. Matthew Passion*.

And so it remained for many years. After a few terms at university, Mendelssohn was permitted to embark on a Grand Tour lasting almost three years, his journey taking him to England, Italy, and France and not only bringing him into contact with many well-known figures from the world of art and politics but allowing him to perform his works and get to know the music of other composers. In Paris, for example, he stumbled upon Meyerbeer's *Robert le diable*, only for him to dismiss it as "cold and heartless." Its music, in particular, was said to lack "warmth and truth."[1]

Wagner, who spent the greater part of his life complaining about the "poverty" of his parental home,[2] found himself in Paris a few years after Mendelssohn, but his journey there was no primrose path, for he was flee-

ing from his Baltic creditors. And even after he had been appointed kapellmeister to the royal court of Saxony in 1843, he continued to lag far behind his rival in terms of his fame and achievements. His elder by only four
years, Mendelssohn was not only principal conductor of the Gewandhaus
concerts in Leipzig but—from June 1841—conductor to the Dresden court,
a post that involved no full-time commitments. But what would have become of Wagner if Mendelssohn had decided at that time to take on a permanent position in Dresden?

During their lifetime, the two men managed to avoid getting in each
other's way. Rather the opposite, in fact: Wagner was full of praise for
St. Paul when it was performed in Dresden in 1843, while Mendelssohn
commented appreciatively on *Der fliegende Holländer* at the time of its first
performance in Berlin in 1844. Two years later he conducted the *Tannhäuser*
overture at one of his Gewandhaus concerts. Moreover, the two composers shared common ground in respect of their views on art and politics:
both of them longed for a new type of German opera that would be taken
seriously. They also promoted serious concert programs. Nor were they
afraid of Beethoven's Ninth. And they did everything in their power to encourage competent professional musicians who were passionate about their
work. In turn this led them to introduce a number of reforms designed to
improve the standing of professional musicians.

It was only when Mendelssohn died in 1847 that this situation changed
in unedifying ways. In 1850, in his essay "Jews in Music," Wagner held up
his colleague as a classic example of the way in which "a Jew may have the
amplest store of specific talents, may claim as his own the finest and most
varied culture and the highest and most delicate sense of honor, and yet
never be able—even with the help of all these advantages—to call forth in
us that deep and affecting effect that we surely expect from art."[3] During
his Bayreuth years, when he was never at a loss for a crude and coarse expression, Wagner compared Mendelssohn to "certain apes who, so gifted
when young, become stupid as their strength increases."[4] Even so, he continued to praise his rival's concert overtures as finely wrought genre scenes.
A particular passage in the *Fingal's Cave* overture, for example, he found
"tremendously beautiful, ghostly."[5] And there was a certain irony to his
comment in 1871, when he was working on a "big aria for Hagen, but only
for the orchestra": "It is incredible what a bungler I am—I can't transcribe
at all. [. . .] Mendelssohn would raise his hands in horror if he ever saw me
composing."[6]

Two years earlier, in 1869, Wagner had expressed the view that

Mendelssohn's complicated position in the musical life of his age entitled him to a certain sympathy, which was not the case with "today's musical bankers who are sprung from the school of Mendelssohn or who are commended to the world by dint of his personal patronage." Despite—or because of—their "elegant polish,"[7] these were conductors who banked on the music's outer brilliance and ultimately, therefore, on their own success. Like real-life bankers, they produced nothing of value but merely kept music in circulation as if it were some commodity. As a result, music was of value only as a form of exchange—above and beyond the disagreeable anti-Semitic context, this remains a sore point in terms of every kind of commercial concert-giving today.

By way of a contrapuntal rejoinder, we may end by quoting a critical comment made by Mendelssohn when discussing the soprano soloist in the acclaimed first performance of his oratorio *Elijah*: "Everything was sung so daintily, so pleasingly, so elegantly, so messily, so soullessly and so mindlessly that the music acquired a kind of charming expression that drives me mad even to think about it now."[8]

A caricature by one of Wagner's friends in Paris, Ernst Benedikt Kietz, dating from 1840–41 and anticipating basic themes of later cartoons of the composer: his imperious attitude, the woman's long-suffering role, financial difficulties, the material power of music, and the imaginative nature of the total artwork. A playbill held by demons predicts that by 1950 there will have been 3,790 performances of Wagner's works, a figure far outstripped by reality. (Photograph courtesy of the Nationalarchiv der Richard-Wagner-Stiftung, Bayreuth: N 2468.)

CHAPTER TWO

The Blandishments of Grand Opera

DAS LIEBESVERBOT AND *RIENZI*

Wagner conducting "loose-limbed fashionable French
operas" — *Das Liebesverbot* — His later attempt to distance
himself from this early work — A "frivolous" plot in the spirit of
"Young Germany" — Minna Planer — "Political" compositions —
Enthusiasm for "mass outbursts" of popular anger in the years
between 1830 and 1848 — The tragic "archetypal scenario" and
the comic *Liebesverbot* — The opera's disastrous premiere in
March 1836 — Wagner and Minna married in Königsberg —
Minna runs away — Bulwer-Lytton's novel *Rienzi* — Wagner
and his wife reconciled — Musical director in Riga — Debts —
Escape from the Baltic — Rienzi, a charismatic tribune of
the people — Hitler's admiration for the role — "A political
game of cowboys and Indians" — Wagner's characterization
of his hero — His aversion to "singing idiots" — Wilhelmine
Schröder-Devrient as his ideal singer — His views on singers
and actors — Meyerbeer and grand opera — *Les Huguenots* as a
"drama of ideas" — Cosima's failed attempt to turn *Rienzi* into
a music drama — Papo whistling a tune from *Rienzi* — Rienzi's
Prayer — Adriano's bravura aria — Adriano as a trouser role

The "sacred seriousness" of *Die Feen* was immediately followed by the
"frivolousness" of *Das Liebesverbot* (The Ban on Love) — or so Wagner
was to view the situation from the standpoint of two decades later. Back
in 1835, the then twenty-two-year-old musical director of Heinrich Bethmann's touring opera troupe was working on his third opera. The company
was based in Magdeburg but was visiting Bad Lauchstädt when Wagner
made his debut in the August of that year. It was a difficult time for all
concerned, albeit one that was typical of the age, for at this date in the
country's history there were permanent companies only in the larger towns
and cities. Wagner, too, was soon to be thrown in at the deep end. New
singers were hired and fired at short notice, and he was required to bring

to Bethmann's provincial company something of the glamour of the Paris Opéra described in such enthusiastic terms in the arts pages of the German newspapers of the period. "Rehearsing and conducting those loose-limbed fashionable French operas, with the piquant prurience of their orchestral effects, often gave me childish pleasure when, from my position at the conductor's desk, I was able to let go," Wagner recalled in *A Communication to My Friends*, his account lacking nothing in graphic realism.[1]

By the time he was working on *Parsifal*, his earlier memories were colored by a sense of reserve that almost smacks of bigotry, at least as transmitted by Cosima:

> When I say I like the Overture to *Die Feen* better, R. observes that the other (*L.-Verb.*) shows more talent. He searches out a few passages, but apart from the "*Salve Regina*" [the duet, no. 3, that anticipates the religious worlds of *Tannhäuser* and *Parsifal*] he finds it all "horrible," "execrable," "disgusting."—It is well orchestrated, he says—"That I could do in my mother's womb."[2]

One would dearly like to know if Wagner really expressed himself in such dismissive terms or whether Cosima somehow added to the acerbic quality of his comments in the pages of her diary. This is certainly possible, but so, too, is the alternative explanation, whereby Wagner was particularly keen to distance himself from his early opera in the presence of the high priestess of his art.

Anyone listening to *Das Liebesverbot* in the light of one hundred and eighty years of musical history may be reminded not so much of the title of Shakespeare's *Much Ado about Nothing* but rather of his comedy *Measure for Measure*, which was the source of Wagner's libretto. In other words, the work is more than passably written when compared with the efforts of his contemporaries. The "flickering, prickling restlessness" that he later associated with the score and that he ascribed to French and Italian models[3] was a quality he still found so appealing in 1840 that he sought by every means in his power to have the work performed in the Paris of Meyerbeer, Halévy, and Donizetti. While he was working on *Das Liebesverbot*, he was clearly fascinated by Auber's *La muette de Portici* and Bellini's *I Capuleti e i Montecchi*, although little would be gained by scouring vocal scores in search of passages that might have served as detailed models for Wagner's comic opera, for even at this early date he was already adept at skillfully incorporating heterogeneous elements into his works. According to his own much later admission, even the final scene of *Tristan und Isolde* contains traces of Bellini (music example 1).[4]

1. Bars 3–5 of Alaide's *Scena e romanza* ("È sgombro il loco") from act 1 of Bellini's *La straniera*.

Wagner's aim in writing his new opera was to sound modern and elegantly cosmopolitan, for he had only recently turned his back on the provincialism of German romantic opera in an essay published in the *Zeitung für die elegante Welt* on June 10, 1834. Here he had argued that neither Spohr nor Weber knew "how to treat song."[5] In spite of this, *Das Liebesverbot* not only breathes a French and Italian spirit that in the overture sounds even a little effortful and overexcited, it also contains numbers that are emphatically "German" in character. Note, for example, the Beethovenian and Weberian passage for Mariana in A-flat major in the second-act finale (music example 2):

> Welch wunderbar' Erwarten,
> Gefühl voll Lust und Schmerz,
> ich zieh' für eine andre
> den Gatten an mein Herz.

[What wondrous expectation, a sense of joy and smart, I draw for another woman my husband to my heart.]

2. Mariana's A-flat major solo from the second-act finale of *Das Liebesverbot*.

In writing *Das Liebesverbot*, Wagner hoped to throw open the gates on another world while avoiding the danger of being branded French or Italian. His music was not to be instantly pigeonholed as an example of grand opera or *opéra comique* but to display his original genius. His lifelong fear of being misunderstood in this respect emerges from a nightmare that he suffered in June 1872, when he dreamed about a performance of *Tannhäuser* in Vienna:

> Suddenly, after Elisabeth's exit, he heard a cabaletta being sung which he had found inserted in the theater score and had cut; speechless with rage, he leaped onto the stage and there encountered his sister-in-law, Elise Wagner, who said to him, "But it all sounds very lovely," while he, searching desperately for words, at last said loudly and clearly, "You swine!" and woke up.[6]

As for the plot of *Das Liebesverbot*, the later Wagner simply dismissed it all as "frivolous." His "grand comic opera," he insisted, dated from a period when he had broken free from his family's sheltering hearth and, sensing the bohemian in himself, was enjoying the "motley life of the theater,"[7] indulging in intimate relationships with singers in his company and courting its most attractive and successful leading actress, Minna Planer. Initially spurned, he still found it in him to boast to his friend Theodor Apel: "You should also get Fräulein *Planer*—she has already given me a couple of moments of sensual transfiguration."[8] A year later, when he was feeling more confident of victory, he asked Apel: "What do you think? If I were to deceive her on purpose, would that not be a masterpiece of deception on my part? Or should I become a philistine?"[9]

That in spite of its adolescent aspects, this liberal attitude also had a political dimension to it is clear from the exclamation "Long live Young Germany" that occurs in an earlier letter to Apel.[10] Associated with artists and intellectuals, the Young Germany movement had not only nailed its colors to the mast of greater liberalism, it also proposed the idea of social reform in general. One of the movement's spokesmen was Heinrich Laube, a friend of the family and editor in chief of the influential *Zeitung für die elegante Welt*, whose support of the politically active student societies of the time and attempts to foment discontent with the reactionary German Confederation resulted in periodic stretches in prison, prompting Wagner to inquire of Apel: "How are things with *Laube*?—I think of him constantly and am very much afraid for his wellbeing."[11]

The power of censorship was something that Laube had to face every day of his working life and which was shortly to affect Wagner, too. According to his much later account in his autobiography, the municipal authorities in Magdeburg agreed to the first performance of his new opera, *Das Liebesverbot oder Die Novize von Palermo* (The Ban on Love, or The Novice of Palermo) only on condition that it was staged under the abbreviated title of *The Novice of Palermo*. Although there is some doubt as to the reliability of Wagner's recollection of these events,[12] what is beyond question is that it accurately reflects the political climate of an age when a title such as *The Ban on Love* could trigger a defensive response on the part of the authorities.

If the official in question had looked at Wagner's libretto in detail, he would indeed have found reasons to be suspicious, for the ban is enacted by Friedrich, a German governor on the island of Sicily who is depicted in an altogether unsympathetic light: during the annual carnival he calls down the full rigor of the law on all illicit liaisons and amorous goings-on, only to be exposed in turn as a hypocrite and lawbreaker. But in response to his fatalistic demand "Judge me according to my own law," the populace exclaims: "No! The law is repealed! We mean to be more merciful than you!" And since the opera is concerned with glorifying "free love," the novice Isabella is allowed to renounce her life as a nun and sink into the arms of her admirer, Luzio.

In Shakespeare's *Measure for Measure*, the conflict is resolved thanks to the intervention of the Duke of Vienna. In Wagner's case, conversely, the denouement is brought about by a popular revolution, a change that Wagner specifically stressed as a feature of his libretto[13] and that is significant for two reasons. First, he reveals himself in this way as a champion of the July Revolution that broke out in Paris in 1830, prompting him to write in his autobiography: "The world of history came alive to me from that day on; and naturally I became a fervent partisan of the revolution, which I now regarded as an heroic, popular and victorious struggle, unstained by the terrible excesses of the first French revolution."[14] When the effects of the July Revolution first made themselves felt in Saxony, Wagner wrote his "Political Overture" (WWV 11), a work that is no longer extant, and shortly afterward he composed two polonaises for the piano (WWV 23) as an expression of his enthusiasm for the wars of liberation waged by the Poles in their attempt to throw off the czarist yoke. Conversely, an opera on the subject of the Polish freedom fighter Tadeusz Kościuszko that Laube had suggested came to nothing.

In all of this, Wagner was a true child of the *Vormärz*—the period in German history between the Congress of Vienna of 1814–15 and the March Revolution of 1848. He was born to the sound of cannon fire during the Napoleonic Wars of Liberation and sympathized with the many volunteers who freed their princes from the burden of Napoleonic tyranny but who were now waiting in vain for the fruits of their actions: instead of liberty, equality, and fraternity they knew only despotism, repression, and censorship, a state of affairs all too familiar to composers such as Beethoven, Schubert, Liszt, and Schumann. At the same time, however, Wagner's sympathy for the revolutionary movements of the period was very much in line with the tenets of Young Germany, being anything but concerned with class warfare or even social change, but representing a kind of student cultural revolution with a streak of libertine sensuality.

This interpretation of the situation is confirmed by Wagner's own account of political conditions in Leipzig in 1830:

> The undergraduates, who had been in a state of turmoil for some days, assembled one night in the market square [. . .], the proceedings being marked by a certain measured solemnity that impressed me deeply: they sang *Gaudeamus igitur*, formed columns, and marched determinedly off, reinforced by all other young men who sympathized with them, heading for the university building to spring the arrested students from their cells there. My heart beat wildly as I marched with them to this storming of the Bastille.[15]

Fascinated by the "purely demonic element in such mass outbursts," the seventeen-year-old Wagner also took part in the storming of a brothel that enjoyed the protection of an unpopular local councilor. The next day he woke up "as if from a hideous nightmare," only the sight of a "trophy in the form of a tattered red curtain" reminding him of the previous night's events.[16]

Wagner's youthful advocacy of "free love" seems like a theatrical prelude to *Das Liebesverbot*, the subject matter of which reflects the progressive thinking of the Young Germans: art and culture were well suited to promoting the social trend toward freedom and progress, ideals that would then be taken up by the nation and invested with a whole new sense of dynamism. It is because of this that *Das Liebesverbot* is the first and last of Wagner's stage works to manage—by and large—without a hero. Instead, it relies above all on the common people to resolve the conflict that is inherent in its plot.

This essentially optimistic idea for social change is clad in the guise of a comedy whose music echoes the fashionable style of the age. Other composers would have regarded this approach as self-evident, but for the later Wagner it represented a fall from grace and a departure from the straight and narrow path of his true vocation, with its commitment to higher ideals and its quest for metaphysical truth. Although this may strike some readers

as inflated, it is impossible not to admire the resolve with which Wagner
went on to pursue this belief in his own mission and to rise above the level
of the ideas contained in *Das Liebesverbot*.

Free love was, of course, to play a triumphant role in Wagner's later
works, not least in the fate of the siblings Siegmund and Sieglinde.
But whereas tragedy was later to become the dominant mode, in *Das
Liebesverbot* Wagner resolves the contradiction between desire and fulfillment inherent in his archetypal scenario by opting for a happy ending in the
spirit of the traditional *commedia dell'arte*. And in the character of the prud-
ish governor Friedrich he holds up a German to public ridicule. In short,
the Wagner of the post-*Holländer* period was no longer interested in the
"un-German" frivolousness of *Das Liebesverbot*.

The Magdeburg premiere of *Das Liebesverbot* took place in adverse
circumstances in March 1836. According to Wagner's later account in *A
Communication to My Friends*, the first-night audience failed to understand
the subject matter—so important to the composer at this time—because
of its "wholly unclear presentation,"[17] and, according to *My Life*, a second
performance was prevented from taking place by a fistfight among the
cast.[18] Although this version of events may be anecdotally exaggerated, it
does at least reflect Wagner's disgust at the thought of having to work with
third-rate actors for any length of time. It was at this juncture that by a
fortunate coincidence Minna Planer received an attractive offer of work in
Königsberg, whither Wagner accompanied her, only to find himself unemployed. The couple were married in November 1836, although this served, in
fact, to make the situation worse, for Minna—almost four years older than
Wagner—now had to accept liability for her husband's debts and stand by
while the local court impounded their furniture, leaving her feeling so buf-
feted by the ill wind of fate that after six months of married life she fled to
her parents in Dresden—apparently in the company of an admirer.

Falling lamentably short of the ideals of the permissive Young Germans,
Wagner set off in pursuit of his errant wife, his personal misfortune paradoxically bearing artistic fruit when he began to read Edward Bulwer-
Lytton's novel *Rienzi: The Last of the Roman Tribunes* and felt impelled to
turn it into a new "grand heroico-tragic opera." Writing retrospectively, he
claimed that

> from the misery of our private lives in the modern world, from which I
> could glean not even the slightest subject suitable for artistic treatment,
> I was carried away by the idea of a grand historical and political event, in

savoring which I would surely find a salutary distraction from cares and conditions that could strike me only as utterly fatal to art.[19]

In the autumn of 1837 the Wagners—now back together again—moved to Riga, where Wagner took up the post of musical director at the town's recently reorganized theater. In general, the conditions seemed tolerable, although he was required to cut his cloth according to the tastes of his superior, Karl von Holtei, a writer famous in his day as the inventor of the popular genre of the *Liederspiel*, a kind of sentimental comedy with vocal numbers. It was to please Holtei that Wagner drafted the libretto for a comic opera, *Männerlist größer als Frauenlist oder Die glückliche Bärenfamilie* (Men's Cunning Greater Than Women's, or The Happy Family of Bears, WWV 48). He even began to set the opening numbers to music—the sketches have recently resurfaced in the form of an autograph short score—but then he realized "with horror that I was once again on the way to composing music à la Auber; my spirit and my deeper feelings were desperately hurt by this discovery."[20]

This was the beginning of the end for Wagner, who now not only turned down commissions that seemed unworthy of him but was even reluctant to perform the duties that he shared with a second conductor. In spite of a handful of interesting productions, including Bellini's *Norma*, Meyerbeer's *Robert le diable*, and Joseph Weigl's *Die Schweizerfamilie*, his position grew steadily worse. In his heart of hearts he saw himself not as a kapellmeister but as the composer of a grand opera that would eclipse all that had gone before it and outstrip the resources of a provincial house like Riga's. He had brought with him to the town his prose draft of his new work, *Rienzi, der Letzte der Tribunen* (Rienzi, the Last of the Tribunes), and now he set about working it up into a libretto and setting it to music. By the time he arrived in Paris in September 1839, two of the opera's five acts were essentially complete.

Initially intended for Berlin, the opera was modeled on Spontini's *Fernand Cortez*. It was a bold idea on Wagner's part to challenge Berlin's general music director on his own home ground, and when such a scheme proved impracticable, Wagner adopted the no less impudent alternative of throwing down the gauntlet to Giacomo Meyerbeer, the absolute ruler of the genre of grand opera. Since this meant moving to Paris, Wagner had the libretto of *Rienzi* translated into French while he was still working on the score.

Holtei's retirement offered the directors of the Riga theater the welcome chance to dispense with the services of their music director, whose one desire was now to establish himself in Paris and overcome Minna's "shocked" reaction to his plan.[21] She was now appearing only infrequently in Riga and took her leave of local audiences with four guest performances, while Wagner himself took French lessons. Throughout this period, however, his debts had been building up and by then had reached the point where only flight and subterfuge could help, a flight that turned out not only to be adventurous but also protracted and extremely dangerous, not least when Minna was thrown from their carriage and "robbed of the joys of incipient motherhood,"[22] to quote from the reminiscences of Minna's illegitimate daughter Natalie, who throughout her life was passed off as Minna's younger sister.

Their escapade began in the Russian resort of Mitau (now Jelgava), where the Riga company was holding its summer season. The season ended on July 7, 1839, and the very next day Wagner and his wife set off to cross the closely guarded Russian border with the help of a friend from Königsberg. The presence of their Newfoundland, Robber, meant that they were unable to travel by stagecoach, and so they persuaded the captain of a topsail schooner to smuggle them aboard in the port of Pillau in East Prussia. Since Wagnerians also include experts on maritime history, we know that the *Thetis* was carrying a cargo of 192.7 tons of oats and peas, with a seven-man crew under a Captain Wulff.[23]

But instead of rearranging deckchairs on the deck of the *Thetis*, we would do better to glance at the creative miracle of the period that Wagner spent in Königsberg and Riga, for however skeptical we may be about Wagner's constant attempts to massage our view of his own creativity, it is fascinating to observe the extent to which the "wildest anarchy" of his existence and the extreme "misery" of his "private life in the modern world" not only failed to frustrate his mission but positively inspired him. Of course, the word "mission" is particularly problematical in the case of *Rienzi*, given Hitler's well-known fondness for the work and his alleged claim, following a performance of the piece in Linz: "In that hour it began."[24]

Needless to add, a work about a charismatic tribune of the people cursing the scene of his failure and, with it, his whole nation at the very moment of his downfall, was very much after Hitler's own heart. And even if we take account of the fact that from a modern democratic perspective Wagner's *Rienzi* is a figure of total integrity, it is still hard to free the work from the contamination of National Socialist ideology.

Wagner's art is certainly not located in a world beyond good and evil, and, turning on its head a remark by Goethe's Mephistopheles, we may even be tempted to toy with the notion that we are dealing with a force that aspires to good but ends up creating evil. And yet we cannot deny that Wagner was forever seeking "good," and this is also true of the period when he was working on *Rienzi*, when he tired overnight of the Young German belief in the here and now and demanded a more nutritional sustenance for his soul. Even so, it is not the quest itself that is so interesting, but the manner in which Wagner found what he was looking for, especially in terms of his subject matter and libretto.

It is significant that in general Wagner did not invite an experienced librettist such as Eugène Scribe to choose and elaborate his texts—throughout this period Scribe worked on all of Meyerbeer's international successes, from *Robert le diable* and *Les Huguenots* to *Le prophète* and *L'africaine*, as well as collaborating on Boieldieu's *La dame blanche*, Auber's *La muette de Portici* and *Fra Diavolo*, Verdi's *Les vêpres siciliennes* and Halévy's *La juive*, in every case contributing to their composers' lasting fame. True, Wagner himself tried to make contact with Scribe in 1836 when he was planning *Die hohe Braut* (The High-Born Bride, WWV 40) and would certainly have been happy to have received Scribe's support at this early date in his career. But the contact came to nothing. This approach did not, however, affect his impulse to rely above all on his own resources and to choose subjects that reflected his own view of the world, a view best understood as the one expressed by Friedrich Schleiermacher, who was writing in the spirit of early romanticism and who categorized such a conviction as "the totality of all the impressions that contribute toward a single entity in our consciousness when raised to the highest degree."[25]

Two of Wagner's German contemporaries, Schumann and Mendelssohn, emulated him to the extent that they, too, declined to accept offers from outside but turned German literature upside down in their attempts to find an attractive, ethnically cleansed subject. The basic difference between them is that Schumann's endless search culminated in an opera—*Genoveva*—that is important more for its music than for its plot, while Mendelssohn foundered endlessly on scruples such as these.

Wagner's approach was very different, and there was something almost reckless about the way he tackled Bulwer-Lytton's novel, a work that coincidentally also inspired the twenty-year-old Friedrich Engels to draft a scenario at this time. In Engels's case, however, the play remained unfinished. For Wagner, the historical figure of the fourteenth-century people's tribune was a great tragic hero who fought not only for himself but for the freedom of his people as well. Even more so than with *Das Liebesverbot*,

Wagner's archetypal scenario is politically colored: "Rome is the name of my bride," Rienzi proclaims as he names the only love of his life. But it is a love that remains unrequited. Again the difference with *Das Liebesverbot* is instructive, for here the common people, egged on by the aristocracy and cowed by the church, stabs the hero in the back, leading ultimately to disaster when the Capitol goes up in flames. Just before Rienzi and his sister are killed by a falling beam, our hero curses the Eternal City and its "degenerate people." The similarities with the end of *Götterdämmerung* are plain, for here, too, Wagner examines the question of apparently selfless political endeavor, this time against an all-encompassing mythic background: Rienzi is reborn and then slain in the figure of Siegfried.

Of course, it should not be forgotten that the leading representatives of grand opera—Spontini and Meyerbeer—were similarly setting store by major historical themes at this time and applying their by no means negligible skill to examining individual fates within the context of overriding historical movements. The age and its audiences demanded such grandiose designs. In 1841 the Braunschweig writer Wolfgang Robert Griepenkerl published a musical narrative under the title *Das Musikfest oder die Beethovener* (The Music Festival or The Beethovenians). For all its fantastical ideas, it contains a coherent program: "Art, then, is no longer the condemned man's little bell but the great bell of nations echoing across the centuries."[26] As a result, the unconventional Griepenkerl praised Meyerbeer's operas for want of any alternative—he had not yet heard of Wagner.

Like his rivals, Wagner naturally wanted *Rienzi* to attract an audience, but he refused to sell himself in order to achieve this aim. As a result, his Rienzi is not painted in garish colors but is a subtly drawn psychological portrait, more of an unstable if charismatic figure than a political leader capable of getting what he wants. Joachim Kaiser's witticism to the effect that Rienzi is a "fantastic tenor role in a political game of cowboys and Indians on the operatic stage" fails to do justice to Wagner's portrayal and to his critical view of politics.[27] According to Udo Bermbach, we are dealing, rather, with the impressive "theatricalization of a fundamental conflict between personal and institutional rule" and even with an artistic line of argument "about the classic political understanding of revolution." With the exception of the *Ring*, Wagner "never again treated politics in so direct a manner."[28]

Against this background—and it matters little whether, like Bermbach, we adopt a charitable view of the work or strike a note of mockery like Kaiser or allow the opera's reception history to color our critical response to it—the somber ending is inevitable. For all the idealism with which Wagner invests his hero, the mere fact that we are dealing with a historical drama that is very much of this world means that there is no scope for transcendental redemption. Such redemption is conceivable, at best, in myth, and even *there* it can come only from the music. Wagner's wife Cosima was so embarrassed by the notion that an opera she loved could end with Rienzi's curse on Rome that after Wagner's death she brought out the first engraved edition of the full score in a version that changed the wording of the ending, so that instead of cursing Rome, Rienzi now gives it his blessing:

> So lang die sieben Hügel Romas stehn,
> So lang die ew'ge Stadt nicht soll vergehn,
> Sollt ihr Rienzi wiederkehren sehn!

> [As long as Rome's seven hills still stand and the Eternal City does not perish, you shall see Rienzi return!]

This is the version that is usually performed today, a wording that does not occur in the edition of his writings that Wagner himself superintended in 1871.

And yet it was in fact Wagner himself who revised the wording when he staged the opera in Berlin in 1847—the change seems to have been made with this production specifically in mind, for both the *Berliner Figaro* and the *Dresdner Tageblatt* report an Italian diplomat complaining about "the opera's dangerous references to conditions in Italy."[29] It is entirely possible that Wagner gave in to pressure from the Berlin court and changed the text accordingly. Even during the negotiations for the first performances in Dresden he had already signaled his willingness to alter passages to which the Catholic court might take exception. And he may also have thought that in cutting Rienzi's curse he was not losing anything substantial. That he evidently felt that the work's ideological heart lay elsewhere emerges from the detailed description of the title role that he sent to the tenor Albert Niemann on the occasion of a production of the opera in Hanover in 1859, while Wagner himself was living in Venice. With the hindsight granted by almost two decades, Wagner writes about the role in terms which, however emotionally overwrought, remain moving in their reading of the part. Describing Rienzi's end, Wagner insists that

> Rome, the fatherland, & freedom now exist in him & him alone. The nation itself knows none of this. [. . .] His downfall is therefore certain. The great purity that he has now gained & his transfigured majesty help to delay

it, but they cannot prevent it from happening. Scarcely has he won over the conspirators outside the church by his all-powerful grandeur & inspiration when everyone recoils before him, appalled & aghast at his excommunication. For he now sees that only his ideal was real, not the nation & its people. He remains great & noble but stands rooted to the spot like a statue, his gaze fixed firmly in front of him in sublime & rapt contemplation, just like his idea, which has likewise turned to stone like some monument that the world cannot understand. But once again the marble melts; Irene throws herself upon his breast. He sees that he is not alone; smiling gently he recognizes his sister & now knows that there is, after all "a Rome." — In his prayer in the 5th act he communes with the God who once spoke to him and who has always spoken to him about that noble idea. It is, as it were, the "idea" that the whole world has failed to understand that now speaks to itself. Nobility, purity, deeply felt religious fervor, the desire for dissemination, finally to be lost entirely within himself, to be totally self-absorbed:—during the postlude to the prayer, therefore, he should incline his head and his whole body to the ground.[30]

I have quoted this passage at length because in many respects it says more about Wagner's artistic intentions than individual stilted sentences from his theoretical writings. Above all, it makes it clear that we cannot draw a distinction between the "political" and the "human." Human beings are politicians, and politicians are human beings. This truism will become even more important when we turn to the characters of the *Ring*, especially Wotan. And the fact that Wagner was already laying the ground for his insight in *Rienzi* helps to make its protagonist more sympathetic than he otherwise appears against the background of the "papier-mâché romanticism" attributed to the opera by the acerbic Italian critic Mario Bortolotto.[31]

At the same time, Wagner's letter to Niemann is a good example of the loving detail with which he portrayed his characters. Mozart, Verdi, and Richard Strauss undoubtedly achieved some wonderful things in terms of the scenic element in their stage works, but on one point Wagner surpasses them all. Whether we interpret it as a strength or a weakness of his art, he depicts his characters step by step, move by move, gesture by gesture. It is clear from the ideas that he proposed to Niemann in 1859—this was when he was working on *Tristan und Isolde*—that his characters needed to be psychologically convincing right down to the very last detail and that they had to be portrayed in a similar fashion. And one can understand why, in spite of his financial problems, he preferred his works not to be performed at all, rather than see them inadequately staged. His fear—expressed on countless occasions—that his works might be badly performed relates less to their musical aspect than to their actual staging. It was in this sense that he repeatedly complained about the "incredible mindlessness and stupidity of our singers and conductors."[32] Even when he was living in Bayreuth and singers were falling over themselves to audition for him, he remained concerned to the point of permanent agitation that he would not be able to find adequate singers for the roles that he had created. "Where am I to find my Hagen with his echoing, bragging voice?" he asked Cosima on July 28, 1871. "The fellows who have such voices turn out to be blockheads."[33] Conversely, he used his essay *On Actors and Singers* to characterize the singer Wilhelmine Schröder-Devrient, whom he had idolized since his youth, with the provocative phrase: "No! She had no 'voice' at all; but she knew how to use her breath so beautifully and to let a true womanly soul stream forth in such wondrous sounds that we never thought of either voice or singing!"[34]

For Wagner, a singer needed to *embody* his or her part, and for this it was not just a question of the singer's professional skills as an actor. Paradoxical though this may sound, it was a question, rather, of metaphysics. What fascinated him about Wilhelmine Schröder-Devrient was her inspired capacity for total "self-surrender."[35] By this, he did not mean the sort of attitude that is explored in modern encounter groups but the ultimate ability to merge as one with the message being presented onstage. This approach demanded that the actor "not only *represents* the action of the fêted hero, but *repeats* its moral lesson; insomuch as he proves by this surrender of his personality that he also, in his artistic action, is obeying a dictate of Necessity which consumes his whole individuality."[36] Such a performer represents not himself but the "free artistic community" of the whole nation; and this nation experiences its own inner life in all its variety in the medium of an art that is interpreted as something religious. Such art is not at odds with life but allows us to experience our physicality and sensuality to their very highest potential.

The cultic nature of this view of the role of the actor and singer reflects Wagner's understanding of Attic tragedy. We do not need to share it ourselves to suspect what it meant for him. If the singing actor was unable to depict something in the spirit of the musical drama, then this "something" was also worthless and, indeed, insignificant as an "idea." A letter that Wagner wrote to Liszt in May 1852 still echoes the sense of outrage he had felt in October 1845 when Joseph Tichatschek had proved so ineffectual in the title role of *Tannhäuser*. Having "no inkling of his task as a dramatic performer," he was unwilling or unable to sing the top A on the words "Erbarm' dich mein" (Have pity on me) in the second act with the necessary "ecstatic contrition,"[37] with the result that Wagner was obliged to cut a passage that he felt was "central to the whole drama."

Wagner was not angry with Tichatschek for any lack of "material means" with which to sing this passage but because thanks to his "preternaturally small cranial capacity" he failed to grasp its meaning. In consequence the tenor lacked the ability "to pour out the text with his entire being—regardless of whether it was by vocal means or any other." Seven years after the event Wagner was still able to get worked up at this failing: "I don't possess even a fraction of his voice, yet I can produce a splendid A at this point! Of course this A doesn't demand to be *sung* but must be hurled forth by the singer straining every sinew of his breast, like a sword with which Tannhäuser intends to kill himself." "All attempts to parley" with the singer having failed, Wagner simply gritted his teeth and cut the passage in question.[38] But once he had assumed control in Bayreuth, he had more success in persuading his singers to regard the drama, the music, and the staging as integral parts of a single whole and to demonstrate the requisite passion in committing themselves to the decisive moments in the drama in their role as singing actors.

By examining this subject in my chapter on *Rienzi*, I hope to do justice to the opera within the context of Wagner's creative development. Whimsical dismissals of the work as "a political game of cowboys and Indians" and as "papier-mâché romanticism" completely miss the point, for Wagner gave far more serious thought to the political background of the plot than we normally expect from a librettist or a composer. From this point of view he was very much a political animal.

On the other hand, the opera fails to pack any punch at all if it is dissected along politological lines, no matter how well-meaning such a surgical incision may be. Until he began to work on the *Ring*, Wagner invariably placed the human above the political and set the greatest store by an effective drama. This was his starting point when he set out to explain the role of Rienzi to Niemann or accused Tichatschek of failing to understand the part of Tannhäuser. Here, too, we find Wagner's strengths: as we have already noted, Rienzi is far more subtly drawn as a character than a superficial observer may realize. And only by ensuring that his characters and the situations in which they find themselves are credibly portrayed in compelling psychological detail could Wagner motivate his performers to be consumed by the truth of their roles in terms of their singing, acting, and gestures. The large number of crowd scenes in *Rienzi* tends to obscure our appreciation of the fact that from this point of view, the work is closer to its successor, *Der fliegende Holländer*, than it is to its predecessor, *Das Liebesverbot*.

What is it, then, that *Rienzi* lacks to make it truly great? In comparison to its potential rivals, the answer is not very much. The quip—attributed to Hans von Bülow—that *Rienzi* is Meyerbeer's best opera is nothing if not shallow, for if we regard Meyerbeer's *Les Huguenots* of 1836 as competition, then this last-named work, which was hugely successful in its day, is by no means lacking in ideas in the sense that Wagner understood this term.[39] Moreover, a glance at Meyerbeer's letters and diaries indicates the depth of his interest in the historical background and the extent to which he discussed the precise characterization of the various roles with his distinguished librettist, Eugène Scribe.[40] It is also worth asking whether Scribe and Meyerbeer, working as a team, showed more skill in handling the different strands in the plot and in arranging the crowd scenes than the still inexperienced Wagner was able to do in the case of *Rienzi*.

At best this question can be answered only theoretically, for both *Rienzi* and *Les Huguenots* are bound to strike today's operagoers as historical monstrosities that can no longer be salvaged as dramas of ideas, no matter what twenty-first-century directors may do to cast them in a more interesting light. And if Wagner himself had not recognized this for himself, his next opera would not have been *Der fliegende Holländer*. For it is very much in the nature of grand opera that the pomp and circumstance of its plot and music—Wagner's own description of the onstage music in *Rienzi*[41]—are just as likely to kill the ideas as the lavishness of the sets. And all of this has the explicit approval of audiences who are willing to countenance lofty ideas only so long as they do not impair their enjoyment.

In the twenty-first century this enjoyment is above all musical. And, like it or not, it is concentrated for the most part not on any coherent musical structures but on individual passages of striking beauty and originality. Such passages may be found in both Meyerbeer and Wagner, with Wagner banking in particular on Italianate melodies. Cosima Wagner's decision to champion *Rienzi* after her husband's death was undoubtedly well intentioned, and she was certainly right to claim that "I feel great affection for the work. With it, opera died the love-death of an over-abundance of melody."[42] She was less fortunate when it came to producing the version of the opera that is still usually performed today and that represents an attempt on her part to turn the opera into a music drama by means of clumsy changes to the score, not least the severely mechanical cuts to virtuoso solo passages and the attacca links between numbers designed to blur the outlines of what Wagner had intended as a number opera.

It is not just from today's perspective that such an undertaking is wholly unnecessary, for Wagner himself had already conceived the opera along dramaturgical lines, casting the opening act in the form of a single great scene and largely dispensing with large-scale arias and duets in favor of word-based melodies and succinct musical gestures, while tending to embed the hero's entrances in crowd scenes. That he even shows signs of what Werner Breig has termed a "symphonic technique for the dialogue"[43] does nothing, however, to alter the fact that it is the work's highlights that retain a toehold in the present-day repertory in the form of two solo numbers and the overture. The overture features a "festive theme" that Wagner's Dresden parrot, Papo, used to whistle when he heard his master returning home from work. Perhaps it is the following passage, which sounds strangely disjointed, especially in the wordless overture (music example 3).[44] In the overture this theme is combined with the Rienzi theme in the manner of a development section. Here good old German counterpoint raises its head in the midst of the work's Italianate melodies and verve (music example 4). But almost at once it is whistled back by Papo. Shortly after the first night Wagner cut this contrapuntal passage.

3. Bars 155–58 from the overture to *Rienzi* and (beneath it) bars 1248–51 of the finale to act 2.

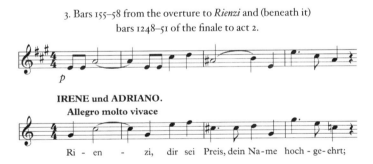

Of the two solo highlights, one is Rienzi's Prayer, "Allmächt'ger Vater" (music example 5) which was a favorite of Berlioz's. In spite of—or because of—its old-fashioned turn (in the musical sense), it is Wagner's first brilliantly inspired idea in a genre that from then on was to be an integral part of his musical thinking: the hymn-like number that raises the onstage action to a higher plane of quasi-religious ecstasy at a prominent point in the score. Of course, such a device is familiar from an earlier period in operatic

Philipp Stölzl's 2010 production of *Rienzi* at the Deutsche Oper in Berlin was inspired by the fact that this was one of Hitler's favorite operas. Not all National Socialists shared that enthusiasm. Indeed, to the extent that the educated middle classes shared a love of Wagner's music dramas, it was his Germanic heroes with whom they tended to identify rather than the Roman tribune. As a result, the idea of locating the entire opera within a National Socialist setting seems a little forced, and the distorted picture of the work presented by Stölzl's production is hard to reconcile with the libretto. The present image depicts the führer's bunker, with its associations of the hero's downfall. (Photograph courtesy of Ullstein Bild—Lieberenz.)

4. Bars 251–58 of the composition draft of the overture to *Rienzi*, showing
a contrapuntal passage that Wagner later struck out, reproduced here
from the appendix to the critical commentary of the score.

history—one thinks of Agathe's "Leise, leise, fromme Weise" from *Der Freischütz*. And it recurs in the later period in Desdemona's "Ave Maria" in Verdi's *Otello*, to cite just a single example. What is original here is that it is a *man* who prays.

The counterpart of this prayer is Adriano's aria "Gerechter Gott." This role was written for a dramatic soprano and was evidently intended from the outset for Wilhelmine Schröder-Devrient, who had particularly impressed Wagner as Romeo in Bellini's *I Capuleti e i Montecchi*. In his later works he would presumably have found it impossible to cast a woman in this "youthfully impassioned man's role," as he called it.[45] But such alienation in terms of vocal casting is all part and parcel of grand opera, a genre in which characters may express their joy in "abstract" coloratura. It is no accident that Wagner's stage action has no genuine "lovers"—Adriano cannot really be regarded as Irene's lover, as she worships her brother above all else, her

5. Bars 67–70 of Rienzi's Prayer from act 5, with the turn written
out in full, first from above, then from below.

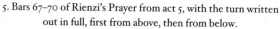

adulation transcending death and, indeed, finding its ultimate expression in her demise. And Rienzi loves only his sister and his "bride," Rome. In creating this character, Wagner explicitly admitted to having "stepped outside the circle of received opinion" and questioned "whether the tenor voice is exclusively suited to the character of a lover." Instead, he wanted a hero "in the fullest sense of the word,"[46] a claim that heralds the birth of what was to become the proverbial "heldentenor."

In answer to the question as to what *Rienzi* lacks as an opera for it to be truly great, we might reply that against the background of French grand opera, it lacks nothing. Only in the context of the demands that Wagner made of himself and of his mission may it be said to lack a good deal, if not everything.

A Word about Giacomo Meyerbeer

An entry in Cosima Wagner's diary for March 30, 1869, mentions the recent republication of her husband's diatribe on "Jews in Music": "R. tells me he recently read somewhere that he had written [the essay] because he envied Mendelssohn his genius and Meyerbeer his success," prompting him to ask: "What, not Hiller his wife?—for he could envy Hiller neither for his genius nor for his success."[1]

As far as Wagner's personal animosities were concerned, this is rich: Ferdinand Hiller was the son of a Jewish businessman and highly regarded throughout Europe as a composer, conductor, and pianist, even being granted a patent of nobility for his services to music, and yet he was no competition for Wagner in the way that Mendelssohn and Meyerbeer were. And it was Meyerbeer's successes that rankled most with Wagner. When the latter sought to gain a foothold in Paris in 1839, it was Meyerbeer—his elder by twenty-two years—who did what he could to help his compatriot. Already internationally renowned as the composer of *Robert le diable* and *Les Huguenots* and the holder of the Prussian order Pour le mérite, Meyerbeer had yet to enjoy his greatest triumph, which did not come until 1849 with the world premiere of *Le prophète*, the receipts for the first ten performances of which at the Paris Opéra amounted to almost 100,000 francs, while the publishing rights brought in another 44,000.

Further honors were quick to follow, including the titles of Chevalier de la
Légion d'honneur, Knight of the Saxon Order of Merit and of the Austrian
Order of Franz Joseph, Commander of the Order of the Württemberg
Crown, Commander (First Class) of the Order of Duke Ernst of Saxony,
an honorary doctorate from the University of Jena, and membership of the
Senate of the Berlin Academy of the Arts.

Meanwhile, Wagner had written a series of letters to Meyerbeer, their
obsequious tone barely mitigated by ironic exaggerations: "The feelings
of gratitude that inspire me toward you, my high-minded patron, know
no bounds. I foresee that from age to age I shall pursue you, stammering
my thanks," we read in a letter written in February 1840.[2] It was at around
this time that Wagner sent his patron a copy of his essay on *Les Huguenots*
that may in fact reflect his genuine admiration for the work: "Meyerbeer
wrote world history, the history of hearts and emotions, he demolished the
barriers of national prejudice, and destroyed the confining boundaries of
linguistic dialects, he wrote deeds of music."[3]

Even as late as 1846, by which date he was working in Dresden as kapellmeister to the royal court of Saxony, Wagner was still writing to Meyerbeer
and professing his "most loyal gratitude and admiration."[4] Secretly, however, his feelings had cooled, and those feelings turned to sheer hatred when
he arrived in Paris in June 1849 as a failed revolutionary with a price on his
head and discovered a city in a state of frenzy inspired by Meyerbeer's new
opera. It was, he believed, a symptom of a capitalist music industry that was
rotten to the core and where there was no place for works like *Tannhäuser*
and *Lohengrin*. In the course of a further flying visit to Paris in February
1850, he attended a performance of *Le prophète*, summing up his reaction in
a letter to one of his Dresden friends, Theodor Uhlig, and holding out the
work's hero, John of Leyden, as the true "prophet of the new world": "I felt
happy and exalted, abandoned all my subversive plans, which struck me as
profane now that the pure, noble, and most holy Truth, together with the
divinely human, lives so directly and warmly in the blessed and immediate
present. [. . .] I can see that I am becoming increasingly fanatical when I
recall that evening of revelation: forgive me!"[5]

Astonishingly, it seems as if practically everyone who has ever written
about Wagner has taken this at face value.[6] But what we find here is pure
contempt, which is why Wagner was able to write to Liszt the following year describing Meyerbeer as "this perpetually kind and obliging man
[who] reminds me of the darkest—I might almost say the most wicked—

period of my life, a period of connections and back-staircases, when we were treated like fools by patrons whom we inwardly despised."[7]

At least to the extent that he was familiar with Wagner's operas, Meyerbeer was not uncomplimentary about them, while Wagner, too, retained a high opinion of certain aspects of his rival's works, even in later years. In *Opera and Drama*, for example, he praises the "wonderfully affecting melody in G-flat major" in the love duet for Raoul and Valentine in act 4 of *Les Huguenots*. It has sprung, he wrote, "like the most fragrant flower from a situation that stirs every fiber of the human heart with blissful anguish."[8] On the other hand, this did not prevent Wagner from striking out two bars in the score of *Parsifal* when they reminded him too clearly of Isabelle's cavatina "Robert, toi que j'aime" from *Robert le diable*.[9]

It remains only to mention one of Wagner's dreams from his years in Bayreuth. He had seen himself in Paris, "walking arm in arm with Meyerbeer, and M. had smoothed for him the paths to fame."[10] By then, Wagner's antithesis had been dead for eight years: Meyerbeer's final diary entry relating to Wagner is dated 1855 and refers to a chance encounter in London: "We greeted each other coldly and without speaking."[11]

This pencil drawing by Ernst Benedikt Kietz depicts Wagner wearing a dressing gown—a favorite piece of apparel—and sporting side whiskers. Completed in June 1842, it was reproduced in newspaper articles in 1843 and on wanted posters in 1849. While living in exile in Switzerland, Wagner arranged for the original to be lithographed and sent copies to friends and admirers in Germany whom he was unable to visit in person. He regarded the expedient as no more than a makeshift solution in view of what he described as his "laboriously and powerfully changed appearance" (SB 4:208). (Photograph courtesy of the Nationalarchiv der Richard-Wagner-Stiftung, Bayreuth: Bi 2321.)

CHAPTER THREE

"Deep shock" and "a violent change of direction"

DER FLIEGENDE HOLLÄNDER

Paris between 1839 and 1842: futile attempts to stage *Das Liebesverbot* and *Rienzi* — Hackwork for the music publisher Maurice Schlesinger — Liszt, Heine, and the Saint-Simonians — *Der fliegende Holländer* — An "outsider" as an alternative to fashionable French grand opera — Heine's *Memoirs of Herr von Schnabelewopski* as the inspiration for the opera — "Redemption through destruction" as a leitmotif — The godless ending of the original — Wagner engaging with the ideas of Baudelaire and Byron — The Dutchman as Senta's vision — Wagner distancing himself from the traditional formal language of opera — Senta's "stage ballad" as the heart of the opera — Wagner's leitmotif technique in embryo — A sense of musical time dictated by myth — Inspired ideas in the overture — Naturalism in the orchestral tone painting — Wagner later distancing himself from his early masterpiece — The freshness and actuality of the opera

There were few other times in Wagner's life when he reacted with such seismographic sensitivity to the conditions in his life and in the age in general as he did with *Der fliegende Holländer*. He had moved to Paris in September 1839 in the hope of finding his fortune in a city that has been described as the "capital of the nineteenth century" but failed to discover it there. Anyone inclined to read an autobiographic element into two of the short stories that he wrote in Paris, "An End in Paris" and "A Happy Evening," will no doubt dismiss their critique of a music industry run along exclusively economic lines as the self-pity of a misprized genius. Yet behind the description of individual fates lie the problems of the age. In his article "On the Situation of Artists and Their Condition in Society" (1835) Liszt had already lamented the "brutal preponderance of material interests," the "petty mercantile egoism" of a large number of artists, and their "lack of faith." It was these ills, he concluded, that were "the great scar on our age."[1] Two decades later Wagner's admirer Charles Baudelaire was to bewail the decline of the modern artist to the point where he became the prostitute of his public.

Between Liszt the Parisian by choice and Baudelaire the archetypal Frenchman, Wagner, newly arrived from the Baltic, cuts an unusual figure. Preferring the company of his fellow countrymen to having his pitiful French ridiculed by the city's prominent musicians, he nonetheless put his shoulder to the wheel, initially trying to capitalize on Meyerbeer's letters of recommendation but quickly being put off or shot down with his ambitious operatic plans, which involved performances of *Das Liebesverbot* and *Rienzi*—he had hurriedly completed the latter in a French translation. All that remained was hackwork in the form of feature articles for Maurice Schlesinger's *Gazette musicale* and August Lewald's *Europa*. He also turned his hand to arranging the latest operas (WWV 62), preparing piano transcriptions for two and four hands, and arranging individual numbers for piano, string or flute quartet, and two violins. In this way he came to know intimately Donizetti's *La favorite* and Halévy's *Le guitarrero* and *La reine de Chypre*. A particularly droll commission, an instruction manual for the *cornet à pistons*, remained unfinished.

Wagner was now twenty-six and felt called to greater things, with the result that he regarded this wearisome labor as a humiliation requiring him to serve the current stars of the operatic scene and present himself at Schlesinger's offices to deliver his completed commissions and receive a new advance. This drudgery continued even after Wagner had taken up his new post as assistant conductor in Dresden, for not all the advance payments that he had received had been worked off, and the arm of his French employers was long.

From the standpoint of operatic history, Wagner's galley years in Paris were by no means unusual, with the result that they deserve neither pity nor gleeful gloating on our part. Anyone wanting to gain a foothold as an opera composer in what was then the cultural capital of Europe could not reckon on doing so overnight. It took Halévy eight years to make his breakthrough in his home city with *La juive* in 1835, while the two non-French composers Meyerbeer and Donizetti had both enjoyed successful careers in Italy before they made a name for themselves in Paris.

Nor do we necessarily have to admire Wagner for reacting to his own failures in the city by criticizing the whole of the Paris musical scene. In this he had at least two distinguished predecessors in Liszt and, to a certain extent, Heinrich Heine. Both Liszt and Heine had been impressed by the Saint-Simonians, who took their name from their *père suprême*, Claude-Henri de Rouvroy, comte de Saint-Simon. Throughout the 1830s everyone who was anyone in Paris flocked to the Salle Taitbout, the headquarters of the movement, where they swore their allegiance to a doctrine aimed at belatedly realizing the goals of the French Revolution. These goals included a greater degree of social responsibility, moral commitment, true religious beliefs, and a love of art. At least in theory the Saint-Simonians demanded the redistribution of property in order to ensure that no one person was exploited by his or her fellow human beings.

It would be interesting to know if Wagner was ever directly involved in the activities of a movement whose ideas he undoubtedly found sympathetic. More fascinating, however, is the show of artistic strength that allowed him to drag himself out of the morass and transcend his "deep shock" at prevailing conditions, leading to a "violent change of direction" as an artist.[2] Of course, *Der fliegende Holländer* does not mark Wagner's definitive farewell to the world of grand opera, for his libretto to *Die hohe Braut* (WWV 40) stills draws on this tradition, and he continued to champion *Rienzi*. But within his output *Der fliegende Holländer* has a revolutionary force comparable only to that of the *Ring* and *Tristan und Isolde*.

Today's music industry appropriates and absorbs whatever it wants, making it hard for us to imagine what it meant for a composer to break out of the order of things with a work like *Der fliegende Holländer* and to swim, as it were, against the tide. Every age has its own specific rhythm, and grand opera was part of the underlying rhythm of the years between 1830 and 1850 in France, when a spirit of restlessness and motley color typified French society. With *Der fliegende Holländer* Wagner abandoned this complex design completely. As he was later to explain in his essay "Music of the Future," "the glamour of the Paris ideal" was now "fading" before his eyes, "and I began to draw the laws of form from a source other than the sea that was spread far and wide before me for general public use."

Even while he was writing the poem, he went on, he had "no longer felt" as he had done when "tossing off the libretto for *Rienzi*, where the only thing I had in mind was an 'opera text' that I could fill as far as possible with all the pre-existent, normative forms of actual grand opera—namely, introductions, finales, choruses, arias, duets, trios and so on." At the same time his choice of subject meant turning his back on the sort of "historical convention" that demanded untold "circumstantial" and "abstruse" details. Instead, he embraced the world of "legend," with its "purely human content": "A ballad, a popular refrain is enough to acquaint us with this character in its most vivid form, and to do so, moreover, in the twinkling of an eye."[3]

In short, Wagner spurned the sort of historical subjects on which grand opera drew its themes in an attempt to demonstrate its seriousness of purpose, an attempt motivated by its desire not just to pay homage to the world of beautiful appearances but to treat "authentic" historical events and in that way provide contemporary society with ample food for thought that would contribute to its own understanding of itself. From this point of view the libretto to *Les Huguenots* is no historical monstrosity. To take a single example: the tragic figure of Marcel indicates the hopelessness and risibility of the defiant attempt to cling to Jacobin ideals in the bourgeois, liberal world of 1830.[4]

The Wagner of *Der fliegende Holländer*, conversely, not only despised the bombast of grand opera, he also refused to share its general tendency to lard its librettos with historical details. Rather, he sought truth in the oceanic depths of legend, where he was drawn to the fate of the mariner who because of his godless existence is obliged to sail the seven seas until the Day of Judgment. Wagner calls him the "Ahasuerus of the seas."[5] His source was Heinrich Heine's version of the legend in his fragmentary picaresque novel *From the Memoirs of Herr von Schnabelewopski*, according to which the Dutchman is redeemed by the love of a woman. But if Wagner borrowed from Heine, he did not do so slavishly. For him, it would have been unthinkable to echo Heine's cynical comment on the climactic redemption motif: "The moral of the tale is that women should beware of marrying a Flying Dutchman; and we men should see from the piece that at best we shall be destroyed by women."[6]

But even for Wagner the "redemption" that the Dutchman is vouchsafed lacks a utopian element: in keeping with his artistic leitmotif, it is "redemption through destruction" that is the work's underlying message. In the original one-act version of the piece this ultimately dark ending is brought out more clearly than in the version that is generally familiar today, lacking, as it does, the harp sonorities that cast the later endings in a more transfigured light. In the original version, the action, too, is similarly bleak — the prose draft of spring 1841 ends with Anna, as Senta is still described here, "calling after the departing Dutchman: 'I know full well that you can be redeemed only by a woman who is faithful to you unto death! Behold! I have been faithful to you until now, until my death!' She leaps into the sea, and at that moment the Dutchman's ship sinks in a trice."[7] Even a decade later, in *A Communication to My Friends*, Wagner was still stressing that Senta was able to redeem the Dutchman "only through her own destruction and his."[8]

In this early version, then, the Dutchman draws Senta down into the watery depths, whereas their roles are later reversed: "Senta raises the Dutchman, pressing him to her breast and pointing heavenward with one of her hands and also with her gaze. The rock has continued to move slowly upward, imperceptibly assuming the shape of a cloud." Thus Wagner's revised stage direction.[9] And yet the harps that enter at this point cannot persuade us that this new ending is anything other than questionable, for the action of the opera includes no sense of development that might justify an apotheosis. Quite the opposite: the existential shock that it triggers is based on a single factor—namely, the doom of the Flying Dutchman, who until then has been condemned to a life of endlessly restless wandering.

Writing to one of his friends in Dresden, Ferdinand Heine, Wagner insisted that the work was "copied from that same nature of which we are all a part" and that it had nothing in common with "modern requirements for piquant situations and unexpected surprises." The result was "so unlike anything we now understand by the term opera" that he had "difficulty explaining" how such an anti-opera might ever find favor with an audience.[10]

Wagner eschews every kind of intrigue of the sort that was felt indispensable in stage works at that date and that was to be an important element of his own later output—at least to the extent that we interpret the term *intrigue* to mean a bringing together of the various strands in a plot and building to a climax. In *Der fliegende Holländer*—a work whose libretto was bound to be regarded by all connoisseurs of French grand opera as démodé—Wagner was uniquely concerned with the truth about modern men and women and, hence, about himself. He says little about the failing that led the Flying Dutchman to curse God but describes him variously as a "fallen angel,"[11] an "Odysseus" figure, and an embodiment of the "Wandering Jew."[12] It is this last-named characterization that probably suits the Flying Dutchman best. All of these metaphors describe members of a society that has lost its way and, plagued by sundry feelings of guilt and anxiety, is good for nothing except its own annihilation. This was a subject that was bound to fascinate Wagner in the "swamps and billows" of his own life.[13] Even during his Zurich period, while Liszt was preparing to give the Weimar premiere of the opera, Wagner was still able to write to his friend: "Good luck with the 'Flying Dutchman'! I can't get this melancholy hero out of my head! I keep hearing 'Ah, spectral man, who can tell when you'll find her!' together with 'One chance remains to gain this poor man his peace and salvation!' But it's too late for this now! For me there's no longer any possibility of redemption, except in *death*!'"[14]

It is in *Der fliegende Holländer* that Wagner's artistic leitmotif of "redemption through destruction" is first formulated in all its clarity. Although he still avails himself of the legendary motif of the redemptive woman who brings about his hero's death, this motif progressively loses its force in the following operas and music dramas. And yet even here the phrase about Senta as the "woman of the future"[15] seems like a bill of exchange that is redeemed neither in the *Ring* nor in *Parsifal*. Unlike their counterparts in *Tannhäuser*, *Lohengrin*, and *Tristan und Isolde*, neither the Dutchman nor Senta demonstrates one jot of affection or love for the other person. Rather, they are at each other's mercy, their only aim being to die together. And whereas the Dutchman remains from start to finish in his state of existential impotence, Senta's "feat" in this initial version of the opera consists simply in leaping after him and throwing herself in the sea. If Senta is the glorious "woman of the future," is it only because she finds fulfillment in perishing, spectacularly, with the Dutchman rather than engaging in a "worldly" affair with Erik?

Baudelaire was unequivocal in welcoming Wagner's decision to opt for a somber ending, and in his essay on *Tannhäuser*—his artistic testament—he describes the creator of *Der fliegende Holländer* as a kindred soul, cut off from God, torn between the world of dreams and real life, and condemned to achieve at best a negative goal in the guise of death.[16]

That in his revisions to the work, Wagner—afraid of his own courage—at least hints at the possibility of a visionary ending does nothing to alter the fact that there is a magnificent godlessness to the earlier version that has its counterpart in Byron's monodrama *Manfred*, a work which Schumann was later to set to music and, much to Nietzsche's annoyance, likewise invest with a conciliatory ending by having God-fearing monks recite the words "Requiem aeternam" over the eponymous hero as he dies a godless death.[17] In Wagner's *Ur-Holländer*, "black" romanticism is taken to such lengths that if the work were to be staged in this spirit all sense of metaphysics would vanish as if into a black hole—in the hundreds of other adaptations of the subject there is ultimately at least a faint trace of a merciful or just God looking down on all the horrors of the story.

We can propose a psychological interpretation of the story of the Flying Dutchman, as Liszt did in 1854 when he drew a parallel between Wagner's

Senta and Honoré de Balzac's Marie-Angélique de Vandenesse in his novel *Une fille d'Ève*: "Each is bound to a kind and loving man whose qualities appear as if they must surely contribute to her happiness," and yet both women abandon themselves

> first to a dreamy sympathy, but then to a violent passion for a human being who, feared by all and shunned like some doom-laden apparition, stands outside their own particular world, offering them only fear, anguish, and renunciation, his bold spirit holding them in thrall as if by some spell so unbreakable that they are willing to suffer pain and misery and even death for him.[18]

The reader may care to go a step further and see the Dutchman as "Senta's vision," as the director Harry Kupfer has done. When staging the work in Berlin in 2001, he argued that "the piece is a psychological bourgeois drama, not a grand romantic opera."[19] But is this anything more than a bon mot? After all, Wagner knew very well why—in spite of his opposition to the current operatic scene—he described the work as a "romantic opera" in his autograph libretto, his autograph score, the first lithographed edition, and consistently thereafter: for him, the character of Senta was just as much a part of the legend as the Dutchman, a legend whose truth is independent of the fate of a single individual. In writing *Der fliegende Holländer*, Wagner made no attempt to invest the plot or the music with a psychological dimension, as he was to do in the *Ring*. And if it *is* a "psychological bourgeois drama," how would it be if we were to reverse the roles and stage the work in such a way that the Dutchman appears wearing Wagner's mask and Senta is seen as his "vision"? And if we are to believe a study published in 1911 by one of Freud's pupils, Max Graf, Senta would have to appear wearing the mask of Wagner's mother, Johanna Rosine, whom Graf claims was the object of the young Wagner's Oedipal desires, desires that the adult artist then transferred to the figure of Senta.[20]

Ultimately attempts to distinguish between dreams and reality do not advance us one iota, for the bewildering interaction between two categories that are only apparently unequivocal is all part of the romantic outlook to which Wagner subscribed in *Der fliegende Holländer* more uncompromisingly than at any other time of his life. Which of the characters is "more true to real life" in E. T. A. Hoffmann's unfinished novel *Tomcat Murr*: the bigoted tomcat grumbling about education or the insane kapellmeister Johannes Kreisler, who sports a collar in E major to go with the wardrobe disaster of his coat in C-sharp minor?

Finally, the music comes into play—and for Hoffmann and for Wagner's contemporaries, music was the romantic art par excellence. According to the romantics, paintings had the disadvantage of being a mere copy of nature, while the idea of an alternative "as if" invariably and inevitably colored our views of every stage presentation. Music, conversely, was simply that which it was at the very moment it was heard. And it was in the immediacy of its presence that its higher reality was to be found. For now, Wagner was still unable to translate this conviction into actions in the fullest sense of the term, but even so—and for the first time in his output—he glimpsed an idea to which he was to give theoretical expression only a few years later in *Opera and Drama*, where he writes that no one wanting to create a musical drama should abide by the conventions of "opera" as a genre and pour his or her musical ideas into the rigid forms of recitative, aria, duet, ensemble, and so on. Rather, such an artist is faced by the challenge of bringing the action to the listener's "feeling" in a way that is both more direct and more flexible than can be achieved by either the spoken theater or by traditional opera, with all its formal, shackling requirements.

Wherein lies the difference between *Der fliegende Holländer* and pre-Wagnerian operas like those by Mozart? On the one hand, Wagner pays almost unqualified homage to a composer whom he described as "the spirit of light and love,"[21] insisting that in his eyes works like *Le nozze di Figaro* and *Don Giovanni* were "perfect" in every way[22] and never for a moment tiring of the arias that Lilli Lehmann would sing for him at musical soirées in Bayreuth in the 1870s.[23] On the other hand, much about Mozart's operas is conventional. On those occasions where this conventionality "suits the subject" and reflects the "noisy confusion of the high-spirited comedy of intrigue,"[24] as it does in *Le nozze di Figaro*, then it is not disruptive. But a composite work like *Die Zauberflöte*, created for a suburban theater in Vienna and thus a product of its age, could no longer be galvanized back into life: "To what torments of existence is the departed soul of such a masterpiece exposed when dragged back to earth by a modern theatrical medium for the delectation of a later generation!"[25] And in the case of *Der fliegende Holländer*, Wagner found it altogether impossible to revel in traditional forms: no one wanting to stage not just *one* particular message but the *only* message capable of moving the world should rely on outmoded, schematic models.

In 1871, in conversation with his second wife, Wagner explained that "the so-called genius of form" planned everything in advance and knew how one thing would follow another, allowing the genius to work "with ease," whereas he saw himself in the more difficult role of the "improviser," who "belongs entirely to the present moment" and who would be lost if he had to keep thinking about what came next: "The peculiar thing about me as an artist, for instance, is that I look on each detail as an entirety and never say to myself, 'Since this or that will follow, you must do thus and such, modulate like this or like that. [. . .] And yet I know I am unconsciously obeying a plan.'"[26]

A glance at the nineteenth-century symphony helps to clarify this idea: in Wagner's view, as well as that of the New German school, it was impossible to add anything of any significance to Beethoven's music, which traded in ideas, at least as long as the traditional four-movement framework was retained and, with it, the use of sonata form, with its predictable sequence of exposition, development section, and recapitulation, for every new idea, however novel, would be lost within the old-fashioned packaging. Moreover, the traditional symphony in the post-Beethovenian period flirted with an emotionality and even a sentimentality whose fluctuating feelings left the objective listener puzzling over what it was all about:

> Our symphonies and the like are now all about world-weariness and disaster; we are gloomy and grim, then courageous and daring; we yearn to see our youthful dreams come true; demonic obstacles inconvenience us; we brood and even rage; but finally the world-weariness's tooth is drawn, and we laugh and in a fit of high spirits show the world its missing tooth, hale, hearty, honest, Hungarian or Scottish—alas, to others it is simply boring![27]

Symphonic poems à la Liszt were certainly an improvement on this, because they did not obey prescribed "architectural" forms but only individual "psychological" models.[28] But even these left Wagner feeling dissatisfied: despite his sympathy for his friend and later father-in-law, he could not get round the fact that the programs on which such works were based did not allow the listener's feelings to be guided in any plausible direction: no matter what images the music might conjure up, the listener quickly lost the thread. For all his sympathy for the illustrative "formal motifs" of program music,[29] he nonetheless doubted their power, for it was only in connection with a performance onstage that such motifs could have any real impact.

And how does Wagner succeed in squaring the circle and invent a musical drama that avoids a traditional formal language in favor of an improvisatory art that makes sense at every moment, while not neglecting the wider picture and the long line? Even a modernist like Arnold Schoenberg had to compromise in this respect: when it became clear to him that his method of free-tonal composition could invest only very short pieces with the degree of comprehensibility that he felt was indispensable, he "invented" the method of twelve-tone composition that was intended to guarantee the formal stability that was needed.

Wagner, too, was prepared to compromise: in its treatment of melody and harmony, *Der fliegende Holländer* is in many ways more conventional than Berlioz's *Symphonie fantastique* of a decade earlier. And although he clearly develops the melodic lines out of the speech patterns of the libretto, he does not yet break completely with traditional musical syntax, with its tendency to create structures based on periods of multiples of two bars (2 + 2 = 4, 4 + 4 = 8, 8 + 8 = 16 bars, and so on). Nor can it be denied that in spite of its sense of drama, *Der fliegende Holländer* is no less made up of "numbers" than other operas of the time—operas that Wagner looked down on. He persuaded his Dresden publisher to issue nine individual numbers in arrangements for voice and piano, and it is even possible that he himself prepared these "Morceaux favoris," as they were known. At all events, titles such as the Steersman's Song ("Mit Gewitter und Sturm"), the Dutchman's Aria ("Die Frist ist um"), Senta's Ballad ("Traft ihr das Schiff"), the Spinning Chorus ("Brumm und summ, du gutes Rädchen"), and the Sailor's Song ("Steuermann, lass die Wacht") were undoubtedly better known in the years following the first performance of the opera in 1843 than the work's message, for all that that message was of decisive, and far greater, importance for Wagner.

Even so, there are good reasons for adopting Carl Dahlhaus's terminology and describing *Der fliegende Holländer* not as a "number opera" but as a "scene opera," since the practice of running together a series of numbers and creating a larger complex is now extended to the entire work, rather than just the act finales, as had been the case in the earlier period.[30] The singspiel elements that commentators claim to find in the figure of Senta's father and in the ostensible coziness of the spinning room are in fact less conventional than they appear to be at first sight, for Wagner consciously uses this "idyllic" quality as a contrast with the Dutchman's more somber world, and his art consists precisely in emphasizing the clash between them.

This last point is particularly well illustrated by Senta's Ballad, which Wagner later insisted was the nucleus from which the rest of the opera grew, a claim which is difficult to sustain in the light of what we know about the work's genesis but which makes sense in terms of its underlying thrust. For if we regard the work as a whole as a "stage ballad" in a single act,[31] then this central number is like a Russian doll nestling inside another Russian doll. In other words, Wagner eschews process and development not only in staging the work but also in composing it, painting one and the same seascape which, however much it may vary on points of detail, has only one center to it: Senta's vision of "redemption through destruction." In this regard it is significant that in Senta's Ballad the external action comes to a standstill, while the inner action reaches its high point.

This is the moment when music comes into its own—music which by definition can depict the invisible. As a result, Senta's Ballad is composed of a concentrate of quintessential motifs that have nothing to do here in terms of the outer action but which reflect Senta's inner reality. We hear the howling winds even though we are in the comfort of the spinning room: the hum of the spinning wheels is overlaid by the imaginary calls of the sailors as they go about their work. And the Dutchman is present even though there is really only the portrait of a wan-featured man hanging on the wall. Finally, the redemption motif from the overture is heard, as if as a matter of course. It represents Senta's innermost driving force and in its relationship to the complete ballad functions as a doll within a doll within a doll.

The reader will be reminded of Wagner's later handling of his leitmotifs. In spite of occasional claims to the contrary, not even in the *Ring* are they used to replicate the action onstage by acoustic means but tend, rather, to hint at what is *not* being shown there—namely, the inner lives of the participants in the drama or the deeper meaning of symbolic objects such as the sword, spear, or ring. Liszt was one of the first writers to draw attention to the fact that even in *Der fliegende Holländer* there are many examples of the practice of "characterizing prominent persons or situations in the drama by means of specific musical motifs that keep recurring."[32]

Instead of criticizing Liszt for slightly exaggerating, we would do better to admire the perspicacity with which he was able to assess Wagner's method of superimposing motifs to create a musical unity that avoids processual parataxis in favor of the simultaneity of different sensorial impressions and emotional states. By replacing the abstraction of argument and juxtaposition by a concrete interplay that we can actually experience for ourselves, Wagner reveals himself—from today's perspective—as an excellent psychologist. Of course, he himself had something different in mind, for he wanted his listeners to experience myth through their emotions, myth which, innocent of the concept of time advancing in a particular direction, tells us what was and is and will be—all at once. In what kind of time do myths about the end of the world take place? In the past, which is where they belong according to our own enlightened view of such matters? In the present, which is when they affect us? Or in the future, which they describe to us for our own greater good?

This new feeling of musical time to which Wagner abandons himself leads away from the subjective, teleological actions of its participants, which had influenced opera until then, to a type of action rooted in the superpersonal and, however graphic, motivated only within itself. The turbulent sea is a good example of this: if the view that the main character in *Der Freischütz* is the German forest is vaguely condescending, the same is no longer true of the elemental force of the sea in *Der fliegende Holländer*. Ernst Bloch saw in Wagner's characters "tossing ships that unresistingly comply with the suffering, the struggle, the love and the longing for redemption of their subhuman ocean and over which, in every decisive moment, instead of the encounter toward one another and toward the depth of an individual fate, breaks only the universal wave of Schopenhauer's Will."[33] This is certainly true of the Dutchman, who does not struggle; and it is also true of Senta, who obeys the dictates of her destiny as if she is in a trance.

Wagner's myth about the Flying Dutchman lacks the ethical dimension found in Beethoven's *Fidelio*, in which a loving couple is inspired to make a supreme effort that ultimately leads to their victory. As a result, the "signal" that leaves such an indelible impression on listeners in each of these operas has a very different function. In *Fidelio* the trumpet fanfare signals the arrival of the Minister and a sudden shift in the characters' fortunes that paves the way to the happy ending, entering the hermetically sealed world of the prison from without and—its repetition notwithstanding—remaining a singular occurrence unrelated to the inner action. By contrast, the Dutchman's horn motif pervades the opera like some primeval symbol that exerts its magic force from first to last and places its seal on the action as a whole.

The overture opens with an inspired idea: as at the start of Beethoven's Ninth Symphony—and it is surely no accident that both works open in D minor—archaic fifths ring out, their mysterious character further underscored by the string tremolando. But unlike Beethoven, Wagner introduces into this unstable environment an extremely striking figure that enters after only two bars and that consists of two intervals of a fourth followed by a fifth to the upper octave. The repeat of this interval of a fifth is not some tasteful echo but is marked "sempre più forte," passing into a series of repeats of the note A stated no fewer than fourteen times on the natural horns. The valve horns add to the impact of this passage by not only playing in unison with the natural horns but adding an appoggiatura to each of the notes and in that way giving rise to an irrational sense of friction (music example 6).

6. Bars 1–7 of the overture to *Der fliegende Holländer* in full score.

Ouvertüre

Although problematical in a number of ways, the opening of the Ninth Symphony is at least an internally coherent melodic, harmonic, and rhythmic structure that makes sense even to anyone simply looking at the score. The opening of *Der fliegende Holländer*, conversely, can be interpreted only as a musical event that owes its existence not to a structure determined in advance but as one that from the outset is conceived along material lines. Starting with *Der fliegende Holländer*, Wagner regarded his scores as functional, not so much representing the substance of the composition as serving a different purpose: the precise timing of musical events within the context of the action onstage.

As a result, we do not need to linger over the question as to whether the Dutchman's motif is capable of development in the sense in which Beethoven understood that term or whether it is vocal in the spirit of Rossini. What matters, rather, is that it works *within the context of the drama*: with the title of the opera before us and, ideally, with the plot already in our heads, we should be able—on hearing these opening bars—to imagine only "the dreadful ship of the Flying Dutchman scudding before the tempest," as Wagner himself prescribed and described it.[34]

This detail also allows us to pin down exactly what it is that Wagner was able to achieve on a more general level—namely, a musical language that can claim to introduce a mythic dimension into our world of emotions in a way that does justice to the situation that is being portrayed. What is novel here are not those elements that make up the music's formal language but the way in which those elements are used and combined. In a letter to Liszt, Wagner explained that "every bar of a piece of dramatic music is justified only to the extent that it expresses something that relates to the action or to the character of the dramatis persona."[35] Although he was referring to *Tannhäuser*, his comment applies equally well to *Der fliegende Holländer*— and not just to the music but, more especially, to the staging:

> The first scene of the opera must create the mood that allows the audience to grasp for itself the strange phenomenon of the Flying Dutchman. [. . .] The sea between the skerries must be as wild as possible; the treatment of the ship cannot be naturalistic enough: little touches such as the tossing of the ship when struck by a powerful wave (between the two verses of the Steersman's Song) must be graphically brought out.[36]

Although this may still represent a duplication of what the music depicts, the coordination of music and staging emerges as sheer naturalism in the Dutchman's monologue:

> The first note of the aria's ritornello (the low E sharp in the basses) is accompanied by the Dutchman's first step on dry land; his rolling gait, typical of seafarers who set foot on terra firma for the first time after a long sea voyage, is accompanied in turn by the wave-like figure in the violoncellos and violas; with the first crotchet of the third bar he takes his second step,

still with folded arms and lowered head; his third and fourth steps coincide with the notes of the eighth and ninth bars.[37]

From our present standpoint, this description reveals glaring weaknesses in what we might term the "Dutchman system": a production that follows the stage directions bar by bar would now seem stiff and even risible, and it is inconceivable that in 2013 any director would approach the music in such a detailed manner, emphasizing every gesture, in the way that Wagner—his views conditioned by the acting style of his own day—imagined this scene. And yet even Wagner himself must have found this concept increasingly problematical, for the naturalistic style presupposed by *Der fliegende Holländer* was harder and harder to reconcile with the increasing interiority that we find in his later works.[38] At the very least he was bound with the passage of time to realize that not even the most willing singers were capable of reacting with thespian conviction to the nuanced gestures of the music. "Don't look too much," Wagner advised Malwida von Meysenbug at the time of the first Bayreuth Festival; "just listen instead!"[39] And in the run-up to *Parsifal*, he even expressed a desire to invent "the invisible theater" to go with his "invisible orchestra."[40]

It is no wonder that on hearing the work for the first time in Dresden in 1843, Wagner found its instrumentation brutal in the extreme, notably at Senta's "surprised scream" in act 2: "The brass and timpani created too coarse and material an impact at this blow," he reported, self-critically, to Liszt in 1853, while the latter was preparing to stage the opera in Weimar: "One should be startled by Senta's scream on seeing the Dutchman, not by the timpani and brass."[41]

Although Wagner had already retouched the score and toned down the instrumentation by this date, he continued to have misgivings about the work. In 1881, for example, he went through the score with the Dresden conductor Ernst von Schuch and was saddened "to note so much in it that is just noise or repetition, that is to say, so many things that spoil the work."[42] On the other hand he had expressed the view only a few years earlier that "from *Holländer* to *Parsifal*—how long the path and yet how similar the character!"[43] In the wake of the 1864 Munich production he had even set about revising Senta's Ballad, perhaps with the aim of removing extraneous elements from it in the form of quotations from other sections of the work. After all, the libretto makes it clear that the ballad is a part of the repertory of Senta's old nursemaid, Mary, and so it does not entirely reflect Senta's state of mind at this decisive point in the action.

This scene from act 2 of Harry
Kupfer's Bayreuth production of
Der fliegende Holländer—first
seen in 1978—could be the inspiration for a nineteenth-century
canvas painted in the spirit of
"real idealism." As such, it reflects
the director's view of the opera
as a "psychological bourgeois
drama." Senta is seen as an Ibsen-
esque figure trapped by her bourgeois environment. The present
image dates from the 1980 revival.
(Photograph courtesy of the
Nationalarchiv der Richard-
Wagner-Stiftung, Bayreuth:
L80-48-5.)

But we would be guilty of falling into Wagner's own trap if we were to take over his own private philosophy and regard his later total artworks as being on a "higher" level than a "mere" opera. For if we adopt this attitude, alleged "weaknesses" in *Der fliegende Holländer* would acquire a weight that would otherwise not have been the case. And the researcher will then feel called upon to look for "borrowings" from other composers and to record in detail those passages that have been taken over from the world of the singspiel or grand opera and so on.[44]

After all, it is by no means certain that the total artwork is the last word on the subject. That Senta's Ballad, for example, is not such an accurate reflection of her emotional state as is the case with analogous passages in the roles of Isolde and Kundry is actually an advantage in the context of *Der fliegende Holländer*. By emphasizing the archetypal and the nonindividual, Senta's performance of the ballad makes it clear that she is under a fatal compulsion to perform her act of heroic self-sacrifice. And even though modern directors may invest the character with tremendous psychological depth, that is not how Wagner himself conceived the part. Rather, he saw her as a mythic figure who performs the role demanded of her by the myth. And the same is true by analogy of the Dutchman himself. That the two main characters do not communicate with one another for long stretches of the opera but commune only with themselves is surely eloquent: in the world of myth and legend there is no room for mutual, soul-baring confidences.

Quite apart from this, Wagner's later "total artworks" will confront us with very different contradictions from those that we find in the case of the rough diamond that is *Der fliegende Holländer*. Did Wagner ever again write an overture of such elemental freshness or a choral scene of such dramatic intensity as the one that occurs at the start of act 3, with its increasingly eerie confrontation between the chorus of Norwegian sailors and young women on the one hand and the Dutchman's crew on the other? In later years he would presumably not have been quite so carefree in composing the constant comings and goings which, however well structured from a dramaturgical point of view, are otherwise redundant: they would surely have struck him as lacking in balance and insufficiently focused on the end of the story. And yet it is very much the formal awkwardness of this scene that gives it its depth. And it is precisely because of its plot, which resembles nothing so much as a popular woodcut, and because of its exuberant orchestral gestures and its lack of what Wagner was later to term his "art of transition," that the whole opera has an immediacy that can effortlessly hold its own in the face of the greater refinement of the later works. Above all, its subject is easily explained: the existential feeling of being damned and the uncontrollable desire to leap after a damned soul are both emotions that are part of our collective unconscious, hidden away beneath the veneer of contemporary civilization.

In Wagner's case, the gloomy and eerily morbid scenario is combined with the blissful transcendence of music that lends a greater luster to the human experience of adventure and love than the subject matter would suggest. Whether or not we agree with Ernst Bloch and hail it as the utopian power of all great music or—again echoing Bloch—respond to it as "conveying a sensational message in the best sense,"[45] it is no accident that *Der fliegende Holländer* remains a powerful draw even among non-Wagnerians.

In future, too, Wagner would succeed in clothing a mood of universal destruction in music of beguiling beauty. But never again would he be able to invest his music with such wild freshness. No doubt he was able to do so only because he was a young and literally hungry composer who, however much he may have despaired of the conditions in which he found himself, believed almost naïvely in his own future. Even by *Tannhäuser* he was already striking a more measured note—it is enough to compare their two overtures to appreciate the truth of this claim.

A Word about Heinrich Heine

Until the 1840s, when Wagner moved back to Dresden, relations between him and Heinrich Heine were amiable in the extreme—otherwise it is simply not possible to explain how he was able to write the following passage in a review that he submitted to the Dresden *Abend-Zeitung*, to which he began to contribute in February 1841:

[In Germany] much has been written about an embarrassing affair affecting the poet *Heinrich Heine*; it seems that people are extraordinarily pleased about what has happened. [. . .] We Germans are clearly a generous nation! We see a talent rise up in our midst, the like of which is rare in Germany. [. . .] But we clap our hands for very joy when this same Heine finally receives the kind of treatment that we practice at home on our penny-a-liners! And in Germany we do so with such a rabid desire for scandal that we do not even have the time to ascertain the facts of so sad an affair, preferring to see in it, rather, the poet's just deserts.[1]

The affair in question became known in Germany as the *Ohrfeigenaffaire*—literally, "the affair of the cuff on the ear." In an invective directed at Ludwig Börne, Heine had made fun of a relationship between Börne, his lady friend Jeanette Wohl, and Salomon Strauß, whom she later married. Strauß immediately took Heine to task and may even have struck him in the street. But it was above all the ensuing duel, from which both participants escaped with only minor injuries, that excited the ridicule of the press. Wagner even suggested to his readers in Dresden that as a result of the duel Heine was close to death.

It is entirely possible that it was Heine himself who prompted Wagner to go on the attack, for the two men were personally acquainted, having been introduced to each other by Heinrich Laube. Both had elected to live in Paris, and they shared a bond in their sympathy for the political and artistic theories of the Young Germany movement. Moreover, Wagner had not only modeled *Der fliegende Holländer* on one of Heine's writings but had even set to music Heine's poem *The Two Grenadiers*—though out of regard for local audiences in Paris, he used a French translation of the poem.

On his return to Germany in 1842, Wagner had no qualms about submitting an autobiographical sketch to Laube's *Zeitung für die elegante Welt*, from which it is clear that he had found in Heine's *Memoirs of Herr von Schnabelewopski* everything he needed to transform the legend into the basis of an opera. Only after 1849 and the failure of the Dresden Uprising did Wagner change his tack. Neither in his autobiography, *My Life*, nor in the version of his autobiographical sketch that he prepared for publication as part of his collected writings in 1871 is Heine's name mentioned in the context of *Der fliegende Holländer*. Instead, Wagner claims that the opera marked his Pauline conversion from a "critical man of letters" to an "artist," allowing him to cast aside the frivolous features of *Das Liebesverbot* once and for all.[2] At the same time, he insisted that it was a "folk poem" about the Dutchman that had been his most important source.[3] This was a claim that he owed to his newfound faith in the mythopoeic power of the people.

At the same time, the anti-Semitism that Wagner espoused after 1848–49 played its part, with the result that Heine—a writer he had formerly admired—was now tarred with the same brush. Although he had earlier set *The Two Grenadiers*, Wagner now vented his spleen on those composers who set Heine's "versified lies" to music.[4] In spite of these strictures, Wagner continued to find "things of incomparable genius" in Heine's writings: on the one hand, they represented "the bad conscience of our whole era, [. . .] the most unedifying and demoralizing matters one can possibly imagine," while at the same time "one feels closer to him than to the whole clique he is so naïvely exposing."[5]

This "clique" inevitably included Meyerbeer, whom Heine had no hesitation in attacking in a particularly undignified way: the beneficiary of Meyerbeer's financial largesse, he began by praising *Les Huguenots*, while simultaneously demonstrating his power as a journalist by means of little digs at his benefactor. But when Meyerbeer—known for his generosity and, like most members of his profession, open to bribery—began to withhold his payments, Heine threatened to humiliate him publicly. And even after Heine's death in 1856, his widow, Mathilde, extorted a large sum of money from the pathologically insecure Meyerbeer in return for the assurance that she would withhold a number of lampoons that were directed against him.

Wagner's bust has been in Walhalla—the temple to German art near Regensburg—since 1913, Heine's since 2010.

Photographed in the spring of 1860 in the Paris studio of Pierre Petit & Trinquart, this is the first surviving photographic portrait of Wagner. Even at this date Wagner already preferred to cast himself in the role of Wotan, prompting him to write to Mathilde Wesendonck on May 23, 1860: "Without my being aware of it, the brute of an artist thought it appropriate to force me into a highly affected pose, with my eyes cocked sideways: I loathe the resulting portrait and told him that it made me look like a sentimental Marat" (SB 12:164). (Photography courtesy of the Nationalarchiv der Richard-Wagner-Stiftung, Bayreuth: N 1279.)

CHAPTER FOUR

Rituals to Combat Fear and Loneliness

TANNHÄUSER UND DER SÄNGERKRIEG AUF WARTBURG

Wagner's return to Germany—Discovery of the subject of
Tannhäuser—Manifold strands in the plot—The ideological
gulf between *Der fliegende Holländer* and *Tannhäuser*—The
German Middle Ages as a source of nationalist ideas—Catholic
elements—Contradictions in the redemption motif—The
Venusberg: natural or perverted sexuality?—Wagner's
dream about Nietzsche's contempt for the work—The Paris
version—Baudelaire's *décadent* view of the opera—Attempts
at deconstruction: Tannhäuser as a man driven to extremes
and finding support in ritual—Adolescent enthusiasm for
Tannhäuser on the part of Schweitzer and Brecht—Specific
features of the score—Advanced harmonic writing and the use
of sonority—The Bacchanal from an aesthetic point of view and
as a commodity—The genre of "tone painting"—Tannhäuser's
Pilgrimage and the Rome Narration as the work's artistic and
dramatic high points—On the road to the musical drama

W hat dismal experiences Herr Richard Wagner was forced to endure when, heeding the voice of reason and of his stomach, he sensibly abandoned his dangerous project of gaining a foothold on the French stage and fluttered back home to the land of German potatoes."[1] Who could have written these lines but Heinrich Heine, a man never at a loss for a wounding witticism? And he was right. Wagner had been forced to admit that no Paris theater was interested in either *Rienzi* or *Der fliegende Holländer* and that he could no longer bear to remain in the capital of European culture, to which he had been powerfully drawn only a few years earlier. And when two German court theaters—Berlin and Dresden—signaled their interest in these two operas, there was no holding him back any longer. He and his wife left Paris on April 7, 1842, and returned to Dresden, still so heavily in debt that his relatives in the city had to advance his travel expenses.

He no longer coveted international fame but wanted only to be German—to think like a German and to serve the cause of German art. Even in Paris he had already drawn inspiration from the subject of Tannhäuser—not in the modernized adaptation by Ludwig Tieck, whom he accused of "coquettish mysticism and Catholic frivolity,"[2] but in the form of a simple "chapbook" like the version found in Ludwig Bechstein's collection of Thuringian legends. Fired by the "involuntary urge" to embrace all that he felt to be "German" "with an increasingly inner warmth and desire," Wagner alighted on "the simple account of this legend based on the ancient, well-known ballad of Tannhäuser."[3]

On passing the Wartburg castle "during the only sunlit hour" of his journey back to Dresden, he "constructed" the relevant scene in the final act of his new opera—or so he later claimed in his autobiography.[4] Soon afterward he had the idea of combining the legend of Tannhäuser at Venus's court in the Venusberg with that of the song contest at the Wartburg but needed more time to examine the various sources before he drafted his libretto in the early part of 1843. By then both *Rienzi* and *Der fliegende Holländer* had been staged in Dresden. *Rienzi*, indeed, was so successful that in February 1843 Wagner was appointed court kapellmeister—a good enough reason to embrace the German national, Catholic mentality of the local court, a shift in outlook that may not have been as opportunistic as it seems to us now but which could certainly not have been predicted after *Der fliegende Holländer*.

Tannhäuser tells of a medieval bard, or minstrel, who, sated with his life of voluptuous pleasure in the Venusberg, returns to the real world. But at the traditional song contest at the Wartburg Castle he again steps out of character, and while the other contestants sing of the nature of love in eloquent, well-turned phrases, he recalls his experiences in the Venusberg, holding them up as an expression of true—purely physical—love. The apostate is exiled from Wartburg society but is persuaded by the landgrave's niece, Elisabeth, who loves him in secret, to go to Rome and seek forgiveness from the pope. When the pope refuses to grant him clemency, Tannhäuser returns to his native Thuringia a broken man. Only with difficulty can Wolfram prevent him from seeking refuge once more in the Venusberg, which appears before him shrouded in a seductive "roseate dusk." Dying,

Tannhäuser sinks down beside the body of Elisabeth, who in the meantime has died a saint. Her intercession with the Virgin Mary may finally allow him to find "the peace of the blessed."

This brief summary of the opera's contents fails to bring out the explosive nature of the subject matter, which emerges only from its biographical and conceptual context. In reconstructing his artistic development Wagner drew a clear line between *Rienzi* and *Der fliegende Holländer*. We do not have to question this assessment to see a further momentous caesura between *Der fliegende Holländer* and *Tannhäuser*, even if such a break remained more or less hidden from the composer himself. The *Ur-Holländer* is as concise as it is inspired: it tells the story of a man driven from pillar to post and under a curse, a man who discovers "redemption through destruction" only as a result of a woman's willingness to sacrifice her own life for his. The narrative avoids all superfluous flourishes: the nature of the Dutchman's curse is not explained, and no attempt is made to invest the couple's leap into oblivion with any psychological depth. The "myth"—which is how Wagner classifies these events—is unmotivated and ahistorical. It is the myth of Ahasuerus, the Wandering Jew, a myth no less lapidary than that of Prometheus, who is punished by the gods for his pride.

We may also be reminded of Sisyphus, who for the rest of time was made to atone for his guile and treachery. And we may further recall the philosophy of the theater of the absurd that Camus defined by reference to this figure: in a nonsensical world, we humans seek in vain to invest our lives with a sense of meaning. Wagner's solution to the problem was to believe that we may be pleased when death finally releases us from our sufferings. Ever since the days of the early romantics, it had been possible to identify with this vague feeling of negative sublimity. Every individual fate could be effortlessly incorporated into it, something of the absurdity of existence continuing to resonate in the twentieth century in the characters of Kafka and Beckett.

From this point of view, Tannhäuser may be seen as a second Dutchman, for he too is a man hounded by destiny and, dependent on a woman's willingness to sacrifice herself for him, able to find redemption only in death. But the timeless and unfathomable events that unfold in *Der fliegende Holländer* and that evince the simplest of structures are given a historical and social context in *Tannhäuser* and located within a space in which the depicted phenomena are brightly lit. But the more basic this process, the more obviously the action becomes caught up in contradictions, the more ideological its context becomes, and the more the music has to struggle not to lose sight of the overall drama as a result of the sheer variety that informs its manifold episodes.

First and foremost there is the matter of the work's "Germanness." Scarcely had Wagner set foot on German soil and, having acquired the status of a well-paid kapellmeister, started to enjoy a run of early successes in German opera houses, when his artistic leitmotif of "redemption through destruction," which had previously been grounded in the purely existential, acquired a nationalist dimension. We are no longer dealing with a Dutchman wandering through world history under the impulse of timeless instinctual drives in the spirit of Schopenhauer. No, Tannhäuser is "a German from head to toe," as Wagner insisted in a letter to the Berlin critic Karl Gaillard, before going on: "May he be capable of winning me the hearts of my fellow Germans in far greater numbers than my earlier works have succeeded in doing!"[5]

This nationalist impulse also helps to explain why Wagner combined the legend of Tannhäuser in the Venusberg with the legends surrounding the song contest at the Wartburg. Carl Dahlhaus has pointed out that the contest, which makes up most of act 2, would be nothing more than an "effective tableau" "filled with theatrical parades" of no real consequence to the action if the relationship between Tannhäuser and Elisabeth were not spelt out and defined here.[6] By declaiming his offensive song in praise of Venus, Tannhäuser "stabs" Elisabeth "to the heart," "exulting" as he does so. In that way he prepares the ground for her assumption of a martyr's crown and his own ability to find peace in death. It is entirely possible that Wagner would have been able to present this dramaturgically important element in the story without a song contest, if he had not needed the contest to stress the German aspects of his opera. In his autobiography, he noted retrospectively that a monograph on *Der Wartburgkrieg*—a didactic poem from the late thirteenth century—had shown him "the German Middle Ages in a significant coloring," a quality of which he had by his own admission been ignorant until that date.[7]

As a result, the second act is set in the great banqueting hall of the venerable Wartburg, where the Landgrave of Thuringia, apostrophized as the "protector of art," acclaims the assembled knights and minstrels:

> Wenn unser Schwert in blutig ernsten Kämpfen
> stritt für des deutschen Reiches Majestät,
> wenn wir dem grimmen Welfen widerstanden

und dem verderbenvollen Zwiespalt wehrten:
so ward von euch nicht mind'rer Preis errungen.

[When in deathly earnest battles our sword fought for the majesty of the
German Empire and we resisted the grim-hearted Guelf and prevented
disastrous discord, you won no less praise for yourselves.]

The doyen of aristocratic singers, Wolfram von Eschenbach, rises to this
challenge in the opening lines of his reply:

Blick' ich umher in diesem edlen Kreise,
welch' hoher Anblick macht mein Herz erglüh'n!
So viel der Helden, tapfer, deutsch und weise, —
ein stolzer Eichwald, herrlich, frisch und grün.

[When I gaze around me in this noble circle, what a lofty sight sets my
heart ablaze! So many heroes, doughty, German and wise—a proud forest
of oaks, glorious, fresh and green.]

In writing these lines, Wagner was echoing the spirit of the age at a time
when it was fashionable to appeal to German history and glorify Germanic
virtues in a language in which the "German oak" figured prominently. And
this was true of every ideological and philosophical camp. It is no accident
that in 1842 Schumann, for example, admitted to the critic Carl Koßmaly:
"Do you know my morning and evening prayer as an artist? It is *German
opera*."[8] And yet it is impossible not to be impressed by the resolve with
which Wagner invested the subject matter—still called *The Mount of Venus*
in the prose draft of 1842—with a markedly "German" component by introducing the Wartburg song contest. And this had consequences for the
music: in Wagner's hands the world of the Wartburg was transformed into
a tableau with positive, affirmative features familiar from the grand operas
that he affected to despise. An onstage band, elaborate choruses, and in-
sertion arias are entirely comparable in their basic outline to Meyerbeer's
Robert le diable,[9] and as such they have always appealed to their audiences.
Of course, Wagner achieves far more than that in *Tannhäuser*, but the
largely unquestioning display of pomp and pageantry in act 2 undoubtedly
confirms the impression left on Max Maria von Weber—the son of the
composer of *Der Freischütz*, Carl Maria von Weber—at the Dresden premiere in 1845: "Not even the most willing and most lively imagination of a
later generation can conceive the extent to which this work struck its early
listeners as a mixture of the great, the sublime, and the beautiful and, at the

same time, the bizarre, the artistically well-nigh impossible, and even the trivial and almost laughable."[10]

There is another instance of the "significant color" with which the German Middle Ages is invested in *Tannhäuser*—this is a quality that Wagner called the "purely human" and that was gaining increasing importance in his thinking. Ultimately the sinful hero receives absolution not from the pope in Rome who, in keeping with the traditional narrative, remains implacable, but from Elisabeth, a German saint, who finds a way out of the impasse and—or so the libretto would seem to imply—intercedes with Heaven and gains forgiveness for Tannhäuser.

Such speculations have no place in the *Ur-Holländer*, for the Dutchman does not find mercy, but only redemption, through his own annihilation. *Tannhäuser* is the first and—with the exception of *Parsifal*—the last work in which Wagner uses the motif of grace, and as a result it almost goes without saying that he draws on a whole range of devotional rituals. Of course, such rituals are an inevitable aspect of a legend grounded in Christian Catholicism, and there is little doubt that they will have been well received by the Catholic court that had Wagner on its payroll. And yet it was by no means a foregone conclusion that a composer brought up in the Protestant faith would have warmed to his subject to such an extent, treating the Virgin Mary and the pope as key figures in his narrative and at the end inviting his audience to share in the spectacle of Elisabeth—once motivated by feelings of earthly love—becoming a saint. Sieghart Döhring has pointed out that the appeal to the Virgin Mary is a part of the world of ideas associated with the utopian socialism that Wagner could have discovered in Paris,[11] but, quite apart from the fact that this appeal is already found in Ludwig Bechstein's version of the Tannhäuser Ballad, we have to ask ourselves whether it is really necessary to know such an arcane context to understand that Wagner needed the figure of the Virgin Mary to intercede and bring out the contrast between pure and sinful love in the opera.

Writing in 1851, in his *Communication to My Friends*, Wagner speaks somewhat cryptically of his own "deeply trivial encounters" and subsequent "disgust" at all that "our modern world has to offer by way of sensuality and life's pleasures in general."[12] And, as we have already seen, he told Liszt that the following passage represents the "nub of the entire drama":

> Zum Heil den Sündigen zu führen,
> die Gott-Gesandte nahte mir:
> doch, ach! sie frevelnd zu berühren

hob ich den Lästerblick zu ihr!
O du, hoch über diesen Erdengründen,
die mir den Engel meines Heil's gesandt,
erbarm' dich mein [...].

[To guide the sinner to his weal, the God-sent woman drew close to me:
but, ah! to touch her sinfully I raised my impious eyes to her! O God who
high above this earth sent me the angel of my salvation, have mercy
upon me.]

The first phrase is directed at Elisabeth, the second at the immaculate
Mother of God as intercessor. Both imply the extreme condemnation of
all forms of sexuality.

Even in *Der fliegende Holländer*, redemption had been possible only because the couple, infatuated with one another, has renounced sexuality and
is content to be united in death. But this falls a long way short of the situation in *Tannhäuser*, which explores almost every aspect of the topic of sinful
love. Not only is the "love" that Tannhäuser feels in the Venusberg sinful,
so too is the "impious" look that he casts at Elisabeth in act 2. In his letter
to Liszt, Wagner explained that Tannhäuser's "whole nature" is crystallized
in these lines as he becomes conscious of his "dreadful crime."[13] Perhaps
Tannhäuser should have followed the lead of his alter ego, Wolfram, who in
his song about the nature of love warns against sullying the waters of love's
fountain with "impious temerity" and counsels his audience to worship it,
instead, in a spirit of rapt contemplation and prayer.

But was Tannhäuser's "sinful" gaze not directed, rather, at a loving woman
who at this point in the opera was still hoping for a life of earthly happiness
with him? This question leads us to a deeper level of the action, where the
superficial, black-and-white contrast between sinful and pure heavenly love
no longer exists. Let us start with the Venusberg, the world ruled over by
the self-styled "goddess of love." It remains unclear how Tannhäuser found
his way here, and yet we are manifestly not dealing with a bordello but
with a place of unending pleasure appropriate only to the gods. Does this
make it a place of natural innocence or one of decadence? A scene of un-
censored sexuality or one that is remote from God? Are the bowels of the
earth a place whose denizens can live out their natural instincts to the full,
instincts that pose a threat to "society," however we choose to picture such
a society? Or is all this chthonic physicality so compulsive and so obsessive
that it needs to be tamed by civilization and turned into "love," a process
that is tantamount to ennobling it?

Wagner's treatment of this scene leaves the question open, and even Tannhäuser's own attitude is contradictory, for his insistent entreaty that Venus should release him from her realm is not one that he seeks to justify by means of moral arguments. Rather, he claims that he has grown weary of a life of luxury and pleasure. While promising to continue to sing the goddess's praises, he longs to escape from this timeless paradise and return to real life, with its temporal limitations, a life in which "battle" and "death" await him instead of "rapture and delight." Only when his lover has risen to a paroxysm of anger at his rejection of her and cursed him does he finally speak of "atonement." To the sound of what the stage directions describe as a "terrible crash," he quits the Venusberg with the words: "Mein Fried,' mein Heil ruht in Maria!" (My peace, my salvation rests in Mary!)[14]

How are we to interpret this turn of events? After all, Tannhäuser has just announced that even in the outside world he will continue to play the part of Venus's "bold warrior." And he does in fact keep his promise when he first reappears at the Wartburg and Elisabeth asks him: "Heinrich! What have you done to me?" "You should praise the god of love," he replies; "he plucked the strings and spoke to you from my songs, bringing me back to you!" In other words, only by meeting Venus has he learned to feel love in an all-encompassing way. Elisabeth is to be the first beneficiary of this new-found attitude. In the song contest, too, he champions the uninhibitedly sensual love that he enjoyed in the Venusberg—initially with Elisabeth's "bashful" approval.

But how is it possible that having launched into his song in praise of Venus, singing "in extreme rapture" and reducing his audience to a state of outrage at his blasphemous behavior, Tannhäuser should suddenly prostrate himself and, using words that Wagner himself called the "nub of the drama," describe his changed attitude to Elisabeth as base and criminal? How is it that, losing all sense of self-esteem, he regards himself as "mired in sin" and calls on the Virgin Mary to intercede on his behalf?

One explanation is that in combining the two disparate legends of Tannhäuser in the Venusberg and the song contest at the Wartburg Wagner tied himself in a knot.[15] This would be the price that he paid for abandoning the single-stranded plot of *Der fliegende Holländer* and seeking, instead, to create a piece that would be dramatically effective onstage. As we have already observed, Wagner's central message—physical fulfillment in love is impossible to find in this world of ours, where we are lucky to discover only self-sacrificial love at best—could have been explored without the need for an elaborate song contest. But can this really be Wagner's central message for audiences today?

There is no doubt that *Tannhäuser* can be read as a "Catholic," antisensualist, bigoted work and, as such, a forerunner of *Parsifal*. It is no accident that in September 1878, while he was working of *Parsifal*, Wagner had a nightmare in which Nietzsche—with whom he had already fallen out at this date—"said a lot of malicious things to him and poured scorn on the melody of the 'Pilgrims' Chorus' in *Tannhäuser*, that is to say, sang a lampoon on it."[16] By this time Nietzsche had not yet written his poem "Is That Still German?" that was to end his 256th aphorism in *Beyond Good and Evil*. And yet, as Dieter Borchmeyer has noted with some amusement, the poem can "with a little effort be sung to the tune of the Pilgrims' Chorus":[17]

> Aus deutschem Herzen kam dies schwüle Kreischen?
> Und deutschen Leibs ist dies Sich-selbst-Entfleischen?
> Deutsch ist dies Priester-Händespreitzen,
> Dies weihrauch-düftelnde Sinne-Reizen?
> Und deutsch dies Stocken, Stürzen, Taumeln,
> Dies ungewisse Bimbambaumeln?
> Dies Nonnen-Äugeln, Ave-Glocken-Bimmeln,
> Dies ganze falsch verzückte Himmel-Überhimmeln?
> —Ist Das noch deutsch?—
> Erwägt! Noch steht ihr an der Pforte:—
> Denn, was ihr hört, ist *Rom,—Rom's Glaube ohne Worte*!

[Out of a German heart, this sultry screeching? / a German body, this self-laceration? / German, this priestly affectation, / this incense-perfumed sensual preaching? / German, this halting, plunging, reeling, / this so uncertain bim-bam pealing? / this nunnish ogling, *Ave* leavening, / this whole falsely ecstatic heaven overheavening? / —Is this still German?— / You still stand at the gate, perplexed? / Think! What you hear is *Rome—Rome's faith without the text*.]

Although these lines were written with *Parsifal* in mind, they can also be applied to *Tannhäuser*—and not just with malice aforethought, for even the best-intentioned of directors will find it difficult to stage *Tannhäuser* as a superior version of the "Oberammergau Passion Play," as Wagner jokingly referred to his Dresden oratorio *Das Liebesmahl der Apostel* (The Love-Feast of the Apostles).[18] It will be hard for any director to avoid all mention of the world of religion, still less to ignore the alternative world of the non-sacred and profanely secular, a point already made by Baudelaire in 1861: "*Tannhäuser* represents the struggle between the two principles that have chosen the human heart for their chief battlefield; in other words, the struggle between flesh and spirit, Heaven and Hell, Satan and God."[19]

Described by René Wellek as "an atheist and modern Dante,"[20] the *décadent* Baudelaire was acutely critical of Catholic romanticism, so that his response to *Tannhäuser* was not theological but existential. What was at stake was not morality but the most intense experience of all conceivable sense stimuli. In the face of the habitual tedium that he felt was the basic attitude of his age and embodied in grand opera,[21] he was fascinated by the "serious" nature of the work, which demanded "sustained attention" with its "fiery and peremptory music" that seemed to "recapture the dizzy perceptions of an opium-dream." In the music associated with the Venusberg, Baudelaire heard "the overflowing of a vigorous nature, pouring into Evil all the energies which should rightly go to the cultivation of Good; it is love unbridled, immense, chaotic, raised to the level of a counter-religion, a Satanic religion."[22]

For Baudelaire, the work's "religious theme" forms a fascinating alternative to its "ineluctable Satanic logic":

> an ineffable feeling [. . .] when Tannhäuser, having escaped from Venus's grotto, will find himself once again amid the realities of life, between the holy sound of his homeland's bells, the shepherd's rustic song, the pilgrims' hymn and the cross planted by the road, a symbol of all those crosses which must be carried on every road. In this latter case there is a power of contrast which acts irresistibly on the mind.[23]

Wagner's profoundly philosophical opera is ruthlessly aestheticized by Baudelaire, who also commits the mistake of treating it as a total artwork in the spirit of his own aesthetic ideal, with its goal of absolute expression. In February 1860, Baudelaire—inspired by the concerts that Wagner had just conducted in the city—wrote a letter to the composer in which he claimed to imagine the music as a "vast surface of dark red." (According to Wagner's later recollection, the music in question was the prelude to act 1 of *Lohengrin*.)[24]

> If this red represents passion, I see it gradually passing through all the stages of red and pink to the point where it acquires the incandescence of flames. One would think it difficult, if not impossible, to achieve anything

more fiery; and yet a final flare casts an even whiter trace across the white of the background. If you like, it is the ultimate cry of a soul in a moment of paroxysm.[25]

Baudelaire's aestheticizing view of *Tannhäuser* as a work inhabiting a world between good and evil was expounded in an essay that appeared under the title "Richard Wagner" in the pages of the *Revue européenne* on April 1, 1861. Since it represents a complete reversal of the values that Wagner's opera proclaims both superficially and on a much deeper level, it is all the more remarkable that the composer responded to the poet's approaches with such sincere civility in his reply of April 15, 1861. Only once before, a clearly jealous Nietzsche complained in the context of his own *Birth of Tragedy*, had Wagner written "a letter of such gratitude and even enthusiasm."[26]

Of course, we need to remember that Wagner felt indebted to Baudelaire as one of the few Parisians willing to out himself as a Wagnerian prepared to champion *Tannhäuser*. At the same time there is much to be said for the suggestion that Baudelaire had brought out an aspect of the opera that Wagner may have felt had been underexplored in responses to it in Germany, not least because it was not until 1861 that he had rewritten the Venusberg music for Paris and raised it to a compositional level that according to Adorno has turned this scene into "the phantasmagoria par excellence."[27]

In the words of Baudelaire, the worlds of "Heaven and Hell, God and Satan" meet as equals here, for all that they are scarcely comparable. Even after he had revised the score for Paris, Wagner remained dissatisfied with the result, and at the very time that he had just started working on the score of *Parsifal* he told Cosima of his intention of "shortening the new first scene considerably, it weighs the rest down too much, there is a lack of balance, this scene goes beyond the style of *Tannhäuser* as a whole."[28] And although he was delighted by the Venusberg music whenever Josef Rubinstein played it to him, Cosima famously noted in her diary only a few weeks before her husband's death: "Chat in the evening, brought to an end by R. with the 'Shepherd's Song' and 'Pilgrims' Chorus' from *Tannhäuser*. He says he still owes the world *Tannhäuser*."[29]

In general, Wagner's later comments on *Tannhäuser* sound like nothing so much as a desire to return to his roots in Dresden and to a version of the opera that was marked by Christian ideology, with the opening Venusberg scene rewritten as a prelude whose siren sounds would not be sufficiently magical to distract attention from the soteriological events that are later celebrated onstage. When the German musicologist Hans-Klaus Jungheinrich suggests that *Tannhäuser* may "also" be seen "as a Christian mystery,"[30] he is not going as far as this, and yet his reading of the piece is still more plausible than that put forward by the social scientist Udo Bermbach, who sees in our hero "an artist at odds with society and prone to interpret every organizational tie as an obligation that risks destroying his freedom and autonomy." According to Bermbach, Tannhäuser is ultimately destroyed by his opposition to church and state and dies a martyr's death.[31] Although Wagner himself inveighed against those "foolish" critics who wanted to impute "a specifically Christian and impotently pietistic drift" to the work, he wrote these lines in 1851, when, as a failed revolutionary, he felt only contempt for the institutions of church and state and was keen to insist that in creating the character of Tannhäuser he had been driven only by the "yearning for love, a very real kind of love seeded in the soil of the fullest sensuality."[32]

Regardless of this remark, to which Bermbach, too, refers, there is no denying that Tannhäuser ultimately feels that he belongs to the world of "institutions" and that although his redemption does not have the pope's approval, it is achieved through the intercession of two saints: the Virgin Mary and Elisabeth. And Wagner depicts the faith of those pilgrims who *have* been absolved by the pope in an entirely positive light. Not even the Wartburg is seen as a negative entity: although the court and its followers may be appalled at a crime from which Wagner himself increasingly distances himself in the course of the second act, there are signs of their greater understanding. And if we ignore the bleak ending of the very first version of the opera, which Wagner revised almost straightaway, it is clear that the Wartburg finally makes its peace with the rebel, albeit only after he has been humbled:

> Der Gnade Heil ward dem Büßer beschieden,
> nun geht er ein in der Seligen Frieden!

[The salvation of grace has been granted the penitent, and now he finds the peace of the blessed.]

No one, surely, will think that Wagner was trying to distance himself from this statement. Such an act of deconstruction must be left to today's audiences.

When seen through Wagner's eyes, the work's message raises many questions. If the opera is about "redemption," then the action seems to me to be far less coherent than the relatively simple tale of the Flying Dutchman as a Wandering Jew in search of salvation, quite apart from the grand operatic ballast that threatens to weigh it down: among these features are the Chorus of Sirens, the Pilgrims' Chorus, the song contest, the *preghiera*, the magical reappearance of Venus and her retinue to the strains of onstage music that is merely illustrative in character, the death knell, the miracle of the burgeoning crosier, and so on.

This wealth of images and metaphors helps to set *Tannhäuser* apart not only from its predecessor but also from its successor, *Lohengrin*, in which the action is concentrated on a single otherworldly apparition in the guise of the eponymous hero. And his miraculous appearance is more skillfully incorporated into an otherwise realistic, historical plot than is the case with *Tannhäuser*. Whether as doubters or believers, we are confronted in *Tannhäuser* with Christian truths, whereas *Lohengrin* offers us a coherent fairy-tale motif within an otherwise rational plot: we accept that motif and empathize with it without being obliged to take a stand on it. And, according to *Opera and Drama*, we do so involuntarily in that the action is presented to our feelings through the agency of the music.

The plot of *Tannhäuser* can best be salvaged if we view the hero as a man driven by forces beyond his control and if we see his actions as the result of his compulsive adherence to certain rituals. Although this interpretation of the work may not reflect Wagner's own intentions, it does not—on the other hand—presuppose any act of deconstruction on our part. In his extended set of instructions on how to perform the opera, Wagner described as follows the principal feature of his hero's character:

> an active and extreme willingness to be consumed by the present situation, while the liveliest contrast that is produced by the violent changes in his situation is revealed through the ways in which he expresses that sense of fulfillment. Tannhäuser is nowhere and never "a little" anything, but is always everything, fully and entirely. He has luxuriated in the arms of Venus in a state of utter ecstasy; and it is only with the keenest feeling of the need to break free from her that he severs the bonds that had fettered him to her, without for a moment railing at the Goddess of Love.[33]

It requires little or no effort to reinterpret this image in psychoanalytical terms and see Tannhäuser as a man who from first to last is driven by figments of an unrealizable imagination. First he wishes to enter a paradise that will meet all his erotic needs and help him to find endless pleasure. When he tries to escape from this "paradise" and compete with his rivals in order to win the hand of the woman he desires most of all, he needs another's help to break free from Venus's embrace, which is when—completely without motivation—he calls on the Mother of God. In the company of his potential rivals for Elisabeth's hand, he initially reacts with supercilious arrogance but, following his hymn to Venus, he becomes acutely conscious of his guilt. When Wartburg society demands that he go to Rome, where he is sent packing by the pope, he vacillates with almost unconscious irresolution between the different possibilities that are open to him: should he return to the Venusberg, as the folk tale demands in consequence of what the stage directions describe as his "appalling lasciviousness," or should he entrust his salvation to Elisabeth, who is already with the saints in heaven? Demonstrating the same lack of will as he must have shown in the Venusberg at the start of the opera, he finally allows Elisabeth to intercede for him.

Tannhäuser is no active hero but a passive, anxious figure torn between self-destruction and delusions of grandeur, and able to invest his existence with a semblance of stability only by following certain rituals: his dealings with Venus have been ritualized, and the competition at the Wartburg, which is about a true understanding of the world, is specifically laid out along the lines of another such ritual. The pilgrimage to Rome is a single extended ritual, and even Tannhäuser's end, which recalls the final scene of *Parsifal*, has ritual features to it.

If we ignore the "happy ending," which seems to have been imposed on the work from outside, and examine the figure of Tannhäuser from a biographical point of view, then we shall see parallels between him and Wagner himself, a man who, as an unsuccessful bohemian artist in Paris, suffers from an identity crisis. Fleeing from this hotbed of godlessness, he seeks to regain that sense of identity in the German Catholic ritual of the Middle Ages but ends up in a medieval world marked by the pagan ritual of the cult of Venus, forcing him unexpectedly to side with Baudelaire, who not unreasonably was to see in Wagner a brother in arms in the spirit of an atheistic, albeit amoral, aestheticism.

It is no accident that Tannhäuser's ambivalence as a character fascinated two such different individuals as Albert Schweitzer and Bertolt Brecht, in each case during their turbulent adolescence. Schweitzer recalled that

> together with my veneration for Bach went the same feeling for Richard
> Wagner. When I was a schoolboy at Mülhausen [*sic*] at the age of sixteen,
> I was allowed for the first time to go to the theatre, and I heard there

Wagner's *Tannhäuser*. This music overpowered me to such an extent that it was days before I was capable of giving proper attention to the lessons in school.[34]

Brecht was probably fifteen when he attended a performance of *Tannhäuser* in 1913—the centenary of Wagner's birth—and was inspired to write a poem to which he gave the title "Autumn Mood from Tanhäuser [*sic*]." Unsurprisingly, he was attracted above all by the hero's feeling of homelessness:

> Oft ritt er mit gesenktem Speer
> In dem schwarzen, trauernden Kleid
> Durch herbstliche Felder und Wälder weit
> Versunken schwer
> In Leid. [. . .]
> So ritt er dahin jetzt bald sieben Jahr
> Und immer stumpfer wurde das Licht
> Der Augen.
> Und die weißen Schläfen sanken ein.
> Grau wurde der Stirne blendendes Weiß
> Und feine Furchen zogen sich leis
> In das Gesicht mit Fleiß.
> Die Stirne schien ganz grau versteint
> Und die Augen waren stumpf verweint
> Da glomm ein Sehnen nach Frieden heiß
> Nach Frieden.[35]

[He often rode with lowered spear in sable mourning garb through autumn fields and woods, his head bowed low in grief. [. . .] And so he rode for almost seven years, and ever duller grew the light within his eyes. And temples that had once been white were sunken, his forehead's dazzling white turned gray, and lightly furrowed was his face. His brow seemed turned to grayish stone, his eyes were dull and tearful, and yet there glowed in them a burning wish for peace, for peace.]

The mixture of fear, loneliness, inhibition, and ritualized action that marks long sections of *Tannhäuser*, including each and every one of its characters, would be difficult to endure if it were not for the music. Of course, we can appreciate this music only if we recognize that Wagner wrote a romantic opera, not a music drama. Whereas the *Ring, Tristan und Isolde, Die Meistersinger*, and *Parsifal* can all claim to be effective as coherent musical structures, *Tannhäuser* fascinates us thanks to the intensity of its individual numbers and tableaus and its sophisticated mixture of tone colors. There is as yet no trace of the "art of transition" that Wagner was to see as his ideal from the time of *Tristan und Isolde*; and his leitmotif technique plays an even less significant role here than it had done in *Der fliegende Holländer*. As Carl Dahlhaus has pointed out, the score "does not explain or connect but asserts and establishes," and yet in spite of—or because of—"the lack of dramatic coherence," the work "succeeds in giving the appearance of necessity to what is unmotivated, and credibility to what is absurd and inconsequential."[36]

We should not be doing the opera a disservice if we were to attend a performance in much the same way that we might visit the Louvre, moved by individual pieces that produce an overall impression but which are not related to one another in any logical way. It is no accident that in September 1842, just after he had completed the prose draft of *Tannhäuser*—still called *Der Venusberg* at this date—Wagner wrote to his friend Ernst Benedikt Kietz in Paris:

> In the parish church at Aussig I asked to be shown the Madonna by Carlo Dolci: it is a quite extraordinarily affecting picture, & if Tannhäuser had seen it, I could readily understand how it was that he turned away from Venus to Mary without necessarily having been inspired by any great sense of piety.—At all events, I am now firmly set on Saint Elisabeth.[37]

In short, not even Wagner himself was able to explain the contradictions in his hero, and so an external image was required to make it clear to his emotional understanding what exactly was involved here. Later, when he started work on the score, this external image was replaced by music that likewise eschews all rational arguments but uses its own inherent power to triumph effortlessly over all argumentative doubts.

Paradoxically, Wagner achieves this aim not simply through musical numbers that can be described as crowd-pleasers in a positive sense—namely, Tannhäuser's Hymn to Venus ("Stets soll nur dir mein Lied ertönen"), Elisabeth's Greeting to the Hall of Song ("Dich, theure Halle"), the Entry of the Guests ("Freudig begrüßen wir die edle Halle"), the Pilgrims' Chorus ("Beglückt darf nun"), Elisabeth's Prayer ("Allmächt'ge Jungfrau"), and Wolfram's Ode to the Evening Star ("Wie Todesahnung"). Of course, Wagner banked on the effectiveness of these numbers and had no objections when his Dresden publisher, C. F. Meser, brought out arrangements of them for voice and piano. But, as he told Hans von Bülow in the context of his "Lyric Pieces for Voice from *Lohengrin*," he ultimately regarded such publications simply as "fripperies" designed "to make some money."[38]

And yet the music of *Tannhäuser* has more to offer than this—namely, a use of color that for long stretches operates with novel refractions, shadings, and shifting hues. In this, the score reveals a degree of refinement appreciably greater than anything found in *Der fliegende Holländer*. And it is a feature that from now on was to be a hallmark of Wagner's music. In his chapter "Sonority" in his book on Wagner, Adorno looks briefly at the "unstable" and "ambiguous" aspects of Wagner's use of sonority,[39] but he is guilty of neglecting the significance of tone color in its relation to the harmonic writing and of ignoring Wagner's own insistence that "anyone who, when judging my music, separates the harmony from the instrumentation does me as great a wrong as the man who separates my music from my poem and my vocal line from the word."[40] But this is precisely what Adorno is guilty of doing when he complains that Wagner was not really master of his own compositional handiwork and that he often confused the progressive with a hankering after empty, superficial effects designed to dazzle his audience. In short, it was the triumph of appearance over substance.

Of course, Wagner was the great illusionist even in *Tannhäuser*. And yet today's audiences are more skeptical toward the sort of "true" or "great" music said to have crystallized in the works of Bach, Beethoven, and Schoenberg and as a result are more likely to dismiss *Tannhäuser* on aesthetic grounds than accuse its composer of charlatanism. And even those listeners who quickly tire of Wagner's music and especially of *Tannhäuser* will scarcely deny that the overture, for all its Teutonic coarseness, affords evidence of great refinement: "expressive elements of anguish and suffering" merge in complex ways with the "ecstatic experience of strength and confidence."[41] We do not have to agree with Adorno when he refers dismissively to "enjoyment of pain" and to "pleasure as sickness"[42] but instead may admire the cloudy admixture of the tonally pure and the distorted as an expression of the fact that human existence is damaged beyond repair.

Such mixtures have something searing and seething about them and have left their mark on whole sections of the score, drawing into their sway listeners who are as responsive as Baudelaire evidently was, so that we forget the inconsistencies in the action and allow our attention to be drawn, instead, to the complex psychological stirrings about which we would have remained unaware, had they not found expression in the music.

This is true not least of the Bacchanal that opens the Paris version of the opera. Wagner's aim was to create an archetypal picture of orgiastic excess, and by drawing on the musical idiom of *Tristan und Isolde* he is strikingly successful, at least from a purely musical point of view. Of course, it can be argued whether a phantasmagoria of action, singing, and dancing can in fact be realized as grippingly as Wagner may have imagined, but for the most part the music can meet these expectations as it does not have to be pinned down to concrete images but can inhabit a world beyond good and evil and play with sound figures to which we can all apply our own individual ideas of just what constitutes an orgy. In this context, Wagner's harmonic writing is innovative and even avant-garde. Thanks to its chromatic and enharmonic procedures it is in a state of constant change, forever modulating to other tonalities and giving listeners—not least Wagner's own contemporaries—the feeling that the ground is being taken from under their feet.

The traditional theory of harmony naturally offers pointers to ways of incorporating these novel sounds into the existing system, so that the D-sharp on the first syllable of "Strande" in the Chorus of Sirens, "Naht euch dem Strande," may be analyzed as a suspension of the chord of a diminished seventh over a pedal point on B. And yet this suspended chord, which is made up of a major and a minor triad, acquires so much weight as a result of its length that its sheer idiosyncrasy leaves a far greater impression on the listener than its subsequent resolution. To borrow from the language of arithmetic, the sirens' sound is both real and imaginary, or, to quote the Wagner scholar Werner Breig, it is "a simultaneous pulling away and an urge to rest."[43]

7. The sirens' call from act 1 of *Tannhäuser*.

Naht euch dem Stran - - de!

As enthusiastic Wagnerians, we may regard this art of illusion as the ne plus ultra of the genre, or we may follow Adorno and claim the moral high ground by accusing Wagner of "ambiguity" and, hence, untruthfulness.[44] Yet again we may agree with Walter Benjamin and Claus-Artur Scheier when they claim that the artistic product is being "technologically produced" here in a way that turns Wagner's idea of metaphysical redemption into a commodity that as such negates itself, while "restoring" that quality "and, as it were, raising it to a higher power."[45] This comes close to the media theory of Marshall McLuhan, according to which the medium is the message, which in the present case would mean that Wagner's music conveys no "higher" meaning of the kind that we find in the score of Beethoven's *Fidelio*, for example, but that the stimuli of the music, when divorced from the visual spectacle, are devoid of meaning and capable, therefore, of docking with all possible synapses. But leaving aside all modern media theory, we can still express astonishment at the unique ideas that Wagner presents here in drawing his listeners into the undertow of the action and lending an entire scene a wholly distinctive and unmistakable color.

The same is true of the introduction to act 3, a passage often described as "Tannhäuser's Pilgrimage." It represents an inspired attempt to depict Tannhäuser's failed journey to Rome and his feelings up to his return to the Valley of the Wartburg in autumn not as those events might unfold onstage but as a purely instrumental tone painting, a term that Wagner was not in fact to use until the time of the prelude to *Lohengrin*. Toward the end of his life, he was fond of asking Josef Rubinstein to play such tone paintings—especially those drawn from the *Ring*—on the piano. According to a much later reminiscence by Wagner's publisher, Ludwig Strecker, the composer explained that such tone paintings "give people the essence of the drama and, indeed, everything, to the extent that it is not only interesting without words but also intelligible."[46]

The original version of Tannhäuser's Pilgrimage was 155 bars long and included "recitative-like orchestral phrases." In writing it, Wagner already had in his head a complete "picture of the events" that take place during his hero's journey to Rome.[47] But in the light of the first performance of the opera, Wagner cut more than a third of it because he felt that many of its details would inevitably remain unclear. And yet even in its shorter version, for which he set out a detailed "program" in a note he wrote for a series of performances of this orchestral introduction in Zurich in May 1853,[48] Wagner plays eloquently with motifs from the earlier acts that help to characterize Tannhäuser's state of mind. These include Elisabeth's appeal "ich fleh' für ihn, ich flehe für sein Leben" (I plead for him, I plead for his life), phrases from the Pilgrims' Chorus such as "Zu dir wall' ich, mein Jesus Christ" (To you I come, my Jesus Christ) and the atonement motif already heard in the overture and later set to the words "Ach schwer drückt mich der Sünden Last" (Ah, the weight of sin weighs heavily on me). But there is also a pre-echo of a phrase later found in the closing scene of the opera at the words "Erlösung ward der Welt zu Theil" (Redemption was granted to the world) and previously used to underpin Tannhäuser's Rome Narration: it recalls the "Dresden Amen" that will later acquire significance as the Grail motif in *Parsifal*.

8–10. The motifs associated with penance, redemption, and contrition. The redemption motif looks forward to the Grail motif from *Parsifal*.

Wagner demonstrates supreme artistry in combining these motifs and adding a new one in the form of a theme associated with remorseful contrition,[49] thereby granting listeners a glimpse of Tannhäuser's emotions during his pilgrimage to Rome, as fear and despair contend with a sense of hope that ultimately becomes euphoric. The sophistication of this tone painting may be illustrated by at least one detail: the chromatic motif associated with atonement and first heard in the overture in bar 17 creates an impression more especially by dint of its eccentric harmonies (E minor—G minor—B-flat minor—the area of E major).[50] In bars 23–30 of Tannhäuser's Pilgrimage it then migrates in a curiously tentative and brooding manner from the horns via the clarinets to the first oboe, while being subjected to a remarkably nuanced treatment even within the horns: the second valve horn enters first of all with the motif, after which the sequencing continues with the second natural horn, while a further sequence is entrusted to the first valve horn. This process leads to a constant recoloring of the sound and creates the impression that the mood is perpetually changing in a subtle and almost indefinable way. (That modern orchestras draw no distinction between natural horns and rotary valve horns means that this effect is considerably impaired.)

To the true composer music willingly reveals its secrets. He grasps its talisman and with it commands the listener's imagination, so that at his summons any scene from life may pass before the mind's eye, and one is irresistibly drawn into the colourful swirl of fantastic images. It may well be that it is in the knowledge of these mysterious charms and their proper application that the true art of musical painting lies. Melody, choice of instruments, harmonic structure—all must work together. [. . .] On the other hand there are certain melodies which suggest solitude, or pastoral life, for example; a certain combination of flutes, clarinets, oboes, bassoons will intensify this feeling with extreme vividness.[51]

These reflections on "musical painting" were penned by E. T. A. Hoffmann in 1812, but not until Wagner arrived on the scene was the compositional promise contained within them finally made good, not least in Tannhäuser's Pilgrimage, which on the one hand represents a traditional entr'acte, while on the other anticipating Wagner's later "orchestral melody." When he discussed this last-named concept in *Opera and Drama* and declared that it conveyed the inner action of his musical drama, Wagner will have had not only the future *Ring* in mind but also those passages in *Tannhäuser* that reflect this ideal—in other words, episodes such as the Rome Narration, which even Adorno was willing to acknowledge as "music of the greatest power."[52]

Even in Tannhäuser's Pilgrimage, Wagner's use of orchestral melody already adumbrates the procedures found in the *Ring*, and this is even more true of the Rome Narration, for here we have not only the orchestral part with its illustrative elements that plainly look forward to Wagner's later use of the leitmotif, but above all the listener is held in thrall by the vocal line, the declamatory nature of which clearly anticipates the later *Ring*. Although this section of the score begins like a song or aria, it quickly becomes—in Carolyn Abbate's words—the "voice of musical anarchy."[53] Not only does Tannhäuser report on the failure of his pilgrimage in melodramatic and gestural terms, but Wagner even reflects his foundering on ecclesiastical institutions in his actual composition of this scene, the "institution" of traditional harmony and periodicity being deconstructed to such an extent that the failure of Tannhäuser's enterprise and the resultant chaos are palpable in the music.

The process of disorientation gets under way only gradually, before culminating in Tannhäuser's hallucinatory vision of Venus. But this makes

The end of act 2 in Jan Fabre's 2010 production of *Tannhäuser* at the Théâtre Royal de la Monnaie in Brussels depicts Elisabeth as a bellicose mater dolorosa protecting Tannhäuser from the unforgiving members of the Wartburg court. (Photograph courtesy of the Archives of the Théâtre Royal de la Monnaie, Brussels. Photographer: Johan Jacobs.)

perfect sense from a dramaturgical point of view, for whereas Tannhäuser initially addresses Wolfram in well-ordered verse, he is increasingly overwhelmed by his own memories and by the associations bound up with them, until madness finally breaks out. We need only to compare Tannhäuser's Rome Narration with Lohengrin's Grail Narration to appreciate its avant-garde nature. In both cases the verse consists of iambic pentameters, but Lohengrin is an ambassador from a world beyond our own, and so his narration has many of the formal qualities of a song or aria, whereas the Rome Narration tends in the direction of the eccentricity of musical prose of a kind that is the exception in Wagner's work. Listeners should harbor the illusion that the Rome Narration was not composed by Wagner but is being ecstatically improvised by Tannhäuser. In this context it is worth reminding ourselves of Wagner's own admission in this regard: "The peculiar thing about me as an artist, for instance, is that I look on each detail as an entirety and never say to myself, 'Since this or that will follow, you must do thus and such, modulate like this or like that. [. . .] And yet I know I am unconsciously obeying a plan.'"[54] It makes perfect sense in this context that Wagner struggled to find singing actors who had not only learned the standard gestures and facial expressions but were able to practice "the art of sublime illusion," an art that in Wagner's view had nothing to do with mere acting but involved "truthfulness" first and foremost.[55]

By examining the "tone paintings" of the Bacchanal and Tannhäuser's Pilgrimage, together with the Rome Narration, from one and the same standpoint, we may be reminded of a passage from Nietzsche's posthumously published writings: "Wagner knows what effects opiates and narcotics can have, and he uses them to combat the nervous distractedness of his powers of musical invention, a distractedness of which he is very well aware."[56] Although Nietzsche was thinking of *Lohengrin*, his comment can be applied equally well to *Tannhäuser*, at least if we ignore the popular crowd-pleasers such as the two Pilgrims' Choruses, Tannhäuser's Hymn to Venus, the Entry of the Guests, Elisabeth's Prayer and Wolfram's Ode to the Evening Star. Whether these numbers would have sufficed to guarantee the work a prominent place in an operatic history of the nineteenth century must remain an open question, but it is a part of Wagner's genius that he was able to incorporate these popular numbers within a context that lacks nothing in musicodramatic verve. Even his rival Meyerbeer, who stopped off in Hamburg in 1855 specially to hear a performance of the opera and who was critical of the work's "formlessness and lack of melody," praised the "great flashes of genius in the conception and orchestral color." In particular, he was impressed by the instrumental passages, including, no doubt, Tannhäuser's Pilgrimage.[57] And it is no accident that the anti-Wagnerian Schumann admitted to Felix Mendelssohn: "*I have to take back much* of what I wrote after reading through the score; from the stage, everything looks very different. I was very moved by much of it."[58]

When Schumann saw *Tannhäuser*, it was in a production that reflected Wagner's own intentions, which ensured that plot, stage action, and music were fully synchronized. Modern directors would find themselves in extreme difficulty if they were to attempt to replicate every aspect of Wagner's aesthetic approach to staging his works. But at least their modern approach would register the losses that ensue when Wagner's music tries to illustrate something that is neither shown onstage in many modern productions nor depicted by the gestures of his performers—or "mimes," as he preferred to call them. A Rome Narration performed by a singer introspectively cowering on the ground considerably circumscribes the gestural range of the music. Something that would have been unthinkable to Wagner should at least give modern directors pause for thought.

A Word about Josef Rubinstein

 As pianist in residence at the Villa Wahnfried, Josef Rubinstein often performed the "tone painting" *The Venusberg*, reminding Wagner on one such occasion of the rehearsals for *Tannhäuser* in Paris during the winter of 1860–61 and of a comment made by Otto Wesendonck, who had been present at that time: "What utterly voluptuous sounds these are!" "I suppose he was afraid I had been dancing something like that in front of his wife," Wagner quipped to Cosima.[1] In general, Wagner was happy with these tone paintings from his own works—characteristic excerpts suitable for the piano. Wagner, who spent most of his evenings in Bayreuth with his family or a small circle of friends, would then revel in the past, while also finding new ideas for future projects and seeing himself above all as a *musician* who traded in sounds. But he also enjoyed hearing Rubinstein performing Bach's *Well-Tempered Clavier* and *Chromatic Fantasy*, piano sonatas by Beethoven, a polonaise by Chopin, a waltz by Johann Strauß, and much else besides. The repertory even included pieces by Rossini, Berlioz,

and Auber. In particular he was fond of playing arrangements of operas and symphonies for piano duet with his "pet Israelite," as Rubinstein was called by way of a joke within the family circle.[2] But was it really just a joke?

Supported by his wealthy father, Rubinstein, who had previously worked as chamber pianist to the Grand Duchess Elena Pavlovna of Russia, no less, spent a whole decade trailing in the wake of the vast ocean liner that was Wagner before finally being sucked beneath the waves. His name occurs frequently in the pages of Cosima's diaries, beginning with an entry dated March 7, 1872: "Letters arrive, among others a very remarkable one from Josef Rubinstein, beginning 'I am a Jew' and demanding salvation through participation in the production of the Nibelungen. R. sends him a very friendly reply."[3]

Within weeks the twenty-five-year-old Rubinstein was knocking at Wagner's door, acting as *répétiteur* at the rehearsals for the *Ring*, and even preparing a copy of the short score of act 3 of *Götterdämmerung* to be presented to Ludwig II. He then spent some time giving concerts with Liszt, before returning to Bayreuth in 1874 and working as a copyist in the "Nibelung chancellery," while once again demonstrating his proficiency as a rehearsal pianist. In the spring of 1876 an article appeared in the popular periodical *Über Land und Meer* describing life at Wahnfried and mentioning Rubinstein by name. But Rubinstein left Bayreuth before the first festival opened in the summer of that year, mortified that Wagner had used a speech thanking his assistants for their help to expatiate on his xenophobic racist theories in the presence of the whole company.[4]

But Rubinstein found it impossible in the longer term to survive without Wagner, and by the following year he had written to ask forgiveness for his behavior the previous summer. By 1878 he had not only been restored to favor but had become a part of the Wagners' entourage, performing each evening at Wahnfried for weeks at a time. He was also invited to accompany the family to Naples, Palermo, and Venice. Back in Bayreuth, he joined Wagner over a drink at the local hostelry, and—just as Nietzsche had helped to decorate the Christmas tree at Tribschen—so he was coerced into playing whist with Hans von Wolzogen and, more frequently, drawn into conversation with Wagner about God and the world. A letter from Rubinstein prompted Wagner to speak of his "extraordinary culture."[5] Even more surprisingly, Wagner prevailed on Rubinstein to write three articles on the aesthetics and politics of music for the *Bayreuther Blätter*, the in-house journal from which Jewish writers were later to be banned.

At the same time, however, it is clear from Cosima's diaries that Rubinstein was cast in the role of the outsider, who, according to Siegfried Wagner's reminiscences, was loved only by the family's English governess.[6] "If he knew how difficult we find him," Wagner told his wife in 1881, "he would make things easier for us."[7] There were times when the Wagners found Rubinstein's interpretation of the "Hammerklavier" Sonata impressive, while on other occasions they felt it was misconceived. One day the young man was incorrigibly fixed in his views; the next day those views were entirely other people's. Of course, everything and everyone at Wahnfried was the subject of carping criticisms, but what makes it all the more disagreeable in Rubinstein's case is the reason that the Wagners gave: the "poor man" simply couldn't help it because he was Jewish.[8] This rendered him just as incapable of coping with life's pressures as of mastering the triplets in the *Siegfried Idyll*. Throughout all this he was nonetheless useful as a lightning conductor. If Wahnfried had not had its "pet Israelite," it would have had to invent him.

Clearly subject to bouts of depression and suffering from an inferiority complex, Rubinstein went on tour after Wagner's death, only to shoot himself near Lucerne on August 23, 1884. Cosima had his body brought back to Bayreuth and placed a simple tombstone over his grave in the town's Jewish cemetery.

This crayon portrait of Wagner is the work of Ernst Benedikt Kietz and dates from the spring of 1850, when Wagner was briefly visiting Paris. Within days of its completion, Wagner had left for Bordeaux, where he fell hopelessly in love with Jessie Laussot née Taylor and presented her with the original. This original is now believed lost, but a daguerreotype prepared from it has survived and has served as the basis of all later reproductions. (Photograph courtesy of the Nationalarchiv der Richard-Wagner-Stiftung, Bayreuth: Bi 151-l.)

CHAPTER FIVE

A Bedtime Story with Dire Consequences

LOHENGRIN

The old theme in a new context — Christian romanticism: just
a front? — Lohengrin as Wagner: a stranger in the here and
now — The historical and political dimension: "For German
lands with German swords" — Wagner's utopian vision of a
popular monarchy — His medieval studies — *Lohengrin* and
its consequences: Thomas and Heinrich Mann contest the
moral high ground — Hitler as Lohengrin reborn — Is the opera
damaged beyond repair? — Ideas on staging the work — Elsa:
condemned to remain a woman? — Wagner as director of
Lohengrin — The work's musical innovations: leitmotifs and
musical fabric illustrated by the scene between Friedrich and
Ortrud — Liszt: "A single chord" says all that needs to be said
about Wagner — The prelude: "Utopia in A major" — Wagner's
Lohengrin: a literary fairy tale about black and white magic —
Can Wagner's music heal the wounds that the work has been
dealt? — Elsa's "Einsam in trüben Tagen" as an illustration of
Wagner's "subtle art of transition" — The lyricism of *Lohengrin*

In each of his self-styled "romantic" operas Wagner reacted directly to
his own situation as man and artist — this is something that we find not
only in *Der fliegende Holländer* and *Tannhäuser* but also in *Lohengrin*. True,
the opera appears at first sight to be a purely romantic fairy tale remote
from all current concerns, but on closer inspection we can discover in it a
whole nexus of motifs drawn from Wagner's life and times. Some of them
complement one another, while others run counter to each other.

It is hard not to be impressed by the persistence with which Wagner,
having completed *Tannhäuser*, remained true to his basic theme: *Lohengrin*
deals with the corruption of modern society that no longer has time for
"purely human" love, condemning obvious outsiders to failure and even

encouraging them in their death wish. Of course, Lohengrin is not Tannhäuser "sinking to his ruin in all that the modern world has to offer by way of sensuality and hedonism," but the Christian morality that underpins the piece is impossible to ignore. As with *Tannhäuser*, Wagner vigorously resisted all attempts to reduce *Lohengrin* to the "category" of "Christian romanticism."[1] And yet Christian miracle and pagan magic are so clearly contrasted in the work that the figure of Ortrud, whose magic is pagan in origin, has negative associations. Elsa even feels obliged to win over her rival to her own faith, hoping in that way to teach Ortrud true charity and what she calls "happiness without remorse." And in a passage that Wagner finally decided against setting to music, Lohengrin, having been driven away by Elsa's curiosity about his background, was for a time intended to say:

> O Elsa! Was hast du mir angethan!
> Als meine Augen dich zuerst ersahn,
> Fühlt' ich, zu dir in Liebe schnell entbrannt,
> Mein Herz des Grales keuschem Dienst entwandt!
> Nun muß ich ewig Reu' und Buße tragen,
> Weil ich von Gott zu dir mich hingesehnt, —
> Denn ach! der Sünde muß ich mich verklagen,
> Daß Weibeslieb' ich göttlich rein gewähnt![2]

[O Elsa! What have you done! When first my eyes beheld you, I felt inflamed at once by my love for you, my heart abjured the Grail's chaste service! Forever must I now repent and atone for having turned from God, for, ah! the shameful sin I must confess of deeming woman's love divinely pure!]

These lines not only look forward to the "sinful worlds" that Lohengrin's father, Parzival, will have to resist in Wagner's last completed music drama, it also, and above all, recalls the "blasphemous gazes" that Tannhäuser once cast at Elisabeth. Of course, Lohengrin has taken a further step down the road that leads to the renunciation of women's love for he has been sent by God, and, as such, his problem differs from Tannhäuser's. On this occasion we are only peripherally concerned with resisting the temptations of insidious sensuality. Rather, "the tragedy of the situation of the true artist in the present age" consists in the fact that his "most necessary and most natural desire to be unconditionally accepted and understood by feeling" is constantly frustrated.

The modern artist is under a "*constraint* to communicate not to the emotions but almost entirely to the critical intellect."[3] Wagner is keen to apply this to the figure of Lohengrin, arguing that his hero could have saved Elsa and, indeed, the whole of Brabant if she had trusted him on an emotional level and listened to her "unconscious, involuntary" nature instead of her "critical intellect," which made her insist on asking him about his origins. In this context it is worth recalling Nietzsche's polemical remark that "Wagner thus represents the Christian concept, 'you ought to and must *believe*.' It is a crime against what is highest and holiest to be scientific."[4]

Although a certain amount of caution is advisable in this context, it may be possible to interpret Wagner's standpoint here as a reflection of his own mission as he saw it particularly while he was working on *Lohengrin* between 1845 and 1848. He was no longer the stranger that he had been in Paris, when his role had been similar to that of the homeless Flying Dutchman. But nor was he like Tannhäuser, fighting against his country's institutions, wanting on the one hand to comply with them, while on the other hand opposing them. The sufferings caused by society were of a higher order but also—by his own lights—more "tragic." Although Wagner was now an established composer, he still felt that he and his mission were misunderstood, for the prevailing music industry in Germany had no time for the sort of music theater whose task was to allow its audiences to experience metaphysical truths for themselves. (In order to make any headway institutionally, Wagner would have to found the Bayreuth Festival.) Although Dresden audiences had not rejected *Der fliegende Holländer* and *Tannhäuser* out of hand, they had been less than fulsome in their praise of either piece, and while it is not possible to attribute their lack of enthusiasm to an excess of "critical intellect," it was undoubtedly due, in Wagner's eyes, to a lack of feeling and a lamentable absence of blind faith in his message, according to which art was the new religion.

In February 1879, Wagner's pianist in residence in Bayreuth, Josef Rubinstein, claimed that in his youth he had not known where to begin with *Tannhäuser* and *Lohengrin*, prompting Wagner to comment, ironically, that "it is intellect which has brought this poor man to his feeling for these works," by which he evidently meant that in exceptional cases even the calculating Jew could see that in Wagner's music dramas what mattered was the "emotionalizing of the intellect," to quote from *Opera and Drama*.[5] If this assessment seems above all to be an example of Wagner's paranoid

conviction that he was regularly misunderstood by the emotionally cold
Jewish intelligentsia, another detail throws significant light on the limited
intelligence of Wagner's professional colleagues at the time of the work's
Dresden premiere. At the very end of his life, Wagner recalled that the theater's general administrator, Baron August von Lüttichau, had suggested in
all seriousness that "Tannhäuser should be pardoned in Rome and should
marry Elisabeth."[6]

No, for as Wagner observed in the very same breath, *Lohengrin* is his
"most tragic" work. It also, if not exclusively, reflects his current feelings about life: as court kapellmeister and as an opera composer of some
distinction in a relatively powerful position, he saw himself as a hero like
Lohengrin, and yet ultimately he felt he was misunderstood in terms of his
message to humanity. Wagner aka Lohengrin was not of this world.

Would this situation ever change? During the years when he was working on *Lohengrin*, Wagner began to cherish the hope that political upheaval
might create a social climate in which a renascent Lohengrin might have the
chance to be unconditionally accepted and understood on the strength of
feeling. This leads us on to the political dimension of the work, a dimension
that ill consorts with its fairy-tale, legendary aspect and presents the modern opera director with serious difficulties. The situation is complicated
above all by the fact that the political element failed to inspire Wagner as
a composer but is nonetheless integral to the plot, which requires a historical framework or, to be more specific, the attempts by King Henry the
Fowler to win over the "dear men of Brabant" for his campaign against the
Hungarians. And so the listener is assailed in the very first scene by military fanfares on four army trumpets, a pep talk from the King, and valiant
calls of welcome on the part of the Brabantine nobles as they clash their
weapons together. In later scenes, too, we hear brass fanfares, shouts of
"Hail" and vassals vowing to fight "for German lands with German swords!
So may the empire's might be preserved!" And when Lohengrin returns
to the world of the Grail, the King and his nobles appeal to him with the
words: "Oh, stay! Oh, do not leave! Your vassals await their leader [*Führer*]."
Although Lohengrin refuses to be swayed by their entreaty, he offers them
a prophetic vision of the future:

> Doch, großer König, laß mich dir weissagen:
> dir Reinem ist ein großer Sieg verlieh'n.
> Nach Deutschland sollen noch in fernsten Tagen
> des Ostens Horden siegreich niemals zieh'n!

[But, great King, let me foretell: a great victory will be granted you in your purity. Not even in the remotest future will Eastern hordes overrun Germany.]

We must resist the temptation to interpret these lines as the harbinger of a nationalistic or even a National Socialist desire for territorial expansion, for Wagner was operating within the political climate of his time. In terms of domestic politics Lohengrin's victory over the intrigue fomented by Ortrud and Telramund may be seen to reflect the imaginary triumph of a new and highly desirable form of bourgeois rule over the corrupt system then in existence. From the standpoint of foreign policy, Wagner had been a champion of Polish independence since the 1830s and, like many other artists and intellectuals, he was sympathetic to the manifold aspirations of the Polish people in their wish to throw off the yoke of czarist Russia. Although the Holy Alliance between Russia, Austria, and Prussia still existed at this period, at least as a formal arrangement, czarist Russia was currently exerting considerable pressure on Western Europe in general and on Prussia in particular, so that Wagner's reference to "Eastern hordes" could well have been interpreted as an allusion to the threat that was posed by Russia at this time.

No matter whether it was Hungary or Russia that was being pilloried here, the warning about these "Eastern hordes" was still sufficiently explosive even as late as 1876 for Wagner to have to omit the relevant passage in a performance that he himself conducted in Vienna in March of that year. Undertaken at the request of the director of the Vienna court opera, the cut was intended to spare the sensitivities of the Hungarian half of the imperial and royal dual monarchy.[7]

Regardless, however, of such details, it is only the libretto of *Lohengrin* that has any political connotations, for in Wagner's eyes there could be no such thing as political *music*: "that which is to be expressed in the language of music is limited to *emotions* and *feelings*," with the result that the task facing the "word-tone poet" was to express *"the purely human as freed from all convention."*[8] And above and beyond such theoretical considerations, it is surely not the "political" parts of *Lohengrin* that make it the musical event that it is, but the "poetical" sections: the "white" romanticism embodied by the lovers Lohengrin and Elsa and the "black" romanticism of the two conspirators, Friedrich and Ortrud, who inspired Wagner to write music so advanced that the world of Henry the Fowler pales into insignificance in comparison. (It is also worth adding parenthetically that many a Bayreuth conductor has cursed Wagner for the military music played by the onstage band in *Lohengrin*, the particular acoustics of the Festspielhaus making it well-nigh impossible to position the players correctly and even more difficult to coordinate them with the orchestra in the pit.)

Musically speaking, then, the piece would not suffer if the work's "politics" were disregarded, and yet—as we have already noted—these "politics" remain an indispensable part of the action. Wagner consciously constructed his plot around the idea of an encounter between reality and a fairy-tale realm that he himself preferred to describe as the world of "legend." The date at which the action takes place can be determined with some precision: it is the reign of Henry the Fowler (ca. 912–36), who was the Duke of Saxony and king of East Franconia. He defeated the Hungarians—previously believed to be invincible—in 933. Wagner was merely repeating received opinion when he made Henry the "German" king of a "German empire" that was still in its infancy. But this does not alter the fact that in his own eyes he was setting out from a historically authenticated position to which his response was to introduce a miracle. Of course, this use of miracles has precedents in early romantic literature, which often featured the irruption of the miraculous into the everyday secular world, but at the same time there is no doubt about Wagner's own inspired coup: by locating his fairy tale within a concrete historical context, he is able to present us with an apparently optimistic *political* utopia, while his utopian vision of successful *human* relationships is postponed *sine die*.

It would not be wrong to conclude from this that Wagner believed that political upheaval must precede any changes to the human heart, an attitude reflected in, and confirmed by, his own situation at this time. He wrote *Lohengrin* during the years leading up to the bourgeois revolution of March 1848, a decisive period in German history generally known as the *Vormärz*. Nor was he indifferent to the political developments that were taking place at this period. He numbered himself among the progressives whose agenda included the idea of a German nation, while stressing its roots in the Middle Ages. On long walks in Dresden and the surrounding area, he would discuss the current political situation with his music director August Röckel, who understood more about politics than music and who helped to organize the Dresden Uprising in May 1849, an act of insurrection for which he was sentenced to death, although the sentence was commuted to life imprisonment in Waldheim. That Wagner was fired by Röckel's optimism is clear from the memoirs of the professional revolutionary Alfred Meißner, who was introduced to the composer during an outing to the Dresden Waldschlößchen arranged by local artists and literary figures in September 1846: "I remember his words exactly: a revolution had already taken place in people's heads, the new Germany was ready and waiting, like a bronze cast that needed only a hammer blow on its clay shell in order for it to emerge."[9]

Writers on Wagner have spilled much ink over the question of whether he was really a political animal or, rather, an artist who wanted to further his own particular cause with the aid of politics. But this is splitting hairs. Wagner was interested only in his own individual mission. In November 1847 he complained in no uncertain terms to the Berlin critic Ernst Kossak about the "poor impression of Berlin" that he had formed during a series of performances of *Rienzi* in the city: "There is a dam that must be broken down here, and the means we must use is Revolution! [. . .] A single sensible decision by the King of Prussia with regard to his opera house, and all will be well again!"[10]

But Wagner's peculiar blend of egocentricity and naïveté did not prevent him from becoming a revolutionary overnight. Whatever misgivings one may harbor about this label, it is one that Wagner emphatically deserves, whereas he does not deserve to be described as a democrat in the spirit of the bourgeois revolutions of 1848–49. Even if he advocated the violent overthrow of the existing order in the anonymous articles that he is believed to have contributed to Röckel's *Volksblätter*, he continued to uphold the romantic tradition of dreaming of a king who was directly legitimized by his people. He wanted a popular monarchy that could bestow its blessings without regard for a "state" that was represented by the nobility and military on the one hand and by "capital" on the other. Under these "ideal" conditions, Wagner could propagate his notion of art as the new religion without having to take account of a hierarchy of sclerotic civil servants or having to compete with a music industry geared merely to making a profit. He would receive his commissions from the king and execute them in the name of the people. If they had still been living in ancient Greece, then Attic tragedy from the time of Aeschylus and Sophocles—an age in which Wagner likewise took an intense interest—would have served as his standard of comparison. In the nineteenth century the idea of a German popular monarchy was the most obvious alternative.

We may legitimately mock Wagner for proposing a utopian vision that may sometimes enjoy the sympathetic, if ironic, support of today's men and women of the theater, motivated, as they are, by anger at the lack of understanding of their own cultural institutions. But equally clearly we should admire Wagner for the creative way in which he sought to integrate his master plan into a stage work, namely, *Lohengrin*. For here, too, we find a popular monarchy and a hero whom Wagner explicitly hailed as an "artist" and who comports himself in the work as a kind of state-appointed artist. In the course of the opera he unites the people of Brabant, who are "without a prince" and living "in discord." And he gives them a ruler in the person of the young Duke Gottfried, who in future will reign with the Grail's blessing, Lohengrin having turned him back into human form after the wicked witch Ortrud cast a spell on him and transformed him into the swan that had brought our hero from the kingdom of the Grail to the banks of the Schelde in Antwerp.

It is said that this aspect of the work reflects Wagner's own "political" view of the situation: if artists like him had any influence over the state, they would be able to hold a protecting hand over young heirs to the throne, with the result that revolutions would no longer be necessary. *Lohengrin* is supposed to demonstrate that although such a notion is utopian, it still remains desirable. Such writers also argue that Wagner did not feel uncomfortable in the role of a political redeemer and that he later attempted to play the part of an intuitive political adviser to King Ludwig II of Bavaria, who bears a number of similarities with the young Duke Gottfried, for all that he himself would have preferred to be an otherworldly Lohengrin than a temporal ruler.

On the other hand, it has also been claimed on a similar basis that Wagner himself felt that on a personal level he had to live without the hope of ever finding fulfillment in love, at least under the social conditions existing at that time. Lohengrin/Wagner remains a stranger in the world and seems to anticipate the maxim of Theodor Adorno—a later critic of Wagner—in his *Minima moralia*: "Wrong life cannot be lived rightly."[11]

It is with a certain fascination that the reader notes the skill with which Wagner has introduced into *Lohengrin* his own situation as man and artist as well as his engagement with the politics of his day. No less impressive is his skill in integrating a fairy-tale motif into a historical framework that has much in common with real life, for all that it has been adapted to suit his own view of the world. Indeed, so successful has he been in this regard that an important political message emerges: we need artists of genius as pure in spirit as Lohengrin to provide our country, torn apart as it is by political intrigue, with the prospect of a better future.

Wagner's interest in *Lohengrin* went hand in hand with a detailed study of the Middle Ages. In the case of *Der fliegende Holländer* and *Tannhäuser* he had been able to seek inspiration in the writings of romantic poets such as Tieck and Heine, but he was unable to do so with *Lohengrin*, which had not been reworked by these writers. Instead, he had recourse to the late thirteenth-century *Lohengrin* epic, a poem for a long time attributed—erroneously—to Wolfram von Eschenbach and one which the books on the Middle Ages that he consulted retold in various ways. Here he found most of his *Lohengrin* motifs as well as the characteristic combination of history and fairy tale. The version of the Lohengrin narrative that dates from around 1280 tells how Henry the Fowler won his battle against a hundred thousand Hungarians with the help of only four thousand Christian knights thanks to the supernatural strength of his vassal Lohengrin.[12] However mysterious this emissary of the Grail may be, he marries Elsa in the medieval sources and they have children together before she finally asks him the fatal question about his origins. This episode is described as follows by San-Marte in his translation of Wolfram von Eschenbach's *Parzival*:

> Nachts ward das Beilager gefeiert,
> Und er am Morgen ausgesteuert
> Mit der Krone von Brabant,
> Die Hochzeit wird mit Pracht begangen,
> Und die Fürsten und Baron' empfangen
> Ihre Lehen von seiner Hand. [. . .]
> Aus ihrer hochbeglückten Ehe
> Wurden schöne Kinder geboren;
> Jedoch der Freude folgte Wehe.
> Wie sie gewonnen, ward sie verloren.[13]

[At night their nuptials were celebrated, and in the morning he was invested with the crown of Brabant. The wedding was marked with pomp, and the princes and barons received their fiefs from his hand. [. . .] From their most happy marriage beautiful children were born; but joy was followed by pain. As it was won, so it was lost.]

Nietzsche was one of the first writers to mock Wagner for cleaning up the narrative, arguing that the "Master" had taught us "that it may have the direst consequences if one doesn't go to bed at the right time."[14] But Lohengrin's refusal to sleep with Elsa underscores a message that was bound to be alien to the Middle Ages: although there may be hope for the German nation, this is not the case for the heroic individual who can fulfill his mission only by renouncing personal happiness. For Wagner himself this topos may well have seemed convincing, but in the light of subsequent German history it is bound to strike today's observers as troubling. A century ago it had positively explosive force when the brothers Thomas and Heinrich Mann found themselves at loggerheads over the opera, a disagreement that even found expression in their respective writings, albeit in encoded form.

The younger of the brothers, Thomas, had been an ardent admirer of *Lohengrin* since his youth, and according to his "Essay on the Theater" of 1908 he had attended performances of all Wagner's works at the Stadttheater in Lübeck, where he had been entranced by "this vast and questionable *oeuvre*, [. . .] this clever and ingenious wizardry, full or yearning and cunning, this fixed theatrical improvisation."[15] He could hardly remain indifferent, then, when his elder brother attacked one of his favorite works in his novel *Der Untertan* (variously translated as *The Patrioteer* and *Man of Straw*), which he completed in 1914. Its hero, Diederich Heßling, attends a performance of *Lohengrin* and exults in the nationalist fervor of the work. Unlike his fiancée Guste, he

> sided more with the King beneath the oak tree, since this was clearly the most prominent person. His entrance was not particularly dashing, [. . .] but what he said was to be welcomed from a national standpoint. "Protect the honor of the Reich in East and West." Bravo! Each time he sang the word "German," he stretched out his hand, and the music emphasized it accordingly. Elsewhere, too, the music powerfully underlined those lines that one should listen to. Powerful, yes, that was the word.

Diederich is particularly struck by the woman playing Elsa, an "emphatically German type, with billowing blonde hair and a lively temperament," only to be told by Guste that the soprano is in fact an "emaciated Jewess." For Diederich, Lohengrin himself embodies "supreme power, flashing in a magical way. [. . .] It was no accident that there were higher powers." As he later informed Guste, the moral of the story was that "next to God, the supreme master is answerable only to his conscience."[16]

It was not only brain-dead members of the petty bourgeoisie like Diederich Heßling who harbored such thoughts under Kaiser Wilhelm II. Max Koch, for example, was not only a self-confessed Wagnerian, he also taught the history of modern German literature in Breslau. In his reminiscences he recalls that "when war broke out, King Henry's promise that the country's enemies 'should never again dare to draw near from the desolate East' seemed like a comforting prophecy that was to come true at Tannenberg, causing us to echo his cries of 'For German lands the German sword! So may the empire's might be preserved!'"[17]

For Thomas Mann's repudiation of a nationalist interpretation of *Lohengrin*, whether such a view was meant to be taken seriously, as with Max Koch, or clothed in satire, as in the case of Mann's brother Heinrich, we must turn to his *Reflections of a Non-Political Man*, which he conceived during the First World War and published in 1918. Here Mann drew a distinction between an aesthetic and a political view of the world and reckoned it to the credit of the older type of Germans that they insisted on the former and refused to be dragged into politics. Although there were political artists, they represented a type of artistry that was "half-hearted, intellectual, willful and artificial," because the politician demanded political consequences from all forms of art. Turning to *Lohengrin*, Mann noted that

> As far as Wagner is concerned, it is clear that he was a revolutionary all his life, both as artist and as thinker. But it is equally certain that this champion of national cultural revolution did not intend political revolution, and never felt at all at home in the climate of 1848–9. [. . .] *Lohengrin* and 1848—two worlds apart, with at most only one thing in common: their national pathos. And the liberal critic [i.e., Heinrich Mann] is guided by a sure instinct when he makes fun of *Lohengrin* in satirical social novels by translating them into the political sphere. Wagner could probably hear the fine bass of his own King Henry in his mind when he made that thoroughly bizarre speech before the Dresden Fatherland Association, in which he proclaimed himself an ardent royalist and a despiser of constitutionalism in all its forms, and called upon Germany to cast out "alien, un-German notions"—by which he meant Western democracy—and to re-establish the one true saving and Old-Germanic relationship between the absolute monarch and the free people.[18]

Here Mann could clearly be accused of pussyfooting around the topic of Wagner and politics, because from Wagner's point of view there *was* a close connection between *Lohengrin* and the revolutions that swept across Germany in 1848, and if he admitted his support of a popular monarchy, this was no bizarre whim on the part of an unpolitical artist but an expression of the "conservative revolution" with which Mann, too, sympathized at this time. It is with some astonishment, moreover, that we read that Wagner's rejection of "Western democracy" was a passing eccentricity, not least because Mann himself largely shared that view, and it was not until some years later that in the wake of a positively Pauline conversion Mann began to champion the ideas of Western democracy.

We may well interpret Mann's reaction as an expression of his mortification—in his diary he complains in no uncertain terms about the "hateful cultural ridicule" heaped on *Lohengrin* by his brother and about the latter's generally "dissolute political tittle-tattle directed at Wagner."[19] But perhaps, too, his complaints are a reflection of his own attempt to suppress his doubts about his own position. After all, is it really possible to draw such a clear distinction between the political and aesthetic messages in *Lohengrin* as Mann would like to have done? And was he not obliged to concede that his brother was right at least to the extent that most audiences see *Lohengrin* through the eyes of that nationalist philistine, Diederich Heßling?

The story of *Lohengrin* does not end with Heinrich and Thomas Mann. Adolf Hitler was twelve when he stood through a performance of the opera in Linz. Recalling the occasion in *Mein Kampf,* he wrote that he was "captivated at once. My youthful enthusiasm for the master of Bayreuth knew no bounds."[20] Later, Hitler prepared set designs for an opera that he must have known almost by heart,[21] with the result that he reacted with surprise when, attending a performance of the work in Bayreuth on July 19, 1936, under Wilhelm Furtwängler, he heard the second half of Lohengrin's Grail Narration, a passage that Wagner himself had cut even before the work's first performance in Weimar in 1850. Mann listened to this same performance on the radio from his home in Küsnacht near Zurich—it was broadcast as part of the celebrations marking the one-thousandth anniversary of the founding of the German Reich—and evinced a knowledge of the score in no way inferior to that of the Führer who had forced him into exile. He, too, was surprised to hear the extended version of the Grail Narration.

Hitler was presumably not the only self-appointed leader to identify with Lohengrin, but he was undoubtedly the only one to be hailed by his people—excluding, of course, the émigré Mann—as a reincarnation of Lohengrin and King Henry.[22] The idea that Hitler was a Lohengrin-like leader who, with the blessing of the mysterious Grail, was sent to Germany directly by Heaven to restore his people to their former glory as long as they believed in him implicitly was not imposed on the Germans against their will but had for generations been an ingrained belief in many of them as the result of a process of socialization.

For me, *Lohengrin* is incapable of concealing its affinities with nationalism and National Socialism, for its ideological aspects not only affect its "political" dimension in the person of King Henry but are inextricably bound up with the action that is centered around Lohengrin. It is Lohengrin, after all, who installs the young Duke Gottfried as "Führer." It was Lohengrin, too, who provided Kaiser Wilhelm II with his motto "I know no more parties" and who was able to serve as a model for the National Socialists' attitude of "You are nothing, your people is everything." However much we may care to stress that it is in Lohengrin's "nature" to fail in his relationship with Elsa and that this has nothing to do with "politics," it remains the case that politically speaking he appears as a God-sent savior who—in the name of the "Providence" that Hitler never tired of invoking—unmasks and destroys the "false" leader of the people in order to install the "right" one.

This interpretation is not intended as an indictment of Wagner. After all, his political ideas had a different significance in the years before 1848 than they did after 1871 or at the time of National Socialism. Nor was it possible to have predicted the disastrous turn that they would take. If it *had* been possible to do so, then we should also have to condemn the hundreds of thousands and even millions of Germans who, attending performances of *Lohengrin* in the spirit of Diederich Heßling, made Wagner's ideological construct their own and treated it as a mainstream idea. After all, it needs only to be remembered that if the work's reception had developed along different lines, then it would have been possible to stress those alternative elements in the work that filled Thomas Mann with such great enthusiasm.

Wagner will not have thought along the lines of physical annihilation. He wanted his son Siegfried to be spared military service and toward the end of his life wrote a sentence that could be interpreted as a rejection of the killing machine set in motion by the National Socialists: "Heroism has bequeathed to us nothing but blood-letting and butchery—without all heroism—but everything with discipline."[23] At the same time, it seems to me impossible to rid *Lohengrin* of its ideological taint without emasculating the work completely. Rather, this is an example of the more general point made by Walter Benjamin to which I referred in my introduction: when surveying cultural treasures, the objective observer will "without exception" note that they "have an origin that he cannot contemplate without horror."

Is this a case of the curtain falling and leaving all questions open? Present-day opera directors can try, of course, to play down the political element in the work or—adopting the opposite extreme—emphasize it unduly. In his 2010 Bayreuth Festival production, for example, Hans Neuenfels was making a valid point when he dressed the Brabantine chorus as laboratory rats, implying that they can be manipulated. And at the end of the opera, when Lohengrin introduces the young Duke Gottfried to the Brabantines as their future leader in their war on Hungary, it may also be legitimate to present him as a boy soldier wearing a steel helmet and toting a machine gun, as Peter Konwitschny did in his Hamburg State Opera production in 1998. Any director wanting to instill a sense of productive unease in his audience could do worse than replicate the production that was seen for the first time in Bayreuth on July 19, 1936, in the sets and costumes of the time, and with Hitler exchanging knowing remarks with Siegfried Wagner's widow, Winifred, about the extended Grail Narration. Clips of Thomas Mann listening to the broadcast from his exile in Switzerland might also be intercut with the action. The conductor might wear a Furtwängler mask, and several members of the orchestra would be sporting swastika armbands. Or the action might be frozen at the relevant moments in order to present *tableaux vivants* by a group of dancers, thereby allowing us to appreciate the distance that exists between us and the nationalist tendencies that are inherent in the plot. Audience members could then judge for themselves whether these tendencies also affect the music. (The choreographer Sasha Waltz adopted this principle when she staged Pascal Dusapin's opera *Medea* at the Berlin State Opera in 2007.)[24]

Whereas other works by Wagner are able to resist this kind of one-sided ideological appropriation, *Lohengrin* remains permanently overshadowed by these unfortunate aspects of its reception. And yet even objects that are damaged beyond repair may still retain their charm as audiences can appreciate them in spite of everything. And this means a great deal in the case of *Lohengrin*: for here is a gripping fairy-tale narrative in which modern man's basic sensitivities can be effortlessly incorporated.

First and foremost there is the battle between the forces of good and evil. On the one hand we have those two beacons of light, Lohengrin and Elsa, while on the other there are the conspirators Ortrud and Friedrich. And yet the relationship between these four figures is far from being crassly black and white, for in spite of their nobility of outlook, Lohengrin and Elsa are not without fundamental weaknesses, while Ortrud, however evil, is a fascinatingly powerful woman. It was in this sense that Wagner wrote to Liszt in 1852:

A *male* politician disgusts us, a *female* politician appalls us: it was this appallingness that I had to portray. [. . .] Her whole passion reveals itself in the scene in act 2 when—following Elsa's disappearance from the balcony—she leaps up from the minster steps and calls out to her old, long-vanished gods. She is a reactionary, a woman concerned only for what is outdated and for that reason is hostile to all that is new—and hostile, moreover, in the most rabid sense of the word: she would like to eradicate the world and nature, simply in order to breathe new life into her decaying gods. But this is no idiosyncratic, sickly whim on Ortrud's part, rather does this passion consume her with the whole weight of a woman's longing for love—a longing that is stunted, undeveloped, and deprived of an object: and that is why she is so fearfully *impressive*.[25]

The reader senses Wagner working himself up into a rage at the very idea that his characters might be dismissed as operatic stereotypes remote from real life rather than being valued for what they are: reflections of actual social trends clothed in myth and fairy tale. This is also true of the figure of Lohengrin. Time and time again Wagner stressed that he had written not only *Der fliegende Holländer* and *Tannhäuser* but also *Lohengrin* to hold up a mirror to the triviality of his age. In view of the "unnatural state" of the world, the "absolute artist" was unable to assert his desire to be "*understood through love*" and express his need for "*the utmost physical reality*": "Lohengrin was looking for the woman who would *believe* in him and who would not ask who he was nor whence he came but who would love him as he was and because he was whatever she deemed him to be."[26]

Herman van Campenhout has objected that the Middle Ages were innocent of the whole concept of the "absolute artist," so that Wagner's interpretation of his own opera is like a "romantic picture invented by the bourgeoisie," a picture for which there is not even any evidence within the work itself.[27] But it is very much this that adds a certain spice to the piece in that Wagner presents us with a fairy tale that does not have to be given a present-day gloss but which certainly allows for one. Nor is he so naïve as to identify completely with a narcissistically world-weary Lohengrin: in referring to his hero's "egoism," he touches on the failings of an individual who is destroyed by his own demands. Conversely, Elsa is not a failure simply because she worships Lohengrin, rather than understanding him, for "there clings to him the tell-tale halo of his 'higher' nature,"[28] and this positively invites her to worship him. At the same time, however, she can become what Wagner calls "a woman of the future" only by dint of her insistent questioning. In this way she becomes a Brünnhilde figure who "knows everything" and to whom "everything is revealed" in turn.[29] But even an Elsa who wants to know everything cannot really be free as long as she tries to possess Lohengrin, for, as Wagner told Cosima, "the Knight of the Grail is sublime and free became he acts, not in his own behalf, but for others."[30] Here we encounter contradictions that for the most part rest not on moral failings, as they still do in *Tannhäuser*, but which are an integral aspect of human existence in general, at least in modern society.

"Nie sollst du mich befragen": "Never shall you question me." Readers are simply being taken in by Wagner if they try to throw light on every aspect of the characters in *Lohengrin*. We then become caught up in contradictions similar to those that beset Wagner himself in his pronouncements on the piece. There was "no escape from the longings of individuality except in death," he summed up his feelings in 1873.[31] It is impossible to imagine a remark as straightforward and yet as ambiguous. In a letter to August Röckel, he had earlier claimed that the "high tragedy of renunciation" was the "underlying poetic feature" of all three of his romantic operas.[32] Although the differences between the Dutchman, Tannhäuser, and Lohengrin are plain to see, they are only inadequately explained by reference to philosophy, the history of the mind, and even depth psychology.

Rather, they become apparent above all when we examine the roles and their representatives, representatives whose actions are ultimately unfathomable, and one can understand why Wagner, as a man of the theater, was furious whenever he saw his "message" threatened by performances characterized by routine or slovenliness. Whenever he could, he tried to show his singing actors how to perform their roles by identifying completely with them. In *Lohengrin*, the impresario Angelo Neumann recalled that when he was rehearsing the work in Vienna in 1875, Wagner

> demonstrated every move and gesture to Lohengrin, Telramund, and the King. Even his rapt expression when he delivered the line "Nun sei bedankt, mein lieber Schwan" [Accept my thanks, beloved swan] remains deeply etched in my memory. But it is altogether impossible to describe the inwardness with which he sang the part of Lohengrin. As for Elsa, he showed her every expression, every arm movement from her very first entry right through her whole long scene with the King. [. . .] But it was the third act that was the most extraordinary of all, for here Wagner acted and sang almost the entire scene in the bridal chamber. I shall never forget the expression of increasingly profound sadness that suffuses Lohengrin's features as he realizes that Elsa is coming ever closer to breaking her vow, and there was something almost otherworldly about his features when, with matchless grace and transfigured expression, he drew Elsa over to the

casement and, gently opening it with his left hand, sang the words "Atmest du nicht mit mir die süßen Düfte" [Can you, too, not smell the sweet perfumes?] while supporting Elsa in his right arm.[33]

By wanting to ban performances that were unauthorized or, he believed, inadequate, Wagner was behaving very much like Lohengrin and treating his audience as his hero treats Elsa: audiences should not use their critical intellect to ask what the emissary Lohengrin was nor whence he came but should love him just as he was and just as they deemed him to be. But this would work only in the case of performances in which the performers, having first made the roles their own, were able to identify with those roles to the maximum possible extent.

And the work's creator had already made this clear to his singers not just as its director but also as its composer. In his letter to Liszt he offers a detailed characterization of the wayward figure of Ortrud, revealing in the process a secret love of the character. Later, too, he spoke of the way in which the "wretchedness of two outcasts"—Ortrud and Telramund—had motivated him to produce such a "moving" account.[34] Clearly Ortrud had fascinated him as a musician and inspired him to write some of his finest music. This brings us—and how could it be otherwise?—to the heart of the matter, namely, the essential role of the music. Wagner could show his singers how to play their parts as often as he liked, but it would all be to no avail if they were not guided by the music, for it is the music that presents the action to our feelings. And it does so in a double sense. First, it "supports" the singers' actions onstage, actions that would have no authority without such a "net" but would seem arbitrary and, from today's standpoint, even absurd. And, second, it opens up a deeper dimension by clarifying things that words and gestures are incapable of expressing or which they are prevented from expressing at this particular point in the action.

It is above all this new depth that reveals just how much progress Wagner has made in *Lohengrin* when compared with *Tannhäuser*. In terms of his compositional technique, this advance may be summed up in two words: *leitmotif* and *fabric*. Although it was not until many years later that Wagner himself used the term *leitmotif*—and then only with great misgivings—and although it was not until the time of *Opera and Drama* that he referred to motifs of "presentiment" and "recollection," the facts of the matter already entitle us to use the word *leitmotif* in the context of *Lohengrin*. Even the prelude, which is intended to provide a musical description of the "wonder-working descent of the Grail in the company of a host of angels" and its "transfer to the most blessed of all mortals,"[35] is concentrated on a single central motif—this, too, is a novel feature of the work (music example 11). But because Wagner composed the prelude last of all, "elements of the later development of the motif also find their way into it. Once Wagner had become conscious of this process, he made the links more precise, allowing the initial motif to continue to resonate just as it echoes in the main characters. In this way the prelude already tells us obscurely about Lohengrin and Elsa."[36]

11. Bars 5–12 of the prelude to *Lohengrin*.

Another of the leitmotifs to command our attention is Ortrud's inasmuch as it looks forward structurally to the *Ring*, its metrical freedom and "lack of any tonal relationship" allowing Wagner to use it in varying forms and different compositional contexts.[37] At the same time, its individual sections are also sufficiently eloquent to have an associative effect when used as brief quotations. Here is the Ortrud motif at its most discursive (music example 12). In more general terms, the role of Ortrud is associated with the notion of a particularly modern compositional style. In the opening scene of act 2, in which Ortrud and Friedrich conspire to bring about Lohengrin's downfall, the American musicologist Graham G. Hunt has rightly noted a "complexity never before encountered in an operatic role."[38] Among the novel features is not only the motivic writing, which serves to characterize Ortrud's darkly demonic nature, but also the tendency for the whole of the compositional fabric to become much denser. Within only thirty-four bars at the start of act 2, we hear not only the Ortrud motif but also two other important motifs, namely, those associated with the forbidden question and with the idea of revenge. In this way Wagner invests the orchestral writing—which serves, as it were, as the background for Ortrud's and Telramund's subsequent exchange—with a specific dramaturgical function clearly anticipating procedures that were later used in the *Ring*. Wagner wants not only to introduce Ortrud in general terms but also to shed light on her insidious plans: she is plotting revenge and by persuading Elsa to ask the forbidden question, she hopes to cause the downfall of her rival, who is currently reveling in her feelings of newfound bliss. The orchestra already allows us to suspect what Ortrud is planning even before she has sung a single note.[39]

12. Bars 35–52 of the introduction to act 2 of *Lohengrin*.

Wagner himself seems to have been struck by the subtleties inherent in this compositional method only after he had already completed work on *Lohengrin*. At all events, it is not until December 28, 1851—by which time he was planning the *Ring*—that we find him writing to Theodor Uhlig:

> Apropos the vocal score, I have again been glancing briefly through the music of Lohengrin:—might it not be of interest to you [. . .] to expatiate on the work's formal thematic web and explain how it is bound to lead to ever new formal structures along the road that I myself have opened up? This struck me at various points in the score, including the opening scene of act 2. Right at the start of the second scene of this act—Elsa's appearance on the balcony—in the woodwind prelude—it struck me that a motif is heard here for the first time in the 7th, 8th, and 9th bars of Elsa's nocturnal appearance, which is later developed and broadly and brilliantly executed when, in broad daylight and in all her glory, Elsa makes her way to church. I realized from this that the themes I write always originate in the context of, and according to the character of, some visual phenomenon on the stage.[40]

Such semantic links are also apparent at other points in the opera, so much so that according to the German musicologist Klaus Döge the two-dimensional image of a "single thread" now needs to be abandoned in favor of the idea of a more complex fabric.[41] In all, it is possible to identify six motifs whose "weft" informs large sections of the score. These motifs and their metamorphoses cover six thematic groups: the Grail, the King, Elsa,

Lohengrin, the forbidden question, and Ortrud. In this way "there is not a single motif in the auratic realm of the Grail that is not connected with the main theme."[42] With the exception of the motif associated with the forbidden question, each motif has its own key and instrumentation. Elsa's music, for example, is in A-flat major, Lohengrin's in A, a semitone higher. Wagner thus suggests the image of a woman looking up to her savior, while also implying a degree of tension between the sexes.

A similar process may be observed in the opening movement of Beethoven's "Eroica" Symphony, where the third theme in E minor that appears—contrary to custom—in the development section likewise seems like a voice from above in relationship to the initial key of E-flat major. This parallelism does not mean that while working on *Lohengrin* Wagner was thinking of the "Eroica," for all that he held the last-named work in high regard. Rather, it illustrates the reason why Wagner thought so highly of the "poetic" features in Beethoven's instrumental music—in other words, those features that go beyond any purely formal calculations. By the same token, Mahler, too, praised Beethoven for the fact that, unlike his predecessors and successors, he always had "something specific" to say in his development sections.[43] Here we have an example of constants in the way in which composers have thought about music over several generations and how they have composed their music in specific semantic contexts.

In his 1879 essay "On the Application of Music to the Drama," Wagner examined this notion from a theoretical standpoint, drawing attention to a motif from *Lohengrin* as one example among many. It is the motif that is heard for the first time when Elsa enters, "immersed in the memory of her blissful dream." This motif, Wagner explains, "consists almost entirely of a tissue of harmonies progressing into the distance." In a symphonic movement this would seem studied and confusing, but within the context of the present scene it is convincing:

> Elsa has slowly approached, in modest grief, her head bashfully lowered; one glance at her raptly transfigured eyes tells us what is in her soul [music example 13]. Questioned, she replies only by recounting her vision of a dream that fills her with the sweetness of hope: "Mit züchtigem Gebaren gab Tröstung er mir ein" [With his courteous bearing he inspired me with comfort]. That glance had already told us something of the kind. Now, boldly passing from her dream to her assurance that it will all come true, she goes on to announce: "Des Ritters will ich wahren, er soll mein Streiter sein" [That knight I shall await: he shall be my champion]. And after fur-

ther modulations, the phrase returns to the key from which it started out [music example 14].[44]

13. Bars 294–97 of act 1 of *Lohengrin* as reproduced by Wagner in his 1879 essay "On the Application of Music to the Drama": GS 10:191; PW 6:189.

14. Bars 370–77 of act 1 of *Lohengrin* as transcribed by Wagner in his essay "On the Application of Music to the Drama": GS 10:192; PW 6:190.

As Wagner went on to admit, many music theorists—and it is with a certain irony that he uses the term "professors" in this context—may regard this "poetic-musical period," as he later termed these structures, as an "eyesore" on account of their many accidentals, but what we are in fact dealing with is the subtlest psychological characterization that finds expression on the printed page in the form of abstract notes. It will be clear from this why Wagner was also thinking at that time of rewriting Senta's Ballad in *Der fliegende Holländer*, where his heroine now seemed to him to quote excessively from popular tradition and to convey too little of her own personal psychological state.

In general we are dealing here with the ideal of articulating every last detail of the musical material and ensuring that even the smallest compositional elements are fully imbued with the meaning demanded at every single moment by the work's overall dramatic concept. In *Lohengrin* this ideal was still an aspiration rather than an actual achievement. Surprising as it may sound, the influence of both Bach and Beethoven is palpable here. Bach's art of counterpoint, which Wagner was increasingly coming to love during the time that he worked on *Lohengrin*,[45] was designed to allow everything to develop out of a single entity and to discover unity in all things. From his youth Wagner had been familiar with Beethoven's motto "Never lose sight of the whole." He also knew the late string quartets, which take to its furthest extreme the principle of ensuring that every detail is fully articulated as part of a dialectical engagement with what might be termed the bigger picture.[46]

Wagner felt that Beethoven's subtle motivic and thematic writing represented the ne plus ultra in the field of instrumental music. It was an ideal that he himself was not to make his own until the time of *Tristan und Isolde*. In his view, everything that the writers of symphonies had achieved in this field since Beethoven was willful, studied, and, as far as the public at large was concerned, unintelligible. Although a Brahms symphony might provide an opportunity for "brooding" and "raging," its "aesthetic forms" lacked the significance that only drama could give them.[47] We may be tempted to share Carl Dahlhaus's view that in *Lohengrin* Wagner strove to achieve the "kind of unity associated with a symphonic movement," except that Wagner used different means. As a result, the idea of "music drama as a symphonic opera" was already in the air.[48] At the same time—as Dahlhaus is fully aware—*Lohengrin* remains a transitional work.

Is there any point, however, in lingering over such specific details and wondering which passages in *Lohengrin* are still a part of the German romantic opera tradition, which ones are inspired by French grand opera, and which are already examples of the later musical drama? By the same token, does it make sense to ask what still constitutes an aria or a scene in the traditional meaning of those terms and which passages are already dominated by an overriding dramaturgical concept? Here it is all too easy to succumb to Wagner's own belief in progress, a belief that we do not need to share in order to enjoy his music. And if we are looking for progress, we should not concentrate unduly on the new quality of Wagner's motivic writing and in the process overlook his innovations in the field of harmony: "A single chord brings us closer together than any number of phrases," Liszt wrote to Wagner under the immediate impression of *Lohengrin*,[49] referring to the sophisticated progression with which Wagner has created a magical transition between the first two scenes of act 3, in other words, from the Bridal Chorus, "Treulich geführt," to the intimate dialogue between Lohengrin and Elsa, starting with the words "Das süße Lied verhallt, wir sind allein" (The sweet song has died away, we are alone) (music example 15). Liszt was referring here to the progression from B-flat major to the chord of the dominant seventh on F-sharp, whereby the suspension on the sixth, D, which in the chord of the dominant seventh delays the fifth, C-sharp, creates that dreamy atmosphere in Wagner's music that fascinated Liszt but which he himself was not fully capable of recreating—take, for example, the main theme of his A-Major Piano Concerto, where the suspension on the sixth is missing. Such idiosyncratic harmonies, which were to continue to leave their mark on later composers such as Scriabin and Webern, are just as typical of the "progressive" Wagner as his novel ability to combine motifs and produce ever new derivatives from them.

15. Bars 305–9 of act 3 of *Lohengrin*.

It scarcely needs to be added that the one cannot be separated from the other and that it would be wrong to underestimate the element of a dramaturgical use of sonority that is often fascinating in its own right, above and beyond the sophistication of the harmonic writing.[50] Nietzsche was one of the first writers to express his admiration and gratitude for Wagner's discovery of "how much magic is still possible with music that has been dissolved and, as it were, made *elementary*. His consciousness of that is downright uncanny, no less than his instinctive realization that he simply did not require the higher lawfulness, *style*. What is elementary is sufficient—sound, movement, color, in brief the sensuousness of music."[51]

Nothing throws a clearer light on these lines than the prelude to *Lohengrin*. Even though this "Utopia in A major," as Hans Mayer called it,[52] is above all a series of eight-bar periods juxtaposed with one another and, harmonically speaking, content to make do with the tonic, dominant, and subdominant, it succeeds in becoming one of the most exciting compositions of the nineteenth century thanks to its specific instrumentation and dramaturgical handling of sonority, impressing other composers, such as Berlioz and Tchaikovsky, who were likewise fascinated by sonority, but also inspiring Liszt, Baudelaire, and Thomas Mann to comment on it in terms of rapt effusiveness.

A scene from Hans Neuenfels's 2010 Bayreuth production of *Lohengrin*. The Brabantine chorus is cast as laboratory rats: creatures that can be manipulated. As such, they are willing to torment Elsa whenever their superiors require them to do so. (Photograph courtesy of the Bayreuth Festival/Enrico Nawrath.)

Is the romanticism of *Lohengrin* that is exuded not least by the prelude no more than a stage prop, as Hans Mayer would have us believe?[53] And if a director puts a swan onstage, does he have some explaining to do? Should Lohengrin, on his arrival, at least carry the bird under his arm in a gesture that is recognizably ironic, as Jonas Kaufmann did in Richard Jones's 2009 production in Munich? In his 1991 Bayreuth production Werner Herzog, working on the principle that he should "risk showing the naïveté of the fairy tale," demonstrated how it is possible for Lohengrin to arrive with his swan and for the solution to be both beautiful and at the same time modern. A production of *Lohengrin*—with or without the swan—would be intolerable without the music, of course, for there is no doubt that it is the music alone that has ensured the opera's survival. There is nothing, therefore, to prevent directors from staging it as a fairy tale about a swan knight—not necessarily a romantic fairy tale, but at least a German one.

Central to the "typical" fairy tale are a hero and a characteristic miracle. There are other fantastical elements such as magic spells and talking animals. And ultimately the work is notable for its strict division between good and evil. When judged by these criteria, the plot of *Lohengrin* is closer to a fairy tale than any of Wagner's other stage works, at least if we exclude the operas he wrote in his youth. By rehabilitating its fairy-tale elements, one would help the music above all, for the latter would then be able to cast its magic spell and reveal subtleties of which the medieval tale of Lohengrin would never have dared to dream. Thanks to Wagner's score, the popular fairy tale has become a literary fairy tale.

We may interpret it, then, as a literary fairy tale in terms of its contents, too: as a tale about a "melancholy hero"[54] whose silver armor is resistant to feminine wiles; and as the tale of a young German who is not of this world but who imagines that he can save it nonetheless, until he is roundly rejected and thrust back into the splendid isolation of his own inner world. And *Lohengrin* also, of course, tells the terrible tale of a German nation that will not perish as long as it relies on God-sent leaders who are willing to sacrifice themselves for their people.

Each of these fairy tales or narratives contains certainties deeply rooted in our collective unconscious. Music means that they do not have to be dissected piece by piece but may be allowed to flourish as part of our inner reality—even if only in their virtuality. *Lohengrin* does not have to be deconstructed at all costs, when the composition already presents the hero as a relatively melancholic figure of light and when the music already reveals the C major of the King's fanfares as banal to a fault. Perhaps admirers of

Wagner's music should respond as Thomas Mann did when—in spite of all his reservations about the composer's Teutonic aspects—he wrote in his diary: "Went outside until supper and sang Lohengrin to myself."[55]

Any listener who is not sent into raptures by every note that Wagner wrote must, of course, be prepared to make certain compromises when listening to the music of *Lohengrin*. To take a single example: the valiant exclamations by the King and Herald that repeatedly interrupt Elsa in her opening scene ("Einsam in trüben Tagen") may be indispensable in terms of the action, but musically speaking they are hardly the last word in refinement. All the more, then, will the listener admire the subtlety of the orchestral writing accompanying Elsa's initially wistful but then increasingly rapt and visionary statement.[56] Even the best orchestras have difficulty doing justice to Wagner's intentions here, for his aim was to create a dreamlike, fairy-tale mood in which the mixture of tone colors changes imperceptibly: the listener must not be aware of the entry of the oboe, english horn, flute, high strings, and so on. Rather they should strike him or her like a ray of light whose angle of incidence shifts only slowly.

Even in *Lohengrin* it is already possible to speak of the "art of transition" that Wagner himself so admired in *Tristan und Isolde*. Moreover, while that art acquires almost suggestive features in his later works and produces an undertow that some music lovers prefer to resist, the mystical changes of color in *Lohengrin*—and not just in the scene under discussion—may be enjoyed like a nonrepresentational painting to which we commit ourselves without abandoning ourselves completely. Here closed eyes are as useful as ears that do not ask too insistently about the meaning of what they can hear. Paul Valéry described the language of poetry as a "prolonged hesitation between sound and meaning."[57] In this context it is worth noting that at the time he was working on *Lohengrin* Wagner was also toying with the idea of writing symphonies:[58] the score of *Lohengrin* is the work not only of a music dramatist striving for semantic clarity and nonambiguity, it also opens the door to an indulgent delight in sonority divorced from all meaning.

A Word about Arnold Schoenberg

"A single chord brings us closer together than any number of phrases!"[1] It is no accident that Liszt was referring here to the harmonic writing in *Lohengrin*, the subtlety of which filled Arnold Schoenberg with no less enthusiasm than it had done in the case of Liszt. At all events, the score of *Lohengrin* was the only one in his extensive Wagner library that contains his handwritten sketch of an harmonic analysis. Moreover, it is the passage that precedes the chord so admired by Liszt: the Bridal Chorus.[2] It comes as no surprise, therefore, to find that in *Style and Idea* Schoenberg demonstrates the "thrill of novelty" that characterizes "all great masterpieces" by reference to the "expressive power of the third, A-flat to C-flat, at Ortrud's lamenting cry of 'Elsa.'"[3]

Schoenberg told his American pupil and biographer Dika Newlin that by the age of twenty-five he had already attended twenty or thirty performances of each of Wagner's operas.[4] In *Style and Idea* he adds that this was by no means exceptional for ordinary music lovers in Germany and Austria at that time.[5] The claim is entirely plausible, for Schoenberg, who was born in Vienna in 1874, grew up in a world of musical culture dominated by Wagnerism. Unsurprisingly, therefore, the works of his tonal period— the Two Songs, op. 1; the sextet *Verklärte Nacht;* and, above all, the *Gurre-Lieder*—are clearly indebted to Wagner's late style.

The "original epigone"[6] later distanced himself from Wagnerism— which was by no means the same as denigrating his former idol. When *Die literarische Welt* asked Stravinsky, Egon Wellesz, and others for their views on Wagner fifty years after the latter's death, Schoenberg, who was by then writing twelve-tone music, responded to the paper's questionnaire:

> For me, Wagner is an ageless phenomenon, entirely independent of all fashionable trends. It is not even possible to describe his world of ideas as outdated or old-fashioned for no thought can grow old once it has been thought—it is a part of the structure of the world. The general public is evidently so corrupted by bad music that it no longer has ears for good music. On the other hand, Wagner's art is not a part of our everyday lives.[7]

Wagner was one of the great composers who guaranteed that German music enjoyed a privileged position in the world, its international standing

one that Schoenberg himself was keen to maintain as a twelve-tone composer, even in adverse times. In terms of the philosophy of history, he regarded the line Bach-Beethoven-Brahms-Schoenberg as more important
than the line Beethoven-Wagner-Schoenberg, although he would have been
the first to agree that Wagner's music, too, represented a milestone not just
in the history of composition but also in the history of ideas. Naturally he
drew attention first and foremost to the innovative features in Wagner's
music, features that served to authenticate his own creative output, which
he strove to categorize not as part of some transitory avant-garde movement but as timelessly classical.

With regard to the theory of music, the salient terms in this context
are "expanded tonality," "quartal harmony," "wandering chords," and "func-
tionless harmonies." And yet Schoenberg also found his own "musical
prose" prefigured in Wagner's music, and even his principle of "developing
variation" has precedents in Wagner's leitmotif technique. By clearly out-
lining the progressive features in Wagner's music, Schoenberg was also able
to clarify our own understanding of Wagner.

In his freely tonal stage work *Die glückliche Hand* (The Fortunate Hand)
Schoenberg continued to champion Wagner's idea of a synthesis of the
arts, not least by writing his own libretto and taking an active part in staging the piece. Conversely, his unfinished opera *Moses und Aron* may be regarded as a conscious attempt to create an alternative universe: Moses is
the Jewish antithesis of Wagner's Germanic heroes. And yet even here
Joseph Kerman—one of the most original thinkers on music—advises us to
study Wagner if we want to understand Schoenberg.[8]

In 1933 Schoenberg typed out a memorandum headed "Program to Help
and Build Up the [Jewish] Party." It contains the following sentence: "I
am sacrificing my art to the Jewish cause."[9] At that time, Wagner's anti-
Semitism played only a minor role in Schoenberg's line of argument, and it
was not until 1935, in a lecture delivered at the Ebell Club in Los Angeles
and beginning with the words "When we young Austrian-Jewish artists
grew up," that he inveighed against Wagner's "Jews in Music"—and yet
even here his comments are astonishingly temperate.

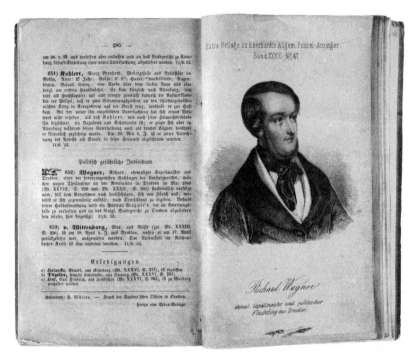

am 30. v. M. aus derselben aber entlassen und an das Landgericht zu Coburg, behufs Einleitung einer neuen Untersuchung, abgeliefert worden. 11/6. 53.

651) **Kahlert**, Georg Bernhard, Webergeselle aus Reustädtl bei Gotha, Alter: 27 Jahr; Größe: 5' 8"; Haare: dunkelblond; Augen: braun. Besond. Kennz.: eine Narbe über dem linken Auge und eine dergl. am rechten Handknöchel. Er kam kürzlich nach Altenburg, trat dort als Hochstapler auf und erregte zunächst dadurch die Aufmerksamkeit der Polizei, daß er zwei Erinnerungszeichen an den schleswigholsteinischen Krieg in Kreuzesform auf der Brust trug, weshalb er zur Haft kam. Bei der wider ihn eingeleiteten Untersuchung hat sich etwas Näheres nicht ergeben, als daß Kahlert, wie auch seine Heimathsbehörde ihn bezeichnet, ein Vagabond und Schwindler ist; er zeigte sich aber in Altenburg während seiner Untersuchung auch als frecher Lügner, weshalb er körperlich gezüchtigt wurde. Am 30. Mai d. J. ist er unter Anrechnung des Arrests als Strafe, in seine Heimath abgeschoben worden. 11/6. 53.

Politisch gefährliche Individuen.

652) **Wagner**, Richard, ehemaliger Kapellmeister aus Dresden, einer der hervorragendsten Anhänger der Umsturzpartei, welcher wegen Theilnahme an der Revolution in Dresden im Mai 1849 (Bd. XXVIII, S. 205) steckbrieflich verfolgt wird, soll dem Vernehmen nach beabsichtigen, sich von Zürich aus, woselbst er sich gegenwärtig aufhält, nach Deutschland zu begeben. Behufs seiner Habhaftwerdung wird ein Portrait Wagner's, der im Vertretungsfalle zu verhaften und an das königl. Stadtgericht zu Dresden abzuliefern sein dürfte, hier beigefügt. 11/6. 53.

653) v. **Wittenburg**, Max, aus Reisse (vgl. Bd. XXXIII, S. 230), ist am 18. April d. J. aus Breslau, wohin er am 17. April zurückgekehrt war, ausgewiesen worden. Der Aufenthalt im Reichenbacher Kreise ist ihm verboten worden. 11/6. 53.

Erledigungen.

a) **Heinecke**, Eduard, aus Eisenberg (Bd. XXXVI, S. 217), ist ergriffen.
b) **Töpfer**, Amalie Antoinette, aus Leipzig (Bd. XXXVI, S. 231).
c) **Huth**, Carl Friedrich, aus Irmbschen (Bd. XXXVI, S. 265), ist zu Marburg verhaftet worden.

Redacteur: H. Müller. — Druck der Teubner'schen Officin in Dresden.

Hierzu eine Extra-Beilage.

Richard Wagner

ehemal. Capellmeister und politischer Flüchtling aus Dresden.

Wagner's wanted notice, reproduced here from the supplement to *Eberhardt's Allgem. Polizei-Anzeiger* of June 1853, more than four years after Wagner had fled Germany. The head is reproduced the wrong way around, as it is taken from a daguerreotype of Kietz's 1842 original pencil drawing (Cf. p. 46 above). (Photograph courtesy of the Nationalarchiv der Richard-Wagner-Stiftung, Bayreuth: N 3791.)

CHAPTER SIX

The Revolutionary Drafts

ACHILLES, *JESUS OF NAZARETH*, *SIEGFRIED'S DEATH*, AND *WIELAND THE SMITH*

Prerevolutionary activities — *Draft for the Organization of a German National Theater* under the patronage of the king — Radical political recommendations to Franz Wigard — Address to the left-wing Fatherland Association: can revolution produce a popular monarchy? — Viennese adventure — Friendship with Mikhail Bakunin — Wagner's revolutionary dramas "in celebration of heroes" — *Frederick Barbarossa* — *Achilles* — *Jesus of Nazareth* — Activities during the May Uprising — Revolution and aesthetics — A dream of the end of the world as a source of fear and pleasure — Beethoven's "Eroica" as the conceptual model for Wagner's "celebration of heroes" — *Siegfried's Death* — Comparison with *Jesus of Nazareth* — The optimistic ending of *Siegfried's Death* — *Wieland the Smith*: an unique example of redemption without destruction — The artistic fruits of Wagner's revolutionary period

Wagner was a spur-of-the-moment kind of person who nevertheless entertained long-term goals. Few would argue with the claim that he gave thought to the future — one thinks, for example, of his ability to pursue over the course of half a century his plans for a religion of art through the medium of the musical drama. His spontaneity, conversely, emerges with particular force from the revolutionary period of 1848–49. He spent the first four months of 1848 devoting all his energies to completing the full score of *Lohengrin*, while the wider world was exercised by the February revolution in Paris and the March revolution in Germany. No wonder, then, that after putting the finishing touches to the full score on April 28, 1848, he threw himself heart and soul into the world of political agitation.

His initial plans were entirely pragmatic and aimed at least in the shorter term at ensuring his own artistic survival: in view of the uncertainty of the age, he was understandably afraid that any prospect of a production of *Lohengrin* was quickly disappearing "into the remote and mystic distance."[1] The court opera's board of directors will hardly have been keen to stage a lavish new opera by a member of its music staff who was becoming ever more politically compromised in the eyes of the Saxon court. At the same time, however, the revolutionary forces that might come to power in Saxony might well regard the subsidized court theater as a feudal relic that should be closed down without further ado. Wagner evidently felt that the best way to counter this twin danger was to put forward a series of reform proposals of his own, proposals that were both concerned with the existing court theater and also designed to suggest a change of direction in the future: the revolutionaries would find an institution adept at cultivating the arts to which they could not possibly take exception. But if Wagner was to square this particular circle, he needed to find a solution that would leave the king in full possession of his existing powers, while also making it clear that the spoken theater and the opera belonged to the "people" and to the artists who worked there.

Wagner felt that his time had come when the king of Saxony, unsettled by the March revolution, offered some early concessions to the rebellious estates and reshuffled his cabinet by introducing a number of more liberal ministers. On May 11, 1848, barely two weeks after completing the score of *Lohengrin*, Wagner duly submitted an extensive "Draft for the Organization of a German National Theater for the Kingdom of Saxony," a text that fills forty-one pages in the second volume of his collected writings, where it is wrongly dated to the period immediately before the outbreak of the Dresden Uprising of May 1849. Wagner was astute enough to say little about his own position, but pleaded, rather, for improvements to be made to the lot of the company as a whole, the general tenor of his remarks being aimed—sensibly and thoughtfully—at "ennobling taste and improving morals" by means of art.[2]

At the same time, however, he put forward suggestions that were not only financially unrealistic but also politically foolhardy. The conductor, for example, was to be elected by the musicians and by members of an "association of patriotic composers" and would be responsible not to the general administrator but to the minister in charge of the theater. Looking down on it all, the king must deem it an honor to approve "the success of the nation's free agency."[3] In this way, the administration at the court opera whose officials had made life so difficult for Wagner was effectively sidelined, for now it was the artists themselves who decided who would represent them and influence the way in which the repertory was planned.

Wagner's decision to leave the theater under the patronage of the king was in part a reaction to the actual balance of power in May 1848, but there is no doubt that he was also attached to the idea of a popular monarchy. And conceivably he was keen to show his superiors that his ideas could be put into practice without delay—and without the violent overthrow of the existing order. Although this may sound naïve, we should not forget that Wagner did indeed succeed in achieving a similar aim sixteen years later in the Munich of Ludwig II, when his plans for reform came true, at least for a time. On that occasion, it was not only his own works that benefited from this development, for his efforts to raise the level of musical culture also came to fruition.

Back in 1848, it was not long before Wagner sought to add his voice to the more general political debate on the questions of the day. By May 19 he was writing to the left-wing Catholic physician Franz Jacob Wigard, one of the Saxon deputies in the recently convened parliament in Frankfurt. His letter constitutes a truly revolutionary program involving the "introduction of a people's militia," a "defensive and offensive alliance" with republican France, and a restructuring of the German states so that in future there would be "no states with fewer than three million inhabitants and none with more than six."[4] Behind such precise proposals we may well suspect the influence of August Röckel. It was Röckel who ensured that a piece Wagner contributed anonymously to the *Dresdner Anzeiger* on June 15, 1848, was also declaimed by him in person at a gathering of some three thousand members of the left-wing Fatherland Association.

Wagner's theme—"How do republican aspirations stand in relation to the monarchy?"—produced a line of argument that was necessarily riven by self-contradiction, for on the one hand he professed to sharing the demands of the radicals for abolishing the aristocracy and court and for introducing universal suffrage, the replacement of the standing army by a people's militia, and, last but not least, the overthrow of the rule of money:

> God will give us the light to find the rightful *law* to put this principle into practice; and like a hideous nightmare this demonic idea of money will vanish, taking with it its whole loathsome retinue of open and secret usury, paper-juggling, percentage interest, and bankers' speculations.

This, Wagner insisted, had nothing to do with "Communism," which he defined as "the most tasteless and meaningless doctrine" for the "mathematical division of property and earnings." No, what he meant was the *fulfillment of Christ's pure teaching*, which is jealously hidden away from us behind dazzling dogmas invented long ago to bind the uncouth world of simple barbarians."[5]

We need only turn to the diaries of Karl August Varnhagen von Ense—an astute observer of the age who held relatively moderate views—to see how ideas not dissimilar to Wagner's had gained ground among wide sections of the population at this time. Shortly before the Dresden Uprising broke out, Varnhagen reported with horror on the "trembling rage" of the king of Prussia in the face of the "Frankfurt rabble" that had had the "temerity" to offer him the imperial crown.[6]

On the other hand—and regardless that similar ideas may be found in the writings of Kant, Friedrich Schlegel, and Julius Fröbel—Wagner's profession of faith in the Saxon monarchy can be regarded only as culpably naïve: was it really conceivable, after all, that reform or even revolution should come to pass under the patronage of a king who, as "the man of Providence," would proclaim a republic for his adoring people? "I declare Saxony a free state," he was to say. As Wagner went on to explain to his listeners, the majority of whom must have been astonished at what they heard: "*Let the first law of this free state provide the finest guarantee that it will survive: the highest executive power rests in the Royal House of Wettin and passes from generation to generation by right of primogeniture.*"[7]

Wagner's protestations of his loyalty to the crown did nothing to prevent his position at court from growing increasingly precarious, and in July 1848 he sought leave of absence in order to take soundings in Vienna and try to find a new field of endeavor—no doubt, too, he was motivated by the vague hope of shifting his oppressive burden of debt. And he was positively elated by the mood of political ferment in Vienna and by the offers that he received as a composer, offers that were naturally noncommittal. On his return to Dresden, he found that his position was even less secure than before, and although the general administrator, August von Lüttichau, felt too inhibited by the explosive political situation to dismiss him out of hand, he ensured that during the early months of 1849 Wagner's duties at the court opera were for the most part limited to conducting performances of Friedrich von Flotow's comic opera *Martha*.

It was during this time that Wagner became friendly with the Russian anarchist Mikhail Bakunin, who was living in Dresden under the assumed name of "Dr. Schwarz" and whom Wagner could still recall three decades later as a "wild, noble fellow."[8] It was no doubt under Bakunin's influence that Wagner contributed an article to Röckel's *Volksblätter* in February 1849 calling not only for the overthrow of the regime but for "man's struggle against existing society."[9] In a second article he predictably hymned "the sublime goddess Revolution."[10] His decision to elevate "Revolution" to the status of a goddess is significant, for however clearly he drew a distinction between the common "mob," bourgeois "philistines," and cultured "epicures,"[11] the object of the longed-for revolution continued to appear to him in only the vaguest outlines, persuading him to believe that it would be simplest if he were to deify her.

And such a goddess was best served by means of active involvement in the Dresden Uprising that broke out on May 5, 1849, and although Wagner did not man the barricades or join the ranks of the communal guard, he nonetheless played his part, printing posters with the words "Are you with us against foreign troops?" and in all likelihood helping the brass founder Carl Wilhelm Oehme to prepare hand grenades.[12] Above all, however, he was keen to discuss his ideas about the goddess whenever the opportunity presented itself—at least until such time as the real-life rebellion was bloodily suppressed by Prussian auxiliaries after only a few days and Dresden's court kapellmeister was obliged to flee the city with a substantial price on his head.

There are good reasons why the present chapter begins with such a detailed account of the biographical background to this period in Wagner's life, for his later works, with their rejection of romantic opera in favor of the musical drama, can be understood only if we are aware of the seriousness with which he explored the political situation before tackling the artistic project of the *Ring*.

Not only are Wagner's life and times—in other words, the revolutionary years in Dresden—part of the prehistory of the *Ring*, so too are the theatrical projects that paved the way for the cycle: *Siegfried's Death*, *Achilles*, and *Jesus of Nazareth*. All three projects are linked by the same idea, that of seeing the future cycle as the "celebration of a death" that would allow the tragic hero to rid himself of his "personal egoism" and merge "with the generality." In that way his exemplary life would become a model for others.[13] Although it was not until October 1849 that Wagner was to express himself in such terms in *The Artwork of the Future*, these sentences throw the clearest possible light on his preoccupations between *Lohengrin* and the *Ring*, when he was both waiting for the coming revolution and at the same time forging ahead in terms of his whole thinking about art: both of these levels are dialectically interlinked.

Wagner was no longer satisfied with the eponymous heroes of his three romantic operas, all of whom were too self-centered and interested only in their own redemption. Thus they were not "purely human" characters striving "with tremendous force to come to grips with the wider picture, only to be overwhelmed by the circumstances in which they find themselves."[14] Wagner was looking for something that Elsa had failed to find in Lohengrin—namely, "a human being in the most natural and blissful fullness of his physical life," a man whose movements were restricted by neither his "historical garb" nor by any other political or cultural constraints.[15] Instead, he radiated life and love and did not even have to fear death since he had already given the world everything he could. This "man of the future whom we desire and long for"[16] and whom Wagner had learned to understand above all through his reading of Ludwig Feuerbach was bound to fail in real life, and yet he left behind him a seed that would flourish in the future, bringing forth a new and better race of human beings.

In spite of his commitment to the politics of the day, it was inconceivable that Wagner would seek his new hero in politics, history, or society. But not even fairy tales and legends could satisfy his demands any longer— at least to the extent that they failed to penetrate to the very foundations of myth, where the most basic questions concerning humankind lay deep in a well, hidden there not by any individual poet but by the folk. At the end of 1848 he briefly dusted down an earlier project about the life of Frederick Barbarossa (WWV 76) that he had discarded in favor of *Lohengrin*. The legend of the ancient emperor asleep in the Kyffhäuser Mountains until the day he wakes and restores the empire to its former glory would have been timely. Eduard Devrient, the stage director at the Dresden court theater, whom Wagner regularly regaled with readings from his works, thought that Barbarossa—as featured in Wagner's essay *The Wibelungs: World History from Legend*—was "the mightiest vehicle for this whole idea, an idea of tremendous, wondrous beauty."[17]

Ultimately, however, Wagner was discouraged by the "vast mass of historical events and relationships," a detailed account of which would obscure the "wider picture." Instead, he was carried back "through the poems of the Middle Ages" to the deeper layers of myth.[18] In this renewed quest of his, Wagner adopted a thoroughness that not only went beyond all his previous studies but which is almost certainly without equal in the whole history of libretto writing. After all, more was at stake than finding a suitable subject for the ordinary music theater: in keeping with his solemn pronouncement

"I shall write no more *operas*,"[19] which Wagner announced to his friends in 1851, he was now eager to explore themes that satisfied the demands of art as a new religion. And the artist may have recourse to such themes only if he sees himself as the plenipotentiary of the folk in whose midst these myths arose. In short: the more deeply and broadly a myth was rooted in the people, the better it was for Wagner.

We would be doing Wagner an injustice if we were to accuse him of "Teutonicism" in this context. After all, he drew not only on Old Icelandic mythology, for all that this was to play a determinative role in *Siegfried's Death* and the *Ring*, but also on the Greek and Judaic-Christian traditions. For a time, all three traditions held his interest, for in spite of what might be termed his Germanophilia, he was motivated first and foremost by the desire to exhaust the best possible sources for his new synthetic myth. Even after he had completed the poem of *Siegfried's Death*, he continued to toy with the idea of writing works about Achilles (WWV 81) and Jesus of Nazareth (WWV 80).

Wagner had already immersed himself in all three parts of the *Oresteia* (*Agamemnon*, *The Libation Bearers*, and *The Eumenides*) during the summer of 1847—in other words, even before the subject of the Nibelungs had become the focus of his interest. Twenty years later, he could still recall his enthusiasm for Aeschylus:

> There was nothing to equal the exalted emotion evoked in me by Agamemnon; and to the close of *The Eumenides* I remained in a state of transport from which I have never really returned to become fully reconciled with modern literature. My ideas about the significance of drama, and especially of the theater itself, were decisively moulded by these impressions.[20]

A handful of notes discovered among Wagner's unpublished papers may relate directly or indirectly to his plans for a three-act drama on the life of Achilles: "Achilles to Agamemnon: / If you seek joy in dominion, / May wisdom teach you to love."[21] Here the theme of love in conflict with power, which dominates the *Ring*, is already clearly adumbrated. And we may well believe that if Wagner had completed this drama, as he planned to do not only in Dresden in 1849 but later, too, in Paris, it would have constituted "a celebration of the hero," with Achilles as the "desired and longed-for man of the future." Like Siegfried, Achilles is not afraid of death since he has previously devoted the whole of his life to fullness and freedom. According to *My Life*, Wagner had already settled on the outlines of the action on May 5, 1849, during a "leisurely stroll" through the barricaded streets of Dresden—presumably the Prussian troops had yet to occupy the town.[22]

The surviving evidence allows us to do little more than speculate about a possible drama on the life and death of Achilles, whereas Wagner's interest in the Judaic-Christian tradition is well documented in the form of a complete prose draft for a five-act "tragedy" to be called *Jesus of Nazareth* and flanked by what one writer has termed a "theological impromptu"[23] and by reflections on Christ's role in Hebrew society. Under the heading "Christ in the nave," Wagner even sketched eleven bars of music, while his correspondence indicates that as late as December 1849 he was still thinking of completing the opera for a performance in Paris.[24] His preliminary work on the opera dates from the early months of 1849 and belongs, therefore, to the period immediately before the outbreak of the Dresden Uprising.

The timing of these events lends weight to the idea proposed by Martin Gregor-Dellin and taken up by Alan David Aberbach that the hero of *Jesus of Nazareth* is portrayed "purely as a social revolutionary."[25] And yet such a suggestion misses the point. True, Wagner's Jesus opposes the constraints of the law and champions the commandment to "love thy neighbor as thyself," allying himself with the dispossessed and powerless at the expense of those in power. And, no less than Siegfried—the son of the Norse god Wotan—he embodies an idea that Wagner had expressed in his fragmentary, Feuerbach-inspired jottings on the subject of Achilles: "Man is god raised to his highest perfection. The eternal gods are the elements that beget man. In humankind Creation thus finds its ultimate expression."[26]

But Wagner's Jesus is neither a politician nor a social revolutionary but a spiritual figure and, together with Apollo, one of the two "most sublime teachers of humankind." As such, he shows us that "men are all the same and that they are brothers." In keeping with Christ's teachings in his Sermon on the Mount, human beings do not have to worry about what they will eat and drink as their "heavenly father will give them everything himself." This heavenly father, Wagner explains in *Art and Revolution*, "will be none other than the social wisdom of mankind, which takes nature and its fullness for the welfare of us all."[27] Of course, Wagner believed that Jesus was able to become an outstanding teacher only because he sacrificed himself and suffered and died for humankind, for death is "the last ascension of the individual life into the life of the whole" and, hence, "the ultimate and most definite end of egoism."[28] In this sense Wagner regarded both *Siegfried's Death* and *Jesus of Nazareth* as works that celebrated the life and death of their heroes, proclaiming the advent of the man of the future who was desired and longed for and doing so, moreover, in a drama based in no small way, he believed, on the cultic character of Attic tragedy.

It is instructive to see how Wagner, at this particular juncture in his life, took such an intense interest in the entirely unpolitical figures of Siegfried and Jesus of Nazareth, both of them exemplary characters with neither the ability nor the will to engage in day-to-day politics, but condemned, rather, to founder on the perversity of a society dominated by the quest for power and by misguided laws. Only through their self-sacrificial deaths can they prepare the way for the longed-for new. This, after all, was the very time that Wagner saw himself as an active revolutionary. It is no wonder, then, that Bakunin felt only well-meaning contempt for *Jesus of Nazareth* and advised the composer to abandon his existing text and replace it with something rather more direct: "The tenor was to sing: 'Off with his head!,' the soprano 'To the gallows,' and the basso continuo 'Fire, fire!'"[29]

In later life Wagner sought to dismiss his contribution to the Dresden Uprising as the apolitical and unreflecting action of a man fired by drunken high spirits. Appealing to Goethe's famously aestheticizing account of the cannon attack on Valmy, he invests his description of the uprising in the Postplatz near to Semper's fountain with all the trappings of an operatic spectacle:

> The whole scene before me seemed bathed in a dark yellow, almost brown light, similar to a color I had once experienced at Magdeburg during a solar eclipse. My most pronounced sensation was one of great, almost extravagant well-being; I suddenly felt the desire to play with something I had hitherto regarded as useless; I thus hit upon the idea, no doubt because it was near the square, to go to Tichatschek's residence and inquire after the guns kept there by this ardent weekend hunter.[30]

We do not need to see this as a belated attempt to gloss over the true facts of the matter for the benefit of King Ludwig II, for whom these reminiscences were for the most part intended, for Wagner—who during his years in exile still hoped that the whole of Paris would be "burned to the ground"[31]—was inclined to play with fire, a game that was both fantastical and at the same time utterly serious. This may well be typical of every genius with a borderline personality. But this game is not only a reflection of Wagner's anarchic ideas, it also mirrors his perpetual dream of world destruction, which was a source of both fear and pleasure. And it also expresses the quintessentially Christian motif of the "eschatological annihilation of the world" that must necessarily precede the advent of a state of eternal bliss.[32] Hans Magnus Enzensberger described this as follows in *The Sinking of the Titanic*:

> Damals glaubten wir noch daran (wer: "wir"?) —
> als gäbe es etwas, das ganz und gar unterginge,
> spurlos verschwände, schattenlos,
> abschaffbar wäre ein für allemal,
> ohne, wie üblich, Reste zu hinterlassen.

[There was a time when we still believed in it / (What do you mean by "we"?), as if anything / were ever to founder for good, to vanish / without a shadow, / to be abolished once and for all, / without leaving the usual traces.][33]

The complex social and personal situation in which Wagner found himself during the late 1840s in Dresden makes it difficult to draw any binding conclusions about what he "believed" at that time. Like many revolutionaries, he had a clear idea of what he disliked, while being unable to offer a straightforward answer to Lenin's well-known question "What's to be done?" It is not even possible to distinguish between what he felt was achievable in real political terms and what he fantasized about as desirable — presumably he never sought to give an account of himself. Theoretically and practically he was an eclectic in the political sciences, convinced only that his own answer to the problems of the day lay in the field of art. The Canadian philosopher Charles Taylor has speculated on what it was that linked "the powerful personalities of the Romantic era," among whom he lists Wagner, Bakunin, Marx, Berlioz, and Hugo: it was, he argues, their protest at "the emptiness, lack of beauty, division from self and nature, atomism, and injustice of the contemporary world."[34] From this point of view it would be wrong to underestimate the strength of the impulses which, critical of the age, emanated from as powerful a personality as Bakunin: Wagner did not have to "understand" the Russian anarchist's political theory to value him as a fellow sufferer and fellow revolutionary.

We shall find ourselves on firmer ground when we turn to the question of the sources on which the revolutionary Wagner drew his literary ideas. In preparing the way for *Jesus of Nazareth* he took an astonishingly detailed interest in the whole of the New Testament and was evidently also familiar with the writings of religious socialists such as Wilhelm Weitling, whose *Poor Sinner's Gospel* was published in 1845, and Pierre Leroux, who is credited with inventing the word "socialism." Nor should we overlook Wagner's private conversations with Bakunin.[35] A recent study by Rüdiger Jacobs explores Wagner's "metapolitical thinking" from so many different angles that the reader's head starts to spin.[36] And yet, however much one may respect such scholarly exercises, a certain degree of skepticism is surely in order in the face of such oversubtle analyses of Wagner's theoretical views.

Although Wagner's "revolutionary" writings contain much that is intelligent, creative, and thoughtful, it is also clear that the more critical one's reading of them, the more it becomes apparent that his "grand narrative" lies not in the commentaries that prefaced his music dramas or that provided them with a post hoc rationalization but only in those works themselves. This is particularly striking in the case of *The Wibelungs* (1848), an essay that Wagner intended as a conceptual precursor of the *Ring* and that he regarded as sufficiently important not only to publish in booklet form in 1850 but to include in his collected writings more than two decades later, long after the libretto of the *Ring* had been completed.

Our admiration of the intensity and imagination that Wagner brought to the field of Norse mythology in the run-up to the *Ring* should not be allowed to discourage us from concluding that this essay tends more in the direction of brain-spun whimsy than of a convincing exercise in the history of philosophy. How would it help us if—as is the case with *Jesus of Nazareth*— we had only Wagner's essay on the *Ring*, rather than the *Ring* itself, and if this were the only object of our analysis? The fascination exerted by the cycle lies in the fact that Wagner leaves far behind him the swagger and bombast that make *The Wibelungs* such effortful reading for the nonspecialist and finds a form of expression that is compelling and inexhaustibly rich, combining, as it does, modern myth and contemporary social criticism.

It is above all nonmusicians among Wagnerians who are keen to reduce Wagner's thinking to a coherent system. In the process they rarely acknowledge that Wagner's thinking is thinking about *music*. And this also affected his aim of staging the exemplary death of a "man of the future whom we desire and long for" as the "celebration of a hero." This aim inevitably recalls the "Eroica" Symphony, a work that Wagner held in high regard from an early age and later conducted on frequent occasions, including one of his subscription concerts in Dresden on January 22, 1848. When he performed the symphony in Zurich in 1851 he explained what and who it was that he believed Beethoven wanted to characterize as "heroic" in the opening movement of the work: it was no "military hero" but "the whole, complete *man* in whom are present all the purely human feelings of love, grief, and strength in their greatest fullness and force."

We are inevitably reminded of Wagner's own Siegfried, a figure who had by this date been conceived but not yet born—if we wish to adopt Wagner's own image of myth as the progenitor and music as the childbearing mother of the music drama. And this figure is accorded a funeral in the second movement of the "Eroica" that could not be more "exalting." At the same time our grief gives rise to a "new strength" that in the final movement is "finally" able to present us with "the whole man in harmony with himself [. . .] in all his divinity" and in that way "reveal the overwhelming force of *love*."[37] Here we have Wagner's revolutionary dramas and drafts in a nutshell, albeit with the important difference that this "celebration of the hero" presents his utopian vision at best as an imaginary ideal, whereas Beethoven's idealism savors that utopia in every possible variant.

Be that as it may, I am convinced that Wagner, who saw himself as the living embodiment of Beethoven in an almost mystic sense, was far more profoundly inspired by the "Eroica" Symphony and by Beethoven's music in general than by any "philosophical" writings and the like. And this is all the more true in that the tradition in question goes back far beyond Beethoven: the funeral march as an expression of heroic adulation was an integral part of the religious festivals associated with the French Revolution. Beethoven, who toyed with the idea of moving to Napoleon's Paris, not only followed with close interest these early stages in the emergence of a modern religion of art but consciously alluded to the music of the French Revolution in the funeral march in his "Eroica" Symphony. And just as it was entirely typical of Beethoven to incorporate these semantically unequivocal elements into the vast structure of his "absolute" symphonic style, so it was typical of Wagner to develop Beethoven's idea in his own music dramas.

As yet, however, this development still lay in the future, for the first draft of the libretto for *Siegfried's Death* that Wagner completed on November 28, 1848, and that was to be the basis of the later *Götterdämmerung* (Twilight of the Gods) is still explicitly described as a "grand heroic *opera* in three acts." At this date Wagner evidently still thought that it was possible to stage his great theme on a single evening in the opera house. And unlike *Achilles* and *Jesus of Nazareth*, he did more than simply draft the libretto; in August 1850 he even made a start on a musical sketch of the prologue.

We shall take a closer look at *Siegfried's Death* in our chapters on the *Ring*. What concerns us here is an aspect of the work that is of particular interest within the context of Wagner's other drafts from his revolutionary period: Siegfried is an idiosyncratic version of Jesus of Nazareth. Although Wagner describes Jesus first and foremost as a man, he is of divine descent, his death allowing him to redeem humankind. Exactly the opposite is the case with Siegfried's self-sacrificial death, for Siegfried not only frees the Nibelungs from their servitude, he also lifts the curse on the gods in favor of "boundless might," allowing Brünnhilde to proclaim at the end of *Siegfried's Death*:

> Nur Einer herrsche:
> Allvater! Herrlicher du!
> Freue dich des freiesten Helden!
> Siegfried führ' ich dir zu:
> biet' ihm minnlichen Gruß,
> dem Bürgen ewiger Macht!

[One alone shall rule: All-Father! Glorious god! Rejoice in the freest of heroes! Siegfried I bring to you now: grant him a loving greeting, the bondsman of boundless might!]

There is, however, one final "heroic opera in three acts" from this revolutionary period that demands no sacrifice of its hero: *Wieland the Smith* (WWV 82). Wagner prepared two prose drafts on the subject in the early months of 1850, by which date he was already living in exile in Switzerland. On March 13, 1850, he wrote to Theodor Uhlig: "Now all that I still have to do is write the verse for my Wiland [*sic*], otherwise the whole poem is finished—German! German!"[38] But what exactly is so "German" about this unfinished project? Above all, Wagner wanted to make it clear that he no longer intended his work to be presented to a French audience, since he had by this date abandoned his "rummagings in French art"—the brouhaha surrounding Meyerbeer's *Le prophète*, while undeniably impressive, had put him off France for good: there was no room in such a work for the "pure, noble, most holy Truth" and "the divinely human" that he demanded of his own works and which, writing to Uhlig with bitter irony, he imputed to *Le prophète*.[39]

The detailed prose draft of *Wieland* combines elements from the traditional legends associated with both Wieland (also known in English as Wayland) and Siegfried. One aspect that bears heavily on the plot is the motif of the skillful smith whose tendons have been severed to prevent him from fleeing but who still manages to escape from his servitude at King Neiding's court by flying away on a pair of wings that he has crafted for

The final scene of Joachim Herz's production of *Das Rheingold* originally staged in 1973 and seen here in its 1976 revival as part of Leipzig's centennial *Ring*. It represents the director's answer to Brecht's "question of a literate worker": "Who built seven-gated Thebes?" Paid for with stolen gold, Valhalla is an architectural collage quoting elements of the Palais de Justice in Brussels, the Niederwald Memorial with its statue of Germania, the Galleria Vittorio Emanuele II in Milan, and the imperial stairway at Vienna's Burgtheater. Among those who witness this magnificent spectacle are all who toiled to build it—not just the site foremen, but an entire team of masons, whose costumes are modeled on those of English dockworkers of the period. Other powerless onlookers include the Nibelungs, who are held in check by Alberich and by his chief engineer Mime and seen here as the unemployed subproletariat. On either side are ordinary people who may be acclaiming the gods or simply looking on in silence. Downstage center are the Rhinedaughters lamenting the loss of their gold and, center stage, Loge, an intellectual who wisely keeps himself apart. (Photograph courtesy of the Leipzig Opera. Photograph by Helga Wallmüller.)

himself. Wagner had already anticipated this scene at the end of his earlier essay *The Artwork of the Future*:

> He did it: he fulfilled the task that *the greatest need had inspired in him*. Borne aloft on the *object created by his own art*, he flew up on high and from there fired his deadly dart into Neiding's heart, before soaring away through the air on his blissfully bold flight to where he found the loved one of his youth.——*O unique and glorious folk! This is the song that you have fashioned, and you yourself are this Wieland! Forge your wings and soar aloft!*[40]

Here Wagner was attempting to come to terms with his disappointed revolutionary hopes in keeping with a motto later formulated by Nietzsche: "*We have art* so as not to be destroyed by the truth."[41] On this occasion, then, the celebration of a hero is not the result of a sacrificial death that is needed to bring about a new order. Instead, it is the apotheosis itself that is staged here. An individual hero is no longer required when the folk itself steps into the breach. As Wagner makes clear in his multistrophic poem *Die Noth* (Need), which he wrote in 1848, the folk has already suffered so much that this in itself amounts to a sacrifice. Did Wagner, writing in the wake of the failed revolution, really believe in the mission of this folk—possibly the German folk, as implied by his letter to Uhlig? Or is the whole exercise no more than a defiantly credulous about-face? Whatever the answer, it is surely significant that this draft was to be followed within a matter of months by an outburst of hatred in the form of the article "Jews in Music" that appeared in the *Neue Zeitschrift für Musik* in September 1850. By now there was no longer any mention of the "glorious folk" but only of the nefarious Jews causing the body of the people to decompose, a body, let it be said, that was already doomed to destruction.

Wieland the Smith is unique in Wagner's output, the only example of a work that not only hints at a positive utopian vision—at least to the extent that such a vision can be detected in his works at all—but ends, according to the stage directions, in the "brilliant radiance of the sun."[42] This was the only time, then, that Wagner contradicted his own artistic leitmotif of "redemption through destruction." Of course, his volte-face did not find expression in one of his musical dramas, for he turned his attention instead to the *Ring* and—to Nietzsche's lasting annoyance—revoked the promise of a better future that provides *Siegfried's Death* with its rhapsodic, hymnlike ending.

In a book concerned above all with Wagner's music theater, a chapter like this would not be worthwhile if it were not ultimately validated by the

Ring. Of course, even the *Ring* can be interpreted without a knowledge of the conditions that led up to it; and yet such a reading would be one-dimensional without the context and intertext, a black-and-white picture compared to one in full color. The *Ring* remains a contentious work of such unparalleled richness and intensity that we need to know the contemporary background and the conditions in Wagner's life at the time he was working on it. Only then will we be able to scale its peaks and plumb its depths and relate it to our own lives.

From the standpoint of this central work, Wagner needed this revolutionary period, with its flights of fancy and subsequent disappointments, in order to clarify his own position and in that way free himself up for the works that he wanted and was able to compose in the future. As Paul Bekker noted in the 1920s, striking a note of almost foolhardy boldness, Wagner had to "become a politician, a revolutionary, a socialist, an atheist—not because these questions as such interested him personally but because his art depended on the answers to them."[43] Without this dry run, there would be no *Ring*—and certainly not this particular *Ring*. Wagner would simply not have succeeded in forging this particular variant of his artistic leitmotif of "redemption through destruction" if he had not passed through the purgatory of politics and tried his hand at "heroic operas" in the spirit of the revolution, experiments that opened his eyes to what was possible and impossible in his art, and doing so, moreover, in a way that commands our respect for its sheer magnificence.

A Word about Paul Bekker

Art and Revolution is the title of a lecture that Paul Bekker published in 1919 on paper that wartime exigencies meant was of inferior quality. It appeared as part of a longer series of monographs under the imprint of the well-respected *Frankfurter Zeitung*, for which Bekker edited the music pages. He was a well-read writer and five years later was to publish a study of Wagner that went through several editions and was also translated into English. In short, it was almost certainly no accident that he chose the title *Art and Revolution* in conscious emulation of Wagner's identically titled pamphlet, even though Wagner's name is not in fact mentioned in it. This is unimportant, however, for what concerns us here is that Bekker developed his theories about the link between art and revolution before applying them to Wagner only a short time afterward.

The liberal Bekker had no sympathy for the kind of political revolution that had just taken place in Russia but hoped for a revolution in the service of "human values" through "a thoroughgoing organic reorganization of our artistic lives."[1] In order to create an "artistic community unified by its feelings for human values," artists themselves and their audiences needed to be "revolutionized," an aim that could be achieved, for example, by abolishing subscription performances and the star system.[2]

This program is by no means as innocent as it may appear at first sight, not least because it remains an unrealized goal even today. Essentially it reflects the ideas on reform that Wagner had never tired of promoting throughout his entire life. Even so, one wonders if Wagner the Dresden revolutionary would have been satisfied with the realization of this particular program. Rather, it seems to have been Bekker's own ideal, for in his subsequent book on Wagner he declared the composer a political "visionary" whose program of reform contained only a single "positive" element—namely, the "reformation of the theatre."[3] And Wagner's flight from Dresden in the wake of the failed uprising in the city receives only the most laconic of comments: "His future was even more insecure than when he embarked at Pillau for London, but he was content with the knowledge that he had finally escaped from forces which had sought to enslave him."[4]

Bekker's standpoint represents a "radical aestheticization of the artist in all his manifestations."[5] "Wagner's nature," he wrote, was "governed by emotion. He was primarily neither musician nor poet, but like Berlioz, Liszt, Schubert, Mendelssohn, and Schumann, he was primarily an expressionist."[6] His art was thus the expression of an emotional experience, with the result that his life "cannot rightly be described as 'tragic' or 'fatal' in the primary sense of those terms, for it was passed in the *use* of tragedy and fatality for the purposes of creative art."[7] For Bekker, Wagner's life and thinking, with all their highs and lows, their insights and their aberrations, were ultimately an organic process, serving as the platform for an artistic oeuvre whose standing is never in doubt.

Against this background even Wagner's anti-Semitism "was as far removed from practical politics as the 'communism' of his Dresden days." Wagner needed this "idea of Judaism, adopted simply for its practical artistic use," as a background for characters such as Alberich, Loge, Hunding, Mime, and Hagen, all of whom express "the dark side of the world of

Wagner's imagination." "He was pleased to call this dark phase of his nature 'Jew,' just as he called the bright phase 'Hero.'"[8]

Such comments on the part of a writer and thinker who was responsive to currents in contemporary music and by no means unworldly create a distinctly sinister impression when we recall how Bekker was rewarded for them: he was dismissed from his post as general administrator of the Wiesbaden State Theater in 1933 and forced to emigrate to the United States, where he died only four years later at the age of forty-four. Every fate suffered by an émigré is tragic, but in this case it struck down a generous, noble-minded individual who tried to adopt a humane approach to works that his destroyers would soon appropriate for their own inhuman ends.

Clementine Stockar-Escher's watercolor dates from the spring of 1853 and was the result of several sittings. The amateur portraitist, who was a sister of Alfred Escher, the president of the Swiss National Council, painted Wagner against the backdrop of Lake Zurich, his delicate facial features somewhat belied by a pose more normally associated with figures of authority. Wagner commissioned the portrait in order to have it lithographed and distributed in Germany as a way of keeping himself in the public eye during his years of exile in Switzerland. (Photograph courtesy of the Nationalarchiv der Richard-Wagner-Stiftung, Bayreuth: Bi 3229.)

CHAPTER SEVEN

"*We have art* so as not to be destroyed by the truth"

THE *RING* AS A NINETEENTH-CENTURY MYTH

The scenario of the failed revolutionary: "destruction" and
"self-annihilation" — "Jews in Music" — Wagner's abandonment
of work on the score of *Siegfried's Death* — His vision of a
theater "of wooden boards" — *Opera and Drama* as a provisional
stocktaking — Traditional operas as a "wanton," a "coquette,"
and a "prude" — Attic tragedy and the Oedipus myth — *The
Artwork of the Future* — The Greek chorus and the modern
orchestra — The semantics of the leitmotifs — The philosophy
and philology of alliterative verse — The "poetic-musical period"
as a formal constituent of the *Ring* cycle — *A Communication
to My Friends* as a statement of Wagner's current thinking
as a composer — Reading the poem of the *Ring* — The *Ring*
as an artistic miracle — Wagner's unwavering faith in his
own work — A comparison with *Faust*, part 2 — The *Ring* as a
nineteenth-century myth — Martin Luther and Walter Benjamin
as the chief witnesses for Wagner's pessimism — The *Ring*
as the expression of a coherent view of the world? — Various
attempts to interpret the *Ring* — Moments of happiness
in the work in spite of its mood of universal doom

Even after Wagner had landed unceremoniously in Zurich in late May
1849 with a price on his head following the failure of the Dresden
Uprising, he continued to fire off barbs in the direction of the well-armored
establishment, an exercise conducted with considerable passion but ultimately futile. In his quiver were belligerently aesthetic and political tracts
such as *Art and Revolution* and *The Artwork of the Future*, a sketch for an
opera on the life of Wieland the Smith, and a maliciously polemical article
published under the title "Jews in Music." With the exception of the unpublished *Wieland*, these writings caused a great stir in Germany. But soon

Wagner's arsenal was empty, and the situation remained unchanged—how could it be otherwise in view of the prevailing conditions? Wagner's greatness emerges from the fact that, far from lapsing into self-pity, he continued along his chosen course. Much, however, had changed.

He began work on the score of *Siegfried's Death* but broke off after only a scene. By now he had lost his faith in a "heroic opera" in which the sacrificial death of an outstanding individual would free humankind from its shackles under the supreme command of Wotan, who continued to be worshipped as the "most glorious" of gods. As Wagner could now see, not only had humankind failed in its revolutionary mission, but the gods were not on their side. And so Wotan had to abdicate and by self-destructing prepare the way for something new, something that was no longer a concrete utopia but at best a vague hope, and even this hope would for a time be abandoned under the influence of Wagner's reading of Schopenhauer and of the latter's Buddhist beliefs. Now he was convinced that we must *all* abdicate, for all that remains to us humans is redemption through destruction. Wagner's old artistic leitmotif returns here with a new and unsuspected power. That it could also assume a threatening aspect is clear from "Jews in Music."

However maliciously mean-spirited Wagner's tirade may be, it would be wrong to see in him an advocate of the physical annihilation of the Jews. True, the Jews were in particular need of "redemption through destruction," as they had proved to be the essential cause of the ruin of humankind, which Wagner believed was damaged beyond repair. But it was humankind in general that was doomed to perish.[1] In this context the words "destruction" and "annihilation" are to be understood as metaphors—in *Opera and Drama* Wagner uses the latter to attack the genre of opera, which, he claims, had proved to be a historical "aberration." Only once it had been destroyed and swept away would the way be open for something new to replace it.

In both cases, the undeniably well-read Wagner may have been thinking subliminally of the philosophical categories of his age: in *Faith and Knowledge*, for example, Hegel speaks of a "subjectivity" that has "sought refuge in destruction" in the guise of faith—the notion is typical of Hegel's dialectic thinking and may well have appealed to Wagner.[2] In his conception of the musical drama, the category of destruction was to become even more significant, for the subject matter of such dramas, like that of Greek tragedy, can only be described as negative: in his social isolation, the present-day artist is incapable of creating an artwork of the future, since this presupposes the restoration of a sense of social and communal cohesion that modern society has forfeited. As an alternative he could chose as his subject matter only the "self-annulment of the egoistical individual" as the necessary precondition for a future sense of community.[3] Wagner had already proposed this idea in *Jesus of Nazareth* and *Siegfried's Death*, although in those two cases he had still been fired by the revolutionary hope that the utopian age that each foretold in its different way would shortly dawn. By the end of 1849, however, he was striking a substantially more pessimistic and disillusioned note in a letter to Theodor Uhlig:

> Works of art cannot be created at present, they can only be prepared for by means of revolutionary activity, by destroying and crushing everything that is worth destroying and crushing. That is our task, and only people totally different from us will be the true creative artists.[4]

In spite of its radical language, this, too, is meant to be read metaphorically. In the course of a conversation held twenty years later with Cosima, Wagner expressly regretted that Schopenhauer's philosophy might exert "a bad influence on young people" like Nietzsche because "they apply his pessimism, which is a form of thinking, contemplation, to life itself, and derive from it an active form of hopelessness."[5]

But let us return to *Siegfried's Death*. In theory Wagner could have incorporated his new nihilistic scenario, dramatically intensified in the wake of his disenchantment with the whole idea of revolution, into the existing libretto without the need for any far-reaching changes. Simply by removing the optimistic ending, he could almost certainly have achieved that aim. He would not even have needed to rewrite the earlier scenes, which had come to seem increasingly indispensable for a proper understanding of his Siegfried tragedy as this prehistory is already mentioned in the Norns' scene that introduces *Siegfried's Death*. Of course, there is space in this scene for only a condensed account of these earlier events, with the result that it immediately became clear to Wagner when he started work on the score that he would have to begin the opera with a lengthy, recitative-like exchange between the Norns expatiating on Siegfried's past. Not only did this fly in the face of Wagner's own maxims about not beginning a new stage work with a mass of undiluted information, but he would be unable to launch the piece with a musical opening that would carry the audience forward with an irresistible sense of momentum. In short, it would impair his aim of conveying his myth to his audience's emotions by means of music capable of speaking for itself within the context of this opening scene.

A glance at the Norns' scene that Wagner set to music twenty years later at the start of *Götterdämmerung* helps to throw light not only on the problem itself but also on its subsequent resolution. By then Wagner had already completed the first three parts of the *Ring*, resulting in a whole series of leitmotifs that could now form the basis of the Norns' scene. As a result he was no longer obliged to think in terms of a dry recitative but could create a musical scenario teeming with richly allusive motifs that would impinge directly on listeners already in the know.

When Wagner set about writing the music for *Siegfried's Death* in August 1850, these motifs did not yet exist. But even if they had existed, their use would have been unmotivated and premature. As a result, Wagner—no doubt with his own highly artificial music to *Lohengrin* still ringing in his ears—was stymied, while continuing to cling to the project, which he now planned to write for an "audience of the future" that would be convened at short notice for a performance, directed by himself, in a theater made from "wooden planks": "I would then send out invitations far and wide to all who were interested in my works, ensure that the auditorium was decently filled, and give three performances—free, of course—one after the other in the space of a week, after which the theater would be demolished and the whole affair would be over and done with."[6] This is the first time in his correspondence that Wagner mentions the idea of a festival, although for the present it lacked all material basis, as Wagner had yet to complete the work and did not have the sum of ten thousand thalers that he believed was necessary to fund the project.

Once again he reacted to his apparently hopeless situation with an impressive show of strength, neither obsessing over the completion of a work that threatened to be stillborn nor abandoning the plan for good. Instead, he launched into a large-scale exercise that sought to clarify the situation for himself and others, an exercise that was to go down in history as *Opera and Drama*. In a total of 641 printed pages he explained to the world where his problems lay and how he planned to solve them. Once again the "necessity" that he had invoked so often in the writings of his revolutionary period proved to be the mother of invention.

Described by Richard Strauss as "the book of books about music,"[7] *Opera and Drama* is undoubtedly one of the most important writings on the theory of music to emerge from the nineteenth century, even though Nietzsche, while admiring certain aspects, was critical of a "disturbing" quality, an "irregularity of rhythm," and the suggestion that Wagner was "speaking in the presence of enemies."[8] Thomas Mann, by contrast, was not afraid of Wagner's more challenging texts and praised the "astonishing perspicacity and intellectual vigour" of *Opera and Drama*, while not overlooking that "there is something difficult to read" in this and Wagner's other prose writings, and "a certain woolliness and stiffness."[9] And it is undoubtedly true that the reader needs to warm to Wagner's disjointed and eclectic style to appreciate the uncommonly creative intelligence that lies behind the text. Shortly after completing it, Wagner read it aloud to an invited audience in Zurich, apparently with such conviction that with each passing day his listeners were increasingly fired by the theses that he was expounding.

Even without a recording of the occasion, one can sense the passion with which Wagner—drawing now on the colorful language of populist demagoguery, now on convoluted philological and theoretical arguments—brought home to his listeners the "error in opera as a genre," whereby "a means of expression (music) has been made the end, while the end of expression (the drama) has been made a means."[10] In the Attic tragedies of Aeschylus and Sophocles, which Wagner imagined constituted a unity of words, music, and gesture, everything had still had its well-ordered place, whereas modern opera had been turned increasingly into a vocal spectacle against the background of commercial interests: Italian opera was a "wanton," her French sister a "coquette," and German opera a "prude."[11]

True, there had been countercurrents—notably with Gluck and Mozart. And, as we have seen, Wagner regarded his own works as a part of the Beethovenian tradition: in the Ninth Symphony, above all, Beethoven had restored the balance between words and music after music had reached "the pinnacle of madness" by wanting "not only to bear, but also to *beget*." In the case of the Ninth Symphony, Schiller's ode was to be regarded as the "fertilizing seed" that "supplies the musical organism with its ability to give birth." This line of argument reflects Wagner's general view of music as a "woman" who needs the "poet's power of begetting" in order to be effective within "the drama of the future."[12]

Conceptually speaking, this "drama of the future" is rooted in the past—namely, in myth, which Wagner famously defined as being "true for all time, its content, however densely compressed, inexhaustible throughout the ages."[13] Since this myth sprang from "the folk's common poetic power,"[14] the Greek poet had but a single task—that of interpretation. Wagner cites the myth of Oedipus as an example of this process, a myth that "presents us with an intelligible picture of the whole history of humankind from the beginnings of society to the inevitable downfall of the state."[15] Oedipus's daughter Antigone buries her brother Polyneices even though King Creon of Thebes has forbidden her to do so. Instead of placing reasons of state above the "purely human nature" that demanded the observance of certain religious rites, she sacrifices her life and ultimately touches the heart of Creon, who is "the state personified": "Wounded deep within, *the state* fell crashing to the ground to become in death a *human being.—Holy Antigone! I call on you! Let your banner wave in order that beneath it we may destroy and redeem!*"[16]

These are Wagner's "old" ideas, which on this occasion are expressed not only in highly concentrated form but in a highly emotive manner. At the same time, however, there is already a clear indication of the ideas underpinning the *Ring.* Moreover, the third part of *Opera and Drama* includes an outline of Wagner's thoughts on music drama in that he begins by retracing the journey that he has taken in his earlier works before sketching out his "drama of the future." In terms of his concept of a total artwork with religious connotations, this drama would take up the tradition of ancient Greek tragedy, but otherwise it would go its own way. The function of the Greek chorus, for example, had been "to express the inexpressible," but this function would in future be entrusted to the orchestra.[17] The orchestra turns listeners into "constant accessories to the deepest secret of the poet's aim" by offering them motifs of "presentiment" and "reminiscence"—these were later to become known as *leitmotifs*—as "emotional signposts" to guide them "through the whole labyrinthine design of the drama."[18]

It was this idea that lay behind Wagner's later comment to Cosima while he was working on the Funeral March in *Götterdämmerung*:

> I have composed a Greek chorus, but a chorus which will be sung, so to speak, by the orchestra; after Siegfried's death, while the scene is being changed, the Siegmund theme will be played, as if the chorus were saying: "This was his father"; then the sword motive; and finally his own theme; then the curtain goes up, Gutrune enters, thinking she has heard his horn. How could words ever make the impression that these solemn themes, in their new form, will evoke? Music always expresses the direct present.[19]

To the extent that these motifs of presentiment and reminiscence are interwoven with each other throughout the whole of the drama, communicating with one another in this way, they ensure that the action appears not as intellectually arid—Wagner, striking a critical note, calls it "novelistic"—but as something sustained by a continuous floodtide of emotion.

It is above all the orchestra, therefore, that ensures that the drama is experienced as a "unified artistic form" "bound together as a coherent whole" and prevents listeners from having to work out the message for themselves by means of elaborate thought processes. In this way two levels of under-standing interlock: the conceptual post hoc rationalization and the emo-tional response that accompanies the aesthetic experience at the instant it occurs. In his later writings Wagner was to draw an explicit distinction between his own compositional aims and those of contemporary sympho-nists, arguing that although a Brahms symphony might invite its listeners to experience it emotionally at the time of its performance and afterward to think about what they have heard, these two processes are unconnected, for it is the symphony's form alone that can be grasped conceptually, whereas feeling does not know what it can feel or why but is merely carried along aimlessly by the waves of the music. In Wagner's eyes this is a kind of music that lacks a message, an example of decadent art.

Greek tragedy had such a message, which is why it alone could serve as a conceptual model for the musical drama that had to be created anew. Readers familiar with Wagner's orchestra, either by seeing it in front of them or by conjuring up its sounds in their mind's ear, will find Wagner's comparison with a Greek chorus farfetched and certainly abstract, but we may also regard it as an original metaphor that illustrates the extent to which the innovation that Wagner was striving to achieve was not merely compositional and technical, perhaps as the result of some progress within the material itself, but a new way of thinking about the music theater as such. His comparison between the orchestra and the Greek chorus illus-trates two different points at once: the institution of "music theater" was intended to present dramas that were *musical* but still *dramas*. Although the music may be of secondary importance, it is nevertheless vastly enhanced in value, for, like the Greek chorus, it plays onstage, albeit invisibly. In short, Wagner's orchestra no longer serves to accompany the dramatis personae but is itself a dramatis persona.

Italian bel canto opera would continue to exist, of course, in spite of Wagner's aesthetic intervention; but no one outside its immediate sphere of influence would be able to maintain the naïve belief that opera func-tioned according to the simple rule of thumb of "plot + singing + orchestral accompaniment = opera." Instead, Wagner would find audiences more or less willing to believe his claim that in music theater, too, there must be a grandly conceived dramatic idea to which action, music, and staging must be subordinated at every moment of the onstage drama. In Wagner's eyes opera was a hybrid form that could mutate into a total artwork only if it adopted this course.

This approach clearly demanded that singers be vocally less self-regarding and less egotistical, a demand which in Wagner's day was far from self-evident. And to the extent that singers gained in importance as astute and credible performers, they must step back from their musically leading role in favor of an orchestra that was not only more "knowing" in respect of the plot's mysterious profundities but which also had at its disposal a far great musical variety and richness. It is no accident that Wagner entrusted his leitmotifs to the orchestra first and foremost.

As we noted in the case of *Rienzi*, the singers continued nonetheless to be central to the action as visible embodiments of Wagner's grand idea, proclaiming the message of his myth, their singing elevated to the status of the "life-giving focus of the dramatic expression."[20] At the time of *Opera and Drama* Wagner was not yet entirely clear in his own mind about the details of this singing, which he described as "verse melody," and even while he was working on the score of *Das Rheingold* he continued to experiment with the different possibilities of treating the melodic line as recitative, arioso, and song. In the case of two other formal elements, conversely, he already had firm ideas: *Stabreim*, or alliteration, and what he termed the "poetic-musical period." The former imposes a formal structure on the libretto, while the latter guarantees the musical form of the work.

It is easy to ridicule Wagner's use of *Stabreim*, and there is little doubt that if the *Ring* were declaimed as a spoken drama over the course of four separate evenings, even dyed-in-the-wool Wagnerians would find this something of a trial. At the same time, however, alliterative lines, whether formulated with serious or satirical intent, tend to engrave themselves on our memories. Who, after reading Thomas Mann's *Confessions of Felix Krull*, can forget the words of Diane Houpflé, a novelist married to a factory owner, as the dashing lift attendant helps her out of her mink coat: "You'd undress me, doughty drudge?" There is no doubt that Mann was consciously striking a note halfway between seriousness and parody, and the reader who wearies of Wagner's use of alliterative meters might well apply this same attitude to their use in the *Ring*—while not ignoring the masterly and even coruscating examples with which the libretto teems and which impressed even a realist writer like Gottfried Keller: "Ihrem Ende eilen sie zu, / die so stark im Bestehen sich wähnen": thus runs Loge's mocking commentary as the gods enter their new fortress of Valhalla. The only English translator to seek to reproduce every aspect of Wagner's meter and alliterative patterns was Alfred Forman, whose version of these lines reads: "To their end they fleetly are led, / who believe themselves founded for ever."

No less striking is Fricka's critique of male hegemony: "Was ist euch Harten / doch heilig und werth, / giert ihr Männer nach Macht!" (What to you men / for worship is meet, / when your minds are on might?) Or take Wotan's later remonstration:

> Als junger Liebe
> Lust mir verblich,
> verlangte nach Macht mein Muth:
> von jäher Wünsche
> Wüthen gejagt,
> gewann ich mir die Welt.

[When love its young / delight had allayed, / I longed in my mind for might, / and worked, in reinless / reach of my will, / to win myself the world.]

He sums up his sense of frustration and resignation in the lines:

> Zum Ekel find' ich
> ewig nur mich
> in Allem was ich erwirke!
> Das And're, das ich ersehne,
> das And're erseh' ich nie.

[I see to sickness / always myself / at last wherever I labour! / I waste for what shall be other—/ no way what is other I win.]

It is fair enough to mock the Rhinedaughters' "Weia! Waga! Woge, du Welle" (Weia! Waga! Waver, thou water), for these children of nature would have done far better to lecture Alberich on the bane of gold than play word games based on the Old High German *Heilawâc*. We can, of course, speak of "Teutonic" diction in this context, at least if we eschew the note of mockery that usually accompanies this term, for the "Teutonic" element in Wagner's verse is not the result of some nationalistic, hyper-German whimsy but the product of literary studies and conceptual experimentation of quite exceptional breadth and depth. Wagner specifically described his librettos as "poems," determined, as he was, that they should not be regarded as prose, for in his eyes there was something redolent of the modern novel about prose. It was, he believed, simply arbitrary. If his poems were to be universally understood, they needed the formal element of verse to round them off. He rejected end rhyme in which the final syllables of two or more lines rhyme with each other according to more or less complex verse patterns, arguing that this was a purely formal device and pointing out that few poems escape from the constraints of such a scheme, whereby it is not the meaning that produces the rhyme but the rhyme that results in the meaning. Writing from the standpoint of a German medievalist, the Swiss scholar Max Wehrli criticized end rhyme as a "game with sonority, independent of meaning and concerned only with imposing a second structure on the poetic text."[21] Of course, it is clear from countless examples of post-medieval literature that verse based on end rhyme can produce magnificent poetry. And, theoretically at least, Wagner could also have fallen back on the verse forms of Greek tragedy, including, for instance, the iambic trimeters that Schiller uses in a number of scenes in his stage play *The Maid of Orleans*.

But Wagner took a conscious decision to use Old Icelandic *Stabreim*, which gave way to the end rhyme of early medieval hymnology in the wake of the Christianization of Europe, only to re-enter the field of interest of nineteenth-century philologists and scholars. Wagner's attempt to restore it to high office represents an implicit critique of the manner in which early Germanic subjects had either been suppressed altogether or typically depicted and experienced. Norse myth is characterized by its unity of action, feeling, and thinking; and this unity was more effectively embodied by head rhyme than by end rhyme since the listener is not distracted by incidental final syllables but is forced, rather, to focus on the semantically important root syllables.

Stabreim is used to forge together the semantically significant words of Wagner's "poetic-musical period" and to create a unity that can be perceived not just intellectually but directly by the senses. When Siegmund, in *Die Walküre*, sings the words "Winterstürme wichen dem Wonnemond" (Winter storms have waned at the wakening May), he is not only describing antithetical phenomena in the world of nature but, more importantly, drawing attention to the unity that prevails in nature when we see it as a meaningful entity. And this structure is present in Wagner's musical drama not just in the abstract but—thanks to the *Stabreim*—on a physical and even childlike level.

In *Opera and Drama* Wagner illustrates his aim by reference to the line "Die Liebe bringt Lust und Leid, doch in ihr Weh auch webt sie Wonnen," quaintly if serviceably rendered by William Ashton Ellis as "Love gives delight to living, but with her woe she weaves things winsome." According to Wagner, "Liebe," "Lust," and "Leid" all derive from the same root: although they express very differing emotions, they are all stages in one and the same process in life. Alliterative verse makes use of this fact, representing phe-

nomena in their totality, rather than intellectually fragmented or individu-
alized. The composer can underscore this holistic experience by setting the
alliterative phrase as a single melodic line. Even better, he or she can use
"harmonic modulation" to "exert a binding constraint on the sensuous feeling such as no other art can achieve."[22]

Whereas the poet can do no more than express the fact that "pleasure"
and "pain," "weal" and "woe" are related, the composer is able to demonstrate that all these emotions may be subsumed beneath the overriding idea
of "love" by modulating back to the key in which that love was first hymned.
Of course, the idea of a return to an earlier key presupposes that in the
meantime the composer has modulated to a different key, which he does
not simply to ensure that his music is more varied from a purely musical
point of view, but to clarify the contrast between pleasure and pain, weal
and woe. The path from pleasure to pain will be traced by a modulation to
a different key, the return from woe to weal by a corresponding modulation back to the home key. This phrase modulating away from, and back
to, the initial key was described by Wagner as a "poetic-musical period."
While earlier writers argued that such periods could cover several hundred
bars, there is now general agreement that the term applies only to shorter
semantic units of the kind just described.

At the time of *Opera and Drama*, Wagner was undoubtedly not yet aware
of the difficulty of giving musical expression to his own compositional principles, which he had had to devise from scratch and which he himself described a decade later as the "abstract expression of the artistically creative
process that was taking place within me."[23] Still less will he have been able
to foresee the amount of imagination necessary to present each element
in the action to the audience's emotions in a way that was both creative
and appropriate to the specific situation onstage without losing sight of the
whole. But this is not our present concern. Here we can only admire the
intelligence and perspicacity with which Wagner assembled his theoretical
tools in advance, tools, let it be added, that were to be used not in elabo-
rately ingenious works such as Bach's *The Art of Fugue* or Stockhausen's
Studie II but in music dramas that in spite of their metaphysical dimensions
and ideological garb teem with sensuality and that can be heard entirely in
the here and now.

We may remind ourselves at this point that in August 1850 Wagner broke
off *Siegfried's Death* after only two pages in order to write *Opera and Drama*
and sort out in his own mind his future concept of the drama. Theory and
the tools of his trade were now ready "for new feats"—to quote from the

prologue to *Siegfried's Death*. It would be a modern myth; its theme was to be love and power; the poem would be in alliterative verse; poetic-musical periods would create the musical drama, guaranteeing unity in multiplicity; motifs of "presentiment" and "reminiscence" would ensure that the action was presented to the audience's feelings at every moment of the work; and the musical "fabric" produced by all the work's different interwoven elements would be presented by the orchestra commenting on the stage action in the manner of an omniscient Greek chorus.

But Wagner had still not worked out how to give practical expression to his newly developed concept. While waiting impatiently for *Opera and Drama* to appear in print and managing to persuade his publisher to increase his fee for five hundred copies from 100 to some 260 thalers, he wrote the poem for *Young Siegfried* between June 3 and 24, 1851, since it now struck him that two evenings were necessary to realize his Siegfried project: *Young Siegfried* and *Siegfried's Death*.

Only then did he take the decisive step that was to lead to the four-part *Ring*. During July and August 1850 he wrote *A Communication to My Friends*, an autobiographical text extremely important for what it has to say about Wagner's political, philosophical, and artistic position. It ends with the announcement that "I plan to perform those three dramas, together with the prologue, *within the course of three days and a preliminary evening* at a festival specially designed for that purpose."[24] The first two parts of the tetralogy that Wagner was announcing in such vague terms were still untitled. Later he vacillated between "The Rhinegold" and "The Rape of the Rhinegold" for the "preliminary evening" and between "Siegmund and Sieglind [*sic*]: The Valkyrie's Punishment" and "The Valkyrie" for the "first evening." Only when the poems of *Das Rheingold* and *Die Walküre* were more or less finished in November 1852 did Wagner's friends discover the cycle's definitive title: *The Nibelung's Ring*. A privately printed edition of the poem, limited to fifty copies, was intended for those members of his circle who were unable to attend the series of readings over four consecutive evenings at the Hôtel Baur au Lac in Zurich.

True, the score still had to be written, a task that was to occupy Wagner for another twenty-two years, and yet what he had produced so far and what he still envisaged was impressive enough: an exile driven from his native Saxony, where he literally had a price on his head, and now living in Zurich under the vigilant eye of the secret police, Wagner was visited by visions that could hardly have been more grandiose. The ancient Greeks remained his model, their tragedies the subject of the following rhapsodic comments in *Art and Revolution*:

> To the Greeks the performance of a tragedy was a religious festival at which the very gods appeared onstage and bestowed their wisdom on humankind. [. . .] The nation, streaming in their thousands from the state assembly, from the agora, from the country, from ships, from camps, from the remotest regions, filled the amphitheater with thirty thousand spectators in order to see the most profound of all tragedies, *Prometheus*, to gather their thoughts in the presence of this mightiest of works, to understand themselves, to rede the riddle of their own activities, and to merge as one with their own nature, with their community, and with their god to create the most intimate unity and in the noblest, profoundest peace to live once again the life that only a few hours earlier they had lived in the most restless excitement and most isolated individuality.[25]

But quite apart from the fact that it was impossible to relate this idealized picture of a Greek polis to Wagner's own age, which he regarded as hopelessly decadent, even the practical realization of his plans presupposed a degree of optimism that was nothing if not hubristic. After all, the Greek tetralogies that undoubtedly lay behind his own concept of the four-part *Ring* had taken place on a single day, whereas Wagner was planning on four whole days. And just as he had allegedly reacted to warnings about the bullets whizzing around him during the Dresden Uprising by claiming "I am immortal,"[26] he was now planning an artistic undertaking that can likewise be described only as foolhardy. A man who, according to Cosima, "should by rights have graced the world in Aeschylus's age," now felt that he had to deal with a theatrical world that resembled nothing so much as a "fairground stall": "He speaks the language of the priest, and shopkeepers are supposed to understand him!"[27]

How could he find a suitable group of performers, raise the necessary money, and conjure the requisite "infrastructure" out of thin air? Not least, how could he find an audience of believers like those who had attended performances of Greek tragedy in their tens of thousands? Even in this apparently hopeless situation, Wagner had specific ideas for his utopian vision, and in the preface to the first official edition of his libretto for the *Ring*, he famously evoked the image of a "prince" who would help to cultivate "a genuine national spirit lacking in all conceit" and set up a foundation designed to mount festival performances of the cycle.[28] And behold! Only a short time afterward a young prince would read this preface and feel that the appeal was addressed to him in person. His name was King Ludwig II of Bavaria.

This was the outward aspect of the miracle. Rather more fascinating, by contrast, is its inner aspect, for Wagner was by no means willing to limit himself to philosophical and theoretical deliberations on the subject of the *Ring*. Still less was he content to study dozens of modern editions and scholarly commentaries on Old Icelandic literature or take a closer interest in the *Nibelungenlied*, the Eddas, and the *Saga of the Volsungs*.[29] Even the attempt by the respected medievalist Karl Simrock to produce "a single great poem"—the *Lay of the Amelungs*—from the mass of disparate sources that had survived from the Middle Ages[30] was insignificant when set beside Wagner's desire to create a universal myth. Above all, Jacob Grimm's *Teutonic Mythology* had made it clear to him that the surviving myths could provide only the building blocks, not the ground plan, that he needed for his task and that he himself would have to become a "creator of myths" in his own right.[31] As a result, any attempt to identify the Attic elements in the *Ring* is little more than an academic exercise, for although there are remarkable parallels, not least with regard to the Oedipus myth to which Wagner gave central importance in *Opera and Drama*,[32] it matters little which motifs he took over consciously or unconsciously and which were already available to him from other contexts as part of the deep structure of myth. Such sources could be of little use to him in developing the large-scale structure of his own particular myth.

Moreover, such a large-scale structure would have been of little avail if he had not been able to write a successful libretto suitable for his musical drama. It is not just the composition of the *Ring* that I find miraculous, but Wagner's ability to thrust aside all theory and literary sources and in under two years to produce a poem that can effortlessly stand comparison with part 2 of *Faust* in terms of its philosophical significance, even if Goethe had no need to take account of his poem's suitability as the libretto for a music drama. In November 1852 Wagner wrote to Liszt, enthusiastically acclaiming his libretto as "the poem of my life and of all that I am and feel."[33] Anyone comparing the monumental nature of the whole undertaking with the chances of its realization is bound to be reminded of a remark by the American dramatist Eugene O'Neill: "The man who pursues the mere attainable should be sentenced to get it—and keep it. [. . .] Only through the unattainable does man achieve a hope worth living and dying for—and so attain himself. He with the spiritual guerdon of a hope in hopelessness is nearest to the stars and the rainbow's foot."[34]

Readers who find this too emotionally overwrought may prefer Nietz-sche's more sober claim that "Wagner is never more Wagner than when difficulties multiply tenfold"[35] or else they may cite Thomas Mann's remark that "the *Ring* remains to me the epitome of the work *per se*. In contrast to Goethe, Wagner was a man wholly concerned with the work in hand, a man devoted absolutely to power, the world and success."[36] This is an approach that views the *Ring* from the standpoint of the artist and does not exclude the possibility that in spite of all its magnificence the *Ring* may be full of inconsistencies and, its affinities with Greek tragedy notwithstanding, may have little to do with the "classical" theory of drama associated with the name of Aristotle, for, as Walter Benjamin has argued, the "nihilism lodged in the depths of the artistic philosophy of Bayreuth nullified—it could do no other—the concept of the hard, historical actuality of Greek tragedy." Benjamin observed such nihilism in both Wagner and Nietzsche and be-lieved that it could never be reconciled with the essence of Attic tragedy and with its "central doctrine of tragic guilt and tragic atonement."[37]

By comparing the ethos of Greek tragedy with Wagner's aestheticiza-tion of myth, Benjamin was conscious of the vast gulf that had opened up between them, although it has to be said that not even the plays of Aeschylus and Sophocles were performed within a cultic context. Yet even the two Aristotelian unities of action and time are invalidated in the *Ring*, for none of the dramatis personae appears in all four parts of the drama. Instead, the times and the places where the action unfolds keep changing between *Das Rheingold* and *Götterdämmerung*.

If Wagner's myth is not a myth in the classical tradition, is it at least timeless as demanded by the philosopher Kurt Hübner in response to Patrice Chéreau's epoch-making Bayreuth *Ring* in 1976?[38] I would find it impossible to write about the *Ring* as a "timeless" myth. Even Wagner him-self was clear on this point when planning the work, as he explained to his friends: "The *absolute work of art*—that is, the work of art that is not bound by time and place nor portrayed by particular people in particular circum-stances for a particular audience for the understanding of that audience—is a complete nonsense, a figment of the aesthetic imagination."[39]

Wagner's principal aim is well illustrated by the title of the tetralogy, for it is not a hero called Siegfried who gives his name to the cycle but a curse-laden ring, a state of affairs undoubtedly due to Wagner's revolutionary experiences, which were anything but timeless. And the idea of starting the work with the theft of the gold from the Rhine and the forging of the ring, with its built-in curse, goes back—according to the German medievalist

Volker Mertens—not to the Old Icelandic *Völuspá* but to Wagner's own imagination and to the *Communist Manifesto*, which Wagner may have known through Georg Herwegh.[40]

Bernard Shaw, who first saw the *Ring* in Bayreuth in 1889 (lack of funds apparently prevented him from attending the cycles staged by Angelo Neumann in London in 1882), was one of the first writers to interpret the work against the background of the nineteenth century. This was a view that inspired Chéreau in his centennial production in Bayreuth. The work, the director insisted, was self-evidently based on a "nineteenth-century myth": "It is the past history of our industrial society, the infancy of our world as it takes its first steps." And he went on: "To want a timeless myth strikes me as a frame without the picture."[41] In advancing this view, he had the support of Michel Foucault:

> On the stage at Bayreuth, where Wagner wanted to create a myth for the nineteenth century, Chéreau and his designer Richard Peduzzi brought back to life the images of this very same century—images that Wagner may have shared not only with Bakunin, Marx, Dickens, Jules Verne, and Böcklin, but also with the architects of the factories and municipal residences, with the illustrators of children's books, and with the agents of anti-Semitism. They showed this mythology, which still rules our world today.[42]

The philosopher Herbert Schnädelbach has summed up this approach in similar terms:

> The *Ring* is the most significant myth of the nineteenth century. What it depicts is not the universally human in general but what nineteenth-century man—that is, Richard Wagner—was bound to regard as the universally human in the wake of idealism and revolution in an age of capitalist modernization, in short, the contemporary truth about the links between love, power, guilt, and redemption.[43]

But how does labeling the *Ring* a "modern" myth help us to understand it? Classical antiquity regarded myth as a narrative invested with a collective, binding authority and, hence, with a religious potential: by partaking of the myth, the individual could be assured that the world and society constituted a meaningful whole. "Das älteste Systemprogramm des deutschen Idealismus" (The Oldest Systematic Program of German Idealism) is the modern title given to a text dating from 1796–97 and believed to be the work of either Friedrich Schelling, Hölderlin, or Hegel. It translates this classical view of myth into the here and now, arguing that once the Enlightenment and the French Revolution had swept aside the old state order but offered nothing in its place that might provide social order with a religious legitimacy, a "new myth" was required to provide a post-Enlightenment blasé society with a new sense of direction, which it would do through the medium of an art that could be physically experienced with the senses.

Manfred Frank has demonstrated the extent to which the revolutionary Wagner was able to learn from early romantic ideas such as these. At the same time, he cites Carl Dahlhaus's insistence on the distance between the ideas of the early Schelling and those underpinning Wagner's conception of the *Ring*, for, as Dahlhaus has written, myth "is not so much restored by Wagner as destroyed, or, rather, it is restored in order to be destroyed."[44] Frank finds an even clearer way of expressing his conviction that Wagner was "revoking" the "new mythology": "Profoundly compromised, irretrievably lost, robbed of all their credibility, certainly not sentimentally glorified, the gods—who justify the status quo on the basis of the highest certainties of faith—abdicate in the most shameful manner. Myth becomes *negative*."[45] This can be allowed to stand as long as it is seen as an *analysis* of Wagner's great historicophilosophical narrative and if the composer is not reproached for not offering a *solution*. For what would such a solution have looked like in the modern world? In a society that has lost its sense of community and its authentic metaphysical values?

This brings us back to Walter Benjamin. In his eyes the modern world is characterized by two factors in particular: a "traumatic shock" and the staging of that shock.[46] This shock stems from the attempts undertaken by Luther and his reformation to replace good works by faith. Since the soul was now dependent exclusively on God's grace, human actions lost their value. "Those who looked deeper saw the scene of their existence as a rubbish heap of partial, inauthentic actions," with the result that "gloominess" filled an "empty world." German tragedy, Benjamin believed, still offered the chance of "enigmatic satisfaction" at the contemplation of that world.[47] And at least its "constant creation of meaning affords the vaguest of hopes that it may be possible to slow down the fate of the empty world, even if that fate cannot be averted altogether."[48]

Inherently critical of the whole concept of progress, Benjamin's ideas may be directly applied to the *Ring*. At the same time they reveal a powerful motif behind Wagner's philosophy of history, which is not just Christian in a general kind of way but also specifically Lutheran. His artistic leitmotif of "redemption through destruction" clearly recalls Luther's Small Catechism, which Wagner was undoubtedly required to recite from memory and which refers to the "Old Adam" who has to be "drowned" every day in order for a "new man" to arise. Luther's Great Catechism refers explicitly to the gradual "destruction" of the old in favor of the new. In much the same way, the question as to the origins and existence of evil—questions of great significance for the relationship between Wotan and Alberich—has roots that are ultimately Lutheran. Although Luther leaves the origins of evil shrouded in darkness, he is in no doubt that by nature mankind tends toward evil.[49]

A second historicophilosophical trace on the road to the *Ring* leads us to Nietzsche, for he too defined the "modern" world in the same sense as that found in the *Ring*—namely, as "'chaos,' a complex fabric of existential and experiential perspectives for which there is no longer an overriding viewpoint, no unifying standpoint afforded by religion."[50] This would be unbearable if it were not that above and beyond all perspectivist variety, there was not a single unifying experience of the *Ring*, which Nietzsche found, quite rightly, in Wagner's music, even if he later came increasingly to criticize that music for becoming bogged down on the level of the suggestive and mimetic instead of soaring aloft to the peaks of "absolute" music whose "existence in sound" would provide a counterweight to the "senseless" aberrations and confusions of the plot.[51]

Anyone wanting to see the *Ring* as a work underpinned by a coherent philosophy will have realized by now that this is impossible, for although Wagner himself clearly laid down the foundations for a reading that involves the depiction of a world rent from first to last by power struggles that leave "purely human" love no chance to develop, thereby leading inevitably to its own downfall, it is clear that as soon as we examine the details of this "philosophy," we are bound to be both fascinated by the unfathomable complexity of its artistic realization and at the same time confronted by the numerous inconsistencies and contradictions that the work contains. Not that there is any lack of attempts to propose an interpretation of the *Ring*. Udo Bermbach has drawn a distinction between "socio-utopian and socialist, mythological and archetypal, philosophical, psychoanalytic, feminist, nationalist and racist interpretations," while adding his own view of the cycle: "The *Ring* is a political parable, telling the story of a world ruined by politics, the story of politicians obsessed with power and with the acquisition of that power, their thinking fired by fantasies about dominion and order, and accepting whatever risks may be involved in the pursuit of their obsessions, even if those risks include their own destruction."[52]

Thus speaks the political scientist, just as it is the philosopher who presents a philosophical reading of the *Ring* and the depth psychologist who proposes a psychoanalytical interpretation. Each commentator proclaims his or her own truth, and each is right—or wrong—in his or her own way. Regardless of the extent to which these readings find greater or lesser favor with individual audiences, these disparate forms of discourse are a necessary elixir for the survival of the *Ring*—assuming we want to see the work not in a mummified form but as the product of intelligent directors onstage. At the same time, however, all these interpretations run the risk of investing a single, partial reading with the status of an absolute, thereby oversimplifying Wagner's message. The *Ring* is most at risk from those interpreters who home in on Wagner's philosophy of history, which is its weakest element, for the cycle's fascination rests in the fact that it unleashes a storm that ultimately leads to the destruction of all that exists, while including scenes of unalloyed happiness that occur, as it were, in the eye of the storm, where there is, as we know, only the most absolute calm. Such scenes include those between the lovers Siegmund and Sieglinde, and between Siegfried and Brünnhilde. The happiness that Siegfried feels with regard to his youthful strength is no less authentic than the violence that accompanies it, whether latently or openly. And—in spite of Loge's mockery—does Wotan not feel genuine happiness in the sight of the mighty castle that the giants have built for him? In this regard, the *Ring* differs from *Tristan und Isolde* and especially from *Parsifal*. For here in the *Ring*, Wagner flies in the face of the ninth of Walter Benjamin's *Theses on the Philosophy of History*: he is not one of the "angels of history" driven from paradise by the storm of progress who turns to face the past, which he sees as "one single catastrophe which keeps piling wreckage upon wreckage and hurls it in front of his feet."[53]

Such moments are significant not just at the point in the narrative where they occur but as a fundamental "counterforce that resists the work's temporal nihilism."[54] By constantly evading its own historical logic, the *Ring* continues to build a new world that can never actually exist. That the moments of happiness vanish, collapsing like a house of cards, serves merely to make them all the more immediate. Wagner's *Ring* is not the "trial" of a Josef K., whom Kafka causes to be swept along by one misfortune after another. Nor does it include characters like Beckett's Krapp rummaging around in the rubbish heap of their own lives, only to suffocate in it. Above all with its positive fairy-tale elements, the *Ring* works against the whole

The fairy-tale final scene in Achim Freyer's 2010 production of *Die Walküre* for the Los Angeles Opera. Writing in the *Wiener Zeitung* on June 8, 2010, the Viennese critic Stephan Burianek noted that "although it proved controversial with local audiences, this was an interpretation that many Wagnerians in Europe would surely have been happy to have seen, namely, a production with a plot that remained close to the text and that was free from socio-political questions, intellectual reinterpretations, and psychological insights." Freyer's "fantastical play of light onstage" quotes from the worlds of pantomime, circus, puppet plays, and fairy tales, generally with a deeper meaning yet also with a tendency to engage in random imagery. (Photograph courtesy of Monika Rittershaus, Berlin.)

concept of a myth of overwhelming destructiveness, and Wagner reveals an advanced understanding of dialectics by both thinking in terms of the ending and enjoying each moment to the full. This is an aspect of the work that can be described by reference to philosophical categories, allowing us to speak of a multiperspective organization of time that distinguishes between a teleological experience of it and an obliviousness to its passage.[55] And yet it seems more obvious to interpret the *Ring* on the basis on our own experience of life, for it is part of our whole approach to life not only to think in terms of the wider picture and to develop long-term goals but to give ourselves up to the moment and in that way forget the universal misery that exists all around us. In that sense, Wagnerians who, listening to and watching the *Ring*, abandon themselves to the happiness of the moment in spite of all that they know about the fate of the characters are undoubtedly closer to Wagner than those thinkers and directors who feel a constant need to prove to themselves and to others that they have not been taken in by the great sorcerer's passing promises. Such writers and directors reveal scant understanding of the dialectics contained in the libretto and the music of the *Ring*. Of course, it can be argued that the reception of the *Ring* has privileged its affirmative and phantasmagorical elements to such an extent that there is now an altogether compelling need to deconstruct it—even the term "deconstruction" seems something of a cliché. But we should never lose sight of the subtle balance that Wagner himself maintains between affirmation and deconstruction. It is a subtlety that Wagner directors ignore at their peril. If they believe it imperative to worship at the shrine of today's event culture, they should at least ensure that their ideas respect Wagner's intentions and do not unfold in parallel universes. The colorful *Ring* that Achim Freyer directed in Los Angeles in 2009–10 is a good example of how to stage the cycle: his images may be surreal in an arbitrarily postmodern manner, but they do not disturb their audiences when assimilating the music.

A Word about Angelo Neumann

If we do not take the matter too seriously, it may offer scope for wry amusement: despite his lofty calling, Wagner was forever beset by Jews wanting to help him, causing him untold agonies of embarrassment. Such self-contradictions also marked his dealings with Angelo Neumann, the impresario of the "Traveling Wagner Theater." In the run-up to the first Bayreuth Festival in 1876 Wagner may well have toyed with the idea of limiting performances of the *Ring* to his own theater on the town's Green Hill, but by the end of the festival it had become clear to him that however many rehearsals he may have held, the artistic results remained disappointing, especially with regard to the staging.

There were times when he was overcome by "a mood of great bitterness" and grew depressed at the failure of his plans for Bayreuth. Since "fragments" from the *Ring* were in any case "being played all over the place," he was inclined to sell the work and "never give any more thought to a theater," especially since the 1876 festival had ended with an enormous deficit that required him to think of ways of generating further income. It was no accident that in April 1877, after casting an eye at her housekeeping books, Cosima noted with some concern "that we spent 14,999 marks in the last quarter"—nearly fifty thousand dollars at today's prices.[1]

By this date no German theater director was willing to risk a production of the whole *Ring*. As Cosima noted in her diary, salvation came "from Leipzig and from Israel" in the guise of Angelo Neumann: "He has come for the *Ring* but would also like to have *Parsifal*! Coaxes R. out of half the royalties for the subscription quota—in short, is just what such gentlemen always are. R. says he has nothing against his coming, insofar as it shows they still need him—and we need money, so agreement is reached!"[2]

A production of all four parts of the *Ring* spread over two seasons in Leipzig in 1878 remained largely unnoticed, which was emphatically not the case with the four cycles that Neumann mounted at Berlin's Victoria Theater in May 1881: they proved a resounding success and at the same time signaled Wagner's breakthrough in the German capital. When he traveled to the city for the opening nights, the hotel porter greeted him as "Your Excellency,"[3] and he was also well received by large sections of the imperial court and upper echelons of bourgeois society. The audience's reaction, too, was positive.

All in all, the press concluded, the success and impact of the Berlin performances were far greater than they had been in Bayreuth five years earlier.

Wagner had no choice but to express his gratitude to Neumann, not
least because the latter had been sufficiently astute to involve him in the
rehearsals. Wagner responded by praising Neumann's commitment, while
at the same time criticizing his work in all manner of petty ways, to say
nothing of the fiasco at the end of the last performance. In his speech after the final *Götterdämmerung*, Neumann began by thanking not Wagner
but the members of the imperial household who had attended the performances, causing the composer to storm offstage in high dudgeon and to
forget in turn to thank the performers. That Neumann, too, felt slighted
is less surprising than that it was Wagner who made the first move in the
direction of a reconciliation, so keen was he not to lose his excellent impresario. But before new negotiations could begin, Wagner and his family had
returned by train to Bayreuth, occupying a private carriage. Waiting for
them at Wahnfried was Joseph-Arthur Gobineau, the author of the four-
volume *Essay on the Inequality of the Human Races* whom Wagner had first
met in Rome in October 1876. Gobineau had in fact been present in spirit
in Berlin, for his theories had been the subject of a lively discussion over a
meal at the home of Count Alexander von Schleinitz, the Prussian minister
of the royal household in the city.

By 1882 Neumann had set off with his Traveling Wagner Theater, performing the more or less complete *Ring* in twenty-three different cities
between September 1882 and July 1883. It was an undertaking that placed
tremendous logistical demands on all concerned: the company numbered
130 singers and instrumentalists, while their sets and costumes filled twelve
separate wagons of a special train that visited not only German cities, but
also Amsterdam, Brussels, Ghent, Antwerp, Basel, Venice, Bologna, Rome,
Turin, Trieste, Budapest, and Graz. Wagner had sold his original sets to
Neumann, as there could no longer be any question of a revival of the cycle
in Bayreuth, although he retained the lighting equipment, which was worth
30,000 marks. Among the props that Neumann acquired was an "armory"
filling forty crates, including the Valkyries' armor and weapons, which
weighed forty-five pounds per singer.[4]

The reduction of the orchestra from 114 to 60 players represented an
unfortunate makeshift, but the cast—with the usual exceptions—was altogether outstanding. The conductor, too, was distinguished: Anton Seidl
was later to take charge of the German repertory at the Metropolitan
Opera in New York.

Photograph of Wagner taken by the Munich court photographer Josef Albert in November 1864. The version reproduced here is a hand-colored copy dedicated to Ludwig II and includes Wagner's autograph signature together with the last two lines of a poem that Wagner wrote for the king in the summer of 1864: "So but from thee my strength to thank is taken, / Through thine own kingly Faith of strength unshaken" (trans. William Ashton Ellis). (Photograph courtesy of the Bayerische Verwaltung der Staatlichen Schlösser, Gärten und Seen, Munich.)

"My music making is in fact magic making, for I just cannot produce music coolly and mechanically"

THE ART OF THE *RING*—SEEN FROM THE BEGINNING

The *Ring*: more art as religion than religion as art—Nietzsche's and Thomas Mann's accusations of dilettantism—Wagner's statement of intent "I shall write no more *operas*" in the light of *Das Rheingold*—The *Rheingold* prelude: art used to create nature—The Rhinedaughters, Erda, and Alberich as seen by present-day directors—Alberich as a "subhuman Jew"—From the wide-angle shot to the narrowest focus—The art of "improvisation"—"Local criteria" in the compositional process and vocal forms that reflect the situation onstage—The perfect arch—Hanslick's narrow critique of *Das Rheingold*—The character of the leitmotifs—From the Rhinegold motif to the Ring and Valhalla motifs—Transfer effects in the listener—The music's "autonomous activity"—The ingenious combination of leitmotifs—"A varied network of melodic and harmonic relationships"—Mixing orchestral colors to produce specific "tone paintings"—The transformation music between scenes 1 and 2 as an example of such "tone painting"—Music as mediator between the fragmentary experience of the moment and the permanent desire for wholeness

The philosopher Georg Wilhelm Friedrich Hegel always thought on the grandest scale and had little time for the individual arts: his interest in the development of the absolute mind or spirit and, hence, in the "whole" that was uniquely "true," meant that the arts—in his view—had outlived their usefulness. It was time for them to be replaced by philosophy, which according to Hegel could provide the key to absolute knowledge, a claim for which Hegel was willing to vouch in person. The "ruse of reason" that he often invoked ensured, of course, that Wagner adopted a highly selective approach to his system and singled out only the one element that he found most appealing—his critique of the individual arts. Wagner had no desire to entrust the concern for the whole to philosophy but, evincing an arrogance no less egregious than Hegel's, regarded his own total artwork as the platform on which to present world-embracing ideas: it was, he believed, not pure thinking or absolute knowledge that could depict the whole in all its greatness but only a new mythology using the medium of art: it was, in short, a religion of art.

Regressive though this may have been from Hegel's perspective, it was an integral part of romantic thinking, with its concern for "ways of depicting the 'absolute' as the ultimate basis on which to anchor our fragile existence and invest it with a sense of assurance." And art was uniquely placed to answer this need since it alone was in a position "to depict something inherently undepictable in a form whose meaning could never be fully understood." Since the artist could not avoid "depicting something specific" but must inevitably fail in revealing "the inexhaustible contents of the absolute," he or she must avoid all "specificity of expression." As Manfred Frank has put it, "They said the finite and meant the infinite. They said something specific and caused it to hang in the balance by means of something else which, equally specific, was not compatible with it. No art can do this better than music, an art revered by the romantics above all others."[1]

This brings us to the *Ring* as a work of art. In other words, the aim of the present chapter is not to discuss whether the cycle offers a coherent view of the world and should be seen as a modern myth or whether it should be rejected as such. Our concern, rather, is Wagner's potential ability to give aesthetic expression to his view of the world in the form of a work of music theater that continues to fascinate us today. *Das Rheingold* will serve to illustrate this point. The intellectual rigor that the composer brought to bear on providing the *Ring* with a solid conceptual foundation may earn our admiration or elicit our contempt, but what matters—in Hegel's terms—is the "material appearance" of these ideas, and this is even more true in a skeptical postmodern age that has made it almost impossible to regard the *Ring* as an example of a religion in art. Instead, we are necessarily obliged to see it as an aesthetic object, with the emphasis no longer on religion but on art. Moreover, the question as to the artistic quality of the total artwork that the *Ring* is or claims to be is not external to the cycle but is the most important issue that singers, instrumentalists, conductors, directors, and designers on the one hand and audiences and critics on the other have to confront. Answers to this question are not to be found in books on Wagner's worldview but time and time again have to be rediscovered in our concrete confrontation with the phenomenon of the *Ring* in performance.

It is, of course, no easy matter to set oneself up as judge of Wagner's art and, more especially, of *Das Rheingold*, for on the one hand the "preliminary evening" of the *Ring*, for which Wagner effectively had to relearn the whole technique of composition, offers many points of access of a formal and aesthetic nature, while on the other hand there is much truth to Nietzsche's remark that "it is all too easy to be proved right with Wagner."[2] And Nietzsche must have known what he was talking about, for he was uniquely placed to understand a man whom he loved and hated, admired and criticized in equal measure. One of his criticisms was directed at the composer's alleged dilettantism, and in his essay "Richard Wagner in Bayreuth"—a text whose perspicacity is in no way compromised by its overemotive language—he invokes

> a spirit of restlessness, of irritability, a nervous hastiness in seizing hold upon a hundred different things, a passionate delight in experiencing moods of almost pathological intensity, an abrupt transition from the most soulful quietude to noise and violence. He was held in check by no traditional family involvement in any particular art: he might as easily have adopted painting, poetry, acting, music as academic scholarship or an academic future; and a superficial view of him might suggest that he was a born dilettante.[3]

Writers on Wagner are inordinately fond of quoting these last five words, while generally overlooking that Nietzsche was essentially describing the intellectual climate of *décadence* within which he was inclined to locate Wagner's art and stressing that only a "superficial" observer would reproach that art for dilettantism. Even so, it will repay our attention to examine the matter more closely. First and foremost, there is the naïve assumption that the age of *décadence*, being restlessly nervous and irritable, was incapable of producing solid, craftsmanlike art. In this context the reader may be reminded of Thomas Mann, who in turn spoke admiringly of Wagner's "infamously inspired dilettantism" in a short story, *Der Bajazzo* (The Clown), that he wrote almost immediately before *Buddenbrooks*. In this last-named work, little Hanno represents the fourth generation of the Buddenbrook family, a youth unsuited to the world of business but also incapable of practicing music professionally, for he could "improvise only a little."

It is clear from this that the accusation of dilettantism went hand in hand with the idea of improvisation, an idea that applied with particular force to an artist like Wagner, who availed himself of several different arts in order to create his total artwork. If we were to question Wagner himself, we would encounter an interesting ambivalence, for on the one hand he tended in later life to stress his conviction that the "symphonic fabric" of his scores need not fear comparison with that of established symphonists, while at the same time he saw himself—as we have already observed—in the difficult role of the "improviser" who "belongs entirely to the moment" and who would be "lost" if he kept having to think of what came next.

At this juncture we may begin to suspect what lies behind the charge of "dilettantism": it is the listener's fear of being forever at the mercy of the music instead of being able to watch its structure unfold in a logically understandable way. That the composer, too, is at the mercy of his music emerges from another remark by Wagner: "My music making is in fact like magic making, for I just cannot produce music coolly and mechanically. [. . .] In a mood of ecstasy I can lead my voices through the most hair-raising contortions without a moment's hesitation; it all pours out so steadily, as if from a machine; but I can do nothing coolly." And in this context he criticized that "donkey" Eduard Hanslick for "speaking of Beethoven's naïveté" but "naturally" with "no idea of the wisdom of genius, which, though it comes and goes like lightning, is the highest there is."[4]

We must also dismiss as "donkeys" those listeners who not only do not like Wagner—for that is their right—but who accuse him of professional incompetence. Great art is incommensurable, and in that sense we can no more compare Wagner with Brahms or Schoenberg than we can compare Monet with Böcklin or Mondrian. Of course, Wagner's musical language may make us feel comfortable or uncomfortable even without our examining his artistic intentions. But to the extent that we are willing to do so, then we need to confront the "poetic aim in all its important elements," as Wagner explained to Liszt when setting forth his plans for the *Ring*.[5] Of course, the audience does not need to understand every aspect of the plot but must be willing to experience music and action as related to one another and commit to this relationship without any preconceived ideas.

In many respects this was already true of Wagner's earlier works and even of Mozart's operas. To take an example: listeners can truly enjoy the Letter Duet in *Le nozze di Figaro* only if they are able to appreciate the niceties of the plot. The Countess is dictating a love letter that Susanna writes down. It takes the form of a *canzonetta* designed to expose the Count as a philanderer. But we can also listen to this number as an "autonomous" duet: its charm and meaning are not entirely lost if we do so. In the *Ring*, too, there are many passages that make sense on a purely musical level and that can be enjoyed in purely orchestral arrangements. As we have already noted, Wagner had nothing against such "tone pictures." While not replacing the stage action, they can at least help to recreate that action before the mind's eye, reminding listeners of what has already happened.

But this does not help us very much in the case of *Das Rheingold*, for here Wagner's statement in *A Communication to My Friends*—" I shall write no more *operas*"[6]—reveals the work's whole revolutionary force: not in relation to its overall compositional level, which is distinctly uneven when compared to the later parts of the *Ring*, but in regard to the innovative manner in which Wagner was able to think primarily in terms of the action and staging and leave behind him the traditional formal world of opera. His decision to forget all that he knew about current systems in the aesthetics of music and the theory of opera before he began work on the score of *Das Rheingold* is vaguely reminiscent of those Renaissance painters who were fully conversant with the new device of a central perspective, which they could handle to virtuosic effect, but who preferred to ignore it in favor of a medieval perspective, a technique well illustrated by Botticelli's *Mystic Nativity*, for example.[7]

The prelude is an excellent illustration of this. Unlike the prelude to *Lohengrin*—to say nothing of the overture to *Tannhäuser*—it can no longer be described as an independent number that could be performed in the concert hall. As Wagner observed at the time of its first performance in 1869, it is completely subsumed by its function of constituting "the world's lullaby,"[8] which it does by dint of its wave-like motion, emerging, as it were, before the listener's ears. A composer relying on his own experience of opera and concerned with his own reputation would probably not have risked opening his *Ring* cycle with a prelude lasting 136 bars of a single E-flat major chord to depict the flowing waters of the Rhine. But what we find here is not an egotistical artist but a *medium* that at the creation of the world knows only about the quality residing in this natural E-flat major. Wagner later claimed that the decisive impulse for his conception of this music came to him during a somnambulistic state after a strenuous walk through the hills surrounding La Spezia. Although this account ill accords with what we know about the outward circumstances of his life at this time, it has an inner truth to the extent that, as we have already noted, Wagner believed that an "insane somnambulistic state" was an integral part of the compositional process.

But this mystification of the creative process was also useful in boosting Wagner's courage: it was not he himself who was forcing his audience to concentrate on a single seething tonality for four whole minutes but the myth. Of course, the conscientious biographer, working to scholarly criteria, has a responsibility to himself and to his readers to get to the bottom of such acts of self-mystification on Wagner's part, and yet this objectivity cannot preclude a sense of admiration for his subject's achievements: how could he have summoned up the reserves of energy needed for such a gigantic project over a period of several decades if he were not constantly able to assure himself of his spiritual reserves? But, regardless of this, even those Wagnerians who are unable to read a note of music are fully aware that the naïveté of the prelude to *Das Rheingold* is achieved only by dint of the greatest sophistication and refinement. Initially, of course, the music cannot modulate in a harmonic sense because Wagner was convinced that such modulations are linked to changes in the underlying emotions within a poetic-musical period. All the more takes place, therefore, in the fields of rhythm and meter, thereby reflecting the arbitrary moods of nature.

What Wagner has created here is an expression not of "the amorphous," as Adorno claimed was the case,[9] but of the impulsive momentum of life, which we can sense in the incessant flow of the Rhine presented in a highly structured form as a sequence of symmetrical groups of bars. But Wagner has also produced an elaborate balance between rest and motion: the pedal point on E-flat that is maintained from start to finish and the triadic figures that rise and fall in changing configurations, while remaining thematically undefined, provide an element of rest within the "billowing waters" that are mentioned in the stage directions. Little rhythmic and metrical shifts and the imperceptible increase in dynamics ensure that the flowing motion is constantly revitalized.[10] Vitality is not the same as chaos, of course, for the clear metrical order and tendency to structure the music in four-bar periods ensures that the apparently infinite space in which Wagner begins his act of creation in E-flat major is soon reduced to the manageable confines of the bed of the river Rhine.

It made sense, therefore, that in his 1976 production of the *Ring* Patrice Chéreau had the waves of the river beating against the foot of a hydroelectric dam, for this pointer to modern technology makes it plain that Wagner treats his orchestra like a complex apparatus that does not simply provide an echo of nature, as suggested by George Steiner, but actually produces it in an extremely up-to-date way, without, however, giving away the details of that production process. Even Wagner's own audiences were unable, of course, to hear such scenes of nature in an entirely naïve way but enjoyed the successful phantasmagoria whose tendency to imply hypothetical alternatives Adorno was to find so troubling.

For Wagner, conversely, music was not "true" or "untrue" in the sense understood by Adorno. For him, all that mattered was whether or not it was suited to the drama, its aim being to convey the contents of the drama to the audience's feelings. In terms of the *Ring*, Wagner was enough of a dialectician to know that at the start of *Das Rheingold* nature appears to be unspoiled only from the standpoint of the Rhinedaughters, whereas the truth of the matter is that it was violated long ago, when Wotan hewed a branch from the World Ash Tree in order to make a spear for himself. The tree then withered, while the god continued to delude himself into believing that the runes carved into the shaft of his spear might guarantee his lasting rule by dint of the one-sided contract that they enshrine. And so Wotan, too, knows that the ululating sounds of the Rhinedaughters guarding their gold are a passing idyll, throwing a spotlight on a world that has long since lost its innocence.

Does this means that the Rhinedaughters have already left their natural innocence so far behind them that it is possible to present them onstage as whores, an interpretation that is now the rule rather than the exception? (In his Essen production of *Das Rheingold* in 2008 Tilman Knabe even thought it appropriate to have the Rhinedaughters couple with Wotan during the prelude.) Here we have an example of the narrow line that is trodden by modern directors, for on the one hand it makes eminent sense to emphasize the actuality of Wagner's characters by placing them in a modern context, even to the point of alienation, while at the same time today's audiences need to see primeval, archetypal figures who affect us in the depths of our collective unconscious.

If the *Ring* contains characters who defy a modern presentation, then they are the two triadic groups of the Rhinedaughters and the Norns, and the figure of Erda. No one has power over them, and although they are ultimately powerless in the face of the power struggles taking place in the world, they are also the only creatures whose timeless existence is unaffected by the great conflagration that engulfs the earth at the end of *Götterdämmerung*. This aspect of the work is well illustrated by Wotan's encounter with Erda, in the course of which Wotan—"the sum total of the [failed] intelligence of the present" who "resembles us to a tee"[11] — conjures up "the eternal world's primeval Vala," as Wagner called her in one of the preliminary drafts for the *Ring*, only for him to dismiss her again and send her back into the primeval depths from which she had emerged.[12]

But let us return to the Rhinedaughters. We may accept Ruth Berghaus's view of them as children who cruelly exploit their charms,[13] but we can also see them as naïvely animalistic women who have no desire to see a "hairy, hunchbacked dwarf" as the father of their offspring, an interpretation that the present author would prefer to resist. But they are emphatically not whores who sell their bodies for money. By contrast, Alberich is not only the natural faun who spends his life pursuing nymphs, but he is also Wotan's shadowy alter ego who gains more from power than from love, and if this power is insufficient to win him love, he can still use "pleasure" to assure him of world dominion. At the same time, we may share Dieter Schickling's belief that Alberich is the leader of a proletariat of dwarfs eager to destroy the ruling gods. As such, he too is guilty of an abuse of power, but he is the only main character to survive the final *Götterdämmerung*, for, according to Schickling's surprising logic, "Wagner wanted Alberich to survive as a liberator."[14]

In November 1848, buoyed up by his mood of revolutionary optimism, Wagner had ended his prose draft *The Nibelung Myth* with the words: "Loosed be the Nibelungs' thralldom, the Ring no more shall bind them. Not Alberich shall receive it; no more shall he enslave you, but he himself be free as ye."[15] When viewed from a nonpolitical standpoint, Alberich is ultimately a despised underdog who, according to Chéreau, would "probably not have cursed love" and traded it for power "if he had not been provoked by the Rhinedaughters."[16] This reading receives some support from an entry in Cosima Wagner's diary: "R. tells me that he once felt every sympathy for Alberich, who represents the ugly person's longing for beauty."[17] It may be added here that Wagner himself does not seem to have toyed with the idea of depicting Alberich as a downtrodden Jew, a view that gained currency only after his death. At all events, a further entry in Cosima's diary for November 17, 1882, reads: "This morning we went through all the characters of the *R. des Nibelungen* from the point of view of race: the gods white; the dwarfs yellow (Mongols); the blacks the Ethiopians; Loge the half-caste."[18]

If we see this largely whimsical comment against the background of the aforementioned interpretations of Alberich, we shall see that it makes no sense to seek to examine every last detail of the dwarf's character, still less to reduce it to a few constants, for Wagner's art was such that he could create characters which, although grounded in myth, reveal such varied features that it is impossible to get a handle on them. Nor should we attempt to do so. Their true lebensraum is the music—music which, for all its mimetic flexibility, is rarely garishly obvious. In a word, it does not tell us how to view a particular character. This art can be understood only by those listeners willing to follow it step by step, like a child implicitly believing the person recounting the fairy tale and being amply rewarded in consequence. Readers who regard this as an imposition will presumably concede that the narrative flow of a Verdi opera guides them in much the same way, the major difference being that Verdi's characters are more clearly drawn, Otello, for example, being neither able nor willing to stand comparison with Alberich or Wotan in terms of his multifaceted personality. And this is true, no matter how subtle the singer's portrayal may be.

This also lays bare a fundamental difference between the two composers, for whereas Verdi regarded the stage as the self-evident setting for a performance of his opera, Wagner felt that the theater was no more than a makeshift solution. Of course, not even *his* music theater can survive without a space in which the stage illusion can unfold, a space enclosed within everyday painted flats and set pieces. But it is the music that creates the true space within which these music dramas are played out, the music that offers the acoustic space in which the singing actors can "improvise" their roles. And there is no part of the *Ring* that illustrates this point as clearly as the "preliminary evening" of *Das Rheingold*. Of course, the prelude is intended to create the illusion of flowing water, an illusion bound up with the concept of time. More important, however, is the creation of a backdrop of sound against which the Rhinedaughters can act. From this point of view it is immediately clear why Wagner increasingly reduces the initially vast space in which this world of sound is created, an aim he achieves by means of increasingly precise rhythms: the orchestral action moves from the wide-angle shot of the opening to the spotlight that focuses on the Rhinedaughters and their initial dialogue.

The first words that the Rhinedaughters sing are "Weia! Waga! Woge, du Welle." They show that the element of improvisation to which we have just referred not only concerns Wagner's *general* demand to his singing actors that they should bring the greatest possible animation to their roles; it is also meant to be taken literally. Neither dramaturgically nor in terms of the work's compositional history is there any formal precedent for the vocal writing for Woglinde, Wellgunde, and Floßhilde, for it does not launch the action in the way that we find with Mozart's accompanied recitative, for example, or with a crowd scene à la *Lohengrin*. Rather, the Rhinedaughters talk among themselves, just as they have been doing since the dawn of time—and presumably they will continue to do so after the action of the *Ring* has come to an end. Wagner needed new compositional resources for such a "conversation": Woglinde's "Weia! Waga! Woge, du Welle" reflects an ancient, primeval language, which is why it is purely pentatonic, without the halftone steps that are an integral part of the major-minor system.

In general, the Rhinedaughters are permitted to revel in natural sounds—derived from the harmonic series—as their vocal line is almost entirely free from individual features, representing, as it does, the principle of unity in triunity. Soon, however, the focus narrows yet further, when a loner—Alberich—introduces a note of unease. Only in the course of the later action does this loner acquire any proper physical contours, although even here, at the very beginning, he is already associated with a number of characteristic motivic particles. By the time he sings the words "Garstig glatter glitschriger Glimmer! wie gleit' ich aus!" (Sleek as slime the slope of the slate is! I slant and slide!), the whole scene has struck a different note and focuses on the disgruntlement of the dwarf as he seeks in vain to capture the Rhinedaughters. He now operates within a totally different set of sonorities notable for their occluded orchestral tone colors and disjointed, dissonant motifs—this is in striking contrast to the "organic" naturalness of the earlier part of the scene. These "disruptive tones," as Tobias Janz has called them,[19] are among Wagner's "motifs of presentiment" even if they are not leitmotifs in the strict sense of the term: listeners experience this initial "disturbance of the existing harmony" as portending threatening events that are yet to be seen onstage.[20] (All of this is a small but typical pointer to the oft-mentioned affinity between Wagner's compositional techniques and those associated with film music.)

The very way in which Wagner notated Alberich's vocal line implies a particular type of delivery for which there was no precedent at that time: although the traditional accompanied recitative had proved itself over the generations as a means of conveying dramatic dialogue, it offered little help when it came to an almost naturalistic treatment of language, ascribing to each performer a specific idiom geared to the particular situation onstage. (We might be inclined to call it "prose melody" if, in *Opera and Drama*, Wagner had not explicitly rejected the kind of vocal style implied by this term.) Compositional elements such as these (music example 16), being naturalistic and illustrative, ran counter to audiences' traditional experience of

opera inasmuch as they were as new to Wagner as they were to his singers.
Even before he had started work on the score of the *Ring*, he explained to
one of his friends in Dresden, Theodor Uhlig, that he was setting foot on un-
charted territory: "I'm telling you—the musical phrases are formed around
these verses and periods without my needing to make the least effort; everything springs up out of the ground like rank vegetation. The beginning is
already sketched out in my head; also a few graphic motifs such as *Fafner*."[21]
A few years later—in his 1861 essay "Music of the Future"—Wagner struck
a more theoretical note, arguing that within the context of the drama, the
music must develop "an entirely new capacity for speech," for this alone
would allow it "to affect our feelings with such certainty that our powers
of reason, being based on logic, are confused and disarmed."[22] In this context, the twenty-first-century composer Claus-Steffen Mahnkopf has spoken of "local criteria."[23] Although they are by no means lacking in logic,
they are effective only in the light of the drama's specific situation.

16. Bars 231–35 of scene 1 of *Das Rheingold.*

This new situation demanded not only improvisatory abilities from the composer but also procedures that can certainly be described as sophisticated. Bars 533–62, for example, can be analyzed as a "perfect arch" in the sense defined by Alfred Lorenz: beginning with the Rhinegold fanfare, Wagner builds to a climax that is then rescinded, returning to the initial fanfare by means of a mirror-like symmetrical structure (music example 17).[24] This form is appropriate to the situation onstage as it reflects the eternal cycle of nature, a cycle that is mirrored in turn in the vocal writ-

17. Bars 533–62 of scene 1 of *Das Rheingold*, demonstrating the perfect arch form of this passage.

ing for the Rhinedaughters. Those readers who are interested in a purely formal musical analysis will find much to enjoy in this passage, as it reveals an interesting structure. At the same time, however, they are bound to be puzzled by the extent to which Wagner was conscious of what he was doing here or whether he was following the "unconscious plan" that he liked to claim was the case. Yet it is part and parcel of his ingenious artistry that we can see its underlying strategy not as some arithmetical game, as may be the case with a Bach fugue, for example, for all that such a piece may also be contingent upon other imponderables.

Especially in the case of *Das Rheingold*, we should not expect to find perfection in this sense, for no matter how elaborate the theories he had already formulated, Wagner was still not clear in his own mind about the exact nature of his "vocal melody" in this preliminary evening. Of course, the practices found in traditional operas, whereby a recitative designed to carry the action forward was followed by an emotionally intense aria, had long been obsolete and in the hands of a composer like Mozart were more of a caricature than a rule of thumb. But how should a composer set a libretto in which every line was equally important for the advancement of a plot that never stands still and which leaves it to the orchestra—heard synchronously with the vocal line—to reflect and comment on events?

This is a question that had already exercised the exponents of early Italian opera, a medium intended to bring about a revival of classical tragedy, for audiences had very quickly tired of the never-ending recitation tone, persuading composers to break up the passages of recitative with more appealing vocal writing based on songs and arias. In turn, these songs and arias soon became the focus of attention, leading to a loss of interest in the actual plot. Wagner was determined to improve on this—which also meant improving on those aspects of his own romantic operas which, however musically gripping, distracted from the developing action.

Wagner's main problem lay in breaking free from the stereotypical forms of traditional opera—unaccompanied and accompanied recitative and arias—and inventing vocal forms appropriate to the situation onstage. The difficulties that this problem initially caused him emerge from Loge's great narration in scene 2 of *Das Rheingold*, starting with the words "Immer ist Undank Loge's Lohn!" (Ingratitude ever is Loge's wage). Wagner begins by adopting the tone of a traditional recitative, something almost entirely inconceivable in later sections of the *Ring*. But during the words "für Weibes Wonne und Werth" (for woman's delights and worth), the mode of performance changes with remarkable suddenness, and at the stage direction "All express astonishment and various forms of consternation," the motif associated with the renunciation of love blossoms not only in the vocal line but also in the orchestra, the function of which had hitherto been limited for the most part to a series of inconspicuous accompanying chords. This motif provides the emotional context, for audiences can still recall its earlier occurrence at the words "Nur wer der Minne Macht" (Only he who forswears love's power). If it is repeated now, it is to remind the assembled gods of what they will be losing by abandoning love, embodied in Freia, for power, symbolized by Valhalla.

When Loge goes on to ask, rhetorically, if there is anything "in water, earth or air that man might deem mightier than woman's delights and worth," his vocal line, now far more expressive in character, encourages the orchestra to add a commentary that becomes an independent strand in the narrative, weaving together the tale of the Rhinedaughters, the Rhinegold, and Alberich's renunciation of love in favor of world domination to produce an independent orchestral melody.[25]

This scene encapsulates the challenges that Wagner faced when composing the *Ring* and demonstrates how he tackled them: it was a difficult balancing act that required him to ensure on the one hand that his musical language revealed the universal validity demanded by the mythical elements in his total artwork, while at the same time being able to react flexibly to the subtleties of the plot. A century before Wagner, composers faced with this situation would have spoken of the well-nigh insoluble task of combining three different styles—"high," "middle," and "low"—within one and the same work. It is certainly possible to argue whether Wagner was as successful in achieving this aim in *Das Rheingold* as he was in the later parts of the *Ring* and whether the stylistic inconsistencies that are found in the vocal writing in *Das Rheingold* are the result of a lack of experience, or whether, conversely, they make sense precisely because the work is set in a strange, archaic world to which a cultured philosophy of beauty cannot be applied. After all, if certain elements of *Das Rheingold* were not so rankly luxuriant, they would not be able to show any signs of degeneration in *Götterdämmerung*.

Be that as it may, Hanslick was being unjust when, in his polemically worded review of the Munich production of *Das Rheingold* in 1869, he complained about the "perversity of Wagner's one-thing-after-another style": "One after the other, the characters have their say, slowly and over-emphatically, while the other characters look on, mute and bored."[26] Here Hanslick is guilty of ignoring not only the sense of drama found in many of the scenes of *Das Rheingold* but also the different kinds of recitative: at one moment Alberich is heard cursing and swearing; at the next Fricka launches into her litany of woes, only for Wotan to strike a note of high emotion—to say nothing of the Rhinedaughters' timeless and weightless vocal lines.

From the standpoint of the vocal lines, the spectator may indeed share Hanslick's view that the world of *Das Rheingold* is unbalanced and even long-winded, but when seen from the perspective of the leitmotifs, it is undoubtedly startling and succinct. Indeed, it takes the breath away to note the assurance with which Wagner finds his leitmotifs, all of which are eloquent in the spirit of the action and characterization, while at the same time being easy to recognize. Moreover, Wagner successfully discovered a succinct musical expression for symbols and archetypal images which, grounded in our collective unconscious, take on material form in specific colors and highlights, depending on the context in which they occur, without their identity suffering in the process.

The motifs in question represent animate creatures such as gods and goddesses, giants, dwarfs, heroes, and villains but also elements and objects such as water, fire, light, a sword, a spear, the ring, and the castle that is home to the gods. Even abstract processes such as brooding and the signing of treaties are reflected in such motifs. Wagner describes them as motifs of presentiment and reminiscence because they serve as pointers to concrete connections within the action of the *Ring*, but they can also allow us to experience what we already know about the world. In this way they are independent of the various strands in the plot.

The triadic motif that dominates the prelude to *Das Rheingold* is a good example of this, for not only does it remind us of a particular river serenely flowing along, but it captures the archetypal experience of flowing water in general. After all, the motifs of presentiment and reminiscence can fulfill their function only by speaking a musical language already familiar to listeners as part of a mimetic tradition that has existed for centuries, if not for millennia. Pentatonic scales and triads carry associations of nature for the simple reason that they are directly derived from the notes of the natural harmonic series, notes that primitive man (and woman) could produce on the simplest of bone flutes. Of course, modern composers, including Wagner, use the triad in very different contexts, and yet it continues to represent the elemental as opposed to the differentiated.

It is no accident, therefore, that the motifs that Wagner himself described as "natural" are based on pentatonic scales and triads: here one thinks, for example, of the motifs associated with the Rhine, the Rhinegold, the rainbow, and Erda. All these motifs are generally close to nature, but each of them also includes a specific gesture. Take the Rhinegold motif (music example 18), an ascending figure notable not least for its striking rhythm and heard on the solo trumpet: almost inevitably it suggests an ele-mentally trail-blazing energy, in this case the positive energy of the earth that becomes a lust for power only when it is misused. Scored for winds, the Valhalla theme (music example 19) is also one of these nature motifs and ac-quires a sense of stolid solemnity, especially in the key of D-flat major, a key which according to the characteristics traditionally associated with the dif-ferent tonalities is relatively remote from nature. As a result, this solemnity is appropriate to the sight of a proud citadel built upon solid foundations. Even so, it is audibly derived from the Rhinegold motif: ultimately, the gi-ants who built Valhalla will receive the Rhinegold as a reward for all their hard work. To the extent that Wotan has to give the giants the ring that has been made from the Rhinegold, it is only logical that the motifs associated with the ring and Valhalla are based on the same musical material: the ring is the symbol of world dominion, Valhalla the symbol of the power of the gods, a power whose material expression—the castle—comes at a very high price. And it is clear from Wagner's music that a curse lies on this ring, for

18 and 19. The Rhinegold motif as it appears in bars 515–17 of scene 1 of *Das Rheingold* and the Valhalla motif in bars 769–70.

although the descending and ascending thirds that make up the motif form
a perfect circle, this circle is formed from thirds which, no longer natural,
are somehow tainted. Taken together, they form the chord of a diminished
seventh, a highly unstable and ambivalent structure (music example 20).

20. The Ring motif as stated in bars 599–604 of scene 1 of *Das Rheingold*.

It was in honor of Valhalla's splendiferous motif that Wagner devised
the tubas that are named after him. Listeners who, on hearing this motif,
are reminded of nationalist or even National Socialist pomp and circumstance or claim that the composer had a positive opinion of power can certainly appeal to the work's reception history. But it is a reception history
that flies in the face of Wagner's own intentions: by deriving the apparently
stable sounds of the Valhalla motif on its first appearance from the unstable
sequence of thirds of the Ring motif, Wagner makes it clear that Valhalla is
built on sand. This is something that any perceptive listener can work out
without studying the score in detail: having in the meantime assimilated
the threatening gesture of the Ring motif, we feel that its transformation
into the resplendent Valhalla motif during the transition between scenes 1
and 2 is all the more magical in consequence. As listeners we feel an almost

archetypal sense of hope that evil may be mysteriously turned to good. Wagner himself is not interested in beautiful appearances, which he exposes in the subsequent course of the *Ring*, but true to his aim of offering his audiences a modern mythology, he presents us with images and ideas that we have carried around inside us from time immemorial.

The reproach that Wagner uses his leitmotifs in blatantly overobvious ways is popular with anti-Wagnerians but is ultimately untenable, while the claim that these motifs merely duplicate the action is vitiated by the nuances of which they are capable. In any case, the transformation of the Ring motif into the Valhalla motif takes place in the orchestra, without any words of explanation, necessitating an independent transfer action on the part of the audience: only then is it possible to appreciate the structural affinity between the two leitmotifs and see the structural similarities with the potential of the ring and Valhalla as instruments of power.[27] That this transfer succeeds, even though it is undertaken not by the intellect but primarily by feeling, represents a triumph that few would begrudge Wagner.

Even within the context of the drama, Wagner's music is sufficiently autonomous to throw listeners back on their own devices. But not only is the listener "active" in this sense, so too is the music, which on this point has no need to fear comparisons with the visual arts. For centuries writers on the visual arts have argued that it is not only the individual who looks at the image but the image that looks at the observer. Philosophers such as Leibniz and Nicholas of Cusa have ascribed an "autonomous activity" to the image inasmuch as it looks "simultaneously at everyone, independently of the position and movements of its observers and, from the standpoint of the individual, at that individual alone."[28] This reflects the way in which Wagner's leitmotifs work and, indeed, the way in which music in general functions: on the one hand motifs send out signals that all listeners can understand in the same or similar ways, while on the other hand they are mostly sufficiently autonomous to affect every listener differently. This ambivalence is already found in the motifs that make up *Das Rheingold*, which are more reminiscent of al fresco painting than the motifs that occur in the later parts of the cycle.

And even these motifs are already remarkable for the variety of ways in which they can be transformed and combined. Let us consider a further detail from Loge's great narration, this time from the standpoint of the music theorist. "Ein Tand ist's / in des Wassers Tiefe, / lachenden Kindern zur Lust" (A toy it is in the watery deep, delighting laughing children), Loge describes the Rhinegold, before going on:

> doch, ward es zum runden
> Reife geschmiedet,
> hilft es zur höchsten Macht,
> gewinnt dem Manne die Welt.

[But once it is forged to a rounded hoop, it confers unending power and wins the world for its master.]

Wotan replies, "reflectively":

> Von des Rheines Gold
> hört' ich raunen:
> Beute-Runen
> berge sein rother Glanz.

[Of the gold in the Rhine I've heard it whispered that booty-runes lie hid in its fiery glow.]

It goes almost without saying that the Rhinedaughters' cantilena and the Ring motif are heard at this point in the orchestra. What is particularly interesting is the way in which this is done. On a purely superficial level, there is nothing unduly striking: the Ring motif appears with importunate frequency, but it remains tonally unaltered, its bass line the same as on its first appearance. On that occasion Wellgunde and Floßhilde had revealed the Rhinegold's secret to Alberich:

> WELLGUNDE
> Der Welt Erbe
> gewänne zu eigen,
> wer aus dem Rheingold
> schüfe den Ring,
> der maaßlose Macht ihm verlieh'.

> FLOSSHILDE
> Der Vater sagt' es,
> und uns befahl er
> klug zu hüten
> den klaren Hort.

[WELLGUNDE: The world's wealth would be won by him who forged from the Rhinegold the ring that would grant him limitless power.
FLOSSHILDE: Father told us and bound us over to guard the bright hoard wisely.]

The opening scene of *Das Rheingold* in Patrice Chéreau's centennial production of the *Ring* in Bayreuth in 1976. The dam on top of which the Rhinedaughters are positioned was intended to illustrate Chéreau's view that the cycle is a nineteenth-century construct, but avoids the sort of explicit political interpretation placed on the work by Joachim Herz in his Leipzig production that was first staged in its entirety that same year. (Photograph courtesy of the Nationalarchiv der Richard-Wagner-Stiftung, Bayreuth: D 1597.)

What is remarkable is that in his exchange with Loge, Wotan claims to have "heard" about the warning concerning the "gold in the Rhine," a warning once issued to his daughters by Father Rhine. But is Wotan really so imperfectly informed about his own world? In offering this information, he merely *pretends* to be expressing himself "reflectively," his expression corresponding with the reciting note F-sharp, which is clearly contradicted by the harmonization of the "orchestral melody" at this point in the score. Moreover, his F-sharp contradicts the reciting note F to which Floßhilde had articulated the words "Der Vater sagt' es." Of course, no listener can possibly recall the harmonic environment of Floßhilde's F when Wotan sings his F-sharp 854 bars later.[29] At the same time, however, the "allusive magic" of Wagner's musical dramas rests on details such as this, details that are so effective precisely because they appear en masse and serve to reinforce each other.

As we have already observed, Wagner succeeds in this aim even in *Das Rheingold*, encouraging Christian Berger to note that a leitmotif "speaks" above all by dint of its function within a "complex network of melodic and harmonic relationships."[30] When such a leitmotif appears in a new context, it serves, therefore, not simply to "illustrate" situations already familiar to us. Rather, the leitmotif—to quote the literary scholar James Treadwell with reference to literary leitmotifs—understands "itself as text, story, myth. In scene after scene, it *tells* itself."[31]

Of course, Wagner must have been unusually clairvoyant to be able to create a set of leitmotifs in *Das Rheingold* that would not only serve him in the as yet unwritten parts of the *Ring* but allow themselves to be woven into an increasingly complex musical texture. Here the reader is inclined to believe Wagner's own tendency to mystify the creative process and regard him less as capable of planning far in advance than of acting as a medium and as an intuitive artist, trusting in his own intrinsic genius.

But it is not only in his handling of his leitmotifs that Wagner reveals his genius in *Das Rheingold*, for this facet also emerges from his ability to combine orchestral colors to produce the most subtly nuanced moods. Of course, there are already examples of this ability in the "tone paintings" in *Tannhäuser* and *Lohengrin*, but the prelude and the transformation music between the four scenes that make up *Das Rheingold* are veritable miracles of music, conjuring up oneiric visions in sound that give way to one another either abruptly or imperceptibly—and always in the sense of pure nature scenes involving no performers onstage.[32] There is something altogether incredible about the orchestral writing while Wotan and Loge descend invisibly from the cloud-girt heights inhabited by the gods through sulfur-filled crevices to the underworld realm of Nibelheim, where they are confronted by the earsplitting din of hammers beating down on eighteen anvils: for what seems a tormenting eternity the music is almost literally choked by the noise of soulless labor; and when it finally catches its breath, it is merely to express the sense of horror-struck oppression that we feel at the sight of Alberich's brutality toward his brother Mime. "Everything to be played with terrible energy of expression," reads one of Wagner's performance instructions from the time of the first Bayreuth *Ring*.[33]

It is insufficient to speak only of illustrative music in a derogatory sense or simply to interpret the work's "message," for what we really need to do here is to provide a proper assessment of the compositional skill that underpins this music—and from this point of view it matters little whether we like the music or not. A book like this, which seeks to engage the general reader, is not a suitable place for a detailed technical analysis. Rather, it aims to adopt the position taken by Carl Philipp Emanuel Bach, who wanted only experts to analyze his works in detail. Not even practicing musicians were to know his tricks—presumably he was afraid of plagiarism and rivalry. Interested music lovers, conversely, were to be shown the "beauty," "risk-taking," and "novelty" that they could admire in "true masterpieces" and the extent to which a composer might "depart from the ordinary and risk something special" in pursuit of originality in art.[34]

These remarks are admirably well suited to *Das Rheingold*, for not even experts have succeeded in understanding this work in the sense of a self-contained, unified system, allowing them to draw conclusions about its individual parts on the basis of the whole, as is possible with Bach's Goldberg Variations, Beethoven's "Eroica" Symphony, and Mozart's *Le nozze di Figaro*. Rather, we need to observe Wagner's novel compositional procedures from the standpoint of the individual details that make up the work. And yet even if it is possible to discover coherent connections extending over longer sections of the work, they remain contingent. In other words: they *may* appear as a unity but do not necessarily have to do so. Wagner's procedure may bewilder and annoy an analyst with a fetish for systematization, but it satisfies amateur music lovers, for whom the combination of a fragmentary experience of the present with the permanent search for wholeness and for a system reflects a common feeling in their lives. And since we know that *Das Rheingold* is merely the "preliminary evening" in advance of the actual events, we shall be encouraged by the incommensurable nature of the work, with its various settings in heaven, earth, and water, its fairy-tale cast of characters, and its wealth of memorable leitmotifs, making us keen to discover how the focus will narrow, how the strands in the plot will unravel, and whether Loge will be proved right when he mockingly prophesies, "They're hurrying on toward their end, / though they think they will last forever."

A Word about George Steiner

In December 1818 the sixty-nine-year-old Goethe was taking the waters at Berka when—as he later recalled—his "mind was in a state of perfect composure and free from external distraction." Listening in this frame of mind to Bach's Preludes and Fugues from *The Well-Tempered Clavier*, he said to himself: "It is as if the eternal harmony were conversing within itself, as it may have done in the bosom of God just before the Creation of the world. So likewise did it move in my inmost soul, and it seemed as if I neither possessed nor needed ears, nor any other sense—least of all, the eyes."[1]

Taking his cue from Goethe, the present-day philosopher George Steiner has defined music as "the soliloquy of being, of the original *fiat* echoing itself."[2] In his later book, *Grammars of Creation*, he discusses Wagner at greater length, describing the "initial chord" of the prelude to *Das Rheingold* as a "rising out of chaos." The "resonance" of this chord, "simultaneously radiant and ominous, poses the question: as we comb the depths, what monsters are we trawling?"[3]

This is a good description of the narrative that constitutes the *Ring*, for there is much—including elements that are far from edifying—that prefigures the rising of the curtain on *Das Rheingold*. Steiner will not have objected, therefore, to Chéreau's idea of damming the Rhine with a hydroelectric dam in his Bayreuth Festival production in 1976, an unmistakable sign that for the children of the modern world there can be no return to nature. Steiner's concern in his *Grammars of Creation* is above all with art and, more especially, music, for although he has a number of objections to Wagner's verbal message, such messages are of little interest to him. Rather, his focus is the music. As he explained in conversation, "There are moments in which one is tempted to say that the human mind has created very little that can compete with Wagner. But a word of caution: all that he did was to express the unfathomable strangeness of music."[4]

Time and again Steiner has referred to the "intimate strangeness" of music,[5] by which he means the "untranslatability of the musical experience": "Even at their most intimate, the relations between music and language bristle with intractabilities."[6] Again: "Organically, human song sets us closer to animality than any other manifestation. [. . .] Song leads us home to where we have not yet been." Steiner calls it *"daimonia* in music."[7] In short, it cannot be explained even by reference to the spiritual experiences that Wagner claimed to have known in La Spezia before he conceived the prelude to *Das Rheingold*: "This is the puzzle: where does the new melody, the novel key-relation [. . .] originate? What, if you will, was there before? Silence, perhaps, but a silence which, in a linguistically inexpressible way, was not mute."[8]

A person who has "no more beginnings" can no longer puzzle over them.[9] And the person who can no longer puzzle over the act of artistic creation abandons all that is best about him to civilization, science, and technology. As a result, Steiner warns us not to try to approach Wagner's music with an ideological scalpel, for although art in general cannot be separated from barbarism, it may arise "for reasons of this barbarism and with this barbarism."[10] At the same time, we would do well to recall another remark by Steiner:

> When the young Hitler heard Wagner's *Rienzi* for the first time, he told one of his young friends that he had a vision of the National Socialist international state. Years earlier, the successful journalist Theodor Herzl had heard the same opera and afterward noted in his diary: "This evening I saw that we shall win back Jerusalem." There is neither good nor evil in music.[11]

And yet we may well be inclined to add that there is militant and less militant music.

This photograph of Wagner was taken in Franz Hanfstaengl's Munich studio in December 1871 and is inscribed "To his Brünnhilde"—the soprano Amalie Materna—by "Wagner-Wotan!" The portrait is now in the Wagner Museum in Bayreuth. (Photograph courtesy of the Nationalarchiv der Richard-Wagner-Stiftung, Bayreuth: Bi 3660).

CHAPTER NINE

"He resembles *us* to a tee; he is the sum total of present-day intelligence"

THE ART OF THE *RING*—WOTAN'S MUSIC

Act 1 of *Die Walküre*: a bourgeois eternal triangle?—Wagner
identifies with Siegmund—Mathilde Wesendonck—Act 2 as
the peripeteia of the whole *Ring*—Wagner's Wotan as
the ne plus ultra of his dialectic characterization—Wotan's
questionable career—His great monologue—Wagner's
sympathy for Wotan—Wotan's downfall hastened by
the orchestral melody—Wagner's own analysis of a detail of the
score—The ingeniously contradictory connection between
plot, vocal line, and orchestral melody—Carolyn Abbate's
narratological comment on Wotan's monologue: "That voice
may *ring false*"—The dialectics of musical logic and intended
meaning—Wotan's Farewell and the Magic Fire Music—Thomas
Mann's admiration of this scene—The sleep motif in Bruckner's
Third Symphony—The sleep motif in terms of music theory—
Wagner as a "thinking" composer—His sympathy for Wotan
and Alberich—*Siegfried*: a new fairy-tale beginning for the
action of the *Ring*? Walter Benjamin's comparison between fairy
tale and myth—Fairy-tale music or deceptive idyll?—Wotan,
as the Wanderer, meeting Mime and Siegfried—Breaking
off composition of *Siegfried* in favor of *Tristan und Isolde*

Wagner's reason for designating *Das Rheingold* a "preliminary evening" will be clear to operagoers by the opening of act of *Die Walküre*, if not before, for the quantitative leap between the two works is enormous. *Das Rheingold* manifestly plays out in an archaic world with a cast of gods, nixies, giants, and dwarfs, and although they evince a number of human qualities, these figures communicate with one another in awkward ways.

Some of them demonstrably dwell "on cloud-girt heights," others "on the bed of the Rhine," and others again "on the earth's broad back" and "in the depths of the earth." The scenes in which the action unfolds span the entire natural world, and it is no accident that the basic elements of fire, water, air, and earth play a crucial role in the plot. And whereas the music of the rest of *Das Rheingold* is not as elemental as it is in the work's opening prelude, it is nonetheless entirely untypical of the nineteenth century.

This all changes with *Die Walküre*, and it changes even before the curtain goes up on its opening act, when the verve of the orchestral prelude, which according to the performance marking is to be played "tempestuously," indicates that we are back in the world of grand opera, a point that applies to the whole of this opening act. While lacking in vocal numbers of a traditional kind, it contains bel canto scenes in which listeners can revel to their heart's content, most notably Siegmund's "Winterstürme," which comes suspiciously close to an aria—in this regard, it is surely significant that Wagner wrote down the earliest melodic sketch while he was still working on the libretto.

But the dynamic markings that Wagner uses with his orchestral melody likewise give the impression that the actions that unfold in this opening act, while impassioned, are human in scale, starting out, as they do, from an "elemental and reduced" range of sonorities gradually invested with more differentiated harmonies before finally "culminating in the sound world of the spring night and the tempestuously erotic final pages with their candid depiction of the twin's act of incest."[1]

The new sense of direction in the musical dramaturgy reflects the drama's concentration on the relationship between Siegmund, Sieglinde, and Hunding. Entering the trammeling confines of Hunding's hut from the vast space of prehistoric time as depicted in *Das Rheingold*, Siegmund has scarcely closed the door behind him when we find ourselves at the heart of a marital drama that clearly relocates Wagner's universal theme of love versus power within the bourgeois present, its mythological garb notwithstanding, as a doughty outsider successfully shakes the very foundations of the institution of forced marriage. The events that unfold in this act could easily be found in a nineteenth-century play or novel on the theme of social justice—German readers will be reminded of Theodor Fontane's novel *L'adultera*, in which the bewitching impact of Wagner's music acts as a catalyst in a way that can hardly be fortuitous. After reading the poems of *Das Rheingold* and *Die Walküre* in 1881, Fontane summed up his opinion of the composer in a letter to his wife, Emilie: "He is entirely Wotan, wanting both money and power but refusing to renounce 'love,' to which end he constantly cheats.—Here, too, the poet lives in his characters."[2]

As a member of the realist school of writers, Fontane avoided taking sides, whereas Wagner clearly identified with Siegmund while working on act 1 of *Die Walküre*. This was a period when the forty-one-year-old composer was passionately in love with the wife of his patron Otto Wesendonck, with the result that the autograph draft of act 1 contains cryptic contractions such as "I. l. d. gr.!!," "L. d. m. M.??," "W. d. n. w., G!!!," "D. l. m. a!!," and "G. w. h. d. m. verl??" generally believed to mean "Ich liebe dich grenzenlos!!" (I love you boundlessly!!), "Liebst du mich Mathilde??" (Do you love me, Mathilde??), "Wenn du nicht wärst, Geliebte!!!" (If it weren't for you, beloved!!!), "Du liebst mich auch!!" (You love me too!!), and "Geliebte, warum hast du mich verlassen??" (Beloved, why have you forsaken me??).[3]

It is one of the piquant imponderables of Wagner's art that although his life is not reflected in his works, the two frequently brush against one another. Specifically, this means that it is likely that Wagner would have written the opening act of *Die Walküre* and been equally successful in investing it with such passion even if he had not been in love with Mathilde Wesendonck, and yet there is something mysterious about the way in which he was able to write scenes whose optimism and passion are not even matched by the final scene of *Siegfried*—and this at a time when his sexual desires appear to have been frustrated.

Equally curious is that neither the second nor the third acts of the complete draft contain any further abbreviations relating to Mathilde Wesendonck. It is possible, of course, that the new set of circumstances in which Wagner found himself had persuaded him to identify with the resigned figure of Wotan rather than the impetuous lover Siegmund. At the same time, however, we may see in this a minor biographical miracle in that this decision—if such it was—was taken at the very moment that Wagner had reached the peripeteia of the *Ring*. And our sense of wonderment will be increased when we recall Wagner's own comment in a letter to Liszt:

> I am worried that the second act is weighed down by its contents—it contains two such important and powerful disasters that they would be enough for two acts, and yet they are so dependent on one another and the second follows on so ineluctably from the first that it was impossible for me to keep them apart.[4]

Nor can we overlook that it was while he was working on act 2 of *Die Walküre* that Wagner became familiar with Schopenhauer's *Die Welt als*

Wille und Vorstellung (*The World as Will and Representation*), which examines the subject of resignation from every possible angle.

Whether or not we choose to speak of chance or providence in this context, there is no doubt that the relationship between the first two acts of *Die Walküre* reveals the same inspired dialectic that informs the *Ring* in general, for on the one hand we have the sibling love that evinces an élan vital unchecked by thoughts of adultery and incest inasmuch as the couple "loves unconsciously," to quote from a passage in the libretto that Wagner did not set to music,[5] while on the other hand we have the disasters invoked by Wagner in his letter to Liszt, namely, Wotan's abdication and Siegmund's execution. Thanks to the music and to Wagner's skill as a composer, these are no thesis and antithesis that would have been followed by a synthesis, but a single entity in which the two are merged imperceptibly.

The scene in which Siegmund and Sieglinde are united in act 1 includes motifs associated with the sword, Valhalla, the contracts carved into Wotan's spear, renunciation, and grief, forcing us to suspect that this euphoric union is no unhistorical, natural coupling between two individuals but part of a doom-laden scenario involving entanglements of every kind. While the intimate drama of the opening act is still unfolding, the actors of the second act's universal drama are already waiting in the wings. At the same time, motifs that in the opening act had had positive, utopian connotations and that include those associated with love, spring, the sword, sibling love, and rapture return in this somber second act, bringing the briefest of rays of light to the action.

In 1876, it is true, some members of the audience complained about the "monotony of expression" caused by the extended passages of dialogue in act 2,[6] and yet it is very much these passages that reveal Wagner at the peak of his powers in terms of his ability to depict characters of astonishing subtlety. This is especially true of Wotan, whom Wagner described in his oft-cited letter to August Röckel as "the sum total of present-day intelligence," adding that the figure "resembles *us* to a tee."[7] For Udo Bermbach, the *Ring* is "Wotan's tragedy," Wotan being "undoubtedly the main character in the tetralogy."[8] And the word "us" in Wagner's letter to Röckel is a clear pointer to the fact that the composer identified with Wotan more than with any other character. It is no wonder, then, that directors have repeatedly staged the *Ring* with Wotan wearing a Wagner mask, notably in Christine Mielitz's 2001 production in Meiningen, a production designed by Alfred Hrdlicka. But when Bermbach describes Wotan as a politician obsessed with power "who rejects all sense of morality" and places his trust entirely in "deception, betrayal, and trickery,"[9] while at the same time arguing that the character—defined exclusively as a political figure—reflects Wagner's own loathing of politics, then the contradiction between the two interpretations—Wotan as a corrupt politician and Wagner as a latter-day Wotan—stretches our credulity to breaking point, for it is scarcely credible that Wagner himself would have recognized himself even at a distance in Bermbach's characterization, to say nothing of the way in which the character is refracted in the mirror of myth.

But the contradiction turns out to be merely apparent, at least when we dispense with dogmatic and naïvely one-sided statements, for Wotan can no more be reduced to the role of a man obsessed with power politics than Wagner can be reduced to the role that he himself created. The mystery of great art consists in the fact that no matter how great the part played by calculation in an artist's work, that art is neither calculable nor capable of being equated with his own life. This is true not just of Wagner. Take Bach's *The Art of Fugue*, for example: although it can be ascribed to a particular theoretical canon and dated with some plausibility to the final years of his life, this says little about the work's true essence. Bach's sovereign command of the rules of counterpoint is no more than the starting point for a method of composition that includes disjointed, playful ideas, surprises, and irregularities of every kind, the composer's ingenuity revealing itself in the dialectic interrelationship between the underlying rules and the arbitrary manner in which they are then applied.

This is even more true of Wagner's music dramas, in which the attempt to merge the different elements of staging, language, and music was bound to lead to contingent processes that may not be entirely illogical but which cannot be controlled by intellect and which therefore have the ability to excite and agitate us. As an astute political scientist, Bermbach does not deny that it is impermissible to write about Wagner without taking account of the music, and yet he cannot gainsay his own nature. For how is it possible to draw a picture of Wotan without examining his music? If we ignore the music, we shall have no difficulty in observing that Wotan appears in *Das Rheingold*, *Die Walküre*, and *Siegfried*, but not in *Götterdämmerung*. But as soon as we turn to the music, we shall see that he is an even greater presence in *Götterdämmerung* than before, for time and again the motifs associated with the sword, the treaties engraved on the god's spear, and Valhalla are woven into the musical fabric. In short, these are the motifs most closely associated with Wotan in the course of the three preceding works. And this list ignores the many other motifs that listeners will likewise have learned to associate with Wotan's actions in the *Ring*. Of course, Wotan does not appear with his own motif in *Götterdämmerung*, but that is because he does not have one.

In the most general terms, the "career" that Wotan pursues between *Das Rheingold* and *Götterdämmerung* can be grasped only through the music, for it is the music that in *Das Rheingold* reveals the chief of the gods' pursuit of power, most notably in the form of the Valhalla motif. This motif is heard in all its glory at the moment when the spectator is confronted by the sight of a "castle with glittering battlements" both at the start of scene 2 and at the end of scene 4. This doubling of onstage image and music is one that Wagner's enemies are fond of criticizing, even though it is far from being the rule in the *Ring*. But in the present case it makes good sense: the Valhalla motif is used in a consciously affirmative way here for it serves as a symbol of power. When the gods enter the castle at the end of the work, it is entrusted to the winds alone, suggesting festive music that Wotan has organized in his own honor in the tradition of the medieval praise of rulers. However much Loge may look forward to the gods' downfall and however heart-wrenching the Rhinedaughters' lament at the loss of their gold, Wotan sees himself as a ruler at this point, a ruler, moreover, in possession of a "grand idea" symbolized by the sword motif that is heard just before this point in the orchestra, implying his hope of a free and fearless hero who will atone for the guilt that weighs on him after he has flouted his own treaties in his ruthless pursuit of power.

A production detail from the 1876 performances of *Das Rheingold* makes clear the extent to which Wagner was keen to have Wotan seen as a man of action, for whereas the libretto and score indicate merely that when the sword motif rings out in the trumpets just before the gods set out for Valhalla, Wotan stands there "very resolutely, as though seized by a grandiose idea," the stage directions indicate that in the course of the rehearsals Wagner decided to spell this out in rather more concrete terms: when the sword motif is heard, Wotan was to "flourish a sword, which Fafner has contemptuously thrown out of the Nibelung hoard because it is not made of gold."[10] We may choose to see this as a meaningful visualization of Wotan's grandiose idea, as a problematical attempt to clarify the action,[11] or as a concession to the naïveté of the audience.[12] But we could also trust Wagner's instinct here and argue that he wanted to show Wotan one last time as a man of action motivated by power politics, in which case the sword motif would no longer imply just the idea of the human race freed from the curse of gold but also a continuation of Wotan's power games using a hero who is to blaze a trial with a sword called Nothung—possibly identical to the one that Wotan flourishes at the end of *Das Rheingold*.

Before examining Wotan's subsequent career as it is reflected in the Valhalla motif, I need to describe the action of the *Ring* in greater detail. When the curtain rises on *Die Walküre*, Wotan still appears to be the very embodiment of youthful vigor. Although invisible, he still seems to be an onstage presence when Siegmund and Sieglinde, whom he himself has sired, in turn produce the new hero—Siegfried—who "lacking godly protection breaks loose from the law of the gods." Although this flies in the face of marital rights and morality, it may well reflect Wotan's own plan for the world's salvation. At the start of act 2, he is still brimming with energy when, "armed for battle," he calls to Brünnhilde, who is "likewise fully armed":

> Nun zäume dein Roß,
> reisige Maid!
> Bald entbrennt
> brünstiger Streit:
> Brünnhilde stürme zum Kampf,
> dem Wälsung kiese sie Sieg!

[Now harness your horse, warrior maid! A furious fight will soon flare up: let Brünnhilde fly to the fray; for the Wälsung let her choose victory!]

But the situation changes in a trice when Fricka enters to insist on her rights and on traditional morality:

> Von Menschen verlacht,
> verlustig der Macht,
> gingen wir Götter zu Grund,
> würde heut' nicht hehr
> und herrlich mein Recht
> gerächt von der muthigen Maid.

[Derided of men, deprived of our might, we gods would go to our ruin were my rights not avenged, nobly and grandly, by your mettlesome maid today.]

As a result, Wotan has to agree—albeit "in terrible dejection" and "gloomy brooding"—to betray his own son in the coming fight with Hunding, even though all his hopes rest on Siegmund. Only moments earlier he had instructed Brünnhilde to fight for the Wälsung, but now he has to explain why she must fight for "Fricka's slaves" and in doing so fly in the face of his own deeper wishes.

In the course of a lengthy monologue that Wagner had approached with great "fear" at a time when he felt "discouraged" and "disillusioned,"[13] Wotan justifies his betrayal of Siegmund, a betrayal that goes hand in hand with his decision to abdicate: he has acquired power over the world through cunning and breach of contract, with the result that he no longer has right on his side. In turn, this means that he is at the mercy of Fafner and Alberich, his greatest fear now being that Alberich will regain the ring that confers world power on its wearer and which Fafner is currently guarding, unused. In order to break free from the present vicious circle and create a new world order based not on power but on love, he needs a hero who, untrammeled by his past, is free to act as he pleases. Wotan had wanted to create such a figure in the person of his son Siegmund, but Fricka exposes his "cunning" in manipulating his son by placing his own sword at his disposal. In spite of his spontaneous love for Sieglinde, Siegmund is not a free hero, then, but a product of Wotan's own lack of freedom. All that is left for Wotan is a sense of self-hatred and the decision to abdicate:

> Zum Ekel find' ich
> ewig nur mich
> in Allem was ich erwirke!
> Das And're, das ich ersehne,
> das And're erseh' ich nie;
> denn selbst muß der Freie sich schaffen —
> Knechte erknet' ich mir nur!
> [. . .]
> Auf geb' ich mein Werk;
> nur Eines will ich noch:
> das Ende —
> das Ende! —
> Und für das Ende
> sorgt Alberich!

[To my loathing I find myself alone in all that I encompass! That other self for which I yearn, that other self I never see; for the free man has to fashion himself—serfs are all I can shape! [. . .] My work I abandon; one thing alone do I want: the end—the end!—And Alberich will see to that end!]

In recalling these events in act 3 of *Siegfried*, Wotan tells Erda how "in furious loathing" he bequeathed the world to the Nibelung dwarf. His actions, then, are the result of a sudden fit of rage.

At this point in the action, an enormous gulf opens up: in *Das Rheingold*, Wotan had still been in control of the situation, in spite of the many crises he had to endure, and he had successfully played his power games, but in *Die Walküre* he changes abruptly from a man of action to a failure with practically no scope for action any longer and capable of conversing only with himself: the world refuses to respond to him. True, he discusses his life with Brünnhilde, but as the libretto makes plain, she is the embodiment of his will, which is why, at the start of his monologue, he says: "With myself I commune when I speak with you." When Wagner dismisses this lonely figure of Wotan as "the sum total of present-day intelligence," this says it all: driven by circumstances, Wotan can do no more than reflect on the hopelessness of his situation and brood on a suitable way of stepping down. In *Das Rheingold*, he had still been able to engage with Alberich and force him to do his will, but in *Die Walküre* he is reduced to calling after his absent successor with bitter irony: "So take my blessing, Nibelung son!"

The radical shift in Wotan's position is one that we can understand only if we take seriously Wagner's description of *Das Rheingold* as the cycle's "preliminary evening," for only then can we imagine that a lengthy period of time has elapsed between this "preliminary evening" and the "first day" of *Die Walküre*, a period during which Wotan's withdrawal from the world's stage has taken place only gradually. At the same time, his monologue in act 2 would seem abrupt and overloaded with arguments if it were part of a spoken drama, for unlike Hamlet, for example, in his monologue "To be or not to be," Wotan does more than offer an insight into his current frame of mind. Rather, he tells a complex tale extending over a mythologically protracted period of time, with the result that it would be impossible to convey its contents to an audience's emotions through the medium of the spoken theater.

Moreover—and notwithstanding our respect for Wagner's inspired ability to tell the story of the *Ring*—it is impossible to avoid noticing that this story leaves many questions unanswered, including ones about Wotan's actions and character. Quite apart from the fact that his past is shrouded in obscurity and his actions generally contradictory, it is unclear how we are to interpret his great narration: is it tragic or merely lachrymose? Is he weeping crocodile tears? Or does he really possess true greatness?

Whenever he wrote about Wotan, Wagner invested him with a high degree of dignity. Even the dismissive remark that we have just quoted is incomplete without its surrounding context, in which Wagner asks Röckel to show greater understanding for the character:

> He is the sum total of present-day intelligence, whereas Siegfried is the man of the future whom we desire and long for but who cannot be made by us, since he must create himself on the basis of *our own annihilation*. In such a guise, Wodan—you must admit—is of extreme interest to us, whereas he would inevitably seem unworthy if he were merely a subtle intriguer, which is what he would be if he gave advice which was *apparently* meant to harm Siegfried but which in truth was intended to help not only Siegfried but, first and foremost, himself: that would be an example of deceit entirely worthy of our political heroes, but not of my jovial god who stands in such need of self-annihilation.[14]

Even toward the end of his life, Wagner was still striking a similar note during a walk through Bayreuth's Hofgarten:

> I know no other work in which the breaking of a will [. . .] is shown as being accomplished through the individual strength of a proud nature [. . .] as it is in Wotan. Almost obliterated by the separation from Brünnhilde, this will rears up again, bursts into flame in the meeting with Siegfried, flickers in the dispatching of Waltraute, until we see it entirely extinguished at the end in Valhalla.[15]

Wotan would be a cardboard cutout if his actions were predictable. The German philosopher Herbert Schnädelbach is not wrong to speak of the "fascination of the incomprehensible" in the *Ring*, even if his language is a little crass:

> It is astonishing that a modern work like the *Ring*, planned and realized with such rational resolve, should reveal this quality, constantly tempting us with the promise of a deeper meaning that no one has yet managed to fathom, only to send us away again empty-handed. On the other hand, the whole thing is not simply the sort of nonsense that we can just ignore. In this sense the *Ring* has a mythic quality that will fascinate only those people who have mythic needs, that is, people who are interested in stories that can be endlessly interpreted and never definitively exhausted.[16]

This also applies to the figure of Wotan. On the one hand, his unpredictability and inconstancy make him the character that Wagner wanted him to be, while on the other hand—and this brings us back to the music—it is the function of the music to turn the myth of the *Ring* into a compelling work of art. Wotan's monologue provides the best possible example of this, not least in terms of the category of time: whereas Wotan's radical volte-face between *Das Rheingold* and *Die Walküre* would inevitably be disconcerting in the spoken theater, the music has no difficulty in bridging vast distances in time. A sung monologue seems to slow down the action not least because in real time it takes much longer than spoken dialogue to convey the same amount of information, while at the same time it is typical of "symphonic" music in the widest sense that it blurs the distinction between past and present: within the fabric of a symphony, the notes that have already been heard are still present in the notes that are currently sounding.

This is especially true of Wagner's own orchestral melody. Take Wotan's great monologue. Most of the leitmotifs that occur here are familiar from *Das Rheingold*—they include the motifs associated with the ring, fear, renunciation, the curse, the sword, Erda, and Valhalla—but these now appear in new guises, sometimes rendered unrecognizable, giving us listeners the impression that we are being drawn into familiar, ancient events but interpreted from Wotan's present point of view. And Wagner's art ensures that these motifs—no longer presented in detail one after the other, as they had been in *Das Rheingold*, but suddenly striking us like individual flashes of inspiration—are fully integrated into a meaningful compositional context. As Bernhard Benz has noted in the context of bars 891 to 950 (from "So nimmst du von Siegmund den Sieg?" to "und für das Ende sorgt Alberich"), this is achieved in part by the "common harmonic feature of an extended third–based relationship in which all the motifs are bound together and, as it were, sucked in."[17]

In his essay "On the Application of Music to the Drama," Wagner himself stressed that his aim was not to clarify Wotan's sequence of associated ideas by means of a "glaring" combination of motifs but to "conceal the strangeness" of such combinations, "either by a suitable slackening of the tempo or a preparatory dynamic compensation." Wotan's feelings were to be brought home to listeners in ways that would allow those listeners to identify with them in spite of all their inherent contradictions. It was not without a certain pride as a composer that Wagner singled out the example of "Wotan's transfer of power to the owner of the Nibelung hoard" at the embittered words "So take my blessing, Nibelung son!" Here, he explained, he had harnessed together the "simple nature motifs" of the Rhinegold and the "gods' citadel of Valhalla, shimmering in the red of dawn, [. . .] with the help of a remote harmony so that, more than Wotan's words, this tone-figure should grant us an insight into the fearful gloom in the soul of the suffering god." At the same time, however, it was important to Wagner to ensure that this process "takes possession of our willing feeling as an artistic element in strict accordance with the laws of nature."[18] Music example 21 is taken from Wagner's essay and shows the passage in question transposed a semitone higher in order to make it easier to read.

21. The Valhalla motif as transcribed by Wagner in his 1879 essay "On the Application of Music to the Drama": GS 10:187; PW 6:186.

In modulating from A-flat minor to E major within the shortest possible time, Wagner uses the device of an enharmonic change. And it is no accident that he does so, for—like such a change—there is something unreal about Wotan's state of mind at the embittered outburst "So take my blessing." At the end of *Das Rheingold*, the Rhinegold motif had accompanied the gods as they were seen entering their magnificent castle, whereas it now appears in a distorted context that makes it clearer than any words could do that Wotan is resolved to hand over Valhalla to his enemy, Alberich, as a possession that has become worthless in his eyes, a mere backdrop to his present concerns. In a silent film, the distance between Wotan's ostentatious entry into Valhalla and his present "grim" renunciation of it would have been bridged by a title link such as "100 years later," but music's circular approach to time allows it to span even greater distances.

Wagner's reference in his essay to this intricate combination of the two motifs associated with the Rhinegold and Valhalla covers no more than a single tiny detail of Wotan's monologue, which is a paragon of compositional skill. A more comprehensive analysis of this passage and its musical context is provided by the musicologist Bernhard Benz.[19] It will be sufficient to refer to his study and, rather than quoting from it, to sum up its findings: in the *Ring* and, indeed, in Wagner's works in general, there is no other "great narration" in which plot, vocal line, and orchestral melody are merged in such an ingenious way as they are in Wotan's monologue, creating a whole which, however contradictory, is nonetheless coherent. On the relatively superficial level of the work's rhetorical language, Wotan delivers his monologue in a "very low voice," beginning with the recitative-like setting of the words "Als junger Liebe / Lust mir verblich" (When youthful love's delights had faded) and building to a series of dramatic outbursts that follow on from one other, each wave more powerful than the last. For a while he grows drunk on his own idea of "gathering hosts of bold warriors in Valhalla's hall," but it is not long before he begins to feel tormented and to express those feelings of oppression, as the stage directions make clear: "Wotan's demeanor passes from an expression of the most terrible anguish to one of desperation," we read just before the lines

> Fahre denn hin,
> herrische Pracht,
> göttlichen Prunkes
> prahlende Schmach!

[Farewell, then, imperious pomp! Godly show's resplendent shame!]

And the singer is instructed to "rise to his feet in bitter anger" at the lines

> So nimm meinen Segen,
> Niblungen-Sohn!
> Was tief mich ekelt,
> dir geb' ich's zum Erbe,
> der Gottheit nichtigen Glanz!

[So take my blessing, Nibelung son! What I loathe most deeply I leave as your legacy.]

In terms of Wotan's vocal writing, this might recall the sort of emotional outburst found in King Philip's aria "Ella giammai m'amò" (She never loved me) in Verdi's *Don Carlo*. But in Wagner's case there are two further layers of interpretation. In the first place, Wotan's narrative is not only emotional but also argumentative: although he desires the "end" and ensures that his monologue builds to a rhetorical climax, his narration deals in the main with the past, a past beneath which he has still not drawn a line. Rather, everything revolves around the question of why the world has taken a turn so unfavorable to the leader of the gods. Behind his reflections, which inevitably contain an element of self-deceit and self-pity, there is clearly the vague hope that it may yet be possible to steer events in a different direction.

A composer like Verdi would never have written anything as complicated as this and would not even have seen any point in doing so. But Wagner is able to risk such an approach by relying on his orchestral melody, investing it with a function that goes beyond anything he had ascribed to it in *Opera and Drama*. In the second act of *Die Walküre*, the orchestra is no longer limited to the task of commenting on the protagonist's remarks in the manner of a Greek chorus or even in revealing his unspoken memories and forebodings. Instead, it acts as a partner, telling its own version of Wotan's story, while keeping half an eye on the global events in which Wotan is caught up. Each party stimulates the other: in the course of his narrative, Wotan is struck by more and more new ideas, which are, of course, old ideas and which he then takes up and discusses, while the orchestra is likewise provoked into drawing its own conclusions by Wotan's line of argument. Ultimately it is impossible to decide which of the two is the more dynamic, the singer or the orchestra. In turn, it is hard to say what is more important here. Is it an impotently egocentric god who cannot decide whether he wants to abdicate or not and who, to quote Wagner, resembles "us intellectuals" to a tee? Or is this god merely the medium for an unending story within which his position could be assumed by any other person? Or, to put it another way, has such a modern character as depicted by Wagner ever found such a home in a myth that deals in eternal verities?

Taking as her starting point a "theory of musical narrative," Carolyn Abbate has argued that in the monologue by this "liar" and "myth-maker," "music's voice" represents "a solipsistic enunciation that originates in an immoral god." In order not to fall into a trap, we need to mistrust it because "that voice may *ring false*." But it is very much in this deceptiveness that Abbate sees one of the reasons for "opera's terrible fascination."[20] But what is the point of judging this duplicity by ethical standards, since it is specific to the *Ring*? True, Wotan is a questionable hero at best in terms of his words and actions, but the music turns him into a mythic figure not without an element of tragedy.

How distorted would Wotan's music have turned out if Wagner had made him obsessed with power politics to the exclusion of all else, as Udo Bermbach claims? Or if he was no more than the starting point for what Manfred Frank has termed "a series of brutal murders"?[21] It is no accident that in the foreword to his edition of his revolutionary writings in his collected works, Wagner advanced ideas that allow for the possibility of investing Wotan's character with utopian features:

> Far though it was from my intent to define the new *political* order that would grow from the ruins of a deceitful world, I nonetheless felt inspired

to sketch the outlines of the *work of art* that should rise from the ruins of a deceitful *art*. To hold up this work of art to life as a prophetic mirror of its future seemed to me to be one of the most important contributions that I could make toward the task of damming the flood of revolution and restoring it to the channel of the calmly flowing river of humanity.[22]

In this sense even the reference to a "series of brutal murders" that Manfred Frank, borrowing an expression of Kafka's, imputes to the myth of the *Ring* is bound to give rise to serious misgivings. Of course, it is true that Fafner kills Fasolt, Hunding kills Siegmund, Wotan kills Hunding "with a contemptuous wave of his hand," Siegfried kills Fafner and Mime, and Hagen kills Siegfried and Gunther. But Frank's suggestion that all the evil in the *Ring* stems from Wotan ignores the fact that for the most part Wagner leaves us in the dark about the cause of the evil that pervades the world of the *Ring*. According to Richard Klein, it would be wrong to locate this cause in the characters of Wotan or even Alberich and equally wrong to echo Frank in his insistence on the "implacable logic" of the events that unfold in the work.[23] Rather, Wagner was at pains to make it clear to us that "the complex underlying actions that are the cause of all that happens are a necessary element in motivating the whole and at the same time a structural force of history."[24]

Wotan may not be a good god, but nor is he a political or criminal monster. "He resembles *us* to a tee," Wagner insisted, and his great-granddaughter, Nike Wagner, likewise argues that Wotan is a "true-to-life figure, true to life in his conflict situation as a man and as a politician."[25] He is both guilty and innocent, disdainful, cynical, and deceitful in his encounters with the giants and dwarfs who threaten his power; he is loving and then cold toward his wife; he brings feelings of great warmth to his dealings with his son Siegmund, while his attitude toward Brünnhilde turns from tenderness to harshness; while wanting to raise his grandson Siegfried as his better self, he reveals himself to be confused by feelings of rivalry; and in confronting his potential adviser Erda, he proves arrogant and high-handed even when forced into a corner. Wagner had good reason for telling Röckel that "in announcing my intentions I was obliged to keep within extremely narrow bounds in accordance with my own feelings on the matter."[26] And in his own subtle analysis of the character, Wolfram Ette has spoken of Wotan's tragic and "increasingly dramatic attempts to pick a fight with himself."[27]

The subtlety with which Wagner shapes Wotan's monologue rests in the fact that it includes different attitudes that we as listeners can not only adopt toward the matter in hand but which we can also observe in ourselves. And what makes this scene so important from an artistic point of view is that music and text move far apart in order to depict this contradiction, while remaining interconnected in the spirit of the total work of art. Wagner himself referred to this dialectic in the essay from which we have already quoted, "The Stage Consecration Festival Drama in Bayreuth in 1882." "Which of us," he asked on that occasion, "can spend his whole life gazing freely and openly at a world of murder and robbery that is organized and legitimized by lying, deceit, and hypocrisy without occasionally having to turn away with a feeling of shuddering disgust?" Happy those people who can see a true reflection of the world in the form of a message that "comes from its innermost soul" and "prophesies redemption."[28]

Wagner gives his listeners a chance to see both the hopeless corruption of this world and the insatiable desire for a better alternative. It seems to have been a kindly fate that decreed that he should have allowed himself to be touched by Schopenhauer's philosophy at the very time that he was working on Wotan's monologue, for the Sage of Frankfurt may well have confirmed him in his decision to equate Wotan's destructive self-will with the will of the world as such, a will that Schopenhauer famously argued was represented by music. In doing so, Wagner equally famously placed a stretch of clear blue water between himself and Schopenhauer, for whom music was as blind as the world-will itself, whereas for Wagner music contained within it an element of hope.

Wotan's monologue is an outstanding example of the high level on which Wagner operated in terms of what he termed the "word-tone relationship." It reveals the unique dialectics of independence and reciprocal dependence between action and music that stems from the flexibility of the relationship: sometimes it is the vocal line and, hence, the text that plays the leading role; at other times it is the orchestra that sets the tone. Sometimes both messages are conveyed together, while on other occasions the individual phrases may be displaced. Sometimes the action onstage and the drama in the orchestra reinforce one another, while at other times there is a standoff between them. And although small and large gestures alternate all the time, the rhetorically logical structure of the monologue ultimately ensures that no matter how open the form may be, the result is coherent according to the motto of "Concordia discors." This is unique in the whole history of opera, for whereas the orchestra may be treated as an independent entity by other composers, it is always a willing partner of the singers. The closest we come to this autonomous involvement of the music within the overall picture is in Schumann's piano-accompanied songs.[29] But Wagner was almost certainly not thinking of Schumann's distinctly marginal innovations when striking out in this direction. He is far more likely to have cast his gaze back to Beethoven's Ninth.

Beethoven's decision to fall back on the sung word in the final movement of his last completed symphony is one that writers usually justify by claiming that he wanted to present the ideas contained in his music in a clearer form than was possible through the medium of pure instrumental music. In this particular case he had recourse to Schiller's *Ode to Joy*. But if we adopt Wagner's standpoint and regard the Ninth as the forerunner of his total artwork, we also need to take into account the sheer size and musical variety of the symphony's final movement, elements that suggest that Beethoven's aim was not only to broadcast a humanitarian message but also to create a new artistic medium and establish a vocal and symphonic field of tension in which the human voices and instruments would unite to form a single, tremendous overall sound. This meant renouncing the traditional distribution of forces within the world of musical genres, according to which instrumental music prevailed in its own particular area but assumed a subordinate role when it came to the aid of singing. The result is a twofold blurring of boundaries in the Ninth. First, there is no longer a clear-cut distinction between poetry, which is committed to expressing a particular idea, and music, which sets the idea only indirectly through the medium of the poem, for in the final movement of his Ninth Symphony, Beethoven is far from abandoning his symphonic ambition of introducing ideas directly through his music. On the other hand, the only music that can do justice to this symphonic ambition is one in which the barriers between vocal and instrumental design are raised in favor of a musical language that combines them both by blending them together and that can engage directly with Schiller's ideas on the level of equals: the hierarchy of idea-word-tone is transformed in this way into a partnership between idea and a word-tone art.

Even those observers who see Beethoven's music as playing a more essential role in the history of music than Wagner's will not overlook the tremendous progress achieved by Wagner when compared with Beethoven, for although the final movement of the Ninth Symphony is ethically impressive and compositionally monumental, it teeters on the brink of aesthetic disaster as the lack of clarity and excessive complexity of the formal musical language scarcely allow the rhetoric to unfold organically, a feature of which Beethoven had previously been so proud in his symphonies. Of course, a choral movement like this is difficult to compare to an excerpt from the *Ring* such as Wotan's monologue, but it is still possible to identify a number of differences on shared points of generic detail. In the case of the final movement of the Ninth, neither the words nor the music escape unscathed, as Beethoven's act of creating his new word-tone language is necessarily a violent process, whereas Wotan's monologue is finely balanced rhetorically, psychologically, and musically. And while the present attempt, however rudimentary, to examine Wotan's monologue in terms of its dialectics of musical logic and intended meaning has proved fruitful, it would be a futile labor of love to adopt a similar approach to the final movement of the Ninth Symphony, a movement that is far more coarsely woven from this point of view or which—at best—is more carefree in its al fresco manner.

Wagner's extremely detailed approach to the character of Wotan continues throughout the rest of *Die Walküre*, especially in the final scene, often performed in the concert hall as "Wotan's Farewell and Magic Fire Music." In a letter to Ferdinand Praeger, Wagner described *Die Walküre* as a whole as "the ne plus ultra of anguish, pain, and despair,"[30] while in an almost contemporary letter to Liszt, he spoke of the final act as "a terrible storm of the elements and of hearts that gradually dies down with Brünhilde's [*sic*] magic sleep."[31] The cycle of confused emotions that is so typical of the *Ring* is briefly brought to a rest here. Thomas Mann was living in Princeton when he noted in his diary on January 3, 1942: "'Walküre' on the radio in the evening. Not for the first time I was forced to think of Erika during the Farewell."[32] According to Nike Wagner, the *Lohengrin* Prelude and Wotan's Farewell were among Mann's favorite pieces of music, a preference she attributes to the fact that in both cases the music succeeds in "creating the idea of pureness."[33] Musically speaking, the idea of purity can be produced in different ways, of course: in the *Lohengrin* Prelude, it is "pure" sounds that dominate, whereas the famous sleep motif, to the sound of which Wotan kisses his daughter "lingeringly on her eyes until she sinks back, with eyes closed, into his arms," is very different in character (music example 22).

It is no accident that Bruckner quotes this motif at the end of the opening movement's development section in the early version of his Third Symphony, where it is gesturally and structurally effective as what Hans-Joachim Hinrichsen has termed a "calming zone."[34] There is no doubt that Bruckner was fascinated by Wagner's ability to create an inimitable atmosphere by a degree of compositional refinement that the listener simply

22. The sleep motif from bars 1617–25 of act 3 of *Die Walküre*.

does not perceive as such, Wagner being a magician whose sleights of hand are by no means as straightforward as the phrase "simple tricks" would imply but which are in fact extremely sophisticated. The listener registers a "dreamlike" flow of "sequences of sound"[35] that create the "impression that they are weaving into each other and disguising themselves" in the presence of a "mysterious figure" that seems "sealed away by a whole range of structural relationships, rather like a magic formula."[36]

These interpretations stem from the writings of music theorists capable of analyzing Wagner's command of the tools of his trade. Ernst Kurth—to quote only one of his least technical observations—speaks of "lines of tension that are interwoven to enhance and deepen" the impression that results from "the interaction between tonally distant chords and a curious iridescence of tone colors that grow brighter and paler by turn."[37] Eckehard Kiem notes, among other things, the existence of a "two-bar model" that descends sequentially in thirds, while at the same time a "bass model ascends four times in sequence."[38]

Conversely, if Thomas Mann was moved by Wotan's Farewell and, hence, by the sleep motif, this was due, above all, to his sensitivities as a poet: what he admired here was Wagner's exemplary ability to achieve his aim of "emotionalizing the intellect."[39] According to *Opera and Drama*, the poet's "inadequate means of expression" obliged him to "divide the content into an emotional and an intellectual component."[40] The "poetic musician," on the other hand, would inevitably be "humiliated to see his drama received by a public that devoted its sole and specific attention to the mechanics of his orchestra."[41] With the best will in the world, then, the spoken theater could do no more than place an actor onstage who, playing the part of Wotan, would kiss the eyes of the actress taking the role of Brünnhilde, whereupon Brünnhilde would "sink back in his arms." It would be the audience's task to go beyond an intellectual understanding of this scene and create a sense of the mythic or fairy-tale element that is inherent in it. Only then would they be able to respond on an emotional level. In the musical drama it is the music that takes over this transfer effect. In the case of the sleep motif, its compositional "mechanics" are extremely complex, but in spite of this it impinges on the listener's feelings as if it were some entirely natural occurrence.

The "natural" impact of the music is further intensified during the final Magic Fire Music by the introduction of the additional element of fire. In his famous Moscow production of *Die Walküre* in 1940, Sergei Eisenstein introduced color into his staging of this section of the score, the only time he did so in the work, for, as he explained,

> Wagner's score is not too rich in its coloration, but it flares up, burns, bathed in light, organically and in the spirit of movement within the music.
>
> In the Magic Fire, Loge's theme runs like a thread of blue through the purple of fire, the underlying element.
>
> Now that theme melts in the fire.
>
> Now it seems to have smothered the fire.[42]

That Wagner was concerned to "conceal intellect from feeling"[43] does not, of course, preclude the possibility that he saw himself explicitly as a rational composer. Notwithstanding the claims of such an intelligent musicologist as Wolfgang Rathert, the complexity of Wagner's "musical fabric" is by no means merely the "product of a mysterious process snatched from the subconscious" but is also the expression of the "rational calculation and aesthetic playfulness" that Rathert associates with Brahms and Schoenberg.[44] On this point Wagner resembles Leonardo da Vinci, whom he described—astutely—as "a man of breeding who could play around with things."[45] In his *Treatise on Painting*, Leonardo argued that

> When the work is equal to the knowledge and judgment of the painter, it is a bad sign; and when it surpasses the judgment, it is still worse [. . .], but when the judgment surpasses the work, it is a perfectly good sign; and the young painter who possesses that rare disposition, will, no doubt, arrive at great perfection.[46]

This can also be applied to the music of Wotan's Farewell in the sense that Wagner knows that even in this deeply moving scene Wotan remains an ambiguous figure, on the one hand showing great tenderness toward his daughter as he banishes her to a fire-girt rock from which only the "fearlessly freest of heroes" can rescue her, while at the same time dreaming a "typically male dream"[47] of winning a "second chance" for himself and his "grandiose idea" by relying on just such a hero.[48] And whereas—according to the surviving record of Wagner's rehearsals of the *Ring* in 1876—Wotan lowers his sword when taking his leave of Brünnhilde as a token of his definitive abdication,[49] he also rebels against the whole idea of any such abdication in *Siegfried*, an irrational reaction that flies in the face of Wagner's own claim that Wotan is "in truth no more than a departed spirit."[50]

Operagoers who attempt to judge Wotan by rational criteria will inevitably find themselves caught up in a descending spiral of ever greater ratiocination, so sympathetic is the inwardly torn leader of the gods. Such an approach may satisfy us intellectually, but this would certainly not be in the spirit of Wagner, who expressly falls back on the medium of music to transform a spoken drama with an intellectual content into a work in which art acquires an altogether religious aura. In 1870, when he broke off work on *Götterdämmerung* to write his essay *Beethoven*, appealing to Schopenhauer in his attempt to propose a "philosophical explanation of music," it is no accident that he introduced into the debate Johann Gottfried Herder's category of "devotion."[51] Music cannot communicate anything that is not "sublime," but only "the character of all the world's appearances according to their innermost essence."[52] Wagner cites the Ninth Symphony as an illustration of this claim:

> Its first movement undoubtedly shows us the idea of the world in its most terrible light. Elsewhere, however, this very work affords us unmistakable evidence of the purposely ordaining will of its creator; we are brought face to face with it when [in the final movement] the composer stops the frenzy of despair that overwhelms each fresh appeasement and, with the anguished cry of one awaking from a nightmare, speaks that actual word whose ideal sense is none other than: "Man, despite all, *is* good!"[53]

The Wagner of the *Ring* is moved by Beethoven's "desperate leap" out of a world of horror into "the new world of light,"[54] but he does not regard this as a model that he himself can emulate, for, like Wotan, modern man is doomed to die. And yet there is one thing that Wagner most emphatically takes over from Beethoven's music: the "most sublime joviality" of this music passes no moral judgment on the world but is, rather, "the world itself" in its interplay of "grief and joy, of weal and woe."[55] Wotan's music, too, attests to the existence of this "world itself" and, hence, to our own existence: avoiding all recriminations, it holds up a mirror in which we can recognize ourselves—in our delusions of grandeur and fears, our noble feelings and base trickeries, our good intentions and our failed actions, our joys and sorrows. Those listeners who, having examined Wagner's music in detail, still cannot abide Wotan's music are bound to ask whether they can live with themselves in all their own contradictions.

Wagner, too, did not always find this easy. While poring over the second complete draft of the third act of *Siegfried*, he told Cosima that "All these primitive hotchpotches (Wotan storming in) I no longer care for at all."[56] In general, however, he was able to identify with the character through the medium of his music, without turning himself into a monster in the process: "Dedicated to his Brünnhilde / Wagner-Wotan," runs the autograph signature on a photographic portrait of him inscribed to his 1876 Brünnhilde, Amalie Materna, and depicting him in a pose that might be deemed appropriate to the ruler of the gods.[57] But that is not the end of the story, for in a letter he wrote to his Dresden friend Theodor Uhlig on November 18, 1852, Wagner signed himself "Your Nibelung prince *Alberich*."[58] Although Wagner may have been striking a note of self-irony here, there is no doubt that his salutation also reflects a certain sympathy for Wotan's antagonist. When Alberich curses love in *Das Rheingold* in his hope of inheriting the world, we hear the renunciation motif, which in the subsequent course of the *Ring* is repeatedly heard at moments of what we might call "noble" renunciation, notably, when Wotan bids farewell to Brünnhilde: this is music that indiscriminately humanizes every form of anguish.[59] In the face of this "naïveté," music can be both comforting and seductive. Wagner's music, in particular, invites us to register both and, therefore, to confront life's contradictions, an aspect of his works that provided Thomas Mann with a lifetime of creative stimulation.

Fortunately, operagoers have a short break between performances of *Die Walküre* and *Siegfried* to prepare inwardly for the fact that following the apocalyptic mood disseminated by Wotan in the course of the earlier work, the action starts up all over again, this time with a young hero called Siegfried, who is to replace Wotan and flourish his sword in token of a better world. Siegfried fills even Alberich with fear, causing the latter to complain to his son, Hagen: "Even my curse grows feeble in the face of the fearless hero; for he does not know what the ring is worth; he makes no use of its coveted power." There is something of a beautiful fairy tale to all of this, and, indeed, Wagner consciously presents it in the form of just such a tale.

In this context it is worth recalling a passage in Walter Benjamin's essay *The Storyteller*, which seems to have been written with *Siegfried* in mind:

> The fairy tale tells us of the earliest arrangements that mankind made to shake off the nightmare which the myth had placed upon its chest. In the figure of the fool it shows us how mankind "acts dumb" toward the myth; in the figure of the youngest brother it shows us how one's chances increase as the mythical primitive times are left behind; in the figure of the man who sets out to learn what fear is it shows us that the things we are afraid of can be seen through; in the figure of the wiseacre it shows us that the questions posed by the myth are simple-minded, like the riddle of the Sphinx; in the shape of the animals which come to the aid of the child in the fairy tale it shows that nature not only is subservient to the myth, but much prefers to be aligned with man.[60]

Wagner takes his time in telling this fairy tale, which he describes in radiant colors: he shows us Siegfried as a strapping youth forging an invincible sword, Nothung, disposing of his scheming foster father, Mime, and finding his way from the Forest Bird to the dragon, Fafner, whom he kills. The dragon's blood allows him to understand the language of the Forest Bird, which tells him to take the ring and magic helmet from the Nibelung hoard. Siegfried then defeats Wotan as he bridles against his destiny, before finding Brünnhilde on her flame-girt rock, then kissing her and coupling with her. The music, too, seems to escape from the weight of myth in these scenes and to assume naïve and fairy-tale qualities. Not only Siegfried's Forging Songs but Mime's whining complaints—described by Siegfried as a squawking "starling's song"—suggest that a naïve form equals an innocent, unspoiled world. Siegfried blows a "merry tune" on his little silver horn; the Forest Bird avails itself by preference of a natural pentatonic scale; and, last but not least, there is the sound of twittering birds in the idyllic scene traditionally known as the Forest Murmurs.

And yet even the Siegfried motif itself hints that this idyll is deceptive, for its characteristics are march-like rather than natural, and the powerful minor-key coloring that it loses only at the moment of Brünnhilde's awakening implies that Siegfried will end his life not as a carefree victor but as a tragic hero.[61] And, indeed, it becomes clear on closer inspection that Siegfried's role as a superior version of Wotan consists for the most part

The opening act of *Die Walküre* in Sergei Eisenstein's 1940 Moscow production. Center stage is the tree of life as a symbol of the all-pervasive world spirit. To the left of the tree are Sieglinde and Siegmund. While she recalls her wedding with Hunding, when "the men from his clan sat here in the hall," a "mime chorus" acts out her narrative, ensuring that the events she recounts are raised to a higher level than that of the merely individual. (Photograph courtesy of VAAP, Moscow. Photographer: Evgeny Fedorovsky.)

in his wrestling with problems inherited from his grandfather. Although he appears on the surface to act spontaneously, he is ultimately no more than a product of that baleful history from which none of the characters in the *Ring* can escape. This history is ever-present in the music, for the characters of *Das Rheingold* and, more especially, the motifs associated with them occur at every turn in *Siegfried*, not least in the riddle scene in act I. Although Wotan demonstrates that he knows more about the world than Mime, who is drawn into their wager against his will, and even though he manages to flaunt the Valhalla motif, it is no longer possible to believe that Valhalla is an important factor in the events that are currently unfolding in the world. While Wotan indulges in all manner of reminiscences, the leitmotifs that are heard in this scene and which include those associated with the World Ash, the treaties carved into Wotan's spear, the giants, the Nibelungs, the Wälsungs, and Nothung open up old wounds. This collage of quotations—the term is legitimate in the face of the many passages recapitulating the action of *Das Rheingold*—makes it clear just how much has gone wrong in the past.[62]

To what extent Wotan undermines his own position by painting an unduly rosy picture of his past in his scene with Mime becomes clear from his confrontation with his grandson in the final act of *Siegfried*. Although Siegfried is supposed to be his better half, Wotan responds in a way that reveals his delusions of grandeur in no uncertain terms, for instead of directing him to Brünnhilde, he bars his way, albeit in vain. On a superficial level, Siegfried's triumph over the unknown Wanderer is also Wotan's triumph signaling the necessary "fratricide" that frees him from the weight of the past, but on a deeper level Wotan's irrational behavior means that his grandson can have no future. By allowing his longed-for heir to go his own way, blind to history and oblivious to the world, instead of passing on his own unproductive knowledge of the world in a way that will benefit Siegfried, he sends him off down a cul-de-sac. Lacking the complex, circumspect understanding that the Greeks termed μῆτις and gave to the Titan Pro-Metheus ("fore-thinker"), Siegfried is mercilessly exposed to all the intrigues of the world.

The encounter between Wotan-Wanderer and Siegfried may be vaguely reminiscent of Oedipus's meeting with Laius, whom Oedipus unwittingly murders. More important than this parallel, however, is the observation that as the action unfolds, *Siegfried* changes from a naïve fairy tale to a myth gravid with portents of destiny, a sea change which, according to Carl Dahlhaus, must have contributed to Wagner's decision to set aside the score until further notice and write *Tristan und Isolde* and *Die Meistersinger von Nürnberg* instead.[63] In order to illustrate the startling nature of the break between the existing sections of the *Ring* and those parts that were yet to be written, I shall introduce a break of my own at this point in my narrative and, thrusting aside this chapter on Wotan, turn instead to *Tristan und Isolde* and, thence, *Die Meistersinger von Nürnberg*.

A Word about Sergei Eisenstein

Writing in his—never fully authenticated—memoirs, Dimitri Shostakovich dismissed as shameful Sergei Eisenstein's acceptance in November 1939 of an invitation to stage *Die Walküre* at Moscow's Bolshoi Theater: the famous film director, Shostakovich argued, was simply too afraid of crossing swords with senior Soviets, perhaps even with Stalin himself.[1] The project was certainly political through and through: in the wake of the nonaggression pact signed by Germany and the Soviet Union in August 1939, the two countries intensified their cultural exchange program. With hindsight we can see that there was something distinctly macabre about the Soviet Union's attempt to make political and cultural capital out of *Die Walküre*, not least because only a short time later the Ride of the Valkyries was to play such an inglorious role in German war films and newsreels.

But Eisenstein, who at this date in his career was by no means universally acclaimed as a film director in the Soviet Union, thought along very different lines when he started work on his production, noting in a mixture of German and English:

> I expect our interpretation will turn out like this: *from the inhuman to the human.* [. . .] The theme of humanity. At the center: Brünnhilde opens up to human feelings [. . .] when she sees how human beings love each other: their love is characterized by compassion and self-sacrifice. *What is fascistic about this play, I wonder?!!!*[2]

Eisenstein was fascinated not by the compassion that comes "from above" and that Hanns Eisler found so objectionable in *Parsifal*,[3] but by the kind of compassion that draws Brünnhilde away from the implacable world of the gods and to the sentient section of humanity. In adopting this approach, Eisenstein was giving one of the principal messages of the *Ring* its due, a message summed up in the redemption motif with which the cycle ends. Even more importantly, he was rehabilitating Wagner and defending him against the exaggerated charge of inhumanity.

The invitation to stage *Die Walküre* found the uncommonly well-educated Eisenstein by no means unprepared, for his mentor Vsevolod Meyerhold had already drawn his attention to the cinematic features in Wagner's works. Later Eisenstein explained that Stuart Gilbert's book on James Joyce, which he read in 1930, had encouraged him to explore the similarities in the leitmotif techniques of the Irish writer and of Wagner. In his essay "The Incarnation of Myth," which appeared in the periodical *Teatr* in the run-up to his production of *Die Walküre*, Eisenstein reveals a knowledge and understanding of Wagner that are impressive by any standards. He had also read the Poetic Edda, of course, and argued that the tree that appears in the opening act of *Die Walküre* represented "a *system* of the world; *a principle of life in general, an image of the process of life.*"[4]

Dominating his sets, the tree was a "pantheistic emblem of the creation" embodying "the *spirit of nature* that is all-pervasive." A powerful stage prop became one of the pillars of the plot: "The tree's—Wotan's—performance reaches its climax when it merges with the theme of spring in an image of the creation of the world, and opens up its centre for Siegmund and Sieglinde's ecstasy of love."[5]

Eisenstein was profoundly sympathetic to Wagner's revolutionary views and it was entirely in their spirit that he hoped that a future post-individualistic society would rediscover the sense of unity that he believed had existed in prehistoric times, when everything was still connected to everything else. As a result he was keen to rid *Die Walküre* of all individualisms and psychologisms. To take an example: in her role as the guardian of restrictive moral laws, Fricka is surrounded by a collective in the form of what Eisenstein described as "the golden-fleeced chorus of half-rams, half-people, neither wild animals nor human beings, who have betrayed their personal passions and voluntarily assumed subject status instead."[6] These "mime choruses" mediate between "the individual human and his milieu" and in that way illustrate a state in which humankind is not yet completely separated from nature.[7]

Nature's sympathetic concern for the plight of human beings was to be illustrated above all by the final scene of *Die Walküre* through the image of the Magic Fire: "Here the emotion of the characters, poured into the element of music, is personified by a fire which engulfs the entire firmament."

Following in the footsteps of Wagner's total artwork, Eisenstein speaks of the "synthetic merging of emotion, music, action, light and colour" as one of the basic ideas underpinning his production.[8]

Die Walküre opened on November 21, 1940, fifteen years after the launch of Eisenstein's film *Battleship Potemkin*. Within months, the Hitler-Stalin pact had been consigned to the rubbish bin of history, the ensuing war offering ample cause for "compassion" of the kind found in *Die Walküre*, but all too little opportunity for any demonstrations of that quality.

This photograph of Wagner was part of a series taken in Franz Hanfstaengl's Munich studio in the second half of 1865 and is inscribed to an otherwise unidentified acquaintance of his uncle Adolf Wagner. In general, this set of images documents Wagner's increasing fondness for the purely decorative, the former revolutionary having become—at least superficially—a member of the upper classes eager to impress his fellow citizens while not feeling entirely comfortable with that role. The Wotan pose that he adopted in the later series of photographs taken by Hanfstaengl suited him rather better. (Photograph courtesy of the Nationalarchiv der Richard-Wagner-Stiftung, Bayreuth: N 2828.)

CHAPTER TEN

"A mystical pit, giving pleasure to individuals"

TRISTAN UND ISOLDE

The biographical and artistic background — Mathilde
Wesendonck as Wagner's muse — The *Ring* set aside in favor
of *Tristan und Isolde* — The original conception of the work:
happiness may be found in love even if it ends in tragedy —
Return to the archetypal scenario of "redemption through
destruction" — Does there have to be a third act after the
love duet of act 2? — The "defeatist" productions of Heiner
Müller and Christoph Marthaler — The dialectics of the
score: unsatisfied longing and momentary fulfillment — More
than in the *Ring*, Wagner able to "push himself to the limit
musically" — Eros and Thanatos — Wagner's efforts to win over
Arthur Schopenhauer to his concept of sexual love — *Tristan
und Isolde* as a work beyond all metaphysical speculations —
Wagner's ability to imagine emotional landscapes — His
"endless melody" — The stimulus of specific sonorities — The
"traurige Weise" as an example of the difficulty of putting
music into words — Wagner not only as a sorcerer but also as a
constructor — Nietzsche's description of the work as Wagner's
"opus metaphysicum" applicable above all to the music

On March 2, 1859, shortly before completing the second act of *Tristan
und Isolde*, Wagner wrote to Mathilde Wesendonck:

My friend, things are difficult for me, oh so difficult. But my guardian angel
is beckoning. He consoles me and gives me peace whenever I need it most.
So I shall thank him and tell myself: "This is how it had to be in order that
it could be so!" Only he who has worn the crown of thorns knows the palm;
and this palm rests so gently, floating in our hands and arching over our
heads like the airiest angel's wings cooling and refreshing us by fanning us.[1]

Wagner's letters strike a poetic note whenever he needs to describe his current feelings. In this case he appears to have availed himself of motifs from a fairy tale that his muse, who had poetic ambitions of her own, had only recently sent to him.

Wagner's situation at that time throws so much light on the subject of "art and life" that it deserves to be examined here in somewhat greater detail. The letter from which we have just quoted was written in Venice, whither Wagner had fled in the wake of the "neighborly embarrassment" that had repeatedly made life difficult for him in Zurich.[2] Wagner and his wife had been living cheek by jowl with Otto and Mathilde Wesendonck on Zurich's "Green Hill" since the end of August 1857, the Wesendoncks and their three children—Myrrha, Guido, and Karl—in their newly built luxury villa, the Wagners in an outbuilding in the villa's grounds. Given the intensity of the friendship that bound Wagner to his muse of many years' standing, marital tensions could hardly be avoided, with the result that within a year Wagner had abandoned his self-styled "refuge" and repaired to Venice, where he remained for seven months, occupying a suite of rooms in the Palazzo Giustiniani on the Grand Canal. By coincidence, another of the buildings on the Grand Canal, the Palazzo Corner Spinelli, had been built, in part, by Giorgio Vasari, the Renaissance artist and art historian who helped to create the myth of the modern artist as a *divino artista*, a figure who, no longer serving as a paid craftsman, was handsomely rewarded by his patron as an artistic genius.

The palatial dimensions of Wagner's music room reflected his own view of himself as an artist: in his current straitened circumstances he saw himself in the grand tradition of the quintessential *divino artista* within the realm of music. And yet his situation was hardly comparable to that of the painters of the Renaissance: the demands that he placed on his art were a source of suffering to him; he suffered with his characters in a manner reminiscent of the tormented Savior; and he railed at a fate that had brought him to Venice not as a fêted hero but as a political refugee under the watchful gaze of the Austrian secret police. At the same time, however, he saw himself as the representative of a religion of art achieving superhuman feats and in consequence demanding not only generous patronage but, like his contemporary Giuseppe Verdi, aspiring to the artist's ancient right to a muse as well as a wife.

And this brings us neatly to *Tristan und Isolde*. In May 1857, after completing the opening act of *Siegfried*, Wagner tried to convince both himself and his benefactress Julie Ritter that he could still complete the *Ring* within two years. Indeed, he even had ideas on casting the roles in the finished cycle. Within two months, however, we find him admitting that it was "only after a great deal of effort" that he had persuaded himself to "abandon Siegfried in the forest for a year" and "catch his breath by writing a 'Tristan & Isolde.'"[3] Evidently Wagner felt that the world was closing in on him—there is a certain irony to his living at this time in a part of Zurich known as "Enge," literally "a narrow defile," but the word also includes a sense of straitened circumstances and the feeling of having been driven into a tight corner. First and foremost, there were artistic problems, Wagner having spent three and a half years laboring over the *Ring*, and while he did not feel that he had burned himself out, he was nonetheless exhausted. Working on the vast cycle was like a game of chess that became more complicated with each successive move. The mythological plot that Wagner was striving, Sisyphus-like, to shove uphill involved a wealth of leitmotifs, each of which demanded to be treated with proper regard not only for the moment but also for the overall context. This required extreme concentration and threatened to cramp his creative imagination. At the risk of oversimplification, we could say that Wagner needed to keep on presenting the same material in more and more new ways.

Conversely, Wagner will not have been particularly keen to see himself cast in a role that was subsequently assigned to him by Claude Lévi-Strauss—namely, that of a structuralist who, however ingeniously, set out to force music into a prescribed pattern. Rather, his aim was creativity in the compositional process. Fourteen years later, when he was once again in harness to his work on the *Ring* after a twelve-year break, he complained to Cosima: "How easy it would be if I could just write arias and duets! Now everything has to be a little musical portrait, but it must not interrupt the flow—I'd like to see anybody else do that!"[4] Against the background of this comment, it is no wonder that Wagner broke off work on the *Ring* during the second act of *Siegfried*, even if he then went on to finish the second complete draft, for it was here that the difficulty of finding his way back from fairy tale to myth was at its most daunting. The opening act contains not only a number of "portraits" that do not "interrupt the flow" but also a series of numbers that the "naïve" Siegfried is able to trumpet forth like so many miniature arias without regard for the mythological context, whereas the rest of the action threatens to be overwhelmed by myth, with its dead weight of the past. And, of course, Wagner knew that *Götterdämmerung* still awaited him and, with it, the need to elaborate an increasingly dense fabric of leitmotifs and "tangled passions" that Nietzsche was later to describe as "confused."[5]

But there were also entirely practical material reasons for setting aside the *Ring*: Wagner was heavily in debt, and his present publisher, Breitkopf & Härtel, was proving reluctant to pay 10,000 thalers—in itself, not an unreasonable fee—for an unfinished work. "What is the opposite of Breitkopf & Härtel?" Wagner asked Hans von Bülow at this time, before providing his own answer to his question: "Liszt-Vass und Meskirug."[6] In a letter he wrote to Liszt on New Year's Eve 1858, Wagner was reduced to begging: "Money! Money!—It doesn't matter how you get it and where you find it. Tristan will repay it all!"[7] Wagner may have thought of his appeal as a desperate joke, but on this occasion the long-suffering Liszt was disinclined to see the funny side of it.

Wagner had first announced his *Tristan* project to Liszt in December 1854, two months after his initial "conception" of the subject:[8]

> Since I have never in my life enjoyed the true happiness of love, I intend to erect a further monument to this most beautiful of dreams, a monument in which this love will be properly sated from start to finish: I have planned in my head a *Tristan* and *Isolte* [sic], the simplest, but most full-blooded musical conception; with the "black flag" that flutters at the end, I shall then cover myself over in order—to die.[9]

In other words, Wagner had already been toying with the idea of writing a music drama on the subject of Tristan and Isolde long before he set aside the *Ring*. And yet, in spite of his having been introduced to Schopenhauer's *Die Welt als Wille und Vorstellung* by 1854 at the latest and possibly as early as 1852,[10] his initial concept of the work—which, notwithstanding the version of events peddled by his autobiography,[11] was almost certainly not set down on paper at this time—was barely affected by the philosopher's quietistic views, which Wagner initially found "repellent."[12] Quite the opposite, in fact: at this date he evidently wanted to raise a monument to absolute love in all its uncompromising intensity, an interpretation confirmed not only by his reference in his letter to Liszt to the "most full-blooded musical conception" but also to his allusion to a particular motif from the medieval corpus of poems on the Tristan legend—that of the white and black flags. In the version by Gottfried von Straßburg that was familiar to Wagner from his days in Dresden with Ulrich von Türheim's ending, Tristan and Isolde do not regard their absolute love as a source of unending torment, but of temporary fulfillment. (This was evidently a view of love that puzzled and even alienated medieval readers whose values were based on a clear distinction between Platonic *hôhe minne* and the sexual attraction of *nidere minne*.)

After King Marke's discovery of the relationship between his nephew and his wife, Tristan seeks refuge in the haven of marriage by marrying Isolde of the White Hands in her native Brittany. In one of his many battles he is dealt a fatal wound by an envenomed glaive and sends word to his former lover in Cornwall, appealing to her to come and heal him, just as she did when he was injured by Morold. Isolde's safe arrival in Brittany is to be heralded by a white sail, but his jealous wife tells him that the sail on the approaching vessel is black, whereupon Tristan, robbed of all hope, dies.[13] Although this version of events ends tragically, Tristan's life up to that point had certainly not been unremittingly gloomy, and it was no doubt this aspect of the medieval narrative that Wagner had in mind when in his letter to Liszt he enthused about the "happiness of love" as "the fairest of all dreams" and spoke of a passion on which he planned to "sate" himself. At all events, it was initially not the torments of love that were to form the subject of his music drama,[14] and although this torment was to be one of the main motifs in his definitive poem, Wagner was content for the present to focus on the idea of fulfillment in love, a fulfillment which, even if it was denied to him in real life, was at least to come true in the field of the musical drama.

But what exactly did Wagner mean when in December 1854 he told Liszt with a sense of resignation that he had "never enjoyed the true happiness of love"? How can this be reconciled with his infatuation for Mathilde Wesendonck, whom a number of his biographers even credit with the inspiration behind *Tristan und Isolde*? He had always felt that his wife, who, however much she may have "deserved his respect," was in his eyes "completely unsuited" to him[15] and lacked all understanding for his art: "What will you say," he asked Liszt in March 1853,

> when I tell you that I have never enjoyed the true happiness of love? I now spend my life poised between privation and a resigned regard for the limitations of the people who are closest to me, people who with each passing day are less and less able to understand and comprehend me! I cannot and will not cause open offence here (since my own heart would suffer as a result—habit is an undeniably potent force!), but I must at least be able to acquire the means to withdraw from this desolation from time to time in order to unfold my wings unhindered and unchecked.[16]

Mathilde Wesendonck promised to requite Wagner for this feelings of desolation. She was twenty-two when she arrived in Zurich in 1851 and the following year heard Wagner conduct Beethoven's Sixth Symphony and his own *Tannhäuser* Overture: "I shall never forget the impression of the first rehearsal [. . .] in the darkened auditorium of the old Company Hall in Zurich," she wrote enthusiastically. "It was a veritable frenzy of happiness, a revelation."[17] The young Frau Wesendonck wanted to be more than just a mother, more than just a trophy wife in tourist centers and elegant spas. Rather, she saw herself as a patron of the arts, with poetic aspirations of her own, and in this respect she exerted a powerful appeal on Wagner. Until the Wesendonck Villa was completed in the summer of 1857, the family occupied a suite of rooms in Zurich's fashionable Hôtel Baur au Lac, so it cannot have appeared unseemly if Wagner visited her there on a regular basis over an extended period of time. As she was later pleased to recall: "What he composed in the morning he would play on my grand piano in the afternoon, checking over what he had written."[18]

Friendly contacts between the two couples were slowly forged, the Wesendoncks inviting Wagner to various functions that Minna, too, often attended. Two years were to pass before Wagner began work on the first complete draft of act 1 of *Die Walküre*, the sketches of which contain the infatuated abbreviations to which we have already referred. As we have seen, this draft, which was completed on September 1, 1854, is the only one to contain these coded messages, although it may be worth mentioning in this context that in September 1855 Mathilde gave birth to a son, Guido. A second son, Karl, followed in April 1857. In neither case does this suggest that the Wesendoncks were drifting apart as a couple. Conversely, Wagner's "Annals"—the brief outline of his life that he kept between Easter 1846 and the end of 1868—contain an entry for September 1855: "Foul temper, especially toward the Wesend[oncks]. Refused to be a godfather because it would be unlucky."[19]

Events such as these appear to have done little to undermine the friendship between artists on the part of Wagner and Mathilde Wesendonck. Indeed, the continuing closeness of that friendship is reflected in a single detail: throughout the time that he was in Zurich, Mathilde would ink over large sections of the composition sketches of Wagner's works, which he himself had prepared in pencil. This task, which was later assumed by Cosima, required both a sympathetic understanding of the nature of the work and a good deal of patience. At this point it is worth mentioning a curious entry in the composition sketch for the third act of *Tristan und Isolde*, on which Wagner began work in April 1859: "One has to help the child a little." Later corrections had made this passage difficult to decipher, obliging Wagner to intervene and correct Mathilde's inking over of the notes. This, at least, is the interpretation proposed by Ulrich Bartels, who has devoted an entire study to these sketches.[20] But how can this be so? By April 1859, Wagner and Mathilde Wesendonck were living hundred of miles apart, with no real contact between them. More likely is the hypothesis that it was Wagner who inked over this passage and that he imagined himself back in the days when he and his muse had still been in very close physical contact.

Of course, he hoped that this intense relationship between artists would develop into a no less passionate affair, but it seems highly unlikely that his dream came true—not that this may have prevented Mathilde from occasionally playing with fire.[21] While writing out the score of *Das Rheingold* using Mathilde's gold pen, Wagner may still have harbored concrete hopes reflected in his outburst in one of his letters to Liszt: "Everything is seething inside me and making music. It is—oh! I am in *love!*—and such a divine *faith* inspires me that I myself no longer have need of *hope!*"[22] But it seems likely that Wagner's hopes will have faded after his initial enthusiasm had passed. More importantly, his art, too, was increasingly being drawn down into the eddying waters of world-denial in the course of his years in Zurich. During the long period when *Tristan und Isolde* lay fallow in his thoughts—in other words, from the autumn of 1854 to the late summer of 1857—Wagner not only took a detailed interest in the philosophy of Schopenhauer but drew up a prose sketch for a stage work, *Die Sieger* (The Victors, WWV 89), that was inspired by the theme of redemption through renunciation.[23] A single musical theme has also survived. This period additionally found Wagner toying with the idea of introducing Parsifal into the third act of *Tristan und Isolde*. In the event, this idea was not pursued any further, not least because Wagner was already thinking of an independent work on the subject of Parsifal's quest for the Grail.

By now Wagner was once again powerfully drawn to his old subject of "redemption through destruction": love was no longer synonymous with fulfillment, as it presumably had been in his initial conception of *Tristan und Isolde*, but was associated above all with torment. Here, too, Wagner's desire to distance himself from *Siegfried* makes sense, for what would have been the point of ending the third act with an impassioned love duet for Siegfried and Brünnhilde on the sun-drenched heights of the Valkyries' rock, when all would be set at naught in the ensuing *Götterdämmerung* in keeping with Wagner's Schopenhauerian view that in the course of the *Ring*, love, initially hailed as "uniquely capable of bringing us love," had come to be seen as "utterly and completely annihilating."[24] A similar degree of skepticism is found in a more or less contemporary pencil sketch that contains a revised version of Brünnhilde's peroration: here, too, there is the same Buddhist tendency to deny the world.

We need to take seriously Wagner's own interpretation of the prelude to act 1 of *Tristan und Isolde*, which dates from 1859: "Yearning! Yearning, insatiable longing ever reborn, thirsting and repining! The only release was to die, to perish, to fade away, nevermore to awaken!" And further:

> The musician who chose this theme to introduce his love drama was bound to feel entirely at one with that most absolute and unrestricted element that is music, so that his sole concern was how he might best restrict *himself*, inasmuch as the theme he had chosen could never be wholly exhausted. And so he depicted that sense of insatiable longing which, rising to but a single climax in a single long-drawn breath, passes from the most timid confession and tender attraction to anxious longing, hope and apprehension, plaints and desires, rapture and torment and, finally, to the most powerful impulse, the most violent attempt to find that breach in the dyke that might open a way for the inexhaustible craving heart to enter the sea of love's endless delight. In vain![25]

It was no accident that Wagner was at this point pursuing the plan of following up this definitive "In vain!" with the denial of the self-tormenting will in *Die Sieger*, as he explained to Liszt in July 1856: "You must first have digested my *Tristan*, especially its third act [. . .], for only then will *Die Sieger* become clearer to you."[26] Instead of writing *Die Sieger*, Wagner composed *Parsifal* and in doing so killed two birds with one stone, Parsifal's motto ("Strong is the magic of him who desires, but stronger is that of him who renounces")[27] being his response not only to *Tristan und Isolde* but also to the *Ring*.

Mathilde Wesendonck would have preferred *Die Sieger* to *Parsifal*. When she heard this last-named work in Bayreuth in 1882, she was afraid "that the world would revert to Catholicism! You can laugh at me if you like, but I'd rather have had 'nirvana.'"[28] And so she went on to write her own verse legend on the theme of compassion, calling it *Unter schatt'gen Mango-Bäumen* (Under shady mango trees) and turning Parsifal into Devadatta and Gurnemanz into the Buddha.[29] As for *Tristan und Isolde*, however, Wagner regarded his muse as irreplaceable: she was an actual or virtual confidante, without whose help he may never have been able to tell what he called this "terrible tale."[30]

Writers have asked why this "terrible tale" does not end when the curtain comes down on act 2. "Why," wonders Nike Wagner—and her question is more than merely theoretical—

> do we need a third act in this opera? Why must we—and the singer—endure the anguish and shouts, the ravings and delirium of such a badly injured man? [. . .] The story, after all, is finished, the two of them discover love in the garden and enjoy the ecstatic vision of death now that there is no longer any help for them on earth: "Now banish fear, lovely death, yearningly longed-for love-death!" sing Tristan and Isolde, rising to a paroxysm of passion at the words: "Glowing white-hot in our breast, love's supreme delight!" Brangäne's scream then rends the night air, the music's tempo and temperature change, and "desolate day" irrupts in the form of Marke, Melot, and their attendants, all of them dressed for a hunt. The rest of act 2 provides, as it were, the consummation of this process as the lovers are unmasked, the king reveals his helpless dismay in the face of his favorite vassal's betrayal, and Tristan throws himself on Melot's sword, precipitating the final curtain.[31]

Even the mystic union with the universe invoked by Isolde in her final words in act 3

> In dem wogenden Schwall,
> in dem tönenden Schall,
> in des Welt-Athems
> wehendem All—
> ertrinken—
> versinken—
> unbewußt—
> höchste Lust!

> [In the surging swell, in the echoing sound, in the world-breath's wafting universe—to drown—to sink—unaware—highest bliss!]

is already adumbrated in act 2:

> O sink' hernieder,
> Nacht der Liebe,
> gieb Vergessen,
> daß ich lebe;
> nimm mich auf

in deinen Schooß,
löse von
der Welt mich los!

[O sink upon us, night of love, let me forget that I am alive; take me to your bosom and release me from the world!]

Thus the lovers sing, before continuing with the words

wonne-hehrstes Weben,
liebe-heiligstes Leben,
nie-wieder-Erwachens
wahnlos
hold bewußter Wunsch.

[Weft of joy most sublime, life of holiest love, sweetly conscious wish that we may nevermore awake.]

In this context it is no accident that Isolde's "Transfiguration" (the traditional term "Liebestod" is not Wagner's), beginning with the words "Mild und leise wie er lächelt" (How gently and softly he smiles), harks back to a passage in the Love Duet in act 2:

So starben wir,
um ungetrennt,
ewig einig,
ohne End',
ohn' Erwachen,
ohne Bangen,
namenlos
in Lieb' umfangen,
ganz uns selbst gegeben
der Liebe nur zu leben.

[And so we died in order that undivided, one forever, without end, never waking, never fearing, namelessly embraced in love, given wholly to one another, we might live for our love alone!]

In his encomiastic tribute to *Tristan und Isolde*, Ernst Bloch makes no secret of his belief that

one has already heard all this in the great final duet of Act Two, so much more beautifully than in the orchestral writing at the end of the third act.

[. . .] It must be said, with all due respect, that the so very deliberately inserted and seemingly discrete final orchestral piece "Isoldens Liebestod" begins to decline into insufferable softness, into unmystical sweetness, which—as with the arpeggiated triads, with the sixty-fold celebration at the conclusion of *Parsifal* that refuses to end—threatens to drop all the more steeply from its tremendous height as a proper, theatrical ending tries to ally itself with the entirely different definitiveness of the birth of redemption from the spirit of music.[32]

If Wagner—an astutely intelligent man of the theater—had stuck to his original conception, however problematical such a reconstruction may be, he might have written a musical drama in two acts, with Tristan and Isolde dying in each other's arms at the end of the second act, which would then have ended in the pitch-black garden in the spirit of early romanticism. Evidently such an ending struck Wagner as too positive in the wake of his conversion to Schopenhauer. As a result, he needed the third act to articulate his thoughts on the "curse of love" to which he refers in one of his sketches for the later libretto.[33] As Egon Voss has written, hitting the nail on the head, "The monument that Wagner wanted to raise to love in writing *Tristan und Isolde* was intended as a deterrent."[34] Only after act 3 has demonstrated this point in the most graphic terms can Isolde's "Transfiguration" bring the work to an end in the spirit of a homecoming myth.

No matter how much or how little Wagner was influenced by Schopenhauer's magnum opus, which he read "like one of the Scriptures,"[35] there is no denying the consistency with which he continued to explore his theme of "redemption through destruction," for the penitent Tannhäuser who ultimately finds salvation through the Virgin Mary is here transformed into a desperate figure breathing his last in a feverish delirium without any obvious sign of divine grace. Whether we follow Ernst Bloch in seeing Isolde's beatific transfiguration as a concession to the world of the theater or whether we interpret it as second-degree metaphysics in the spirit of the redemption motif that appears at the end of *Götterdämmerung*, the events that unfold in the castle courtyard at Kareol exhibit a painful realism that first and foremost affects our experience of time: Tristan's wait for the ship that is coming to save him lasts around fifty minutes, including the introduction. As a result, it is no longer possible to speak of time onstage speeding up, since the listener experiences Tristan's impatience in real time with an intensity that is almost unbearable. The gesturally loaded music that accompanies his delirious fantasies has a different, but equally realistic dynamism.

It makes sense in this context that neither Heiner Müller (1993) nor Christoph Marthaler (2005) made any attempt to stage the work in Bayreuth in a historicist medieval setting or in the tradition of Wieland Wagner's timeless mystery play about love and death. Each of them emphasized the experience of isolation, alienation, and decline, Müller expressly welcoming the fact that his reading of act 3 evoked associations of the "end of time" and "devastation" redolent of the world of Samuel Beckett.[36] In Marthaler's production, Tristan ends his life in a hospital bed, with no suggestion of any union between the lovers, whether ecstatic or "mild and gentle." Quite the opposite, in fact: Marthaler's aim was explicitly to exclude the utopian vision of the original.

Just as society in Wagner's day was riven by contradictions, so the music of *Tristan und Isolde* is laid out along dialectic lines, for on the one hand it expresses the perpetually dissatisfied longing to which Wagner referred in his note on the prelude, while on the other hand it possesses a utopian element implying the momentary fulfillment of that longing. Such ambivalence has always enabled listeners to find heaven on earth in music, a belief abundantly illustrated by countless examples from Ovid to Gottfried and Shakespeare. Or take the Baroque poet Paul Fleming: "The voluptuous sound bewitches our senses and makes us sick with longing, yet by a woe that is sweet."[37] A musical equivalent would be the Christmas cantata on the late medieval carol *In dulci jubilo* by Fleming's Baroque contemporary, the composer Dietrich Buxtehude, which ends with the line "Eya, wär'n wir da" (Oh, if only we were there). The words merely register the hope of heavenly joys to come, whereas the musical setting by the organist of Lübeck's St. Mary's Church treats the final word "da" (there) in an altogether unusual manner, repeating it a dozen times as if he wanted to cast the singers in the role of little children by a Christmas tree, their hopes having become a reality.

Wagner tackled this same dialectic in a very different way, of course, explaining to Mathilde Wesendonck that the final act of *Tristan und Isolde* was a "real intermittent fever—the deepest and most unprecedented suffering and yearning, and, immediately afterward, the most unprecedented triumph and jubilation."[38] He characterized the completed second act with the words "Life's utmost fire flared up in it with such unspeakable ardor that it almost burned and consumed me."[39] And, commenting with hindsight, he described the work as a whole to Cosima:

You can understand that I felt the need, after writing these parts of the *Nibelungen* [i.e., *Das Rheingold*, *Die Walküre*, and the first half of *Siegfried*], to leave this element of dreadfulness and write *Tristan und Isolde*, which was, so to speak, just a love scene; indeed, I thought of it as an Italian opera, that is to say, to be sung by Italian singers—and in Rio de Janeiro.[40]

Wagner was referring here to the fact that he briefly toyed with the idea of composing *Tristan und Isolde* for the Italian opera company of Dom Pedro II of Brazil, a Wagnerian who later attended the first Bayreuth *Ring* in 1876. But his playful expression conceals behind it a serious impulse, for on completing *Die Walküre* Wagner came increasingly to view the *Ring* as a "terrible" onus of superhuman proportions. The cycle was turning into a game of mythological chess involving a multiplicity of pieces that was threatening to overwhelm him. Perhaps only an artist can judge what must have been going through Wagner's head at this time. After all, he was living in and through all his characters and was constantly concerned for their future.

Although the poem was complete, it was the music that determined the weal and woe of these characters. They had to be believable at every single moment and in every situation. Yet even if he had wanted to, the German composer could only dream of depicting his Siegfried, Wotan, and Brünnhilde in such a straightforward way as Verdi depicted characters such as Otello and Desdemona. Wagner returned to this subject on numerous occasions: while working on *Parsifal*, for example, he spoke to Cosima of his "need to push himself to the limit musically, since in the *Nibelungen* the requirements of the drama frequently forced him to restrict the musical expression."[41]

Commentators who adopt a less insistently philosophical view of *Tristan und Isolde* than they do of the *Ring* certainly have Wagner on their side, and this begins with the characters: Brangäne, Kurwenal, and Melot are subsidiary figures of a kind that simply do not exist in the *Ring*, for although they propel the plot forward, they are largely irrelevant to the inner action. Even Marke, the deceived husband, can do little more than raise his hands in calm dismay, before lowering them again with equal ineffectuality. Everything revolves around the lovers. There are hundreds of books and articles on the nature of their love. Portentous terms such as "atheistic metaphysics," "deathly erotic undertow," "mystic union," "metaphysics of fusion," "return to archetypal oneness," "oceanic feeling," "erotic solipsism," and "apotheosis of fulfillment," as well as negative expressions such as a "symptom of decadence" and the "rigorous blueprint for a union between two neurotic individuals doomed in advance to fail" haunt the literature on *Tristan und Isolde*, spanning a range of interpretations of which it is hard to gain any overview.[42] One writer even offers a clinically matter-of-fact analysis: "Tristan's pathological characteristics, which we have related structurally to those of a borderline personality, acquire a degree of differentiation through the component of [Heidegger's] existential philosophy that entitles us to coin the term 'Tristan syndrome' to describe this particular psychopathological type."[43]

This analysis may be compared with the crass formulation by the German-American cultural historian Peter Gay, who locates the delirium associated with the work in the whole attitude to life of the bourgeois fin de siècle, noting that

> its music heavily underscores its story, especially in the love scenes with its luxuriant themes and flowing rhythms rising, rising, and those final satiated moments with Tristan breathing his last in Isolde's arms; it evokes the thrilling journey to what the French call the little death, which seals sexual intercourse happily completed. In such representations, the regressive pull toward primitive feelings is almost irresistible, sublimation far from complete, with the erotic sources of the composition unmistakable, consciously exploited.

The Wagnerian's task, Gay goes on, is to sublimate his or her musical experience and "elevate the Master's explorations of sensual appetites into the sphere of the sublime."[44]

Readers may be tempted to distill a heady brew from all of these quotations and use it to create a coherent narrative, but they may also adopt the opposite course of singling out a particular theory and seeking to interpret the work on the basis of this one hypothesis alone, but in neither case will they get very far. Rather, we need to recognize that various approaches intersect here, and that although these lead to contradictions, this does not detract from *Tristan und Isolde* as a work of art. Among its most important motifs is that of Eros and Thanatos, a motif stretching back over several millennia to which Wagner himself alluded when describing the night of love in act 2: "Even the ancients placed a lowered torch in the hand of Eros as the genius of Death!"[45] Wagner was sufficiently familiar with classical myth to have read about the primeval womb of the earth goddess Gaia and to know that everything emerges from this womb, only to return to it in the end: Eros symbolizes becoming, Thanatos fading away, the two of them merging in the cycle of creation.

Writing in his classic study *Pagan Mysteries in the Renaissance*, Edgar Wind argued that "to die was to be loved by a god and partake through him of eternal bliss."[46] The gods' amorous kisses had something fatal about them. Wagner drew a similar conclusion when discussing the final scene of *Siegfried*: "The kiss of love is the first intimation of death, the cessation of individuality, that is why a person is so terrified by it."[47] But it is precisely this dissolution of the self that is central to *Tristan und Isolde*: "You Isolde, Tristan I, no more Isolde," Isolde sings, while Tristan—in one of the few "duets" that Wagner felt able to acknowledge in the light of his aesthetic views at this period—replies: "Tristan you, I Isolde, no more Tristan!" And both of them conjure up the "ardently longed-for love-death."

This brings us to Schopenhauer, who may not have influenced the work's entire philosophical substructure but who certainly provided Wagner with the support that he needed while working on the score. Schopenhauer, too, regarded death as "the great opportunity no longer to be I."[48] Conversely, the idea of a love-death certainly did not have his approval. For him, sex was no more than an animalistic instinct designed to propagate the species. When it came to glorifying love, Wagner could not have found it easy to argue, knowing that Schopenhauer was looking over his shoulder. But, self-confident to a fault, he thought of writing to the Sage of Frankfurt at the end of 1858 and acquainting him with his conviction that "sexual love" offered "a means to salvation, leading to self-knowledge and denial of the will—and not just the individual will."[49]

Schopenhauer would presumably have shaken his head in disbelief at this suggestion, but it seems that Wagner never sent his letter, for it survives only in the form of a draft. Nonetheless, Wagner's "Venice Diary," the entries of which were addressed to Mathilde Wesendonck, likewise refers to his intention of writing to Schopenhauer and persuading him to "correct his system" by pointing out the "path to salvation [. . .] which involves a total pacification of the will through love, and not through any abstract human love, but a love engendered on the basis of sexual love, i.e., the attraction between a man and a woman."[50] This conviction merely serves to point up the yawning gulf not only between Schopenhauer's "system" and Wagner's but also within Wagner's own system, a gulf impossible to bridge even with the best will in the world. If the work were to have ended with act 2 and the love-death of its two main characters, it might have been possible to speak of love leading to a pacification of the will. But the third act then follows, bringing with it all its desolation and torment. And even if we choose to interpret Isolde's "Transfiguration" as an example of the "pacification of the will," this "love-death," as it is erroneously called, has nothing to do with sex. Rather, it resembles a happy ending which, according to Wagner's intentions, should really not exist at all, since Tristan's self-lacerating torments, which *are* the result of sexual love, should be followed not by "supreme bliss" but by nirvana at best.

Andreas Dorschel claims that behind *Tristan und Isolde* lies an "infatuated enthusiasm" for the sort of "return to archetypal oneness" that Wagner shared with the German romantics, but which was bound to be repellent to a writer like Schopenhauer.[51] According to Dorschel, this contradiction is inherent in the very subject: "Perhaps the music, *as art*, conjuring up the moment of supreme happiness in Isolde's love-death, is forced to say 'yes' where in order to be *philosophically* logical, it should have said a most emphatic 'no.'"[52] In this sense Wagner's music presents us with the force of a love that motivates the action, keeping it moving forward from first to last.

The composer has no need to be ashamed of such contradictions, of course, for although *Tristan und Isolde* cannot be salvaged as a coherent philosophical work, we are under no obligation to rescue it in this way. Unlike the *Ring*, the fascination it exudes rests not on the depiction of a baleful system but on an underlying message that we would do best not to examine too closely. Rather, we should simply allow the work's powerful images to impinge upon us, for few of today's audiences will regard the world of Tristan and Isolde as a fascinating and viable alternative to the deceitful contemporary world in the way that they may have done in Wagner's day, when moral pressures in terms of marriage were arguably so great that attempts to break free could plausibly be accepted as rash and in some cases fatal, as they are in *Tristan und Isolde* and in Fontane's *Effi Briest*. If we look more closely at Wagner and at his own marriage with Minna, he appears to have been more than just the philanderer that his enemies are fond of claiming but he was also a husband who, while occasionally deluding himself about his own motives, clearly thought in terms of strict moral categories and, where the subject of infidelity was concerned, wrestled with his conscience.

Such is the liberalism of today's society that the subject of adultery can no longer be invested with a metaphysical dimension in the way that Wagner was able to do. Even so, *Tristan und Isolde* contains more than a mere disquisition on marital infidelity: it examines our longings for something different, for the sanctity of absolute love and self-surrender. Wagner's attempt to give this longing a voice through the medium of his quasi-religious approach to art has lost little of its fascination, even though the emphasis must now lie on the element of "art" rather than on "religion." In other words, we allow the longing for the absolute to affect us on an aesthetic level and are less drawn to this theme than to a work of art that allows us to experience for ourselves archetypal scenes that no longer have any real place in today's enlightened society.

It is not unimportant, of course, that in *Tristan und Isolde* two such existential aspects of our lives as love and death are at stake and revealed in all their nakedness with a rawness found in few other stage works. But it is sufficient to know their essential stages: the love potion is used in act 1 to fuel the dramatic action, followed by the impassioned night of love in act 2 and, in act 3, by the hero's slow and painful death as a consequence of his unbridled passion and by the transfiguration of self-sacrificial love in the form of the culminating apotheosis.

The love potion that Brangäne serves up instead of the poison that the lovers are expecting is not what Thomas Mann described as a "mere device for liberating a passion that already exists (in fact the lovers might as well be drinking plain water)."[53] It also has a number of important functions in terms of the listener's perception of the action, for we no longer need to follow and understand the complex tale that until now has prevented Tristan and Isolde from falling into each other's arms but can instead embrace a myth for which "absolute passion" is a given. Yet it is also a myth that ends in disaster or, at best, in disillusionment and which is therefore far from being timeless. In short, it is both an ancient, primeval myth and at the same time a myth for today, one that all listeners carry around within them.

This is enough for us to be able to follow the work, which ultimately is not about logically intelligible processes or even a rigorous juxtaposition of events. Taken to its extreme limits, this implies that the individual elements that make up the plot—the folly of love, its fulfillment, and its inevitable torment—could be presented to us in a different order in keeping with the law of *bricolage* that Claude Lévi-Strauss has imputed to most mythological narratives: what matters is not the way in which the individual structural elements follow on from one another but that they occur at all. In the case of *Tristan und Isolde*, this means that we are not held in a state of breathless suspense by the unfolding action, because far too little happens for this to be a viable possibility. No, we are fascinated, rather, by Wagner's magnificent ability to tease the subtlest of moods from an altogether extreme relationship. He himself stressed that while working on the subject he plunged "into the inner depths of mental processes," where "life and death, the whole import and existence of the outer world, hang on nothing but the inner stirrings of the soul."[54] In his edition of Wagner's collected writings, Julius Kapp argued prosaically but aptly that Wagner's language is marked by a "brevity restricted to a few key words," thereby taking him "to the very limit of what is dramatically permissible" and frequently appealing "more to his listeners' presentiment and feelings than to their intellect."[55]

This is true of all operas, of course, and yet a comparison between *Tristan und Isolde* and Wagner's other stage works reveals just how extreme his approach has become in this particular case. It is no accident that the French symbolists made such great play of the libretto of *Tristan und Isolde*, finding in it an ideal model for the *poésie pure* that implies a type of verse based on the actual sounds of the language. Stéphane Mallarmé's poems, for example, are concerned with the magic of language and its sonorities rather than objects and concepts. Of course, Wagner's libretto cannot avoid recounting the action of the drama, but the words are clearly not intended to bridge the gap between action and music. Rather, they form an alliance with the music that is unusual and novel even for a musician as fond of experimentation as Wagner was.

Mallarmé even dubbed Wagner a "poète français" and sought to create a kind of poetry that would be "not unlike the multiplicity of cries in an orchestration."[56] For his part, Wagner entrusts his "cries" to a real orchestra, but for whole stretches of the work he merges poem and music, voices and orchestral sounds to create a single entity. When a willing listener hears the phrases "Ohne Wähnen sanftes Sehnen, ohne Bangen süß Verlangen; ohne Schmachten hold Umnachten" (Without illusion, gentle yearning; without fear, sweet desire; without pining, lovely dusk enfolding us), he or she may find it hard to distinguish between words and music but will surrender instead to the flood of a single all-encompassing sensation such as an infant might experience when hearing a lullaby.

It is no accident that Mallarmé's "Hommage" to Wagner refers to "hiéroglyphes,"[57] "divine symbols" in the sense understood by Friedrich Schlegel. Such hieroglyphic symbols are not deciphered in the manner of a script but require a "particular interpretation through the medium of art."[58] When, at the end of act 2, Tristan replies to Marke's remonstrations, "My king, that I cannot say; and what you ask, you can never discover," this is entirely in keeping with Wagner's tendency to privilege the unspoken and inexpressible, which he does not least through the medium of music: "In truth the greatness of a poet is mostly to be measured by what he leaves unsaid, letting us say to ourselves in silence the thing that is unspeakable," Wagner wrote in "Music of the Future." "It is the musician who makes what has been kept silent ring out aloud, and the unmistakable form of his sounding silence is his *endless melody*."[59] In the private diary that he kept for Mathilde Wesendonck, Wagner likewise referred to the "profound art of resonant silence" found in act 2 of *Tristan und Isolde*.[60]

By describing the work simply as a "Handlung" (action), Wagner made it abundantly clear that the term "musical drama" that he used, albeit reluctantly, elsewhere was no longer possible here: what matters is not the dramatic construction but events that transcend the meager onstage action and raise that action to a level at which acting and being acted upon merge to create an "action" that cannot be reduced to a single concept but tends, rather, to follow the flood of musical sounds. Ernst Bloch felt that he was in the presence of a "tremendous adagio into which almost nothing antithetical penetrates from the outside such that Tristan or Isolde could even become aware of it as conflict, catastrophe."[61]

Bloch compares this "profoundly inward dreaming," which he experiences as "our own," with a different kind of unconsciousness, namely, that of the *Ring*, which he attacks with some virulence in his early *Spirit of Utopia*: "The music here goes almost completely over into vacuity and dismal animality. Any prospect within this work that could lead out of the narrowness of personhood does so only by serving up a world of cardboard, greasepaint, and irredeemable heroic posturing."[62] But by taking as its subject the "metadramatic lyricism of redemption,"[63] *Tristan und Isolde* makes up for an objectification lacking any historical, philosophical, or metaphysical dimension.

In this, Bloch reveals himself as a true romantic—very much in the spirit of Wagner himself, for Wagner, too, asks whether existence has any meaning: within an apparently meaningless world, is there anything that might offer us redemption and provide "ultimate assurance and a place of refuge within our fragile existence"?[64] For the romantics, such a haven was conceivable only in art, and even *then* it could exist only in the form of a paradox: the infinite—the philosophical sign of "redemption"—can be demonstrated only in confrontation with the finite. And it was here that music came into play. Musical figures are finite, but to the extent that they can be constantly transformed, they tend toward the infinite. Music gives us an inkling of the infinite, but without ever actually attaining it.

Compositions in which the mutability of the musical material is raised to the level of the highest structural principle are particularly well suited to this paradigm. Long before *Tristan und Isolde*, Wagner had struck out in the direction of what we might call the "liquefaction" of musical processes: by turning his back on rigid traditional structural principles at an early date and using constantly mutating leitmotifs in the *Ring*, he had prepared for *Tristan und Isolde* in not unimportant ways, even if Bloch was reluctant to acknowledge this. And yet Bloch's polemical attack on the *Ring* is by no means unjustified, for it highlights decisive differences between the *Ring* and *Tristan und Isolde*, even if the language that he uses is overemphatic. These are differences of which Wagner, too, was aware. Whereas the constant changes to the *Ring*'s motifs are so closely bound up with the action that the music may be said to be fettered to the drama, the music can unfold more freely in the later work. As Roger Scruton has observed, "The motives in *Tristan* are quite unlike the characteristic motives of the *Ring* cycle, being devoted to the expression of an inner life rather than to the depiction of an epic mythological saga."[65] Not only are there no graphic leitmotifs directly related to the plot, including those associated with the sword, the ring, and Valhalla, but the leitmotif technique found in the *Ring* is no longer as obvious, having been replaced by a flood of sound that rarely abates and that Wagner hailed as his "endless melody."

Sebastian Urmoneit has claimed that the two "archetypal motifs of the action" are Eros and Thanatos and that these are reflected in two "basic melodic motifs" from which everything else proceeds, the motifs in question being "the descending chromatic line which, stated at the very beginning, expresses suffering" and "the rising line of the yearning motif that stands in opposition to it."[66] His claim is undoubtedly oversimplistic, and yet the difference between *Tristan und Isolde* and the *Ring* is plain to see: in the *Ring*, "nature," as depicted in the prelude to *Das Rheingold*, develops into an increasingly complex "social" structure, whereas the action in *Tristan und Isolde* is complex from the very outset, a point illustrated by the combination of the motifs associated with suffering and yearning in the opening bars of the work. It remains related, however, to the same simple underlying conflict between desire and abstention and, as such, is entirely in the spirit of the "endless" theme that affects society in its almost proverbial way and produces nothing that is truly new.

This is not to say that Wagner's "endless melody" ignores the course of the action. Quite the opposite, in fact, for the subtlety of the links between the music and the events that are simultaneously unfolding onstage goes beyond anything achieved in the *Ring*. We need merely glance at the countless corrections that Wagner made in his composition sketch to Tristan's melancholy reference to his parents' fate ("When he sired me and died, she, dying, gave birth to me") to appreciate the extent to which he struggled to find the right musical expression for every single moment in the action, especially at those points where this expression is hard to grasp not just textually but musically too.[67]

An entry in Cosima Wagner's diary is worth quoting in this context: "In the evening R. sang something from *Tristan* and said, 'This *Tristan* has a color all its own, it is mauve, a sort of lilac.'"[68] (Proust, for whom Wagner was "a constituent part of his creativity," wrote *À la recherche du temps perdu* "in pink."[69]) And *Tristan und Isolde* is all about color and changes of color that are sometimes abrupt but more frequently subtle. Ernst Kurth has provided a technical description of the "iridescent change of color" of many sequences of chords.[70] That Wagner uses predominantly rare color mixtures, introducing a note of greater purity only at particular climaxes such as "O sink' hernieder," "So starben wir," and "Mild und leise," is well illustrated by the opening bars of the prelude, where the motif heard here expresses a complex mixture of feelings in the form of the *dulce malum* of which we have already spoken.

These mixtures stem from a specific combination of harmony and instrumentation. In order to be able to present them convincingly, Wagner—like every great artist—had his sights fixed firmly on a characteristic polarity. In order to be understood, he used a traditional musical rhetoric that ascribes specific musical idioms to specific human emotions. And in order to say something new, he expanded its range of expression to a degree that even today remains unprecedented. Previously, composers and their audiences had been able to get by with the admittedly naïve view that music reflected specific emotions, whereas the sounds of *Tristan und Isolde* alerted listeners to emotional states of greater complexity, states of whose existence they had hitherto been unaware. This is not only true of *Tristan und Isolde*, of course, but also applies to other works by Wagner and to the music of other composers. But in the case of *Tristan und Isolde*, the listener has a greater chance—or, in the eyes of Wagner's detractors, runs a greater risk—of being enticed into a web of diffuse emotional and psychological states on which the music alone can impose any sense of order. For, on the one hand, the plot is insufficiently taut to provide a firm support, allowing the music, which might otherwise be mere background music of a kind found in the cinema, to assume control. And on the other hand there are no readily recognizable musical structures such as recitatives and arias that might provide any objective support—even the "poetic-musical periods" that impose a sense of order on the score of the *Ring* are far less evident here.

It is easy to draw a parallel between the plot of *Tristan und Isolde*, with its metaphor of Eros and Thanatos, and Freud's theory of the unconscious, but it would be more profitable to examine the music and see to what extent its irrational nature predisposes it to invite associations with Freud's id and Schopenhauer's blind world-will. Wagner knew why, as a composer, he was drawn to Schopenhauer's worldview and why he was able to write to Mathilde Wesendonck shortly after completing the work:

> Just consider my music, with its delicate, oh so delicate, mysteriously flowing humors penetrating the most subtle pores of feeling to reach the very marrow of life, where it overwhelms everything that looks like sagacity and the self-interested powers of self-preservation, sweeping away all that belongs to the delusive madness of personality and leaving behind it only that wondrously sublime sigh with which we confess to our sense of powerlessness—: how shall *I* be a wise man when it is only in such a state of raving madness that I am altogether at home?[71]

To achieve this aim, Wagner needed to employ the sort of effects that had previously not existed, since they tested to their very limits existing theories of harmony and instrumentation, and while it makes no sense to dub the composer of *Tristan und Isolde* the father of atonal music, not least because in the work's most rhapsodic moments he largely eschews the chromatic writing and enharmonic procedures traditionally associated with the score, we may undoubtedly describe him as the father of new music, inasmuch as he takes to its furthest extreme the textbook, school-based thinking of the time: in the years around 1860 he may not have been the first or only composer to go down this particular road, but he was certainly the most influential.

The use of chromaticisms and enharmonic modulations had long been established by Wagner's day, even as modest a composer as Schubert taking us to the remote regions of E-double-flat major in the opening movement of his late Piano Sonata in B-flat Major. In order to simplify things for himself and the pianist he turns this E double flat into D-flat and treats the following C double flat as B-flat major, so that he is already back in the tonic by the start of the recapitulation. But this point perfectly illustrates the difference between Schubert and Wagner, for whereas Schubert—only sixteen years older than the composer of *Tristan und Isolde*—explored the major-minor system in the certainty that he could end up back in the home key when the time came, Wagner places almost unbearable strain on the leading notes of this major-minor system: in the spirit of his "endless melody" they are not resolved in the traditional way (or at least only at particularly striking points in the score) but taken in the direction of a new leading-note chord combination which for its part leads to another such new combination, and so on. This procedure is well illustrated by the opening bars of the prelude, with its famous "Tristan" chord (music example 23).

23. The opening bars of the prelude to act 1 of *Tristan und Isolde.*

Scores of books and articles have been written by scholars keen to prove or disprove the theory that this chord can be analyzed in terms of traditional harmony. Or should we treat it, rather, as sui generis?[72] The obvious response is that it depends on the analyst's standpoint. A more substantial answer might be that the "Tristan" chord is just one of a whole range of examples in which Wagner achieves a precarious balance between psychological insight and musical logic. According to the contemporary composer Claus-Steffen Mahnkopf, the score is "a miracle of existential and emotional urgency and formal concision."[73]

In order to prove this point, we do not necessarily need complex examples that make little sense to the layman. Even the monophonic "traurige Weise" (sad tune) that the Shepherd plays on his pipe—nowadays normally an english horn—at the start of the final act speaks for itself (music example 24).[74] Although this passage clearly reworks elements of the traditional *ranz des vaches* that Wagner will have heard on his many walks through the Swiss Alps,[75] it is not intended to provide any sense of naïve local color redolent of folk music. It is possible, of course, to describe the effect of these forty-two bars by recourse to technical categories and analyze it as an attempt to render the natural language of music unrecognizable by means of arbitrary melodic writing, rhythmic and metrical freedom, and harmonic ambiguity. In this context Thomas Grey has noted the combination of the "artificial *naïveté* of the folk-like material with the highly modern, 'sentimental' artifice of the *Tristan* idiom itself."[76] We may also agree with Carl Dahlhaus when he argues that in the spaciousness of the pipe's notes Wagner's "endless melody" becomes conscious of "its archaic origins."[77] As

24. The english horn solo in bars 52–77 of act 3 of *Tristan und Isolde.*

(Engl. Horn auf der Bühne.)

listeners, finally, we may also feel that we are hearing the "traurige Weise" through the ears of the dying Tristan before he himself recognizes in its strains the tragic "primal sound and basic note of his life."[78]

But none of this is of much use in helping us to put into words the underlying gesture and character of the "traurige Weise," a passage admired by Proust, among others, in his magnum opus, for the sounds of the Shepherd's pipe express more than merely the idea of time standing still, the desolation of the landscape, and the unbearable torments of a man incapable of either living or dying, even if they fall short of evoking the "apotheosis of the Void," as Mario Bortolotto has claimed.[79] Rather, the listener is aware of a hidden optimism that characterizes the carefree nature of the Shepherd playing his pipe, a man who sympathizes with Tristan's fate but who is by no means obsessed with death: Tristan will die, but the sounds of the pipe will continue to be heard, embodying Ernst Bloch's "principle of hope" almost more convincingly than Isolde's "Transfiguration." Proust describes this passage as follows:

> Before the great orchestral movement that precedes the return of Isolde, it
> is the work itself that has attracted toward itself the half-forgotten air of a
> shepherd's pipe. And, no doubt, just as the orchestra swells and surges at the
> approach of the ship, when it takes hold of those notes of the pipe, trans-
> forms them, imbues them with its own intoxication, breaks their rhythm,
> clarifies their tonality, accelerates their movement, expands their instru-
> mentation, so no doubt Wagner himself was filled with joy when he discov-

ered in his memory the shepherd's tune, incorporated it in his work, gave it its full wealth of meaning. This joy moreover never forsakes him. In him, however great the melancholy of the poet, it is consoled, transcended.[80]

Of course, the mood remains ambivalent: Wagner allows his fatally wounded hero to become one with nature, which, like him, suffers and longs for redemption. "For we know that the whole creation groaneth and travaileth in pain together until now," we read in St. Paul's Epistle to the Romans (8:22). And despair and hope is interwoven in an altogether unique way here, as Tristan hovers on the cusp of a return to a world marked in turn by suffering and hope.

Wagner admired Dürer's copper engraving *Melencolia I*, a copy of which he owned in the form of a reproduction left by Nietzsche on one of his visits to Tribschen in June 1870. Looking at the print, he was moved to draw a comparison between Dürer and Bach: "Both [were] endowed with this rich and mysterious imagination, dispensing with beauty but achieving sublimity, which is greater than all beauty."[81] It is the ambivalence of the precise detail of the craftsmanship and the fantastical imagination of the content that even today continues to provide a link between Dürer's engraving and Wagner's "traurige Weise," which share the same quality of melancholy. Perhaps we could speak of a mystic fire that lights up the darkness of melancholy and offers us the certainty that in spite of everything the earth will continue to turn on its axis. Only the siren call and its repeated echo (music example 25) allow us to glimpse this. But we do not need to return quite so far back in the past to see links between music and the visual arts, for many of the Harlequin figures that Picasso painted during his Cubist period treat the subject of melancholy with the same ambivalence of precision and ambiguity.

25. Bar 56 of the prelude to act 3 of *Tristan und Isolde*.

One of Wagner's greatest admirers was Richard Strauss, a composer inimitable in the field of illustrative music. But while Strauss's naturalism tended in the direction of materialism, in Wagner's case realism consorts with metaphysics independently of the action and the poem. Thomas Mann knew very well why his enthusiasm for Wagner extended beyond the heroic and rhapsodic side of the composer and embraced little gems like the

CHAPTER 10 [254]

"traurige Weise." By using a clearly and intelligibly articulated melody in which one note follows another with strict precision in order to throw a sharp light on the scene while leaving that situation indescribable, he brought together being and existence, essence and existence in an altogether inspired way, creating a link more succinct than any poet could have done.

Mann's virtual opposite was Martin Heidegger, who in his book on Nietzsche complains about music's increase in power:

> The dominance of music is intentional, bringing with it the dominance of a state of pure emotion: the raging and rutting of the senses, the great convulsion, the blissful horror of melting away in enjoyment, the sinking into the "bottomless sea of harmony," the plunging into a frenzy of passion, and dissolving in pure feeling as a form of redemption: the "experience" as such becomes decisive. The work is no more than a stimulant designed to excite that experience. All that it depicts is intended to create the impression of something superficial, a façade aimed at leaving an impression and creating an effect by churning up the emotions—in short, "theatre."[82]

Aimed exclusively at Wagner, Heidegger's rhetoric anticipates comments made a generation later by the German writer Peter Härtling, who was no less critical of *Tristan und Isolde*:

> The monomaniacal music distracts me and fails to explain the images. It is long gone, overreaching itself, its hideously glorious excesses reminding me yet again that it is open to any interpretation, any mystification, and every form of megalomania. Those people who unthinkingly and unresistingly join forces with it just want to puff themselves up like the diminutive Saxon.[83]

Is this really the case? Of course, this particular Wagner existed—a self-publicist who stage-managed his own life. And equally certainly his music contains floodtides of sound that wash away the difference between singers and instrumentalists and turn the musicians into one vast orchestra. Wagner himself speaks of "the ceaseless play of musical motifs, emerging, unfolding, uniting, severing, blending anew, waxing, waning, battling with each other, at last embracing and well-nigh engulfing one another." And he invites his listeners to reflect that "these motifs have to express a life of the emotions that ranges from the extreme desire for bliss to the most resolute longing for death and therefore requires a harmonic development and an independent motion such as could never be planned with this kind of variety in any purely symphonic piece."[84]

At this point it is less Wagner the sorcerer whom we should be admiring than Wagner the constructor, a figure who once advised his later adversary Eduard Hanslick: "Do not underestimate the power of reflection; the unconsciously created work of art belongs to periods remote from our own: the work of art of the most advanced period of culture can be produced only by a process of conscious creation."[85] Even if Wagner was himself responsible for promoting the myth that he composed intuitively, it is impossible to ignore the element of rigorous planning that went into the composition of *Tristan und Isolde*. Indeed, it is enough to note the consistency with which the composer retained the same number of bars in his orchestral sketch and full score as he had already employed in his very first composition sketch to appreciate this point.[86] And just as everything is in its rightful place here in this initial sketch, the individual scenes likewise attest to a rare degree of "structural cohesion and common ground in terms of their motivic substance."[87] This is confirmed even by a writer like Eric Chafe, who sees Wagner through the eyes of a scholar versed in Bach's music and who has examined in detail the Love Duet in act 2.[88]

Even a writer as critical of Wagner as Adorno might not have dissented from this view, although he would undoubtedly have dismissed as specious and superficial Wagner's motivic writing and grasp of structure when seen against the background of symphonic developments in the Viennese classical tradition. But instead of taking his cue from Beethoven, Brahms, Mahler, and Schoenberg, he might also have considered Verdi, where the problem of symphonic development through lack of any corresponding substance simply does not arise. And whereas Wagner's supporters have little reason to wax enthusiastic about a "symphonic opera,"[89] the champions of "absolute music" have even less need to demand that the symphonic writing of the musical drama should display any sense of inner unity.

Nietzsche will hardly have described *Tristan und Isolde* as "the actual *opus metaphysicum* of all art" simply because he saw the work as the ne plus ultra of "absolute music." Rather, he was attempting to sum up a work whose "insatiable sweet longing for the mysteries of night and death" and "mystery of death in life" are so "distant from life" that it almost inevitably acquires a metaphysical dimension and in doing so raises questions that lie beyond our empirical world. He called this "philosophizing in sound," thereby cultivating his own particular view of the total artwork.[90] But however we choose to define this "total artwork," it remains a fact that one hundred and fifty years after the work's first performance, it is no longer the grandiose idea of finally granting equality to music alongside its sister arts but, at

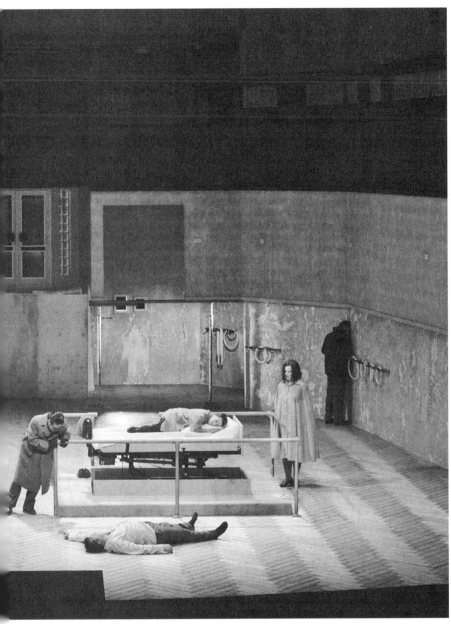

The final scene of Christoph Marthaler's 2005 Bayreuth production of *Tristan und Isolde*. Tristan dies alone in a hospital ward in an image of extreme sobriety, leaving the music alone to provide the emotional charge with which Wagner invested this scene. The question is whether the scene is enhanced or reduced in consequence. (Photograph by courtesy of the Richard Wagner-Stiftung, Bayreuth, Zustiftung Wolfgang Wagner. Photographer: Jochen Quast. WS6Q4045-JQ.)

best, an aesthetic concept that still has to defend itself against the charge of dilettantism.

In terms of the respective weighting of the action and the music, I agree with Wagner on this point. Although he laid so much emphasis on the libretto that he had two thousand copies of it printed before the score was published, he still regarded the music as the truly exceptional aspect of the work—even more so than in the case of the *Ring*. It was above all in the music that he was able to "push himself to the limit" and usher in a revolution in the history of composition. For the philosopher Bryan Magee, the subject of the work—"the fundamentalities of feeling and experiencing and relating"—is, as such, something that is genuinely musical: "So it is now the music that is the drama."[91]

From this point of view, it seems pointless to examine the plot in detail and draw attention to possible inconsistencies or explore alternatives of a philosophical or dramaturgical kind. The subject of Eros and Thanatos is now so all-pervasive in any number of impressive variants in stage plays, poems, and novels that it is little more than an intellectual game to ask, as Slavoj Žižek does, "What if, toward the end of Act I, when Tristan and Isolde discover their love for each other and simultaneously acknowledge the hopelessness of their situation, they were to drink the cup of poison?"[92] Such games can ultimately have only one aim, which is to score points off Wagner. What if—instead—we were to accept the plot of *Tristan und Isolde* as it is and if, above all, we were to examine the *music* from an intellectual standpoint? This music remains so unique that Alban Berg, when confronted by a precocious anti-Wagnerian, retorted: "Yes, you can talk like that—you're not a musician."[93]

All that has to be effortfully distilled from the libretto and plot finds wordless expression in the music. It is the music that guarantees transcendence in a godless *opus metaphysicum* of all art, the music that stands for the unfathomable nature of human experience and the "perpetual spirals of power and pleasure,"[94] the music whose sheer lack of moderation reflects the violation of the rules of self-control, the music that runs the whole gamut of emotion from megalomania to fatal despair, the music that describes the continuing destruction of the personality and yet proclaims the "principle of hope," and the music, finally, that illustrates both the constant fluctuation of all living things and the physical theory of entropy, which describes the heat death caused by the exhaustion of all kinetic energy.

During his years in Bayreuth, Wagner referred to *Tristan und Isolde* as "a mystical pit, giving pleasure to individuals."[95] It would be wrong to criticize him for patting himself on the back in this way, for his remark is related to a work which, unlike most of his other music dramas, requires no ideological correction. We may choose to reject its over-inflated language, or else we may agree with the Wagner director Hans Neuenfels that "most of the writings that seek to interpret Wagner amount to little more than an expression of the fear, shored up by information, that if we allow a composer or poet to get too close to us, we may end up feeling confusion, devastation, even rapture—and yet it must be said in advance that there is no art without conflict and no work of art without an anarchistic impulse."[96]

A Word about Ernst Bloch

Now we advance into ourselves, just as quietly as deeply. The others are agitated and always lead back out again. Tristan and Isolde have fled the bustling day, they do not act. It is our own inmost dreaming, to be found where words and steps no longer hasten. It is we who go along, we obscure ourselves chromatically, we move in a state of yearning and float toward the dream taking shape in the advancing night.[1]

These are sentences of an altogether expressionist power, and they have affected readers—Wagnerians and non-Wagnerians alike—over several generations. And yet these comments are without any musicological or aesthetic relevance to the matter in hand. Rather, their author—Ernst Bloch—avails himself of a series of powerful metaphors. And it is these alone which, according to Umberto Eco, are capable of producing the shock that we need to bring us closer to the work that we are trying to interpret. And, their vagueness notwithstanding, they are not as noncommittal as they may appear at first sight to Bloch's critics. If we were to attempt to apply them to *Parsifal*, *La forza del destino* or *Die Zauberflöte*, we would see how specific they are. First published in 1923, *The Spirit of Utopia* is an early work that deals with music in general. Allotted a "primacy in what is otherwise unsayable,"[2] music, for Bloch, had a particular metaphysical dignity. This seems to suggest an affinity with Schopenhauer, whom Bloch nonetheless criticizes for his "utterly false definition of music as 'Will generally.'" For although such a definition may "apply to Wagner here and there,"³ its regressive tendency denies the utopian element in all great music. Such music is part of a constant journey undertaken "in the darkness of the lived moment," the "docking of our dream boat with ourselves." By dint of its "central magic," music allows us to encounter ourselves, an encounter that is otherwise restricted to a utopian world.⁴ The overheated language of this radical return to basics may be deemed untimely, but it certainly offers little scope for listeners anxious to dismiss Wagner's music as musty or antiquated. Above all, it invites us to listen to this music closely.

Bloch was anything but an uncritical Wagnerian content to luxuriate in the music's sonorities. In his late essay—the austerely titled "Paradoxes and the Pastorale in Wagner's Music"—he adopts a distinctly wayward approach to this music by avoiding all reference to passages that might be described as sentimental or mawkish. Instead, he displays an astonishing knowledge of these scores by throwing light on the paradoxes that they contain and by examining the "seemingly incidental" and "surprising," in other words, passages that "transmit a sense of surprise even after repeated hearings, often a delight in the fragment, and an abundance of tricks, capers and subtleties that go against the ordinary grain."⁵ Bloch is no longer concerned with Wagner's "total artwork" but with "musico-scenic subtleties" and "incidental episodes" that reveal how "a Wagner who had been all too clandestine obtained his freedom."⁶

Bloch is able to cite examples that can teach even experts a thing or two, *Tristan und Isolde* being a particularly fertile field of inquiry in this regard. Here, Bloch claims, it is easier to hear the unusual than the merely appropriate:

> Take Brangäne's song from the tower, buoyantly extended over the rhythmic or even polyrhythmic unit as though separate, along with "that ascent of the violins that passeth all understanding" (T. Mann). In its musical *ekstasis*, this goes against the fear and warning it signifies within the framework of the opera. "Habet acht" is sung from up in the tower, and from this song, of Brangäne's warning, "Lausch, Geliebter" is registered by Isolde in total contradiction to the song itself, though not to its slow, immeasurably long, arching lines, which do everything to suggest arrival.⁷

And Bloch goes on:

> Brangäne perceives the horn fanfare from the nearby hunt merely at its face value as C major jostles with F major, but when Isolde is listening, the horns are replaced by violins, *una corda*. First there is the sound of rustling

leaves and then of a stream trickling in the nocturnal hush: "What did I hear?" Isolde asks, "was that the horns again?"[8]

Friedrich Nietzsche, Thomas Mann, Ernst Bloch, and Marcel Proust: these philosopher-writers and writer-philosophers were all enthusiastic about Wagner. And all of them knew his works—often far better than his detractors.

Wagner in 1868 at the time of *Die Meistersinger von Nürnberg*, seen here in a classic pose in an oil painting by the eminent portraitist Joseph Bernhardt. Wagner was initially reluctant to sit for Bernhardt, whom Ludwig II had commissioned to produce a portrait, preferring to be painted by Franz von Lenbach, but in the event he was pleased with the result. A pupil of Joseph Stieler, Bernhardt depicted Wagner not in some heroic attitude but as a thoughtful, visionary artist. (Photograph by the Nationalarchiv der Richard-Wagner-Stiftung, Bayreuth: Bi 3255.)

CHAPTER ELEVEN

"A magnificent, overcharged, heavy, late art"

DIE MEISTERSINGER VON NÜRNBERG

Between a "grand comic opera" and the theater of ideas—
Marke as Sachs, Tristan as Walther, and Isolde as Eva—Lydia
Goehr's theory of "the opera's secret": Wagner denies his
own idea of reconciliation—The opera in the context of
contemporary events—Art and politics—The affinities
between the opera and contemporary trends in realism—Hans
Sachs: a contradictory figure—Old Nuremberg as a "life
form" and "utopian setting"—Wagner's wish to be hailed as
a "German artist"—*Die Meistersinger von Nürnberg* as "music
about music"—Playing with irony—Deep structure and
Bachian counterpoint—Nietzsche's inspired characterization
of the prelude—Stravinsky's interest in the harmonic
writing of the opera—Folk music in the opera as more than
mere local color—The music as a historicophilosophical
construct—Beckmesser as an anti-Semitic caricature?

In *Tristan und Isolde* Wagner had championed uncontrolled desire in
the face of the terror of rationality, and even when it was required to
tell of the torments of passion, the work was still permeated by rhapsodically frenzied sounds. But after Wagner had "pushed himself to the limit,"
there was now the need for self-restraint. Two months after the first performance of *Tristan und Isolde*, he noted in his *Brown Book*: "Strong is the
magic of him who desires, but stronger is that of him who renounces."[1]
These words are taken from his extended prose draft for *Parsifal*, which
was set down in August 1865. Although Wagner was referring to his final
Bühnenweihfestspiel—literally, a festival drama for consecrating a stage, the
stage in this case being the Bayreuth Festspielhaus—his words can also be

applied to the figure of Hans Sachs, the main character in *Die Meistersinger von Nürnberg*, on which he was likewise working at this time.

Die Meistersinger differs from *Parsifal*, of course, in that in the earlier work there is still scope for a sense of fulfillment in the matter of profane love, although even here it is acceptable only because in the course of the action Walther and Eva learn to control the anarchical element of their passion in favor of the bourgeois ideal of marriage. This inevitably suggests a comedy with a happy ending and reflects the fact that back in Dresden Wagner originally planned to write a "grand comic opera." According to *A Communication to My Friends*, it would have taken the form of a "comic satyr play as a pendant" to the tragedy of *Tannhäuser*,[2] but in the end it turned into a work full of ideas and was labeled simply an "opera." Listeners expecting only entertainment, however, will find themselves sold short, for while it contains moments of situation comedy and genuine wit in addition to what Carl Dahlhaus has termed "an untrustworthy sense of humour,"[3] its principal characters exude not only wit and irony but also a great deal of earnestness.

Tristan und Isolde has not been forgotten but continues to leave its mark on *Die Meistersinger von Nürnberg*, with Sachs as a second Marke. According to the German writer on music Gerd Rienäcker, Walther von Stolzing could also have been called Tristan, while Eva could have been named Isolde: "Both are attempting to escape from a bourgeois existence." But, Rienäcker argues, Walther does not achieve Tristan's greatness, and in the tailor-made Prize Song that leads to his being elected a middle-class mastersinger, he is no more than a "domesticated Tristan."[4] The American philosopher and musicologist Lydia Goehr goes a step further and points out that before he finally agrees to wear the mastersingers' chain of honor, Walther initially rejects the guild's insignia: "No Master! No! I mean to be happy without being a Master!" The "opera's secret," Goehr claims, lies in Walther's final words, for they indicate the way in which Wagner, after superficially promoting the idea of reconciliation in the work, denies that message on a deeper level, the idea of a reconciliation between genius and convention containing "a promise it deliberately does not keep so that it could tell us that the promise was being kept elsewhere."[5]

For Goehr, "elsewhere" is *Tristan und Isolde*. It is not the relatively conventional *Die Meistersinger* that deserves to be hailed as a song in praise of German art but the exceptional *Tristan und Isolde*. This, at least, is how Goehr interprets Wagner's secret message. Wagner disavows the role of Hans Sachs, who is ultimately concerned only with compromise, but identifies, rather, with the iconoclast Walther von Stolzing and his Trial Song ("Fanget an"), which Walther sings in the presence of the mastersingers' guild. For although his singing encounters incomprehension, it reveals more "emancipatory potential" and more "Tristanesque chromaticism" than the more conventional Prize Song to which Sachs later gives his explicit approval.[6]

We do not have to subscribe wholeheartedly to this view to see that it contains much of interest and value by offering an original counterweight to the thoughtlessly two-dimensional interpretations of *Die Meistersinger* that include crude attempts to dismiss the work as nationalistic or even proto-National Socialist. True, Sachs invites his audience to honor "German art" and "German masters" in his final address, and it is no accident that in his very next breath he inveighs against "Romance dross."[7] But his words reflect the spirit of the age: for all their fundamental differences, composers such as Mendelssohn, Schumann, Brahms, and Bruckner were all convinced at this time that the Germans had a historic mission. And although the idea of a German national state no longer had the same appeal between the failed revolutions of 1848–49 and the foundation of the Reich in 1871 as it had done before 1848, it had not yet acquired the craving for status typical of the Wilhelminian age, the dawn of which Wagner viewed with mistrust and even hostility.

Ultimately we must be able to differentiate between Wagner's actual political activities and an operatic project stretching back to his years in Dresden and, therefore, to a time when the question of German national identity bore entirely progressive features. At that date no one would have thought of dismissing the *Deutschlandlied* by the freedom fighter Hoffmann von Fallersleben, with its lines "From the Maas to the Memel and from the Etsch to the Belt," as an example of blatant chauvinism: in 1841 these words reflected a desire on the part of progressive Germans to establish a nation united in its freedom from the self-interested ambitions of the country's particularist rulers.

And while the fate of *Die Meistersinger* is closely bound up with the patronage of the King of Bavaria, its libretto and whole sections of its score were written before Wagner met Ludwig. And yet it is impossible to overlook that throughout the time he was working on the piece, Wagner was keen to forge a link between politics and art. It was as a political adviser that he offered his services to his young admirer, not least in his series of articles *German Art and German Politics*. He also suggested that the king should consider moving his seat of government from Munich to Nuremberg, an idea that Ludwig was far from dismissing out of hand. It was in Nuremberg, Wagner argued, that "my 'Walther' knows he is at home."[8]

"Walther" was the name that Ludwig had chosen for himself at a politically difficult time when he would far rather have been an artistic genius than king and supreme commander of his country's armed forces. But it was as the latter that he was needed most of all by Wagner, a fatherly friend who cast himself in the role of Sachs and who required the backing of a politically and militarily powerful king, a goal he pursued so single-mindedly that in early 1867 he replaced a "pacifist" passage in the libretto of *Die Meistersinger* with some far more bellicose lines. In 1862 Sachs's final address had included the words:

> Welkt manche Sitt' und mancher Brauch,
> zerfällt in Schutt, vergeht in Rauch, —
> Lasst ab vom Kampf!
> nicht Donnerbüchs' noch Pulverdampf
> macht wieder dicht, was nur noch Hauch!
> Ehrt eure deutschen Meister:
> dann bannt ihr gute Geister![9]

[Though many a habit and custom may wither, crumbling into dust and going up in smoke, you should stop fighting! It is not the blunderbuss or gunpowder smoke that will restore substance to what is now a mere breath! Honor your German masters and you will then conjure up kindly spirits.]

In the full score, these lines were redrafted in order to ensure that the dilatory Ludwig would not have an excuse for any defeatist capitulation before the Prussians in the politically confused situation that then existed:

> Habt Acht! Uns dräuen üble Streich':—
> zerfällt erst deutsches Volk und Reich,
> in falscher wälscher Majestät
> kein Fürst bald mehr sein Volk versteht;
> und wälschen Dunst mit wälschem Tand
> sie pflanzen uns in deutsches Land.
> Was deutsch und ächt wüßt' Keiner mehr,
> lebt's nicht in deutscher Meister Ehr'.
> Drum sag' ich euch:
> ehrt eure deutschen Meister,
> dann bannt ihr gute Geister!

[Beware! Evil tricks threaten us: if the German people and empire should one day fall apart under false Romance rule, soon no prince will understand his people any longer; and they will plant empty Romance ideas and Romance dross in our German land. No one would know any more what is German and genuine if the country did not honor its German masters. And so I say to you: honor your German masters and you will then conjure up kindly spirits!]

A comment by Hans von Bülow, who conducted the work's first performance in Munich in 1868, indicates that its "political" dimension is more far-reaching than this opportunistic attack on non-German elements in art and politics: in a letter that he wrote in 1862 to Ferdinand Lassalle, the leader of the Socialist Workers' Party, he described the libretto as an example of "thoroughly healthy realism in a poetically transfigured light."[10]

The term "realism" was used between 1849 and 1871 to refer to a pioneering trend in politics, literature, and art whose principal newspaper in Germany was *Die Grenzboten*, which boasted contributors of the eminence of Gottfried Keller, Gustav Freytag, Theodor Fontane, and Berthold Auerbach. The central aim of these German-speaking realists was a critique of romanticism as an expression of the German mind and of German art whose flower had faded, its critics stigmatizing it as lachrymose, otherworldly, and stylistically overwrought. In general, the shift from romanticism to realism marks a significant change in the history of ideas, for whereas romantic writers had restricted their discourse to poetry, lyricism, religion, and the individual, the realists took as their starting point philosophy, epic, drama, and the concept of the folk, or nation. And politics, too, was an inevitable part of this debate, the failure of the bourgeois revolutions of 1848–49 having necessitated a radical shift in emphasis and, with it, a repositioning involving new goals for the whole of society.

Instead of whining about the failure to achieve political progress through revolution and instead of pursuing unattainable ideals, the realists who wrote for *Die Grenzboten* argued in favor of a positive approach to the challenges of the day and a determination to place their bourgeois lives in the service of universal social progress. In the field of literature and art, realism aspired to what it termed "real idealism"—Fontane defined this as a "reflection of all real life [. . .] in the element of art."[11] This aim was not to be achieved, however, through any naturalistic imitation of life but should take the form of the "prospective possibility of a harmonious order that could be recognized in real life."[12] Such prospects did not preclude backward glances at moments of happiness in Germany's past, for these examples of the transfiguring standpoint of "real idealism" demonstrated the feats of which the *Volksgeist*—the "spirit of the nation," a vague category much valued by the nineteenth century—was capable. It was no accident that Wagner himself described his figure of Hans Sachs as "the last manifestation of the artistically creative spirit of the nation."[13] Within the context of a role laid out along "real idealistic" lines, Sachs is admirably successful in resolving the contradictions that arise and in presenting the communal lives of his beloved Nurembergers as altogether exemplary on no fewer than three different levels: on those of love, art, and politics.

Thanks to Sachs's wisdom, fateful passion, whose claims to be treated as an absolute have no place in this society, can be channeled in a "healthier" direction. An emotion that initially smacked of dangerous passion and irrational instinct and that Eva had summed up in the words "It was obligation, compulsion" is transformed into the ideal of marital love as the shoemaker-poet prevents the hotheaded Walther from eloping with Eva and thereby losing his chance as an "impoverished"[14] knight of marrying into the house of the well-to-do patrician Veit Pogner and laying the foundations for a middle-class career. In his future role, we may take Wagner's premise a stage further and imagine Walther encouraging art and artists in the same way that his father-in-law once did. After all, Pogner—with Eva's approval—gives his daughter's hand in marriage not to the richest man in Nuremberg but to the one with the greatest appreciation of art. As a widower, Sachs has enough common sense to know not to throw his hat into the ring. We shall not go far wrong in assuming that in future he will content himself with the role of godfather to the children of Walther and Eva, while finding satisfaction in his art above all else.

Within the work itself, Sachs's actions are designed to promote a "German art" of a kind very dear to Wagner. This involves, first and foremost, the reconciliation of art and life and, second, the reconciliation of old and new. It is not only with ideas such as these that Wagner aligned himself with current thinking in "real idealism" but also with his whole decision to tackle the subject of *Die Meistersinger* at all. In a study that he published in 1849 on the "socialist elements" in Goethe's *Wilhelm Meister*, Ferdinand Gregorovius—later to make a name for himself as a historian—examined the art of the mastersingers and saw in it a historical model for a "sense of a social community" needed in the present day to mitigate class divisions.[15]

Wagner does not ridicule mastersong as such but only its "narrow-minded, petty bourgeois" aspects. Above all, the "marker" Sixtus Beckmesser has negative connotations thanks to his "absurd pedantry, with its insistence on prosody and the rules of the *Tabulatur*."[16] Hans Sachs, who was ultimately reconciled with Beckmesser in Joachim Herz's 1960 production of the work in Leipzig,[17] is not only a mastersinger himself, but also does everything in his power to persuade a reluctant Walther von Stolzing to accept the title of mastersinger, a title that Walther had aspired to acquiring only in order to win the hand of Eva, not because of its artistic implications. It is no accident that Wagner summed up his intentions in a program note on the overture to the opera: "The love song is heard at the same time as the mastersongs: pedantry and poetry are reconciled."[18]

By the end of the opera, both pedantry and poetry have been forced to compromise. On the one hand, the mastersingers have been obliged to see that the townspeople no longer accept Beckmesser, who is a pedant of the worst possible kind. Instead, they welcome Walther into their ranks, even though his grasp of the rules cannot keep pace with his poetry. And on the other hand, Walther has demonstrated with his Prize Song that he can control his artistic temperament in the service of the tradition that the mastersingers have long been cultivating. After his initial, distinctly rash attempt to become a mastersinger without any knowledge of the guild's rules, his second attempt—made with the help of his generous mentor Hans Sachs—produces a song that with some effort on our part may be said to satisfy the prescribed rules. In Sachs's view Walther's concession to tradition is not only artistically meaningful but also socially responsible: the "bar form" that he has taught Walther is presented as a symbol of bourgeois family life, the poetic and musical model of two *Stollens* followed by an *Abgesang* mirroring the three-member family of two parents and a child.

Sachs, too, appears in a new light at the end. The shoemaker-poet initially played a particularly base trick on his adversary Beckmesser and even precipitated the nighttime riot that left the town clerk badly beaten by his fellow Nurembergers. Moreover, in his Cobbling Song he had vented his frustration at the drudgery of his work as a shoemaker, and in his "Wahn" Monologue he had expressed his doubts about the power of reason in general. But in the final scene of the opera he is able to cast aside the features of an outsider that have been discernible in him until this point in the work. Fully at peace with himself, he will henceforth be an ideal champion of a traditional, self-confident "German art" and at the same time a worthy representative of Nuremberg as an "intellectual and spiritual form of life," to quote the phrase coined by Thomas Mann in the context of his own birthplace of Lübeck. But in the final version of the libretto, with its concession to contemporary political developments, Sachs also and above all appears as a propagandist promoting a sense of national resentment, causing the nationalist element that in the earlier version of the libretto had been relatively harmless to become "profoundly problematical."[19] Is this Sachs, too, a suitable advocate for Nuremberg's artistic scene?

In more general terms, is Sachs really such a "wonderful figure" and "truly a democratic personality," as the German director Harry Kupfer sees him?[20] On closer inspection, Sachs's character turns out to be decidedly ambivalent. Indeed, the semantic change undergone by individual elements in the plot takes place with a speed more appropriate to a comedy than a philosophical work. As the opera's librettist, Wagner inevitably found himself in what for him was an unusual situation, for in his previous works, which had been geared to myth and legend, the motivation of the individual stages in the action, while not unimportant, was nonetheless secondary inasmuch as in myth and legend essential matters evolve in the way they do because this is precisely how they are fated to unfold, while the characters, far from controlling their fates, tend, rather, to be driven by destiny. But a "realistic" subject also requires a logical approach to every single detail. Wagner does his best here and presents us with a plot within which many examples of "Wahn" (folly and illusion) are purged of their irrational element. And yet this approach works only on a superficial level, for in the background questions are raised similar to those that Lydia Goehr poses in the article mentioned earlier. Can a composer who in the rest of the work wrestles endlessly with the problem of "Wahn" really identify with the positive ending of *Die Meistersinger*?

Joachim Herz is only one of many writers to point out that *Die Meistersinger* discusses "art" above all else.[21] In advancing this argument, he can of course appeal to Wagner himself, for, as we have already observed, the composer singled out the reconciliation between pedantry and poetry as integral to the work's happy ending. But can we—as Lydia Goehr rightly asks—regard Walther's Prize Song and Sachs's demand that we "honor" our "German masters" as the be-all and end-all of the work's underlying message? Does this appeal to such mastery not seem distinctly innocuous against the background of Wagner's other works, every single one of which—*Der fliegende Holländer, Tannhäuser, Lohengrin*, the *Ring, Tristan und Isolde*, and, later, *Parsifal*—reveals a mythic depth conspicuously absent here?

German literary scholars have sought to see this alleged "innocuousness" in a rather more relative light. Walter Jens, for example, praises "Sachs's poetological reflections as a valid and exemplary pointer to a synthesis of 'art' and 'nature' in the spirit of those timeless rhetorical traditions dating back to a classical writer like Horace."[22] Conversely, Hans Mayer empha-sizes the contradictory elements in the makeup of the shoemaker-poet and points out that if we ignore the affirmative ending, Sachs is far from resolv-ing the conflict between craft and art but leads a "romantic double life" in the manner of E. T. A. Hoffmann, with "on the one hand the crude materi-alism of the empirical and on the other the idealism of the surreal."[23] Peter Wapnewski sees Hans Sachs as a "skeptical Schopenhauerian sage" and even speaks of him in the same breath as Baudelaire and Stefan George.[24] Dieter Borchmeyer, on the other hand, argues that the "splendour of the final scene is doubtless overshadowed by a sense of resignation. Utopian-ism and pessimism, always intermeshed in Wagner's view of the world, overlap on this occasion, too."[25] A glance at Sachs's antithesis, Beckmesser, even calls to mind the German absurdist poet Christian Morgenstern: Ernst Bloch hails the linguistic temerities of Beckmesser's garbled Prize Song as "an early example of Dadaism."[26] Many stage directors have fol-lowed Bloch's lead and treated the Nuremberg town clerk as an avant-garde artist. And yet it is clear from the history of comedy as a genre that such interpretations need to be seen within a wider picture, for even in Shakespeare's *A Midsummer Night's Dream* Bottom the weaver garbles his text when playing the part of Pyramus.[27]

To sum up: literary scholars may have shed light on a number of origi-nal aspects of the opera, but their endeavors also resemble a Dance around the Golden Calf aimed at exploring Wagner's genius from every conceivable angle. Instead, it might make more sense to concentrate on essentials in the form of Wagner's genius as a man of the theater, for with the exception of the longueurs in act I Wagner demonstrates an exceptional feel for a plot whose construction would be to the credit of an experienced writer of com-edies. Avoiding all shallowness, he shows great skill in balancing the conflict-ing aims of poetry and situation comedy, pathos and persiflage. Hugo von Hofmannsthal is only one of many writers to admire the inspired decision to treat the "genuine, complete world" of Nuremberg as the decisive element in the plot—a decisiveness comparable to that of the Vienna of Maria Theresa in *Der Rosenkavalier*.[28] Scarcely less inspired is the idea of concentrating the action on the St. John's Day celebrations and drawing on the fund of ecclesi-astical rituals and secular customs associated with that particular festival.

Of course, we can argue over the extent to which Wagner's Nuremberg is "authentic," or merely a "utopian setting" for his imaginary view of a mu-nicipal community.[29] What mattered for Wagner as a theater practitioner, however, was the repositioning of the work's horizon, the vast expanse of myth, which is crucial in the case of his other stage works, being restricted in time and place to a particular historical moment that does not represent an interchangeable allegory for certain social ideals but speaks, as it were, for itself. According to Hofmannsthal, "even a picturesque detail like the Beckmesser-Hanslick equation is only possible, after all, because the institution of the 'marker' was already inherent in the given old setting."[30]

This particular strength is also offset, of course, by a specific weakness— if we choose to regard it as such: in terms of the work's interpretation and staging, *Die Meistersinger von Nürnberg* is not as elastic as the *Ring* or *Tristan und Isolde*. Rather, there are really only two interpretive approaches that are possible here, the first of which involves treating the work as an example of the "real idealism" outlined above. This does not necessarily mean stressing its nationalist features but it requires us to accept the opera as Wagner's profession of faith in a life-affirming art meaningfully embedded in real-life society. This is a legitimate approach as it respects the work's obvious intentions and also the ideals that Wagner developed in 1849 in his two essays *Art and Revolution* and *The Artwork of the Future*.

In order to explore the second possibility, we need to examine the wider picture. By nature, Wagner was no Gottfried Keller, whose "real idealism" was admirably suited to the age in which he lived. Although the original version of Keller's novel *Der grüne Heinrich* ends on a note of pessimism, his short story *Hadlaub* takes as its theme a youthfully impetuous *Minnesänger* who as if of his own accord matures into a master of his art before renouncing that art in favor of marriage and a belief in shared middle-class values and public-spiritedness. It is clear from this that Wagner's true picture of the world means that he constantly undercuts his own optimistic conception of *Die Meistersinger*; with the exception of his rebellious revolutionary period he always doubted that life and art could be balanced. And Sachs's technical understanding of musical form and of a congruent social order has little to do with his own artistic output.

That Alfred Lorenz filled several volumes analyzing Wagner's scores in an attempt to demonstrate how the "secret of Wagner's form" could be found in the formal structures of the "quintessentially German" bar does not mean that this form—which Sachs commends to his "pupil" Walther as the first and last word in composition—will bring us any closer to Wagner's own understanding of form, with its manifold multiple perspectives. Even the merger of old and new, which Wagner raises to the level of an aesthetic principle in *Die Meistersinger*, may add a number of original elements and provide some stirring music, notably in the overture. But it would be presumptuous to claim that such a maxim can be applied to the whole of the opera, still less to the rest of Wagner's oeuvre by analogy with similar interpretations of Brahms, Max Reger, and Schoenberg.

What, ultimately, are we to make of Nuremberg as a "utopian place with which Wagner hoped to show how a new community might arise through an art tied to the people and emerging naturally from it, an art, moreover, that has no need of politics"?[31] We may choose to follow Udo Bermbach's lead and interpret *Die Meistersinger* in this way, but at the same time we are bound to question whether the opera can provide a "concrete model" for this blueprint.[32] It would also be good to know if Wagner felt that a "state free from politics,"[33] as he imagined Nuremberg to have been in the sixteenth century, was possible or even desirable in Ludwig II's day. For today's audiences, at least, Wagner's Nuremberg proves on closer inspection to be altogether unpalatable: Hans Rudolf Vaget may be guilty of exaggeration, but he is certainly not wrong when he describes Wagner's Nuremberg as a "repressive community ever ready to exclude unwanted elements," a comment made above all with reference to Beckmesser.[34] Warren Darcy suggests that such contradictions are inherent in the clinically pure but ultimately unadventurous C major in the final act of the opera, a claim that is likewise not altogether groundless: this key is said to express "the repression of the individual will for the good of society and the expulsion from that purified society of all undesirable elements."[35] It is no wonder, then, that Wagner's Nuremberg, painted in the colors of the "real idealism" of the middle of the nineteenth century, was obliged to exclude all the real power structures and social conflicts of the sixteenth century, to say nothing of its obsession with the power of money.

As soon as we seek to fathom the underlying message of the opera, rather than glossing it over, we shall stumble upon inconsistencies. Such inconsistencies are not comparable to those built into the *Ring* and *Tristan und Isolde*, for example, where they are grounded in the unfathomability of myth, but rest on the fact that in writing *Die Meistersinger* Wagner was eager not only to play-act but also to hold forth on the subject of public life. And a glance at the work's genesis indicates that his thinking was not always consistent. As we have already observed, he jotted down the first prose draft in 1845 as a "satyr play" designed as a pendant to *Tannhäuser* but at that date did not elaborate the draft because what he called the "unnaturalness of public life" meant that "irony" was the only effective form of comedy. But he was unwilling to commit himself to this irony lest he lost the "power" of his "comedic instinct."[36] That he turned instead to the "myth of the people" and entered the world of *Lohengrin* and its hero's longing to aspire to "the highest sphere"[37] hardly suggests that Wagner was thinking in terms of realpolitik at this time.

When Wagner returned to the subject of *Die Meistersinger* in 1861, it was — as he repeatedly announced — in the hope not least of finding the sort of quick success that was eluding him with *Tristan und Isolde*, already dismissed as "unperformable." His claim that the decision to take up the work again was inspired by Titian's *Assunta* in Venice cannot be supported by what we know about the opera's genesis but is evidently another of his conscious attempts to surround it with an aura of mystery. As Bernhard Schubert has observed, the claim is nonetheless revealing: Wagner's "*Assunta* experience represents the fruits of his reading; it is like a legend, a new theatrical role for the great actor and, as such, no different from the theatrical costumes that he wore at this time, including his beret and artist's jacket."[38]

In this particular case, such an act of self-mystification was particularly necessary as Wagner had no wish to give the impression that he had abandoned his whole mythological baggage simply out of opportunism. And we should not be treading on the composer's toes or offending his amour propre by noting that he planned to complete the score of *Die Meistersinger* as quickly as he could. According to the German musicologist Jörg Linnenbrügger, the sketches for the first act reveal "that not every recourse to existing motivic and thematic material relating to individual characters or specific elements in the plot can be explained by reference to the rules of Wagner's 'leitmotif technique,'" but they reflect the fact that the composer was trying to be as economical as possible.[39] At all events, he abandoned the approach that he had adopted with *Tristan und Isolde* and instead used "compositional building blocks" notated on individual pages and correspondingly easy to find and assemble.

Only during the final stage of the work's genesis did Wagner's relations with Ludwig II acquire any real significance. Nothing would have made the king happier than to live in an artists' colony with Wagner, as a single detail may illustrate:

According to his diary Ludwig should have spent May 22 [1866] opening the new session of parliament, but instead he slipped away from Johann von Lutz, a member of the supreme court who was looking after him at Schloss Berg, and rode via Polling and Peißenberg to Peiting, where he caught the mail coach to Biessenhofen, then took the scheduled train to Lindau, crossing Lake Constance by steamboat and disembarking at Romanshorn, from where he traveled to Zurich and thence by special train to Lucerne, where, dressed as Walther von Stolzing in a blue Byronic cape and a large hat with ostrich feathers, he arrived in the early afternoon and, to Wagner's infinite surprise, congratulated the "God-sent" composer on his birthday.[40]

Wagner could do nothing with a king who was tired of ruling and afraid of conflict, and so he kept reminding Ludwig of his responsibility to the world of pan-German politics, advising him first to side with Prussia, then with Austria, concerned, as he was, to keep his king's hands from slipping from the reins of state. It was against this background—and not least in response to Cosima's nagging—that Wagner incorporated into Sachs's closing speech the monitory lines that we quoted earlier: "Beware! Evil tricks threaten us: if the German people and empire should one day fall apart under false Romance rule, soon no prince will understand his people any longer." When seen against the background of Nuremberg's position in the sixteenth century, such a warning to beware of succumbing to Romance influences may well have made sense, but it is unclear what a ruler like Ludwig II was supposed to make of this advice, not least because Wagner, following the lead of a writer like Friedrich Schiller, has his Sachs hail "holy German art" as the one thing that might survive as an example of German greatness.

By the end of a long latent period when Wagner's views on *Die Meistersinger* kept changing, only one thing remains clear from an ideological standpoint, namely, that he himself wanted to be acclaimed as a "German artist" and as the guardian of "holy German art." This ultimately seems a trifle unjust toward a work that is about far more than crude nationalism but contains a degree of culture of which many of the opera's detractors, versed in ideological criticism, can only dream. But a glance at the tributes that Wagner received at the end of the first performance, which he watched from the royal box in Munich's National Theater, and an examination of the caricatures that appeared in the local and national press at this time suggest that at least in June 1868 it was Wagner himself as an artist who created far more of a sensation than any vague national or nationalist message that the work may be deemed to have contained.

In short, there is not exactly an abundance of alternatives to staging *Die Meistersinger* as a "real idealistic" fairy tale, leaving it hard for directors to find an overriding idea that could bring together all the conflicting and contradictory strands in the plot.[41] It seems more sensible, therefore, to examine the character of the individual scenes and present them as an open-ended sequence in the hope that the ingenuity of the action and the genius of the music will sustain the piece and its audiences over a period of five and a half hours. The guiding principle might be an ironic view of the work that avoids satire and slapstick but emphasizes the human limitations and limited humanity of all the characters in the spirit of a good comedy and at the same time makes clear the distance that exists—or should exist—between us and Wagner's vague concept of a community.

This would effectively be a play within a play. In 1845 Wagner was still unable to accept irony as a specific form of comedy, and it was not until twenty years later that he was prepared to take this step, a risk he was willing to undertake not least because with *Tristan und Isolde* he had just written a work that could hardly be less ironic and less concerned with the whole idea of distance. Instead, he approached *Die Meistersinger* with very different eyes, as "sentiment" became "resentment" in the sense of "feeling something again afterward." As he himself put it, he had "pushed himself to the limit" in *Tristan und Isolde* and was no longer interested in exploring a world of total obsession, preferring to examine the varied and shifting emotional states of his various characters. And by presenting his beloved Sachs as a man in all his contradictions, he was able to maintain a greater sense of distance than had been the case in *Der fliegende Holländer, Tannhäuser, Lohengrin*, and *Tristan und Isolde*.

Wagner was still in his fifties when he worked on the score of *Die Meistersinger*, so it is difficult to describe this as a late piece. At the same time, however, there is a clear tendency to abandon the worm's-eye view of subjective experience and replace it with the bird's-eye view that allows the observer to see the whole picture. This trend was continued in *Götterdämmerung* and *Parsifal*, in each case in a very specific way: the final evening of the *Ring* is marked by the attempt to keep control of a semantic structure that had by now grown overcomplicated until the coup de grâce was inevitable, while in *Parsifal* Wagner's principal concern was the renunciation of individual instinct in favor of a higher wisdom, hence Wagner's comment to Cosima that in the case of *Parsifal* it had "not been possible to avoid a certain restriction of feeling; this does not mean that it is churchlike in tone, he says, indeed there is even a divine wildness in it, but such affecting emotions as in *Tristan* or even the *Nibelungen* would be entirely out of place." And he concluded by informing his wife: "You will see—diminished sevenths were just not possible!"[42]

According to traditional theories on musical rhetoric, the diminished seventh was used, by preference, for states of emotional effusiveness, as in the first two notes of Marke's line "Sieh' ihn dort, den Treu'sten aller Treuen" (See him there, the truest of the true). Wagner's reference to this interval positively invites us to examine all of his works in terms of their specific musical semantics. In the case of *Die Meistersinger*, this aim cannot be achieved by making the musicological point that the advanced chromatic writing of *Tristan und Isolde* has been subverted in favor of pseudo-archaic diatonic writing in keeping with the historical subject matter. Rather, Wagner writes "music about music" on a grand scale, and this also involves juggling with various styles, not with a copy of those styles.

"Music about music" existed long before *Die Meistersinger*. On the very highest level we may be reminded of Beethoven's late string quartets, works much admired by Wagner in which the older composer offers a nostalgic but defiant summation of his own "heroic" phase. On a more concrete level, there are the many scenes that emerge naturally from the action of the work and that have always been typical of opera. Among such scenes, which are responsible for creating a sense of local color and involve songs and music making in general, are the serenades in Mozart's operas, the trumpet fanfare at Don Fernando's arrival in *Fidelio* and the Huntsmen's Chorus and Bridesmaids' Chorus in *Der Freischütz*, to name only works drawn from Wagner's favorite repertory. He himself continued to work in this same tradition, most notably with Senta's Ballad, Wolfram's Ode to the Evening Star, the Bridal Chorus from *Lohengrin*, Siegfried's Forging Songs, and the song of the Young Sailor and the "traurige Weise" in *Tristan und Isolde*.

But all of this now acquires a new quality, for whereas the foregoing examples—with the exception of Senta's Ballad—play little part in driving the action forward, *Die Meistersinger* may be regarded from start to finish as an opera about music. That it features an ongoing discussion about the ideological element of "German art" tends to obscure that it is German *music* that is, as it were, the work's invisible leading lady. The number of occasions when music is presented onstage speaks for itself, beginning with the congregation singing a chorale in St. Katharine's Church ("Da zu dir der Heiland kam"), followed later in the act by the Apprentices' round ("Das Blumenkränzlein aus Seiden fein") and culminating at the end of the act with Walther's Trial Song ("Fanget an"). Indeed, the action of the first act as a whole is largely laid out along the lines of a discussion about music and, more especially, the rules and customs of the mastersingers' guild in Nuremberg.

The second act is no different: the Apprentices begin by singing their song about St. John's Day. Later, Sachs performs his Cobbling Song ("Als

Eva aus dem Paradies") and Beckmesser sings his serenade ("Den Tag seh'
ich erscheinen"), while the Night Watchman blows his horn three times in
the course of the act. The final act includes not only a trial run of Walther's
Prize Song ("Morgenlich leuchtend") but also a final tableau that resembles
a music festival matinee, starting with the entrance of the guilds, continuing with the "Wach' auf" chorus, and ending with the two songs with which
Beckmesser and Walther seek to win Eva's hand in marriage ("Morgen ich
leuchte" and "Morgenlich leuchtend"). It scarcely needs adding that the
action in general revolves about music and its social function. In short,
around a third of the opera is taken up with scenes in which the plot requires singing in the true sense of the term (rather than simply as a setting
of a prescribed text). A further third is reserved for aspects of the plot that
bear some relation to the subject of music. And only the remaining third is
a setting of words that are not primarily concerned with music.

I am uncertain whether Wagner was already aware, while writing out the
libretto, that the preponderant role of music in the story would have such
far-reaching consequences for the score, as such an approach required him
to demonstrate entirely new qualities as a composer. Normally a composer
is required to find the right "tone" for particular elements in the plot and
for specific atmospheric situations. Here the composer relies on his feeling for what those situations express. But if he has to find the right tone
for what is effectively pre-existent music, then his range of expression is
limited, for the tone is a function of the message that the existing music is
intended to convey.

The song contest in act 2 of *Tannhäuser* already gives us a foretaste of
this problem, but no more than that, for this scene is not designed to characterize the art of the *Minnesänger* but only to present us with different
views of love. And for this, Wagner uses a modern musical language, the
only exception being the harp accompaniment indicative of each of the
contributions to the contest. The situation is very different in the case of
Die Meistersinger, for although Walther's Trial Song and Prize Song are both
about love, the main focus of interest is the actual technique of songwrit-
ing—not the what, but the how. Against this background Wagner could
not avoid engaging with the mastersingers' traditional type of singing not
just on the level of plot and text but also through the medium of music. To
be specific: what should the music of the Nuremberg mastersingers sound
like? As we have already observed, Wagner initially intended to write the
opera as a satyr play that would have provided a counterpart to *Tannhäuser*
but then shied away from this idea on account of the degree of irony that

would have been necessary. Presumably his original concept involved a certain mockery of mastersinging.

But instead of indulging in idle speculations on this point, we would do better to see what Wagner actually achieved after 1862—namely, irony of a superior kind that includes the odd sideswipe at some of the quirks of mastersong but which is generally at pains to reconcile the old and the new. In short, irony is only rarely synonymous with mockery. One such occasion is the scene in which David instructs Walther in the rules and "tones" of mastersinging using musical gestures of exceptional vividness or when Kothner declaims the *Leges Tabulaturae*, ending each of its clauses with a grotesquely old-fashioned coloratura flourish. In general, however, irony means simply rising above the matter in hand and writing music about music.

At this point it must have become clear to Wagner that it was not enough to play off the old against the new or craftsmanship against genius. To have done so would not only have contradicted his view of history, according to which "masters" or "artists" occupied an important position, it would also have overtaxed him as a composer because it would have meant always working with negations, resulting in an opera which, at least when seen against the aesthetic background of the nineteenth century, was neither logical nor coherent. From a musical point of view, his idea of reconciling the old and the new and of creating a harmonious balance between pedantry and poetry in *Die Meistersinger* was a necessary precondition for his ability to write music about music.

Wagner's brilliance as a composer lay in his ability to take his decisions on two different levels at once: that of a comedy and that of a drama of ideas. On the level of the comedy, the local color of mastersong offered him a chance to poke fun at its eccentricities in a particularly vivid and even graphic way, while at the same time exposing the failing of uncreative pomposity in the figure of the town clerk. And on the level of the play of ideas, Wagner chose as his starting point a type of "early" music that he regarded as above criticism on account of its timeless, masterly character and that he believed was particularly well suited to reconciling the old and the new: Bachian counterpoint.

The composer Peter Cornelius highlighted these parallels at the time of the first performance of *Die Meistersinger*:

> Just as the theme or themes of a fugue by Bach contain within them the seed of the whole, so here, too, the introduction, exposition, and the whole of the musical picture are no more than a constant unfolding of the wealth

contained within them, while the ever more intense return of the main motifs goes hand in hand with the manner in which the main poetic idea builds
to a triumphant climax.[43]

During his Bayreuth period, Wagner too repeatedly forged a link between
the music of Bach and his score of *Die Meistersinger*. At one of the family's
regular soirées in December 1878, for example, Josef Rubinstein played the
Prelude in F-sharp Minor from part 1 of *The Well-Tempered Clavier*, a piece
not notable for any great harmonic subtleties. It reminded the Wagners
of *Die Meistersinger* and prompted the composer to refer to the assembly
of the mastersingers as a "continuation of Bach."[44] Only a few days later
Wagner explained fugue technique to his children using the example of *The
Well-Tempered Clavier*, then turned to the overture to *Die Meistersinger* as an
instance of "applied Bach."[45] And in June 1882 he worked through Cantata
18, *Gleichwie der Regen und Schnee vom Himmel fällt*, with Hermann Levi, the
work striking him as "rather mastersingerish, clumsy."[46] Presumably he
was referring to the unison introduction and *falsobordone* quotations from
the Lutheran liturgy.[47] It is also possible that Wagner knew the Second
Brandenburg Concerto, the first subject of which recalls a motif in *Die
Meistersinger* often referred to by German writers on music as the "Motif of
burgher mastery" (music example 26).[48]

26. The opening bars of the first movement of Bach's Second Brandenburg Concerto,
transposed from the original F major to C major, and, beneath them, the
opening bars of the overture to *Die Meistersinger von Nürnberg*.

It is not enough, however, to draw attention to such details, which are in
any case merely atmospheric. Nor shall we come any closer to understanding the work by agreeing with Cornelius's pointedly worded claim that the
"musical form" of the work is a "fugue that has become an opera."[49] Rather,
Bach and counterpoint symbolize Wagner's aim of investing the work with

a very specific deep structure. This aim is not new in Wagner's output but springs from his desire to create a musical drama that does more than merely juxtapose individual moments designed to please the listener in that it constantly allows a hidden world of meaning to be glimpsed beneath the surface: the hidden world of myth. Rudimentary examples of this may be read into Wagner's three romantic operas, but it is only in the *Ring* and in *Tristan und Isolde* than the aim emerges with any real clarity. In the *Ring*, alliterative verse, leitmotif technique, and orchestral melody—to name only the principal elements—ensure that all its events are bathed in an aura that makes them seem as if they have always been there, whereas in *Tristan und Isolde* it is above all Wagner's "endless melody" and the motivic density of the quasi-symphonic writing that promote the idea of a fabric of altogether impenetrable mythic complexity. Here the actual plot seeks nothing more nor less than to decode this archetypal text. (The "traurige Weise" is the best example of this, impinging on the present as if from an age long past.)

In short, the problem that we are discussing is not unique to *Die Meistersinger*. But it appears here in a different guise, the tragic events of the earlier works having become something essentially comic, while archaic myth has been replaced by the myth of the German nation, German art, and, specifically, German music. This demands a specific deep structure characterized by "counterpoint"—in this case the term has a philosophical as well as a technical dimension to it. During the second half of the nineteenth century it came to be used in Germany as a shorthand way of referring to virtues believed to be typically German, including "a sense of community in the face of individualism and subjectivism," "tradition in contradistinction to the merely fashionable," "the spiritual as opposed to the purely material," "a profound impression rather than a superficial impact," "transcendence instead of metaphysical decline," and "persistence and strength of will rather than quick solutions."[50] In *Opera and Drama* Wagner had adopted a highly critical view of counterpoint and dismissed medieval vocal polyphony as an aberration for rejecting the original naïveté of Christian hymnology, but his view of history had changed with his increasing admiration of Bach, with the result that by the 1860s counterpoint and Bach were synonymous with the ostensible German virtues sketched out above—at least to the extent that these virtues were to be distinguished from "Romance dross."

This, then, was the background against which Nietzsche, in a passage headed "Peoples and Fatherlands," could write so perceptively about the contrapuntal procedures used by Wagner in his overture to *Die Meistersinger von Nürnberg*:

> It is magnificent, overcharged, heavy, late art that has the pride of presupposing two centuries of music as still living, if it is to be understood: it is to the credit of the Germans that such pride did not miscalculate. What flavors and forces, what seasons and climes are not mixed here! It strikes us now as archaic, now as strange, tart, and too young, it is just as capricious as it is pompous-traditional, it is not infrequently saucy, still more often coarse and rude—it has fire and courage and at the same time the loose dun skin of fruit that ripens too late. [. . .] Altogether, no beauty, no south, nothing of southern and subtle brightness of the sky, nothing of gracefulness, no dance, scarcely any will to logic; even a certain clumsiness that is actually stressed, as if the artist wished to say to us, "that is part of my intention"; [. . .] something German in the best and worst senses of the word, something manifold, formless, and inexhaustible in a German way; a certain German powerfulness and overfulness of the soul.[51]

It is entirely possible to describe the overture to *Die Meistersinger* in terms other than these, but it is surely not possible to write any better than this, for Nietzsche has observed a dialectic that Wagner enthusiasts are barely able to see. Wagner does not write "beautiful" music in the spirit of traditional aesthetics, but nor does he transfigure the older style. Rather, his art consists in placing the old in an affectionately ironic light. The music appears to be telling us that although it may no longer be possible to write like this, there is no need to look down on the contrapuntal strength and assurance of the older composers or on their naïve way of throwing together heterogeneous themes in the manner of a popular quodlibet. It is significant in this context that Heinrich Schenker, whose commitment to solid "German" counterpoint had a self-confessed ethical component, described the combination of themes at the end of the overture as "nonsense,"[52] indicating that he was unable to appreciate Wagner's use of irony and delectable sleight of hand.

But it is very much these elements that constitute Wagner's modernity, a modernity that increased music's linguistic power in a very different way from the one found in *Tristan und Isolde*. Now the provocation lies not in the breakdown of the usual musical forms or the undermining of traditional harmony but in the introduction of what we might call doubletalk: music looks over its own shoulder, commenting on itself and reflecting on its own particular design. It is inconceivable that Wagner would have added a programmatic explanation to one of his earlier works similar to the one he provided for *Die Meistersinger*: "The love song is heard at the same time as the mastersongs: pedantry and poetry are reconciled." This is the first time that listeners had been confronted by a technical element that they previously did not need to know about since they were concentrating entirely on the myth. Indeed, they were not even supposed to know about it at all. True, we are still dealing with a myth, but on this occasion it is the myth of German art that can be approached only through the medium of artistic understanding. Although it is not yet the case with Wagner that the technique is the message, it is undoubtedly true that in writing *Die Meistersinger* he had struck out in a direction that was to lead directly to the twentieth century: to Richard Strauss, Stravinsky, and far beyond.

In a piano scherzo dating from 1902, the young Stravinsky reflected explicitly on the "characteristic harmony" of the overture to *Die Meistersinger*,[53] metaphorically pointing the way to the aesthetics of the opera, a work that plays constantly with all manner of styles and types of writing. This aspect of the opera has nothing to do with historicism or eclecticism but is a direct result of its subject matter. In *Die Meistersinger*, Wagner aimed to depict the musical life of the nation in as many facets as possible and in that way draw a distinction between a genuinely German art of the theater and the hothouse blooms of French and Italian opera, which he regarded as the epitome of a corrupt society. In consequence, the chorale sung by the congregation in St. Katharine's Church, the assembly of the mastersingers in the same building, the stylistically authentic appearance of the Night Watchman and the "Wach' auf" chorus inspired by a poem by the historical figure of Hans Sachs are anything but picturesque set pieces but instead are historically significant examples of the life of the German people. The songs that drive the action forward and that include Walther's Trial Song and Prize Song and Sachs's Cobbling Song likewise reflect the richness of German song as sung by the people—in this case, Walther, too, can be regarded as a man of the people because he is no product of an aristocratic education but a naturally talented artist who has learned his songs "from finches and titmice" and who ultimately succeeds in reconciling his art with the rules of middle-class mastersong. This does not mean, however, that in writing *Die Meistersinger*, Wagner concentrated on a "middle style," by which I mean an account of middle-class normality. Instead, the score strikes out in a number of different directions. The riot scene at the end of act 2, for example, not only functions as a dramaturgically skillfully constructed finale in which masters, journeymen, and apprentices come to blows in Nuremberg's nighttime alleyways but also recalls the *turba* scenes in Bach's Passions, scenes which, familiar to Wagner, feature a rabble-rousing crowd. In *Die Meistersinger*, too, the good people of Nuremberg, provoked by a relatively trivial incident, steadily become an aggressive mob. (This analogy remains true even though the writing in the riot scene is entirely untypical of Bach.)

As with the overture, so the earthiness of this scene can be seen as "applied Bach," while we may also identify two examples of "applied Beethoven" as a lyrical counterpoint to it. The first such example is the prelude to act 3, the opening of which recalls Beethoven's late style and, in particular, the imitative opening of the C-sharp Minor String Quartet, op. 131. Even so, this is a reminiscence that is "felt," not one we can demonstrate by means of specific details. The second example is the quintet, beginning with Eva's cantilena "Selig, wie die Sonne meines Glückes lacht" (Blissful as the sun of my happiness laughs). This is a number that Wagner would surely not have written if he had not been familiar with the quartet "Mir ist so wunderbar" from *Fidelio*, which served not just as a technical model but also as an inspiration for the idealistic and, hence, "German" attempt to bring together the disparate feelings of the individual characters and express the absolute nature of love beyond all individual feelings, thus coming closer to the oft-cited notion of "absolute" music. And, last but not least, we also find an instance of "applied Wagner" in the form of a striking quotation from *Tristan und Isolde* in Sachs's scene with Eva in act 3, where the famous "Tristan" chord is contrapuntally structured.

It can hardly be fortuitous that in Bach, Beethoven, and himself, Wagner was quoting three composers who according to his own historicophilosophical construct had brought to the history of music a dynamism found in the case of no other musician. Although he was no nationalist, Nietzsche hit the nail on the head when he observed that if music was ever again to be what it had been in the remote Dionysian past, then "it would have to rediscover itself through Bach, Beethoven, and Wagner and free itself from the service of civilization."[54] The opposite of a culture of "civilization" is music with a deep structure to it, a demand that the score of *Die Meistersinger* is able to meet with its contrapuntal interweaving of historical, social, compositional, and ideological contexts. As a work of music, *Die Meistersinger* amounts to far more than those of its elements that draw upon folk music and caricature—and certainly more than any straightforwardly ideological features. In order to judge the work properly, we need a certain appreciation of its unique multilayered qualities, which are apparent not only in its earthier moments but also in those passages which, with their filigree textures, are more easily overlooked.

This brings us to the notion of a "satyr play" and, in particular, the idea of Beckmesser as a character designed to provoke us. For a time Wagner planned to call his town clerk Veit Hanslich and in that way to insult his bête noire, Eduard Hanslick, the music critic of the *Neue Freie Presse*. For Wagner, Hanslick was the prototypical critic, narrow-minded, limited in his outlook, capable of judging a work only from a purely formal standpoint, skeptical toward the new, and constitutionally incapable of demonstrating even the most basic creativity. As their marker, familiar with the rules of their guild, Beckmesser enjoys the respect of his fellow mastersingers, but he cuts a ridiculous figure with the townsfolk when competing with Walther in his attempt to win Eva's hand in marriage. In the opera's final scene he regales his listeners with a grotesquely garbled version of a song that he stole from Sachs's workshop in the belief that it had been written by the shoemaker-poet himself.

Beckmesser is also seen as a figure of fun in act 2, when the serenade that he sings at night in the hope of impressing Eva creates a pitiful impression as a result of its lack of orchestral support, its vocally uningratiating staccato passages, wayward coloratura writing, and incorrect textual emphases. According to Egon Voss, Wagner is not only poking fun at the critic's artistic impotence but also caricaturing a traditional operatic aria.[55] But is there also a third aspect here, namely, an anti-Jewish element? After all, Cosima Wagner's diary contains the following entry for March 1870 in connection with the Viennese premiere of *Die Meistersinger*:

> Among other things the J[ews] are spreading a story that "Beckmesser's Song" is an old Jewish song which R. was trying to ridicule. In consequence, some hissing in the second act and calls of "We don't want to hear any more," but complete victory for the *Germans*. R. says, "That is something none of our fine historians of culture notice: that things have reached the stage of Jews' daring to say in the imperial theater, "We do not want this."[56]

Wagner's comment could hardly be more anti-Semitic, and yet it ignores the reproach that he had been attempting to parody a Jewish song. Nor is there a single suggestion of anti-Semitism in any of his other remarks on the role of Beckmesser.

There are good reasons for this silence. It is conceivable that when Wagner wrote Beckmesser's garbled serenade, he could hear in his mind's

Die Meistersinger von Nürnberg in Wieland Wagner's 1956 Bayreuth production. Wagner's grandson was keen to avoid any reference to the historical city of Nuremberg in this final tableau, as he wanted to rid the work of its associations with the recent past, when the city had been the scene of National Socialist party rallies and *Die Meistersinger* had been performed in the local opera house as a part of those official celebrations. Intentionally or otherwise, Wieland's production still features totalitarian images in the guise of the chorus treated as a well-regimented crowd. (Photograph courtesy of the Nationalarchiv der Richard-Wagner-Stiftung, Bayreuth: N 3605.)

ear the sort of synagogue chanting that he roundly dismisses in his essay "Jews in Music." It is also conceivable that he wanted to expose Beckmesser's handling of God's gift of music as foreign and, hence, implicitly Jewish. And yet it would have made no sense in the context of the plot of the opera to have made Beckmesser—highly regarded in Nuremberg through his office as town clerk—a Jew.[57] Still less would such an approach have validated Wagner's claim that his message was universally valid. We would be guilty of limiting the role of Beckmesser by seeking to reduce it to anti-Semitic rancor. As a criticaster and confirmed bachelor, Beckmesser is part of a long tradition of comic characters who ultimately come a cropper and in the process forfeit our sympathy.

Some of Beckmesser's fellow mastersingers fare no better. Kothner the baker, for example, offers an extraordinarily silly critique of Walther's Trial Song: "And he even leapt up from his chair!" And the Night Watchman, too, is subjected to Wagner's ridicule, the final note of his song "Hört ihr Leut," F, being followed by a dissonant G-flat on his horn, implying a particularly inept official. Of course, this foray into the world of atonality is not only intended to caricature the Night Watchman but also aims to render the elements of reality and ghostly apparition inextricably linked in a way entirely appropriate to an eventful Midsummer's Eve in Nuremberg. This is merely one tiny example of Wagner's use of multiple perspectives throughout the whole of the score, starting with the overture, which, as we have already indicated, offers no mixture of festive and comic elements free from any sense of conflict but uses eccentrically weighty counterpoint at times of particular parody,[58] without itself descending into parody in the process.

If we examine the remaining parts of the *Ring* and the whole of *Parsifal* from this point of view, we shall surely be obliged to concede that *Die Meistersinger* already contains signs of a "late" work. The idea of a lack of distance characteristic of long sections of *Tristan und Isolde* gives way to the impression of an artist standing over his subject and reflecting on it, while remaining entangled with it. It is the contradiction of old age to be always taking one's leave while not wanting to do so at all.

A Word about Berthold Auerbach

By the time the writer Berthold Auerbach stopped off in Dresden in 1846 for a series of public readings from his works, his *Schwarzwälder Dorfgeschichten* (Village Tales from the Black Forest) of three years earlier had already been translated into English, Italian, and Swedish. Auerbach was a relatively well-known figure at this time, and Wagner got on well with a man who was only a year older than he was: "Within the last few days I've become very friendly with *Auerbach*," Wagner wrote to Alwine Frommann, reader to Princess Augusta of Prussia and responsible for drawing the composer's attention to the writer's *Village Tales*. "He read us his latest short story & I regaled him with *Tannhäuser*, the first time he'd heard it. He's an excellent poet, & what pleasure he takes in himself & his poetry!"[1]

A member of a liberal student organization, Auerbach had been imprisoned for two months in the fortress of Hohenasperg, accused of activities hostile to the state, and must have seemed a sympathetic figure to Wagner, whose own outlook was becoming increasingly revolutionary at this time. "If it hadn't been for my child, I would undoubtedly have fallen on the barricades in Vienna," Auerbach wrote.[2] It would be good to know if in 1846 the two men had discussed Auerbach's 1837 progressive novel *Spinoza*, which turns on its head the motif of Kundry's kiss that we later find in *Parsifal*: Ahasuerus is released from his curse by kissing the sleeping philosopher who, repudiated by Jews but revered by Christians, ushers in a new age marked by a new kind of truth.[3] But we can be certain that in the light of the success of Auerbach's *Village Tales*, Wagner will have been thinking about his own draft for *Die Meistersinger* from the previous year—perhaps he even declaimed the text to Auerbach. The two men, after all, were united by their interest in popular themes in the spirit of the "real idealism" of the period.

They remained in contact for a number of years. When Auerbach visited Wagner in Zurich in August 1852, the composer read to him from the poem of the *Ring*, on which he was working at that time. Auerbach seems to have responded so positively that seven years later Wagner wrote to one of his friends in Dresden, Anton Pusinelli, asking him to lend Auerbach a copy of the limited private edition of the poem as a matter of some urgency. He had heard that Auerbach, now an even more successful writer and friendly with Gottfried Keller and Gustav Freytag, among others, was living just outside Dresden. Wagner hoped that Auerbach might prove a useful literary advocate.

It remains unclear whether Auerbach ever received a copy of the poem, but his failure to follow up his initial interest rankled with Wagner to such an extent that in 1869, when publishing his open letter, "Some Explanations Concerning 'Jews in Music,'" he described the unnamed but nonetheless readily identifiable Auerbach as "a very gifted, truly talented, and intellectual writer of Jewish origin who seems almost to have come to embody the most distinctive characteristics of the life of the German folk" but who continued to demonstrate typically Jewish character flaws. Privately he had spoken "with warm appreciation and clear understanding" about the poems of *Tristan und Isolde* and the *Ring* but had not dared to express his views in public.[4] As a result the Wagners adopted a far cooler response to Auerbach's work as a writer: in July 1869, for example, they described Keller's short stories as "much more significant" than Auerbach's.[5] And only a few months later we find another entry in Cosima Wagner's diary: "An article by Berthold Auerbach (no such genius he!) about woods is printed in the newspaper; R. says he found it unreadable on account of its affected closeness to Nature: 'These fellows are a real nuisance' (the Jews)."[6]

As a passionate and in many ways courageous pioneer of Jewish emancipation, Auerbach was shocked by the republication of "Jews in Music" in 1869. Even though his name does not appear in it, he seriously toyed with the idea of penning a public riposte, as he did in *Die Gegenwart* in 1876 in response to an anti-Semitic article by Brahms's friend Theodor Billroth. Although he decided in the end to refrain from making any public statement on the matter, he followed Wagner's rising star in international circles with undiluted displeasure. Months before his death he thought of calling on the Jews in Berlin, where he was then living, and asking them to boycott the *Ring* that Angelo Neumann staged in the city's Victoria Theater in May 1881. Among the unpublished manuscripts found among his papers at the time of his death was one headed "Richard Wagner and the Self-Respect of the Jews."[7]

In August 1875 Adolph von Menzel attended the rehearsals for *Siegfried* in Bayreuth and produced a number of pencil sketches depicting Wagner sitting at a production desk next to the prompt box. On his desk is a copy of the score lit by a paraffin lamp with a green shade. Reproduced here is a replica of one of these drawings with an original vignette that Menzel presumably gave as a present to Wagner, dating it "Berlin, May 5, 1876." (Photograph courtesy of the Nationalarchiv der Richard-Wagner-Stiftung, Bayreuth: RP 612.)

"They're hurrying on toward their end, though they think they will last for ever"

THE ART OF THE *RING*—SEEN FROM THE END

Resumption of work on the *Ring* and the resultant stylistic
break — Taking over musical idioms from *Tristan und Isolde* and
Die Meistersinger von Nürnberg — A compositional comparison
of the love between Siegmund and Sieglinde with that
between Siegfried and Brünnhilde — The new *Ring* tutti and
the increasing complexity of the writing — The omnipresence
of the leitmotifs ensuring that the plot of *Götterdämmerung*
also has a mythological dimension — Compositional scope
for greater liberties in spite of all the constraints — Hagen as
villain and victim — On the genealogy of the topos of "Nibelung
loyalty" — The scene between Hagen and Alberich: "Wagner
at his best"? — Hagen's cynicism — On the musical design of a
background of menace — A shattering moment: Brünnhilde's
cry of "Deceit" — The end of *Götterdämmerung*: shipwreck as
a launch? — Wagner's claim that Wotan's guilt is treated as in
a "peasant's trial" — The different endings of the *Ring* — The
interpretations of Nietzsche, Hans Mayer, Adorno, and Udo
Bermbach — The role of the redemption motif at the end
of the *Ring* — The redemption motif intertwined with the
Siegfried and Valhalla motifs — The end of *Götterdämmerung*
as a reflection of Wagner's espousal of nationalism and the
new Reich? — The real utopia of the *Ring* heralding *Parsifal*,
the misgivings of Nietzsche and others notwithstanding

Twelve years were to pass before Wagner returned to the *Ring* on a
permanent, rather than a sporadic, basis, following the interruption
caused by his decision to write *Tristan und Isolde* and *Die Meistersinger*

von Nürnberg. Few writers on Wagner have foregone the opportunity to comment on the stylistic break between those sections of the *Ring* that predate the break and those that were written later. Indeed, even the most innocent listener registers the greater "weight" of the second half of *Siegfried* and the whole of *Götterdämmerung* when compared with the freshness of *Das Rheingold*, the verve of *Die Walküre*, and the color of the early scenes of *Siegfried*. Wagner had no choice but to take over into his compositional arsenal certain subtleties of the harmonic writing in *Tristan und Isolde* and the sumptuous instrumentation of *Die Meistersinger*. And we also encounter regular assonances.[1] To take an example: when Siegfried reaches the summit of Brünnhilde's rock and sings the words "Wie mild erzitternd mich zagen er reizt" (Gently trembling it lures me on, fainthearted that I am) we hear the chord of the diminished seventh with a suspended major seventh over a pedal point on F. Exactly the same device, this time starting out from E, is found in the third act of *Tristan und Isolde* in the context of Tristan's delirious fantasy at the words "Ach Isolde! Wie schön bist du!" (Ah, Isolde, how beautiful you are). The same gesture ensures that on both occasions both listener and character are painfully drawn into this sound world only to withdraw again afterward.

Wagner's recourse to the full-bodied, full-blooded sounds of *Tristan und Isolde* reflects the increasing pressure now placed on the plot. Although Siegfried and Brünnhilde may be united in jubilant love at the end of the music drama that bears his name, this can hardly blind us to the events that are to follow, for, as Loge says of the gods at the end of *Das Rheingold*, Siegfried and Brünnhilde, too, are hurrying on toward their end.

A comparison between the music that Wagner wrote for the love scene between Siegmund and Sieglinde and that which he composed for Siegfried and Brünnhilde helps to shed light on the difference between them: the earlier scene exudes the feeling of an outpouring of sensuality and private happiness, whereas the later scene suggests a public display of almost religious ecstasy lacking in any real warmth. As the German writer on music Gregor Herzfeld has noted, "The sensual eroticism inherent in music is here transformed into a sensual sublimity that seeks to overwhelm us."[2] In the opening act of *Die Walküre* the music reflects a passion opposed to all social constraints, whereas its function in the final act of *Siegfried* is to depict a love already doomed to be destroyed by those very same social forces. Both Sieglinde and Brünnhilde express an all-or-nothing mentality, but the union of Siegmund and Sieglinde is followed by new life, whereas the "hour" in which Brünnhilde's world is lit by "Siegfried's star" gives way to a "night of annihilation."

The figure of Siegfried likewise changes dramatically as the youthful and carefree fairy-tale hero fearlessly thrusting aside all his enemies and once hailed as the freest of the free is progressively turned into a tragic hero driven to his death in the tradition of classical tragedy, incurring guilt through no fault of his own. Although only the last part of the *Ring* deals with Siegfried's death—*Siegfried's Death* was the original title of *Götterdämmerung*—the final scene of *Siegfried* already brings with it the peripeteia of Siegfried's tragedy, for the hero who forces his way through the fire to Brünnhilde's rock seems to be drawn by unseen strings or at the very least to be driven by a higher calling.

With the strikingly symbolic union of the ideal couple of Siegfried and Brünnhilde, the action of the *Ring* allows itself an idealistic flight of fancy entirely alien to the spirit of Attic tragedy, making a sudden fall all the more inevitable and precipitous. It is significant that on completing the *Ring*, Wagner told Cosima: "Siegfried ought to have turned into Parsifal and redeemed Wotan, he should have come upon Wotan (instead of Amfortas) in the course of his wanderings—but there was no antecedent for it, and so it would have to remain as it was."[3] This would imply that the kiss with which Siegfried wakes Brünnhilde is not unrelated to the kiss with which Kundry awakens desire in Parsifal, bringing disaster in its wake: "Strong is the magic of him who desires, but stronger is that of him who renounces."[4]

Shaw was one of the first writers to note that while he was working on the score of *Götterdämmerung*, Wagner had already "accepted the failure of Siegfried and the triumph of the Wotan-Loki-Alberic trinity as a fact" and conceived a "new protagonist" in Parsifal: "The change in the conception of the Deliverer could hardly be more complete."[5]

First of all, however, existing society has to confront its own state of bankruptcy: until it has become clear that even the most hallowed and sublime love is bound to have what Wagner himself called an "annihilating" effect on a hopelessly corrupt community,[6] it is not yet time for Parsifal to step up to his new position as ruler of the kingdom of the Grail.

Is it any wonder that it was so difficult for Wagner to find his way back into the *Ring* and that it was particularly hard for him to deal with the transition from the euphoric ritual at the end of *Siegfried* to the mood of apocalyptic doom that imbues the whole of *Götterdämmerung*? He also had to portray the still ebullient Siegfried as the plaything of fate, without depriving his hero of all his remaining dignity. And then there was the character of Hagen, who had to be depicted with greater detail and clarity than an agent of evil is normally worth. There is a difference between dealing with such opposites as a poet and doing so as a composer who may have to spend days on end wrestling with only a handful of bars while he gets under the skin of his protagonists.

It is surely not necessary to dismiss the Siegfried of *Götterdämmerung* as an "idiot," as Slavoj Žižek has done.[7] Nor do we need to take the fashionable view of him as a guileless fool with a hobbyhorse meant to represent Grane. Least of all is it necessary to have him staggering across the stage as a slovenly dropout. And yet it is undoubtedly true that he is only a shadow of his former self, so that it is hardly surprising to find that by his own admission Wagner—already with half an eye on the Siegfried of *Götterdämmerung*—felt "no pleasure" at the prospect of having to work on the instrumentation of the jubilant final duet in *Siegfried*.[8]

When he started work on *Götterdämmerung* only shortly afterward, Wagner complained at having to ensure that "every note" needed to "convey the end of the world,"[9] but this should not be invested with undue importance, for it may merely be an expression of the fifty-six-year-old composer's general disgruntlement at his lot as a music dramatist and head of a family. It is nonetheless significant that he had done everything in his power to procrastinate and to defer the herculean task of completing the *Ring*.

The projects that had provided him with a degree of distraction between *Die Meistersinger* and his resumption of work on the *Ring* speak for themselves: they include a theme headed "Romeo & Juliet" (WWV 98), a series of prose sketches for a play about Martin Luther (WWV 99), and a prose draft titled simply "Comedy" (WWV 100) featuring characters such as a theater prompter Barnabas Kühlewind, a "dissolute student and debutant actor" by the name of Kaspar Schreiblich, and a "heroic actor" called Napoleon Baldachin.

And last but not least, there was the dramatic shift in the whole design of the *Ring* project. In September 1850 Wagner had still been pursuing the idea of presenting *Siegfried's Death* to a hand-picked audience in a "rough-hewn theater made of planks and beams."[10] After three exemplary performances, to which the audience would have been admitted free of charge, the theater would have been torn down. Since then, there had been numerous plans for an architecturally imposing festival theater, initially in Munich, later in Bayreuth. And Wagner had barely started work on the score of *Götterdämmerung* when Emil Heckel founded the first Wagner Society in Mannheim. It was no accident that this event took place so soon after the founding of the second German Reich. In keeping with a motto that was then doing the rounds, the society may be said—not without a certain malice—to have been established under the banner "Singers, gymnasts, and riflemen all support the Reich."[11]

By the time Wagner resumed work on the *Ring*, he was indeed already well on his way to denying his past as an exiled political outlaw and becoming a "state musician," as Karl Marx mockingly dismissed him at the time of the first Bayreuth Festival.[12] How can this new "statesman-like" role be reconciled with the scenario of doom and destruction that is to be found in *Götterdämmerung*? (We shall have more to say on this point at the end of the present chapter.)

We have already quoted Thomas Mann's answer to this question: Wagner, he wrote, was "a man wholly concerned with the work in hand, a man devoted absolutely to power, the world and success."[13] But in view of the contradictions that we have already noted, it is entirely possible that Wagner would not have found the mental reserves needed to complete the *Ring* if, like some tempestuously youthful Siegfried, he had not already laid down the compositional outlines of the work sixteen years earlier, an aim he achieved by means of the leitmotif technique that governs the cycle from start to finish and which time and again came to the composer's rescue.

Even before his lengthy interruption, Wagner had already transferred whole passages from *Das Rheingold* to *Siegfried* in the sense of what Tobias Janz has described as a "collage of quotations."[14] But whereas he proceeded along such mechanical lines in the prelude to act 1 of *Siegfried* that he was able to write out the orchestral sketch in ink without the need for a preliminary sketch in pencil, his whole approach to the older material became positively playful once he resumed work on the score in 1869. Among other things, he took advantage of the experience he had gleaned in dealing with the brass choir while working on *Tristan und Isolde* and *Die Meistersinger*: whereas the "great *Ring* tutti" is used almost exclusively as a "special sonority" in *Das Rheingold* and *Die Walküre*,[15] it becomes an almost permanent feature of the later sections of the *Ring*, where it appears in all its luxuriant splendor.

Although being at the mercy of his leitmotifs until the bitter end meant that Wagner's leeway as a composer was limited, the *Ring* was in any case conceived in such a way that by the end its actors increasingly forfeit their freedom to act and can operate only within certain limits. Is it a disadvantage that the composer, too, has to bow to these constraints or at least groans beneath the task of having to find the right music for the increasingly complex web of past, present, and future?

In one of his posthumously published fragments on *Götterdämmerung*, Nietzsche noted: "In many a sequence of harmonies in Wagner's music I find something agreeably resistant, like turning a key in a complicated lock."[16] Here Wagner is held up as a master not of primary invention but of the brilliant organization of nonsimultaneous procedures as if they were simultaneous. The score of *Götterdämmerung* contains barely a note that is not derived from the existing store of leitmotifs. In this way it reflects reminiscence and presentiment within one and the selfsame process.

This sometimes makes the writing so complex that as listeners we cannot always follow all the details. Wagner would undoubtedly have condoned this, for it means we must entrust ourselves completely to the emotional impression. And an impenetrable structure turns abruptly into blindly sensual sounds—a highly modern aspect of Wagner's music. Which of us can hear in the somber transitional passage after the episode known as Hagen's Watch in the first act of *Götterdämmerung* that the following motifs are overlaid and for the most part interwoven: the motifs associated with anguish, the dominance of gold, the Nibelung's hatred, Hagen, the ring, Siegfried's horn, Siegfried himself, the treaties carved into Wotan's spear, Brünnhilde, and the curse?

But the omnipresence of the leitmotifs ensures that the mythic dimension of the *Ring* is preserved, even though the plot seems superficially to have been reduced to an intrigue dealing with human concerns. Although Wotan no longer appears in person, he continues to play an important role as what Carl Dahlhaus terms "a phantom of the imagination by the grace of the music."[17] And, as Bernhard Benz has observed, "the action of the heroic tragedy that is visible onstage collapses beneath the weight of the myth about the gods, which controls and guides it on a subliminal level."[18] In short, there is no reason to try to turn *Götterdämmerung* back into what it once was when it was still called *Siegfried's Death*: an ordinary heroic opera with a plot geared to a logical goal. Instead, the music ensures that the different layers of time flow into one another as they do in myth: the whole manifests itself in the moment, and the moment is refracted in the mirror of the whole. Such art is unique in the whole history of musical theater—and this is true whether we regard the result as authentic or merely as self-serving.

In completing the *Ring*, Wagner was at the mercy of specific constraints that were both determined by the history of the work's creation and at the same time inherent in the work itself. All the more impressive, therefore, are the freedoms that he was able to create for himself and the new impulses that he was still able to give the work. The best example of this is his treatment of the character of Hagen, who appears for the first time in *Götterdämmerung*, with the result that the composer had a relatively free hand in fleshing him out. We have already quoted Wagner's complaint to his wife in July 1871, at a time when he was just starting work on act 2: "Where am I to find my Hagen, with his echoing, bragging voice?"[19] As always, he had half an eye on the theatrical impact of his characters from the very outset. Hagen was to be full of himself, without ever appearing to be a mere peasant. After all, he wields a spear—albeit not Wotan's spear—as a token of his rule. And it is he who pulls the strings, at least until he is dragged down into the depths of the Rhine by the Rhinedaughters as a result of his uncontrollable desire to gain possession of the ring.

Wagner reveals exceptional mastery in using music to invest Hagen with features of nonidentity and exposing him as both a villain and a victim, an authentic individual and cunning intriguer or cynical seducer. In his monologue, Hagen's Watch, we meet the antihero alone in the Gibichung Hall—Siegfried and Gunther have left in high spirits with the intention of using trickery to bring Brünnhilde back to Gunther's court as the Gibichung ruler's future wife. Ignobly born, he is deeply unhappy by nature and strikes a powerful note in his monologue:

> Ihr freien Söhne,
> frohe Gesellen,
> segelt nur lustig dahin!
> Dünkt er euch niedrig,
> ihr dient ihm doch—
> des Niblungen Sohn'.

[You freeborn sons, carefree companions, merrily sail on your way!
Though you think him lowly, you'll serve him yet, the Nibelung's son.]

But the music shows us another Hagen, a Hagen who, according to Dieter Schickling, represents a "ravaged human race without parents."[20] By his own admission, his blood "curdles" within him, "stubborn and cold," while his monologue is accompanied by dull and hesitant chords that are difficult to make any logical sense of in terms of their meter and rhythm. His vocal line, too, attests to a lack of direction, becoming more coherent only when he seizes control of Siegfried's motif and recalls the "doughty hero" who is to bring his "own bride" to Gunther's court and, in doing so, bring him closer to Alberich's ring. The reference to Siegfried as a "doughty hero" is, of course, contemptuous.

But is this also true of his appropriation of Siegfried's motif? After all, this is not the only leitmotif heard during Hagen's Watch, where the orchestral melody features a veritable floodtide of such motifs. As with so many other passages in the *Ring*, it resembles a dreamlike, speeded-up traversal of the whole action of the cycle. Hagen, it is true, has his own motif in the form of a falling diminished fifth, but this is perceived more as a harmonic foundation to this episode than as a musical figure in its own right, not least because it is often harnessed together with a variant of Siegfried's horn motif that "mutilates the original in the most dreadful way imaginable" (music example 27).[21]

In other words, it is only superficially that Hagen is able to play the part of the intriguer hoping ultimately to triumph over everyone and everything. On a deeper level he longs to be a second Siegfried. When the real Siegfried loses all knowledge of his origins as a result of the potion that Gutrune serves him, Hagen is the only person at the Gibichung court who knows about the dark tale of the Nibelung's ring and, more especially, about his father, Alberich, who once forged this ring and then lost it to Wotan. Two scenes later, Alberich recalls that he brought up his only son "to feel stubborn hatred: now he'll avenge me and win the ring in contempt of the Wälsung and Wotan."

Hagen is indeed a second Siegfried to the extent that both men ultimately perish. Both, moreover, think that they are in control of their actions, whereas they are merely figures caught up in mythic events and, as such, driven by those events. Hagen's cry of "To me, though, he'll bring the ring"—Wagner wanted the final *g* on *Ring* to be articulated almost like a *k*—is far from being a triumphant outburst, for, as Gerd Rienäcker observes, "the coveted object is perverted in the most appalling way imaginable, collapsed into a shrill dissonance before being resolved in a gesture that sinks down plaintively."[22]

The difference between Siegfried and Hagen is not so much moral as existential, Siegfried being the naïve individual who thinks positively but is impervious to any deeper understanding, while Hagen has been conditioned by his father into clinging to his historical knowledge about the

27. Bars 870–77 of act I of *Götterdämmerung* ("Hagen's Watch"), with
Hagen's motif indicated in the bass line of the first bar.

baleful conditions that obtain in a world ultimately concerned only with
who will acquire the accursed ring. This knowledge also includes the Norns'
primeval presentiment that this world is coming to an end, with the result
that even Hagen's scheming at the Gibichung court will ultimately merely
contribute to its downfall.

In consequence, Alberich must browbeat Hagen into winning back
the ring. In his Stuttgart production of *Götterdämmerung* in 2000, Peter
Konwitschny brought out this aspect of the plot in a particularly impressive way: when Alberich encounters his son asleep, it is the troubled
sleep of one who most of all would like to throw off the burden of history
and forget his obligation to avenge his father. But the old man becomes

increasingly agitated as he reminds his son of his duty, his role suggesting a
"delirious dream" on Hagen's part: "The tempo and intonation of what he
says, together with the orchestral comment on the primeval events that he
evokes, obey a logic that catches us off guard, linking together the damaged
and barely recognizable motifs by means of a collage effect."[23]

Hagen is not confident that his mission will succeed and is reluctant, therefore, to swear allegiance to his father. In German, the term
Nibelungentreue was first used in the early years of the twentieth century by
the then chancellor, Bernhard von Bülow, who was referring, in fact, not
to Wagner's ignoble Nibelungs, Alberich and Hagen, but to the heroes of
the original *Lay of the Nibelungs*. Even so, it is not inappropriate to speak of
Hagen's "Nibelung loyalty" to his father in the baleful sense that it was to acquire at the time of the National Socialists. And there is a certain piquancy
to Slavoj Žižek's description of the oneiric encounter between Hagen and
Alberich as "the mother of all Wagnerian scenes" and as "Wagner at his
best,"[24] and to turn Hagen—and arguably Wagner, too—into a "protofascist"[25] in keeping with the SS watchword, "Our honor is loyalty."

It would, of course, be wrong to equate Wagner with one of his characters. Nor should we overlook the fact that Žižek has singled out an ideological factor that is found almost everywhere in nationalist circles in the
nineteenth and twentieth centuries and that can look back on a tradition
lasting thousands of years: even Tacitus was already hailing kinship, loyalty,
honor, and the worship of women as Germanic virtues, while implicitly cas-
tigating the moral decline of his own Roman *civitas*. The *Sachsenspiegel*—a
compendium of medieval laws compiled between 1220 and 1235—likewise
invests qualities such as honor and loyalty with an importance tantamount
to that of the law itself. And Wagner's contemporary, Julius Langbehn,
whose *Rembrandt as Educator* was a cult book of the German youth movement, wrote that "noble is he whose right hand never breaks the oath of
loyalty that it has sworn."[26]

Wagner substantially altered the character of Hagen as he discovered
him in his Old Icelandic and Middle High German sources. In the *Lay of
the Nibelungs*, for example, Hagen is a hero in spite of his murderous deeds,
whereas the *Ring* casts him first and foremost in the role of a traitor. Even
so, Wagner avoids stereotypes and presents the character as a multifaceted
figure capable of springing a number of surprises. In his scene with Alberich,
for instance, Hagen seems to vacillate and to be almost introverted, and yet
only a few moments later he develops a hyperactive streak, summoning his
vassals with a grimly resolute call to arms: "Woe! Woe! To arms! To arms!

To arms throughout the land! Goodly weapons! Sturdy weapons, sharp for the fray! Danger is here! Danger! Woe! Woe!"

This is one of the most remarkable passages in the whole of the *Ring*, for what kind of "danger" can be involved in inviting the vassals to the wedding of Gunther and Brünnhilde and instructing them to offer up sacrifices to the gods? They are to bring down a wild boar for Froh, slay a goat for Donner, and slaughter sheep for Fricka "so that she gives a goodly marriage." That Hagen adds an elaborate Baroque ornament to the word "gives" makes it clear beyond a doubt that he feels only mockery and contempt for the ceremonies that are about to take place. And this is no accident, for although Wagner's stage directions indicate that altar stones to Wotan, Fricka, and Donner are located close to the Gibichung Hall, no one seriously believes in the power of the gods any longer, least of all Hagen himself. But how does he justify his dramatic shouts of "Woe" and "To arms"? And why does he want to make his vassals drunk? For Lawrence Kramer, this is "the one moment in the opera when Hagen 'lets himself go' expressively."[27] In order to assure himself of his men's loyalty and provide them with a fix in the form of a mixture of power fantasies, grim joviality, and alcohol, he briefly adopts their own coarse lifestyle, with its close connection between alarmism and crude jokes.

Wagner's ability to use music, too, to create a sense of menace here is remarkable. Until now, Hagen has largely been a background figure and a loner, a gloomy, lowering figure on the edges of the action, but now, in the third scene of act 2, he and his vassals represent brute force as such. Symptomatic of this development is the writing for the steerhorns, which in Bayreuth were simple natural instruments until the 1940s. Rumor has it that American GIs then carried them off as trophies. Hagen plays the note C on his steerhorn, while those of his vassals reply to his right and left with a D and a D-flat, producing a sinister sound in keeping with the macabre and aggressive jollity of the chorus. No less eerie is this episode as a whole. It is dominated by the brass, whose harshness is broken from time to time by nervous strings resembling nothing so much as will-o'-the-wisps, while the harmonic writing—quite apart from the dissonance in the steerhorns—is so implacably brutal that the major-key consonance of the repellent boisterousness of the vassals' response to Hagen's "jokes" is bound to seem even more shocking.

The same is true of the crass tribute paid shortly afterward by the chorus of vassals to the bridal couple Gunther and Brünnhilde. The couple, after all, is hardly in the best of spirits: Gunther is bringing home a bride whom he has won only through cunning on Siegfried's part, while Brünnhilde's spirit has been broken by suffering and humiliation. As a result, the vassals' cry of "Hail to you, Gunther! Hail to you and your bride" sounds cynical in the extreme, and the leitmotifs in the orchestra point constantly to such discrepancies. At the same time Wagner operates on what might be called a meta-level by playing with the popular genre of the wedding chorus: as dusk falls on the gods, so the traditional forms of opera grow increasingly desperate and the listener's expectations are thereby rendered futile.

Instead of adopting the problematically extreme and extremely problematical view of Hagen as a protofascist, we might do better to admire Wagner's ability to breathe life into the character, more especially within the context of the drama. Claus-Steffen Mahnkopf has argued that the brutality of this scene is necessary "to prepare the ground musically for Brünnhilde's subsequent anger, which is filled with hate and bent on thoughts of revenge" and "to desensitize the listener, making us deaf to psychological subtleties, so that the negative emotion of the doubly betrayed ex-Valkyrie acquires the musical force needed for the all-important peripeteia of *Götterdämmerung*."[28]

This peripeteia begins with Brünnhilde's cry of "Deceit! Deceit! Most shameful deceit! Betrayal! Betrayal—as never before avenged!" Siegfried's erstwhile lover is torn apart by grief and transformed into a vengeful fury. Taken together with the turbulent writing in the orchestra, this passage is one of the most shocking in any of Wagner's music dramas, making it hard to believe that it was written by a composer who claimed to be weary of emotional outbursts. It reveals mature craftsmanship, but none of the routine occasionally found elsewhere in the score. In its piling up of negative emotions, it looks ahead to what half a century later would be called "new music," so that it is easy to understand why Wagner's contemporaries had such difficulties with this second act of *Götterdämmerung* and its "displays of brute force"[29] and why Alban Berg—as we have already noted in our chapter on *Tristan und Isolde*—was able to say to a tyro critic: "Yes, you can talk like that—you're not a musician."

What is left at the end of the cycle—apart from Father Rhine and his daughters rejoicing in the ring that they have finally regained? From a material point of view, we are left with the ruins of the Gibichung Hall and, from a conceptual standpoint, there remains the so-called redemption motif (music example 28) that has been interpreted as a "symbol of birth and—here—the rebirth of a state of paradisal innocence."[30] But can these

28. Bars 1594–95 of act 3 of *Götterdämmerung*, with the motif
generally described as the "redemption motif."

two elements be reconciled? In other words, can a shipwreck become a relaunch?

Let us first examine the shipwreck—viewed here not from a lofty philosophical vantage point but in entirely pragmatic terms. The final part of the *Ring* is called *Götterdämmerung* because it describes the downfall of the gods. In the last scene of all—according to the stage directions—"bright flames flare up in the hall of the gods, finally hiding them from sight completely." None of the main actors in the drama—Siegfried, Brünnhilde, Gunther, Gutrune, or Hagen—survives this apocalypse. Only nature remains in the form of the Rhine and the Rhinedaughters, together with the men and women of the Gibichung court, and perhaps also Alberich, who does not, however, appear at the end.

The conclusion is clear enough: the gods perish, as they had always been intended to do. In December 1870, when he was working on *Götterdämmerung*, Wagner told Cosima that *Das Rheingold* "has the one advantage—that as in a peasant's trial it does clearly show us Wotan's guilt and fatal error and the urgent need for his renunciation."[31] Peasant's trials were legal proceedings instituted by farmers and other simple folk against the authorities when they felt that they had been unjustly treated. In the context of the *Ring*, the unjust gods bear responsibility for the state of the world, a point confirmed by Wagner's comment in his letter to August Röckel in January 1854, when he wrote that "Alberich and his ring could not harm the gods if the latter had not already been susceptible to evil."[32] A comment that Wagner made to Cosima in May 1877 when seeing London's docklands indicates what he thought the world would have looked like under Alberich's rule. The weather in London that day was "mild and gray," the impression left by the docks "tremendous": "This is Alberich's dream come true—Nibelheim, world dominion, activity, work, everywhere the oppressive feeling of steam and fog."[33] Even more explicit is a comment from February 1881: "Recently R. expressed his pleasure at having provided in

Der Ring des Nibelungen a complete picture of the curse of greed for money, and the disaster it brings about."[34] That same year, within the framework of his essay "Know Thyself," Wagner noted that "'Property' has acquired an almost greater sanctity in our social conscience than religion."[35]

Although key words such as "property," "power," and "world domin-ion" are defined in different and even contradictory ways in the *Ring* and in Wagner's own comments on the work, the cycle's basic message remained unchanged over the decades: the gods may not have caused the human race to founder, but they did nothing to prevent it. Only through the downfall of the gods can something new arise in their place.

We have already seen that in Wagner's view Wotan represented "the sum total of the [failed] intelligence of the present day" and that he "re-sembles *us* to a tee."[36] His descendants—Siegmund, Sieglinde, Siegfried, and Brünnhilde—are ultimately doomed to perish. But what happens af-terward—always assuming that everything does not start up all over again, with Alberich stealing the ring once more, a new Wotan wresting it from Alberich before having to cede it to the giants, and so on? Wagner has no answer to this question. As we know, he left four different endings to the *Ring*, each of which differs from the others in terms of its underlying tenor.

At the end of *Siegfried's Death* there is no cosmic conflagration, no destruction of Valhalla, but, rather, the optimistic prospect of an end to humankind's slavery. And yet it remains unclear how this act of libera-tion will come about. In the light of all that has previously happened at the Gibichung court, Brünnhilde's final assertion that "the bravest of men's most mighty deed must now be blessed by my knowledge" seems unduly starry-eyed, and Wagner, too, came to see this for himself in the wake of the failed bourgeois revolutions of 1848–49. When he revised the work, he allowed the world to be destroyed, a decision which, as far as visions of the future are concerned, could hardly be less equivocal. And yet he still felt the urge to equivocate, for the world was not to be destroyed in its entirety: something had to remain. Of course, Wagner found it hard to say exactly what this "something" was. Was it "love" that could be the start of some-thing new? In her 1852 peroration, Brünnhilde had insisted that "blessed in joy and sorrow love alone can be," but by August 1856 Wagner's exposure to Schopenhauer had convinced him that "in the course of the myth this love had emerged as fundamentally annihilating."[37]

Or is this really the end of everything, as the so-called Schopenhauer version of 1856 implies? "Grieving love's profoundest suffering opened my eyes for me: I saw the world end." Or should we trust in the vague sense of hope that we find in the definitive version of the work, where the gods do indeed perish, but, as we have already noted, "men and women" watch these events unfold "in speechless dismay." In the full score, Wagner changed this yet again: here the men and women are "moved to the very depths of their being," suggesting that a dream on the part of the human race has here come true. We could also adopt a similar interpretation of the ending of Patrice Chéreau's Bayreuth production of the *Ring* between 1976 and 1980, the final tableau of which was vaguely reminiscent of Delacroix's canvas *Liberty Leading the People*.

In the sixth volume of his collected writings, which appeared in print in 1872, before the first Bayreuth *Ring*, Wagner included all three versions of the end of *Götterdämmerung*, merely adding a note to the effect that the lines that had not been set to music were either superfluous or unhelpful, because they struck a "tendentious" note and "tried in advance to replace" what should be "left to the musical impact of the drama" to express.[38] But can we really reconcile the different endings of the *Ring* in the way that Wagner implies here?

We must in any case wonder at Wagner's decision to publish all these variants in the form of a series of notes in the collected edition of his writings as if they were part of some critical apparatus, but not part of a myth that cannot be rewritten at will. It can hardly be chance that as far as the poem of the *Ring* is concerned, Wagner played only with the ending but otherwise changed practically nothing else in the rest of the libretto, which remained the same over a period of more than two decades.

Although Wagnerians of the old school continue to imply that with his definitive ending to *Götterdämmerung* Wagner found a coherent solution, however we may choose to interpret this, attempts to deconstruct the work had already begun during the composer's own lifetime. In his later, anti-Wagnerian phase, Nietzsche would accept only the life-affirming end of *Siegfried's Death* and dismissed all three endings to *Götterdämmerung* as the product of an unseemly decline into pessimism. In "The Wagner Case," he fulminated against the composer: "What had he transposed into music [in *Siegfried's Death*]? Optimism. Wagner was ashamed." Then, referring to the lines "blessed in joy and sorrow love alone can be," he mocks the new peroration: "Brunhilde [*sic*] was initially supposed to take her farewell with a song in honor of free love, putting off the world with the hope for a socialist utopia in which 'all turns out well'—but now gets something else to do. She has to study Schopenhauer first; she has to transpose the fourth book of *The World as Will and Representation* into verse."[39]

Hans Mayer was merely echoing Nietzsche when he described the *Ring* as a work whose "ultimate meaning evolves before us in three different variants," Wagner "shamefully" traducing his original concept, as found in *Siegfried's Death*.[40] Theodor W. Adorno, conversely, wasted little time examining the different versions of the ending of *Siegfried's Death* and the *Ring* and instead launched into a generalized critique of Wagner's utopias. In his major essay on Wagner, he wrote simply: "In Wagner, the bourgeoisie dreams of its own destruction, conceiving it as its only road to salvation even though all it ever sees of the salvation is the destruction."[41] In 1964 the weekly *Die Zeit* published a piece under the heading "Postscript to a Discussion on Wagner," in which Adorno stated that "it was with Wagner that the destruction of the world first became an unprecedented spectacle." In the final pages of *Götterdämmerung*, in particular, "aesthetic form and social untruth" were intimately connected.[42]

This brings us to the age of Chéreau and Boulez, which in many respects is also our own. Certainly it now almost goes without saying that we will treat the end of *Götterdämmerung* as "one big question mark," as Chéreau put it. Explaining his production concept, he had the following to say about the ending: "I simply wanted everyone present, the whole of present humanity, to listen to the music as if to an oracle that can reach every individual or not, as the case may be, and whose meaning we can understand [or not, as the case may be]."[43]

For Udo Bermbach, such relativism or deconstructionism likewise goes without saying, with the result that he makes no attempt to salvage the ending of the *Ring* in the sense of a "new blueprint for the world" but speaks of "the lack of any future prospect, no matter whether in the sense of 're-demption,' 'self-annihilation,' or even 'resignation.'"[44] Anglo-Saxon readers, at least, have been aware of this debate for over a century, Shaw's covert encomium of the *Ring* in his *Perfect Wagnerite* of 1898 eliciting a response the following year from the music critic and Wagnerian cynic Ernest Newman, who insisted that in writing the *Ring* the composer "was not contributing one iota to the knowledge or the wisdom of mankind."[45]

But is this not just as true of Wagner's description of the status quo as it is of any vague future prospects? After all, he hardly offers a coherent analysis of capitalism, at least of the kind that a socialist like Shaw would like to have seen. In my own view, Wagner does paint an impressive picture of the corrupting influence of power, which is fascinating more especially because he describes not only the structures of power but also the agents of that power and does so in a way that makes his diagnosis seem as topical today as it was in the nineteenth century.

That Wagner becomes entangled in all manner of contradictions is not something we need to hold against the artist that he was. Such condescension on our part is unnecessary, not least because economists and sociologists of the nineteenth or even the twentieth century could scarcely have argued more compellingly. Some decades ago Claude Lévi-Strauss—a self-declared admirer of Wagner—referred to the hubristic view of intellectuals from the years between 1700 and the early nineteenth century that "the social world" was "conceptually intelligible," adding: "I no longer believe that the world is conceptually intelligible, for societies have now become too complicated, too comprehensive, the number of variables has become too great. That is why political actions can take place only as a move and countermove, blow by blow, day by day."[46]

Wagner offers a magisterial description of this particular kind of political action in the figure of Wotan. After all, the Wotan of the *Ring* is a politician who has "recognized the guilt of existence" and who "atones for the error of creation," as Wagner explained to Cosima.[47] His music theater has neither the need nor the ability to offer us anything more than this by way of argumentation, especially when we place the emphasis on the music. "Just wait," Wagner told Cosima on November 14, 1869: "when I write my treatise on the philosophy of music, church and state will be abolished. Religion has assumed flesh and blood in a way quite different from these dogmatic forms—music, that is the direct product of Christianity, as is the saint, like Saint Francis of Assisi, who compensates for the whole church as well as for the whole world."[48] The end of the *Ring*—godless in the truest sense of the term—was already predictable in the Middle Ages: the gods of the old Germanic tribes were dead, and music drew its life force from Christianity only as the latter's "indirect emanation." The young Nietzsche, who visited the Wagners frequently at this period, will have heard such comments and rejoiced at them: for him, too, God was dead, while Wagner's metaphysical art was very much alive. This brings us to the relaunch into which we may—or may not—care to transform the shipwreck of the end of the *Ring*.

Particularly compelling in this context is a comment made by Wagner on July 23, 1872. The previous day he had completed the orchestral sketch for *Götterdämmerung*, adding a final note, "End! All to please Cosel." On the 23rd he informed his wife that "Music has no ending. It is like the genesis of things, it can always start again from the beginning, go over to the opposite, but it is never really complete. [. . .] I am glad that I kept back Sieglinde's theme of praise for Brünnhilde, to become as it were a hymn to the heroine."⁴⁹ The theme in question is the one first heard in act 3 of *Die Walküre* at Sieglinde's words "O hehrstes Wunder" (Sublimest wonder) and refers to Brünnhilde. When it returns at the end of *Götterdämmerung*, it indicates the importance that music has for Wagner's musical drama: to the extent that this task has not already been taken over by the plot, it reveals in an immediate and physical way that the myth of the *Ring* does not depict a linear series of events taking place at a particular point in history and moving inexorably toward a unique ending but describes a circular action that reflects the state and structure of the world in which we live. That which ends at one particular point is still in full swing at another, while at a third point it is still in the process of coming into being.

In other words, the redemption motif that Wagner weaves into the closing bars of the *Ring* does not have to be interpreted in a linear way as a vision of the future or even as a vague pointer to how events may yet unfold. Rather, it should be understood as a clarification of a permanent and at the same time metaphysical demand that Wagner does not abandon even in the face of the catastrophic events depicted in the *Ring*: no one can imagine power without thinking at the same time of its opposite, self-sacrificial love; and it makes no sense to speak of "damnation" unless we also have an inkling of "bliss."⁵⁰ If—to quote Kant's categorical imperative—there is no "starry sky above us," guaranteeing the world order, there is still "the moral law within us." Without such a moral law, Wagner's critique of prevailing conditions in the *Ring* would not only lack any yardstick by which we could measure it, it would also lack a corrective.

Words, of course, are of no avail here. When Nietzsche turned up at Wahnfried in August 1874 flourishing a copy of the *Triumphlied* of Brahms—a composer whom Wagner held in low esteem—Wagner "laugh[ed] loudly at the idea of setting such a word as *Gerechtigkeit* ["justice"] to music."⁵¹ No, music alone can help us here—as an "emanation" of religion. But Wagner would not be Wagner if he did not have a number of concrete hints up his sleeve. In this particular case he had the aforementioned redemption motif at the ready, a motif he had already described as "Sieglinde's theme in praise of Brünnhilde" and which was now entrusted to the orchestra and treated as a "hymn to the heroine." A letter that Cosima Wagner wrote to one of her husband's admirers, the chemist Eduard von Lippmann, provides a further explanation: "Not being in a position to reply to you in person, my husband has asked me to tell you that the motif that Sieglinde sings to Brünnhilde is the glorification of Brünnhilde, which is taken up at the end of the work, as if by the entirety."[52]

Brünnhilde, who has endured so many highs and lows in the *Ring*, is left as Wagner's only figure of hope. Cosima—no doubt echoing her husband—called her "compassionate and loving."[53] To love compassionately would be the categorical imperative to offset the striving for power on the part of the *Ring*'s other characters, most of them men. And that this imperative can be articulated only through music, not words, would reflect Wagner's conviction that transcendence can be imagined only in the language of music. According to Carolyn Abbate, Brünnhilde lives on "in the form of her dematerialized voice, which at the end finds a home for itself in the violins and sings through them."[54] The media theorist Friedrich Kittler has spoken more drastically of the "liquidation of articulated speech": for him, the end of the gods is "the beginning of all sound effects in Wagner. If no one commands it, music remains noise" and becomes the "technology" of pure "ecstasy." We no longer listen attentively but listen, rather, to a "musical noise spectrum."[55]

Kittler, too, alludes to the redemption motif. But this is not the only motif that we hear at the end of *Götterdämmerung*. Others include the Siegfried motif and the Valhalla motif. And herein lies the problem of the ending of the *Ring*, not in the much-discussed function of the redemption motif, for the Siegfried and Valhalla motifs ring out with a splendor that has absolutely nothing to do with the preceding narrative. Indeed, it is scarcely possible to conceive of a more radical dismantling of musical motifs than we find with these two leitmotifs.

What did Wagner once write about the prelude to *Das Rheingold*? It had been impossible, he explained, to "quit the home key" of E-flat, because the plot gave him no reason "to change it."[56] In the second act of *Die Walküre*, when he wanted to provide a "picture of the fearful gloom in the soul of the suffering god" at the words "So nimm meinen Segen, Niblungen-Sohn" (So take my blessing, Nibelung son), he had, conversely, harnessed together various leitmotifs "with the help of a digression in the harmony," using enharmonic change to move from A-flat minor to E major within the shortest possible time. A composer of symphonies would have brought out the "acerbity of such musical combinations" as particularly "bold," whereas he himself had sought to "tone down" the stridency of the writing and present the passage "in accordance with the laws of nature," in other words, in a psychologically credible way.[57]

Did such subtleties in terms of the interplay between plot and music no longer play a role when in the early part of 1872 Wagner jotted down a composition draft for the ending of *Götterdämmerung* that already gives a good idea of the definitive ending? It may be objected that Wagner seems unable to get by without affirmatively transfiguring finales and that these endings are due less to the plot than to the desire to paint as bright a picture as possible of the conciliatory power of music. But there is a difference between interpreting Isolde's "Transfiguration" and the final unveiling of the Grail in this way and writing music for an apocalyptic scene like the end of *Götterdämmerung* that may not be triumphalist in a martial sense but which at least tends in the direction of triumph and frenzied ecstasy.

In this context, a comment made by Wagner in November 1880 is worth noting. This was a time when he resumed work on *Parsifal* after a lengthy interruption and, possibly in this very context, looked at the end of *Götterdämmerung*, prompting him to tell Cosima that "never again will [I] write anything as complicated as that."[58] There is no doubt that Wagner had in fact written even more complicated passages elsewhere in the *Ring*. Indeed, John Deathridge has claimed that the initial sketch for the ending is "perhaps one of the most disconcerting documents in the Bayreuth archives. If one takes an uncharitable view of musical composition, it could have been written by a roughly trained university student doing a paper in tonal composition."[59]

Of course, the corpus of Beethoven's sketches teaches us that early versions of a passage do not always allow us to draw conclusions about its intended final form. Rather, they must be seen as a composer's vague attempts to invest a nebulous idea with a preliminary shape. Is it conceivable that it was not the technical element in his compositional approach that Wagner found complicated and which Deathridge describes as "the usurping of quasi-symphonic development by motivic allegory,"[60] but something completely different? Might he not have asked himself the question whether the frenzy and pomp of the music describing the end of the world might not in fact be appropriate from an *ideological* standpoint?

As the starting point for our assumption we could take the somewhat cynical motto that "inferior reality remains with us while utopias keep on changing." Wagner had already had problems with the ending of the libretto, making it likely that he also found himself in a predicament as a composer having to explain to himself and to others whether he still saw himself as a revolutionary who had once wanted to burn down Paris or as a state composer who had gained respectability during the early years of the new Reich and was satisfied with the symbolism of a fire that burned down Valhalla and that was staged as a frenzy of sounds? When he noted down this particular sketch, the foundation-stone ceremony for the Bayreuth Festspielhaus lay only weeks away, a building which, for all its relative modesty, was far from being the provisional theater of planks and beams that had fired his imagination twenty-two years earlier. Bayreuth was now a project of national importance for which the Wagners were drumming up trade with all the means at their disposal.

The united German Reich had come into being in 1871, a development that Wagner had initially followed with ardent patriotism, even if he was later unable to disguise his disappointment at the way in which the national idea took concrete shape. Like Brahms and Nietzsche and other patriots he avidly supported the Franco-Prussian War of 1870–71. When he was asked for an autograph for an organization set up to help the war-wounded, he added a line of verse inspired by his libretto to *Lohengrin*: "Nie soll der Feind aus seinem öden Osten" (Ne'er shall our foe come from his barren east) but changed the "barren east" to the "windy west." This line of doggerel verse was not meant to be sung to the music of *Lohengrin* but, according to Wagner, was intended "as an alternative"—exactly *how* is not clear—to the patriotic *The Watch on the Rhine*, which famously starts with the bellicose lines: "Es braust ein Ruf wie Donnerhall, / Wie Schwertgeklirr und Wogenprall" (The cry resounds like thunder's peal, / Like crashing waves and clang of steel).[61]

In his poem "To the German Army outside Paris," which he wrote in January 1871, Wagner paid tribute to the King of Prussia, who had been named German kaiser in the Hall of Mirrors at Versailles and whom Wagner renames "Siege-Fried" (A Truce to Victories).[62] Shortly afterward he laid at the kaiser's feet a further act of homage in the form of his *Kaisermarsch* (WWV 104) that culminates in an extended quotation from Luther's *Ein feste Burg ist unser Gott* (A mighty stronghold is our God) and a "folk poem" beginning with the words "Hail! Hail to the kaiser! King Wilhelm!" that was to be sung by the entire army. This was also the work that Wagner chose to launch the official celebrations marking the laying of the foundation stone in Bayreuth on May 22, 1872:

Heil! Heil dem Kaiser!
König Wilhelm!
aller Deutschen Hort und Freiheitswehr!
Höchste der Kronen,

> wie ziert Dein Haupt sie hehr!
>
> Ruhmreich gewonnen,
>
> soll Frieden Dir lohnen!
>
> Der neu ergrünten Eiche gleich
>
> erstand durch Dich das deutsche Reich:
>
> Heil seinen Ahnen,
>
> seinen Fahnen,
>
> die Dich führten, die wir trugen,
>
> als mit Dir wir Frankreich schlugen!
>
> Feind zum Trutz,
>
> Freund zum Schutz,
>
> allem Volk das deutsche Reich zu Heil und Nutz!

[Hail! Hail to the kaiser! King Wilhelm, the hoard and defender of liberty of all Germans! Highest of crowns, how gloriously it adorns your head! Praiseworthily won, peace shall reward you! Like the oak with its fresh green leaves, the German Reich arose through you: hail to its forebears and flags, which guided you and which we bore when we vanquished France with you! Defying our foe and protecting our friend, the German Reich exists for the salvation and benefit of all people!]

Is it possible that the music at the end of *Götterdämmerung* contains an echo of the mood of euphoria that accompanied the establishment of the new German Reich? Was no further utopia needed now that the present age had showed such a friendly face? Was Wagner's dream world now directed less at the future than at what was attainable in the here and now? By now there was not only Wilhelm I — "Siege-Fried" — to ensure good times for all but also Parsifal, who was on hand to demonstrate that things could take a positive turn after *Götterdämmerung*. The question as to whether the *Ring* must inevitably end in destruction or whether it can strike a utopian note now becomes unimportant. If we go back to the cycle's beginnings, we could of course argue that the affirmative ending of the music takes up the heroic gesture of the final tableau of *Siegfried's Death*, which survives the saga of the *Ring* at least in terms of the music.

The idea that the *Ring* may extend into *Parsifal* is not new, of course. As early as 1848, even before he had conceived the notion of an opera on *Siegfried's Death*, Wagner had already written a substantial study to which he gave the title *The Wibelungs: World History from Legend*, the penultimate section of which was headed "Ascent of the ideal content of the hoard into the 'Holy Grail.'" (The "hoard" is, of course, the Nibelung treasure.)

In short, Wagner's reconstruction of the Nibelung myth encompassed the Grail from the outset. And even when he started work on the *Ring*, Wagner never lost sight of *Parsifal*. It is significant, for example, that the earliest prose sketch for *Parsifal* dates from 1857, the very time that Wagner broke off work on the *Ring* for a period of almost twelve years. Is it possible that—already anticipating the failure of his hero Siegfried—he saw Parsifal as a second Siegfried even at this early date? We have already quoted from

Act I of *Götterdämmerung* in Peter Konwitschny's 2000 Stuttgart production. Seen here are Siegfried, Hagen, and Gutrune's legs. The production explored different layers in the work, layers that the conductor Lothar Zagrosek also heard in the score—notably "in the scene for Hagen, Gunther, Gutrune, and, later, Siegfried: if you take out specific layers of the winds—even just held notes—the result would almost be a comic minuet. Of course, it is already poisoned, but there is also something comic about it as it strikes you as so stilted, with a positively 'courtly' character. As Adorno says, there are various levels or layers, and you suddenly sense that behind it all there is something else, something that from the outset tells you that things are going unstoppably wrong. I find this great about Wagner—it is this that is so wonderful and enigmatic about his music": see Eckehard Kiem, "'. . .verschiedene Schichten von Präsenz': Wagnerorchester und Wagnerregie; Gespräch mit Lothar Zagrosek," in Richard Klein, ed., *Narben des Gesamtkunstwerks: Wagners "Ring des Nibelungen"* (Munich: Wilhelm Fink, 2001), 300. (Photograph courtesy of A. T. Schaefer, Stuttgart.)

Cosima Wagner's diary entry for April 29, 1879: "Siegfried ought to have turned into Parsifal and redeemed Wotan, he should have come upon Wotan (instead of Amfortas) in the course of his wanderings—but there was no antecedent for it, and so it would have to remain as it was."[63]

Does this still have to be so? Or can a modern director take Wagner's statement in *The Wibelungs* at face value and end the *Ring* not with the redemption motif but with the faith motif from *Parsifal*? In his Bayreuth production of the *Ring* in 2000, Jürgen Flimm placed the young Parsifal onstage at the end, though the idea was abandoned at subsequent revivals. I myself would like to go a stage further and propose a solution that is not afraid of encroaching on the music: at a Wagner conference organized by the Hamburg State Opera in October 2009 I even presented a collage in which the ending of the *Ring* passed seamlessly into the heroic faith motif from *Parsifal*.[64]

In my own view, this would be the only honest answer that Wagner can give: there is no escaping from the world of the *Ring*—neither into the utopia of a free society nor into the realm of free love nor into a state of nirvana. Although we may be able to choose whether we are buried in the earth, at sea, or on a funeral pyre (Wagner's preference was for cremation and burial at sea), we cannot transcend ourselves. The only alternatives are cultic ritual, the liturgy, and the "incense-perfumed sensual preaching" against which Nietzsche—understandably indignant—fulminated in *Beyond Good and Evil*.[65] I imagine the final scene of the *Ring* transmuting into the Temple of the Grail, with Siegfried as Parsifal and Wotan as Titurel. At the side of the stage, Brünnhilde vegetates as Kundry. And the sounds we hear are those of *Parsifal*. For me, this would be no deconstruction of the "grand narrative" of the *Ring* but would mean getting to the heart of this "grand narrative" in the spirit of Wagner himself.

Eliding the *Ring* and *Parsifal* in this way inevitably has consequences for *Parsifal*, for it will now be difficult to hail this as a *Bühnenweihfestspiel*. Instead, we shall be forced to concede that the hopelessness that marks the events of the *Ring* continues to resonate in *Parsifal*, albeit with the decisive difference that the structural injustice found in the *Ring* becomes the personal guilt of the characters in *Parsifal*. And religion is a panacea for personal guilt, a point illustrated by the Grail bells with a clarity that leaves nothing to the imagination. And so *Götterdämmerung* could end not with the prelude to *Parsifal* but with the inviting peal of the bells. Then the men and women who, "in speechless dismay," watch as events unfold at the end of the *Ring* would know which community they will belong to in the future.

But perhaps we should not insist unduly on the ideological dilemma raised by the end of *Götterdämmerung* and leave the floor instead to Friedrich Kittler with an offer that may well warm the hearts of many Wagnerians inasmuch as it encourages them to "plunge into the ocean of the music" in an altogether elemental way: "In the final moments of the *Ring*, fire, water, and wind—that is, air—contend with each other. [. . .] Wotan represents the storm with the Valhalla motif, the Rhinedaughters are aquatic creatures, and fire is present in the conflagration that destroys Valhalla and also in the person of Loge. These three layers run counter to each other as music." In other words, the end of *Götterdämmerung* does not proclaim a message. Rather, the message is the "world breath"—the *Weltatem*—that lends its powerful voice to the orchestra. Whether listeners are convinced by this multimedia answer to the "question as to how the world can be destroyed or vanish into thin air"[66] or whether they regard it as an example of a postmodern lack of commitment will depend on which generation they belong to.

A Word about Theodor W. Adorno

There is no doubt that when Theodor W. Adorno spoke of the "phantasmagoria" of the ending of the *Ring*,[1] he hit the nail on the head, for it is here that the bourgeoisie celebrates its own demise. Thus a critical observer may judge the situation. But what are we to make of the ideological criticism to which that same observer subjects the whole of Wagner's output? As a philosopher, Adorno championed the idea of "inexorable music" that defiantly represented the "truth of society in opposition to society."[2] At its simplest, the opposite of "inexorable music" is music as a commodity—a type of music that throws itself at the spirit of the age, at audiences, and at the culture industry. Adorno was always in two minds about Wagner, whose music he regarded as "true" at the same time that it was a "commodity," no clear dividing line being discernible between them.[3]

For Ernst Bloch, classical music was above all an occasion to revel in its sounds, for it provided, in his eyes, a unique foretaste of the future, whereas Adorno placed his finger on what were above all its problematical elements, even though he shared Bloch's love of music. He felt, for example, that Bach's artistry "shows a moment of heteronomy, of something not entirely embraced by the subject which, despite his superior 'accomplishment,' places him, in historico-philosophical terms, *below* Beethoven."[4] Beethoven was the composer he revered above all others, a composer whose music, while not free from contradictions, expressed a greater truth than Wagner's, whose much-lauded *Gesamtkunstwerk* was a late offshoot of the great metaphysical systems of the past: "The disintegration into fragments sheds light on the fragmentariness of the whole."[5]

We should, of course, be doing Adorno's great Wagner essay an injustice by one-sidedly taking exception to such terms as "affirmation," "regression," "game of deception," and "context of delusion,"[6] for as a dialectician, Adorno knew very well what Wagner is all about—even in the case of Wagner the myth maker: "We can hear like an echo in the final lines of the *Rhinegold* what the *Ring*, as the luminous facsimile of the great systems, could ultimately see in them: the senseless, jejune, hopeless and solitary hope that nothingness offers to the man who is tragically ensnared."[7] And almost at the end of the same study Adorno praises the "feverish passages in Act III of *Tristan*," referring to "that black, abrupt, jagged music which instead of underlining the vision unmasks it."[8]

But there is no doubt that the dominant tone is critical, and to the extent that it is directed at Wagner as a self-appointed prophet of art, it is easy for us to relate to it, especially when that critique is voiced by a writer who witnessed at first hand the National Socialists' idolization of Wagner as a cult hero, a misappropriation that Adorno must have found particularly unbearable. It is surely no accident that the earliest draft of his Wagner essay dates from 1937–38, when Adorno was living in exile and making a determined effort to decode Wagner's music socially. He interpreted its inflated, hypertrophic features as the symptom of a sick society holding all-night parties in an attempt to forget its own sickness.

The Achilles' heel of Adorno's argument is that whereas it is easy to take offense at Wagner's view of himself as a prophet of art and at his musical gift of gab, it is much harder to criticize him for any actual or alleged inadequacies in terms of his musical craftsmanship. For all its occasional perspicacity, Adorno's polemic also contains a number of serious misunderstandings, and yet it would be wrong to dismiss his criticisms simply on the grounds that opera and music drama must be judged by other laws than those that govern the "autonomous" music of Beethoven and Schoenberg, for example. After all, Adorno was concerned with the truth and actuality of the whole idea of the total artwork, a concern that extended well beyond the confines of any questions about genre and aesthetics. But even here his sometimes unduly apodictic analyses of Wagner's scores do not really get us any further. The actual or alleged illusory nature of the idioms that he criticizes is not an expression of any technical shortcomings on Wagner's part, even in the most comprehensive sense of that term, but an inextricable part of his art in its totality. Here it is possible to criticize Wagner only on an ideological, not a technical, level—however much Adorno, as a connoisseur and composer in his own right, may have wished that the two were dialectically interrelated.

Today's listeners are in any case more tolerant, for every art provides us with its own "context of delusion." And those of us who have a weakness for Wagner as a sorcerer and media virtuoso admire not some coherent concept but the perfection in imperfection. When seen from such a standpoint, Wagner's musical drama resembles nothing so much as a magnificent mirror held up to our own society, with all its contradictions, hopes, and lies.

Adorno's study of Wagner is full of insights and has always fascinated its readers, while also creating the impression of excessive effort, an impression due to the fact that the young Adorno was emotionally drawn to Wagner—when he was sixteen, a performance of *Tristan und Isolde* under Furtwängler had left him "completely overwhelmed."[9] All the greater, then, was his sense of disenchantment on realizing that the genius that Wagner had for a time seemed to him to be had, in his eyes, so fundamentally betrayed the ethos of music. Much the same had already happened to Nietzsche, albeit for very different reasons.

Franz von Lenbach was known as the "prince of painters" on the strength of his portraits of eminent individuals invested with a sense of the self-assurance associated with the early years of Germany's new Reich. Most of these portraits were prepared from photographs, and the same is true of this sketch of Wagner, made in red chalk and based on one of Franz Hanfstaengl's photographs from 1871. It is arguably the most appealing of Lenbach's numerous portraits of Wagner and probably dates from the winter of 1880–81, when Wagner was in Munich and may even have sat briefly for the artist, with whom he was on friendly terms. (Photograph courtesy of the Nationalarchiv der Richard-Wagner-Stiftung, Bayreuth: N 1227a.)

CHAPTER THIRTEEN

"You will see—diminished sevenths were just not possible!"

PARSIFAL

Hermann Levi visits Wahnfried—Wagner's belief in
godliness, not in God—His study of the rituals of the Catholic
Church—*Parsifal* as music with a philosophy—Wolfram von
Eschenbach's *Parzival*—The enigmatic phrase "Redemption
to the Redeemer"—Anti-Semitic interpretations of this
phrase by Gutman and Zelinsky—Harry Kupfer's 1977
Berlin production—Wagner's contemporaries' criticism of
the work's ideology—Structural affinities with Schubert's
short story *My Dream*—Parsifal as a dream machine for
Wagner—Suffering in the work: Thomas Mann, Friedrich
Nietzsche, and Nike Wagner—Alban Berg's admiration for
the music—Innovative elements in terms of the history of
music—*Parsifal* as a pivotal piece—Compositional symbols for
the mix of faith and the search for meaning—The "pure fool"
motif—Symbolism and Jugendstil: a comparison with the work
of Gustav Klimt—"Parsifal's Wanderings": a detailed analysis—
Ambivalence of the music's semantics—Kundry's laughter and
Kundry's music—Sounds as "demons"—"Sorrow in bliss"

Wagner completed the composition sketch of *Parsifal* on April 16, 1879, just after Easter. The orchestral sketch was finished ten days later. Shortly beforehand, he had received a visit from Hermann Levi, Munich's court conductor, so that the two men could work through the finished sections of the score. One such passage was the Good Friday scene in act 3. The following day, Good Friday, Cosima attended Communion with her eldest children—for good Protestants this was an almost obligatory act.

Wagner himself remained at home. Perhaps in an attempt to justify himself, he told his wife that "it was not Christ's death but his resurrection which gave rise to the religion; the death all but destroyed the poor disciples, but the women's not finding the body in the morning, and seeing Christ in their exaltation, created the community."[1] With this interpretation, Wagner was adopting the line taken by the so-called Tübingen school of theology, more especially a study familiar to Wagner and written by Nietzsche's friend Franz Overbeck: *How Christian Is Our Present-Day Theology?*

By then, Levi had already returned to Munich. Wagner would undoubtedly have welcomed it if Levi, too, had attended Communion—having first been baptized, of course. For years he continued to nag his designated *Parsifal* conductor to convert to Christianity, for he—Wagner—was on the horns of a dilemma: it was only with the greatest reluctance that he had been persuaded to let Levi conduct *Parsifal* at all and to entrust his great confessional work to the son of a rabbi from Gießen. An entry in Cosima Wagner's diary for April 28, 1880, reveals her husband's attitude at its most cynical: "I cannot allow him to conduct *Parsifal* unbaptized, but I shall baptize them both, and we shall take Communion together."[2] And yet Wagner knew of no more suitable replacement to conduct the work: on the one hand, his patron, King Ludwig II, saw no reason to distance himself from his Jewish kapellmeister; and on the other, Wagner could think of no more competent conductor and no more suitable team of singers than those of the Munich court opera. His annoyance at his predicament found expression in a particularly unpleasant episode that took place during rehearsals, when he confronted Levi with an anonymous anti-Semitic letter accusing the conductor of having an affair with Cosima.

Levi was so unnerved by this accusation that he left Bayreuth forthwith and demanded to be relieved of his duties, prompting Wagner to write what Cosima—in an appalling lapse of good taste—called a "splendid reply,"[3] in which he in turn accused the deserter of being oversensitive and ended by adding the distinctly ambiguous sentence: "Perhaps this will be a great turning point in your life—but at all events, you are my *Parsifal* conductor."[4] Once again Levi was evidently being invited to consider baptism, only this time the invitation was implied. Such tactlessness toward Levi is in striking contrast to Wagner's open-minded attitude to August Friedrich Gfrörer's *Critical History of Early Christianity*, which had held his attention since 1874, not least on account of a number of striking parallels between Jewish theosophy and the message of his own *Parsifal*.[5]

Wagner himself was neither loyal to the Protestant Church nor a believer in the traditional sense of the term: "I do not believe in God, but in godliness, which is revealed in a Jesus without sin."[6] Dated September 20, 1879, this entry in Cosima Wagner's diary is by no means untypical of Wagner's attitude in general. Only the previous day, for example, he had exclaimed: "If Protestantism had remained on a popular level, completely untheological, it would have been capable of survival; theology was its downfall."[7]

There were times, however, when Wagner adopted a far more critical attitude to the rituals of the Catholic Church: an entry in his *Brown Book*—effectively a diary that he kept for Cosima—includes a passage that dates from September 1, 1865, three days after he had completed the prose draft of *Parsifal*. It was intended first and foremost as a dig at Liszt and was therefore pasted over by Wagner's daughter, Eva Chamberlain, decades later in an attempt to render it unreadable: "To me all this Catholic rubbish is repugnant to the very depths of my soul: anyone who takes refuge in that must have a great deal to atone for. Once you revealed it to me, speaking in a dream: it was dreadful. Your father is repugnant to me.—and when I was able to bear him, there was more Christianity in my blind indulgence than in all his piety."[8]

The very next day—again in the pages of his *Brown Book*—Wagner returned to the subject of his *Parsifal* draft: "What to do about the blood-stained lance?—The poem says the lance is supposed to have been produced at the same time as the Grail, and clinging to the tip was a drop of blood.—Anyway, this is the one which has caused Anfortas' [*sic*] wound: but how does this hang together? Great confusion here. As a relic, the lance goes with the cup; in this is preserved the blood that the lance made to flow from the Saviour's thigh. The two are complementary.—So either this: [. . .] Or this: [. . .] Which is better, Cos?"[9]

For all his criticism of the Catholic Church, Wagner was also at this time visiting the Munich Benedictine priest Petrus Hamp in order to "exchange ideas on the representational aspects of the Catholic Mass." As Hamp recalled in his reminiscences, "a copy of the Missal lay open between us throughout these discussions. Wagner asked probing questions about the tiniest details, including the sense and significance of the ceremonies, especially their origins and age, and the theatrical design of the Mass. Time and again he asked me to sing the *praefationes*, or prefaces." Wagner also expressed an interest in the moment when the act of transubstantiation took place and asked "whether the faithful did not feel a frisson."[10] Twenty-six years later Paul Valéry observed in a letter to André Gide that "we are all little boys when set beside liturgists and theologians since the most brilliant among us, Wagner and Mallarmé, bow before them and *imitate* them."[11]

Some of the "great confusion" that Wagner felt on reading Wolfram von Eschenbach's medieval romance may seem to have left its mark on the opening pages of the present chapter, but the heteroclite character of this section is in fact intentional, for it is meant to indicate that we would be guilty of fundamentally misjudging the composer's creative and conceptual work on *Parsifal* if we were to compare it to the careful planning of a professional librettist. Rather, Wagner kept leaping back and forth between different levels right up to the time of the work's first performance in 1882.

Ever since he had first become acquainted with the subject of *Lohengrin* in 1845, Wagner had been engaged in mythological speculations and studies of the circle of legends surrounding the Grail and Parzival. With the passage of time, theological and philosophical questions became increasingly central to his thinking. At the same time, he was exercised by the concrete question of how he could present what Hermann Danuser has called his "world-view music"[12] in the form of a *Bühnenweihfestspiel* that would be his most important contribution to the religion of art that he was propagating. This required him not only to work on *Parsifal* as a librettist and composer but also to demonstrate uniquely compelling powers of persuasion such that it is almost impossible for us to draw a distinction between Wagner as the "founder of a new religion" and Wagner as a private individual.

After all, Wagner's interest in the debate in conservative circles who had diagnosed a crisis in civilization and were examining the chances of finding a cure was not confined to the public sphere but also found expression within his own private circle. Among the leading figures of this movement, in which a critique of civilization went hand in fist with anti-Semitism, were Paul de Lagarde, Constantin Frantz, and the self-styled Count Joseph-Arthur de Gobineau, all of whom were known to Wagner not just through their writings but also through personal and epistolary contact. Theological and philosophical debates were such a regular feature of daily life at Wahnfried that we may surely claim that Wagner lived every single minute of the creative process surrounding his last great confessional work, suffering and reacting to it with every fiber of his being.

And, miracle of miracles, Wagner managed to ensure that the world premiere of *Parsifal* in 1882 was a cultural event never previously seen in Germany, at least in the field of music. Even more incredible is that the event was a financial success, the quarter of a million marks that the enterprise cost being met by box-office receipts, while donations from the Patrons' Societies worth 140,000 marks additionally helped to support the cause. For the full score and vocal score Wagner's publisher paid 150,000 marks, a sum that no previous German composer had commanded, although, as Wagner was aggrieved to discover, Gounod received a similar sum for his oratorio *La rédemption*.

The press reacted far more positively than had been the case in 1876, when the response had been relatively muted and had revolved in the main around the question of whether or not Wagner had achieved his record-breaking aim. By 1882 a different climate prevailed: now there was applause and publicity wherever one turned. Even Bayreuth's numerous enemies avoided their earlier note of malice, since the subject matter of *Parsifal* was undoubtedly calculated to inspire a mood of national solemnity. Wagner's new work was not as long and complicated as the *Ring*; it lacked its gloomy ending; and it was a drama about redemption, allowing audiences to leave the theater after only a few hours in a suitably elevated mood.

"Whereas it was blood and fire that flowed freely in the *Ring*," we read in a review in the *Nationalzeitung* almost defensive in its critique of the work, "it is now consecrated oil."[13] The age could make use of consecrated oil in the guise of a work imbued with religious and nationalist ideas, whether we view those ideas as Catholic, Protestant, Celtic, Germanic, or Buddhist or attribute them to the tradition of Jewish mysticism or the spirit of animal rights, or see them as an expression of *décadence* — or even if we have no clear idea what the work is ultimately about.

And this brings us to a central point — the lack of any clear message in terms of Wagner's "theology." Hundreds of books and articles have sought to explain whether the "love-feast" should be interpreted as a celebration of the Eucharist and whether the bread, wine, Last Supper, lance, and dove should be seen as Christian symbols and, if so, how. And then there is the role of the Grail, which has inspired esoteric writers of all shades of opinion to indulge in the most lurid speculations.

I have nothing but respect for all interpretations that show commitment and conviction: even a person not inclined to esoteric speculations can sympathize with the view that the Grail satisfies a primal need in us for protection and sustenance. And there is no doubt that Parsifal's journey to greater maturity — "Made wise by pity, the blameless fool" — invites us to identify with the hero in a positive way, while exactly the same is true of the motif of compassion, whether we see it in Buddhist or Christian terms. After all, no less an authority than Claude Lévi-Strauss has described Wagner's libretto as an important "contribution to mythology" and hailed Gurnemanz's lines "You see, my son, here time becomes space" as arguably "the most profound definition of myth in general."[14]

Other writers have sought, rather, to demythologize *Parsifal* in their attempts to salvage the work. Hans Mayer, for example, sees in Parsifal a second Siegfried—"once again a young man who is meant to embody the fate of human freedom but who on this occasion is not destroyed by the curse of some Alberich or other."[15] Udo Bermbach even speaks of an "aestheticization" of religion that began with the *Ring* and is continued in *Parsifal*.[16]

However much sympathy one may have for Wagnerian exegetes who approach the plot of *Parsifal* in a spirit of positive thinking, there remains the question: would Wagner's *Parsifal* have existed if Wolfram's *Parzival* had not done so? Wagner's poem is undoubtedly more coherent and concentrated than Wolfram's rambling and barely logical romance, which runs to almost 25,000 lines. But is the same also true of its message? Wagner's *Parsifal* ends with words that are not only mystical but also baffling: "Miracle of supreme salvation: Redemption to the Redeemer." Wolfram, on the other hand, ends his poem with the lines:

> swes lebn sich sô verendet,
> daz got niht wirt gepfendet
> der sêle durch des lîbes schulde,
> und der doch der werlde hulde
> behalten kan mit werdekeit,
> daz ist ein nütziu arbeit.[17]

[If any man's life ends in such a way that God is not robbed of his soul because of the body's guilt, and if he can retain, with honour, this world's favour, that is a useful labour.][18]

Wolfram's motto might be summed up as "von tumpheit durch zwîfel zur staete" (from folly through doubt to constancy) and represents an attempt on the poet's part to combine two distinct virtues as his template for a chivalric education: worldliness and piety. Although the medieval hero ultimately rules over the Grail community, he is allowed to keep beside him his beautiful wife Condwîrâmûrs, whose name—significantly—derives from the Old French meaning "she who leads to love." There is no such love in Wagner's *Parsifal*. Indeed, Wagner turns on their head Wolfram's ideals, a decision prompted by his own motto, which we have already quoted in other contexts: "Strong is the magic of him who desires, but stronger is that of him who renounces."[19]

In the process, Wagner also rewrote *Tristan und Isolde*, his program note for the prelude having read: "Now there could be no end to love's desire and

yearning, no end to its joy and its misery: the world and all its power, reputation, honor, knighthood, loyalty, and friendship—all had turned to dust
like some insubstantial dream; one thing alone lived on: yearning! Yearning,
insatiable longing ever reborn, thirsting and repining! The only release was
to die, to perish, to fade away, nevermore to awaken!"[20] Instead, Wagner's
concern, as expressed in his program note to the prelude to act 1 of *Parsifal*,
was "charity—faith—hope?"[21]

But what are we to hope for? *Parsifal* ends, as we have already noted,
with the enigmatic words "Miracle of supreme salvation: Redemption to
the Redeemer." We may preempt our discussion of this point by quoting
a malicious insight on the part of the disenchanted Nietzsche: "There is
nothing about which Wagner has thought more deeply than redemption:
his opera is the opera of redemption. Somebody or other always wants to
be redeemed in his work: sometimes a little male, sometimes a little female—this is *his* problem."[22] But this is now a problem for countless writers on Wagner, for whereas the composer's other operas and music dramas
leave us in little doubt about the immediate beneficiary of the intended act
of redemption, the ending of *Parsifal* is nothing if not cryptic. And Wagner
himself, normally so eager to dispense advice and helpful hints, did little
on this occasion to add to the cause of enlightenment. There is a single
sibylline entry in Cosima Wagner's diary in the course of a conversation
on the subject of *Parsifal*: "'I know what I know and what is in it; and the
new school, Wolz[ogen] and the others, can take their lead from it.' He
then hints at, rather than expresses, the content of this work, 'salvation
to the savior'—and we are silent after he has added, 'Good that we are
alone.'"[23]

It is entirely possible that—a year before his death—Wagner saw himself as a redeemer released from all further obligations by the success of his
final confessional work. That, at least, was the interpretation placed on the
work's final line by the Munich Wagner Society, whose wreath on the occasion of his burial bore the inscription "Erlösung dem Erlöser," prompting
Nietzsche to fire off another barb in Wagner's general direction: "Many
(strangely enough!) made the same small correction: 'Redemption *from* the
redeemer!'—One heaved a sigh of relief."[24]

But this phrase is already a part of the 1877 libretto, where logic dictates
that it refers to Amfortas, whose sinful past means that the king of the Grail
community is incapable of bestowing the redeeming power of the Grail on
his knights. As the new king, Parsifal relieves Amfortas of this burden and
releases him from the torments caused by the exercise of his office.

And yet this interpretation is barely calculated to reflect the "content" of the work to which Wagner obliquely referred, encouraging commentators to claim that the redeemed redeemer is "Christ, who is immanent within the Grail."[25] In correspondence with Hans von Wolzogen, Wagner was at this time developing the idea of an "incomparably and sublimely simple and true redeemer who must first be cleansed and redeemed of the distortion that has been caused by Alexandrine, Judaic, and Roman despotism."[26] Brahms's early biographer Max Kalbeck provided a particularly telling summary of these ideas in a review that he wrote of the first production of *Parsifal*: "The modern faith hero has come to realize that the nineteenth century can no longer use a Christian, *Semitic* Savior but has urgent need of a Christian, *Germanic* Redeemer, and the anti-Semites in our midst may therefore thank Wagner for this blond-haired Christ."[27]

A century later, Robert Gutman, one of the elder statesmen of Anglo-Saxon Wagner studies, developed this critique along even more polemical lines, arguing that "in *Parsifal*, with the help of church bells, snippets of the Mass, and the vocabulary and paraphernalia of the Passion, [Wagner] set forth a religion of racism under the cover of Christian legend. *Parsifal* is an enactment of the Aryan's plight, struggle, and hope for redemption."[28]

Following in Gutman's footsteps, the German historian Hartmut Zelinsky has put forward arguments that implicitly accuse Wagner of preparing the way for the Holocaust, arguments that were widely discussed at the time they were first presented.[29] Carl Dahlhaus, at that date the doyen of musicologically oriented Wagner scholars, dismissed Zelinsky's arguments out of hand, claiming that it is insane to regard *Parsifal* as an "anti-Semitic ritual" and as "coded anti-Semitic propaganda" in the sense of a "demand that Christianity be 'purged' of its Jewish elements by means of the root-and-branch destruction of all those aspects."[30] While it is undeniable that members of Wagner's circle flirted with these ideas, it is impossible to make these charges stick to Wagner, who in 1881 famously refused to sign Bernhard Förster's notorious petition against the Jews, a refusal that was arguably dictated by more than just tactical considerations. At the very least, it is ludicrous to attempt to see the intended "content" of his final stage work in this light.[31] Such a content can be found, if at all, only on a range of different semantic levels.

Of course, Dahlhaus's own proposed interpretation is no less problematical, for on the one hand he claims that Parsifal, "as the redeemer of the tormented Amfortas himself needs to be redeemed from past guilt," while at the same time insisting that "Redemption to the Redeemer" is "also a sentence about Christ," inasmuch as Wagner believed "that Christ, the Redeemer, was seeking redemption in order finally to reveal Himself as He actually was."[32] But what exactly was this "actual" Christ like? He can hardly be equated with the Jesus of Nazareth to whom Wagner had devoted an outline scenario during his revolutionary period,[33] even if Jürgen Kühnel is right to argue that in *Parsifal*, Wagner had sought to free "the historical Jesus" and "perfect human being" from his "status as the son of God, a position that theologians had foisted upon him with the aim of allowing him to safeguard his authority and maintain his grip on power."[34]

If Wagner really wanted to establish a private religion in *Parsifal*, then it remains vague to the point of unintelligibility. And I myself see no need to join the long line of exegetes eager to shed light on the line "Erlösung dem Erlöser" in the spirit of biblical hermeneutics. Whatever the implications of the term *Bühnenweihfestspiel*, we are ultimately dealing with a work of art. That its ending is unclear evidently reflects its creator's view that redemption can be expressed neither in words nor in actions but only in music. The spear that alone can close the wound it once dealt is ultimately not the spear in Parsifal's hands but the music flowing from Wagner's pen. The situation is hardly any different in *Tannhäuser*, *Tristan und Isolde*, or the *Ring*, for there, too, it remains to a greater or lesser extent unclear who is redeeming whom and why. What matters is that the act of redemption is celebrated through the music.

It made sense, therefore, that in his 1977 production of *Parsifal* in Berlin, Harry Kupfer eschewed a final tableau suggestive of solemn sanctity: after the eponymous hero had restored the spear to the brotherhood of the Grail, the members of that community were not overcome by "utter rapture," as the stage directions require them to be, but remained lost and bewildered at the sight of their new king carrying spear and Grail out of the hall and signaling the failure of his mission. Kupfer could appeal to Wagner's music in defense of his production concept, for the music, too, leaves Amfortas unredeemed: the augmented triad that lends Amfortas's motif its underlying character is not resolved at the words "Sei heil, entsündigt und gesühnt" (Be whole, forgiven and unstained) but is retained as a dissonance, encouraging Egon Voss to write that "Wagner the composer falls, as it were, into the arms of Wagner the librettist."[35] The moral of the story is that if there is to be any act of redemption, it is still in the lap of the gods—or of God.

The same is true of Diotima, a key figure in Robert Musil's novel *The Man without Qualities*. She uses the "inflated" word "redemption" until General Stumm "is sick and tired of it," not least because he has no real idea what she means by it. Musil's novel is set in Vienna in the years leading up to the outbreak of the First World War and describes a society looking for ideas to guide it in the face of impending crises, ideas that might save the imperial and royal dual monarchy from disintegrating and at the same time help "unredeemed nationalities" to come into their own.[36] In a wider sense the novel deals with an existential crisis on the part of an inwardly ravaged civilization abandoned by God but still wanting to retain its divine soul and, like Diotima, seeking refuge in mysticism and all kinds of spirituality.

Musil offers a magisterial account of the way in which politics and philosophy have become intertwined and in doing so he throws an involuntary light on the debate surrounding *Parsifal*. (It is significant that he does so from the vantage point of 1913, the year in which Bayreuth's exclusive right to perform the work expired, allowing the *Bühnenweihfestspiel* to be staged elsewhere in the world.) Wagner, too, felt that the one true God had been lost sight of, and, like Musil's prewar society, he and his disciples sought "redemption," confusing art, philosophy, and politics. Although *Parsifal* cannot be interpreted solely in terms of narrow anti-Semitic ideas, there is no denying that it contains "the imagined picture of an attempt to regenerate the human race" that Wagner painted in his late essay "Religion and Art."[37]

This picture also had a nationalistic undertone to it. In his essay "What Is German?" of 1865, for example, Wagner had referred to the Celtic origins of the *Parsifal* and *Tristan* legends before noting how these narratives were then "taken up and elaborated by Germans; and whilst the originals have become mere curiosities of no importance except to students of literary history, in their German counterparts we recognize poetic works of imperishable worth."[38] Presumably Wagner regarded his own contribution to the tradition as the ne plus ultra of these reworkings of the old legend. And there is no doubt that he saw himself as part of the predominantly German tradition of "artist-poets" and "poetic priests" who in the past had kept alive the hope that the "human race might yet be regenerated."[39]

And yet this point, too, needs to be qualified, for Wagner's idea of regeneration is based on the concept of compassion, a concept that pervades the whole of the action of *Parsifal*. In "Religion and Art" he expressly inveighs against the "advancing art of war" with its "torpedoes" and "dynamite cartouches."[40] At the same time, however, the reader is bound to balk at the reasons that Wagner adduces in his essay "Heroism and Christianity" for the part that "blood, the quality of race" can play in "equipping us for the exercise of so holy a heroism"[41]—regardless of the fact that such statements create a less macabre impression when quoted in context than they do when cited in isolation.

Parsifal cannot be salvaged as a work that embodies a positive religion of art, for, as Peter Wapnewski has noted, "the troubling core of it is the equation of human purity with sexual asceticism. The messianic state is associated with an immunity to carnal temptation, and sexual desire is associated with sin. One proves one's nobility by resisting sensual urges." And he goes on to claim that "in its hostility to senses and to women, *Parsifal* is a profoundly inhuman spectacle, glorifying a barren masculine world whose ideals are a combination of militarism and monasticism."[42] We may add that it also depicts the journey through life of a man who has been robbed of his childhood and who can escape from his feelings of guilt only by seeking refuge in a virtual higher existence.[43] In Parsifal's world, any female creature who wants to be more than a mother is a disruptive influence. Whereas the women in Wagner's earlier stage works at least had within them the potential to redeem others, the only female characters in *Parsifal* are the Flowermaidens and Kundry, who is herself in need of redemption. But to shy away from eroticism is also to shy away from society, at which point the artificiality and sterility of the Grail community are revealed in all their grim inhumanity.

The work excited ridicule even among Wagner's contemporaries, Nietzsche, for example, mocking it as "operetta material par excellence,"[44] while one of Brahms's female friends, Elisabeth von Herzogenberg, reacted to a Bayreuth performance in 1889 with undisguised contempt, complaining that Wagnerians "go to *Parsifal* just as Catholics visit graves on Good Friday—it has become a church service for them. They are all in an unnaturally heightened, hysterically enraptured state. [. . .] A blood-thirstiness and musty smell of incense, a sultry sensuality with terribly serious gestures, a heaviness, and a bombast otherwise unprecedented in art weighs down on one, its brooding intensity taking one's breath away." What she found in Bayreuth was a "bag of spiritual conjuring tricks" and an "unhealthy ecstasy which, fired by the stigmata, is almost an emetic for stomachs accustomed to a diet of Bach."[45] Today her great-grandchildren would presumably complain that in the final tableau the dead Titurel rises up in his coffin to bless the knights of the Grail as if he were some alien or zombie from the realm of science fiction.

However we look at it, Parsifal bears no resemblance whatever to Siegfried as a suitable mate for Brünnhilde as the "woman of the future." While the characters of the *Ring* constitute a family, albeit one riven by internecine strife, *Parsifal* introduces us to a community of human ghosts. And whereas Wotan reveals features that allow us a glimpse of Wagner's own contradictory personality, there is not a single character in *Parsifal* with whom we could plausibly identify the composer—assuming we are not to ferret around in the recesses of his unconscious: Wagner is not present in his characters but controls them like a director. And while this may be appropriate behavior for the creator of a *Bühnenweihfestspiel*, this does not make him any more convincing as an advocate in his own cause, a cause that in any case seems not a little desperate.

What remains? *Parsifal* offers us a chance to get to know Wagner not only as the self-important founder of a new religion and as a dubious ideologue but also as a committed artist with a specifically romantic understanding of suffering and a longing for redemption. If we judge him by these human standards, then the subject matter of *Parsifal* reveals astonishing similarities with a text by Franz Schubert—his short story *My Dream* of 1822:

> I was the brother of many brothers & sisters. Our father & mother were good people. I was deeply devoted to them all.—Once my father took us to a feast, where my brothers became very merry. But I was sad. My father came over & bade me enjoy the delicious food, but I was unable to do so, whereupon my father, growing angry, banished me from his sight. I left [. . .] and wandered away to a far-off region. [. . .] I then received news of my mother's death. I hastened home, & my father, mellowed by grief, did nothing to stop me from entering. [. . .] We followed her body in mourning, & the coffin was lowered into the earth.—From then on I remained at home. Then my father took me back to his favorite garden. He asked me whether I liked it. But I hated the garden [. . .]. My father then struck me, & I fled. [. . .] One day I received news of a God-fearing maiden who had just died. And a circle formed round her grave in which many youths & old men walked as if in everlasting bliss. [. . .] I too longed to walk there. But I was told that only a miracle could allow one to enter that circle. Yet I slowly walked toward the gravestone with lowered gaze, fired by inner devotion & firm belief, & before I was aware of it, I found myself in the circle, which produced a wondrously lovely sound; & I felt as if eternal bliss were compressed into a single moment. I also saw my father, reconciled & loving. He took me in his arms & wept. But not as much as I did.[46]

The structural affinities between Schubert's *My Dream* and Wagner's *Parsifal* are plain, and it is no accident that as perceptive a musician as Pierre Boulez has observed that in *Parsifal* "Wagner realized the romantics' dream, realized and surpassed it."[47] This may encourage us to examine *Parsifal* not from the standpoint of its complicated and largely disturbing reception history but as a dream machine on the part of Wagner the artist. Describing a performance of the work in Bayreuth in 1909, Thomas Mann wrote, "Although I went there in a spirit of considerable skepticism and felt that I was undertaking a pilgrimage to Lourdes or visiting an oracle or some other place associated with some mildly indecent fraud, I was in the end profoundly shaken by the experience. Certain passages, especially in act 3—the Good Friday music, the baptism, the anointing and so on, and then the unforgettable final tableau—are significant and completely irresistible."

But Mann was even more impressed by the darker aspects of the work: "It is really only here that these accents of contrition and torment that W[agner] spent his whole life working on achieve their ultimate intensity. Tristan's longing pales beside this Miserere, with its piercing details and ardent cruelties."[48]

Even a writer as critical of *Parsifal* as Nietzsche had nothing but admiration for "a synthesis of states which will seem incompatible to many people, even 'loftier people,' with a severity that judges, an 'altitude' in the terrifying sense of the word, with an intimate cognizance and perspicuity that cut through the soul like a knife—and with a compassion for what is being *watched* and *judged*. Something of that sort occurs in Dante—nowhere else."[49]

A century later Nike Wagner homed in on the pathological elements in the work, diagnosing a "universal state of suffering which is all the more modern because no one knows its cause; it remains uncomprehended, nameless and unredeemed."[50] My own attitude to *Parsifal* has changed now that I no longer hear it as music that seeks to express a particular view of the world, an interpretation I would be bound to resist in every shape and form. Now I see it as a musical psychograph, describing twisted and damaged individuals, all of whom are in search of salvation. Here there is, of course, no scope for conciliatory gestures of the kind seen in Wolfgang Wagner's 1975 production, in which Kundry was allowed to live and partake of the Grail. Nor is there any scope for the sort of epiphany hinted at even in Christoph Schlingensief's 2004 production in Bayreuth, a production otherwise obsessed with images of death. We are dealing, rather, with a desperately hysterical fight against the dictates of a fear of death that Wagner's notorious redemptive mysticism strives merely superficially to keep in check even in *Parsifal*. This does not contradict Nietzsche's claim, in which admiration and malice are finely balanced: "Wagner never had better inspirations than in the end. Here the cunning in his alliance of beauty and sickness goes so far that, as it were, it casts a shadow over Wagner's earlier art—which now seems too bright, too healthy."[51]

True, this view does not salvage the work's central religious experience in the way that Wagner wanted. But it asserts itself as *art*. Modern audiences can approach *Parsifal* not through the medium of religion but only through that of its theatricality. Listeners receptive to that theatricality and able to hear "a mystical imprimatur on the temple proceedings"[52] in the final "Erlösung dem Erlöser" sung "barely audibly" by an unseen chorus and to see in this passage a vehicle for beguiling sounds are unlikely to be unimpressed by a performance of the work. Both Debussy and Proust were fascinated by *Parsifal* without abandoning themselves to its ideology. And the young Alban Berg—later to compose the socially critical *Wozzeck*—wrote in 1909, immediately after a performance of the work in Bayreuth: "You would be able to tell from the tears that keep welling to my eyes and from the dreamy otherworldliness of my thoughts how deeply and sublimely I have been moved. Words can say barely half of what I am feeling and can scarcely express the tremendously life-enhancing and shattering impression that the work has left on me. And how futile it would be to try to describe the music—*such* music."[53]

It is no accident that Berg praises the music. We do not need to celebrate the syncretic construct that *Parsifal* represents as an example of "sacred world theater"[54] or to dismiss it as a National Socialist handbook to admire this music as altogether unique. Ideally, I believe the work should be performed as an oratorio with a silent film in the background, clarifying Wagner's point that the music is the "unseen soul" of the action,[55] the action itself being tolerable only in the spirit of the voyeurism that the darkened auditorium of a cinema invites us to share. Like the young Parsifal attending events in the Castle of the Grail and feeling only uncomprehending astonishment, the cinemagoer would be aware of the plot only as a strangely distant expression of fin-de-siècle mysticism that can acquire a private reality only through the eloquence of Wagner's music. Even while still working on the score, Wagner had already noted with a sigh: "Oh, I hate the thought of all those costumes and grease paint! When I think that characters like Kundry will now have to be dressed up, those dreadful artists' balls immediately spring into my mind. Having created the invisible orchestra, I now feel like inventing the invisible theater!"[56] There is something paradoxical about the fact that the work by Wagner most clearly in-

tended to trade in ideas survives today in a form in which philosophy and
ritual are merely peripheral.

Innovative features in terms of the history of music may be found at
every point in the score. Werner Breig, for example, has drawn attention
to the scene between Klingsor and Kundry at the start of act 2 where the
"text declamation is heightened into a veritable psychological image of the
character."[57] According to Wagner's stage directions, Kundry's voice must
sound "rough and disjointed, as if she is attempting to regain the use of language," a type of setting that looks forward to the verismo operas of the future (music example 29). As for Parsifal's cry of "Amfortas!—Die Wunde!—
Die Wunde!—Sie brennt in meinem Herzen" (Amfortas! The wound! The
wound! It's burning in my heart), Adorno notes that Wagner's music is
"poised immediately on the threshold of atonality" (music example 30).[58]

29. Bars 166–79 of act 2 of *Parsifal*.

30. Bars 994–1002 of act 2 of *Parsifal*.

It is by no means certain, of course, that those elements in a work that were once regarded as progressive will ensure its survival in the canon, for every example of avant-garde art is quickly consigned to history. But *Parsifal* deserves to be called a pivotal piece inasmuch as two levels clash in it in an altogether unique way. As a "work" in the classical and romantic sense, *Parsifal* has a hollow form whose content is made up for the most part of what is called "new music"—music that plays at random with elements of that form. It is this dialectic that makes it possible for us to hear *Parsifal* with both traditional and modern ears. Or, rather, listeners receptive to musical nuances will necessarily hear *Parsifal* with two different kinds of ears—in stereo, as it were. And, like it or not, such listeners will be reflecting the attitude of the composer, who on the one hand was absorbed by his confessional work in the nineteenth-century tradition, while on the other hand playing with his own feelings, like an old man in whom sadness at his own emotional involvement consorts with his professional routine as a skilled craftsman. Or like someone who believes not in God but in his own religion of art.

For me, one of the most impressive aspects of Wagner's entire creative output is his music's ability to convey this contradictory attitude—and this is true, no matter whether its creator would have welcomed such an interpretation or not. If the modern catchphrase about the "death of the author" has any meaning at all, then it is in the present case, in which the largely diffuse interaction of a traditional and a progressive musical language ensures that what we have here is a pivotal work that communicates the experiences of modern men and women independently of its author. And although we experience these only on a metalevel by marveling at Wagner's skills as a magician, such experiences, while not making us any happier, at least are closer to reality than any that may be encountered in the field of "idealistic" music. After all, they reflect the inner turmoil of modern men and women: our self-pity in the face of existential insecurity and our ambivalent attitude to the various kinds of redemption that are on offer. We hear the sound of the Grail bells with a frisson, while making no attempt to follow them.

Nothing ever happens in the history of music without some prior warning. Specifically, we can regard *Die Meistersinger* as the model for a method of composition whose interplay between the old and the new anticipates the broken, refracted nature of Wagner's final score, except that in the earlier work that interplay was limited to the world of comedy. And whereas the old was used in *Die Meistersinger* to provide a "real-idealistic" reflection of a particular moment in the history of music, in *Parsifal* it is a synonym for weathering, for sparseness, and for mysteriousness in general. The impact is all the greater in that the corresponding musical figures—one scarcely dares speak of leitmotifs any longer—help to paint the old using modern colors, with the result that it simultaneously appears new and, as such, resembles a newly rediscovered primitive religion. (On a much smaller scale, Robert Schumann had demonstrated how this could be done in his song "Auf einer Burg" from his *Liederkreis*, op. 39.)

The mixture of piety and the search for meaning, of steadfastness and mysteriousness, of closed melodic forms and open harmonic writing typical of the "mantric formula"[59] "Durch Mitleid wissend, der reine Thor, harre sein, den ich erkor" (Made wise by pity, the blameless fool, wait for him whom I have chosen) is achieved by means of a compositional process of rare refinement: on the one hand a textbook sequence of fifths lends the upper voice and hence the writing as a whole a sense of archaic beauty, while on the other, the chromatically modern and distinctly volatile harmonization ensures a feeling of instability (music example 31).

31. The "Pure Fool" motif from bars 737–41 of act 1 of *Parsifal*.

The distance covered by Wagner since the early stages of the *Ring* is clear from a comparison between the above passage ("Durch Mitleid wissend") and the renunciation motif in scene 1 of *Das Rheingold* ("Nur wer der Minne Macht versagt"). In both cases we are dealing with a magic rhyme, but whereas this is set in the *Ring* as a vocally and harmonically unambiguous phrase, it takes the form of a musical puzzle in *Parsifal*. As such, it is able to fulfill its "mantric" function in various contexts, hinting at all manner of allusions in keeping with the unfolding action onstage. Shortly before the end of the work, for example, a variant of the beginning of the phrase turns up as the anacrusis of the Last Supper motif, which in turn is adapted in such a way that it can continue with the final phrase of the theme associated with the words "Durch Mitleid wissend" (music example 32).

32. Bars 1081–84 of act 3 of *Parsifal*.

This comparison helps us to understand why *Parsifal* can be described as a pivotal work in terms of the history of composition. In the good old tradition of the leitmotif, the renunciation motif is semantically unambiguous in that it uses the tried-and-tested language of a minor tonality to express the idea of renunciation in love, an idea that from the Rhinedaughters' point of view is entirely regrettable. Such a use was familiar to listeners from ancient ballads, including the melancholy folk song "Schwesterlein, Schwesterlein, wann geh'n wir nach Haus?" collected by Zuccalmaglio and arranged by Brahms. The setting of the words "Durch Mitleid wissend" is also semantically charged, but on this occasion the listener cannot fall back on any tradition to interpret its meaning but has to rely on the overall context. And if the musical symbols lack any binding meaning that can accrue to them only from a lengthy tradition, their interpretation necessarily becomes localized, with the result that it can change in a trice, and instead of establishing meaning, it merely satisfies ornamental or decorative needs.

Wagner himself would not have referred to the work being poised on a threshold, of course, for his aim was to equip the piece with binding symbols, and he would presumably have refuted Jean Moréas's claim in his "Symbolist Manifesto" of 1886 that the aim of symbolist art was "never to concentrate on the Idea as such."[60] For however much Wagner may have insisted on using music to introduce his ideas to the emotional world of his listeners, he left those listeners in no doubt that it was the *music* that had to convey those ideas. The situation changed only when audiences began to respond to *Parsifal*, for against this background the symbol takes on a life of its own and becomes the res ipsa. When he described the Good Friday music, baptism, anointing, and final tableau as "irresistible," Thomas Mann was not responding to Wagner's private religion but to a series of powerful images *qua images*. If there are ideas in *Parsifal*, music is not their reflection but—in the finest Schopenhauerian tradition—their archetype, an image behind which no listeners can ever hope to go.

Whereas *Parsifal* became a pivotal work only for later generations, the paintings of Gustav Klimt—generally viewed as examples of symbolism and Jugendstil—combine within them the corresponding ambivalence from the outset. The Beethoven frieze that Klimt painted for the Vienna Secession in 1902 and that was directly inspired by Wagner's interpretation of Beethoven's Ninth Symphony demonstrates the artist's interest in ideas, hence his description of one particular scene depicting a knight with a couple kneeling behind him as "The Longing for Happiness. The Sufferings of Weak Humanity: Their Entreaties Addressed to the Well-Armed Stronger Man."[61] On the other hand, Klimt's art aims to aestheticize the artist's ideas, each theme being relatively random—it is enough for it to signal an intellectual flight of fancy. Once this provision has been met, then the theme may take second place to questions of form and artistic treatment. Indeed, this is sometimes true in the literal sense, notably when a human figure disappears behind the painter's brushstrokes.

And yet we may approach the music of *Parsifal* not only in the way that we might approach a painting by Klimt; we could also hear it as a piece by Debussy born before his time. This takes us a stage further, for Debussy had no time for music that seeks to convey a message. Even titles such as *La mer* (The sea) and *Prélude à l'après-midi d'un faune* (Prelude to a faun's afternoon) signal that we are not dealing with existential victories and defeats and that the composer simply wanted his listeners to share what he himself saw and felt and heard before giving it musical form. Even in his symbolist opera *Pelléas et Mélisande*, it is—according to Boulez—the "musical structure that assumes total responsibility for what happens onstage."[62] Essentially this means that the music alone expresses all that we can ever know about Pelléas, Mélisande, Golaud, and Yniold. Or, to put it another way, we hear the music in the context of the action but not as a reaction to it.

In the case of *Parsifal*, we do not need to go as far as this, and yet it remains a viable approach. Boulez, whose appearances in the sunken pit at Bayreuth proved pioneering, has referred to the work as "a kind of 'prism' of Claude Debussy."[63] Conversely, he has compared the opening of act 3, "Parsifal's Wanderings," to an expressive, unsentimental, and nonironic night piece—again his point of reference is clearly Debussy.[64] I would remind readers at this juncture of a comment by Wagner that I quoted in my chapter on *Die Meistersinger von Nürnberg*: "It has not been possible to avoid a certain restriction of feeling; this does not mean that it is churchlike in tone, he says, indeed there is even a divine wildness about it, but such affecting emotions as in *Tristan* or even the *Nibelungen* would be entirely out of place. 'You will see—diminished sevenths were just not possible!' "[65]

Wanderings are an integral part of Wagner's archetypal scenario in terms of his life and art. There are obvious parallels between Tannhäuser's Pilgrimage and Parsifal's Wanderings. Both are "imaginary pictures," to quote Wagner's own taxonomy; both of them open their respective third acts and are performed with the curtains closed; and both of them serve to bridge a considerable period of time. In Tannhäuser's case, the hero goes on a pilgrimage to Rome, his return journey being notable only for its aimlessness, while Parsifal's wanderings take him "through pathless wildernesses" and "countless afflictions, battles, and struggles," to quote from the second prose draft of 1877.[66]

As with *Tannhäuser*, so the orchestral introduction to act 3 of *Parsifal* is intended to replace the action onstage. As a precaution, Wagner reminded himself of Tannhäuser's Pilgrimage while he was working on the compositional draft of Parsifal's Wanderings between October 18 and October 30, 1878. During this time he played the end of act 2 and the beginning of act 3 to Cosima and two of their daughters. And yet, in spite of the fact that Parsifal is more like a reformed Tannhäuser than a reborn Siegfried, and although Tannhäuser's Pilgrimage already contains the Dresden Amen that reappears in Parsifal's Wanderings in the form of the Grail motif, the later introduction is far from being a remake of the earlier interlude. In Tannhäuser's Pilgrimage, the pervasive note of despair includes an element of passion, whereas the dominant impression in the introduction to act 3 of *Parsifal* is one of asceticism, desolation, and emptiness—despite the initial performance marking of "expressively," a marking contradicted by Wagner's own remark during the rehearsals in 1882 that bar 11 should be played "as if without expression."[67] This is reflected in the chromatic melodic writing, in the predominance of ambiguous chord combinations that repeatedly call into question the underlying tonal system, and in contrapuntal writing that creates a curiously emaciated impression. The opening motif, for example, has been described both as the motif of desolation and as that of the grief associated with the Grail and has a long prehistory. Stated by the strings alone, without any support or color from the winds, it was noted down in a rudimentary form at a time when Wagner was preoccupied with *Tristan und Isolde*. Here it appears on a sheet of music manuscript paper intended for Mathilde Wesendonck and headed "Parzival." Underlying the music are the words "Wo find' ich dich, du heil'ger Gral, dich sucht voll Sehnsucht mein Herze" (Where shall I find you, O Holy Grail? Filled with longing, my heart is seeking you) (music example 33).[68]

33. A transcription of the undated sketch that Wagner sent to Mathilde Wesendonck in 1858 in which Parzival tells of his longing to find the Grail.

In 1858 Wagner had briefly toyed with the idea of having Parsifal visit the fatally wounded Tristan in the course of his wanderings. Even at this date, then, the Parsifal project was already affecting him. Twenty years later he returned to this musical idea, but without elaborating it. Instead he told Cosima, before starting on Parsifal's Wanderings, that "he must not introduce anything isolatedly, it must all be in context; and so his prelude to the 3rd act will introduce the theme of Titurel's funeral [. . .]. There is no place, he says, for a big 'independent affair' depicting Parsifal's wanderings."[69] In the end Wagner did not use "the theme of Titurel's funeral"—generally described by writers on Wagner as the funeral chorus motif—and instead we hear the motifs associated with the grief of the Grail, the Grail itself, Kundry, the lance, the pure fool theme, and the lament. Particularly striking is the way in which Wagner combines the pure fool theme with the Kundry motif: after all, Parsifal has set out on his wanderings because he was cursed by Kundry at the end of act 2.

The "context" to which Wagner referred in his conversation with Cosima was nothing if not tricky: "Now I am writing something which should sound like nothing, nothing at all, Robert Schumann, but there

34. The motif associated with Titurel's obsequies in bars 804–8 of act 3 of *Parsifal*.

A preliminary sketch of bars 23–28 of the prelude to act 3 of *Parsifal*, bearing Wagner's date "22. Oct. R." at the end, followed by a note in Cosima's hand: "Written out for me by R. Oct. 22, 1878." (Photograph courtesy of the Nationalarchiv der Richard-Wagner-Stiftung, Bayreuth: NA A III m. 4⁽²⁾, folio 12r.)

must be method in it—the theme of the march would have been much too definite," he observed on October 21, 1878.[70] The "theme of the march" was presumably the rhythmically striking funeral chorus motif that is now heard for the first time during Titurel's obsequies (music example 34). Wagner's surviving sketches and Cosima's diary entries allow us to reconstruct his work on the score on an almost daily basis. A preliminary sketch of bars 23–28 of the prelude ends with a note in Cosima's hand: "Written out for me by R. Oct. 22, 1878."[71]

On October 24, 1878, Wagner spoke of the "sad strains he will now have to compose; they must not contain a single ray of light, he says, for that could lead one far astray. Parsifal's sad wanderings, which must lead up to the situation on Monsalvat."[72] On October 29 we read: "R. says he has composed two bars, but they are very important ones, an addition in the middle of the prelude: they had occupied his mind the minute he awoke in the morning."[73] And on October 31 Cosima noted: "He plays the prelude to me; it is very much altered, even more gloomy! It begins like the lament of an extinguished star, after which one discerns, like gestures, Parsifal's arduous wanderings and Kundry's pleas for salvation. It seems as if none of this could be sung—only the 'elemental' quality can be felt here." And in the

margin Cosima added a further note: "That is to say, not the lament, but the sounds of extinction, out of which lamenting emerges."[74]

Symptomatic of this mood is Wagner's harmonic writing, which flouts the traditional rules of functional harmony and treats the chord of the diminished seventh—a dissonance—as the central sound. The writer and director Einar Schleef, who is anything but a committed Wagnerian, has examined in detail the affinities between Goethe's *Faust* and Wagner's *Parsifal* and in a disturbingly original way ignores the present tendency to fixate on *Parsifal*'s racist elements. He speaks of "notes in which Schoenberg may be glimpsed and even surpassed."[75] In adopting this approach he places these "notes" in the context of music explicitly dismissed by the National Socialists as "degenerate."

But what is astonishing is not just the advanced nature of the compositional means that Wagner uses in Parsifal's Wanderings, for other composers such as Liszt were able to keep pace with him and even outdo him, but rather that, as Mario Bortolotto has written, Wagner was concerned "solely with extending the tonal principle" in his final stage work, whereas Liszt in his *Parsifal* paraphrase *Am Grabe Richard Wagners*, for example— "explored unknown regions with a merely acoustic attentiveness and in an unequivocally experimental way."[76]

And it is this final point that matters here: Wagner's harmonic temerities are not an example of art for art's sake but aim to achieve a rare degree of semantic clarity and vividness in their depiction of the most complex emotional states. In spite of his skepticism toward what he called the "brume wagnérienne," Debussy was so profoundly influenced by this aspect of Wagner's harmonic writing that Robert Craft has described the musical interludes in *Pelléas et Mélisande* as "Xerox copies of *Parsifal*."[77] Wagner needed two weeks of immensely hard work to set down the forty-four bars of Parsifal's Wanderings in their definitive form, a struggle that took place not only in his head but also on paper and at the piano and that sheds light on the passion with which he sought to reconcile the opposing elements of existential sensitivity and compositional structure.

And this brings us back to the notion of a pivotal art. By now—if not sooner—we have come to the end of idealism and romanticism, for on the one hand the expressive language of this "orchestral psychograph"[78] can scarcely be described except in such negative terms as "numb," "inhibited," "lost," "shrouded in gloom," "restlessly encircling," and so on, a language notable for its total lack of closed and rounded forms—qualities which had at least been vaguely discernible as a specific quality of music in even the most advanced works of the nineteenth century.

As a piece of music, Parsifal's Wanderings is even more radical than Tannhäuser's Pilgrimage, the "traurige Weise" from *Tristan und Isolde*, and the prelude to act 3 of *Die Meistersinger von Nürnberg*—all of them key passages at the start of their respective final acts, where purely instrumental tone paintings seem to invalidate the usual time continuum in favor of a melancholic or deeply depressing reflection on all that has happened hitherto. But whereas the sounds of the young shepherd piping his mournful lay in *Tristan und Isolde* seem to encompass an element of hope, and whereas the prelude to act 3 of *Die Meistersinger* features not only the Wahn motif but also the optimistic sounds of the "Wittenberg Nightingale," the introduction to act 3 of *Parsifal* is intended to plumb depths of unprecedented despair. Nowhere else does Wagner reveal himself so unequivocally as a disciple of Arthur Schopenhauer; and as such, nowhere else does his music reflect Schopenhauer's blind world-will as emphatically as it does here—in other words, without recourse to a concrete action. It was no accident that Wagner spoke of "a background of elemental sorrow" that should prevail in Parsifal's Wanderings.[79]

As the choice of leitmotifs indicates, we are dealing here with more than just the fate of the hero himself but also with "Kundry's pleas for salvation" and the "vision" of the unredeemed Grail.[80] In short, Parsifal's Wanderings represent the folly of the world itself. The darkness of the music is, as it were, the black hole of the *Bühnenweihfestspiel*, its remoteness from God casting its shadow over the whole of the rest of the work.

Even the Last Supper motif, for all that it is conceived as a symbol of comfort and promise, has acquired a note of anguish thanks to its minor-key coloring since it was first heard in the prelude to act 1 and is now chromatically "distorted."[81] Superficially, this motif is sermon-like in its simplicity, and yet it turns out on closer inspection to be a disturbing product of the fin de siècle, extraordinarily subtle and yet diffuse in its message. The lines that originally underlay this motif appear in the 1877 edition of the libretto—published before Wagner had started work on the score—and are as follows:

> Nehmet hin mein Blut
> um unsrer Liebe Willen!
> Nehmet hin meinen Leib,
> auf daß ihr mein' gedenkt!

[Take this my blood for the sake of our love! Take this my body that you remember me!]

When he came to set these words to music, Wagner thought that they needed expanding in order to allow him to explore every facet of their message in his music. Unusually for him, he added two more lines to produce two strophes of three lines each:

> Nehmet hin meinen Leib,
> nehmet hin mein Blut
> um uns'rer Liebe Willen!
> Nehmet hin mein Blut,
> nehmet hin meinen Leib,
> auf daß ihr mein gedenkt!

[Take this my body, take this my blood for the sake of our love! Take this my blood, take this my body that you remember me!]

Neither in the Last Supper motif nor anywhere else in the work is it possible to separate the Grail from the Counter-Grail or distinguish between the worlds of positive and negative experience, encouraging William Kinderman to note that "when the Redeemer's gaze falls on Kundry or when Parsifal brandishes the sacred lance in Klingsor's magic garden, two opposing worlds are manifest in one and the same sound, which is highly charged with tension."[82] And John Daverio tends in the same direction when he describes Amfortas's outburst, "Wehvolles Erbe," as a "tortured derivative" of the Last Supper motif (music examples 35 and 36).[83]

35 and 36. A comparison between the Last Supper motif from bars 1–6 of the prelude to act 1 of *Parsifal* and Amfortas's lament in bars 1302–5.

Even the mystic finale has elements of *Uneigentlichkeit* in Heidegger's sense of "that which does not belong to me," a point that applies not least to its musical aspect. Readers may care to recall the dissonant choruses beset by Grail bells whose sound for many years was produced in Bayreuth by four plain metal drums. Presumably money could have been found to cast four actual bells, but a deliberate decision was evidently taken not to do so. At least the dull sound of the drums, with its relatively paucity of upper partials, was more at home in an imaginary crypt as a somber place of repression than in the light-filled dome envisaged by Wagner's stage directions.

The ceremony associated with the Grail is an excellent indication of the way in which certain symbols can emerge from their context and become an example of art for art's sake—not in the sense of "absolute" music but in the wake of a compositional and historical development that removes the religious element from its original context and in the spirit of symbolism and Jugendstil turns it into material that can be freely adapted and reused. In this way, the material retains its spiritual essence but loses all contact with binding rituals such as those of the Catholic Mass and Protestant Communion. Wagner made a start by constructing his own Communion ritual, a ritual which is clearly oriented to the Christian liturgy but at the same time tends in the direction of a private religion.

Writing in the wake of Wagner, Mahler took over the theme of religion for use in his symphonies. The final movement of his First Symphony includes a variant of the Grail motif, while the Adagio of his Fourth Symphony contains a theme that clearly recalls the Grail bells at an exposed point in the musical argument. His tendency to avail himself of "sacred" themes is even more pronounced in his vocal symphonies, especially his

Second and Eighth, both of which deal with the question of redemption that pervades the whole of *Parsifal*. His Second Symphony is also known as his "Resurrection" Symphony, a name that it owes to the choral passage in the final movement, "Aufersteh'n, ja aufersteh'n wirst, du, mein Staub, nach kurzer Ruh!" (Arise, yes you will arise, my dust, after a brief rest), while the Symphony of a Thousand, as the Eighth is also known, deals with the theme of redemption from first to last, both in the form of Hrabanus Maurus's medieval hymn *Veni creator spiritus* and in that of the mystical final scene from part 2 of Goethe's *Faust*.[84]

The qualitative leap from *Parsifal* to Mahler's symphonies lies in the fact that the presentation of the divine, which in Wagner's music drama has already been transferred from a sacred space to the boards of a secular theater, now has to make do with the concert hall. But this means that the religious ideas, however important they may have been for the composer, are now completely dissipated. It is no accident that in 1917, a decade after Mahler completed his Eighth Symphony, the theologian Rudolf Otto published his phenomenological study *The Idea of the Holy* in which he defined the "holy" as the "numinous" experience of something "outside the self."[85]

That this "mysterium fascinans" cannot and should not be explained will be understood at once by listeners familiar with the credo of "absolute" music, and my readers will perhaps understand why I regard *Parsifal* as a pivotal work that mediates between two different understandings of art as a religion: for the nineteenth century the accent lay on religion in the early romantic tradition, whereas by the twentieth century the emphasis had shifted to art. *Parsifal* can be seen against both these horizons.

This is also true of Kundry, arguably the most enigmatic of all Wagner's characters. As the "woman" who laughed at Christ on the road to Calvary, she is "Jewish" by birth; her lord and master Klingsor calls her "Herodias," and Wagner himself compared her to the Wandering Jew in his 1865 prose draft, adding that as a result of her "curse," she is "condemned, in ever new forms, to bring to men the suffering of love's seduction; redemption, dissolution, complete extinction is vouchsafed to her only if the purest and most youthfully radiant of men resists her most powerful blandishments."[86] But the libretto also refers to her as a "heathen," and for Ulrike Kienzle, she allowed Wagner "to illustrate the Indian idea of metempsychosis."[87]

Even during Wagner's own lifetime, the composer's associates were already describing Kundry as a "representative of the Jewish principle" in contrast to Parsifal, who was seen as "the Aryan, Germanic figure of the Christian Redeemer."[88] Writers on Wagner continue to argue over the question as to whether the composer, too, regarded Kundry as an expression of anti-Semitism not just in passing but primarily, and yet it is all too easy to overlook the fact that in Kundry he created a genuinely fascinating character who cannot be reduced to questions of ideology or to interpretations limited to a particular point in history. In short, she cannot without further ado be identified with the decadent movement that was fashionable in Europe at the end of the nineteenth century. From that point of view we may regard it as a compliment that the gender theorist Christina von Braun has seen in the role of Kundry the image of a hysterical woman of a kind that did not exist in reality but which Wagner conjured up onstage in the form of an "artificial woman."[89]

But it is also worth asking whether—as visitors to the *Parsifal* freak show—we feel more comfortable identifying with Klingsor, Amfortas, or Parsifal himself. After all, the cultural historian Elisabeth Bronfen has argued that from the standpoint of a psychopathologist Parsifal's imagination and his "identification" with Amfortas's wound as a "mimetic representation of Christ's wound" are no less "hysterical" than Kundry's "phantasy scenario" whereby her "ecstatic laughter" at Christ's wound triggered the curse that weighs upon her.[90]

Does Kundry—undoubtedly Wagner's most complex and riveting character from a mythological point of view—not deserve our sympathy too? After all, she is not only what Thomas Mann once described as a "desperate woman of split personality, half corrupter, half penitent Mary Magdalene, with cataleptic transitions between these two states of being,"[91] but is also a natural creature who laughs horribly, utters bloodcurdling screams, groans pitifully, and—following her baptism—weeps tears of redemptive release, all of them physical and emotional utterances that do not have to be reinterpreted in any unduly complex, oversophisticated way but which can be associated above all with children.

As far as I can see, all writers on Wagner have ignored the fact that in Kundry our vital component—otherwise frighteningly absent from *Parsifal*—comes into its own. And while its manifestation may be distorted, it is still recognizable. More importantly: once Kundry has given free rein to her provocatively animalistic emotions, she is allowed to appear as a beautiful seductress. But she is also permitted to serve others and finally to be released from her sufferings. Her various characteristics merely need to be shaken, as in a kaleidoscope, and reassembled in order to produce a new and entirely positive Kundry.

In her book *Revolution in Poetic Language*, the French cultural semiologist Julia Kristeva has explored the idea of "chora" that ultimately goes back to Plato and redefined it as the "semiotic bed" of those expressions of very young children, especially those who have not yet learned to talk. These expressions are dictated by physical needs but are only apparently uncoordinated and meaningless, whereas in fact they have their own specific rhythms that are conditioned by the particular situation and as a result are a part of the "genotext" of body language that Kristeva defines as "the only transfer of drive energies that organizes a space in which the subject is not *yet* a split unity."[92] This allows "jouissance" to infiltrate "the social and symbolic order."[93] In the medium of art, this process results in elements of improvisation and in the aphoristic, the disjointed, the fragmentary, the incomplete, the ambiguous, the wildly luxuriant, and the confusing. Kristeva cites examples from Wagner's admirer Stéphane Mallarmé and also from Joyce, but she could equally well have quoted from Wagner himself.[94]

Kundry, too, avails herself of a "genotext" that operates with striking noises, interjections, and interruptions and which, unlike any actual language, knows neither good nor evil, in which respect it reflects Wagner's own composition. In general terms the music of *Parsifal* is less ethically unambiguous than many sections of the *Ring*, which take sides musically, and this is even more true of the role of Kundry. As the composer Bernd Asmus has observed, the "shock gesture" of Kundry's motif is a symbol of expressionism: "As in a scream, the musical energy builds up in a single dissonant chord, before being carried away and continued in a monophonic line that plunges down over the notes of the chord."[95] Compositionally speaking, Kundry's inner disunity assumes the guise of a "split sonority" (music example 37).[96]

37. Kundry's motif from bars 216–20 of act 1 of *Parsifal*.

In the middle of the motif the harmonic fabric suddenly falls apart. What remains is a powerfully expressive gesture, but it is not one that seeks to "evaluate" either Kundry as a person or the situation in which she finds herself. Rather, the motif should be understood in the sense of a genotext that reaches back into deeper layers of experience and is unconditionally no more than what it is. Although he may have used a different technique, it is passages such as these that Alban Berg picks up and elaborates, notably in *Lulu*. It is above all her music that ensures that Kundry—like all the other characters in the work—is not a monster but a genuinely human figure. Although the opposites that she combines within her may be extreme, they nonetheless make clear what each of us carries around with us as baggage.

A quotation from Cosima Wagner's diary may serve to illustrate this point: "R. fetches me for lunch and says, 'Do you know how Kundry calls to Parsifal?' He sings me the phrase, so piercingly tender, with which she names him: 'It is the first time his name is spoken, and thus his mother had called to him! Only music can do that.'"[97] One of the first interpreters of the role of Kundry was Marianne Brandt, who was initially considered unsuited to the character as she appears in act 2, but, as, Hans Bartolo Brand reports: "A sustained note, as if from a little silver bell, a note pure and clear, gradually dying away to the most delicate *pianissimo*. And then the call of 'Parsifal! Tarry!' wafting over the flowery hedge. This wonderful, beguilingly beautiful voice cast its spell on listeners and fellow performers alike, drawing them into its sway."[98] This, too, is a part of Kundry's character. However necessary the debates about Wagner's ideology and current productions of his works, the most precious part of his legacy—his music within the context of the theater—should never be lost from sight.

The French philosopher André Glucksmann, who was the son of Jewish parents, used his ironically titled book *The Master Thinkers* to attack those major figures who in his view had been responsible for leading the West into the byways of ideological totalitarianism. For him, Wagner was the "master thinker" among artists. In mocking its own premises, Glucksmann argues that Wagner's work—and he was thinking specifically of the *Ring* in Patrice Chéreau's Bayreuth production—defies the constraints of the system: "A man sets out upon a stage the grand machinery of modern power: he launches the speeches, prepares the imbroglios, puts the fantasms into action. It works. In his miracle of Bayreuth he realizes the philosophy of Hegel and of Marx, that of the Kremlin, the Pentagon and the Forbidden City. He guffaws in our faces."[99]

It is the laughter of the music, as provocative as Kundry's laughter, provoking all know-it-alls and fanatics addicted to a particular system. As Wagner observed on February 25, 1870: "Concepts are the gods living within a convention, but tones are the daemons."[100] The music of *Parsifal* is likewise demonic, counteracting the theory expressed in this chapter that erotic love was on the point of vanishing. But this disappearance can relate only to Wagner's vision of the perfect *Parsifal* society, not to the experiences of its characters as revealed above all in the music. That, as Wagner explained, a "certain sentimentality" was no longer "possible" does not mean that he was retracting what he had written at the time of *Tristan und Isolde*: "Just consider my music, with its delicate, oh so delicate, mysteriously flowing humors penetrating the most subtle pores of feeling to reach the very marrow of life, where it overwhelms everything that looks like sagacity and the self-interested powers of self-preservation, sweeping away all that belongs to the delusive madness of personality."[101]

The music of *Parsifal* resembles the paintings of Klimt in that both have the same tendency to explore an "exquisitely refined sensuality"[102] that Wagner too recalled while orchestrating *Parsifal*: " 'Oh, music!' he exclaims. 'Here one will be able to see for the first time what potentialities it contains for conveying sorrow in bliss!' "[103] True, Wagner rarely allows "bliss" to express itself freely, for even in the music for the Flowermaidens, there are echoes of the Grail motif, and the music of the "Good Friday Spell" likewise reflects the ambivalence of Parsifal's words: "Du weinest—sieh! es lacht die Aue" (You are weeping—behold! The meadow is smiling). Conversely, Parsifal's despairing cry in act 3, "in Irrniß wild verloren der Rettung letzter Pfad mir schwindet" (lost in the wilderness, deliverance's final path disappears from sight), is followed by a clarinet motif that recalls Venus's words in *Tannhäuser*, "Geliebter, komm'! Sieh' dort die Grotte" (Beloved, come! Behold the grotto). Immediately afterward, the "Tristan" chord is heard repeatedly. Presumably it is only the connoisseur who notices these echoes, whereas every lover of Wagner's music will be aware of the sensuality that keeps that music alive: without it, the static action of *Parsifal* would be barely tolerable.

That this sensuality may be found in manifold guises is a subject that Wagner repeatedly raised in the pages of Cosima's diary. On May 30, 1878, for example, she refers to the "heavenly Flower Maidens' scene, in which R. has conjured up for all time spring and its longing, its sweet complaint. And in the middle of it Kundry's cry, like a mortal soul suddenly giving voice to its suffering and its loving amid the innocence of Nature."[104] In the course of another conversation, Wagner and his wife discussed the scene between Parsifal and Kundry "up to the cry of the former: 'Amfortas!' Indescribably moving! 'A moment of daemonic absorption,' R. calls the bars which accompany Kundry's kiss and in which the fatal motive of love's longing,

No previous Wagner director had regarded himself in quite the same way as Christoph Schlingensief, who saw himself not just as lord and master of his own productions but who even cast himself in the role of a performance artist making an active contribution to those productions—in this case his 2004 Bayreuth Festival staging of *Parsifal*. On the one hand, his reading offered a sympathetic exploration of the Grail community as envisaged by Wagner, but at the same time flooded the stage with so many symbols, images, and visual stimuli that they got in the way of the detailed direction of the singers that Wagner had always placed at the center of his own productions. Seen here is an example from act 2: Schlingensief presented both Kundry and Parsifal simultaneously in several different guises and different media with the result that the two were never able to communicate properly. Still less was Schlingensief able to ensure that their interaction—fraught, as it should be, with tremendous tension—was credible, while the various stages in their evolving relationship were no longer adequately explored in words and music. Three different Kundrys are discernible here: significantly, none is seen interacting with Parsifal. To be fair, it has to be admitted that even in Wagner's original stage work the two characters engage with each other only on a symbolic level, regardless of the psychological sensitivity with which Wagner has invested their scenes together. (Photograph courtesy of the Nationalarchiv der Richard-Wagner-Stiftung Bayreuth: parsifal2-e.)

creeping like poison through the blood, makes a shattering effect [. . .]—all these things, so richly and variously laid out, so ravishing and so painful, form a whole of unfathomable beauty and nobility."[105]

We do not need to set excessive store by such comments, but they may serve to counter the impression that has sometimes been given that *Parsifal* is dominated by some kind of sultry eroticism. But nor shall we do justice to the score by concentrating unduly on its more somber aspects as found, for example, in the entry of the Parsifal motif in act 3, where it appears *pianissimo* in a relatively dark mixture produced by the E-flat trumpet, four horns, and three trombones. ("Horns alone would have been too soft, not ceremonious enough, the trumpet alone too clattery, brassy."[106]) When Pierre Boulez conducted *Parsifal* in Bayreuth in 1966, he was instantly able to demonstrate that Wagner's dark orchestral colors do not have to be ideologically based but can also be lit from the vantage point of French impressionism. And already a light began to gleam in the darkness.

A Word about Gustav Mahler

Mahler was twenty-three when, in 1883, he saw *Parsifal* for the first time in Bayreuth. By then he was already infected by those of Wagner's later writings that were critical of contemporary society and had even become a vegetarian. But these impressions were as nothing when compared to the impact left by the Festival: "It would be hard to describe what is going on in me," he told one of his friends, Fritz Löhr. "When I emerged from the Festspielhaus, incapable of uttering a word, I knew that all that is greatest and most painful had been vouchsafed to me, and that I would carry it around within me, inviolate, for the rest of my life."[1] Mahler returned to Bayreuth on several subsequent occasions, and in 1894 he was even privileged to attend the performances from the Wagner family's private box: Cosima was particularly interested in the talented and successful conductor, although she was never able to bring herself to invite him to conduct at the Festival.

Appointed principal conductor of the Hamburg Opera in 1891, Mahler had already made his mark as a Wagner conductor, and almost every season in Hamburg ended with a cycle of Wagner's works made up of *Rienzi, Der fliegende Holländer, Tannhäuser, Lohengrin, Tristan und Isolde, Die Meistersinger von Nürnberg*, and all four parts of the *Ring. (Parsifal* was still restricted to Bayreuth.) Following his move to Vienna in 1897, his enthusiasm for Wagner's works remained undiminished, and in 1904, for example, we find him writing to his wife, Alma: "Having worked through all of Brahms [in the form of printed scores], I returned to Bruckner. Curiously mediocre figures.—The one spent too long 'in the ladle' [presumably the ladle used with a crucible], the other was in need of that very treatment. Now I've come to rest with Beethoven. *Only he and Richard* [Wagner] are beyond re-proach—and *nobody* else!!"[2]

As an artist who was the victim of aggressive anti-Semitism in fin-de-siècle Vienna, Mahler was, of course, aware of Wagner's feelings on this point. But such was his admiration for Wagner as an artist that he tended in fact to ignore them. In 1898, working on the *Ring* in Vienna, he commented on the figure of Mime: "Although I am convinced that this character is the living parody of a Jew as envisaged by Wagner (in all the features with which he invested him: his petty cleverness, his acquisitive greed, and his whole jargon, which is musically and textually admirable), it really mustn't appear exaggerated here and laid on with a trowel. [. . .] I know only *one* Mime [. . .] and that's *me*! You'd be amazed at what's in this role and how I would bring it all out!"[3]

With his 1903 Vienna production of *Tristan und Isolde*, Mahler began his exemplary partnership with the painter and stage designer Alfred Roller, who was the president of the Vienna Secession and a friend of Klimt. One has an inkling of some of the intensity with which Mahler now pursued the idea of the total artwork. In our chapter on *Parsifal* we noted the way in which, as a mystic and pansophist, he was inspired by the idea of redemp-tion that permeates Wagner's works, but it is worth recalling that in the context of *Parsifal*, Wagner brooded on the ideal of an "invisible theater" and—almost certainly not merely in jest—spoke of his resolve to write only symphonies in future. Mahler may have regarded this as a link with his own creative output, which he saw as a total artwork within the medium of the symphony. It was against this background that his contemporary Thomas Mann admired not only *Parsifal* but also the Symphony of a Thousand: both were examples of art as a form of religion.

It would be wrong, however, to see Mahler's indebtedness to Wagner only on the lofty level of philosophy and world theater, for a more important aspect of Mahler's debt was that of his "musical prose,"[4] even if this term is confined to the level of compositional technique. Where could Mahler find a more compelling legitimization of the disjointed, volatile character of his own symphonic diction than in Wagner's music? After all, there was no precedent for it in the German symphonic tradition and only to a limited extent in that of program music. Instead, he was thrown back on Wagner's "musical prose." In the case of the older composer, this aspect was covered by the context onstage, but as a symphonist Mahler developed his "epic and novel-like"[5] style of writing using semantically charged "vocables."[6]

Mahler must have been particularly fascinated by Wagner's fearless ability to let beauty and ugliness, the sublime and the trivial clash with uncompromising directness, for it lent support to his own aesthetic conviction that contrasts, no matter how abrupt, were legitimate, for all that this was an aesthetic that repeatedly caused him problems.

On seeing this portrait of himself by Auguste Renoir, Wagner complained that it made him look like "the embryo of an angel, an oyster swallowed by an epicure" (CT 2:873; Engl. trans. 2:791; entry of Jan. 15, 1882). Now in the Musée d'Orsay in Paris, it was produced during a thirty-five-minute session in Palermo that Wagner granted the painter on January 15, 1882, when he was completely exhausted from his work on the final pages of the full score of *Parsifal*. Renoir wrote to a friend in Paris to report on his conversation with Wagner prior to the sitting: "We spoke about the impressionists, about music. What nonsense I must have spoken! I ended up shouting, getting completely drunk and turning as red as a rooster. In a word, I was just like any shy person letting himself go and overstepping the mark. But I know I made him happy, though I'm not sure why. He hates the German Jews, including Wolff [Albert Wolff, the critic at *Le Figaro*]. He asked me if we still like [Auber's] *Les diamants de la couronne* in France." See Willi Schuh, *Renoir und Wagner* (Erlenbach: Eugen Rentsch Verlag, 1959), 21–22; and Martin Geck, *Die Bildnisse Richard Wagners* (Munich: Prestel, 1970), 55–56. (Photograph courtesy of Ullstein Bild—Roger Viollet.)

CHAPTER FOURTEEN

Wagner as the Sleuth of Modernism

In the preface to his 1888 "naturalistic tragedy," *Miss Julie*, Strindberg observed that "since they are modern characters, living in an age of transition more urgently hysterical at any rate than the age which preceded it, I have drawn my people as split and vacillating, a mixture of the old and the new. [. . .] My souls (or characters) are agglomerations of past and present cultures, scraps from books and newspapers, fragments of humanity, torn shreds of once-fine clothing that has become rags, in just the way that a human soul is patched together."[1]

Impressed by Théodule Ribot's *Les maladies de la personnalité* and its theory concerning the "multiplicité du moi,"[2] Strindberg—who was familiar with Wagner's output but whose musical icons were Bach and Beethoven—deliberately located his own art in fin-de-siècle, *décadent* Europe. A glance at the interpretations of Wagner's works proposed by modern theater directors suggests that these works are seen as a part of this same environment. And, as our chapter on *Parsifal* will have shown, there is much to be said for this view. Even so, I do not intend to start my final summing up at the end but prefer to return to the roots of Wagner's creativity and begin with Beethoven: after all, Wagner regarded himself as Beethoven's heir in an almost mystical manner.

In his essay *The Artwork of the Future*, which he completed in November 1849 and published the following spring, Wagner referred to Beethoven as a bold seafarer who set out on his "stoutly built and giant-bolted ship" to cross "the endless sea" of absolute music, music said to speak the language of "insatiable, heart-felt longing." On seeing a new continent before him, he had had to decide "whether to turn round and face the bottomless ocean once again or cast anchor on the newfound shore." "Staunchly he threw out his anchor: and this anchor was the *word*"—not just any random word but the one "that the redeemed world-man cries out from the fullness of the world-heart," namely, "joy." The "*universal drama*" that will in future spring from this merger of words and music is one that Wagner describes as the "*human* gospel of the art of the future."[3] It goes without saying that this gospel will be proclaimed primarily by Wagner's own *Gesamtkunstwerk*.

Readers may smile at the lofty tone that Wagner adopts here, and some may even be inclined to ridicule such flights of fancy, but we shall nonetheless have to concede that it chimes with the nineteenth century as a whole: Wagner's century sought a prophet of art; and in the course of his threescore years and ten he succeeded in donning this mantle—he may not have been uncontroversial, but there is no doubt that he was unrivalled.

From a political point of view, Wagner's century began with the French Revolution of 1789, while in terms of cultural history it started with romanticism. And there was a close link between the two. The "Culte de l'être suprême" created by the painter Jacques-Louis David in response to a Jacobin commission and organized by the leaders of the French Revolution in 1794 was intended to lay the foundations of a national religion of art. It may also be seen as a total artwork: the houses of Paris were festooned with flags, the streets were strewn with flowers, men and women garlanded with roses carried sheaves of wheat and baskets of flowers, and Robespierre invoked the "supreme being." And while the musicians from the Institut National de Musique struck up François-Joseph Gossec's anthem *Père de l'univers, suprême intelligence*, Robespierre lit a funeral pyre on which atheism, discord, and ambition were metaphorically consumed as the allegory of Wisdom rose from the ashes.

As we have already noted, Beethoven took over and developed the tone of French revolutionary music in his symphonies. And in using Schiller's *Ode to Joy* in his Ninth Symphony, he offered his own explicit contribution to a religion of art, even though the leading romantics regarded such a religion of art as predominantly apolitical. (Schiller's ode dates from 1785 and is an expression of his enthusiasm for the whole idea of art as a religion in the run-up to the French Revolution, which he initially welcomed.) But the romantics' view of "absolute music" was by no means the one that Carl Dahlhaus claimed, namely, the metaphysical idea of "non-representational and non-conceptual instrumental music": "Music expresses what words are not even capable of stammering."[4] Rather, such "absolute" music was now revealed in the context of poetry, no matter how imperfect that manifestation may be. This had two implications: first, it is invariably accompanied by pictorial ideas and feelings, and, second, it includes the medium of opera—readers will recall E. T. A. Hoffmann's admiration for Mozart's operas.

Nietzsche could have appealed to Hoffmann the early romantic when he described a stage work, *Tristan und Isolde*, as the "actual *opus metaphysicum* of all art."[5] And Wagner himself was entirely right to claim that he was the true heir of "absolute" music, music which is "entirely *itself*" precisely because it really only begins to blossom in the soil that the total artwork offers it.[6] Such considerations are by no means academic but lead to the first crux of "modern" responses to Wagner, for the religion of art of the modern age that emerged from the French Revolution in the form of a political program and that the romantics then espoused as an aesthetic and philosophical concern has always been an ambiguous concept, because on the one hand the message it proclaims is essential to it, otherwise we would not be able to speak of a *religion* of art, whereas on the other hand, it revolves around art, otherwise it would not be a religion of *art*.

It was, of course, Wagner's keenest ambition to merge the two along the lines of an idealized classical Greek model, an ambition underscored by an entry in Cosima Wagner's diary: "He should by rights have graced the world in Aeschylus's age."[7] But in an age when music had acquired a new degree of complexity, Wagner's music almost inevitably took on a life of its own and certainly gained in importance even in works involving both words and music. Wagner himself admitted as much when he stressed that his music was in the tradition of Beethoven, moving "amid its own most quintessential element"[8] in the musical drama that he himself was propagating and being laid out along symphonic lines on an orchestral level.

The contradiction that is discernible here is even more clearly demonstrated, of course, by the reception of Wagner's works. From the outset his stage works were perceived as operas—in other words, works that existed for the sake of their music and their stage magic. As a result, the question as to whether we are dealing with total artworks or even with a religion of art is of secondary importance and certainly does not enjoy the status traditionally accorded to it by secondary—verbal—discourse on Wagner. In the nineteenth century many members of what we might call the "sophisticated" public wanted stage works whose message reflected and respected the major ideas of the period, and there is no doubt that Wagner's underlying idea of redemption made his works particularly attractive to audiences enamored of the notion of art as a religion, allowing them to see in him a figure "who brought joy to the world" in the same way that he himself regarded Beethoven as a figure who had gladdened the world.[9]

And yet a comparison between Wagner and Beethoven the writer of symphonies reveals that what matters are not the specific, concrete ideas contained within this word-tone-art but their powers of persuasion in terms of their function as purveyors of a modern religion. The disciple of a religion of art is no more required to decide in favor of certain ideas than someone who professes his or her faith in a higher being while refusing to acknowledge the concrete tenets of Christian belief is required to provide an account of the nature of that higher being. Indeed, we may even go a stage further and argue that as an enlightened contemporary, which is how any operagoer would at least like to see himself, such a disciple will have misgivings about choosing between possibly rival myths and their respective roads to salvation but will generally be content to cling to myth in general, thereby ensuring a refuge for himself in an age of transience. And yet this leads all too easily to our attaching more importance to the person than to the object, a point made by Peter Wapnewski, when he writes that "the artist as the creative human being, the artist as an autonomous authority is regarded by the modern age as the authentication of human existence in general after religious and metaphysical legitimacy has become dubious and invalid."[10]

This leads me to the title of my final chapter. Although Wagner may not have seen himself as the "sleuth of modernism," he certainly merits this description when judged by objective criteria inasmuch as he served the needs of nineteenth-century society by offering benefits whose drawbacks his audiences evidently preferred to ignore. In wanting to be gratified by Wagner's gifts as a sorcerer, audiences prefer not to have their lives called into question by Wagner the moral preacher.

But what exactly is the secret of Wagner's artistry as a magician? Striking a sympathetically modest note, Lawrence Kramer suggests that it involves no coherent mythology or ideology but impressive "premodern narrative images" combined with the "hypnotic effect" of the music.[11] Thomas Mann was only one of many earlier writers to regard Wagner's music as an opiate: an intoxicating consciousness-expanding drug that was used by almost every fin-de-siècle artist. Mann identified with an art that was subtle and dangerous and no less attractive in consequence. When Gerda Buddenbrook announces her intention of working through the score of *Tristan und Isolde* with Edmund Pfühl, an organist brought up with the music of Bach, the latter groans: "That is not music—believe me! [. . .] This is chaos! This is demagogy, blasphemy, insanity, madness! It is a perfumed fog, shot through with lightning! It is the end of all honesty in art."[12]

This passage also reflects the situation of "modern man" encouraged by countless world fairs and exhibitions to believe that his scientific and technological potential is boundless even while repeatedly striking against his own personal boundaries. Wagner's art tricks us into thinking that individual experience can be delimited and infinitely expanded. It is clear from French responses to Wagner that his mythological message was scarcely affected by all this, for here the boundaries that were crossed remained an essential part of the world of art, Baudelaire, Mallarmé, and Valéry all drinking at the well of art for art's sake and deriving this element from Wagner's music without engaging with the action of his works, fascinated, as they were, by the idea that their German model was able to extend the conventional system of music, expanding its boundaries almost to infinity, while never actually violating them. Even more clearly than with the early romantics, the "what" of art was now eclipsed by the "how." Valéry in particular valued Wagner's music for its "pure sounds":[13] unlike literature, it did not have to wrestle constantly with meanings.

Robert Musil summed up this quality of music in a passage in *The Man without Qualities* in which Diotima, exercised by problems of the heart, reflects in the third person: "Should a woman in Diotima's difficult position make a gesture of renunciation, or let herself be swept into adultery, or take a third, mixed course [. . .]. For this third solution there was as yet no libretto, as it were, only some great harmonic chords."[14]

Diotima would prefer it if the ethical decisions that she feels incapable of taking were raised to a higher aesthetic level that allowed her to feel good about herself. Something similar is felt by Wagnerian audiences: they refuse to engage with the ethical conflicts that these works explore but enjoy the aesthetic solution that is suggested by the music. Although this flies in the face of Wagner's original intentions, it ultimately reflects the composer's own approach to his works—at least to the extent that we see that approach against the background of Nietzsche's aforementioned motto: "*We have art* so as not to be destroyed by the truth."[15] The myth that is music reveals no truths but aestheticizes them.

This is particularly problematical when it is brute force and violence that are aestheticized, a topic that played a role in the reception of Wagner's works from a relatively early date—and not just in the German-speaking world. In *À la recherche du temps perdu*, for example, Proust describes the Wagnerian Robert, Marquis de Saint-Loup—an officer in the First World War—standing on the balcony of a building in Paris and admiring the "great aesthetic beauty" of an air raid by German zeppelins picked out in the night sky by the circles of light of the French anti-aircraft searchlights: in this apocalyptic vision the zeppelins become Valkyries, the noise of the air-raid sirens another Ride of the Valkyries.[16]

It is no accident that this same scene was quoted by Ernst Jünger in his ideologically dubious wartime diary, *Strahlungen*, while the Ride of the Valkyries acquired a very specific popularity thanks to Francis Ford Coppola's anti–Vietnam War film *Apocalypse Now*, one of the US Airborne Cavalry's helicopters having mounted in it a tape recorder blaring out Wagner's music: "We'll come in low out of the rising sun," announces the commanding officer, "and about a mile out, we'll put on the music. Yeah, I use Wagner—scares the hell out of the slopes. My boys love it."[17]

Can Wagner's music really be used to justify this cinematic demonstration of violence? In a wider sense, yes, but in this specific case, no. Wagner's high art involves the ability to offer us tone paintings of the greatest vividness and succinctness. It is an art that benefits the specific atmosphere of the start of *Der fliegende Holländer* as well as the *Lohengrin* prelude. It also affects the "traurige Weise" at the start of act 3 of *Tristan und Isolde* and the whole of the *Parsifal* prelude. And it additionally leaves its mark on the Ride of the Valkyries at the start of act 3 of *Die Walküre*. For his well-developed ability to write music according to "local criteria"[18] and for his decision to bank more on sonority than on an integral compositional structure, Wagner inevitably has to pay a high price—this is the nub of Adorno's critique of Wagner's use of phantasmagoria: music that moves from situation to situation without being integrated into a higher, overriding concept runs the risk of being exploited for other ends.

And yet this is no green light for interpretations that equate the Ride of the Valkyries with fascism or dismiss Wagner's music in general as proto-fascist, for not only is the theme of violence merely one among many in Wagner's work and by no means determinative, but the Ride of the Valkyries is not about violence as such but—conceptually and musically—concerned with what Richard Klein has termed "the synchronization of extremes": "Delimiting lightness clashes with rigidly fixed structures." "Wagner's orchestra anticipates the air-borne steeds of the twentieth century, dreaming them up in advance of their actual appearance."[19]

In his Library of Congress lecture "Nietzsche's Philosophy in the Light of Contemporary Events," Thomas Mann advanced the view that "with his philosopheme of power," Nietzsche "presaged the dawning imperialism and as a quivering floatstick indicated the fascist era of the West." Mann was in fact inclined "to reverse cause and effect and not to believe that Nietzsche created fascism, but rather that fascism created him."[20] What was true of Nietzsche could also be true of Wagner, especially if we replace the "fascist era" by the "modern age" in keeping with Nietzsche's own dictum that "Wagner sums up modernity."[21]

It is, of course, a varied and ambiguous modernity with which Wagner engages, being the product of a civilization that seeks to control itself in every last detail and yet does not know why, refusing to acknowledge its demonic basis, while permanently confronting it. Here is a society that would like to be enlightened but which is exposed to such existential concerns as nature, love, sexuality, guilt, death, and destruction in the same way that every previous society has been. Wagner's works are contradictory, especially in terms of their "great narratives": as Gerd Rienäcker has observed in the context of the *Ring*, "The work is not about people mastering their fate but about the circumstances that turn each and every one of us into the victims of that fate."[22] In this respect Wagner's mythological characters are barely any different from Strindberg's "modern characters." Whether seen from the standpoint of the characters themselves or from that of their audiences, a yawning gulf opens up between ambition and reality, between the subjective desire for emancipation and the objective state of the world, a gulf that no myth, however beautiful, can fill—not even Wagner's myth of redemption through destruction.

And yet Wagner has a specific trump card up his sleeve—his music. Although this cannot fill the gulf, it can shrink it by offering meanings merely by dint of the sounds that it makes, which it is able to do in keeping with what is arguably its most important anthropological function. It is this that renders it the one truly redemptive factor in Wagner's total artwork. In his late essay "Religion and Art," Wagner tells a story to clarify this point:

> The children of a parish priest in Sweden once heard a nixie singing, while accompanying herself on her harp. "Sing as much as you like," they called out to her, "you'll never get to heaven." The nixie sadly lowered her harp and head: the children heard her weeping and ran to tell their father. He counseled them and sent them back to the nixie with glad tidings. "Come, nixie, don't be sad," they called out to her. "Father says that you may get to heaven after all." Then all night long they heard the river echoing with songs so sweet than never man heard sweeter.[23]

In other words: true redemption may be tied to destruction, but the music ensures that we have no need to feel stoic or to be overcome by despair in the face of such destruction. Rather, there is reason to feel "longing, faith, and hope."[24]

Here Wagner reveals himself as a true romantic—just as he does in those passages in his stage works in which music was "never sweeter" and sings as beautifully as the nixie. At the same time, however, he is the sleuth of a fractured modernism, for in its details his music is by no means as affirmative or calming as its reputation. Rather, it displays some of the qualities of Strindberg's psychological realism. It was Nietzsche who first highlighted these contradictions, praising his idol for extending music's potential for language in immeasurable ways,[25] while at the same time mocking the composer for loosening music's tongue only to break its limbs.[26] In both cases we can see Wagner's presumptuous keenness to ensure that his music is psychologically true in every detail and is able "to advance into hitherto inaccessible areas at the very limits of expression and dig deep into the buried depths of our consciousness."[27]

This "attention to detail" goes hand in hand with the "fragmentation of the bigger picture,"[28] prompting Nietzsche to describe Wagner as "the greatest *miniaturist* of music."[29] And there is no doubt that Wagner's art of the theater lacks the authority that would mediate between the lofty superstructure of his music theater and its "naïve" type of localized narrative. As a result—and in spite of his self-proclaimed "art of transition"—constructive and destructive elements clash violently with each other in his scores. And yet which court should we appeal to when complaining that Wagner fails to bring off the contortionist feat of embracing the myth of music while at the same time savoring every last detail of his own compositional dexterity? Building on his theory that music is both autonomous and a "fait social," Adorno was able to claim that Wagner's music is not only phantasmagorically untrue but also and at the same time an expression of social truth: the whole of modernism seeks the big picture while finding only riveting sequences of separate images.

It is in this sense that Gerd Rienäcker has declared Wagner's "strange linguistic construct" a "magnificent failure": "States of narcotic intoxication yield to oddly gleaming brightness and to painful clarity of detail and overall context; the sounds are wan and broken when Hagen lashes out, they break open in the Grail ceremony, and they are dissonant in the face of Valhalla, robbed for long stretches of any unambiguous tonal context."[30]

Wagner's music draws its strength and life force from these contradictions, insisting on the harmony of the world while at the same time bidding it a resolute farewell. It is planned by the composer right down to the very last detail and simultaneously represents a rhizomatic fabric that seems able to survive without the guiding hand of an author. Its leitmotif technique is both hierarchical and anarchic. And although the leitmotifs exist for the sake of their significance within the drama, they also provide the material for an autonomous musical syntax. Wagner's compositional thinking follows traditional Aristotelian logic whereby something can be either A or *not* A—first subject or second subject, theme or accompaniment, theme or interlude, structure or instrumentation—and yet it constantly ignores this logic, for A can also be *not* A, the theme can also be the accompaniment, and the structure can vanish behind the instrumentation.

As a result, anyone who for reasons of ideology or simply to make a rhetorical point insists on the idea of a total artwork will find that his or her access to Wagner's works is barred. The sinister attempts of fascism and Stalinism to inflict the mask of the total artwork on a society aligned with a set of state-imposed norms make it almost impossible to salvage this category for the narrower world of aesthetics, for even here authoritarian structures may still be found in discussions of this theme. On the other hand, it is all too typical of the German tendency to overestimate the importance of the mind and of mental effort to posit artistic heroes such as Wagner as influential figures in the ebb and flow of social processes. His "total art" is nothing more than an enzyme of such a process. And at least it is true of the present day that a free society will listen to its artists but will not allow them to dictate their behavior. Nor does such a society need to keep importuning Wagner with the ultimately unanswerable question as to the extent to which his understanding of art may itself be questionable. Rather, it should be possible for us simply to enjoy the intellectual and sensual stimuli that his art continues to promise us.

Wrestling with such questions is more than postmodernism has to offer in the case of Wagner, for postmodernism no longer checks out Wagner's total artwork for sense and meaning, being or appearance, morality or immortality, coherence or contingency, but examines it for its media competence. According to Jean Baudrillard, "We no longer experience the drama of alienation but the ecstasy of communication," a diagnosis taken over by Sven Friedrich, the director of the Wagner Museum in Bayreuth, in a fashionably titled article "tannhaeuser@venusberg.de: On Wagner's media technology."[31] In keeping with the motto that "the medium is the message," communication can mean anything and everything in this context. The only thing it cannot mean is rational discourse on art. As we have already noted, Friedrich Kittler prefers the term "noise": "With Wagner, music becomes a matter of pure dynamics and pure acoustics."[32] We could choose other images and examine Wagner's music in terms of its different thermal states or drives. And we may even concentrate on the "erotic impulse" of these works[33] or, with reference to *Tannhäuser*, aim our rifle sights at the "virtual hyper-reality of the Venusberg."[34]

The aim, in a word, is to describe Wagner's music as an "acoustic hallucination"[35] and in that way tap into forms of perception associated with our modern media society. At the same time such writers are keen to understand what it is that makes Wagner's music so attractive to audiences who do not approach the composer from the standpoint of classical music and who are not interested in his edifice of ideas. From this point of view, too, Wagner—whether he wants it or not—is a precursor of modernism. Nietzsche was one of the first writers to sense this when he compared Wagner's music to that of his predecessors. "Earlier music," he argued, invited its listeners to "*dance*: in pursuit of which the needful preservation of orderly measure compelled the soul of the listener to a continual *self-possession*." Wagner's "endless melody," by contrast, belonged to a type of listener who "goes into the sea, gradually relinquishing a firm tread on the bottom and finally surrendering unconditionally to the watery element: one is supposed to *swim*."[36]

There is no doubt that current media theory has the ability to offer new readings of important aspects of Wagner's works, but it would represent a loss if all that were left of the idea of the total artwork was the subtle despotism of postmodern media technology. However willingly Wagner's stage works may be adapted to meet the requirements of today's event culture, for all who have eyes and ears they continue to demonstrate the optimistically forward-looking yet desperate contortions of a society which in its search for happiness is by no means as coolly postmodern as it sometimes claims to be. At all events, I myself cannot reflect on the states of intoxication and on the phantasmagorias in Wagner's works without seeing them against the background of the sacred element, or "le sacré," a background against which the art of the modern world in general is set, for all that art may be bashfully coy or refracted.

Nor should we forget that there are many media spectacles—but there is only one Wagner.

NOTES

INTRODUCTION

1. Cosima Wagner, *Die Tagebücher*, ed. Martin Gregor-Dellin and Dietrich Mack (Munich: R. Piper, 1976–77), 1:21; translated into English by Geoffrey Skelton as *Cosima Wagner's Diaries* (London: Collins, 1978–80), 1:27 (entry of Jan. 1, 1869) (hereafter CT).

2. Martin Gregor-Dellin, *Richard Wagner: Sein Leben, sein Werk, sein Jahrhundert* (Munich: R. Piper, 1980), 733; translated by J. Maxwell Brownjohn as *Richard Wagner: His Life, His Work, His Century* (London: Collins, 1983), 443.

3. CT 2:335; Engl. trans. 2:295 (entry of April 22, 1879).

4. CT 1:202; Engl. trans. 1:193 (entry of Feb. 25, 1870).

5. Richard Wagner, *Mein Leben*, ed. Martin Gregor-Dellin (Munich: List, 1976), 512; translated by Andrew Gray as *My Life*, ed. Mary Whittall (Cambridge: Cambridge University Press, 1983), 499 (hereafter ML).

6. But see Warren Darcy, *Wagner's "Das Rheingold"* (Oxford: Clarendon Press, 1993).

7. Arthur Schopenhauer, *Werke in fünf Bänden: Nach den Ausgaben letzter Hand*, ed. Lutger Lütkehaus (Zurich: Haffmans Verlag, 1988), 4:265; translated by E. F. J. Payne as *Parerga and Paralipomena* (Oxford: Clarendon Press, 1974), 1:265.

8. Johannes Fried, *Der Schleier der Erinnerung: Grundzüge einer historischen Memorik* (Munich: C. H. Beck, 2004), 25–32.

9. Gregor-Dellin, *Richard Wagner*, 813–14; this passage was not included in the English translation.

10. Udo Bermbach, *Der Wahn des Gesamtkunstwerks: Richard Wagners politisch-ästhetische Utopie* (Frankfurt: Fischer, 1994), 11.

11. Christian Kaden, *Des Lebens wilder Kreis: Musik im Zivilisationsprozeß* (Kassel: Bärenreiter, 1993), 169.

12. Peter Wapnewski, *Der traurige Gott: Richard Wagner in seinen Helden*, 2nd ed. (Berlin: Berlin Verlag, 2001), 276.

13. CT 1:191; Engl. trans. 1:183 (entry of Jan. 22, 1870).

14. CT 2:684; Engl. trans. 2:616 (entry of Feb. 6, 1881).

15. Walter Benjamin, *Gesammelte Schriften*, ed. Rolf Tiedemann and Hermann Schweppenhäuser (Frankfurt: Suhrkamp, 2009), 1.2:696; translated by Harry Zohn as "Theses on the Philosophy of History," in Benjamin, *Illuminations* (London: Pimlico, 1999), 248.

16. Joachim Kaiser, *Leben mit Wagner* (Munich: Albrecht Knaus, 1990), 15.

17. White's study was first published in 1978 under the title *Tropics of Discourse: Essays in Cultural Criticism* by John Hopkins University Press (Baltimore) and deals, among other

things, with the essentially subjective nature of historiography, a point underlined by the title of the German translation, produced in collaboration with the German historian Reinhart Koselleck and published in Stuttgart in 1999 as *Auch Klio dichtet oder Die Fiktion des Faktischen* (Clio too writes poetry, or the fiction of the factual).

CHAPTER ONE

1. CT 1:409; Engl. trans. 1:386 (entry of July 5, 1871).

2. ML 17–18; Engl. trans. 11.

3. Otto Strobel, ed., *König Ludwig II. und Richard Wagner: Briefwechsel* (Karlsruhe: G. Braun, 1936–39), 3:153 (letter from Wagner to Ludwig II, May 28, 1879).

4. CT 1:714; Engl. trans. 1:664 (entry of Aug. 13, 1873).

5. CT 1:187; Engl. trans. 1:179 (entry of Jan. 11, 1870).

6. ML 15; Engl. trans. 9.

7. ML 23; Engl. trans. 16.

8. Richard Wagner, *Sämtliche Briefe*, ed. Gertrud Strobel and others (Leipzig: VEB Deutscher Verlag für Musik, 1967–2000, and Wiesbaden: Breitkopf & Hartel, 1999–), 1:308 (letter from Richard to Minna Wagner, June 22, [1836]) (hereafter SB).

9. CT 1:627 and 2:645; Engl. trans. 1:583 and 2:581 (entries of Jan. 12, 1873, and Dec. 24, 1880).

10. CT 1:745; Engl. trans. 1:692 (entry of Oct. 29, 1873).

11. ML 19–20; Engl. trans. 13 (emended).

12. ML 11; Engl. trans. 5 (emended).

13. CT 1:186; Engl. trans. 1:178–79 (entry of Jan. 9, 1870).

14. ML 20; Engl. trans. 13–14 (emended).

15. SB 2:358 (letter from Wagner to Karl Gaillard, Jan. 30, 1844).

16. SB 6:56 (letter from Wagner to Julie Ritter, Jan. 20, 1854).

17. SB 5:495 (letter from Wagner to Franz Liszt, Jan. 15, 1854).

18. Marcel Proust, *À la recherche du temps perdu*, ed. Pierre Clarac and André Ferré (Paris: Gallimard, 1973–77), 3:920; translated by C. K. Scott Moncrieff and Terence Kilmartin as *In Search of Lost Time* (London: Folio Society, 2000), 6:499.

19. ML 32; Engl. trans. 25.

20. SB 1:96 ("Autobiographical Sketch").

21. Isolde Vetter, "'Leubald, ein Trauerspiel': Richard Wagners erstes (erhaltenes) Werk," *Die Programmhefte der Bayreuther Festspiele 1988*, vol. 7: *Die Meistersinger von Nürnberg*, ed. Matthias Theodor Vogt (Bayreuth: Emil Mühl, 1988), 1–19. The text of the play is reproduced in German on pp. 95–207.

22. SB 8:153 (letter from Wagner to August Röckel, Aug. 23, 1856).

23. Richard Wagner, *Das Braune Buch: Tagebuchaufzeichnungen 1865 bis 1882*, ed. Joachim Bergfeld (Zurich: Atlantis, 1975), 70; translated by George Bird as *The Diary of Richard Wagner, 1865–1882: The Brown Book* (London: Victor Gollancz, 1980), 61 (emended) (hereafter BB).

24. CT 1:193; Engl. trans. 1:185 (entry of Jan. 31, 1870).

25. CT 1:198; Engl. trans. 1:189 (emended) (entry of Feb. 12, 1870).

26. CT 1:71; Engl. trans. 1:73 (entry of March 12, 1869).

27. Richard Wagner, *Gesammelte Schriften und Dichtungen*, 4th ed. (Leipzig: C. F. W. Siegel's Musikalienhandlung, 1907), 3:316 (hereafter GS); translated by William Ashton Ellis

as *Richard Wagner's Prose Works* (London: Kegan Paul, Trench & Trübner, 1893–99), 2:111 (emended) (hereafter PW) (*Opera and Drama*).

28. John Deathridge, Martin Geck, and Egon Voss, eds., *Wagner Werk-Verzeichnis (WWV): Verzeichnis der musikalischen Werke Richard Wagners und ihrer Quellen* (Mainz: Schott, 1986), 101 (hereafter WWV).

29. Egon Voss, "*Die Feen*: Eine Oper für Wagners Familie," in *"Wagner und kein Ende": Betrachtungen und Studien* (Zurich: Atlantis, 1996), 17–18.

30. Carl Dahlhaus, "Wagners Stellung in der Musikgeschichte," in Ulrch Müller and Peter Wapnewski, eds., *Richard-Wagner-Handbuch* (Stuttgart: Alfred Kröner, 1986), 66; translated by Alfred Clayton as "Wagner's Place in the History of Music," in John Deathridge, ed., *Wagner Handbook* (Cambridge, MA: Harvard University Press, 1992), 104.

31. Werner Breig, "Wagners kompositorisches Werk," in Müller and Wapnewski, eds., *Richard-Wagner-Handbuch*, 364; translated by Paul Knight and Horst Leuchtmann as "The Musical Works," in Deathridge, *Wagner Handbook*, 406.

32. Paul Bekker, *Wagner: Das Leben im Werke* (Stuttgart: Deutsche Verlags-Anstalt, 1924), 89; translated by M. M. Bozman as *Richard Wagner: His Life in His Work* (New York: W. W. Norton, 1931), 79; see also Ludwig Holtmeier, "Von den *Feen* zum *Liebesverbot*: Zur Geschichte eines Dilettanten," in *Richard Wagner und seine Zeit*, ed. Eckehard Kiem and Ludwig Holtmeier (Laaber: Laaber-Verlag, 2003), 38–44.

33. GS 4:255; PW 1:296 (emended) (*A Communication to My Friends*).

34. GS 4:253; PW 1:293 (*A Communication to My Friends*).

35. CT 1:476; Engl. trans. 1:445 (entry of Jan. 3, 1872).

36. Peter Sloterdijk, *Thinker on Stage: Nietzsche's Materialism*, translated by Jamie Owen Daniel (Minneapolis: University of Minnesota Press, 1989), 23.

37. Friedrich Nietzsche, *Sämtliche Werke: Kritische Studienausgabe*, ed. Giorgio Colli and Mazzino Montinari (Munich: Deutscher Taschenbuch Verlag, 1988), 1:479; translated by R. J. Hollingdale as *Untimely Meditations* (Cambridge: Cambridge University Press, 1983), 232.

38. GS 4:264; PW 1:306 (*A Communication to My Friends*).

39. Nietzsche, *Sämtliche Werke*, 13:500.

40. "Erlösung durch Untergang": "Untergang" is a notoriously difficult term to translate, its semantic field extending from the "setting" of the sun and the "decline" of the West (in the Spenglerian sense) to the "sinking" of the *Titanic* and physical or figurative ruin.

41. Nietzsche, *Sämtliche Werke*, 6:16; translated by Walter Kaufmann as "The Case of Wagner," in Nietzsche, *Basic Writings of Nietzsche* (New York: Modern Library, 1968), 616.

42. GS 5:85; PW 3:100 (emended) ("Jews in Music").

43. The traditional translation, "Judaism in Music," was first proposed by Ferdinand Praeger in the *New York Musical Gazette* on February 24, 1855, but seems to the present translator to be potentially misleading, for although the word *Judaism* could be used in the nineteenth century to mean "Jewry," it is nowadays limited to the Jewish religion. Wagner's concern was ethnic rather than religious.

44. SB 6:68–69 (letter from Wagner to August Röckel, Jan. 25–26, 1854). Wagner retained the form *Wodan* until 1860.

45. Richard Wagner, *Sämtliche Werke*, ed. Carl Dahlhaus and others (Mainz: Schott, 1970–), 29.1:54 (hereafter SW) (*Dokumente zur Entstehungsgeschichte des Bühnenfestspiels Der Ring des Nibelungen*).

46. SW 29.1:30 (Eduard Devrient's diary, Dec. 2, 1848).

47. GS 4:72; PW 2:201 (*Opera and Drama*).

48. Christian Kaden, *Des Lebens wilder Kreis: Musik im Zivilisationsprozeß* (Kassel: Bärenreiter, 1993), 169.

49. GS 4:266; PW 1:308 (*A Communication to My Friends*).

50. SB 6:299 (letter from Wagner to Liszt, Dec. [16?], 1854).

51. Dieter Borchmeyer, *Richard Wagner: Ahasvers Wandlungen* (Frankfurt: Insel Verlag, 2002), 142; translated by Daphne Ellis as *Drama and the World of Richard Wagner* (Princeton: Princeton University Press, 2003), 100.

52. GS 10:307–8; PW 6:312 (emended) ("The Stage Consecration Festival Drama in Bayreuth in 1882").

A WORD ABOUT FELIX MENDELSSOHN

1. Paul Mendelssohn Bartholdy and Carl Mendelssohn Bartholdy, eds., *Briefe aus den Jahren 1830 bis 1847 von Felix Mendelssohn Bartholdy* (Leipzig: Hermann Mendelssohn, 1870), 1:230 (letter from Mendelssohn to Carl Immermann, Jan. 11, 1832).

2. CT 2:530; Engl. trans. 2:475 (entry of May 8, 1880).

3. GS 5:79; PW 3:93–94 ("Jews in Music").

4. CT 2:283; Engl. trans. 2:247 (entry of Jan. 3, 1879).

5. CT 2:367; Engl. trans. 2:325 (entry of June 17, 1879).

6. CT 1:404–5; Engl. trans. 1:381 (entry of June 23, 1871).

7. GS 8:266; PW 4:295 ("On Conducting").

8. Mendelssohn, *Briefe*, 2:302 (letter from Mendelssohn to Livia Frege, Aug. 31, 1846). The soprano soloist at the Birmingham performance of *Elijah* on Aug. 26, 1846, was Maria Caradori-Allan (1800–1865).

CHAPTER TWO

1. GS 4:256; PW 1:297 (emended) (*A Communication to My Friends*).

2. CT 2:300; Engl. trans. 2:263 (entry of Jan. 31, 1879).

3. GS 4:256; PW 1:297 (emended) (*A Communication to My Friends*).

4. Egon Voss, "Einflüsse Rossinis und Bellinis auf das Werk Wagners," in Christoph-Hellmut Mahling and Kristina Pfarr, eds., *Richard Wagner und seine "Lehrmeister"* (Mainz: Are Edition, 1999), 115; see also CT 2:508–9; Engl. trans. 2:455 (entry of March 22, 1880).

5. Richard Wagner, "Die deutsche Oper," *Zeitung für die elegante Welt* 111 (June 10, 1834), 441–42; PW 8:55 ("On German Opera").

6. CT 1:541; Engl. trans. 1:505 (entry of June 30, 1872).

7. GS 4:256; PW 1:297 (emended) (*A Communication to My Friends*).

8. SB 1:164 (letter to Theodor Apel, Sept. 15, [1834]).

9. SB 1:223 (letter to Theodor Apel, Oct. 2, 1835).

10. SB 1:160 (undated letter to Theodor Apel, [July 27 or Aug. 3, 1834]).

11. SB 1:158 (letter to Theodor Apel, July 3, [1834]).

12. WWV p. 141.

13. GS 4:254; PW 1:295 (*A Communication to My Friends*).

14. ML 47; Engl. trans. 39.

15. ML 48; Engl. trans. 40.

16. ML 48; Engl. trans. 41.

17. GS 4:256; PW 1:297 (*A Communication to My Friends*).

18. ML 128; Engl. trans. 119.

19. GS 4:257; PW 1:298 (emended) (*A Communication to My Friends*).

20. SB1:104; PW 1:12 (emended) ("An Autobiographical Sketch"). When revising this text in 1871 for inclusion in his collected writings, Wagner replaced "Auber" by "Adam."

21. ML 167; Engl. trans. 157.

22. John N. Burk, ed., *Richard Wagner: Briefe; Die Sammlung Burrell* (Frankfurt: Fischer, 1953), 119–20; translated by Hans Abraham and others as *The Letters of Richard Wagner: The Burrell Collection* (London: Victor Gollancz, 1951), 83 (emended).

23. Siegfried Fornaçon, "Richard Wagners Seereise von Pillau nach London," *Schiff und Zeit* 8 (1978): 1–10.

24. August Kubizek, *Adolf Hitler, mein Jugendfreund*, 6th ed. (Graz: Leopold Stocker, 1995), 118; translated by E. V. Anderson as *Young Hitler: The Story of Our Friendship* (Maidstone: George Mann, 1973), 66.

25. Friedrich Schleiermacher, *Pädagogische Schriften*, ed. Theodor Schulze and Erich Weniger (Düsseldorf: Küpper, 1957), 1:133.

26. Wolfgang Robert Griepenkerl, *Das Musikfest oder die Beethovener*, 2nd ed. (Braunschweig: Eduard Leibrock, 1841), 60.

27. Joachim Kaiser, *Leben mit Wagner* (Munich: Albrecht Knaus, 1990), 82.

28. Udo Bermbach, *"Blühendes Leid": Politik und Gesellschaft in Richard Wagners Musikdramen* (Stuttgart: J. B. Metzler, 2003), 65 and 67–68.

29. Helmut Kirchmeyer, *Das zeitgenössische Wagner-Bild*, vol. 3, *Dokumente 1846–1850* (Regensburg: Gustav Bosse, 1968), col. 395.

30. SB 10:264–65 (letter to Albert Niemann, Jan. 25, 1859).

31. Mario Bortolotto, *Wagner l'oscuro* (Milan: Adelphi, 2003), 75.

32. SB 6:97 (letter to Franz von Dingelstedt, March 20, 1854).

33. CT 1:422–23; Engl. trans. 1:398 (entry of July 28, 1871).

34. GS 9:221; PW 5:219 (*On Actors and Singers*).

35. GS 9:219; PW 5:217 (emended) (*On Actors and Singers*).

36. GS 3:166; PW 1:201 (*The Artwork of the Future*).

37. BB 170; Engl. trans. 142 ("Recollections of Ludwig Schnorr von Carolsfeld").

38. SB 4:377–78 (letter to Franz Liszt, May 29, 1852).

39. Sieghart Döhring and Sabine Henze-Döhring, *Oper und Musikdrama im 19. Jahrhundert* (Laaber: Laaber-Verlag, 1997), 144–46.

40. See Norbert Miller, "Große Oper und Historiengemälde: Überlegungen zur Zusammenarbeit von Eugène Scribe und Giacomo Meyerbeer," in Jens Malte Fischer, ed., *Oper und Operntext* (Heidelberg: Winter, 1985), 45–80.

41. SB 1:589 (undated letter to Ferdinand Heine, [late Jan. 1842]).

42. See Martin Geck, "Rienzi-Philologie," in Carl Dahlhaus, ed., *Das Drama Richard Wagners als musikalisches Kunstwerk* (Regensburg: Gustav Bosse, 1970), 187 (undated letter from Cosima Wagner to Felix Mott, [Sept. 1888]).

43. Werner Breig, "Wagners kompositorisches Werk," in Ulrich Müller and Peter Wapnewski, eds., *Richard-Wagner-Handbuch* (Stuttgart: Alfred Kröner, 1986), 373; translated by Paul Knight and Horst Leuchtmann as "The Musical Works," in John Deathridge, ed., *Wagner Handbook* (Cambridge, MA: Harvard University Press, 1992), 413.

44. John Deathridge, *Wagner's* Rienzi: *A Reappraisal Based on a Study of the Sketches and Drafts* (Oxford: Clarendon Press, 1977), 43–44.

45. SB 1:503 (letter to Gottfried Engelbert Anders, July 13, 1841).

46. SB 1:507 (undated letter to Joseph Tichatschek, [Sept. 6 or 7, 1841]).

A WORD ABOUT GIACOMO MEYERBEER

1. CT 1:78; Engl. trans. 1:80 (entry of March 30, 1869).
2. SB 1:380 (letter to Giacomo Meyerbeer, Feb. 15, 1840).
3. Richard Wagner, *Sämtliche Schriften und Dichtungen* (Leipzig: Breitkopf & Härtel, 1911–14), 12:27 ("On Meyerbeer's *Les Huguenots*") (hereafter SSD).
4. SB 2:481 (letter to Giacomo Meyerbeer, Jan. 15, 1846).
5. SB 3:248–49 (letter to Theodor Uhlig, March 13, 1850).
6. See, for example, Sieghart Döhring, "Die traumatische Beziehung Wagners zu Meyerbeer," in Dieter Borchmeyer and others, eds., *Richard Wagner und die Juden* (Stuttgart: J. B. Metzler, 2000), 271; and Matthias Broszka, "Geschichtsphilosophische Dimensionen in Meyerbeers Grand Opéra," in Hermann Danuser and Herfried Münkler, eds., *Zukunfts-bilder: Richard Wagners Revolution und ihre Folgen in Kunst und Politik* (Schliengen: Edition Argus, 2002), 108. Only Oswald Georg Bauer speaks of "ironic refraction": see Bauer, "Der falsche Prophet," in Borchmeyer, *Richard Wagner und die Juden*, 276.
7. SB 3:545 (letter to Liszt, April 18, 1851).
8. GS 3:306; PW 2:101 (emended) (*Opera and Drama*).
9. Döhring, "Die traumatische Beziehung Wagners zu Meyerbeer," 264–65.
10. CT 1:577; Engl. trans. 1:538 (entry of Sept. 26, 1872).
11. Giacomo Meyerbeer, *Briefwechsel und Tagebücher*, ed. Heinz Becker and others (Berlin: Walter de Gruyter, 1960–2006), 6:567 (entry of June 24, 1855).

CHAPTER THREE

1. Franz Liszt, *Sämtliche Schriften*, vol. 1, *Frühe Schriften*, ed. Rainer Kleinertz (Wiesbaden: Breitkopf & Härtel, 2000), 14 ("De la situation des artistes"); see also Martin Geck, *Von Beethoven bis Mahler: Leben und Werk der großen Komponisten des 19. Jahrhunderts* (Stuttgart: J. B. Metzler, 2000), 216–17.
2. GS 1:3; PW 7:3 ("Introduction").
3. GS 7:120–21; PW 3:328–29 ("Music of the Future").
4. Michael Walter, *Hugenotten-Studien* (Frankfurt: Peter Lang, 1987), 65.
5. SB 1:109; PW 1:17 ("An Autobiographical Sketch").
6. Heinrich Heine, *Sämtliche Schriften*, ed. Klaus Briegleb (Munich: Deutscher Taschenbuch Verlag, 2005), 1:532 ("Aus den Memoiren des Herren von Schnabelewopski").
7. SW 24:180 (*Dokumente und Texte zu "Der fliegende Holländer"*).
8. GS 4:268; PW 1:311 (*A Communication to My Friends*).
9. SW 24:250.
10. SB 1:314–15 (undated letter to Ferdinand Heine, [early Aug. 1843]).
11. GS 5:163; PW 3:211 (*Remarks on Performing the Opera "The Flying Dutchman"*).
12. GS 4:265; PW 1:308 (*A Communication to My Friends*).
13. GS 4:266; PW 1:308 (*A Communication to My Friends*).
14. SB 5:189 (letter to Liszt, Feb. 11, 1853).
15. GS 4:266; PW 1:308 (*A Communication to My Friends*).
16. Charles Baudelaire, *Œuvres complètes*, ed. Claude Pichois (Paris: Gallimard, 1976), 2:803–5.
17. See Martin Geck, *Robert Schumann: Mensch und Musiker der Romantik*, 2nd ed. (Munich: Siedler, 2010), 281; translated by Stewart Spencer as *Robert Schumann: The Life and Work of a Romantic Composer* (Chicago: Chicago University Press, 2012), 245.
18. Franz Liszt, *Sämtliche Schriften*, vol. 5, *Dramaturgische Blätter*, ed. Dorothea Redepenning and Britta Schilling (Wiesbaden: Breitkopf & Härtel, 1989), 71.

19. Harry Kupfer, "'Denken Sie an die Seeräuber-Jenny!' Ein Gespräch mit Harry Kupfer," in Staatsoper Unter den Linden Berlin, ed., *Der fliegende Holländer: Romantische Oper in drei Aufzügen* (Frankfurt: Insel, 2001), 31.

20. Max Graf, *Richard Wagner im "Fliegenden Holländer": Ein Beitrag zur Psychologie künstlerischen Schaffens* (Leipzig: Franz Deuticke, 1911).

21. GS 9:90; PW 5:90 (*Beethoven*); see also Martin Geck, "Richard Wagner und die ältere Musik," in Walter Wiora, ed., *Die Ausbreitung des Historismus über die Musik* (Regensburg: Gustav Bosse, 1969), 137.

22. GS 3:229; PW 2:15 (*Opera and Drama*).

23. Lilli Lehmann, *Mein Weg*, 2nd ed. (Leipzig: S. Hirzel, 1920), 228; translated by Alice Benedict Seligman as *My Path through Life* (New York: G. P. Putnam's Sons, 1914), 211.

24. Hans von Wolzogen, *Erinnerungen an Richard Wagner*, 2nd ed. (Leipzig: Philipp Reclam, 1891), 24.

25. GS 10:96; PW 6:90 (emended) ("The Public in Time and Space").

26. CT 1:433; Engl. trans. 1:407 (entry of Sept. 1, 1871).

27. GS 10:182; PV 5:180 (emended) ("On the Application of Music to the Drama").

28. Hugo Riemann, *Geschichte der Musik seit Beethoven* (Berlin: Spemann, 1901), 442.

29. GS 5:192; PW 3:247 (*On Franz Liszt's Symphonic Poems*).

30. Carl Dahlhaus, *Richard Wagners Musikdramen*, 2nd ed. (Zurich: Orell Füssli, 1985), 18; translated by Mary Whittall as *Richard Wagner's Music Dramas* (Cambridge: Cambridge University Press, 1979), 13.

31. Ibid., 20; Engl. trans. 15.

32. Liszt, *Dramaturgische Blätter*, 68–69.

33. Ernst Bloch, *Geist der Utopie*, 2nd ed. (Frankfurt: Suhrkamp, 1964), 121; translated by Anthony A. Nassar as *The Spirit of Utopia* (Stanford: Stanford University Press, 2000), 92.

34. GS 5:176; PW 3:228 ("The Overture to *The Flying Dutchman*").

35. SB 3:391 (letter to Liszt, Sept. 8, 1850).

36. GS 5:160; PW 3:209 (*Remarks on Performing the Opera "The Flying Dutchman"*).

37. GS 5:161; PW 3:210 (*Remarks on Performing the Opera "The Flying Dutchman"*).

38. Carl Dahlhaus, *Die Bedeutung des Gestischen in Wagners Musikdramen* (Munich: R. Oldenbourg, 1970), 34.

39. Martin Gregor-Dellin, *Richard Wagner: Sein Leben, sein Werk, sein Jahrhundert* (Munich: R. Piper, 1980), 719; this passage was cut from the English translation.

40. CT 2:181; Engl. trans. 2:154 (entry of Sept. 23, 1878).

41. SB 5:162 (letter to Liszt, Jan. 13, 1853).

42. CT 2:793; Engl. trans. 2:717 (entry of Sept. 8, 1881).

43. CT 1:1079; Engl. trans. 1:990 (entry of Oct. 28, 1877).

44. Ulrich Schreiber, *Opernführer für Fortgeschrittene: Das 19. Jahrhundert*, 3rd ed. (Kassel: Bärenreiter, 2002), 467.

45. Ernst Bloch, "Paradoxa und Pastorale bei Wagner," in Karola Bloch, ed., *Zur Philosophie der Musik* (Frankfurt: Suhrkamp, 1974), 227; translated by Peter Palmer as "Paradoxes and the Pastorale in Wagner's Music," in Ernst Bloch, *Essays on the Philosophy of Music* (Cambridge: Cambridge University Press, 1985), 155 (emended).

A WORD ABOUT HEINRICH HEINE

1. SSD 12:101–2; PW 8: 147–8 (emended) ("Letter from Paris," July 6, 1841).

2. GS 4:264; PW 1:306 (*A Communication to My Friends*).

3. GS 4:266; PW 1:307 (*A Communication to My Friends*).

4. GS 5:85; PW 3:100 ("Jews in Music").

5. CT 1:178; Engl. trans. 1:172 (entry of Dec. 13, 1869).

CHAPTER FOUR

1. Heinrich Heine, *Sämtliche Schriften*, ed. Klaus Briegleb (Munich: Deutscher Taschen-buch Verlag, 2005), 5:443.

2. GS 4:269; PW 1:311–12 (*A Communication to My Friends*).

3. ML 223; Engl. trans. 212 (emended).

4. ML 231; Engl. trans. 219.

5. SB 2:434 (letter to Karl Gaillard, June 5, 1845).

6. Carl Dahlhaus, *Richard Wagners Musikdramen*, 2nd ed. (Zurich: Orell Füssli, 1985), 27; translated by Mary Whittall as *Richard Wagner's Music Dramas* (Cambridge: Cambridge University Press, 1979), 23.

7. ML 224; Engl. trans. 213; see also Mary Cicora, *From History to Myth: Wagner's "Tannhäuser" and Its Literary Sources* (Bern: Peter Lang, 1992), 39–63.

8. F. Gustav Jansen, ed., *Robert Schumanns Briefe: Neue Folge*, 2nd ed. (Leipzig: Breitkopf & Härtel, 1904), 220 (letter from Robert Schumann to Carl Koßmaly, Sept. 1, 1842).

9. Sieghart Döhring and Sabine Henze-Döhring, *Oper und Musikdrama im 19. Jahrhundert* (Laaber: Laaber-Verlag, 1997), 170.

10. SW 25:47 (*Dokumente und Texte zu "Tannhäuser und der Sängerkrieg auf Wartburg"*).

11. Sieghart Döhring, "*Tannhäuser* und die Transformation der romantischen Oper," in Klaus Döge and others, eds.,*"Schlagen Sie die Kraft der Reflexion nicht zu gering an": Beiträge zu Richard Wagners Denken, Werk und Wirken* (Mainz: Schott, 2002), 54.

12. GS 4:278–79; PW 1:322 (*A Communication to My Friends*).

13. SB 4:376–77 (letter to Liszt, May 19, 1852).

14. In the "Paris" version, this line has been reduced to "My salvation rests in Mary."

15. Dieter Borchmeyer, *Richard Wagner: Ahasvers Wandlungen* (Frankfurt: Insel, 2002), 195; translated by Daphne Ellis as *Drama and the World of Richard Wagner* (Princeton: Princeton University Press, 2003), 145. For a highly original but oversophistic resolution of the problem, see Heike Harmgart, Steffen Huck, and Wieland Müller, "Strategien der Erlösung: Über Aspekte der Rationalität in Richard Wagners *Tannhäuser*," *wagnerspectrum* 3, no. 1 (2007): 93–106.

16. CT 2:169; Engl. trans. 2:143 (entry of Sept. 5, 1878).

17. Dieter Borchmeyer, *Nietzsche, Cosima, Wagner: Portrait einer Freundschaft* (Frankfurt: Insel, 2008), 102; see also Friedrich Nietzsche, *Sämtliche Werke: Kritische Studienausgabe*, ed. Giorgio Colli and Mazzino Montinari (Munich: Deutscher Taschenbuch Verlag, 1988), 5:204; translated by Walter Kaufmann as "Beyond Good and Evil," in Nietzsche, *Basic Writings of Nietzsche* (New York: Modern Library, 1968), 388.

18. CT 2:367; Engl. trans. 2:325 (entry of June 17, 1879).

19. Charles Baudelaire, "Richard Wagner et *Tannhäuser* à Paris," in *Œuvres complètes*, ed. Claude Pichois (Paris: Gallimard, 1976), 2:794; translated by Jonathan Mayne as "Richard Wagner and *Tannhäuser* in Paris," *The Painter of Modern Life and Other Essays* (London: Phaidon, 1995), 125.

20. René Wellek, *A History of Modern Criticism: 1750–1950*, vol. 4, *The Later Nineteenth Century* (London: Jonathan Cape, 1966), 82.

21. Claus-Artur Scheier, *Ästhetik der Simulation: Formen des Produktionsdenkens im 19. Jahrhundert* (Hamburg: Meiner, 2000), 56.

22. Baudelaire, "Richard Wagner et *Tannhäuser* à Paris," 809, 785, and 796; Engl. trans. 140, 117, and 127.

23. Ibid., 795; Engl. trans. 126 (emended).

24. CT 2:439; Engl. trans. 2:392 (entry of Nov. 10, 1879).

25. Baudelaire, *Œuvres complètes*, 1453 (letter from Baudelaire to Wagner, Feb. 17, 1860).

26. Friedrich Nietzsche, *Sämtliche Briefe: Kritische Studienausgabe in 8 Bänden*, ed. Giorgio Colli and Mazzino Montinari (Munich: Deutscher Taschenbuch Verlag, 1986), 8:264 (letter from Nietzsche to Heinrich Köselitz, Feb. 26, 1888). For Wagner's letter to Baudelaire, see SB 13:107–8.

27. Theodor W. Adorno, *Gesammelte Schriften*, ed. Rolf Tiedemann (Frankfurt: Suhrkamp, 1997), 13:82; translated by Rodney Livingstone as *In Search of Wagner* (London: New Left Books, 1981), 86.

28. CT 1:1083; Engl. trans. 1:993 (entry of Nov. 5, 1877).

29. CT 2:1098; Engl. trans. 2:996 (entry of Jan. 23, 1883).

30. Hans-Klaus Jungheinrich, "Ritter, Bürger, Künstler," in Attila Csampai and Dietmar Holland, eds., *Richard Wagner, Tannhäuser: Texte, Materialien, Kommentare* (Reinbek: Rowohlt, 1986), 22.

31. Udo Bermbach, *"Blühendes Leid": Politik und Gesellschaft in Richard Wagners Musikdramen* (Stuttgart and Weimar: J. B. Metzler, 2002), 101.

32. GS 4:279; PW 1:323 (emended) (*A Communication to My Friends*).

33. GS 5:152; PW 3:198 (emended) (*On Performing "Tannhäuser"*).

34. Albert Schweitzer, *My Life and Thought: An Autobiography*, translated by C. T. Campion (London: George Allen & Unwin, 1933), 23.

35. Bertolt Brecht, *Werke: Große kommentierte Berliner und Frankfurter Ausgabe*, ed. Werner Hecht and others (Frankfurt: Suhrkamp, 1993), 13:37–38.

36. Dahlhaus, *Richard Wagners Musikdramen*, 30; Engl. trans. 26–27.

37. SB 2:153 (letter to Ernst Benedikt Kietz, Sept. 6–10, 1842). The painting in question is now believed to be a copy by Ismael Mengs.

38. SB 5:476 (letter to Hans von Bülow, Nov. 25, 1853).

39. Adorno, *Gesammelte Schriften*, 13:59–67; Engl. trans. 62–70.

40. SB 4:386 (letter to Theodor Uhlig, May 31, 1852).

41. Eckehard Kiem, "Lichtgebung: Aspekte zur Wagnerschen Harmonik," in Eckehard Kiem and Ludwig Holtmeier, eds., *Richard Wagner und seine Zeit* (Laaber: Laaber-Verlag, 2003), 244.

42. Adorno, *Gesammelte Schriften*, 13:64 and 88; Engl. trans. 67 and 93.

43. Werner Breig, "Wagners kompositorisches Werk," in Ulrich Müller and Peter Wapnewski, eds., *Richard-Wagner-Handbuch* (Stuttgart: Alfred Kröner Verlag, 1986), 390; translated by Paul Knight and Horst Loeschmann as "The Musical Works," in John Deathridge, ed., *Wagner Handbook* (Cambridge, MS: Harvard University Press, 1992), 426.

44. Adorno, *Gesammelte Schriften*, 13:64; Engl. trans. 67.

45. Scheier, *Ästhetik der Simulation*, 58.

46. Ludwig Strecker, *Richard Wagner als Verlagsgefährte* (Mainz: B. Schott's Söhne, 1951), 280.

47. GS 5:137; PW 3:183 (emended) (*On Performing "Tannhäuser"*).

48. SSD 16:168–69 ("Tannhäuser's Journey to Rome").

49. Max Burkhardt, *Führer durch Richard Wagners Musikdramen* (Berlin: Schuster & Loeffler, n.d.), 82.

50. For a detailed harmonic analysis, see Kiem, "Lichtgebung," 243–44.

51. E. T. A. Hoffmann, *Sämtliche Werke in sechs Bänden*, ed. Gerhard Allroggen and others (Frankfurt: Deutscher Klassiker Verlag, 2003), 1:613; translated by Martin Clarke as *E. T. A. Hoffmann's Musical Writings*, ed. David Charlton (Cambridge: Cambridge University Press, 1989), 297–98.

52. Adorno, *Gesammelte Schriften*, 13:88; Engl. trans. 93.

53. Carolyn Abbate, "Erik's Dream and Tannhäuser's Journey," in Arthur Groos and Roger Parker, eds., *Reading Opera* (Princeton: Princeton University Press, 1988), 166.

54. CT 1:433; Engl. trans. 1:407 (entry of Sept. 1, 1871).

55. GS 9:221; PW 5:220 (*On Actors and Singers*).

56. Nietzsche, *Sämtliche Werke*, 9:536.

57. Giacomo Meyerbeer, *Briefwechsel und Tagebücher*, ed. Heinz Becker and others (Berlin: Walter de Gruyter, 1960–2006), 6:533.

58. Jansen, *Robert Schumanns Briefe*, 254 (letter from Schumann to Felix Mendelssohn, [Dec.] 12, 1845).

A WORD ABOUT JOSEF RUBINSTEIN

1. CT 2:711; Engl. trans. 641 (entry of March 15, 1881).

2. CT 2:291; Engl. trans. 2:254 (entry of Jan. 14, 1879).

3. CT 1:497; Engl. trans. 1:464–65 (entry of March 7, 1872).

4. Peer Baedeker, "Ein Jude sucht Erlösung bei Richard Wagner: Joseph Rubinstein (1847–1884)," in Bernd Mayer and Frank Piontek, eds., *Jüdisches Bayreuth* (Bayreuth: Ellwanger, 2010), 123.

5. CT 2:1052; Engl. trans. 2:956 (entry of Nov. 18, 1882).

6. Siegfried Wagner, *Erinnerungen* (Stuttgart: J. Engelhorns Nachfolger, 1923), 15.

7. CT 2:776; Engl. trans. 2:701 (entry of Aug. 6, 1881).

8. CT 2:970; Engl. trans. 2:880 (entry of June 26, 1882).

CHAPTER FIVE

1. GS 4:298; PW 1:343 (emended) (*A Communication to My Friends*).

2. SB 2:513 (letter from Wagner to Hermann Franck, May 30, 1846).

3. GS 4:298–99; PW 1:343–44 (emended) (*A Communication to My Friends*).

4. Friedrich Nietzsche, *Sämtliche Werke: Kritische Studienausgabe*, ed. Giorgio Colli and Mazzino Montinari (Munich: Deutscher Taschenbuch Verlag, 1988), 6:17; translated by Walter Kaufmann as "The Case of Wagner," in Nietzsche, *Basic Writings of Nietzsche* (New York: Modern Library, 1968), 617.

5. CT 2:303; Engl. trans. 2:265 (entry of Feb. 4, 1879). The relevant passage from *Opera and Drama* may be found in GS 4:78; PW 2:208.

6. CT 2:1088; Engl. trans. 2:987 (entry for Jan. 6, 1883).

7. SW 26:197 (*Dokumente und Texte zu "Lohengrin"*).

8. GS 4:317–18; PW 1:364 (emended; emphasis in original) (*A Communication to My Friends*).

9. Alfred Meißner, *Geschichte meines Lebens* (Vienna: Karl Prochaska, 1884), 1:169.

10. SB 2:578 (letter from Wagner to Ernst Kossak, Nov. 23, 1847).

11. Theodor Adorno, *Minima moralia*, in Adorno, *Gesammelte Schriften*, ed. Rolf Tiedemann (Frankfurt: Suhrkamp, 1997), 4:43; translated by E. F. N. Jephcott as *Minima moralia: Reflections from Damaged Life* (London: Verso, 1974), 39.

12. Tschang-Un Hur, "Die Darstellung der großen Schlacht in der deutschen Literatur des 12. und 13. Jahrhunderts" (PhD diss., University of Munich, 1971), 77.

13. San-Marte, ed., *Parcival: Rittergedicht von Wolfram von Eschenbach: Aus dem Mittelhochdeutschen zum ersten Male übersetzt von San-Marte* (Magdeburg: Verlag der Creutz'schen Buchhandlung, 1836), 1:571.

14. Nietzsche, *Sämtliche Werke*, 6:17; Engl. trans. 616 ("The Case of Wagner").

15. Hans Rudolf Vaget, *Im Schatten Wagners: Thomas Mann über Richard Wagner*, 2nd ed. (Frankfurt: Fischer, 2005), 22; translated by Allan Blunden as Thomas Mann, *Pro and Contra Wagner* (London: Faber, 1985), 29 ("An Essay on the Theatre").

16. Heinrich Mann, *Der Untertan* (Düsseldorf: Claassen, 1961), 361–67. This whole episode is missing from the Penguin Twentieth-Century Classics translation of 1992, which reduces the 659 pages of the original to a mere 304.

17. Max Koch, *Richard Wagners geschichtliche völkische Sendung* (Langensalza: Beyer & Söhne, 1927), 99. Tannenberg was the site of a battle fought between Aug. 26 and 30, 1914, when the Russian army was completely routed by German troops.

18. Vaget, *Im Schatten Wagners*, 59–60; Engl. trans. from Mann, *Pro and Contra Wagner*, 61–62 (*Reflections of a Non-Political Man*).

19. Vaget, *Im Schatten Wagners*, 67–68 (entries of June 29, 1919, and April 29, 1920).

20. Adolf Hitler, *Mein Kampf* (Munich: Franz Eher Nachfolger, 1934), 15; translated by Ralph Manheim as *Mein Kampf* (London: Pimlico, 2002), 16.

21. Hitler's design for act 2 is reproduced in Frederic Spotts, *Hitler and the Power of Aesthetics* (London: Hutchinson, 2002), 239.

22. Isabella Kreim, "Richard Wagners *Lohengrin* auf der deutschen Bühne und in der Kritik" (PhD diss., University of Munich, 1983), 188.

23. Richard Wagner, *Entwürfe, Gedanken, Fragmente. Aus nachgelassenen Paperien zusammengestellt* (Leipzig: Breitkopf & Härtel, 1885), 120.

24. Horst Bredekamp, *Theorie des Bildaktes* (Frankfurt: Suhrkamp, 2010), 117.

25. SB 4:272 (letter from Wagner to Liszt, Jan. 30, 1852).

26. GS 4:290 and 295–96; PW 1:335 and 341 (emended) (*A Communication to My Friends*).

27. Herman van Campenhout, *Die bezaubernde Katastrophe: Versuch einer Wagner-Lektüre* (Würzburg: Königshausen & Neumann, 2005), 240.

28. GS 4:296; PW 1:341 (emended) (*A Communication to My Friends*).

29. Ursula Link-Heer, "Der 'androgyne Wagner' und die Dramaturgie des Blicks," in Susanne Vill, ed., *"Das Weib der Zukunft": Frauengestalten und Frauenstimmen bei Richard Wagner* (Stuttgart: J. B. Metzler, 2000), 94.

30. CT 1:203; Engl. trans. 1:194–95 (entry of March 1, 1870).

31. CT 1:637; Engl. trans. 1:592 (entry of Feb. 5, 1873).

32. SB 8:152 (letter from Wagner to August Röckel, Aug. 23, 1856).

33. Angelo Neumann, *Erinnerungen an Richard Wagner* (Leipzig: Staackmann, 1907), 11–14. Unfortunately Edith Livermore's 1909 English translation (*Personal Recollections of Wagner*) is too disfigured by arbitrary omissions and errors to be usable or recommendable.

34. SW 26:186 (*Dokumente und Texte zu "Lohengrin"*) (letter from Heinrich Porges to his family in Munich, late Feb. or early March 1870).

35. GS 5:179; PW 3:232 (emended) ("Prelude to 'Lohengrin'").

36. Manfred Hermann Schmid, "Metamorphose der Themen: Beobachtungen an den Skizzen zum 'Lohengrin'-Vorspiel," *Die Musikforschung* 41 (1988): 116.

37. Helga-Maria Palm, *Richard Wagners "Lohengrin": Studien zur Sprachbehandlung* (Paderborn: Wilhelm Fink, 1987), 109.

38. Graham G. Hunt, "Ortrud and the Birth of a New Style in Act 2, Scene 1, of Wagner's *Lohengrin*," *Opera Quarterly* 20 (2004): 68.

39. See Palm, *Richard Wagners "Lohengrin,"* 108.

40. SB 4:241 (letter from Wagner to Theodor Uhlig, Dec. 28, 1851). (Although Uhlig had already published a number of articles on Wagner's theoretical writings in the *Neue Zeitschrift für Musik*, his illness and premature death from consumption on Jan. 3, 1853, prevented him from following up the idea suggested here.)

41. Klaus Döge, "Wagner beim Wort genommen: 'Über das thematische formgewebe' im *Lohengrin*," in Ulrich Konrad and Egon Voss, eds., *Der 'Komponist' Richard Wagner im Blick der aktuellen Musikwissenschaft* (Wiesbaden: Breitkopf & Härtel, 2003), 104.

42. Schmid, "Metamorphose der Themen," 114–15.

43. Josef Bohuslav Foerster, *Der Pilger: Erinnerungen eines Musikers* (Prague: Artia, 1955), 408.

44. GS 10:191–92; PW 6:189–90 (emended) ("On the Application of Music to the Drama").

45. See Klaus Döge, "Wagner—Polyphonie—Kontrapunkt—angewendeter Bach," in Reinmar Emans and Wolfram Steinbeck, eds., *Bach und die deutsche Tradition des Komponierens: Festschrift Martin Geck zum 70. Geburtstag* (Dortmund: Klangfarben, 2009), 181–86.

46. See Klaus Kropfinger, *Wagner und Beethoven* (Regensburg: Gustav Bosse, 1975); translated by Peter Palmer as *Wagner and Beethoven: Richard Wagner's Reception of Beethoven* (Cambridge: Cambridge University Press, 1991).

47. GS 10:182; PW 6:180–81 (emended) ("On the Application of Music to the Drama").

48. Carl Dahlhaus, "'Lohengrin' und die 'Einheit des Symphoniesatzes,' sowie 'Opus metaphysicum': Das Musikdrama als symphonische Oper," in Carl Dahlhaus and Norbert Miller, eds., *Europäische Romantik in der Musik* (Stuttgart: J. B. Metzler, 2007), 2:912–23. For a dissenting view, see Carolyn Abbate, "Opera as Symphony: A Wagnerian Myth," in Carolyn Abbate and Roger Parker, eds., *Analyzing Opera: Verdi and Wagner* (Berkeley: University of California Press, 1989), 92–124.

49. Erich Kloss, ed., *Briefwechsel zwischen Wagner und Liszt*, 3rd ed. (Leipzig: Breitkopf & Härtel, 1910), 1:197 (letter from Liszt to Wagner, Dec. 27, 1852). I am grateful to Eckehard Kiem for his help with the harmonic analysis here.

50. Tobias Janz, *Klangdramaturgie: Studien zur theatralen Orchesterkomposition in Wagners "Ring des Nibelungen"* (Würzburg: Königshausen & Neumann, 2006).

51. Nietzsche, *Sämtliche Werke*, 6:30–31; Engl. trans. 629 ("The Case of Wagner").

52. Hans Mayer, "Lohengrin oder die Utopie in A-Dur," in Mayer, *Richard Wagner: Mitwelt und Nachwelt* (Stuttgart: Belser, 1978), 201–7.

53. Ibid., 203.

54. Egon Voss, "Lohengrin, der melancholische Held," in Voss, *"Wagner und kein Ende": Betrachtungen und Studien* (Zurich: Atlantis, 1996), 77–81.

55. Thomas Mann, *Tagebücher 1918–1921*, ed. Inge Jens (Frankfurt: Fischer, 1979), 534 (entry of June 27, 1921).

56. See Barbara Zuber, "Theater mit den Ohren betrachtet: Klangstruktur und Dramaturgie in Wagners *Lohengrin*," in Hanspeter Krellmann and Jürgen Schläder, eds., *"Die Wirklichkeit erfinden ist besser": Opern des 19. Jahrhunderts von Beethoven bis Verdi* (Stuttgart: J. B. Metzler, 2002), 99–100.

57. Paul Valéry, *Rhumbs* (Paris: Gallimard, 1933), 217: "Le poème—cette hésitation prolongée entre le son et le sens"; see also Albrecht Wellmer, "Werke und ihre Wirkungen: Kein Beitrag zur Rezeptionstheorie des Musiktheaters," in Hermann Danuser and Herfried

Münkler, eds., *Zukunftsbilder: Richard Wagners Revolution und ihre Folgen in Kunst und Politik* (Schliengen: Edition Argus, 2002), 260.

58. WWV pp. 335–36 (WWV 78: Sinfonien).

A WORD ABOUT ARNOLD SCHOENBERG

1. Erich Kloss, ed. *Briefwechsel zwischen Wagner und Liszt*, 3rd ed. (Leipzig: Breitkopf & Härtel, 1910), 1:197 (letter from Liszt to Wagner, Dec. 27, 1852).

2. Constantin Grun, *Arnold Schönberg und Richard Wagner: Spuren einer außergewöhnlichen Beziehung* (Göttingen: V&E unipress Verlag, 2006), 1245–47.

3. Arnold Schoenberg, *Style and Idea*, ed. Leonard Stein, trans. Leo Black (Berkeley: University of California Press, 1984), 374–75 ("On the Question of Modern Composition Teaching [1929]").

4. H. H. Stuckenschmidt, *Schoenberg: His Life, World and Work*; translated by Humphrey Searle (New York: Schirmer, 1978), 33.

5. Schoenberg, *Style and Idea*, 155–56 ("Art and the Moving Pictures [1940]").

6. Grun, *Schönberg und Wagner*, 1279.

7. Arnold Schönberg, "Richard Wagner und die Gegenwart," *Die literarische Welt* 9, no. 6–7 (1933): 3; quoted by Grun, *Schönberg und Wagner*, 1036.

8. Joseph Kerman, "Wagner: Thoughts in Season," in Kerman, *Write All These Down: Essays in Music* (Berkeley: University of California Press, 1994), 271.

9. Michael Mäckelmann, *Arnold Schönberg und das Judentum: Der Komponist und sein religiöses, nationales und politisches Selbstverständnis nach 1921* (Hamburg: Wagner, 1984), 232.

CHAPTER SIX

1. ML 374; Engl. trans. 361.

2. GS 2:269; PW 7:356 ("Draft for the Organization of a German National Theater").

3. GS 2:273; PW 7:359 ("Draft for the Organization of a German National Theater").

4. SB 2:590 (letter to Franz Jacob Wigard, May 19, 1848).

5. Helmut Kirchmeyer, *Das zeitgenössische Wagner-Bild*, vol. 3, *Dokumente 1846–1850* (Regensburg: Gustav Bosse, 1968), cols. 433–34; PW 4:139 ("How Do Republican Aspirations Stand in Relation to the Monarchy?").

6. Karl August Varnhagen von Ense, *Tageblätter*, ed. Konrad Feilchenfeldt (Frankfurt: Deutscher Klassiker Verlag, 1994), 484.

7. Kirchmeyer, *Das zeitgenössische Wagner-Bild*, vol. 3, col. 438; PW 4:143 (emphasis in original).

8. CT 2:134; Engl. trans. 2:110 (entry of July 7, 1878).

9. Kirchmeyer, *Das zeitgenössische Wagner-Bild*, vol. 3, col. 535; PW 8:227 ("Man and Existing Society").

10. SSD 12:245; PW 8:232 ("Revolution").

11. GS 4:306; PW 1:352 (*A Communication to My Friends*).

12. For a recent assessment of the current state of research concerning Wagner's revolutionary activities, see Bernd Kramer, *"Laßt uns die Schwerter ziehen, damit die Kette bricht . . .": Michael Bakunin, Richard Wagner und andere während der Dresdner Mai-Revolution 1849* (Berlin: Karin Kramer Verlag, 1999), 64–67.

13. GS 3:164; PW 1:199 (*The Artwork of the Future*).

14. GS 4:313; PW 1:359 (emended) (*A Communication to My Friends*).

15. GS 4:328; PW 1:375 (emended) (*A Communication to My Friends*).

16. SB 6:69 (letter to August Röckel, Jan. 25–26, 1854).

17. Eduard Devrient, *Aus seinen Tagebüchern*, ed. Rolf Kabel (Weimar: Hermann Böhlaus Nachfolger, 1964), 1:470 (entry of Feb. 22, 1849).

18. GS 4:312–13; PW 1:359–60 (*A Communication to My Friends*).

19. GS 4:343; PW 1:391 (*A Communication to My Friends*).

20. ML 356; Engl. trans. 342–43.

21. Richard Wagner, *Entwürfe, Gedanken, Fragmente: Aus nachgelassenen Papieren zusammengestellt* (Leipzig: Breitkopf & Härtel, 1885), 55.

22. ML 410; Engl. trans. 396.

23. Peter Hofmann, *Richard Wagners politische Theologie: Kunst zwischen Revolution und Religion* (Paderborn: Schöningh, 2003), 137.

24. SB 3:187 (letter to Liszt, Dec. 5, 1849).

25. Martin Gregor-Dellin, *Richard Wagner: Sein Leben, sein Werk, sein Jahrhundert* (Munich, R. Piper, 1980), 254; translated by J. Maxwell Brownjohn as *Richard Wagner: His Life, His Work, His Century* (London: Collins, 1983), 161. See also Alan David Aberbach, *The Ideas of Richard Wagner: An Examination and Analysis of His Major Aesthetic, Political, Economic, Social, and Religious Thoughts*, 2nd ed. (Lanham: University Press of America, 2003), 209.

26. Wagner, *Entwürfe, Gedanken, Fragmente*, 59.

27. GS 3:33; PW 1:57 (emended) (*Art and Revolution*).

28. Richard Wagner, *Jesus von Nazareth: Ein dichterischer Entwurf aus dem Jahre 1848* (Leipzig: Breitkopf & Härtel, 1887), 50–51; PW 8:313 (emended) (*Jesus von Nazareth*).

29. ML 401; Engl. trans. 387.

30. ML 405; Engl. trans. 392.

31. SB 3:460 (letter to Theodor Uhlig, Oct. 22, 1850).

32. Odo Marquard, "Kunst als Antifiktion—Versuch über den Weg der Wirklichkeit ins Fiktive," in Dieter Henrich and Wolfgang Iser, eds., *Funktionen des Fiktiven* (Munich: Wilhelm Fink, 1983), 39.

33. Hans Magnus Enzensberger, *Der Untergang der Titanic* (Frankfurt: Suhrkamp, 1978), 97; translated by Hans Magnus Enzensberger as *The Sinking of the Titanic* (Manchester: Carcanet New Press Limited, 1981), 81. See also Martin Geck, *Richard Wagner* (Reinbek: Rowohlt, 2004), 54.

34. Charles Taylor, *A Secular Age* (Cambridge, MA: Belknap Press, 2007), 390.

35. See Manfred Frank, *Mythendämmerung: Richard Wagner im frühromantischen Kontext* (Munich: Wilhelm Fink, 2008), 148–55.

36. Rüdiger Jacobs, *Revolutionsidee und Staatskritik in Richard Wagners Schriften: Perspektiven metapolitischen Denkens* (Würzburg: Königshausen & Neumann, 2010).

37. GS 5:169–72; PW 3:221–24 (emended) ("Beethoven's 'Heroic' Symphony").

38. SB 3:251 (letter to Theodor Uhlig, March 13, 1850).

39. SB 3:249 (letter to Theodor Uhlig, March 13, 1849).

40. GS 3:177; PW 1:212–13 (*The Artwork of the Future*).

41. Friedrich Nietzsche, *Sämtliche Werke: Kritische Studienausgabe*, ed. Giorgio Colli and Mazzino Montinari (Munich: Deutscher Taschenbuch Verlag, 1988), 13:500.

42. GS 3:206; PW 1:248 (*Wieland the Smith*).

43. Paul Bekker, *Wagner: Das Leben im Werke* (Stuttgart: Deutsche Verlags-Anstalt, 1924), 246; translated by M. M. Bozman as *Richard Wagner: His Life in His Work* (New York: W. W. Norton, 1931), 223.

A WORD ABOUT PAUL BEKKER

1. Paul Bekker, *Kunst und Revolution* (Frankfurt: Frankfurter Societäts Verlag, 1919), 31 and 13.

2. Ibid., 22–23.

3. Paul Bekker, *Wagner: Das Leben im Werke* (Stuttgart: Deutsche Verlags-Anstalt, 1924), 232; translated by M. M. Bozman as *Richard Wagner: His Life in His Work* (New York: W. W. Norton, 1931), 213.

4. Ibid., 235; Engl. trans., 215.

5. Udo Bermbach, *Richard Wagner in Deutschland: Rezeption—Verfälschungen* (Stuttgart: J. B. Metzler, 2011), 27.

6. Bekker, *Wagner*, 10; Engl. trans., 7–8.

7. Ibid., 16; Engl. trans., 13.

8. Ibid., 536; Engl. trans., 473–74.

CHAPTER SEVEN

1. See Martin Geck, "Erlösung durch Untergang: Wagners zerstörerischer Pessimismus," *Musik & Ästhetik* 1, no. 4 (1997): 67–73.

2. Georg Wilhelm Friedrich Hegel, "Glauben und Wissen," in Hegel, *Jenaer Kritische Schriften*, ed. Hartmut Buchner and Otto Pöggeler (Hamburg: Felix Meiner, 1986), 82.

3. Manfred Frank, *Mythendämmerung: Richard Wagner im frühromantischen Kontext* (Munich: Wilhelm Fink, 2008), 61.

4. SB 3:197 (letter to Theodor Uhlig, Dec. 27, 1849).

5. CT 1:199; Engl. trans. 1:191 (entry of Feb. 17, 1870).

6. SB 3:404–5 (letter to Ernst Benedikt Kietz, Sept. 14, 1850).

7. Roland Tenschert, "Richard Wagner im Urteil von Richard Strauss: Aus Briefen und mündlichen Äußerungen des Meisters," *Schweizerische Musikzeitung* 46 (1954): 328.

8. Friedrich Nietzsche, *Sämtliche Werke: Kritische Studienausgabe*, ed. Giorgio Colli and Mazzino Montinari (Munich: Deutscher Taschenbuch Verlag, 1988), 1:502; translated by R. J. Hollingdale as *Untimely Meditations* (Cambridge: Cambridge University Press, 1983), 248 ("Richard Wagner in Bayreuth").

9. Hans Rudolf Vaget, *Im Schatten Wagners: Thomas Mann über Richard Wagner*, 2nd ed. (Frankfurt: Fischer, 2005), 100; translated by Allan Blunden as Thomas Mann, *Pro and Contra Wagner* (London: Faber, 1985), 105 ("The Sorrows and Grandeur of Richard Wagner").

10. GS 3:231; PW 2:17 (*Opera and Drama*).

11. GS 3:317–18; PW 2:112–13 (*Opera and Drama*).

12. GS 3:314–16; PW 2:109–11 (emended) (*Opera and Drama*).

13. GS 4:64; PW 2:191 (emended) (*Opera and Drama*).

14. GS 4:31; PW 2:153 (emended) (*Opera and Drama*).

15. GS 4:65; PW 2:191 (*Opera and Drama*).

16. GS 4:63–64; PW 2:190 (emended) (*Opera and Drama*).

17. GS 4:173; PW 2:316 (*Opera and Drama*).

18. GS 4:200; PW 2:346 (emended) (*Opera and Drama*). For two representative studies on the term *leitmotif*, see Thomas Grey, "'. . . wie ein rother Faden': On the Origins of the 'Leitmotif' as Critical Construct and Musical Practice," in Ian Bent, ed., *Music Theory in the Age of Romanticism* (Cambridge: Cambridge University Press, 1996), 187–210; and Christian Thorau, *Semantisierte Sinnlichkeit: Studien zu Rezeption und Zeichenstruktur der Leitmotivtechnik Richard Wagners* (Stuttgart: Franz Steiner, 2003).

19. CT 1:444; Engl. trans. 417–18 (entry of Sept. 29, 1871).

20. GS 4:190; PW 2:335 (*Opera and Drama*).

21. Max Wehrli, *Literatur im deutschen Mittelalter* (Stuttgart: Reclam, 1984), 196.

22. GS 4:153; PW 2:292 (emended) (*Opera and Drama*).

23. GS 7:118; PW 3:326 (emended) ("Music of the Future").

24. GS 4:343; PW 1:391 (emended) (*A Communication to My Friends*) (emphasis in original).

25. GS 3:23 and 11; PW 1:47 and 34 (*Art and Revolution*).

26. Bernd Kramer, "*Laßt uns die Schwerter ziehen, damit die Kette bricht . . .*": *Michael Bakunin, Richard Wagner und andere während der Dresdner Mai-Revolution 1849* (Berlin: Karin Kramer Verlag, 1999), 60.

27. CT 1:157; Engl. trans. 1:152 (entry of Oct. 4, 1869).

28. GS 6:281; Engl. trans. 3:282 ("Preface to the Poem of the *Ring*").

29. For a detailed account of Wagner's reworking of his mythological and poetic sources, see Elizabeth Magee, *Richard and the Nibelungs* (Oxford: Clarendon Press, 1990).

30. See Volker Mertens, "Richard Wagner und das Mittelalter," in Ulrich Müller and Peter Wapnewski, eds., *Richard-Wagner-Handbuch* (Stuttgart: Alfred Kröner Verlag, 1986), 33; translated by Stewart Spencer as "Wagner's Middle Ages," in John Deathridge, ed., *Wagner Handbook* (Cambridge, MA: Harvard University Press, 1992), 248.

31. Mertens, "Richard Wagner und das Mittelalter," 34; Engl. trans. 248.

32. See Mischa Meier, *Richard Wagners "Der Ring des Nibelungen" und die griechische Antike: Zum Stand der Diskussion* (Göttingen: Vandenhoeck & Ruprecht, 2005); and Daniel H. Foster, *Wagner's "Ring" Cycle and the Greeks* (Cambridge: Cambridge University Press, 2010).

33. SB 5:97 (letter to Liszt, Nov. 9, 1852).

34. Arthur Gelb and Barbara Gelb, *O'Neill: Life with Monte Cristo* (East Rutherford, NJ: Applause Books, 2000), 423, first published in the *New York Tribune* on Jan. 23, 1921.

35. Nietzsche, *Sämtliche Werke*, 1:494; Engl. trans. 243 ("Richard Wagner in Bayreuth").

36. Vaget, *Im Schatten Wagners*, 79; Engl. trans. 82 ("To an Opera Producer").

37. Walter Benjamin, *Ursprung des deutschen Trauerspiels* (Frankfurt: Suhrkamp, 1978), 82–83; translated by John Osborne as *The Origin of German Tragic Drama* (London: Verso, 2003), 103–4.

38. Kurt Hübner, *Die Wahrheit des Mythos* (Munich: C. H. Beck, 1985). For a critique of Hübner, see Wolfram Ette, "Mythos minus Moderne: Zwölf Thesen zu Wagner und der 'modernen Mythosforschung,'" in Richard Klein, ed., *Narben des Gesamtkunstwerks: Wagners "Ring des Nibelungen"* (Munich: Wilhelm Fink, 2001), 150–65.

39. GS 4:234; PW 1:274 (emended) (*A Communication to My Friends*).

40. Mertens, "Richard Wagner und das Mittelalter," 39. This passage was removed from the English translation on the grounds of its dubious reliability.

41. Patrice Chéreau, "Kommentare zu 'Mythologie und Ideologie,'" in Herbert Barth, ed., *Bayreuther Dramaturgie: Der Ring des Nibelungen* (Stuttgart: Belser, 1980), 430.

42. Michel Foucault, "Die Bilderwelt des 19. Jahrhunderts: Boulez' und Chéreaus Bayreuther Ringinszenierung," *Ästhetik und Kommunikation* 56 (Nov. 1984), 129.

43. Herbert Schnädelbach, "'Ring' und Mythos," in Udo Bermbach, ed., *In den Trümmern der eignen Welt: Richard Wagners "Der Ring des Nibelungen"* (Berlin: Dietrich Reimer, 1989), 154.

44. Carl Dahlhaus, *Richard Wagners Musikdramen*, 2nd ed. (Zurich: Orell Füssli, 1985), 111; translated by Mary Whittall as *Richard Wagner's Music Dramas* (Cambridge: Cambridge University Press, 1979), 114.

45. Manfred Frank, "Der *Ring*-Mythos als 'Totschlägerreihe,'" in Klein, *Narben des Gesamtkunstwerks*, 97.

46. Samuel Weber, "Der *Ring* als Dekonstruktion der Moderne: Wagner mit Benjamin," in Klein, *Narben des Gesamtkunstwerks*, 68.

47. Benjamin, *Ursprung des deutschen Trauerspiels*, 119–20; Engl. trans. 139.

48. Weber, "Der *Ring* als Dekonstruktion," 71.

49. Richard Klein, "Der sichtbare und der unsichtbare Gott: Versuch über Wotan," in Klein, *Narben des Gesamtkunstwerks*, 122.

50. Günter Figal, "Der moderne Künstler par excellence: Wagner in Nietzsches philosophischer Perspektive," in Klein, *Narben des Gesamtkunstwerks*, 63.

51. Nietzsche, *Sämtliche Werke*, 1:491; Engl. trans. 240 ("Richard Wagner in Bayreuth").

52. Udo Bermbach, *"Blühendes Leid": Politik und Gesellschaft in Richard Wagners Musikdramen* (Stuttgart: J. B. Metzler, 2003), 165 and 167.

53. Walter Benjamin, *Gesammelte Schriften*, ed. Rolf Tiedemann and Hermann Schweppenhäuser, 1.1:697; translated by Harry Zohn as "Theses on the Philosophy of History," in Benjamin, *Illuminations* (London: Pimlico, 1999), 249.

54. Richard Klein, "Wagners plurale Moderne: Eine Konstruktion des Unvereinbaren," in Claus-Steffen Mahnkopf, ed., *Richard Wagner: Konstrukteur der Moderne* (Stuttgart: Klett-Cotta, 1999), 195.

55. Richard Klein, "Gebrochene Temporalität: Die Revolution der musikalischen Zeit im *Ring des Nibelungen*," in Klein, *Narben des Gesamtkunstwerks*, 171.

A WORD ABOUT ANGELO NEUMANN

1. CT 1:1035 and 1042; Engl. trans. 1:950 and 1:956 (entries of March 3 and April 4, 1877).

2. CT 2:39; Engl. trans. 2:21 (entry of Jan. 21, 1878).

3. CT 2:734; Engl. trans. 2:663 (entry of May 5, 1881).

4. For full details, see Markus Rubow and Susanne Rump, "Das wandelnde Bayreuth: Das Richard Wagner-Theater Angelo Neumanns," in Klaus Hortschansky and Berthold Warnecke, eds., *Der Ring des Nibelungen in Münster: Der Zyklus von 1999 bis 2001* (Münster: Agenda Verlag, 2001), 191–203.

CHAPTER EIGHT

1. Manfred Frank, "Die Dialektik von 'erb' und 'eigen' in Wagners *Ring*: Auch eine Einführung in die *Götterdämmerung*," in Otto Kolleritsch, ed., *Die Musik als Medium von Beziehungsbefindlichkeiten: Mozarts und Wagners Musiktheater im aktuellen Deutungsgeschehen* (Vienna: Universal-Edition, 2002), 99–100.

2. Friedrich Nietzsche, *Sämtliche Werke: Kritische Studienausgabe*, ed. Giorgio Colli and Mazzino Montinari (Munich: Deutscher Taschenbuch Verlag, 1988), 8:591 (Posthumous Fragment 41[51]).

3. Nietzsche, *Sämtliche Werke*, 1:435–36; translated by R. J. Hollingdale as *Untimely Meditations* (Cambridge: Cambridge University Press, 1983), 200 ("Richard Wagner in Bayreuth").

4. CT 1:461; Engl. trans. 1:433 (entry of Nov. 19, 1871).

5. SB 4:186 (letter to Liszt, Nov. 20, 1851).

6. GS 4:343; PW 1:391 (*A Communication to My Friends*).

7. Hans Körner, *Botticelli* (Cologne: DuMont, 2006), 374–53.

8. CT 1:129; Engl. trans. 1:127 (July 17, 1869).

9. Theodor W. Adorno, *Gesammelte Schriften*, ed. Gretel Adorno and Rolf Tiedemann (Frankfurt: Suhrkamp, 1997), 13:51; translated by Rodney Livingstone as *In Search of Wagner* (London: New Left Books, 1981), 53.

10. For a representative cross-section of analyses of this passage, see Peter Ackermann, *Richard Wagners "Ring des Nibelungen" und die Dialektik der Aufklärung* (Tutzing: Hans Schneider, 1981), 23–25; Warren Darcy, *Wagner's "Das Rheingold"* (Oxford: Clarendon Press, 1993), 62–86; Richard Klein, "Gebrochene Temporalität: Die Revolution der musikalischen Zeit im *Ring des Nibelungen*," in Klein, ed., *Narben des Gesamtkunstwerks: Wagners "Ring des Nibelungen"* (Munich: Wilhelm Fink, 2001), 182–87; and Gerd Rienäcker, *Richard Wagner: Nachdenken über sein "Gewebe"* (Berlin: Lukas-Verlag, 2001), 236–58.

11. SB 6:69 (letter to August Röckel, Jan. 25–26, 1854).

12. Susanne Vill, "Erda: Mythische Quellen und musikalische Gestaltung," in Udo Bermbach, ed., *"Alles ist nach seiner Art": Figuren in Richard Wagners "Der Ring des Nibelungen"* (Stuttgart: J. B. Metzler, 2001), 199. The word *vala* derives from Old Icelandic *völva*, meaning "sibyl" or "witch."

13. Vera Nemirova and others, "Ansichten eines Mythos: Zur gegenwärtigen Verortung von Wagners *Ring*," in Isolde Schmid-Reiter, ed., *Richard Wagners "Der Ring des Nibelungen": Europäische Traditionen und Paradigmen* (Regensburg: ConBrio Verlagsgesellschaft, 2010), 215–16.

14. Dieter Schickling, *Abschied von Walhall: Richard Wagners erotische Gesellschaft* (Stuttgart: Deutsche Verlags-Anstalt, 1983), 304.

15. GS 2:166; PW 7:311 ("The Nibelung Myth as Sketch for a Drama").

16. Patrice Chéreau, "Annexe I," in Pierre Boulez and others, *Histoire d'un "Ring": Der Ring des Nibelungen (l'Anneau du Nibelung) de Richard Wagner, Bayreuth 1976–1980*, ed. Sylvie Nussac and François Regnault (Paris: Robert Laffont, 1980), 120.

17. CT 2:52; Engl. trans. 2:33 (entry of March 2, 1878).

18. CT 2:1051; Engl. trans. 2:955 (entry of Nov. 17, 1882).

19. Tobias Janz, *Klangdramaturgie: Studien zur theatralen Orchesterkomposition in Wagners "Ring des Nibelungen"* (Würzburg: Königshausen & Neumann, 2006), 231.

20. Jan Buhr, *"Der Ring des Nibelungen" und Wagners Ästhetik im Fokus struktureller Semantik* (Würzburg: Königshausen & Neumann, 2008), 230.

21. SB 4:99 (undated letter to Theodor Uhlig, [Sept. 3, 1851]).

22. GS 7:110; PW 3:318 (emended) ("Music of the Future").

23. Claus-Steffen Mahnkopf, "Wagners Kompositionstechnik," in Claus-Steffen Mahnkopf, ed., *Richard Wagner: Konstrukteur der Moderne* (Stuttgart: Klett-Cotta, 1999), 180.

24. Werner Breig, "Der 'Rheintöchtergesang' in Wagners 'Rheingold,'" *Archiv für Musikwissenschaft* 37 (1980): 251.

25. See Werner Breig, "Zur musikalischen Struktur von Wagners 'Ring des Nibelungen,'" in Udo Bermbach, ed., *"In den Trümmern der eignen Welt": Richard Wagners "Der Ring des Nibelungen"* (Berlin: Dietrich Reimer, 1989), 57–58.

26. Eduard Hanslick, *Die moderne Oper: Kritiken und Studien* (Berlin: Allgemeiner Verein für Deutsche Literatur, 1875), 310–11.

27. Christian Thorau, *Semantisierte Sinnlichkeit: Studien zu Rezeption und Zeichenstruktur der Leitmotivtechnik Richard Wagners* (Stuttgart: Franz Steiner, 2003), 101.

28. Horst Bredekamp, *Theorie des Bildaktes: Über das Lebensrecht des Bildes* (Frankfurt: Suhrkamp, 2010), 241.

29. For the sake of the general reader's ease of understanding I have simplified the true facts of the matter.

30. Christian Berger, "Leitmotive in den harmonischen Kraftfeldern von Wagners *Rheingold*," in Klaus Hortschansky, ed., *Richard Wagners "Ring des Nibelungen": Musikalische Dramaturgie—Kulturelle Kontextualität—Primär-Rezeption* (Schneverdingen: Wagner, 2004), 46.

31. James Treadwell, "The *Ring* and the Conditions of Interpretation: Wagner's Writing, 1848 to 1852," *Cambridge Opera Journal* 7 (1995): 228.

32. See Klaus Aringer, "'Kunst des Übergangs': Zu den Verwandlungsmusiken in *Rheingold*," in Hortschansky, *Richard Wagners "Ring des Nibelungen."*

33. SW X/1:200. For the general reader, a more accessible source is the Eulenburg reprint of the critical edition, published in London in 2002 (= Eulenburg 8059, pp. 200–201, bars 1852–59).

34. Quoted by Peter Schleuning, *Der Bürger erhebt sich: Geschichte der deutschen Musik im 18. Jahrhundert*, 2nd ed. (Stuttgart: J. B. Metzler, 2000), 131.

A WORD ABOUT GEORGE STEINER

1. Martin Geck, "Es ist wie die Stimme des Ding an sich: Wagners 'Bach,'" in Geck, *"Denn alles findet bei Bach statt": Erforschtes und Erfahrenes* (Stuttgart: J. B. Metzler, 2000), 180; translated by A. D. Coleridge in *The New Bach Reader: A Life of Johann Sebastian Bach in Letters and Documents*, ed. Hans T. David and Arthur Mendel (New York: W. W. Norton, 1998), 499 (letter from Goethe to Carl Friedrich Zelter, June 21, 1827).

2. George Steiner, *Errata: An Examined Life* (London: Weidenfeld & Nicolson, 1997), 75.

3. George Steiner, *Grammars of Creation* (London: Faber & Faber, 2001), 11.

4. George Steiner, "Melodien für Millionen: Über das schwierige und intime Verhältnis von Musik und Politik," *Süddeutsche Zeitung* (Sept. 1, 1998).

5. Steiner, *Errata*, 75.

6. Ibid., 65.

7. Ibid., 67.

8. Ibid., 73.

9. Steiner, *Grammars of Creation*, 1.

10. Jan Brachmann, "Ohne Barbarei gibt es keine große Kunst," *Berliner Zeitung* (July 31, 2004).

11. Wolfgang Rihm, "Gespräch mit George Steiner," *Sinn und Form* 57 (2005): 42.

CHAPTER NINE

1. Tobias Janz, *Klangdramaturgie: Studien zur theatralen Orchesterkomposition in Wagners "Ring des Nibelungen"* (Würzburg: Königshausen & Neumann, 2006), 152.

2. Theodor Fontane, *Briefe an seine Familie* (Berlin: Fontane, 1905), 1:316.

3. Egon Voss, ed., *Richard Wagner: Die Walküre (Textbuch)* (Stuttgart: Reclam, 1997), 122.

4. SB 7:282 (letter to Liszt, Oct. 3, 1855).

5. GS 6:31.

6. Susanna Großmann-Vendrey, *Bayreuth in der deutschen Presse: Dokumentenband 1; Die Grundsteinlegung und die ersten Festspiele 1872–1876* (Regensburg: Gustav Bosse, 1977), 116 (Eduard Schelle's review of the second cycle, published in *Die Presse* on Aug. 25, 1876).

7. SB 6:69 (letter to August Röckel, Jan. 25–26, 1854).

8. Udo Bermbach, "Wotan—der Gott als Politiker," in Bermbach, ed., *"Alles ist nach seiner Art": Figuren in Richard Wagners "Der Ring des Nibelungen"* (Stuttgart: J. B. Metzler, 2001), 47.

9. Ibid., 45.

10. CT 1:988; Engl. trans. 1:909 (entry of May 30, 1876).

11. Christopher Wintle, "The Numinous in *Götterdämmerung*," in Arthur Groos and Roger Parker, eds., *Reading Opera* (Princeton: Princeton University Press, 1988), 206.

12. See Martin Knust, *Sprachvertonung und Gestik in den Werken Richard Wagners: Einflüsse zeitgenössischer Rezitations- und Deklamationspraxis* (Berlin: Frank & Timme, 2007), 309. For an alternative version of this anecdote, as reported by Heinrich Porges, see Knust, *Sprachvertonung*, 308; see also Heinrich Porges, *Wagner Rehearsing the "Ring": An Eye-Witness Account of the Stage Rehearsals of the First Bayreuth Festival*, translated by Robert L. Jacobs (Cambridge: Cambridge University Press, 1983), 39.

13. SB 7:282 (letter to Liszt, Oct. 3, 1855).

14. SB 7:69 (letter to August Röckel, Jan. 25–26, 1854). (Wagner used the form *Wodan* until around 1860.)

15. CT 2:73; Engl. trans. 2:52 (entry of March 29, 1878).

16. Herbert Schnädelbach, "'Ring' und Mythos," in Udo Bermbach, ed., *In den Trümmern der eignen Welt: Richard Wagners "Der Ring des Nibelungen"* (Berlin: Dietrich Reimer, 1989), 145.

17. Bernhard Benz, *Zeitstrukturen in Richard Wagners "Ring"-Tetralogie* (Frankfurt: Peter Lang, 1994), 311.

18. GS 10:187–88; PW 6:186–87 ("On the Application of Music to the Drama").

19. Benz, *Zeitstrukturen*, 319–20.

20. Carolyn Abbate, "Wotan's Monologue and the Morality of Musical Narration," in Abbate, *Unsung Voices: Opera and Musical Narrative in the Nineteenth Century* (Princeton: Princeton University Press, 1991), 204.

21. Manfred Frank, "Der *Ring*-Mythos als 'Totschlägerreihe,'" in Richard Klein, ed., *Narben des Gesamtkunstwerks: Wagners "Ring des Nibelungen"* (Munich: Wilhelm Fink, 2001), 81–101.

22. GS 3:2; PW 1:24 (emended) ("Introduction to Art and Revolution").

23. Frank, "Der *Ring*-Mythos als 'Totschlägerreihe,'" 88.

24. Richard Klein, "Der sichtbare und der unsichtbare Gott: Versuch über Wotan," in Klein, *Narben des Gesamtkunstwerks*, 126.

25. Nike Wagner, "Wotan, eine Warnung," in Klein, *Narben des Gesamtkunstwerks*, 272.

26. SB 6:69 (letter to August Röckel, Jan. 25–26, 1854).

27. Wolfram Ette, "Mythos und negative Dialektik in Wagners Ring," in Klein, *Narben des Gesamtkunstwerks*, 145.

28. GS 10:307–8; PW 6:312 (emended) ("The Stage Consecration Festival Drama in Bayreuth in 1882").

29. Martin Geck, *Robert Schumann: Mensch und Musiker der Romantik* (Munich: Siedler, 2010), 135–59 ("Das Liederjahr 1840" and "Zwielicht"); translated by Stewart Spencer as *Robert Schumann: The Life and Work of a Romantic Composer* (Chicago: University of Chicago Press, 2012), 109–31.

30. SB 7:366 (letter to Ferdinand Praeger, March 28, 1856).

31. SB 7:373 (undated letter to Franz Liszt, [late March 1856]).

32. Thomas Mann, *Tagebücher 1940–1943*, ed. Peter de Mendelssohn (Frankfurt: Fischer, 1982), 373–74 (entry of Jan. 3, 1942).

33. Nike Wagner, "'Es war ein Verhältnis': Thomas Mann und Richard Wagner," in Manfred Papst and Thomas Sprecher, eds., *Vom weltläufigen Erzählen: Die Vorträge des Kongresses in Zürich 2006* (Frankfurt: Vittorio Klostermann, 2007), 54.

34. Hans-Joachim Hinrichsen, "Bruckners Wagner-Zitate," in Albrecht Riethmüller, ed., *Bruckner-Probleme* (Stuttgart: Franz Steiner, 1999), 123.

35. Ernst Kurth, *Romantische Harmonik und ihre Krise in Wagners "Tristan"* (Berlin: Max Hesse, 1923), 226–27.

36. Eckehard Kiem, "Lichtgebung: Aspekte der Wagnerschen Harmonik," in Eckehard Kiem and Ludwig Holtmeier, eds., *Richard Wagner und seine Zeit* (Laaber: Laaber-Verlag, 2003), 244–45 (the music example reproduced here is defective).

37. Kurth, *Romantische Harmonik*, 225–26.

38. Kiem, "Lichtgebung," 244–45.

39. GS 4:78; PW 2:208 (*Opera and Drama*).

40. GS 4:198; PW 2:344 (emended) (*Opera and Drama*).

41. GS 4:224; PW 2:371 (emended) (*Opera and Drama*).

42. Sergei Eisenstein, *Beyond the Stars: The Memoirs of Sergei Eisenstein*, ed. Richard Taylor and trans. William Powell (London: British Film Institute, 1995), 660.

43. Wolfgang Schild, "Hegel und Wagner," in Martin Asiáin and others, eds., *Der Grund, die Not und die Freude des Bewußtseins: Beiträge zum Internationalen Symposion in Venedig zu Ehren von Wolfgang Marx* (Würzburg: Königshausen & Neumann, 2002), 180.

44. Wolfgang Rathert, "Schönberg und der Kontrapunkt," in Ulrich Tadday, ed., *Philosophie des Kontrapunkts* (Munich: edition text + kritik, 2010), 124.

45. CT 2:865; Engl. trans. 2:783 (entry of Jan. 3, 1882).

46. Leonardo da Vinci, *Treatise on Painting*, trans. John Francis Rigaud (London: J. B. Nichols and Son, 1835), 235.

47. Sabine Zurmühl, "Brünnhilde—Tochter im Tode im Leben: Eine feministische Interpretation," in Udo Bermbach, ed., *In den Trümmern der eignen Welt: Richard Wagners "Der Ring des Nibelungen"* (Berlin: Dietrich Reimer, 1989), 188.

48. Bermbach, "Wotan—der Gott als Politiker," 46.

49. Knust, *Sprachvertonung*, 454.

50. SB 6:69 (letter to August Röckel, Jan. 25–26, 1854).

51. GS 9:104–5; PW 5:104–5 (*Beethoven*).

52. GS 9:105; PW 5:106 (*Beethoven*).

53. GS 9:100; PW 5:101 (emended) (*Beethoven*).

54. GS 9:101; GS 5:101 (emended) (*Beethoven*).

55. GS 9:100; PW 5:100–101 (*Beethoven*).

56. CT 1:113; Engl. trans. 1:112 (entry of June 22, 1869). (The misreading in the German text—*dementarischen* for *elementarischen*—has been corrected in Geoffrey Skelton's English translation.)

57. See Martin Geck, *Die Bildnisse Richard Wagners* (Munich: Prestel, 1970), pl. 22B and the caption on 145.

58. SB 5:118 (letter to Theodor Uhlig, Nov. 18, 1852).

59. Klaus Kropfinger, "Wagners 'Entsagungs'-Motiv," in Hermann Danuser and others, eds., *Das musikalische Kunstwerk: Geschichte, Ästhetik, Theorie; Festschrift Carl Dahlhaus zum 60. Geburtstag* (Laaber: Laaber-Verlag, 1988), 247.

60. Walter Benjamin, *Gesammelte Schriften*, ed. Rolf Tiedemann and Hermann Schweppenhäuser (Frankfurt: Suhrkamp, 2009), 2.2:458; translated by Harry Zohn as "The Storyteller," in Benjamin, *Illuminations*, ed. Hannah Arendt (London: Pimlico, 1999), 101.

61. See Egon Voss, "Siegfrieds Musik," in Danuser, *Das musikalische Kunstwerk*, 260–61.

62. Janz, *Klangdramaturgie*, 314.

63. Carl Dahlhaus, "Das unterbrochene Hauptwerk: Zu Wagners Siegfried," in Dahlhaus, *Vom Musikdrama zur Literaturoper: Aufsätze zur neueren Operngeschichte* (Munich: Piper, 1989), 105–8.

A WORD ABOUT SERGEI EISENSTEIN

1. Dimitri Shostakovich, *Testimony: The Memoirs of Dimitri Shostakovich as Related to and Edited by Solomon Volkov*; translated by Antonia W. Bouis (London: Faber and Faber, 1979), 99–100.

2. Quoted by Dieter Thomä, *Totalität und Mitleid: Richard Wagner, Sergej Eisenstein und unsere ethisch-ästhetische Moderne* (Frankfurt: Suhrkamp, 2006), 223.

3. See Thomä, *Totalität und Mitleid*, 203.

4. Sergei Eisenstein, *Writings 1934–1947*, ed. Richard Taylor and trans. William Powell (London: I. B. Tauris, 2010), 158 ("The Incarnation of Myth").

5. Ibid., 159.

6. Ibid., 162.

7. Ibid., 163.

8. Ibid., 161.

CHAPTER TEN

1. SB 10:355 (letter to Mathilde Wesendonck, March 2, 1859).

2. BB 128; Engl. trans. 107.

3. SB 8:361 (letter to Julie Ritter, July 4, 1857).

4. CT 1:415; Engl. trans. 1:391 (entry of July 18, 1871).

5. Friedrich Nietzsche, *Sämtliche Werke: Kritische Studienausgabe*, ed. Giorgio Colli and Mazzino Montinari (Munich: Deutscher Taschenbuch Verlag, 1988), 8:198 and 541 (unpublished fragments from summer 1875 and summer 1878).

6. SB 6:78 (letter to Hans von Bülow, Feb. 3, 1854). (Wagner wrote the words "Schmalarsch und Weichel" upside down in his letter.)

7. SB 10:207 (letter to Franz Liszt, Dec. 31, 1858).

8. ML 524; Engl. trans. 510.

9. SB 6:299 (undated letter to Franz Liszt, Dec. [16], 1854).

10. The earlier date is attested by Wagner's letter to Otto Eiser of Oct. 29, 1877, and by Mathilde Wesendonck's reminiscences: see Curt von Westernhagen, *Richard Wagner: Sein Werk, Sein Wesen, Seine Welt* (Zurich: Atlantis, 1956), 532; and Mathilde Wesendonck, "Erinnerungen," *Allgemeine Deutsche Musik-Zeitung* 23, no. 7 (1896): 91–94.

11. See Egon Voss, "Die 'schwarze und die weiße Flagge': Zur Entstehung von Wagners 'Tristan,'" *Archiv für Musikwissenschaft* 54 (1997): 226.

12. See Wagner's letter to Otto Eiser quoted in Westernhagen, *Richard Wagner*, 532.

13. For a modern German translation of Gottfried's poem, see Dieter Kühn, *Tristan und Isolde des Gottfried von Straßburg* (Frankfurt: Fischer, 2003), 747–57. This final section of the poem is taken from Ulrich von Türheim's continuation, Gottfried having died before he could complete the poem. Ulrich based his narrative on an older version of the tale. For an English translation, see A. T. Hatto, *Gottfried von Strassburg: Tristan. Translated Entire for the*

First Time (Harmondsworth: Penguin, 1960). Hatto completes the narrative by drawing on the twelfth-century Anglo-Norman version of Thomas of Britain.

14. See Voss, "Die 'schwarze und die weiße Flagge,'" 216–17.

15. SB 5:494 (letter to Franz Liszt, Jan. 15, 1854).

16. SB 5:233 (letter to Franz Liszt, March 30, 1853).

17. Eva Rieger, *Minna und Richard Wagner: Stationen einer Liebe* (Düsseldorf: Patmos, 2003), 197.

18. Wesendonck, "Erinnerungen," 92; see also Egon Voss, "Die Wesendoncks und Richard Wagner," in Axel Langer and Chris Walton, eds., *Minne, Muse und Mäzen: Otto und Mathilde Wesendonck und ihr Zürcher Künstlerzirkel* (Zurich: Museum Rietberg, 2002), 123.

19. BB 125; Engl. trans. 105 (emended).

20. Ulrich Bartels, *Analytisch-entstehungsgeschichtliche Studien zu Wagners Tristan und Isolde anhand der Kompositionsskizze des zweiten und dritten Aktes* (Cologne: Studio, 1995), 97.

21. See John Deathridge's balanced assessment in *Wagner Beyond Good and Evil* (Berkeley: University of California Press, 2008), especially 117–32 ("Public and Private Life").

22. SB 5:463 (undated letter to Franz Liszt, [Nov. 14, 1853]). (A play on words involving the biblical "faith, hope, and charity" is lost in English.)

23. See the whole issue of the first issue of *wagnerspectrum* for 2007, "Wagner und der Buddhismus."

24. SB 8:153 (letter to August Röckel, Aug. 23, 1856).

25. SW 27:93 (*Dokumente und Texte zu "Tristan und Isolde"*).

26. SB 8:122 (letter to Franz Liszt, July 20, 1856).

27. BB 70; Engl. trans. 61 (emended).

28. Unpublished papers in the Zurich Central Library.

29. See Dieter Borchmeyer, "'. . . sehnsüchtig blicke ich oft nach dem Land Nirwana . . .': Richard Wagners buddhistisches Christentum," *wagnerspectrum* 3, no. 2 (2007): 27.

30. SB 11:121 (letter to Mathilde Wesendonck, June 5, 1859).

31. Nike Wagner, "'Dem Traum entgegenschwimmen': Zu Richard Wagners *Tristan und Isolde*," in Sabine Borris and Christiane Krautscheid, eds., *O, sink hernieder, Nacht der Liebe: Tristan und Isolde; Der Mythos von Liebe und Tod* (Berlin: Parthas, 1998), 46 and 48.

32. Ernst Bloch, *Geist der Utopie*, 2nd ed. (Frankfurt: Suhrkamp, 1964), 110–11; translated by Anthony A. Nassar as *The Spirit of Utopia* (Stanford: Stanford University Press, 2000), 83–84.

33. Voss, "Die 'schwarze und die weiße Flagge,'" 213.

34. Egon Voss, "Wagner's 'Tristan': 'Die Liebe als furchtbare Qual,'" in Attila Csampai and Dietmar Holland, eds., *Richard Wagner: Tristan und Isolde; Texte, Materialien, Kommentare* (Reinbek: Rowohlt, 1983), 109.

35. Werner Vordtriede, "Richard Wagners 'Tod in Venedig,'" *Euphorion* 52 (1958): 381.

36. Dieter Kranz, "Sinnlichkeit durch Aussparung," *Opernwelt* 45 (Jan. 2004): 18.

37. Paul Fleming, *Deutsche Gedichte*, ed. Johann Martin Lappenberg (Stuttgart: Litterarischer Verein, 1865), 351.

38. SB 11:104 (letter to Mathilde Wesendonck, May 29–30, 1859).

39. SB 11:32 (letter to Mathilde Wesendonck, April 10, 1859).

40. CT 1:206; Engl. trans. 1:197 (entry of March 6, 1870).

41. CT 2:188; Engl. trans. 2:161 (entry of Oct. 1, 1878).

42. The last of these quotations is taken from Petra Urban, *Liebesdämmerung: Ein psychoanalytischer Versuch über Richard Wagners "Tristan und Isolde"* (Eschborn: Dietmar Klotz, 1991), 135.

43. Gabriele Hofmann, *Das Tristan-Syndrom: Psychologische und existenzphilosophische Aspekte der Tristan-Figur Richard Wagners* (Regensburg: Roderer, 1997), 121.

44. Peter Gay, *The Bourgeois Experience: Victoria to Freud*, vol. 2, *The Tender Passion* (New York: Oxford University Press, 1986), 265.

45. Eliza Wille, *Richard Wagner an Eliza Wille: Fünfzehn Briefe des Meisters nebst Erinnerungen und Erläuterungen* (Berlin: Schuster & Loeffler, 1908), 114.

46. Edgar Wind, *Pagan Mysteries in the Renaissance* (New Haven: Yale University Press 1958), 154.

47. CT 1:140; Engl. trans. 1:137 (entry of Aug. 15, 1869).

48. Arthur Schopenhauer, *Werke in fünf Bänden: Nach den Ausgaben letzter Hand*, ed. Ludger Lütkehaus (Zurich: Haffmans Verlag, 1988), 2:590; translated by E. F. J. Payne as *The World as Will and Representation* (New York: Dover Publications, 1969), 2:507.

49. SB 10:208 (undated draft of a letter to Arthur Schopenhauer, [Dec. 1858]).

50. Wolfgang Golther, ed., *Richard Wagner an Mathilde Wesendonk: Tagebuchblätter und Briefe, 1853–1871*, 2nd ed. (Berlin: Alexander Duncker, 1904), 79 (diary entry of Dec. 1, 1858).

51. Andreas Dorschel, "Die Idee der 'Einswerdung' in Wagners *Tristan*," in Heinz-Klaus Metzger and Rainer Riehn, eds., *Richard Wagner: Tristan und Isolde* (Munich: edition text + kritik, 1987), 32.

52. Dorschel, "Die Idee der 'Einswerdung,'" 36.

53. Hans Rudolf Vaget, ed., *Im Schatten Wagners: Thomas Mann über Richard Wagner; Texte und Zeugnisse, 1895–1955*, 2nd ed. (Frankfurt: Fischer, 2005), 92; translated by Allan Blunden as Thomas Mann, *Pro and Contra Wagner* (London: Faber and Faber, 1985), 97 ("The Sorrows and Grandeur of Richard Wagner").

54. GS 7:123; PW 3:330–31 (emended) ("Music of the Future").

55. Julius Kapp, ed., *Richard Wagners Gesammelte Schriften* (Leipzig: Hesse & Becker, [1914]), 5:13.

56. Stéphane Mallarmé, *Œuvres complètes*, ed. Henri Mondor and G. Jean-Aubry (Paris: Gallimard, 1945), 360–61.

57. See Werner Vordtriede, *Novalis und die französischen Symbolisten: Zur Entstehungsgeschichte des dichterischen Symbols* (Stuttgart: Kohlhammer, 1963), 158.

58. Michael Gratzke, *Liebesschmerz und Textlust: Figuren der Liebe und des Masochismus in der Literatur* (Würzburg: Königshausen & Neumann, 2000), 156.

59. GS 7:130; PW 3:338 (emended) ("Music of the Future").

60. Golther, *Richard Wagner an Mathilde Wesendonk*, 68 (diary entry of Oct. 12, 1858).

61. Bloch, *Geist der Utopie*, 110; Engl. trans. 83.

62. Bloch, *Geist der Utopie*, 118; Engl. trans. 90.

63. Bloch, *Geist der Utopie*, 108; Engl. trans. 82.

64. Manfred Frank, "Die Dialektik von 'erb' und 'eigen' in Wagners *Ring*: Auch eine Einführung in die *Götterdämmerung*," in Otto Kolleritsch, ed., *Die Musik als Medium von Beziehungsbefindlichkeiten: Mozarts und Wagners Musiktheater im aktuellen Deutungsgeschehen* (Vienna: Universal-Edition, 2002), 99.

65. Roger Scruton, *Death-Devoted Heart: Sex and the Sacred in Wagner's "Tristan und Isolde"* (New York: Oxford University Press, 2004), 99.

66. Sebastian Urmoneit, *Tristan und Isolde: Eros und Thanatos; Zur "dichterischen Deutlichkeit" der Harmonik von Richard Wagners "Handlung" "Tristan und Isolde"* (Sinzig: Studio, 2005), 106.

67. Bartels, *Analytisch-entstehungsgeschichtliche Studien*, 101–2.

68. CT 2:106; Engl. trans. 2:83 (entry of June 3, 1878).

69. Ronald Perlwitz, "Wagner-Rezeption in *À la recherche du temps perdu*: Ein deutscher Komponist in einem französischen Roman. Okkultierung und Evidenz," in Reinhard

Düssel and others, eds., *Die Macht der Differenzen: Beiträge zur Hermeneutik der Kultur* (Heidelberg: Synchron, 2001), 367.

70. Ernst Kurth, *Romantische Harmonik und ihre Krise in Wagners "Tristan"* (Berlin: Max Hesse, 1923), 266.

71. SB 11:197 (letter to Mathilde Wesendonck, Aug. 24, 1859).

72. For a summary of existing scholarship, see Robert Bailey, *Richard Wagner: Prelude and Transfiguration from "Tristan and Isolde"* (New York: W. W. Norton, 1985).

73. Claus-Steffen Mahnkopf, "*Tristan*-Studien," in Mahnkopf, ed., *Richard Wagner: Konstrukteur der Moderne* (Stuttgart: Klett-Cotta, 1999), 94.

74. Readers who require convincing that the writings on Wagner have reached the point where it is no longer possible to gain a coherent overview of them need look no further than the subject of the "traurige Weise," which was the topic of an interdisciplinary conference held in Uppsala in 1997 devoted exclusively to these forty-two bars (out of a total of 5,698). The papers were published a year later in a special number of the journal *Musicae scientiae*, complemented by a series of other articles on the same subject, all of them seeking to examine these bars not only from various theoretical angles but also from a structuralist, semiological, musicopsychological, psychoanalytic, and hermeneutic standpoint. No matter how much respect one may have for such scholarship, one is bound to ask oneself whether the results of all this research do not say more about the researchers themselves and their attempts to promote their own individual disciplines than they do about Wagner's creativity. Among the other instruments that have been tried by conductors attempting to create the "natural" sound demanded by Wagner are a single-reed Hungarian tárogató, a treble shawm, a soprano saxophone, a muted trumpet, and (Bayreuth's preferred alternative) a straight wooden trumpet with a single valve.

75. Hanspeter Renggli, "'Das drollige Geblase im Kopfe': Schweizer Folklore in Richard Wagners *Tristan* oder Von der Zwiespältigkeit Wagnerscher Ursprungsmythen," in Anselm Gerhard, ed., *Schweizer Töne: Die Schweiz im Spiegel der Musik* (Zurich: Chronos, 2002), 107–21. In spite of Robert Bailey's claim, the singing of Venetian gondoliers was not the model for the "traurige Weise": see Bailey, *Richard Wagner: Prelude and Transfiguration*, 105–6.

76. Thomas Grey, "In the Realm of the Senses: Sight, Sound and the Music of Desire in *Tristan und Isolde*," in Arthur Groos, ed., *Richard Wagner: Tristan und Isolde* (Cambridge: Cambridge University Press, 2011), 79.

77. Carl Dahlhaus, "Ernst Blochs Philosophie der Musik Wagners," in Dagmar Droysen, ed., *Jahrbuch des Staatlichen Instituts für Musikforschung Preussischer Kulturbesitz 1971* (Berlin: Merseburger, 1972), 186–87.

78. Ulrike Kienzle, *. . . daß wissend würde die Welt! Religion und Philosophie in Richard Wagners Musikdramen* (Würzburg: Königshausen & Neumann, 2005), 169.

79. Mario Bortolotto, *Wagner l'oscuro* (Milan: Adelphi, 2003), 324–25.

80. Marcel Proust, *À la recherche du temps perdu*, ed. Pierre Clarac and André Ferré (Paris: Gallimard, 1973–77), 3:161; translated by C. K. Scott Moncrieff and Terence Kilmartin as *In Search of Lost Time*. Revised by D. J. Enright (London: Folio Society, 2000), 5:145–46.

81. CT 1:244; Engl. trans. 1:232 (entry of June 14, 1870).

82. Martin Heidegger, *Nietzsche* (Pfullingen: Günther Neske, 1961), 1:103. For a critique of Heidegger's attack on Wagner, see Dieter Thomä, "Umwertungen der Dekadenz: Korrespondenzen zwischen Richard Wagner, Friedrich Nietzsche und Sergej Eisenstein," in Aram Mattioli and Enno Rudolph, eds., *Nietzsche und Wagner: Geschichte und Aktualität eines Kulturkonfliktes* (Zurich: Orell Füssli, 2008), 120–24.

83. Peter Härtling, *Notenschrift: Worte und Sätze zur Musik* (Stuttgart: Radius, 1998), 31.

84. GS 8:186; PW 4:235 (emended) ("My Recollections of Ludwig Schnorr von Carolsfeld").

85. SB 2:538 (letter to Eduard Hanslick, Jan. 1, 1847).

86. See Bartels, *Analytisch-entstehungsgeschichtliche Studien*.

87. Eckehard Kiem, "Vom Sinn der Motivbeziehungen: *Der Ring des Nibelungen*," in Eckehard Kiem and Ludwig Holtmeier, eds., *Richard Wagner und seine Zeit* (Laaber: Laaber-Verlag, 2003), 136.

88. Eric Chafe, *The Tragic and the Ecstatic: The Musical Revolution of Wagner's "Tristan und Isolde"* (Oxford: Oxford University Press, 2005), 194–230.

89. For a discussion of this term, see Carl Dahlhaus, "'Lohengrin' und die 'Einheit des Symphoniesatzes,' sowie 'Opus metaphysicum': Das Musikdrama als symphonische Oper," in Carl Dahlhaus and Norbert Miller, eds., *Europäische Romantik in der Musik* (Stuttgart: J. B. Metzler, 2007), 2:916–23.

90. Nietzsche, *Sämtliche Werke*, 1:479; translated by R. J. Hollingdale as *Untimely Meditations* (Cambridge: Cambridge University Press, 1983), 232.

91. Bryan Magee, *The Tristan Chord: Wagner and Philosophy* (New York: Metropolitan Books, 2001), 210.

92. Slavoj Žižek and Mladen Dolar, *Opera's Second Death* (New York: Routledge, 2002), 123.

93. Joachim Kaiser, *Leben mit Wagner* (Munich: Albrecht Knaus, 1990), 21. The young critic was Hans Mayer.

94. Michel Foucault, *The Will to Knowledge: The History of Sexuality Volume 1*; translated by Robert Hurley (London: Penguin Books, 1998), 45.

95. CT 2:347; Engl. trans. 2:306 (entry of May 10, 1879).

96. Hans Neuenfels, *Wie viel Musik braucht der Mensch? Über Oper und Komponisten* (Munich: Pantheon, 2011), 156.

A WORD ABOUT ERNST BLOCH

1. Ernst Bloch, *Geist der Utopie*, 2nd ed. (Frankfurt: Suhrkamp, 1964), 110; translated by Anthony A. Nassar as *The Spirit of Utopia* (Stanford: Stanford University Press, 2000), 82.

2. Ibid., 208; Engl. trans. 163.

3. Ibid., 132; Engl. trans. 101.

4. See Arno Münster, *Utopie, Messianismus und Apokalypse im Frühwerk von Ernst Bloch* (Frankfurt: Suhrkamp, 1982), 147–52.

5. Ernst Bloch, "Paradoxa und Pastorale bei Wagner," in Karola Bloch, ed., *Zur Philosophie der Musik* (Frankfurt: Suhrkamp, 1974), 227–28; translated by Peter Palmer as "Paradoxes and the Pastorale in Wagner's Music," in Ernst Bloch, *Essays on the Philosophy of Music* (Cambridge: Cambridge University Press, 1985), 153–56.

6. Ibid., 225–26; Engl. trans. 153–54.

7. Ibid., 224; Engl. trans. 152.

8. Ibid., 237; Engl. trans. 164.

CHAPTER ELEVEN

1. BB 70; Engl. trans. 61 (emended).

2. GS 4:284; PW 1:329 (*A Communication to My Friends*).

3. Carl Dahlhaus, *Richard Wagners Musikdramen*, 2nd ed. (Zurich: Orell Füssli, 1985), 67; translated by Mary Whittall as *Richard Wagner's Music Dramas* (Cambridge: Cambridge University Press, 1979), 65.

4. Gerd Rienäcker, *Richard Wagner: Nachdenken über sein "Gewebe"* (Berlin: Lukas Verlag, 2001), 231.

5. Lydia Goehr, "The Dangers of Satisfaction: On Songs, Rehearsals, and Repetition in *Die Meistersinger*," in Nicholas Vazsonyi, ed., *Wagner's "Meistersinger": Performance, History, Representation* (Rochester, NY: University of Rochester Press, 2003), 69.

6. Ibid.

7. The word "wälsch" that Sachs uses here derives from the name of the Celtic tribe of the Volcae and refers specifically to Romance or Latin nations.

8. SB 18: 198 (letter to Ludwig II, July 24, 1866).

9. Richard Wagner, *Die Meistersinger von Nürnberg: Faksimile der Reinschrift des Textbuchs von 1862*, ed. Egon Voss (Mainz: Schott, 1983), 82.

10. Ferdinand Lassalle, *Nachgelassene Briefe und Schriften*, ed. Gustav Mayer (Stuttgart: Deutsche Verlags-Anstalt, 1925), 5:48 (undated letter from Hans von Bülow to Ferdinand Lassalle, [Aug. 1862]). See also Martin Geck, *Zwischen Romantik und Restauration: Musik im Realismus-Diskurs, 1848 bis 1871* (Stuttgart: J. B. Metzler; Kassel: Bärenreiter, 2001), 164.

11. See Geck, *Zwischen Romantik und Restauration*, 109.

12. Gerhard Plumpe, ed., *Theorie des bürgerlichen Realismus* (Stuttgart: Reclam, 1985), 16.

13. GS 4:284; PW 1:329 (emended) (*A Communication to My Friends*).

14. GS 4:285; PW 1:329 (where the reference to Walther's penury has been removed) (*A Communication to My Friends*).

15. Ferdinand Gregorovius, *Göthe's Wilhelm Meister in seinen socialistischen Elementen* (Königsberg: Bornträger, 1849), 193.

16. GS 4:284–85; PW 1:329 (emended) (*A Communication to My Friends*).

17. Joachim Herz, "Der doch versöhnte Beckmesser: Noch eine Wagner-Polemik (1961)," in Attila Csampai and Dietmar Holland, eds., *Richard Wagner: Die Meistersinger von Nürnberg; Texte, Materialien, Kommentare* (Reinbek: Rowohlt, 1981), 213–15.

18. SS 12:348 (program note written for a performance of the overture on Dec. 2, 1863).

19. Reinhold Brinkmann, "'... einen Schluß machen!' Über externe Schlüsse bei Wagner," in Jürgen Schläder and Reinhold Quandt, eds., *Festschrift Heinz Becker zum 60. Geburtstag* (Laaber: Laaber-Verlag, 1982), 187.

20. Harry Kupfer, "We Must Finally Stop Apologizing for *Die Meistersinger!*" in Vazsonyi, ed., *Wagner's "Meistersinger,"* 39.

21. Joachim Herz, "Musik und Szene in den 'Meistersingern': Diskussion mit einem Kritiker (1961)," in Csampai and Holland, *Richard Wagner: Die Meistersinger von Nürnberg*, 209.

22. This is Bernhard Schubert's summary of Walter Jens's view: see Bernhard Schubert, "Wagners 'Sachs' und die Tradition des romantischen Künstlerverständnisses," *Archiv für Musikwissenschaft* 40 (1983): 244; see also Walter Jens, "Natur und Kunst: Richard Wagner und 'Die Meistersinger von Nürnberg,'" in Jens, *Von deutscher Rede*, 2nd ed. (Munich: Piper, 1988).

23. This is again Schubert's summary of Mayer's article: see Schubert, "Wagners 'Sachs,'" 232; see also Hans Mayer, "Parnaß und Paradies: Anmerkungen zu den 'Meistersingern von Nürnberg,'" in Mayer, *Richard Wagner*, ed. Wolfgang Hofer (Frankfurt: Suhrkamp, 1998).

24. Peter Wapnewski, *Die Szene und ihr Meister*, 2nd ed. (Munich: C. H. Beck, 1983), 61 and 67; see also Lucy Beckett, "Sachs and Schopenhauer," in John Warrack, ed., *Richard Wagner: Die Meistersinger von Nürnberg* (Cambridge: Cambridge University Press, 1994).

25. Dieter Borchmeyer, *Das Theater Richard Wagners: Idee—Dichtung—Wirkung* (Stuttgart: Reclam, 1982), 229; translated by Stewart Spencer as *Richard Wagner: Theory and Theatre* (Oxford: Clarendon Press, 1991), 284.

26. Ernst Bloch, "Über Beckmessers Preislied-Text," in Karola Bloch, *Zur Philosophie der Musik* (Frankfurt: Suhrkamp, 1974), 213.

27. Yvonne Nilges, *"Die Meistersinger von Nürnberg* oder Die Geburt der musikalischen Komödie aus dem Geiste Shakespeares," *wagnerspectrum* 3, no. 1 (2007): 31–32.

28. Willi Schuh, *Richard Strauss, Hugo von Hofmannsthal: Briefwechsel*, 5th edn. (Zurich: Atlantis, 1978), 577–78; translated by Hanns Hammelmann and Ewald Osers as *The Correspondence between Richard Strauss and Hugo von Hofmannsthal* (Cambridge: Cambridge University Press, 1980), 433 (letter from Hugo von Hofmannsthal to Richard Strauss, July 1, 1927).

29. Udo Bermbach, *"Blühendes Leid": Politik und Gesellschaft in Richard Wagners Musikdramen* (Stuttgart: J. B. Metzler, 2003), 248.

30. Schuh, *Strauss, Hofmannsthal*, 577–78; Engl. trans. 434 (letter from Hugo von Hofmannsthal to Richard Strauss, July 1, 1927).

31. Bermbach, *"Blühendes Leid,"* 248.

32. Ibid., 256.

33. Ibid., 257.

34. Hans Rudolf Vaget, "Wehvolles Erbe: Zur 'Metapolitik' der *Meistersinger von Nürnberg,*" *Musik & Ästhetik* 6 (2002): 34.

35. Warren Darcy, "In Search of C Major: Tonal Structure and Formal Design in Act III of *Die Meistersinger,*" in Matthew Bribitzer-Stull and others, eds., *Richard Wagner for the New Millennium: Essays in Music and Culture* (New York: Palgrave, 2007), 124.

36. GS 4:287; PW 1:331–32 (emended) (*A Communication to My Friends*).

37. GS 4:290; PW 1:335 (*A Communication to My Friends*).

38. Schubert, "Wagners 'Sachs,'" 236.

39. Jörg Linnenbrügger, *Richard Wagners "Die Meistersinger von Nürnberg": Studien und Materialien zur Entstehungsgeschichte des ersten Aufzugs (1861–1866)* (Göttingen: Vandenhoeck & Ruprecht, 2001), 404.

40. Martin Geck, *Richard Wagner* (Reinbek: Rowohlt, 2004), 100.

41. The contradictions in the work are well brought out by Marco Bortolotto in *Wagner l'oscuro* (Milan: Adelphi, 2003), 332–70 ("La città, il profumo").

42. CT 2:333; Engl. trans. 2:293 (entry of April 17, 1879).

43. Peter Cornelius, *Literarische Werke*, vol. 3, *Aufsätze über Musik und Kunst*, ed. Edgar Istel (Leipzig: Breitkopf & Härtel, 1904), 181 (review first published in *Die Tonhalle* on Sept. 7, 1868).

44. CT 2:260; Engl. trans. 2:229 (entry of Dec. 15, 1878).

45. CT 2:264; Engl. trans. 2:232 (entry of Dec. 18, 1878).

46. CT 2:961; Engl. trans. 2:872 (entry of June 14, 1882).

47. Martin Geck, "Es ist wie die Stimme des Ding an sich: Wagners 'Bach,'" in Geck, *"Denn alles findet bei Bach statt: Erforschtes und Erfahrenes* (Stuttgart: J. B. Metzler, 2000), 179.

48. Ibid.

49. Cornelius, *Literarische Werke*, vol. 3, *Aufsätze über Musik und Kunst*, 181.

50. Martin Geck, "'Von deutscher Art und Kunst'? Mit Bachs 'nordischem' Kontrapunkt gegen drohenden Kulturverfall," in Ulrich Tadday, ed., *Philosophie des Kontrapunkts* (Munich: edition text + kritik, 2010), 181–82.

51. Friedrich Nietzsche, *Sämtliche Werke*, ed. Giorgio Colli and Mazzino Montinari (Munich: Deutscher Taschenbuch Verlag, 1988), 5:179–80; translated by Walter Kaufmann as *Basic Writings of Nietzsche* (New York: Modern Library, 1968), 363 ("Beyond Good and Evil").

52. Heinrich Schenker, *Neue Musikalische Theorien und Phantasien*, vol. 3: *Der freie Satz*, 2nd ed. (Vienna: Universal-Edition, 1935), 97.

53. Richard Taruskin, *Stravinsky and the Russian Traditions* (Berkeley: University of California Press, 1996), 1:104–5.

54. Nietzsche, *Sämtliche Werke*, 7:285 (unpublished fragment from 1871, 9[36]).

55. Egon Voss, "Wagners 'Meistersinger' als Oper des deutschen Bürgertums," in Attila Csampai and Dietmar Holland, eds., *Richard Wagner: Die Meistersinger von Nürnberg: Texte, Materialien, Kommentare* (Reinbek: Rowohlt, 1981), 27.

56. CT 1:208–9; Engl. trans. 1:199 (entry of March 14, 1870). The new production—the first in the newly built opera house—had opened the previous month.

57. For a useful summary of the thinking on this point, see Vaget, "Wehvolles Erbe."

58. Ludwig Finscher, "Über den Kontrapunkt der Meistersinger," in Carl Dahlhaus, ed., *Das Drama Richard Wagners als musikalisches Kunstwerk* (Regensburg: Gustav Bosse, 1970), 306.

A WORD ABOUT BERTHOLD AUERBACH

1. SB 2:524 (letter to Alwine Frommann, Oct. 9, 1846).

2. Berthold Auerbach, *Briefe an seinen Freund Jakob Auerbach* (Frankfurt: Literarische Anstalt, 1884), 1:66 (undated letter from Berthold Auerbach to Jakob Auerbach, [Nov. 1848]).

3. See Wolf-Daniel Hartwich, *Romantischer Antisemitismus: Von Klopstock bis Richard Wagner* (Göttingen: Vandenhoeck & Ruprecht, 2005), 213–14.

4. GS 8:258–59; PW 3:120–21 ("Some Explanations Concerning 'Jews in Music'").

5. CT 1:128; Engl. trans. 1:125 (entry of July 14, 1869).

6. CT 1:235; Engl. trans. 1:224 (entry of May 28, 1870).

7. First published by Paul Lawrence Rose, "One of Wagner's Jewish Friends: Berthold Auerbach and His Unpublished Reply to Richard Wagner's Antisemitism (1881)," *Leo Baeck Institute Year Book* 36 (1991): 227–28.

CHAPTER TWELVE

1. See Tobias Janz, *Klangdramaturgie: Studien zur theatralen Orchesterkomposition in Wagners "Ring des Nibelungen"* (Würzburg: Königshausen & Neumann, 2006), 311.

2. Gregor Herzfeld, "Verführung—Vereinnahmung—Verderben: Musik bei Søren Kierkegaard, Richard Wagner und Thomas Mann," *Musik & Ästhetik* 15 (2011): 91.

3. CT 2:339; Engl. trans. 2:299 (entry of April 29, 1879).

4. BB 70; Engl. trans. 61 (emended).

5. George Bernard Shaw, *The Perfect Wagnerite: A Commentary on the Niblung's Ring*, 4th ed. (London: Constable, 1923), 94. (This passage does not appear in the three earlier editions of 1898, 1901, or 1913.)

6. SB 8:153 (letter to August Röckel, Aug. 23, 1856).

7. See Tobias Janz, "Wagner, Siegfried und die (post-)heroische Moderne," in Janz, ed., *Wagners Siegfried und die (post-)heroische Moderne* (Würzburg: Königshausen & Neumann, 2011), 20. Žižek was taking part in a masterclass on the *Ring* at the Birkbeck Institute for the Humanities in London in June 2009.

8. CT 1:161; Engl. trans. 1:156 (entry of Oct. 21, 1869).

9. CT 1:170; Engl. trans. 1:165 (entry of Nov. 16, 1869).

10. SB 3:425–26 (undated letter to Theodor Uhlig, [Sept. 20, 1850]).

11. See Dietmar Klenke, *Der singende "deutsche Mann": Gesangsvereine und deutsches Nationalbewußtsein von Napoleon bis Hitler* (Münster: Waxmann, 1998), 20.

12. Saul K. Padover, ed., *The Letters of Karl Marx* (Englewood Cliffs, NJ: Prentice-Hall, 1979), 308 (letter from Karl Marx to Friedrich Engels, Aug. 19, 1876). (The German term "Staatsmusikant" has more derogatory connotations than the English word "musician.")

13. Hans Rudolf Vaget, ed., *Im Schatten Wagners: Thomas Mann über Richard Wagner; Texte und Zeugnisse, 1895–1955*, 2nd ed. (Frankfurt: Fischer, 2005), 79; translated by Allan Blunden as Thomas Mann, *Pro and Contra Wagner* (London: Faber and Faber, 1985), 82. (These lines were originally part of Mann's open letter to an unidentified opera director dated Nov. 15, 1927, but were later repeated verbatim in an article "Wagner and the Present Age" published in *Die Musik* in Feb. 1933.)

14. Janz, *Klangdramaturgie*, 314.

15. Ibid., 319.

16. Friedrich Nietzsche, *Sämtliche Werke*, ed. Giorgio Colli and Mazzino Montinari (Munich: Deutscher Taschenbuch Verlag, 1988), 7:789 (unpublished fragment from Jan.–Feb. 1874, 33[8]).

17. Carl Dahlhaus, *Wagners Konzeption des musikalischen Dramas* (Regensburg: Gustav Bosse, 1971), 43.

18. Bernhard Benz, *Zeitstrukturen in Richard Wagners "Ring"-Tetralogie* (Frankfurt: Peter Lang, 1994), 192.

19. CT 1:422–23; Engl. trans. 1:398 (entry of July 28, 1871).

20. Dieter Schickling, *Abschied von Walhall: Richard Wagners erotische Gesellschaft* (Stuttgart: Deutsche Verlags-Anstalt, 1983), 86.

21. Gerd Rienäcker, *Richard Wagner: Nachdenken über sein "Gewebe"* (Berlin: Lukas-Verlag, 2001), 147.

22. Ibid.

23. Richard Klein, "Rausch und Zeit in Wagners *Ring*," in Thomas Strässle and Simon Zumsteg, eds., *Trunkenheit: Kulturen des Rausches* (Amsterdam: Rodopi, 2008), 120.

24. Slavoj Žižek, "'There Is No Sexual Relationship': Wagner as a Lacanian," *New German Critique* 69 (1996): 15.

25. Ibid., 12.

26. Julius Langbehn, *Langbehns Lieder* (Hamburg: tredition, 2011), 28.

27. Lawrence Kramer, *Opera and Modern Culture: Wagner and Strauss* (Berkeley: University of California Press, 2004), 37.

28. Claus-Steffen Mahnkopf, "Haß und Rache: Zum II. Akt der *Götterdämmerung*," in Richard Klein, ed., *Narben des Gesamtkunstwerks: Wagners "Ring des Nibelungen"* (Munich: Wilhelm Fink, 2001), 232.

29. Heinrich Ehrlich, "Das Bayreuther Bühnenfestspiel," *Die Gegenwart* 10 (1876): 131–34; quoted by Susanna Großmann-Vendrey, *Bayreuth in der deutschen Presse*, vol. 1, *Die Grundsteinlegung und die ersten Festspiele, 1872–1876* (Regensburg: Gustav Bosse, 1977), 148.

30. Sabine Henze-Döhring, "'Liebe—Tragik': Zur musikdramaturgischen Konzeption der Brünnhilden-Gestalt," in Susanne Vill, ed., *"Das Weib der Zukunft": Frauengestalten und Frauenstimmen bei Richard Wagner* (Stuttgart: J. B. Metzler, 2000), 138.

31. CT 1:323; Engl. trans. 1:306 (entry of Dec. 12, 1870).

32. SB 6:69 (letter to August Röckel, Jan. 24–25, 1854).

33. CT 1:1052; Engl. trans. 1:965 (entry of May 25, 1877).

34. CT 2:692–93; Engl. trans. 2:624 (entry of Feb. 15, 1881).

35. GS 10:267; PW 6:267 (emended) ("Know Thyself").

36. SB 6:69 (letter to August Röckel, Jan. 25–26, 1854).

37. SB 8:153 (letter to August Röckel, Aug. 23, 1856).

38. GS 6:255 (*Götterdämmerung*).

39. Nietzsche, *Sämtliche Werke*, 6:20–21; translated by Walter Kaufmann as "The Case of Wagner," in Nietzsche, *Basic Writings of Nietzsche* (New York: Modern Library, 1968), 620.

40. Hans Mayer, "Richard Wagners geistige Entwicklung," in Mayer, *Richard Wagner*, ed. Wolfgang Hofer (Frankfurt: Suhrkamp, 1998), 55 and 52.

41. Theodor W. Adorno, *Gesammelte Schriften*, ed. Rolf Tiedemann (Frankfurt: Suhrkamp, 1997), 13:133; translated by Rodney Livingstone as *In Search of Wagner* (London: New Left Books, 1981), 142.

42. Adorno, *Gesammelte Schriften*, 16:669.

43. Carlo Schmid, Pierre Boulez, and Patrice Chéreau, "Mythologie und Ideologie: Gedankenaustausch über die Neuinszenierung 'Der Ring des Nibelungen' 1976," in Herbert Barth, ed., *Bayreuther Dramaturgie: Der Ring des Nibelungen* (Stuttgart: Belser, 1980), 380.

44. Udo Bermbach, *Der Wahn des Gesamtkunstwerks: Richard Wagners politisch-ästhetische Utopie* (Frankfurt: Fischer, 1994), 305–6.

45. Ernest Newman, *A Study of Wagner* (New York: G. P. Putnam's Sons, 1899), 225.

46. Claude Lévi-Strauss, "Intervista a cura di Marco d'Eramo," *Mondoperaio: Revista Socialisti* 2 (1979): 118–24; translated by Max Looser as "Die strukturalistische Tätigkeit," in *Mythos und Bedeutung: Fünf Radiovorträge*, ed. Adelbert Reif (Frankfurt: Suhrkamp, 1980), 271–72.

47. CT 1:543; Engl. trans. 1:506–7 (entry of July 2, 1872).

48. CT 1:170; Engl. trans. 1:162–63 (entry of Nov. 14, 1869).

49. CT 1:552; Engl. trans. 1:515 (emended) (entry of July 23, 1872.) The German edition contains a mistranscription, Cosima's handwriting having misled the German editors into thinking that she wrote "Helden" (heroes) rather than "Heldin" (heroine).

50. For more on the term "bliss" (German *Seligkeit*), see Wolfram Steinbeck, "Zur Formfrage in Wagners *Ring des Nibelungen*," in Klaus Hortschansky, ed., *Richard Wagners "Ring des Nibelungen": Musikalische Dramaturgie—Kulturelle Kontextualität—Primär-Rezeption* (Schneverdingen: Wagner, 2004), 296.

51. CT 1:843; Engl. trans. 1:779 (entry of Aug. 6, 1874).

52. Egon Voss, "Siegfrieds Musik," in Hermann Danuser and others, eds., *Das musikalische Kunstwerk: Geschichte, Ästhetik, Theorie; Festschrift Carl Dahlhaus zum 60. Geburtstag* (Laaber: Laaber-Verlag, 1988), 267. Here Cosima's correspondent is wrongly identified as Edmund von Lippmann (1857–1940), rather than the older Eduard von Lippmann (1838–1919), who was a prominent member of the Vienna Wagner Society.

53. CT 1:255; Engl. trans. 1:243 (entry of July 9, 1870).

54. Carolyn Abbate, "Mythische Stimmen, sterbliche Körper," in Udo Bermbach and Dieter Borchmeyer, eds., *Richard Wagner, "Der Ring des Nibelungen": Ansichten des Mythos* (Stuttgart: J. B. Metzler, 1995), 79.

55. Friedrich Kittler, "Wagners wildes Heer," in Wolfgang Storch, ed., *Die Symbolisten und Richard Wagner* (Berlin: Edition Hentrich, 1991), 38, 40, 42.

56. GS 10:186; PW 6:185 (emended) ("On the Application of Music to the Drama").

57. GS 10:188; PW 6:186–87 (emended) ("On the Application of Music to the Drama").

58. CT 2:625; Engl. trans. 2:562 (entry of Nov. 25, 1880).

59. John Deathridge, "*Don Carlos* and *Götterdämmerung*: Two Operatic Endings and Walter Benjamin's *Trauerspiel*," in Deathridge, *Wagner Beyond Good and Evil* (Berkeley: University of California Press, 2008), 96.

60. Ibid.

61. CT 1:324; Engl. trans. 1:306 (entry of Dec. 13, 1870).

62. GS9:2; PW 5:2 ("To the German Army Outside Paris").

63. CT 2:339; Engl. trans. 2:299 (entry of April 29, 1879).

64. Martin Geck, "'Eigentlich hätte Siegfried Parsifal werden sollen . . .': Der Schluss des 'Rings' im Focus philosophischer Überlebensstrategien von Nietzsche bis Žižek," in Tobias Janz, ed., *Wagners Siegfried und die (post-)heroische Moderne* (Würzburg: Königshausen & Neumann, 2011), 65–73.

65. Nietzsche, *Sämtliche Werke*, 5:204; translated by Walter Kaufmann as "Beyond Good and Evil," in Nietzsche, *Basic Writings of Nietzsche*, 388.

66. Friedrich Kittler, *Das Nahen der Götter vorbereiten* (Munich: Wilhelm Fink, 2012), 45 and 81–82.

A WORD ABOUT THEODOR W. ADORNO

1. Theodor W. Adorno, *Gesammelte Schriften*, ed. Rolf Tiedemann (Frankfurt: Suhrkamp, 1997), 13:93; translated by Rodney Livingstone as *In Search of Wagner* (London: New Left Books, 1981), 98 ("Versuch über Wagner"). As John Deathridge has pointed out, the English title—foisted on the translator by his publisher—is misleading, as Adorno was not "in search of Wagner," but was convinced that he had found him.

2. Adorno, *Gesammelte Schriften*, 12:116; translated by Robert Hullot-Kentor as *Philosophy of New Music* (Minneapolis: University of Minnesota Press, 2006), 94 (*Philosophie der neuen Musik*).

3. The equation is facilitated and underscored in German by the similarity between the adjective *wahr* (true) and the noun *Ware* (commodity).

4. Theodor W. Adorno, *Beethoven: Philosophie der Musik*, ed. Rolf Tiedemann (Frankfurt: Suhrkamp, 1994), 72; translated by Edmund Jephcott as *Beethoven: The Philosophy of Music* (Cambridge: Polity, 2002), 41–42.

5. Adorno, *Gesammelte Schriften*, 13:101; Engl. trans. 106 ("Versuch über Wagner").

6. Adorno's *Verblendungszusammenhang* is explored in his *Negative Dialectics* and is defined as the link between social being and the misconceptions of the nature of bourgeois society that arise therefrom. Other writers have defined it as the "blinding universal delusion generated by alienation."

7. Adorno, *Gesammelte Schriften*, 13:142; Engl. trans. 152 ("Versuch über Wagner").

8. Adorno, *Gesammelte Schriften*, 13:145; Engl. trans. 156 ("Versuch über Wagner").

9. Adorno, *Gesammelte Schriften*, 19:468 ("Wilhelm Furtwängler").

CHAPTER THIRTEEN

1. CT 2:330; Engl. trans. 2:291 (entry of April 12, 1879).

2. CT 2: 526; Engl. trans. 2: 471 (entry of April 28, 1880). (The other figure whom Wagner was planning to baptize was the banker Mayer Karl von Rothschild, whom the Wagners had just been discussing. The banker is wrongly identified by the German editors of CT as Henri de Rothschild, an error repeated in the English translation.)

3. CT 2:755; Engl. trans. 2:682 (entry of July 2, 1881).

4. SW 30:50 (*Dokumente zur Entstehung und ersten Aufführung des Bühnenweihfestspiels Parsifal*) (letter to Hermann Levi, July 1, 1881); see also Laurence Dreyfus, "Hermann Levi's Shame and *Parsifal*'s Guilt," *Cambridge Opera Journal* 6 (1994): 127.

5. See Wolf-Daniel Hartwich, "Jüdische Theosophie in Richard Wagners *Parsifal*: Vom christlichen Antisemitismus zur ästhetischen Kabbala," in Dieter Borchmeyer and others, *Richard Wagner und die Juden* (Stuttgart: J. B. Metzler, 2000), 107–8.

6. CT 2:411; Engl. trans. 2:367 (entry of Sept. 20, 1879).

7. CT 2:411; Engl. trans. 2:367 (entry of Sept. 19, 1879).

8. BB 75; Engl. trans. 65 (entry of Sept. 1, 1865).

9. BB 75–76; Engl. trans. 65–66 (entry of Sept. 2, 1865). (Wagner retained the spelling Anfortas—derived from the Latin *infirmitas*—until the beginning of 1877.)

10. [Petrus Hamp], *Ein Blick in die Geisteswerkstatt Richard Wagners* (Berlin: Albert Böhler, 1904), 14. (Hamp's memoir was published anonymously "By an old clerical friend of the Master of Bayreuth in memory of his swansong, Parzival.")

11. Robert Mallet, ed., *André Gide–Paul Valéry: Correspondance 1890–1942* (Paris: Gallimard, 1955), 126 (undated letter from Paul Valéry to André Gide, [Sept. 1891]); see also Gert Mattenklott, "Unwiderstehliche Mimik: Valéry über Wagner," in Wolfgang Storch, ed., *Die Symbolisten und Richard Wagner* (Berlin: Hentrich, 1991), 176.

12. Hermann Danuser, "Verheißung und Erlösung: Zur Dramaturgie des 'Torenspruchs' in *Parsifal*," *wagnerspectrum* 4, no. 1 (2008): 35.

13. Karl Frenzel, "Die erste Aufführung des 'Parsifal,'" *Nationalzeitung* 358 (Aug. 3, 1882); reproduced in Susanna Großmann-Vendrey, *Bayreuth in der deutschen Presse*, vol. 2, *Die Uraufführung des Parsifal (1882)* (Regensburg: Gustav Bosse, 1977), 46.

14. Claude Lévi-Strauss, "De Chrétien de Troyes à Richard Wagner," *Die Programmhefte der Bayreuther Festspiele*, vol. 1, *Parsifal* (Bayreuth: Emil Mühl, 1975), 67 and 1; translated by T. A. Willcocks as "From Chrétien de Troyes to Richard Wagner," in ibid., 45 and 22.

15. Hans Mayer, *Ein Denkmal für Johannes Brahms: Versuche über Musik und Literatur*, 2nd ed. (Frankfurt: Suhrkamp, 1993), 104.

16. Udo Bermbach, *Der Wahn des Gesamtkunstwerks: Richard Wagners politisch-ästhetische Utopie* (Frankfurt: Fischer, 1994), 307.

17. Karl Lachmann, ed., *Wolfram von Eschenbach*, 6th ed. (Berlin: Walter de Gruyter, 1926), 388.

18. Ibid., translated by Cyril Edwards as *Wolfram von Eschenbach: Parzival* (Cambridge: D. S. Brewer, 2004), 265.

19. BB 70; Engl. trans. 61 (emended).

20. SW 27:93 (*Dokumente und Texte zu "Tristan und Isolde"*).

21. SW 30:45.

22. Friedrich Nietzsche, *Sämtliche Werke: Kritische Studienausgabe*, ed. Giorgio Colli and Mazzino Montinari (Munich: Deutscher Taschenbuch Verlag, 1988), 6:16; translated by Walter Kaufmann as "The Case of Wagner," in Nietzsche, *Basic Writings of Nietzsche* (New York: Modern Library, 1968), 616.

23. CT 2:866; Engl. trans. 2:784 (entry of Jan. 5, 1882).

24. Nietzsche, *Sämtliche Werke*, 6:41–42; Engl. trans. 638 ("The Case of Wagner").

25. Dieter Borchmeyer, *Richard Wagner: Ahasvers Wandlungen* (Frankfurt: Insel, 2002), 311; translated by Daphne Ellis as *Drama and the World of Richard Wagner* (Princeton: Princeton University Press, 2003), 241.

26. Erich Kloss, ed., *Richard Wagner an seine Künstler* (Berlin: Schuster & Loeffler, 1908), 386 (letter to Hans von Wolzogen, Jan. 17, 1880).

27. Max Kalbeck, "Das Bühnenweihfestspiel in Bayreuth," *Wiener Allgemeine Zeitung* (1882); reproduced by Großmann-Vendrey, *Bayreuth in der deutschen Presse*, 183.

28. Robert W. Gutman, *Richard Wagner: The Man, His Mind, and His Music* (London: Secker & Warburg, 1968), 432.

29. Hartmut Zelinsky, "Rettung ins Ungenaue: Zu Martin Gregor-Dellins Wagner-Biographie," in Heinz-Klaus Metzger and Rainer Riehn, eds., *Richard Wagner: Parsifal* (Munich: edition text + kritik, 1982), 98–106.

30. Carl Dahlhaus, "Erlösung dem Erlöser: Warum Richard Wagners 'Parsifal' nicht Mittel zum Zweck der Ideologie ist," in Attila Csampai and Dietmar Holland, eds., *Richard Wagner: Parsifal; Texte, Materialien, Kommentare* (Reinbek: Rowohlt, 1984), 262, 265, and 269.

31. For a balanced account, see Jens Malte Fischer, *Richard Wagners "Das Judentum in der Musik": Eine kritische Dokumentation als Beitrag zur Geschichte des Antisemitismus* (Frankfurt: Insel, 2000), 187; see also John Deathridge's claim that *Parsifal* "is a rather broader fantasy about race than is generally realised" in Deathridge, "Strange Love; Or, How We Learned to Stop Worrying and Love Wagner's *Parsifal*," in Julie Brown, ed., *Western Music and Race* (Cambridge: Cambridge University Press, 2007), 83.

32. Dahlhaus, "Erlösung dem Erlöser," 264–65.

33. See Peter Steinacker, *Richard Wagner und die Religion* (Darmstadt: Wissenschaftliche Buchgesellschaft, 2008), 135–36.

34. Jürgen Kühnel, *Parsifal: Erlösung dem Erlöser; Von der Aufhebung des Christentums in das Kunstwerk Richard Wagners* (Siegen: Richard-Wagner-Verband, 1982), 40.

35. Egon Voss, "Die Möglichkeit der Klage in der Wonne: Skizze zur Charakterisierung der *Parsifal*-Musik," in Voss, *"Wagner und kein Ende": Betrachtungen und Studien* (Zurich: Atlantis, 1996), 233.

36. Robert Musil, *Der Mann ohne Eigenschaften: Roman*, ed. Adolf Frisé (Reinbek: Rowohlt, 2002), 1:518; translated by Sophie Wilkins and Burton Pike as *The Man without Qualities* (London: Picador, 1995), 565.

37. GS 10:243; PW 6:243 (emended) ("Religion and Art").

38. GS 10:45; PW 4:160 (emended) ("What Is German?").

39. GS 10:247; PW 6:246–47 (emended) ("Religion and Art").

40. GS 10:252; PW 6:252 ("Religion and Art").

41. GS 10:280; PW 6:280 ("Heroism and Christianity").

42. Peter Wapnewski, "Die Oper Richard Wagners als Dichtung," in Ulrich Müller and Peter Wapnewski, eds., *Richard-Wagner-Handbuch* (Stuttgart: Alfred Kröner, 1986), 341; translated by Peter Palmer as "The Operas as Literary Works," in John Deathridge, ed., *Wagner Handbook* (Cambridge, MA: Harvard University Press, 1992), 91.

43. Martin Geck, "Parsifal: A Betrayed Childhood: Variations on a Leitmotif by Alice Miller," *Wagner* 9 (1988): 75–88.

44. Nietzsche, *Sämtliche Werke*, 6:430; translated by Walter Kaufmann as "Nietzsche contra Wagner," in Nietzsche , *The Portable Nietzsche* (New York: Penguin, 1982), 674.

45. Bernhard Sattler, ed., *Adolf von Hildebrand und seine Welt: Briefe und Erinnerungen* (Munich: Callwey, 1962), 327 and 329.

46. Otto Erich Deutsch, ed., *Schubert: Die Dokumente seines Lebens* (Kassel: Bärenreiter, 1996), 158–59; translated by Eric Blom as *Schubert: A Documentary Biography* (London: J. M. Dent, 1946), 226–28 (emended).

47. Pierre Boulez, "Chemins vers *Parsifal*," in Boulez, *Points de repère* (Paris: Christian Bourgois, 1985), 283–84; translated by Martin Cooper as "Approaches to *Parsifal*," in Boulez, *Orientations*, ed. Jean-Jacques Nattiez (London: Faber and Faber, 1986), 258.

48. Hans Rudolf Vaget, ed., *Im Schatten Wagners: Thomas Mann über Richard Wagner; Texte und Zeugnisse, 1895–1955*, 2nd ed. (Frankfurt: Fischer, 2005), 40–41 (letter from Thomas Mann to Ludwig Ewers, Aug. 23 1909). Parts of this letter also reappear verbatim in Mann's letter to Walter Opitz of Aug. 26, 1909: see Thomas Mann, *Pro and Contra Wagner*, trans. Allan Blunden (London: Faber and Faber, 1985), 44–45.

49. Friedrich Nietzsche, *Sämtliche Briefe: Kritische Studienausgabe*, ed. Giorgio Colli and Mazzino Montinari (Munich: Deutscher Taschenbuch Verlag, 1986), 8:12–13; translated by Christopher Middleton as *Selected Letters of Friedrich Nietzsche* (Indianapolis: Hackett, 1996), 260 (letter from Nietzsche to Heinrich Köselitz, Jan. 21, 1887).

50. Nike Wagner, *Wagner Theater* (Frankfurt: Insel, 1998), 233; translated by Ewald Osers and Michael Downes as *The Wagners: The Dramas of a Musical Dynasty* (London: Weidenfeld & Nicolson, 1998), 144.

51. Nietzsche, *Sämtliche Werke*, 6:43; Engl. trans. 640 ("The Case of Wagner").

52. Ryan Minor, "Wagner's Last Chorus: Consecrating Space and Spectatorship in *Parsifal*," *Cambridge Opera Journal* 17 (2005): 36.

53. Alban Berg, *Briefe an seine Frau*, ed. Helene Berg (Munich: Albert Langen, 1965), 107–8 (letter from Alban Berg to Helene Nahowski, Aug. 8, 1909).

54. Ulrike Kienzle, "Sakrales Welttheater: Eine Betrachtung zu den Bühnenbildern des *Parsifal*," in Richard-Wagner-Museum Bayreuth, ed., *Wer ist der Gral? Geschichte und Wirkung eines Mythos* (Munich: Deutscher Kunstverlag, 2008), 25.

55. SW 30:176 (Heinrich Porges's record of Wagner's comments during rehearsals in 1882).

56. CT 2:181; Engl. trans. 2:154 (entry of Sept. 23, 1878).

57. Werner Breig, "Wagners kompositorisches Werk," in Müller and Wapnewski, *Richard-Wagner-Handbuch*, 460; translated by Paul Knight and Horst Loeschmann as "The Musical Works," in Deathridge, *Wagner Handbook*, 477.

58. Adorno, *Gesammelte Schriften*, 13:64; Engl. trans. 67 ("Versuch über Wagner").

59. Breig, "Wagners kompositorisches Werk," 463; Engl. trans. 479.

60. Jean Moréas, "Le Symbolisme," *Le Figaro* (Sept. 18, 1886): 1; see also Hans H. Hofstätter, *Symbolismus und die Kunst der Jahrhundertwende* (Cologne: DuMont, 1965), 228.

61. Fritz Novotny and Johannes Dobai, *Gustav Klimt* (Salzburg: Galerie Welz, 1967), 386.

62. Pierre Boulez, "Lexikon-Artikel Debussy," in Boulez, *Anhaltspunkte*, trans. Josef Häusler (Stuttgart: Belser Verlag, 1975), 51. Originally published in volume 1 of Fasquelle's *Dictionnaire de la musique* in 1958 and translated into German in the German edition of *Points de repère* but not included in either the French original or the English translation.

63. Pierre Boulez, *Wille und Zufall: Gespräche mit Célestin Deliège und Hans Mayer* (Stuttgart: Belser, 1977), 150. (The conversations with Célestin Deliège were translated anonymously and published by Eulenburg in 1976, but the German edition also included interviews with Hans Mayer from which the present quotation is taken.)

64. Ibid.

65. CT 2:333; Engl. trans. 2:293 (entry of April 17, 1879).

66. SW 30:85.

67. SW 30:212.

68. SW 30:13.

69. CT 2:202; Engl. trans. 2:174 (entry of Oct. 18, 1878).

70. CT 2:206; Engl. trans. 2:178 (entry of Oct. 21, 1878).

71. WWW, p. 541 (Musik d folio 12r = NA A III m 4(2)).

72. CT 2:209; Engl. trans. 2:181 (entry of Oct. 24, 1878).

73. CT 2:213; Engl. trans. 2:184 (entry of Oct. 29, 1878).

74. CT 2:214–15; Engl. trans. 2:186 (entry of Oct. 31, 1878).

75. Einar Schleef, *Droge—Faust—Parsifal* (Frankfurt: Suhrkamp, 1997), 404.

76. Mario Bortolotto, *Wagner l'oscuro* (Milan: Adelphi, 2003), 428.

77. Quoted (without a source) by Bortolotto, *Wagner l'oscuro*, 422.

78. Thomas Müller, "Orchesterpsychogramm: Das Vorspiel zum III. Akt des *Parsifal*," in Eckehard Kiem and Ludwig Holtmeier, eds., *Richard Wagner und seine Zeit* (Laaber: Laaber-Verlag, 2003), 291.

79. CT 2:212; Engl. trans. 2:184 (entry of Oct. 30, 1878).

80. CT 2:215; Engl. trans. 2:186 (entry of Oct. 31, 1878).

81. William Kinderman, "Gral und Gegengral: Klangräume des *Parsifal*-Dramas," *wagnerspectrum* 4, no. 1 (2008): 53. For a characterization of this motif, see Gerd Rienäcker, *Richard Wagner: Nackdenken über sein "Gewebe"* (Berlin: Lukas-Verlag), 335–51.

82. Kinderman, "Gral und Gegengral," 67.

83. John Daverio, *Nineteenth-Century Music and the German Romantic Ideology* (New York: Schirmer, 1993), 198.

84. See Constantin Floros, "Studien zur *Parsifal*-Rezeption," in Heinz-Klaus Metzger and Rainer Riehn, eds., *Richard Wagner: Parsifal* (Munich: edition text + kritik, 1982), 47–53.

85. Rudolf Otto, *The Idea of the Holy*, trans. John Wilfred Harvey (London: H. Milford, 1923), 11.

86. SW 30:72; see also Frank Halbach, *Ahasvers Erlösung: Der Mythos vom ewigen Juden im Opernlibretto des 19. Jahrhunderts* (Munich: Herbert Utz Verlag, 2009), 145–81.

87. Ulrike Kienzle, "Komponierte Weiblichkeit im *Parsifal*: Kundry," in Susanne Vill, ed., *"Das Weib der Zukunft": Frauengestalten und Frauenstimmen bei Richard Wagner* (Stuttgart: J. B. Metzler, 2000), 168.

88. Arthur Seidl, "Richard Wagners 'Parsifal' und Schopenhauers 'Nirwana': Ein Jubiläumsbeitrag (1883–88)," in Seidl, *Richard Wagners Parsifal: Zwei Abhandlungen* (Regensburg: Gustav Bosse, [n.d.]), 46 quoted by Ulrich Drüner, *Schöpfer und Zerstörer: Richard Wagner als Künstler* (Cologne: Böhlau Verlag, 2003), 307.

89. Christina von Braun, *Nicht Ich: Logik, Lüge, Libido*, 2nd ed. (Frankfurt: Neue Kritik, 1988), 408.

90. Elisabeth Bronfen, "Kundry's Laughter," *New German Critique* 69 (1996): 159.

91. Vaget, *Im Schatten Wagners*, 124; translated by Allan Blunden as "The Sorrows and Grandeur of Richard Wagner," in Thomas Mann, *Pro and Contra Wagner* (London: Faber and Faber, 1985), 129.

92. Julia Kristeva, *Revolution in Poetic Language*, trans. Margaret Waller (New York: Columbia University Press, 1984), 86.

93. Ibid., 79.

94. See Heath Lees, *Mallarmé and Wagner: Music and Poetic Language* (Aldershot: Ashgate, 2007).

95. Bernd Asmus, "Die Zeit steht still im Fadenwerk: Zu Wagners Knüpftechnik im Parsifal; Unter besonderer Berücksichtigung der Harmonik," in Claus-Steffen Mahnkopf, ed., *Richard Wagner: Konstrukteur der Moderne* (Stuttgart: Klett-Cotta, 1999), 150–51.

96. Hans-Joachim Bauer, *Wagners "Parsifal": Kriterien der Kompositionstechnik* (Munich: Emil Katzbichler, 1977), 69.

97. CT 2:75; Engl. trans. 2:54 (entry of March 31, 1878).

98. Hans B. Brand, *Aus Richard Wagners Leben in Bayreuth: Ernstes und Heiteres* (Munich: G. Hirth Verlag, 1934), 58.

99. André Glucksmann, *The Master Thinkers*, trans. Brian Pearce (Brighton: Harvester Press, 1980), 263.

100. CT 1:202; Engl. trans. 1:193 (entry of Feb. 25, 1870).

101. SB 11:197 (letter to Mathilde Wesendonck, Aug. 24, 1859).

102. Egon Voss, "Die Möglichkeit der Klage in der Wonne," 222.

103. CT 2:841; Engl. trans. 2:762 (entry of Dec. 5, 1881).

104. CT 2:102; Engl. trans. 2:80 (entry of May 30, 1878).

105. CT 2:108; Engl. trans. 2:85 (entry of June 4, 1878).

106. CT 2:853; Engl. trans. 2:773 (emended) (entry of Dec. 18, 1881).

A WORD ABOUT GUSTAV MAHLER

1. Gustav Mahler, *Briefe*, ed. Herta Blaukopf (Vienna: Paul Zsolnay, 1996), 47; translated by Eithne Wilkins and others as *Selected Letters of Gustav Mahler* (London: Faber and Faber, 1979), 73 (emended) (undated letter from Gustav Mahler to Friedrich Löhr, [July 1883]).

2. Henry-Louis de La Grange and Günther Weiß, eds., *Ein Glück ohne Ruh': Die Briefe Gustav Mahlers an Alma* (Berlin: Siedler, 1995), 209; translated by Antony Beaumont as *Gustav Mahler: Letters to His Wife* (London: Faber and Faber, 2004), 168 (emended) (undated letter from Gustav Mahler to Alma Mahler, [July 3, 1904]).

3. Herbert Killian, ed., *Gustav Mahler in den Erinnerungen von Natalie Bauer-Lechner*, 2nd ed. (Hamburg: Karl Dieter Wagner, 1984), 122 (Sept. 1898). (This passage was suppressed from the 1923 edition of Natalie Bauer-Lechner's reminiscences and does not appear, therefore, in Dika Newlin's 1980 English translation.)

4. See Hermann Danuser, *Musikalische Prosa* (Regensburg: Gustav Bosse, 1975).

5. Theodor W. Adorno, *Gesammelte Schriften*, ed. Rolf Tiedemann (Frankfurt: Suhrkamp, 1997), 13:233; translated by Edmund Jephcott as *Mahler: A Musical Physiognomy* (Chicago: University of Chicago Press, 1992), 86.

6. Hans Heinrich Eggebrecht, *Die Musik Gustav Mahlers* (Munich: Piper, 1982), 67.

CHAPTER FOURTEEN

1. August Strindberg, *Miss Julie*, trans. Michael Meyer (London: Methuen, 2009), xci.

2. See Dieter Hensing, "Tankred Dorst: Von der geschlossenen zur offenen Figurenkonzeption," in Gerhard Kluge, ed., *Studien zur Dramatik in der Bundesrepublik Deutschland* (Amsterdam: Rodopi, 1983), 222.

3. GS 3:95–96; PW 1:125–26 (*The Artwork of the Future*).

4. Carl Dahlhaus, *Die Idee der absoluten Musik* (Kassel: Bärenreiter, 1978), 66.

5. Friedrich Nietzsche, *Sämtliche Werke: Kritische Studienausgabe*, ed. Giorgio Colli and Mazzino Montinari (Munich: Deutscher Taschenbuch Verlag, 1988), 1:479; translated by R. J. Hollingdale as "Richard Wagner in Bayreuth," in Nietzsche, *Untimely Meditations* (Cambridge: Cambridge University Press, 1983), 232.

6. GS 3:96; PW 2:126–27 (*The Artwork of the Future*).

7. CT 1:157; Engl. trans. 1:152 (entry of Oct. 4, 1869).

8. GS 3:96–97; PW 1:127 (emended) (*The Artwork of the Future*).

9. GS 9:126; PW 5:126 (emended) (*Beethoven*).

10. Peter Wapnewski, *Die Szene und ihr Meister*, 2nd ed. (Munich: C. H. Beck, 1983), 10.

11. Lawrence Kramer, *Opera and Modern Culture: Wagner and Strauss* (Berkeley: University of California Press, 2004), 112.

12. Thomas Mann, *Buddenbrooks: Verfall einer Familie* (Frankfurt: Fischer, 1960), 423; translated by H. T. Lowe-Porter as *Buddenbrooks* (London: Vintage Books, 1999), 407.

13. See Gert Mattenklott, "Unwiderstehliche Mimik: Valéry über Wagner," in Wolfgang Storch, ed., *Die Symbolisten und Richard Wagner* (Berlin: Hentrich, 1991), 175.

14. Robert Musil, *Der Mann ohne Eigenschaften: Roman*, ed. Adolf Frisé (Reinbek: Rowohlt, 2002), 1:571; translated by Sophie Wilkins and Burton Pike as *The Man without Qualities* (London: Picador, 1995), 623.

15. Nietzsche, *Sämtliche Werke*, 13:500 (unpublished fragment from spring or summer 1888, 16[40]).

16. Marcel Proust, *À la recherche du temps perdu*, ed. Pierre Clarac and André Ferré (Paris: Gallimard, 1973–77), 3:758; translated by C. K. Scott Moncrieff and Terence Kilmartin as *In Search of Lost Time*. Revised by D. J. Enright (London: Folio Society, 2000), 6:334–35.

17. See Richard Klein, "Walkürenritt in Vietnam? Zu Francis Coppolas Wagner," in Ares Rolf and Ulrich Tadday, eds., *Martin Geck: Festschrift zum 65. Geburtstag* (Dortmund: Klangfarben, 2001), 409; see also Sven Friedrich, *Richard Wagner: Deutung und Wirkung* (Würzburg: Königshausen & Neumann, 2004), 88–89.

18. Claus-Steffen Mahnkopf, "Wagners Kompositionstechnik," in Mahnkopf, ed., *Richard Wagner: Konstrukteur der Moderne* (Stuttgart: Klett-Cotta, 1999), 180.

19. Klein, "Walkürenritt in Vietnam?," 412–13.

20. Don Heinrich Tolzmann, ed., *Thomas Mann's Addresses Delivered at the Library of Congress* (Oxford: Peter Lang, 2003), 93–94.

21. Nietzsche, *Sämtliche Werke*, 6:12; translated by Walter Kaufmann as "The Case of Wagner," in Nietzsche , *Basic Writings of Nietzsche* (New York: Modern Library, 1968), 612.

22. Gerd Rienäcker, *Richard Wagner: Nachdenken über sein "Gewebe"* (Berlin: Lukas Verlag, 2001), 180.

23. GS 10:259–50; PW 6:249 ("Religion and Art").

24. GS 10:250; PW 6:249 ("Religion and Art").

25. Nietzsche, *Sämtliche Werke*, 6:30; Engl. trans. 629 ("The Case of Wagner").

26. Nietzsche, *Sämtliche Werke*, 8:188 (unpublished fragment from summer 1875, 10[16]).

27. Eckehard Kiem, "Lichtgebung: Aspekte der Wagnerschen Harmonik," in Eckehard Kiem and Ludwig Holtmeier, eds., *Richard Wagner und seine Zeit* (Laaber: Laaber-Verlag, 2003), 242.

28. Dieter Thomä, "Umwertungen der Dekadenz: Korrespondenzen zwischen Richard Wagner, Friedrich Nietzsche und Sergej Eisenstein," in Aram Mattioli and Enno Rudolph, eds., *Nietzsche und Wagner: Geschichte und Aktualität eines Kulturkonfliktes* (Zurich: Orell Füssli, 2008), 125.

29. Nietzsche, *Sämtliche Werke*, 6:28; Engl. trans. 627 ("The Case of Wagner").

30. Rienäcker, *Richard Wagner*, 9.

31. Reproduced in Friedrich, *Richard Wagner: Deutung und Wirkung*, 74–91.

32. Friedrich Kittler, *Das Nahen der Götter vorbereiten* (Munich: Wilhelm Fink, 2012), 38.

33. Laurence Dreyfus, *Wagner and the Erotic Impulse* (Cambridge, MA: Harvard University Press, 2010).

34. Friedrich, *Richard Wagner: Deutung und Wirkung*, 75.

35. Kittler, *Das Nahen der Götter vorbereiten*, 39.

36. Nietzsche, *Sämtliche Werke*, 2:434; translated by R. J. Hollingdale as *Human, All Too Human: A Book for Free Spirits* (Cambridge: Cambridge University Press, 1996), 244.

BIBLIOGRAPHY

Abbate, Carolyn. "Erik's Dream and Tannhäuser's Journey." In *Reading Opera*, ed. Arthur Groos and Roger Parker, 129–67. Princeton: Princeton University Press, 1988.

———. "Mythische Stimmen, sterbliche Körper." In *Richard Wagner, "Der Ring des Nibelungen": Ansichten des Mythos*, ed. Udo Bermbach and Dieter Borchmeyer, 75–86. Stuttgart: J. B. Metzler, 1995.

———. "Opera as Symphony: A Wagnerian Myth." In *Analyzing Opera: Verdi and Wagner*, ed. Carolyn Abbate and Roger Parker, 92–124. Berkeley: University of California Press, 1989.

———. *Unsung Voices: Opera and Musical Narrative in the Nineteenth Century*. Princeton: Princeton University Press, 1991.

Aberbach, Alan David. *The Ideas of Richard Wagner: An Examination and Analysis of His Major Aesthetic, Political, Economic, Social, and Religious Thoughts*. 2nd ed. Lanham: University Press of America, 2003.

Ackermann, Peter. *Richard Wagners "Ring des Nibelungen" und die Dialektik der Aufklärung*. Tutzing: Hans Schneider, 1981.

Adorno, Theodor W. *Beethoven: Philosophie der Musik*. Edited by Rolf Tiedemann. Frankfurt: Suhrkamp, 1994. Translated by Edmund Jephcott as *Beethoven: The Philosophy of Music*. Cambridge: Polity, 2002.

———. *Gesammelte Schriften*. 20 vols. Edited by Gretel Adorno and Rolf Tiedemann. Frankfurt: Suhrkamp, 1997.

———. *In Search of Wagner*. Translated by Rodney Livingstone. London: New Left Books, 1981.

———. *Mahler: A Musical Physiognomy*. Translated by Edmund Jephcott. Chicago: University of Chicago Press, 1992.

———. *Minima moralia: Reflections from Damaged Life*. Translated by E. F. N. Jephcott. London: Verso, 1974.

———. *Philosophy of New Music*. Translated by Robert Hullot-Kentor. Minneapolis: University of Minnesota Press, 2006.

Aringer, Klaus "'Kunst des Übergangs': Zu den Verwandlungsmusiken in *Rheingold*." In *Richard Wagners "Ring des Nibelungen": Musikalische Dramaturgie—Kulturelle Kontextualität—Primär-Rezeption*, ed. Klaus Hortschansky, 3–17. Schneverdingen: Karl Dieter Wagner, 2004.

Asmus, Bernd. "Die Zeit steht still im Fadenwerk: Zu Wagners Knüpftechnik im Parsifal; Unter besonderer Berücksichtigung der Harmonik." In *Richard Wagner: Konstrukteur der Moderne*, ed. Claus-Steffen Mahnkopf, 129–56. Stuttgart: Klett-Cotta, 1999.

Auerbach, Berthold. *Briefe an seinen Freund Jakob Auerbach*. 2 vols. Frankfurt: Literarische Anstalt, 1884.

Baedeker, Peer. "Ein Jude sucht Erlösung bei Richard Wagner: Joseph Rubinstein (1847–1884)." In *Jüdisches Bayreuth*, ed. Bernd Mayer and Frank Piontek, 119–28. Bayreuth: Ellwanger, 2010.

Bailey, Robert. *Richard Wagner: Prelude and Transfiguration from "Tristan and Isolde."* New York: W. W. Norton, 1985.

Bartels, Ulrich. *Analytisch-entstehungsgeschichtliche Studien zu Wagners Tristan und Isolde anhand der Kompositionsskizze des zweiten und dritten Aktes.* Cologne: Studio, 1995.

Baudelaire, Charles. *Œuvres complètes.* 2 vols. Edited by Claude Pichois. Paris: Gallimard, 1976.

———. "Richard Wagner and *Tannhäuser* in Paris." In *The Painter of Modern Life and Other Essays*, trans. Jonathan Mayne, 111–46. London: Phaidon, 1995.

Bauer, Hans-Joachim. *Wagners "Parsifal": Kriterien der Kompositionstechnik.* Munich: Emil Katzbichler, 1977.

Bauer, Oswald Georg. "Der falsche Prophet." In *Richard Wagner und die Juden*, ed. Dieter Borchmeyer and others, 275–95. Stuttgart: J. B. Metzler, 2000.

BB: *See* Wagner, Richard. *Das Braune Buch.*

Beckett, Lucy. "Sachs and Schopenhauer." In *Richard Wagner: Die Meistersinger von Nürnberg*, ed. John Warrack, 66–82. Cambridge: Cambridge University Press, 1994.

Bekker, Paul. *Kunst und Revolution.* Frankfurt: Frankfurter Societäts Verlag, 1919.

———. *Richard Wagner: Das Leben im Werke.* Stuttgart: Deutsche Verlags-Anstalt, 1924. Translated by M. M. Bozman as *Richard Wagner: His Life in His Work.* New York: W. W. Norton, 1931.

Benjamin, Walter. *Gesammelte Schriften.* 6 vols. Edited by Rolf Tiedemann and Hermann Schweppenhäuser. Frankfurt: Suhrkamp, 2009.

———. *Illuminations.* Translated by Harry Zohn. London: Pimlico, 1999.

———. *Ursprung des deutschen Trauerspiels.* Frankfurt: Suhrkamp, 1978. Translated by John Osborne as *The Origin of German Tragic Drama.* London: Verso, 1998.

Benz, Bernhard. *Zeitstrukturen in Richard Wagners "Ring"-Tetralogie.* Frankfurt: Peter Lang, 1994.

Berg, Alban. *Briefe an seine Frau.* Edited by Helene Berg. Munich: Albert Langen, 1965.

Berger, Christian. "Leitmotive in den harmonischen Kraftfeldern von Wagners *Rheingold*." In *Richard Wagners "Ring des Nibelungen": Musikalische Dramaturgie — Kulturelle Kontextualität — Primär-Rezeption*, ed. Klaus Hortschansky, 33–48. Schneverdingen: Wagner, 2004.

Bermbach, Udo. *"Blühendes Leid": Politik und Gesellschaft in Richard Wagners Musikdramen.* Stuttgart: J. B. Metzler, 2003.

———. *Der Wahn des Gesamtkunstwerks: Richard Wagners politisch-ästhetische Utopie.* Frankfurt: Fischer, 1994.

———. *Richard Wagner in Deutschland: Rezeption — Verfälschungen.* Stuttgart: J. B. Metzler, 2011.

———. "Wotan — der Gott als Politiker." In *"Alles ist nach seiner Art": Figuren in Richard Wagners "Der Ring des Nibelungen,"* ed. Udo Bermbach, 27–48. Stuttgart: J. B. Metzler, 2001.

Bloch, Ernst. *Geist der Utopie.* 2nd ed. Frankfurt: Suhrkamp, 1964. Translated by Anthony A. Nassar as *The Spirit of Utopia.* Stanford: Stanford University Press, 2000.

———. "Paradoxa und Pastorale bei Wagner." In *Zur Philosophie der Musik*, ed. Karola Bloch, 218–55. Frankfurt: Suhrkamp, 1974. Translated by Peter Palmer as "Paradoxes and the Pastorale in Wagner's Music." In Ernst Bloch, *Essays on the Philosophy of Music*, 146–82. Cambridge: Cambridge University Press, 1985.

———. "Über Beckmessers Preislied-Text." In *Zur Philosophie der Musik*, ed. Karola Bloch, 208–13. Frankfurt: Suhrkamp, 1974.

Borchmeyer, Dieter. *Das Theater Richard Wagners: Idee—Dichtung—Wirkung*. Stuttgart: Reclam, 1982. Translated by Stewart Spencer as *Richard Wagner: Theory and Theatre*. Oxford: Clarendon Press, 1991.

———. *Nietzsche, Cosima, Wagner: Porträt einer Freundschaft*. Frankfurt: Insel, 2008.

———. *Richard Wagner: Ahasvers Wandlungen*. Frankfurt: Insel, 2002. Translated by Daphne Ellis as *Drama and the World of Richard Wagner*. Princeton: Princeton University Press, 2003.

———. "'. . . sehnsüchtig blicke ich oft nach dem Land Nirwana . . .': Richard Wagners buddhistisches Christentum." *wagnerspectrum* 3, no. 2 (2007): 15–34.

———. "Vom Kuß der Liebe und des Todes: Eros und Thanatos in der Oper." In *Geist, Eros und Agape: Untersuchungen zu Liebesdarstellungen in Philosophie, Religion und Kunst*, ed. Edith Düsing and Hans-Dieter Klein, 369–81. Würzburg: Königshausen & Neumann, 2009.

Bortolotto, Mario. *Wagner l'oscuro*. Milan: Adelphi, 2003.

Boulez, Pierre. "Approaches to *Parsifal*." In *Orientations*, ed. Jean-Jacques Nattiez; trans. Martin Cooper, 245–59. London: Faber and Faber, 1986.

———. "Lexikon-Artikel Debussy." In Boulez, *Anhaltspunkte: Essays*, trans. Josef Häusler, 35–59. Stuttgart: Belser, 1975.

———. *Points de repère*. Paris: Christian Bourgois, 1985. Translated by Martin Cooper as *Orientations*, ed. Jean-Jacques Nattiez. London: Faber and Faber, 1986.

———. *Wille und Zufall: Gespräche mit Célestin Deliège und Hans Mayer*. Stuttgart: Belser, 1977.

Boulez, Pierre and others. *Histoire d'un "Ring": Der Ring des Nibelungen (l'Anneau du Nibelung) de Richard Wagner, Bayreuth 1976–1980*, ed. Sylvie de Nussac and François Regnault. Paris: Robert Laffont, 1980.

Brachmann, Jan. "Ohne Barbarei gibt es keine große Kunst." *Berliner Zeitung* (July 31, 2004).

Brand, Hans B. *Aus Richard Wagners Leben in Bayreuth: Ernstes und Heiteres*. Munich: G. Hirth Verlag, 1934.

Braun, Christina von. *Nicht Ich: Logik, Lüge, Libido*. 2nd ed. Frankfurt: Neue Kritik, 1988.

Brecht, Bertolt. *Werke: Große, kommentierte Berliner und Frankfurter Ausgabe*. 30 vols. Edited by Werner Hecht and others. Frankfurt: Suhrkamp, 2000.

Bredekamp, Horst. *Theorie des Bildaktes: Über das Lebensrecht des Bildes*. Frankfurt: Suhrkamp, 2010.

Breig, Werner. "Der 'Rheintöchtergesang' in Wagners 'Rheingold.'" *Archiv für Musikwissenschaft* 37 (1980): 241–63.

———. "Wagners kompositorisches Werk," In *Richard-Wagner-Handbuch*, ed. Müller and Wapnewski, 353–470. Translated by Paul Knight and Horst Loeschmann as "The Musical Works." In *Wagner Handbook*, ed. Deathridge, 397–482.

———. "Zur musikalischen Struktur von Wagners 'Ring des Nibelungen.'" In *In den Trümmern der eignen Welt: Richard Wagners "Der Ring des Nibelungen,"* ed. Udo Bermbach, 39–62. Berlin: Dietrich Reimer, 1989.

Brinkmann, Reinhold. "'. . . einen Schluß machen!' Über externe Schlüsse bei Wagner." In *Festschrift Heinz Becker zum 60. Geburtstag*, ed. Jürgen Schläder and Reinhold Quandt, 179–90. Laaber: Laaber-Verlag, 1982.

Bronfen, Elisabeth. "Kundry's Laughter." *New German Critique* 69 (1996): 147–61.

Broszka, Matthias. "Geschichtsphilosophische Dimensionen in Meyersbeers Grand Opéra." In *Zukunftsbilder: Richard Wagners Revolution und ihre Folgen in Kunst und Politik*, ed. Hermann Danuser and Herfried Münkler, 108–15. Schliengen: Edition Argus, 2002.

Buhr, Jan. *"Der Ring des Nibelungen" und Wagners Ästhetik im Fokus strukturaler Semantik.* Würzburg: Königshausen & Neumann, 2008.

Burk, John N., ed. *Richard Wagner: Briefe; Die Sammlung Burrell.* Frankfurt: Fischer, 1953. Translated by Hans Abraham and others as *Letters of Richard Wagner: The Burrell Collection.* London: Victor Gollancz, 1951.

Burkhardt, Max. *Führer durch Richard Wagners Musikdramen.* Berlin: Schuster & Loeffler, n.d.

Campenhout, Herman van. *Die bezaubernde Katastrophe: Versuch einer Wagner-Lektüre.* Würzburg: Königshausen & Neumann, 2005.

Chafe, Eric. *The Tragic and the Ecstatic: The Musical Revolution of Wagner's "Tristan and Isolde."* Oxford: Oxford University Press, 2005.

Chéreau, Patrice. "Kommentare zu 'Mythologie und Ideologie.'" In *Bayreuther Dramaturgie: Der Ring des Nibelungen*, ed. Herbert Barth, 419–37. Stuttgart: Belser, 1980.

Cicora, Mary A. *From History to Myth: Wagner's* Tannhäuser *and Its Literary Sources.* Bern: Peter Lang, 1992.

Cornelius, Peter. *Literarische Werke.* 4 vols. Edited by Carl Maria Cornelius and Edgar Istel. Leipzig: Breitkopf & Härtel, 1904–5.

CT: *See* Gregor-Dellin and Mack, eds., *Cosima Wagner.*

Dahlhaus, Carl. "Bach und der romantische Kontrapunkt." In *Bach-Tage Berlin 1989: Kapellmeister Bach*, ed. Verband Deutscher Musikerzieher und Konzertierender Künstler, 78–84. Berlin: Landesverband, 1989.

———. "Das unterbrochene Hauptwerk: Zu Wagners *Siegfried*." In *Vom Musikdrama zur Literaturoper: Aufsätze zur neueren Operngeschichte*, 105–8. Munich: Piper, 1989.

———. *Die Bedeutung des Gestischen in Wagners Musikdramen.* Munich: R. Oldenbourg, 1970.

———. *Die Idee der absoluten Musik.* Kassel: Bärenreiter, 1978.

———. "Erlösung dem Erlöser: Warum Richard Wagners 'Parsifal' nicht Mittel zum Zweck der Ideologie ist." In *Richard Wagner: Parsifal. Texte, Materialien, Kommentare*, ed. Attila Csampai and Dietmar Holland, 262–69. Reinbek: Rowohlt, 1984.

———. "Ernst Blochs Philosophie der Musik Wagners." In *Jahrbuch des Staatlichen Instituts für Musikforschung Preussischer Kulturbesitz 1971*, ed. Dagmar Droysen, 179–88. Berlin: Merseburger, 1972.

———. "'Lohengrin' und die 'Einheit des Symphoniesatzes,' sowie 'Opus metaphysicum': Das Musikdrama als symphonische Oper." In *Europäische Romantik in der Musik*, 2 vols., ed. Carl Dahlhaus and Norbert Miller, 2:916–23. Stuttgart: J. B. Metzler, 2007.

———. *Richard Wagners Musikdramen.* 2nd ed. Zurich: Orell Füssli, 1985. Translated by Mary Whittall as *Richard Wagner's Music Dramas.* Cambridge: Cambridge University Press, 1979.

———. *Wagners Konzeption des musikalischen Dramas.* Regensburg: Gustav Bosse, 1971.

———. "Wagners Stellung in der Musikgeschichte." In *Richard-Wagner-Handbuch*, ed. Müller and Wapnewski, 60–85. Translated by Alfred Clayton as "Wagner's Place in the History of Music." In *Wagner Handbook*, ed. Deathridge, 99–117.

Dahlhaus, Carl, and Egon Voss, eds. *Wagnerliteratur—Wagnerforschung: Bericht über das Wagner-Symposium München 1983.* Mainz: Schott, 1985.

Danuser, Hermann. *Musikalische Prosa.* Regensburg: Gustav Bosse, 1975.

———. "Verheißung und Erlösung: Zur Dramaturgie des 'Torenspruchs' in *Parsifal.*" *wagnerspectrum* 4, no. 1 (2008): 9–39.

Darcy, Warren. "In Search of C Major: Tonal Structure and Formal Design in Act III of *Die Meistersinger.*" In *Richard Wagner for the New Millennium: Essays in Music and Culture*, ed. Matthew Bribitzer-Stull and others, 111–28. New York: Palgrave, 2007.

———. *Wagner's "Das Rheingold."* Oxford: Clarendon Press, 1993.

Daverio, John. *Nineteenth-Century Music and the German Romantic Ideology.* New York: Schirmer, 1993.

David, Hans T., and Arthur Mendel, eds. *The New Bach Reader: A Life of Johann Sebastian Bach in Letters and Documents.* New York: W. W. Norton, 1998.

Deathridge, John. *Wagner Beyond Good and Evil.* Berkeley: University of California Press, 2008.

———. "Strange Love; Or, How We Learned to Stop Worrying and Love Wagner's *Parsifal.*" In *Western Music and Race*, ed. Julie Brown, 65–83. Cambridge: Cambridge University Press, 2007.

———. *Wagner's* Rienzi: *A Reappraisal Based on a Study of the Sketches and Drafts.* Oxford: Clarendon Press, 1977.

Deathridge, John, Martin Geck, and Egon Voss, eds. *Wagner Werk-Verzeichnis (WWV): Verzeichnis der musikalischen Werke Richard Wagners und ihrer Quellen.* Mainz: Schott, 1986. (Abbreviated WWV; numbers are work numbers unless page numbers are indicated by *p.* or *pp.*)

Deliège, Irène, ed. *Tristan und Isolde, "cor anglais" solo. Musicae Scientiae* (1998) (unnumbered special issue).

Deutsch, Otto Erich, ed. *Schubert: Die Dokumente seines Lebens.* Kassel: Bärenreiter, 1996. Translated by Eric Blom as *Schubert: A Documentary Biography.* London: J. M. Dent, 1946.

Devrient, Eduard. *Aus seinen Tagebüchern.* 2 vols. Edited by Rolf Kabel. Weimar: Hermann Böhlaus Nachfolger, 1964.

Döge, Klaus. "Wagner beim Wort genommen: 'Über das thematische formgewebe' im *Lohengrin.*" In *Der "Komponist" Richard Wagner im Blick der aktuellen Musikwissenschaft*, ed. Ulrich Konrad and Egon Voss, 95–104. Wiesbaden: Breitkopf & Härtel, 2003.

———. "Wagner—Polyphonie—Kontrapunkt—angewendeter Bach." In *Bach und die deutsche Tradition des Komponierens: Festschrift Martin Geck zum 70. Geburtstag*, ed. Reinmar Emans and Wolfram Steinbeck, 181–86. Dortmund: Klangfarben, 2009.

Döhring, Sieghart. "Die traumatische Beziehung Wagners zu Meyerbeer." In *Richard Wagner und die Juden*, ed. Dieter Borchmeyer and others, 262–74. Stuttgart: J. B. Metzler, 2000.

———. "Kontinuität und Entwicklung: Wagners Tannhäuser und seine Metamorphosen." In *Mit Fassung: Fassungsprobleme in Musik- und Text-Philologie; Helga Lühning zum 60. Geburtstag*, ed. Reinmar Emans, 123–39. Laaber: Laaber-Verlag, 2007.

———. "*Tannhäuser* und die Transformation der romantischen Oper," In *"Schlagen Sie die Kraft der Reflexion nicht zu gering an": Beiträge zu Richard Wagners Denken, Werk und Wirken*, ed. Klaus Döge and others, 48–61. Mainz: Schott, 2002.

Döhring, Sieghart, and Sabine Henze-Döhring. *Oper und Musikdrama im 19. Jahrhundert.* Laaber: Laaber-Verlag, 1997.

Dorschel, Andreas. "Die Idee der 'Einswerdung' in Wagners *Tristan.*" In *Richard Wagner: Tristan und Isolde*, ed. Heinz-Klaus Metzger and Rainer Riehn, 3–45. Munich: edition text + kritik, 1987 (= Musik-Konzepte 57–58).

Dreyfus, Laurence. "Hermann Levi's Shame and *Parsifal*'s Guilt." *Cambridge Opera Journal* 6 (1994): 125–45.

———. *Wagner and the Erotic Impulse*. Cambridge, MA: Harvard University Press, 2010.

Drüner, Ulrich. *Schöpfer und Zerstörer: Richard Wagner als Künstler*. Cologne: Böhlau Verlag, 2003.

Eggebrecht, Hans Heinrich. *Die Musik Gustav Mahlers*. Munich: Piper, 1982.

Eisenstein, Sergei. *Beyond the Stars: The Memoirs of Sergei Eisenstein*. Edited by Richard Taylor. Translated by William Powell. London: British Film Institute, 1995.

———. *Über Kunst und Künstler*. Translated by Alexander Kaempfe. Munich: Rogner und Bernhard, 1977.

———. *Writings 1934–1947*. Edited by Richard Taylor. Translated by William Powell. London: I. B. Tauris, 2010.

Enzensberger, Hans Magnus. *Der Untergang der Titanic*. Frankfurt: Suhrkamp, 1978. Translated by Hans Magnus Enzensberger as *The Sinking of the Titanic*. Manchester: Carcanet New Press, 1981.

Ette, Wolfram. "Mythos und negative Dialektik in Wagners Ring: Mit einem Anhang zur 'modernen Mythosforschung.'" In *Narben des Gesamtkunstwerks: Wagners "Ring des Nibelungen,"* ed. Richard Klein, 133–65. Munich: Wilhelm Fink, 2001.

Figal, Günter. "Der moderne Künstler par excellence: Wagner in Nietzsches philosophischer Perspektive." In *Narben des Gesamtkunstwerks: Wagners "Ring des Nibelungen,"* ed. Richard Klein, 53–63. Munich: Wilhelm Fink, 2001.

Finscher, Ludwig. "Über den Kontrapunkt der Meistersinger." In *Das Drama Richard Wagners als musikalisches Kunstwerk*, ed. Carl Dahlhaus, 303–12. Regensburg: Gustav Bosse, 1970.

Fischer, Jens Malte. "'Erlösung dem Erlöser': Richard Wagners letztes Wort." In *Jahrhundertdämmerung: Ansichten eines anderen Fin de siècle*, 177–89. Vienna: Paul Zsolnay, 2000.

———. *Richard Wagners "Das Judentum in der Musik": Eine kritische Dokumentation als Beitrag zur Geschichte des Antisemitismus*. Frankfurt: Insel, 2000.

Fleming, Paul. *Deutsche Gedichte*. Edited by Johann Martin Lappenberg. Stuttgart: Litterarischer Verein, 1865.

Floros, Constantin. "Studien zur *Parsifal*-Rezeption." In *Richard Wagner: Parsifal*, ed. Heinz-Klaus Metzger and Rainer Riehn, 14–57. Munich: edition text + kritik, 1982 (= Musik-Konzepte 25).

Foerster, Josef Bohuslav. *Der Pilger: Erinnerungen eines Musikers*. Prague: Artia, 1955.

Fontane, Theodor. *Briefe an seine Familie*. 2 vols. Berlin: Fontane, 1905.

Fornaçon, Siegfried. "Richard Wagners Seereise von Pillau nach London." *Schiff und Zeit* 8 (1978): 1–10.

Foster, Daniel. *Wagner's "Ring" Cycle and the Greeks*. Cambridge: Cambridge University Press, 2010.

Foucault, Michel. "Die Bilderwelt des 19. Jahrhunderts: Boulez' und Chéreaus Bayreuther Ringinszenierung." *Ästhetik und Kommunikation* 56 (Nov. 1984): 127–29.

———. *The Will to Knowledge: The History of Sexuality Volume 1*. Translated by Robert Hurley. London: Penguin, 1998.

Frank, Manfred. "Der *Ring*-Mythos als 'Totschlägerreihe.'" In *Narben des Gesamtkunstwerks: Wagner's "Ring des Nibelungen,"* ed. Richard Klein, 81–101. Munich: Wilhelm Fink, 2001.

———. "Die Dialektik von 'erb' und 'eigen' in Wagners Ring: Auch eine Einführung in die *Götterdämmerung*." In *Die Musik als Medium von Beziehungsbefindlichkeiten: Mozarts und Wagners Musiktheater im aktuellen Deutungsgeschehen*, ed. Otto Kolleritsch, 89–110. Vienna: Universal-Edition, 2002.

———. *Mythendämmerung: Richard Wagner im frühromantischen Kontext*. Munich: Wilhelm Fink, 2008.

Fried, Johannes. *Der Schleier der Erinnerung: Grundzüge einer historischen Memorik*, Munich: C. H. Beck, 2004.

Friedrich, Sven. *Richard Wagner: Deutung und Wirkung*. Würzburg: Königshausen & Neumann, 2004.

Gay, Peter. *The Bourgeois Experience: Victoria to Freud*, vol. 2, *The Tender Passion*. New York: Oxford University Press, 1986.

Geck, Martin. "Bach und Tristan—Musik aus dem Geiste der Utopie." In *Bach-Interpretationen*, 190–96. Göttingen: Vandenhoeck & Ruprecht, 1969.

———. *Die Bildnisse Richard Wagners*. Munich: Prestel, 1970.

———. "'Eigentlich hätte Siegfried Parsifal werden sollen . . .': Der Schluss des 'Rings' im Focus philosophischer Überlebensstrategien von Nietzsche bis Žižek." In *Wagners Siegfried und die (post-)heroische Moderne*, ed. Tobias Janz, 65–73. Würzburg: Königshausen & Neumann, 2011.

———. "Erlösung durch Untergang: Wagners zerstörerischer Pessimismus." *Musik & Ästhetik* 1, no. 4 (1997): 67–73.

———. "Es ist wie die Stimme des Ding an sich: Wagners 'Bach.'" In *"Denn alles findet bei Bach statt": Erforschtes und Erfahrenes*, 170–90. Stuttgart: J. B. Metzler, 2000.

———. "Parsifal: A Betrayed Childhood: Variations on a Leitmotif by Alice Miller." *Wagner* 9 (1988): 75–88.

———. *Richard Wagner*. Reinbek: Rowohlt, 2004.

———. "Richard Wagner und die ältere Musik." In *Die Ausbreitung des Historismus über die Musik*, ed. Walter Wiora, 123–46. Regensburg: Gustav Bosse, 1969.

———. "Rienzi-Philologie." In *Das Drama Richard Wagners als musikalisches Kunstwerk*, ed. Carl Dahlhaus, 183–96. Regensburg: Gustav Bosse, 1970.

———. *Robert Schumann: Mensch und Musiker der Romantik*. 2nd ed. Munich: Siedler, 2010. Translated by Stewart Spencer as *Robert Schumann: The Life and Work of a Romantic Composer*. Chicago: University of Chicago Press, 2012.

———. *Von Beethoven bis Mahler: Leben und Werk der großen Komponisten des 19. Jahrhunderts*. Stuttgart: J. B. Metzler, 2000.

———. "'Von deutscher Art und Kunst'? Mit Bachs 'nordischem' Kontrapunkt gegen drohenden Kulturverfall." In *Philosophie des Kontrapunkts*, ed. Ulrich Tadday, 178–200. Munich: edition text + kritik, 2010 (= Musik-Konzepte: Sonderband).

———. *Zwischen Romantik und Restauration: Musik im Realismus-Diskurs, 1848 bis 1871*. Stuttgart: J. B. Metzler and Bärenreiter, 2001.

Gelb, Arthur, and Barbara Gelb. *O'Neill: Life with Monte Cristo*. New York: Applause, 2000.

Glasenapp, Carl Friedrich. *Das Leben Richard Wagners in sechs Büchern*. Leipzig: Breitkopf & Härtel, 1905–11.

Glucksmann, André. *The Master Thinkers*. Translated by Brian Pearce. Brighton: Harvester Press, 1980.

Goehr, Lydia. "The Dangers of Satisfaction: On Songs, Rehearsals, and Repetition in *Die Meistersinger*." In *Wagner's "Meistersinger,"* ed. Vazsonyi, 56–70.

Golther, Wolfgang, ed. *Richard Wagner an Mathilde Wesendonk: Tagebuchblätter und Briefe, 1853–1871*. 2nd ed. Berlin: Alexander Duncker, 1904.

Graf, Max. *Richard Wagner im "Fliegenden Holländer": Ein Beitrag zur Psychologie künstlerischen Schaffens.* Leipzig: Franz Deuticke, 1911.

Gratzke, Michael. *Liebesschmerz und Textlust: Figuren der Liebe und des Masochismus in der Literatur.* Würzburg: Königshausen & Neumann, 2000.

Gregor-Dellin, Martin. *Richard Wagner: Sein Leben, sein Werk, sein Jahrhundert.* Munich: R. Piper, 1980. Translated by J. Maxwell Brownjohn as *Richard Wagner: His Life, His Work, His Century.* London: Collins, 1983.

Gregor-Dellin, Martin, and Dietrich Mack, eds. *Cosima Wagner: Die Tagebücher.* 2 vols. Munich: R. Piper, 1976–77. Translated by Geoffrey Skelton as *Cosima Wagner's Diaries.* 2 vols. London: Collins, 1978–80. (Abbreviated CT)

Gregorovius, Ferdinand. *Göthe's Wilhelm Meister in seinen socialistischen Elementen.* Königsberg: Bornträger, 1849.

Grey, Thomas. "In the Realm of the Senses: Sight, Sound and the Music of Desire in *Tristan und Isolde*." In *Richard Wagner: Tristan und Isolde*, ed. Arthur Groos, 69–94. Cambridge: Cambridge University Press, 2011.

———. "'. . . wie ein rother Faden': On the Origins of the 'Leitmotif' as Critical Construct and Musical Practice." In *Music Theory in the Age of Romanticism*, ed. Ian Bent, 187–210. Cambridge: Cambridge University Press, 1996.

Griepenkerl, Wolfgang Robert. *Das Musikfest oder die Beethovener.* 2nd ed. Braunschweig: Eduard Leibrock, 1841.

Großmann-Vendrey, Susanna. *Bayreuth in der deutschen Presse.* Vol. 1, *Die Grundsteinlegung und die ersten Festspiele, 1872–1876.* Regensburg: Gustav Bosse, 1977.

———. *Bayreuth in der deutschen Presse.* Vol. 2, *Die Uraufführung des Parsifal (1882).* Regensburg: Gustav Bosse, 1977.

Grun, Constantin. *Arnold Schönberg und Richard Wagner: Spuren einer außergewöhnlichen Beziehung.* 2 vols. Göttingen: V&E unipress Verlag, 2006.

GS: *See* Wagner, Richard. *Gesammelte Schriften und Dichtungen.*

Gutman, Robert W. *Richard Wagner: The Man, His Mind, and His Music.* London: Secker & Warburg, 1968.

Halbach, Frank. *Ahasvers Erlösung: Der Mythos vom ewigen Juden im Opernlibretto des 19. Jahrhunderts.* Munich: Herbert Utz Verlag, 2009.

[Hamp, Petrus.] *Ein Blick in die Geisteswerkstatt Richard Wagners: Von einem alten geistlichen Freunde des Meisters von Bayreuth zur Erinnerung an dessen Schwanengesang.* Berlin: Albert Böhler, 1904.

Hanslick, Eduard. *Die moderne Oper: Kritiken und Studien.* Berlin: Allgemeiner Verein für deutsche Literatur, 1875.

Harmgart, Heike, Steffen Huck, and Wieland Müller, "Strategien der Erlösung: Über Aspekte der Rationalität in Richard Wagners *Tannhäuser*." *wagnerspectrum* 3, no. 1 (2007): 93–106.

Härtling, Peter. *Notenschrift: Worte und Sätze zur Musik.* Stuttgart: Radius, 1998.

Hartwich, Wolf-Daniel. "Jüdische Theosophie in Richard Wagners *Parsifal*: Vom christlichen Antisemitismus zur ästhetischen Kabbala." In *Richard Wagner und die Juden*, ed. Dieter Borchmeyer and others, 103–22. Stuttgart: J. B. Metzler, 2000.

———. *Romantischer Antisemitismus: Von Klopstock bis Richard Wagner.* Göttingen: Vandenhoeck & Ruprecht, 2005.

Hatto, A. T. *Gottfried von Strassburg: Tristan; Translated Entire for the First Time.* Harmondsworth: Penguin, 1960.

Hegel, Georg Wilhelm Friedrich. *Jenaer Kritische Schriften.* 4 vols. Edited by Hartmut Buchner and others. Hamburg: Felix Meiner, 1968–86.

Heidegger, Martin. *Nietzsche*. 2 vols. Pfullingen: Günther Neske, 1961.

Heine, Heinrich. *Sämtliche Schriften*. 6 vols. Edited by Klaus Briegleb. Munich: Deutscher Taschenbuch Verlag, 1996.

Hensing, Dieter. "Tankred Dorst: Von der geschlossenen zur offenen Figurenkonzeption." In *Studien zur Dramatik in der Bundesrepublik Deutschland*, ed. Gerhard Kluge, 177–223. Amsterdam: Rodopi, 1983.

Henze-Döhring, Sabine. "'Liebe—Tragik': Zur musikdramaturgischen Konzeption der Brünnhilden-Gestalt." In *"Das Weib der Zukunft": Frauengestalten und Frauenstimmen bei Richard Wagner*, ed. Susanne Vill, 124–52. Stuttgart: J. B. Metzler, 2000.

Herz, Joachim. "Der doch versöhnte Beckmesser: Noch eine Wagner-Polemik (1961)." In *Richard Wagner: Die Meistersinger von Nürnberg; Texte, Materialien, Kommentare*, ed. Attila Csampai and Dietmar Holland, 213–15. Reinbek: Rowohlt, 1981.

———. "Musik und Szene in den 'Meistersingern': Diskussion mit einem Kritiker (1961)." In *Richard Wagner: Die Meistersinger von Nürnberg. Texte, Materialien, Kommentare*, ed. Attila Csampai and Dietmar Holland, 207–12. Reinbek: Rowohlt, 1981.

Herzfeld, Gregor. "Verführung—Vereinnahmung—Verderben: Musik bei Søren Kierkegaard, Richard Wagner und Thomas Mann." *Musik & Ästhetik* 15 (2011): 79–96.

Hinrichsen, Hans-Joachim. "Bruckners Wagner-Zitate." In *Bruckner-Probleme*, ed. Albrecht Riethmüller, 115–33. Stuttgart: Franz Steiner, 1999.

Hitler, Adolf. *Mein Kampf*. Munich: Franz Eher Nachfolger, 1934. Translated by Ralph Manheim as *Mein Kampf*. London: Pimlico, 2002.

Hoffmann, E. T. A. *E. T. A. Hoffmann's Musical Writings*. Edited by David Charlton; translated by Martin Clarke. Cambridge: Cambridge University Press, 1989.

———. *Sämtliche Werke in sechs Bänden*. Edited by Gerhard Allroggen and others. Frankfurt: Deutscher Klassiker Verlag, 2003.

Hofmann, Gabriele. *Das Tristan-Syndrom: Psychoanalytische und existenzphilosophische Aspekte der Tristan-Figur Richard Wagners*. Regensburg: Roderer, 1997.

Hofmann, Peter. *Richard Wagners politische Theologie: Kunst zwischen Revolution und Religion*. Paderborn: Schöningh, 2003.

Hofstätter, Hans H. *Symbolismus und die Kunst der Jahrhundertwende*. Cologne: DuMont, 1965.

Holtmeier, Ludwig. "Von den *Feen* zum *Liebesverbot*: Zur Geschichte eines Dilettanten." In *Richard Wagner und seine Zeit*, ed. Eckehard Kiem and Ludwig Holtmeier, 33–73. Laaber: Laaber-Verlag, 2003.

Hübner, Kurt. *Die Wahrheit des Mythos*. Munich: C. H. Beck, 1985.

Hunt, Graham G. "Ortrud and the Birth of a New Style in Act 2, Scene 1, of Wagner's *Lohengrin*." *Opera Quarterly* 20 (2004): 47–70.

Hur, Tschang-Un. "Die Darstellung der großen Schlacht in der deutschen Literatur des 12. und 13. Jahrhunderts." PhD diss., University of Munich, 1971.

Jacobs, Rüdiger. *Revolutionsidee und Staatskritik in Richard Wagners Schriften: Perspektiven metapolitischen Denkens*. Würzburg: Königshausen & Neumann, 2010.

Jansen, F. Gustav, ed. *Robert Schumanns Briefe: Neue Folge*. 2nd ed. Leipzig: Breitkopf & Härtel, 1904.

Janz, Tobias. *Klangdramaturgie: Studien zur theatralen Orchesterkomposition in Wagners "Ring des Nibelungen."* Würzburg: Königshausen & Neumann, 2006.

———, ed. *Wagners Siegfried und die (post-)heroische Moderne*. Würzburg: Königshausen & Neumann, 2011.

Jens, Walter. "Natur und Kunst: Richard Wagner und 'Die Meistersinger von Nürnberg.'" In Jens, *Von deutscher Rede*. 2nd ed., 147–62. Munich: Piper, 1988.

Jungheinrich, Hans-Klaus. "Ritter, Bürger, Künstler." In *Richard Wagner: Tannhäuser; Texte, Materialien, Kommentare*, ed. Attila Csampai and Dietmar Holland, 9–29. Reinbek: Rowohlt, 1986.

Kaden, Christian. *Des Lebens wilder Kreis: Musik im Zivilisationsprozeß*. Kassel: Bärenreiter, 1993.

Kaiser, Joachim. *Leben mit Wagner*. Munich: Albrecht Knaus, 1990.

Kapp, Julius, ed. *Richard Wagners Gesammelte Schriften*. 14 vols. Leipzig: Hesse & Becker, [1914].

Kerman, Joseph. *Write All These Down: Essays in Music*. Berkeley: University of California Press, 1994.

Kiem, Eckehard. "Lichtgebung: Aspekte der Wagnerschen Harmonik." In *Richard Wagner und seine Zeit*, ed. Eckehard Kiem and Ludwig Holtmeier, 237–60. Laaber: Laaber-Verlag, 2003.

———. "Vom Sinn der Motivbeziehungen: *Der Ring des Nibelungen*." In *Richard Wagner und seine Zeit*, ed. Eckehard Kiem and Ludwig Holtmeier, 123–44. Laaber: Laaber-Verlag, 2003.

Kienzle, Ulrike. . . . *daß wissend würde die Welt! Religion und Philosophie in Richard Wagners Musikdramen*. Würzburg: Königshausen & Neumann, 2005.

———. "Komponierte Weiblichkeit im *Parsifal*: Kundry." In *"Das Weib der Zukunft": Frauengestalten und Frauenstimmen bei Richard Wagner*, ed. Susanne Vill, 153–90. Stuttgart: J. B. Metzler, 2000.

———. "Sakrales Welttheater: Eine Betrachtung zu den Bühnenbildern des *Parsifal*." In *Wer ist der Gral? Geschichte und Wirkung eines Mythos*, ed. Richard-Wagner-Museum Bayreuth, 17–26. Munich: Deutscher Kunstverlag, 2008.

Killian, Herbert, ed. *Gustav Mahler in den Erinnerungen von Natalie Bauer-Lechner*, 2nd ed. Hamburg: Karl Dieter Wagner, 1984.

Kinderman, William. "Gral und Gegengral: Klangräume des *Parsifal*-Dramas." *wagnerspectrum* 4, no. 1 (2008): 41–67.

Kirchmeyer Helmut. *Das zeitgenössische Wagner-Bild*. Vol. 3, *Dokumente 1846–1850*. Regensburg: Gustav Bosse, 1968.

Kittler, Friedrich. *Das Nahen der Götter vorbereiten*. Munich: Wilhelm Fink, 2012.

———. "Wagners wildes Heer." In *Die Symbolisten und Richard Wagner*, ed. Wolfgang Storch, 37–43. Berlin: Hentrich, 1991.

Klein, Richard. "Der sichtbare und der unsichtbare Gott: Versuch über Wotan." In *Narben des Gesamtkunstwerks: Wagners "Ring des Nibelungen,"* ed. Richard Klein, 103–32. Munich: Wilhelm Fink, 2001.

———. "Gebrochene Temporalität: Die Revolution der musikalischen Zeit im *Ring des Nibelungen*." In *Narben des Gesamtkunstwerks: Wagners "Ring des Nibelungen,"* ed. Richard Klein, 169–214. Munich: Wilhelm Fink, 2001.

———, ed. *Narben des Gesamtkunstwerks: Wagners "Ring des Nibelungen*." Munich: Wilhelm Fink, 2001.

———. "Rausch und Zeit in Wagners *Ring*." In *Trunkenheit: Kulturen des Rausches*, ed. Thomas Strässle and Simon Zumsteg, 101–25. Amsterdam: Rodopi, 2008.

———. "Wagners plurale Moderne: Eine Konstruktion des Unvereinbaren." In *Richard Wagner: Konstrukteur der Moderne*, ed. Claus-Steffen Mahnkopf, 185–225. Stuttgart: Klett-Cotta, 1999.

———. "Walkürenritt in Vietnam? Zu Francis Coppolas Wagner." In *Martin Geck: Festschrift zum 65. Geburtstag*, ed. Ares Rolf and Ulrich Tadday, 409–17. Dortmund: Klangfarben, 2001.

Klenke, Dietmar. *Der singende "deutsche Mann": Gesangsvereine und deutsches Nationalbewußtsein von Napoleon bis Hitler*. Münster: Waxmann, 1998.

Kloss, Erich, ed. *Briefwechsel zwischen Wagner und Liszt*. 3rd ed. Leipzig: Breitkopf & Härtel, 1910.

———, ed. *Richard Wagner an seine Künstler*. Berlin: Schuster & Loeffler, 1908.

Knust, Martin. *Sprachvertonung und Gestik in den Werken Richard Wagners: Einflüsse zeitgenössischer Rezitations- und Deklamationspraxis*. Berlin: Frank & Timme, 2007.

Koch, Max. *Richard Wagners geschichtliche völkische Sendung*. Langensalza: Beyer & Söhne, 1927.

Körner, Hans. *Botticelli*. Cologne: DuMont, 2006.

Kramer, Bernd. *"Laßt uns die Schwerter ziehen, damit die Kette bricht . . .": Michael Bakunin, Richard Wagner und andere während der Dresdner Mai-Revolution 1849*. Berlin: Karin Kramer Verlag, 1999.

Kramer, Lawrence. *Opera and Modern Culture: Wagner and Strauss*. Berkeley: University of California Press, 2004.

Kranz, Dieter. "Sinnlichkeit durch Aussparung." *Opernwelt* 45 (Jan. 2004): 18.

Kreim, Isabella. "Richard Wagners *Lohengrin* auf der deutschen Bühne und in der Kritik." PhD diss., University of Munich, 1983.

Kristeva, Julia. *Revolution in Poetic Language*. Translated by Margaret Waller. New York: Columbia University Press, 1984.

Kropfinger, Klaus. *Wagner und Beethoven*. Regensburg: Gustav Bosse, 1975. Translated by Peter Palmer as *Wagner and Beethoven: Richard Wagner's Reception of Beethoven*. Cambridge: Cambridge University Press, 1991.

———. "Wagners 'Entsagungs'-Motiv." In *Das musikalische Kunstwerk: Geschichte, Ästhetik, Theorie; Festschrift Carl Dahlhaus zum 60. Geburtstag*, ed. Hermann Danuser and others, 241–58. Laaber: Laaber-Verlag, 1988.

Kubizek, August. *Adolf Hitler: Mein Jugendfreund*, 6th ed. Graz: Leopold Stocker, 1995. Translated by E. V. Anderson as *Young Hitler: The Story of Our Friendship*. Maidstone: George Mann, 1973.

Kühn, Dieter. *Tristan und Isolde des Gottfried von Straßburg*. Frankfurt: Fischer, 2003.

Kühnel, Jürgen. *Parsifal: Erlösung dem Erlöser; Von der Aufhebung des Christentums in das Kunstwerk Richard Wagners*. Siegen: Richard-Wagner-Verband, 1982.

Kupfer, Harry. "'Denken Sie an die Seeräuber-Jenny!' Ein Gespräch mit Harry Kupfer," In *Der fliegende Holländer: Romantische Oper in drei Aufzügen*, ed. Staatsoper Unter den Linden Berlin, 25–32. Frankfurt: Insel, 2001.

———. "We Must Finally Stop Apologizing for *Die Meistersinger!*" In *Wagner's "Meistersinger": Performance, History, Representation*, ed. Nicholas Vazsonyi, 39–49. Rochester: University of Rochester Press, 2003.

Kurth, Ernst. *Romantische Harmonik und ihre Krise in Wagners "Tristan."* Berlin: Max Hesse, 1923.

Lachmann, Karl, ed. *Wolfram von Eschenbach*. 6th ed. Berlin: Walter de Gruyter, 1926. Translated by Cyril Edwards as *Parzival*. Cambridge: D. S. Brewer, 2004

La Grange, Henry-Louis de, and Günther Weiß, eds. *Ein Glück ohne Ruh': Die Briefe Gustav Mahlers an Alma*. Berlin: Siedler, 1995. Translated by Antony Beaumont as *Gustav Mahler: Letters to His Wife*. London: Faber and Faber, 2004.

Langbehn, Julius. *Langbehns Lieder*. Hamburg: tradition, 2011.

Lassalle, Ferdinand. *Nachgelassene Briefe und Schriften*. 6 vols. Edited by Gustav Mayer. Stuttgart: Deutsche Verlags-Anstalt, 1921–25.

Lees, Heath. *Mallarmé and Wagner: Music and Poetic Language.* Aldershot: Ashgate, 2007.

Lehmann, Lilli. *Mein Weg.* 2nd ed. Leipzig: S. Hirzel, 1920. Translated by Alice Benedict Seligman as *My Path through Life.* New York: G. P. Putnam's Sons, 1914.

Leonardo da Vinci, *Treatise on Painting.* Translated by John Francis Rigaud. London: J. B. Nichols and Son, 1835.

Lévi-Strauss, Claude. "De Chrétien de Troyes à Richard Wagner." In *Die Programmhefte der Bayreuther Festspiele,* vol. 1, *Parsifal,* 1–9, 60–67. Translated by T. A. Willcocks as "From Chrétien de Troyes to Richard Wagner," ibid., 22–26, 41–45. Bayreuth: Emil Mühl, 1975.

―――. "Intervista a cura di Marco d'Eramo." *Mondoperaio: Revista Socialisti* 2 (1979): 118–24. Translated by Max Looser as "Die strukturalistische Tätigkeit." In *Mythos und Bedeutung: Fünf Radiovorträge,* ed. Adelbert Reif, 252–74. Frankfurt: Suhrkamp, 1980.

Link-Heer, Ursula. "Der 'androgyne Wagner' und die Dramaturgie des Blicks." In *"Das Weib der Zukunft": Frauengestalten und Frauenstimmen bei Richard Wagner,* ed. Susanne Vill, 84–94. Stuttgart: J. B. Metzler, 2000.

Linnenbrügger, Jörg. *Richard Wagners "Die Meistersinger von Nürnberg": Studien und Materialien zur Entstehungsgeschichte des ersten Aufzugs (1861–1866).* 2 vols. Göttingen: Vandenhoeck & Ruprecht, 2001.

Liszt, Franz. *Sämtliche Schriften.* 9 vols. Edited by Detlef Altenburg and others. Wiesbaden: Breitkopf & Härtel, 1989―.

Mäckelmann, Michael. *Arnold Schönberg und das Judentum: Der Komponist und sein religiöses, nationales und politisches Selbstverständnis nach 1921.* Hamburg: Wagner, 1984.

Magee, Bryan. *The Tristan Chord: Wagner and Philosophy.* New York: Metropolitan Books, 2001.

Magee, Elizabeth. *Richard Wagner and the Nibelungs.* Oxford: Clarendon Press, 1990.

Mahler, Gustav. *Briefe.* Edited by Herta Blaukopf. Vienna: Paul Zsolnay, 1996. Translated by Eithne Wilkins and others as *Selected Letters of Gustav Mahler.* London: Faber and Faber, 1979.

Mahnkopf, Claus-Steffen. "Haß und Rache: Zum II. Akt der *Götterdämmerung.*" In *Narben des Gesamtkunstwerks: Wagners "Ring des Nibelungen,"* ed. Richard Klein, 231–36. Munich: Wilhelm Fink, 2001.

―――. "*Tristan*-Studien." In *Richard Wagner: Konstrukteur der Moderne,* ed. Claus-Steffen Mahnkopf, 67–127. Stuttgart: Klett-Cotta, 1999.

―――. "Wagners Kompositionstechnik." In *Richard Wagner: Konstrukteur der Moderne,* ed. Claus-Steffen Mahnkopf, 159–82. Stuttgart: Klett-Cotta, 1999.

Mallarmé, Stéphane. *Œuvres complètes.* Edited by Henri Mondor and G. Jean-Aubry, Paris: Gallimard, 1945.

Mallet, Robert, ed. *André Gide–Paul Valéry: Correspondance 1890–1942.* Paris: Gallimard, 1955.

Mann, Heinrich. *Der Untertan.* Hamburg: Claassen, 1961.

Mann, Thomas. *Buddenbrooks: Verfall einer Familie,* Frankfurt: Fischer, 1960. Translated by H. T. Lowe-Porter as *Buddenbrooks.* London: Vintage Books, 1999.

―――. *Tagebücher 1918–1921.* Edited by Inge Jens. Frankfurt: Fischer, 1979.

―――. *Tagebücher 1940–1943.* Edited by Peter de Mendelssohn. Frankfurt: Fischer, 1982.

Marquard, Odo. "Kunst als Antifiktion―Versuch über den Weg der Wirklichkeit ins Fiktive." In *Funktionen des Fiktiven,* ed. Dieter Henrich and Wolfgang Iser, 35–54. Munich: Wilhelm Fink, 1983.

Mattenklott, Gert. "Unwiderstehliche Mimik: Valéry über Wagner." In *Die Symbolisten und Richard Wagner*, ed. Wolfgang Storch, 175–78. Berlin: Hentrich, 1991.

Mayer, Hans. *Ein Denkmal für Johannes Brahms: Versuche über Musik und Literatur*. 2nd ed. Frankfurt: Suhrkamp, 1993.

———. *Richard Wagner*. Edited by Wolfgang Hofer. Frankfurt: Suhrkamp, 1998.

———. *Richard Wagner: Mitwelt und Nachwelt*. Stuttgart: Belser, 1978.

Meier, Mischa. *Richard Wagners "Der Ring des Nibelungen" und die griechische Antike: Zum Stand der Diskussion*. Göttingen: Vandenhoeck & Ruprecht, 2005.

Meißner, Alfred. *Geschichte meines Lebens*. 2 vols. Vienna: Karl Prochaska, 1884.

Mendelssohn Bartholdy, Paul, and Carl Mendelssohn Bartholdy, eds. *Briefe aus den Jahren 1830 bis 1847 von Felix Mendelssohn Bartholdy*. Leipzig: Hermann Mendelssohn, 1870.

Mertens, Volker. "Richard Wagner und das Mittelalter," In *Richard-Wagner-Handbuch*, ed. Müller and Wapnewski, 19–59. Translated by Stewart Spencer as "Wagner's Middle Ages." In *Wagner Handbook*, ed. Deathridge, 236–68.

Meyerbeer, Giacomo. *Briefwechsel und Tagebücher*. 8 vols. Edited by Heinz Becker and others. Berlin: Walter de Gruyter, 1960–2006.

Miller, Norbert. "Große Oper und Historiengemälde: Überlegungen zur Zusammenarbeit von Eugène Scribe und Giacomo Meyerbeer." In *Oper und Operntext*, ed. Jens Malte Fischer, 45–80. Heidelberg: Winter, 1985.

Minor, Ryan. "Wagner's Last Chorus: Consecrating Space and Spectatorship in *Parsifal*." *Cambridge Opera Journal* 17 (2005): 1–36.

ML: *See* Wagner, Richard. *Mein Leben*.

Mösch, Stephan. *Weihe, Werkstatt, Wirklichkeit: "Parsifal" in Bayreuth 1882–1933*. Kassel: Bärenreiter, 2009.

Mozart, Wolfgang Amadeus. *Briefe und Aufzeichnungen*. Edited by Wilhelm A. Bauer and others. 8 vols. Kassel: Bärenreiter, 1962–2005.

Müller, Thomas. "Orchesterpsychogramm: Das Vorspiel zum III. Akt des *Parsifal*." In *Richard Wagner und seine Zeit*, ed. Eckehard Kiem and Ludwig Holtmeier, 291–305. Laaber: Laaber-Verlag, 2003.

Müller, Ulrich, and Peter Wapnewski, eds. *Richard-Wagner-Handbuch*. Stuttgart: Alfred Kröner, 1986. Translated as *Wagner Handbook*, ed. John Deathridge. Cambridge, MA: Harvard University Press, 1992.

Münster, Arno. *Utopie, Messianismus und Apokalypse im Frühwerk von Ernst Bloch*. Frankfurt: Suhrkamp, 1982.

Musil, Robert. *Der Mann ohne Eigenschaften*. 2 vols. Edited by Adolf Frisé. Reinbek: Rowohlt, 2002. Translated by Sophie Wilkins and Burton Pike as *The Man without Qualities*. London: Picador, 1995.

Nagel, Ivan. *Gemälde und Drama: Giotto, Masaccio, Leonardo*. Frankfurt: Suhrkamp, 2009.

Neuenfels, Hans. *Wie viel Musik braucht der Mensch? Über Oper und Komponisten*. Munich: Pantheon, 2011.

Neumann, Angelo. *Erinnerungen an Richard Wagner*. Leipzig: Staackmann, 1907.

Newman, Ernest. *A Study of Wagner*. New York: G. P. Putnam's Sons, 1899.

Nietzsche, Friedrich. *Basic Writings of Nietzsche*. Translated by Walter Kaufmann. New York: Modern Library, 1968.

———. *Human, All Too Human*. Translated by R. J. Hollingdale. Cambridge: Cambridge University Press, 1996.

———. *The Portable Nietzsche*. Translated by Walter Kaufmann. New York: Penguin, 1982.

————. *Sämtliche Briefe: Kritische Studienausgabe in 8 Bänden*. Edited by Giorgio Colli and Mazzino Montinari. Munich: Deutscher Taschenbuch Verlag, 1986.

————. *Sämtliche Werke: Kritische Studienausgabe in 15 Einzelbänden*. Edited by Giorgio Colli and Mazzino Montinari. Munich: Deutscher Taschenbuch Verlag, 1988.

————. *Selected Letters of Friedrich Nietzsche*. Translated by Christopher Middleton. Indianapolis: Hackett, 1996.

————. *Untimely Meditations*, trans. R. J. Hollingdale. Cambridge: Cambridge University Press, 1983.

Nilges, Yvonne. "*Die Meistersinger von Nürnberg* oder Die Geburt der musikalischen Komödie aus dem Geiste Shakespeares." *wagnerspectrum* 3, no. 1 (2007): 7–34.

Novotny, Fritz, and Johannes Dobai. *Gustav Klimt*. Salzburg: Galerie Welz, 1967.

Otto, Rudolf. *The Idea of the Holy*. Translated by John Wilfred Harvey. London: H. Milford, 1923.

Padover, Saul K., ed. *The Letters of Karl Marx*. Englewood Cliffs, NJ: Prentice Hall, 1979.

Palm, Helga-Maria. *Richard Wagners "Lohengrin": Studien zur Sprachbehandlung*. Munich: Wilhelm Fink, 1987.

Perlwitz, Ronald. "Wagner-Rezeption in *À la recherche du temps perdu*: Ein deutscher Komponist in einem französischen Roman; Okkultierung und Evidenz." In *Die Macht der Differenzen: Beiträge zur Hermeneutik der Kultur*, ed. Reinhard Düssel and others, 327–68. Heidelberg: Synchron, 2001.

Plumpe, Gerhard, ed. *Theorie des bürgerlichen Realismus*. Stuttgart: Reclam, 1985.

Porges, Heinrich. *Wagner Rehearsing the "Ring": An Eye-Witness Account of the Stage Rehearsals of the First Bayreuth Festival*. Translated by Robert L. Jacobs. Cambridge: Cambridge University Press, 1983.

Proust, Marcel. *À la recherche du temps perdu*. 3 vols. Edited by Pierre Clarac and André Ferré. Paris: Gallimard, 1973–77. Translated by C. K. Scott Moncrieff and Terence Kilmartin as *In Search of Lost Time*. 6 vols. Revised by D. J. Enright. London: Folio Society, 2000.

PW: *See* Wagner, Richard. *Richard Wagner's Prose Works*.

Rathert, Wolfgang. "Schönberg und der Kontrapunkt." In *Philosophie des Kontrapunkts*, ed. Ulrich Tadday, 121–34. Munich: edition text + kritik, 2010 (= Musik-Konzepte: Sonderband).

Renggli, Hanspeter. "'Das drollige Geblase im Kopfe': Schweizer Folklore in Richard Wagners *Tristan* oder Von der Zwiespältigkeit Wagnerscher Ursprungsmythen." In *Schweizer Töne: Die Schweiz im Spiegel der Musik*, ed. Anselm Gerhard, 107–21. Zurich: Chronos, 2002.

Rieger, Eva. *Minna und Richard Wagner: Stationen einer Liebe*. Düsseldorf: Patmos, 2003.

Riemann, Hugo. *Geschichte der Musik seit Beethoven*. Berlin: Spemann, 1901.

Rienäcker, Gerd. *Richard Wagner: Nachdenken über sein "Gewebe."* Berlin: Lukas-Verlag, 2001.

Rihm, Wolfgang. "Gespräch mit George Steiner." *Sinn und Form* 57 (2005): 42.

Rose, Paul Lawrence. "One of Wagner's Jewish Friends: Berthold Auerbach and His Unpublished Reply to Richard Wagner's Antisemitism (1881)." *Leo Baeck Institute Year Book* 36 (1991): 219–28.

Rubow, Markus, and Susanne Rump. "Das wandelnde Bayreuth: Das Richard Wagner-Theater Angelo Neumanns." In *Der Ring des Nibelungen in Münster: Der Zyklus von 1999 bis 2001*, ed. Klaus Hortschansky and Berthold Warnecke, 191–203. Münster: Agenda Verlag, 2001.

San-Marte, ed. *Parcival: Rittergedicht von Wolfram von Eschenbach: Aus dem Mittelhochdeutschen zum ersten Male übersetzt von San-Marte*. 2 vols. Magdeburg: Verlag der Creutz'schen Buchhandlung, 1836.

Sattler, Bernhard, ed. *Adolf von Hildebrand und seine Welt: Briefe und Erinnerungen*. Munich: Callwey, 1962.

SB: *See* Wagner, Richard. *Sämtliche Briefe*.

Scheier, Claus-Artur. *Ästhetik der Simulation: Formen des Produktionsdenkens im 19. Jahrhundert*. Hamburg: Meiner, 2000.

Schenker, Heinrich. *Neue Musikalische Theorien und Phantasien*, vol. 3: *Der freie Satz*. 2nd ed. Vienna: Universal-Edition, 1935.

Schickling, Dieter. *Abschied von Walhall: Richard Wagners erotische Gesellschaft*. Stuttgart: Deutsche Verlags-Anstalt, 1983.

Schild, Wolfgang. "Hegel und Wagner." In *Der Grund, die Not und die Freude des Bewußtseins: Beiträge zum Internationalen Symposion in Venedig zu Ehren von Wolfgang Marx*, ed. Martin Asiáin and others, 157–84. Würzburg: Königshausen & Neumann, 2002.

Schleef, Einar. *Droge—Faust—Parsifal*. Frankfurt: Suhrkamp, 1997.

Schleiermacher, Friedrich. *Pädagogische Schriften*. 2 vols. Edited by Theodor Schulze and Erich Weniger. Düsseldorf: Küpper, 1957.

Schleuning, Peter. *Der Bürger erhebt sich: Geschichte der deutschen Musik im 18. Jahrhundert*. 2nd ed. Stuttgart: J. B. Metzler, 2000.

Schmid, Carlo, Pierre Boulez, and Patrice Chéreau. "Mythologie und Ideologie: Gedankenaustausch über die Neuinszenierung 'Der Ring des Nibelungen' 1976." In *Bayreuther Dramaturgie: Der Ring des Nibelungen*, ed. Herbert Barth, 375–402. Stuttgart: Belser, 1980.

Schmid, Manfred Hermann. "Metamorphose der Themen: Beobachtungen an den Skizzen zum 'Lohengrin'-Vorspiel." *Die Musikforschung* 41 (1988): 105–26.

Schmid-Reiter, Isolde, ed. *Richard Wagners "Der Ring des Nibelungen": Europäische Traditionen und Paradigmen*. Regensburg: ConBrio Verlagsgesellschaft, 2010.

Schnädelbach, Herbert. "'Ring' und Mythos." In *In den Trümmern der eignen Welt: Richard Wagners "Der Ring des Nibelungen,"* ed. Udo Bermbach, 145–61. Berlin: Dietrich Reimer, 1989.

Schoenberg, Arnold. *Style and Idea*. Edited by Leonard Stein. Translated by Leo Black. Berkeley: University of California Press, 1984.

Schopenhauer, Arthur. *Parerga and Paralipomena*. 2 vols. Translated by E. F. J. Payne. Oxford: Clarendon Press, 1974.

———. *Werke in fünf Bänden: Nach den Ausgaben letzter Hand*. Edited by Ludger Lütkehaus. Zurich: Haffmans Verlag, 1988.

———. *The World as Will and Representation*. 2 vols. Translated by E. F. J. Payne. New York: Dover, 1969.

Schreiber, Ulrich. *Opernführer für Fortgeschrittene: Das 19. Jahrhundert*. 3rd ed. Kassel: Bärenreiter, 2002.

Schubert, Bernhard. "Wagners 'Sachs' und die Tradition des romantischen Künstlerver-ständnisses." *Archiv für Musikwissenschaft* 40 (1983): 212–53.

Schuh, Willi. *Renoir und Wagner*. Erlenbach: Eugen Rentsch Verlag, 1959.

———. *Richard Strauss, Hugo von Hofmannsthal. Briefwechsel*. 5th ed. Zurich: Atlantis, 1978. Translated by Hanns Hammelmann and Ewald Osers as *The Correspondence between Richard Strauss and Hugo von Hofmannsthal*. Cambridge: Cambridge University Press, 1980.

Schweitzer, Albert. *My Life and Thought: An Autobiography*. Translated by C. T. Campion. London: George Allen & Unwin, 1933.

Scruton, Roger. *Death-Devoted Heart: Sex and the Sacred in Wagner's "Tristan und Isolde."* Oxford: Oxford University Press, 2004.

Seidl, Arthur. "Richard Wagners 'Parsifal' und Schopenhauers 'Nirwana': Ein Jubiläumsbeitrag (1883–88)." In Seidl, *Richard Wagners Parsifal: Zwei Abhandlungen.* Regensburg: Gustav Bosse, n.d.

Shaw, George Bernard. *The Perfect Wagnerite: A Commentary on the Niblung's Ring.* 4th ed. London: Constable, 1923.

Shostakovich, Dimitri. *Testimony: The Memoirs of Dimitri Shostakovich as Related to and Edited by Solomon Volkov.* Translated by Antonia W. Bouis. London: Faber and Faber, 1979.

Sloterdijk, Peter. *Thinker on Stage: Nietzsche's Materialism.* Translated by Jamie Owen Daniel. Minneapolis: University of Minnesota Press, 1989.

Spotts, Frederic. *Hitler and the Power of Aesthetics.* London: Hutchinson, 2002.

SSD: *See* Wagner, Richard. *Sämtliche Schriften und Dichtungen.*

Steinacker, Peter. *Richard Wagner und die Religion.* Darmstadt: Wissenschaftliche Buchgesellschaft, 2008.

Steinbeck, Wolfram. "Zur Formfrage in Wagners *Ring des Nibelungen.*" In *Richard Wagners "Ring des Nibelungen": Musikalische Dramaturgie—Kulturelle Kontextualität—Primär-Rezeption,* ed. Klaus Hortschansky, 279–97. Schneverdingen: Wagner, 2004.

Steiner, George. *Errata: An Examined Life.* London: Weidenfeld & Nicolson, 1997.

———. *Grammars of Creation.* London: Faber and Faber, 2001.

———. "Melodien für Millionen: Über das schwierige und intime Verhältnis von Musik und Politik." *Süddeutsche Zeitung* (Sept. 1, 1998).

———. "Vom Schicksal Europas: Über die Erschöpfung oder die Renaissance eines geistigen Elans (Gespräch mit Olivier Mongin)." *Lettre International* 64 (2004): 26–30.

Strecker, Ludwig. *Richard Wagner als Verlagsgefährte.* Mainz: B. Schott's Söhne, 1951.

Strindberg, August. *Miss Julie.* Translated by Michael Meyer. London: Methuen, 2009.

Strobel, Otto, ed. *König Ludwig II. und Richard Wagner: Briefwechsel.* 5 vols. Karlsruhe: G. Braun, 1936–39.

Stuckenschmidt, H. H. *Schoenberg: His Life, World and Work.* Translated by Humphrey Searle. New York: Schirmer, 1978.

SW: *See* Wagner, Richard. *Sämtliche Werke.*

Taruskin, Richard. *Stravinsky and the Russian Traditions.* 2 vols. Berkeley: University of California Press, 1996.

Taylor, Charles. *A Secular Age.* Cambridge, MA: Belknap Press, 2007.

Tenschert, Roland. "Richard Wagner im Urteil von Richard Strauss: Aus Briefen und mündlichen Äußerungen des Meisters," *Schweizerische Musikzeitung* 46 (1954): 328.

Thomä, Dieter. *Totalität und Mitleid: Richard Wagner, Sergej Eisenstein und unsere ethisch-ästhetische Moderne.* Frankfurt: Suhrkamp, 2006.

———. "Umwertungen der Dekadenz: Korrespondenzen zwischen Richard Wagner, Friedrich Nietzsche und Sergej Eisenstein." In *Nietzsche und Wagner: Geschichte und Aktualität eines Kulturkonfliktes,* ed. Aram Mattioli and Enno Rudolph, 103–37. Zurich: Orell Füssli, 2008.

Thorau, Christian. *Semantisierte Sinnlichkeit: Studien zu Rezeption und Zeichenstruktur der Leitmotivtechnik Richard Wagners.* Stuttgart: Franz Steiner, 2003.

Tolzmann, Don Heinrich, ed. *Thomas Mann's Addresses Delivered at the Library of Congress.* Oxford: Peter Lang, 2003.

Treadwell, James. "The *Ring* and the Conditions of Interpretation: Wagner's Writing, 1848 to 1852." *Cambridge Opera Journal* 7 (1995): 207–31.

Urban, Petra. *Liebesdämmerung: Ein psychoanalytischer Versuch über Richard Wagners "Tristan und Isolde."* Eschborn: Dietmar Klotz, 1991.

Urmoneit, Sebastian. *Tristan und Isolde: Eros und Thanatos; Zur "dichterischen Deutlichkeit" der Harmonik von Richard Wagners "Handlung" "Tristan und Isolde."* Sinzig: Studio, 2005.

Vaget, Hans Rudolf. "'Du warst mein Feind von je': The Beckmesser Controversy Revisited." In *Wagner's "Meistersinger": Performance, History, Reception,* ed. Nicholas Vazsonyi, 190–208. Rochester: University of Rochester Press, 2002.

———, ed. *Im Schatten Wagners: Thomas Mann über Richard Wagner; Texte und Zeugnisse, 1895–1955.* 2nd ed. Frankfurt: Fischer, 2005. Partially translated by Allan Blunden as Thomas Mann, *Pro and Contra Wagner.* London: Faber and Faber, 1985.

———. "Wehvolles Erbe: Zur 'Metapolitik' der *Meistersinger von Nürnberg.*" *Musik & Ästhetik* 6 (2002): 23–39.

Valéry, Paul. *Rhumbs.* Paris: Gallimard, 1933.

Varnhagen von Ense, Karl August. *Tageblätter.* Edited by Konrad Feilchenfeldt. Frankfurt: Deutscher Klassiker Verlag, 1994.

Vetter, Isolde. "'Leubald, ein Trauerspiel': Richard Wagners erstes (erhaltenes) Werk." In *Die Programmhefte der Bayreuther Festspiele,* vol. 7: *Die Meistersinger von Nürnberg,* ed. Matthias Theodor Vogt, 1–19, 95–208. Bayreuth: Emil Mühl, 1988.

Vill, Susanne. "Erda: Mythische Quellen und musikalische Gestaltung." In *"Alles ist nach seiner Art": Figuren in Richard Wagners "Der Ring des Nibelungen,"* ed. Udo Bermbach, 198–224. Stuttgart: J. B. Metzler, 2001.

Vordtriede, Werner. *Novalis und die französischen Symbolisten: Zur Entstehungsgeschichte des dichterischen Symbols.* Stuttgart: Kohlhammer, 1963.

———. "Richard Wagners 'Tod in Venedig.'" *Euphorion* 52 (1958): 378–96.

Voss, Egon. "Die 'schwarze und die weiße Flagge': Zur Entstehung von Wagners 'Tristan.'" *Archiv für Musikwissenschaft* 54 (1997): 210–27.

———. "Die Wesendoncks und Richard Wagner." In *Minne, Muse und Mäzen: Otto und Mathilde Wesendonck und ihr Zürcher Künstlerzirkel,* ed. Axel Langer and Chris Walton, 117–29. Zurich: Museum Rietberg, 2002.

———. "Einflüsse Rossinis und Bellinis auf das Werk Wagners." In *Richard Wagner und seine "Lehrmeister,"* ed. Christoph-Hellmut Mahling and Kristina Pfarr, 95–118. Mainz: Are Edition, 1999.

———, ed. *Richard Wagner: Die Walküre (Textbuch).* Stuttgart: Reclam, 1997.

———. "Siegfrieds Musik." In *Das musikalische Kunstwerk: Geschichte, Ästhetik, Theorie; Festschrift Carl Dahlhaus zum 60. Geburtstag,* ed. Hermann Danuser and others, 259–68. Laaber: Laaber-Verlag, 1988.

———. "Wagners 'Meistersinger' als Oper des deutschen Bürgertums." In *Richard Wagner: Die Meistersinger von Nürnberg; Texte, Materialien, Kommentare,* ed. Attila Csampai and Dietmar Holland, 9–31. Reinbek: Rowohlt, 1981.

———. "Wagners 'Tristan': 'Die Liebe als furchtbare Qual.'" In *Richard Wagner: Tristan und Isolde; Texte, Materialien, Kommentare,* ed. Attila Csampai and Dietmar Holland, 101–11. Reinbek: Rowohlt, 1983.

———. *"Wagner und kein Ende": Betrachtungen und Studien.* Zurich: Atlantis, 1996.

Wagner, Nike. "'Dem Traum entgegenschwimmen'. Zu Richard Wagners *Tristan und Isolde.*" In *O, sink hernieder, Nacht der Liebe: Tristan und Isolde; Der Mythos von Liebe und Tod,* ed. Sabine Borris and Christiane Krautscheid, 45–71. Berlin: Parthas, 1998.

———. "'Es war ein Verhältnis': Thomas Mann und Richard Wagner." In *Vom weltläufigen Erzählen: Die Vorträge des [Thomas-Mann-]Kongresses in Zürich 2006,* ed. Manfred Papst and Thomas Sprecher, 43–62. Frankfurt: Vittorio Klostermann, 2007.

———. *Wagner Theater.* Frankfurt: Insel, 1998. Translated by Ewald Osers and Michael

Downes as *The Wagners: The Dramas of a Musical Dynasty*. London: Weidenfeld & Nicolson, 1998.

———. "Wotan, eine Warnung." In *Narben des Gesamtkunstwerks: Wagners "Ring des Nibelungen,"* ed. Richard Klein, 265–72. Munich: Wilhelm Fink, 2001.

Wagner, Richard. *Das Braune Buch: Tagebuchaufzeichnungen 1865 bis 1882*. Edited by Joachim Bergfeld. Zurich: Atlantis, 1975. Translated by George Bird as *The Diary of Richard Wagner, 1865–1882: The Brown Book*. London: Victor Gollancz, 1980. (Abbreviated BB)

———. *Die Meistersinger von Nürnberg: Faksimile der Reinschrift des Textbuchs von 1862*. Edited by Egon Voss. Mainz: Schott, 1983.

———. *Entwürfe, Gedanken, Fragmente: Aus nachgelassenen Papieren zusammengestellt*. Leipzig: Breitkopf & Härtel, 1885.

———. *Gesammelte Schriften und Dichtungen*. 4th ed. 10 vols. Leipzig: C. F. W. Siegel's Musikalienhandlung, 1907. (Abbreviated GS)

———. *Jesus von Nazareth: Ein dichterischer Entwurf aus dem Jahre 1848*. Leipzig: Breitkopf & Härtel, 1887.

———. *Mein Leben*. Edited by Martin Gregor-Dellin. Munich: List, 1976. Translated by Andrew Gray as *My Life*, ed. Mary Whittall. Cambridge: Cambridge University Press, 1983. (Abbreviated ML)

———. *Richard Wagner's Prose Works*. 8 vols., trans. William Ashton Ellis. London: Kegan Paul, Trench, & Trübner, 1893–99. (Abbreviated PW)

———. *Sämtliche Briefe*. 30 vols. Edited by Gertrud Strobel and others. Leipzig: VEB Deutscher Verlag für Musik, 1967–2000 and Wiesbaden: Breitkopf & Härtel, 1999–. (Abbreviated SB)

———. *Sämtliche Werke*. 31 vols. Edited by Carl Dahlhaus and others. Mainz: Schott, 1970–. (Abbreviated SW)

———. *Sämtliche Schriften und Dichtungen: Volks-Ausgabe*. 16 vols. Leipzig: Breitkopf & Härtel, [1911–14]. (Abbreviated SSD)

Wagner, Siegfried. *Erinnerungen*. Stuttgart: J. Engelhorns Nachfolger, 1923.

Walter, Michael. *Hugenotten-Studien*. Frankfurt: Peter Lang, 1987.

Wapnewski, Peter. *Der traurige Gott: Richard Wagner in seinen Helden*. 2nd ed. Berlin: Berlin Verlag, 2001.

———. "Die Oper Richard Wagners als Dichtung." In *Richard-Wagner-Handbuch*, ed. Ulrich Müller and Peter Wapnewski, 223–352. Translated by Peter Palmer as "The Operas as Literary Works." In *Wagner Handbook*, ed. John Deathridge, 3–95. Cambridge, MA: Harvard University Press, 1992.

———. *Die Szene und ihr Meister*. 2nd ed. Munich: C. H. Beck, 1983.

Weber, Samuel. "Der *Ring* als Dekonstruktion der Moderne: Wagner mit Benjamin." In *Narben des Gesamtkunstwerks: Wagners "Ring des Nibelungen,"* ed. Richard Klein, 65–79. Munich: Wilhelm Fink, 2001.

Wehrli, Max. *Literatur im deutschen Mittelalter*. Stuttgart: Reclam, 1984.

Wellek, René. *A History of Modern Criticism, 1750–1950*. Vol. 4, *The Later Nineteenth Century*. London: Jonathan Cape, 1966.

Wellmer, Albrecht. "Werke und ihre Wirkungen: Kein Beitrag zur Rezeptionstheorie des Musiktheaters." In *Zukunftsbilder: Richard Wagners Revolution und ihre Folgen in Kunst und Politik*, ed. Hermann Danuser and Herfried Münkler, 257–73. Schliengen: Edition Argus, 2002.

Wesendonck, Mathilde. "Erinnerungen." *Allgemeine Deutsche Musik-Zeitung* 23, no. 7 (1896): 91–94.

Westernhagen, Curt. *Richard Wagner: Sein Werk, sein Wesen, seine Welt.* Zurich: Atlantis, 1956.

White, Hayden. *Tropics of Discourse: Essays in Cultural Criticism.* Baltimore: John Hopkins University Press, 1978.

Wille, Eliza. *Richard Wagner an Eliza Wille: Fünfzehn Briefe des Meisters nebst Erinnerungen und Erläuterungen von Eliza Wille.* Berlin: Schuster & Loeffler, 1908.

Wind, Edgar. *Pagan Mysteries in the Renaissance.* New Haven: Yale University Press, 1958.

Wintle, Christopher. "The Numinous in *Götterdämmerung.*" In *Reading Opera,* ed. Arthur Groos and Roger Parker, 200–234. Princeton: Princeton University Press, 1988.

Wolzogen, Hans von. *Erinnerungen an Richard Wagner.* 2nd ed. Leipzig: Philipp Reclam, 1891.

WWV: *See* Deathridge, Geck, and Voss, eds. *Wagner Werk-Verzeichnis.*

Zelinsky, Hartmut. "Rettung ins Ungenaue: Zu Martin Gregor-Dellins Wagner-Biographie." In *Richard Wagner: Parsifal,* ed. Heinz-Klaus Metzger and Rainer Riehn, 74–115. Munich: edition text + kritik, 1982 (= Musik-Konzepte 25).

Žižek, Slavoj. "'There Is No Sexual Relationship': Wagner as a Lacanian." *New German Critique* 69 (1996): 7–35.

Žižek, Slavoj, and Mladen Dolar. *Opera's Second Death.* New York: Routledge, 2002.

Zuber, Barbara. "Theater mit den Ohren betrachtet: Klangstruktur und Dramaturgie in Wagners *Lohengrin.*" In *"Die Wirklichkeit erfinden ist besser": Opern des 19. Jahrhunderts von Beethoven bis Verdi,* ed. Hanspeter Krellmann and Jürgen Schläder, 96–102. Stuttgart: J. B. Metzler, 2002.

Zurmühl, Sabine. "Brünnhilde—Tochter im Tode im Leben: Eine feministische Interpretation." In *In den Trümmern der eignen Welt: Richard Wagners "Der Ring des Nibelungen,"* ed. Udo Bermbach, 181–200. Berlin: Dietrich Reimer, 1989.

GENERAL INDEX

RW = Richard Wagner
WWV = *Wagner Werk-Verzeichnis*

Abbate, Carolyn (b. 1955): on Brünnhilde's peroration, 309; on Tannhäuser's Narration, 89; on Wotan's Narration, 212

Abend-Zeitung, 65

Aberbach, David Alan (1932–2010), 134

Adam, Adolphe (1803–56), 371n20

Adorno, Theodor W. (1903–69), xiv, 313, 315–17; ambivalence toward RW, 255, 315–17; as disappointed admirer, xvii; on the ending of the *Ring*, 306; innovation in *Parsifal*, 333; phantasmagoria, 79, 315, 362, 364; on the prelude to *Das Rheingold*, 178, 179; sonority in *Tannhäuser*, 85; on Tannhäuser's Rome Narration, 89; and "untruthfulness" in *Tannhäuser*, 86

Writings: *In Search of Wagner*, 315–17, 398n1; *Minima moralia*, 104; "Postscript to a Discussion on Wagner," 306

Aeschylus (525–456 BC), 103, 151, 159, 161, 359

Works: *Oresteia*, 133; *Prometheus*, 159

Ahasuerus myth, 17, 50, 51, 71, 81, 288, 345

Albert, Josef (1825–86), 172

Amsterdam, 170

anti-Semitism: as a nineteenth-century phenomenon, 93, 162, 289, 320, 322, 353; its relationship to Wagner's music dramas, xvi–xvii, 285–87, 326, 328; and Schoenberg, 124; in Wagner's life, 18, 94, 100, 144, 169, 289, 320, 326; in Wagner's writings, 14, 19, 20, 43, 66, 124, 142, 147–48, 287, 289

Antwerp, 104, 170

Apel, Theodor (1811–67), 26

Aristotle (384–322 BC), 161, 365

Asmus, Bernd (b. 1959), 347

Auber, Daniel-François-Esprit (1782–1871), 11, 30, 93, 371n20

Works: *Diamants de la couronne, Les*, 358; *Fra Diavolo*, 32; *Muette de Portici, La*, 24, 32

Auerbach, Berthold (1812–82), 267, 288–89

Works: "Richard Wagner and the Self-Respect of the Jews," 289; *Schwarzwälder Dorfgeschichten*, 288; *Spinoza*, 288

Augusta, Princess of Prussia (1811–90), 288

Aussig (Ústi nad Labem), 84

Avenarius, Cäcilie née Geyer (1815–93), 2, 3, 4

Bach, Carl Philipp Emanuel (1714–88), 195

Bach, Johann Sebastian (1685–1750), xvi, 82, 85, 117, 124, 185, 203, 253, 255, 316, 329, 357, 360; and *Die Meistersinger von Nürnberg*, 279–81, 284

Works: *Art of Fugue, The*, xvi, 157, 203; Brandenburg Concerto no. 2, 280; Cantata 18, 280; *Chromatic Fantasy*, 92; Goldberg Variations, 195; *St. Matthew Passion*, 18; *Well-Tempered Clavier, The*, 92, 196, 280

Bad Lauchstädt, 23

Bakunin, Mikhail (1814–76), 130, 135, 137, 162

Balzac, Honoré de (1799–1850): *Fille d'Ève, Une*, 53

Bartels, Ulrich (b. 1965), 235

Basel, xv, 170

Baudelaire, Charles (1821–67): as artist figure, 271, 361; correspondence with RW, 78–79; and the creative process,

Baudelaire, Charles (1821–67) (cont.)
5–6; on *Der fliegende Holländer*, 52;
on the ills of modern society, 48; on
Lohengrin, 78, 119; and *Tannhäuser*,
78–79, 82, 85
Writings: "Richard Wagner et
Tannhäuser à Paris," 52, 78–79
Baudrillard, Jean (1929–2007), 365
Bayreuth; Festspielhaus, 101–2, 263, 294, 311;
Hofgarten, 208; Jewish Cemetery, 94;
Nibelung chancellery, 93; Wagner in,
xi, 17, 19, 36, 37, 45, 54, 92, 93, 99, 170,
258, 280; Wagner Museum, 198, 310, 365;
Wahnfried, 17, 92, 93, 94, 170, 308, 322
Bayreuth Festival, 17, 37, 62, 99, 109, 110,
120, 121, 161, 162, 240, 257, 286, 301,
305, 311, 314, 320, 323, 328, 329, 331, 332,
337, 344, 348, 350, 352, 353; in 1876, xi,
61, 169–70, 195, 241, 290, 295; in 1882,
236, 322–23, 338; in 1976, 161, 162, 192,
196, 305, 348; and Hitler, 108; New
Bayreuth, xii
Bayreuther Blätter, 93
Beaumarchais, Pierre-Augustin Caron de
(1732–99), 9
Bechstein, Ludwig (1801–60), 70, 74
Beckett, Samuel (1906–89), 71, 165, 240
Beethoven, Ludwig van (1770–1827): early
influence on RW, 9, 25, 117, 357, 359;
and genius, 176; and the German
symphonic tradition, 60, 85, 124, 255,
284, 316, 357, 359; and Klimt, 337; and
Mahler, 116, 353; and *Die Meistersinger
von Nürnberg*, 284; motivic writing in
late string quartets, 118, 277; as the
ne plus ultra of four-movement symphonic form, 55; "poetic features," 116;
and revolutionary music, 138, 358; RW
as the living embodiment and heir, 138,
151, 357, 359; sketches, 310; as victim of
repression and censorship, 28
Works: *Fidelio* op. 72, 58, 87, 277;
"Hammerklavier" Sonata op. 106, 94;
Incidental Music to Goethe's *Egmont*
op. 84, 9; piano sonatas, 92; String
Quartet in C-sharp Minor op. 131, 284;
Symphony no. 3 op. 55 ("Eroica"), 116,
137–38, 195; Symphony no. 6 op. 68,
233; Symphony no. 9 op. 125, 19, 58, 151,
215–16, 219–20, 337, 358
Beidler, Franz (1872–1930), ix
Beidler, Isolde née von Bülow (1865–1919), ix
Beijing: Forbidden City, 348

Bekker, Paul (1882–1937), 143–45
Bellini, Vincenzo (1801–35), 11
Works: *Capuleti e i Montecchi*, 24, 42;
Norma, 30
Benjamin, Walter (1892–1940): and histori-
cal materialism, xvii, 109; and myth,
221; on RW's view of Greek tragedy,
161, 163; on *Tannhäuser*, 86
Writings: *Storyteller, The*, 221; *Theses on
the Philosophy of History*, 165
Benz, Bernhard, 209, 210, 296
Berg, Alban (1885–1935): admiration for
RW's music, 258, 302, 332
Works: *Lulu*, 348; *Wozzeck*, 332
Berger, Christian (b. 1951), 194
Berghaus, Ruth (1927–96), 180
Berka, 196
Berlin, 290; Academy of the Arts, 44;
Court Opera, 69; critics in, 72, 103;
Deutsche Oper, 40; *Der fliegende Hol-
länder* in, 19; Mendelssohn's revival of
the *St. Matthew Passion*, 18; and *Rienzi*,
30, 34, 103; Royal Orchestra, 18; State
Opera, 53, 110, 327; Victoria Theater,
169–70, 289
Berliner Figaro, 34
Berlioz, Hector (1803–69), 92, 136, 144;
fondness for Rienzi's Prayer, 39; and
Lohengrin, 119
Works: *Symphonie Fantastique*, 56
Bermbach, Udo (b. 1938), xiv; on *Die Meis-
tersinger von Nürnberg*, 273; on *Rienzi*,
33; on *Parsifal*, 324; on the *Ring* 164,
202–3, 212, 306; on *Tannhäuser*, 80
Bernhardt, Joseph (1805–85), 262
Bethmann, Heinrich (1774–1857), 23
Biessenhofen, 274
Billroth, Theodor (1829–94), 289
Birmingham Festival, 370n8
Bloch, Ernst (1885–1977), 259–61, 315; on
Der fliegende Holländer, 58, 65; on *Die
Meistersinger von Nürnberg*, 271; on the
Ring, 248; on *Tristan und Isolde*, 238,
239, 247, 248, 252, 260–61
Writings: "Paradoxes and the Pastorale
in Wagner's Music," 260; *Principle of
Hope*, 252; *Spirit of Utopia, The*, 247, 259
Böcklin, Arnold (1827–1901), 162, 176
Böhme, Rudolf (Wagner's landlord in
Dresden), 2
Bohr, Niels (1885–1962), xiii
Boieldieu, François-Adrien (1775–1834):
Dame blanche, La, 32

Bologna, 170

Bonfantini, G. A., xv

Borchmeyer, Dieter (b. 1941), 17, 77, 271

Bordeaux, 96

Börne, Ludwig (1786–1837), 66

Bortolotto, Mario: on *Parsifal*, 341; on *Rienzi*, 35; on *Tristan und Isolde*, 252

Botticelli, Sandro (1444/45–1510): *Mystic Nativity*, 177

Boulez, Pierre (b. 1925), 306, 330, 337, 352

Brahms, Johannes (1833–97): and Billroth, 289; and German patriotism, 311; and the German symphonic tradition, 124, 176, 218, 255, 265, 273; and Herzogenberg, 329; and Kalbeck, 326; and Mahler, 353; RW on, 118, 153 Works: "Schwesterlein, Schwesterlein, wann geh'n wir nach Haus?" 336; *Triumphlied*, 308

Brand, Hans Bartolo (1854–1945), 348

Brandt, Marianne (1842–1921), 348

Braun, Christina von (b. 1944), 346

Braunschweig, 33

Brecht, Bertolt (1898–1956), 82, 83, 140

Breig, Werner (b. 1932), 39, 86, 333

Breitkopf & Härtel, 232

Breslau, 106

Brockhaus, Ottilie née Wagner (1811–83), 2

Bronfen, Elisabeth (b. 1958), 346

Bruckner, Anton (1824–96), 265, 353 Works: Symphony no. 3, 216

Brussels: Palais de Justice, 140; Théâtre Royal de la Monnaie, 90

Budapest, 170

Buddhism, 148, 236, 323; metempsychosis, 345; nirvana, 236, 244, 314

Bülow, Bernhard von (1849–1929), 300

Bülow, Hans von (1830–94), 232; as legal father of Isolde Beidler, ix; and "Lyric Pieces from *Lohengrin*," 84–85; on *Die Meistersinger von Nürnberg*, 267; and *Rienzi*, 38

Bulwer-Lytton, Edward George Earle Lytton, first Baron Lytton (1803–73): *Rienzi: The Last of the Roman Tribunes*, 29, 32

Burianek, Stephan, 166

Burrell, Mary (1850–98), xv

Büsching, Johann Gustav Gottlieb (1783–1829): *Ritterzeit und Ritterwesen*, 10

Buxtehude, Dietrich (ca. 1637–1707): *In dulci jubilo*, 240

Byron, George Gordon, sixth Baron (1788–1824): *Manfred*, 52

Campenhout, Herman van (b. 1943), 111

Camus, Albert (1913–60), 71

Caradori-Allan, Maria (1800–65), 370n8

Castelli, Ignaz Franz (1781–1862): *Waise und der Mörder, Die*, 4

Chafe, Eric (b. 1946), 255

Chamberlain, Eva (1867–1942), ix, 321

Chéreau, Patrice (b. 1944), 161, 162, 178, 180, 192, 196, 305, 306, 348

Chopin, Frédéric (1810–49), 92

Christianity: Christ as a social revolutionary, 134–35; Christian Catholicism, 74; Christianization of Europe, 156; and eschatological annihilation, 135–36; Judaic-Christian tradition, 133, 134, 320, 326; RW's views on, 79, 80, 130, 163–64, 281, 307, 319–21, 323, 326–27, 328, 344, 345. See also the entries under *Lohengrin*, *Parsifal*, and *Tannhäuser* in the Index of Works

Cola di Rienzo (ca. 1313–54), 32

commedia dell'arte, 29

Communism, 15, 129–30, 144

Coppola, Francis Ford (b. 1939): *Apocalypse Now*, 362

Cornelius, Peter (1824–74), 279, 280

counterpoint, 39, 117, 203, 279, 280, 281, 282, 284, 287

Craft, Robert (*1923), 342

Dahlhaus, Carl (1928–89): on "absolute music," 358; on *Die Feen*, 11; on *Der fliegende Holländer*, 56; on *Lohengrin*, 118; on *Die Meistersinger von Nürnberg*, 264; on *Parsifal*, 326; on the *Ring*, 163, 224, 296; on *Tannhäuser*, 72, 84; on *Tristan und Isolde*, 251

Dante Alighieri (1265–1321), 78, 331

Danuser, Hermann (b. 1946), 322

Darcy, Warren, 273

Daverio, John (1954–2003), 343–44

David, Jacques-Louis (1748–1825), 358

Deathridge, John (b. 1944), 310, 398n1

Debussy, Claude (1862–1918), 332, 337, 342 Works: *Mer, La*, 337; *Pelléas et Mélisande*, 342, *Prélude à l'après-midi d'un faune*, 337

décadence, 75, 78, 153, 175, 241, 323, 346, 357

deconstruction, 80, 81, 89, 121, 168, 305, 306, 314

Delacroix, Eugène (1798–1863): *Liberty Leading the People*, 305

Devrient, Eduard (1801–77), 132

Dickens, Charles (1812–70), 162

Döge, Klaus (1951–2011), 115
Döhring, Sieghart (b. 1939), 74
Dolci, Carlo (1616–86), 84
Dom Pedro II, emperor of Brazil (1825–91), 241
Donizetti, Gaetano (1797–1848), 24; establishes a name for himself in Paris, 48
    Works: *Favorite, La*, 48
Dorschel, Andreas (b. 1962), 244
Dresden, 2, 66, 130, 183, 220, 288, 289; Court Opera, 34, 61, 69, 70, 73, 99, 100, 132; "Dresden Amen," 88, 338, 344, 349; Dresden Uprising, 15, 66, 102, 128, 130, 131, 134, 135, 136, 144, 147, 159; Fatherland Association, 107, 129; Kreuzschule, 2; Mendelssohn's role in, 19; Minna flees to in 1837, 29; Postplatz, 135; RW as Kapellmeister to the Royal Court, 39, 44, 48, 51, 56, 77, 79, 84, 130, 131, 133, 144, 232, 264, 265; RW moves to in 1814, 1; RW returns to in 1822, 2; RW settles there in 1842, 65, 70; subscription concerts, 137; Waldschlößchen, 103
Dresdner Anzeiger, 129
Dresdner Tageblatt, 34
Dürer, Albrecht (1471–1528): *Melencolia I*, 253
Dusapin, Pascal (b. 1955), 110

Eberhardt's Allgem. Polizei-Anzeiger, 126
Eco, Umberto (b. 1932), 259
Edda (Poetic and Prose), 160, 226. See also *Völuspá*
Eike von Repgau (fl. 1209–33): *Sachsenspiegel*, 300
Eisenstein, Sergei (1898–1948), 218, 223, 225–27
    Works: *Battleship Potemkin*, 227; "Incarnation of Myth, The," 226–27
Eiser, Otto (1834–98), 388n10
Eisleben, 2
Eisler, Hanns (1898–1962), 225
Elena Pavlovna, Grand Duchess of Russia (1807–73), 93
Ellis, William Ashton (1853–1919), 156, 172
Engels, Friedrich (1820–95), 32
    Writings: *Communist Manifesto*, 162
Enzensberger, Hans Magnus (b. 1929): *Sinking of the Titanic, The*, 136
Escher, Alfred (1819–82), 146
Essen, 179
Ette, Wolfram (b. 1966), 213
Europa, 48

Fabre, Jan (b. 1958), 90
Feuerbach, Ludwig (1804–72), 132, 134
Figaro, Le, 356
Fleming, Paul (1609–40), 240
Flimm, Jürgen (b. 1941), 314
Flotow, Friedrich von (1812–83): *Martha*, 130
Fontane, Emilie (1824–1902), 200
Fontane, Theodor (1819–98), 201, 267
    Writings: *L'adultera*, 200; *Effi Briest*, 244
Forman, Alfred (1840–1925), 154
Förster, Bernhard (1843–89), 326
Foucault, Michel (1926–84), 162, 258
Francis of Assisi (1181/82–1226), 307
Franco-Prussian War, 311
Frank, Manfred (b. 1945), 163, 174, 212, 213
Frankfurt: National Assembly, 129, 130
Frankfurter Zeitung, 143
Frantz, Constantin (1817–91), 322
Freud, Sigmund (1856–1939), 53, 250
Freyer, Achim (b. 1934), 166, 168
Freytag, Gustav (1816–95), 267, 289
Fried, Johannes (b. 1942), xiii
Friedrich, Sven (b. 1963), 365
Friedrich August II, king of Saxony (1797–1854), 128–29
Friedrich Wilhelm IV, king of Prussia (1795–1861), 103, 130
Fröbel, Julius (1805–93), 130
Frommann, Alwine (1800–75), 288
Furtwängler, Wilhelm (1886–1954), 108, 110, 317

Gaillard, Karl (1813–51), 5, 72
Gautier, Judith (1845–1917), xi
Gay, Peter (b. 1923), 242
Gazette musicale, 48
Gegenwart, Die, 289
George, Stefan (1868–1933), 271
Gesamtkunstwerk, xvii, 9, 22, 64, 78, 124, 152, 153, 176, 186, 215, 227, 260, 316, 353, 358, 359, 363, 365, 366; and Hegel, 174; in life as well as art, xiii–xiv; Nietzsche's backing for, 12, 255
Geyer, Cäcilie. *See* Avenarius, Cäcilie
Geyer, Karl (1791–1831), 2
Geyer, Ludwig (1779–1821), 8; influence on RW's early life and career, 1–2, 3, 4
Gfrörer, August Friedrich (1803–61): *Critical History of Early Christianity*, 320
Ghent, 170
Gide, André (1869–1951), 321
Gießen, 320

Gilbert, Stuart (1883–1969), 226
Gluck, Christoph Willibald (1714–87), 151
Glucksmann, André (b. 1937), 348
Gobineau, Joseph-Arthur de (1816–82),
170, 322
    Writings: *Essay on the Inequality of the
    Human Races*, 170
Goehr, Lydia (b. 1960), 264, 270
Goethe, Johann Wolfgang von (1749–1832):
and Bach's *Well-Tempered Clavier*, 196;
friend of Adolf Wagner, 3; friend of
Friedrich Wagner, 3; and Mendels-
sohn, 18; Thomas Mann compares to
RW, 161; and Valmy, 135
    Writings: *Egmont*, 9; *Faust*, xiv, 3, 31–32,
    160, 341, 345; *Götz von Berlichingen*, 6;
    Wilhelm Meister, 268
Gossec, François-Joseph (1734–1829), 358
Gottfried von Strassburg (fl. 1210), 232, 240,
388n13
Gounod, Charles (1818–93): *La rédemption*,
323
Gozzi, Carlo (1720–1806): *Donna serpente,
La*, 11
Graf, Max (1873–1958), 53
grand opera, 25, 30, 33, 38, 42, 43, 49–51, 64,
73, 78, 81, 118, 200
Graz, 170
Greek antiquity as an inspiration, 6, 7, 18,
103, 133, 148, 151, 152, 153, 156, 158–59,
161, 224, 359; Greek chorus, 152, 153,
158, 212
Gregor-Dellin, Martin (1926–88), xi, xiv, 134
Gregorovius, Ferdinand (1821–91), 268
Grenzboten, Die, 267
Grey, Thomas, 251
Griepenkerl, Wolfgang Robert (1810–68):
Musikfest oder die Beethovener, Das, 33
Grimm, Jacob (1785–1863): *Teutonic
Mythology*, 160
Gutman, Robert W. (b. 1925), 326

Halévy, Jacques-Fromental (1799–1862),
24, 48
    Works: *Guitarrero, Le*, 48; *Juive, La*, 32,
    48; *Reine de Chypre, La*, 48
Hamburg: Hamburg Opera, 91, 110, 314, 352
Hamp, Anton [Pater Petrus], 321
Hanfstaengl, Franz (1804–77), 198, 228, 318
Hanover, 34
Hanslick, Eduard (1825–1904), 176, 186–87,
255, 272, 285
Härtling, Peter (b. 1933), 254

Heckel, Emil (1831–1908), 295
Hegel, Georg Wilhelm Friedrich (1770–
1831), 148, 163, 348; critique of the
individual arts, 173–74
    Writings: *Faith and Knowledge*, 148
Heidegger, Martin (1889–1976), 242, 254
Heine, Ferdinand (1798–1872), 51
Heine, Heinrich (1797–1856): critical of
artistic conditions, 49; and RW, 65–
67, 69
    Writings: *Aus den Memoiren des Herren
    von Schnabelewopski*, 50, 66, 105; *Beiden
    Grenadiere, Die*, 66
Heine, Mathilde née Mirat (1815–83), 67
Heisenberg, Werner (1901–76), xiii
heldentenor, 43
Hell, Theodor (1775–1856) and Joseph
Schubert (1757–1837): *Beiden
Galeerensklaven, oder Die Mühle von
Saint Alderon, Die*, 4
Henry I ("Henry the Fowler"), duke of
Saxony and king of East Franconia
(ca. 876–936), 100, 101, 102, 105
Herder, Johann Gottfried (1744–1803), 219
Herwegh, Georg (1817–75), 162
Herz, Joachim (1924–2010): on *Die Meis-
tersinger von Nürnberg*, 269, 270; pro-
duction of the *Ring* in Leipzig, 140, 192
Herzfeld, Gregor (b. 1975), 292
Herzl, Theodor (1860–1904), 197
Herzog, Werner (b. 1942), 121
Herzogenberg, Elisabeth von (1847–92), 329
Hiller, Antolka née Hogé (1820–96), 43
Hiller, Ferdinand (1811–85), 43
Hinrichsen, Hans-Joachim (b. 1952), 216
Hitler, Adolf (1889–1945): and *Lohengrin*,
108–10; pact with Stalin, 227; and
Rienzi, 31, 40, 197
    Writings: *Mein Kampf*, 108
Hoffmann, E. T. A. (1776–1822): admiration
for Mozart, 358; friend of Friedrich
Wagner, 3; as Hans Sachs-like figure,
271; on "musical painting," 89; music as
the Romantic art par excellence, 54
    Writings: *Tomcat Murr*, 53; *Kreisleriana*,
    53
Hoffmann von Fallersleben, August
Heinrich (1798–1874), 265
Hofmann, Leopold Friedrich von (1822–85),
101
Hofmannsthal, Hugo von (1874–1929), 271,
272
    Works: *Der Rosenkavalier*, 271

Hohenasperg, 288
Hölderlin, Friedrich (1770–1843), 3, 163
Holtei, Karl von (1798–1880), 30
Homer (probably 8th century BC): *Odyssey*, 6
Horace (65–8 BC), 271
Hrabanus Maurus (ca. 776–856): *Veni creator spiritus*, 345
Hrdlicka, Alfred (1928–2009), 202
Hübner, Kurt (b. 1921), 161
Hugo, Victor (1802–85), 136
Hunt, Graham G., 114

Ibsen, Henrik (1828–1906), 62
Impressionism, 352, 356

Jacobs, Rüdiger, 137
Janz, Tobias (b. 1974), 182, 295
Jens, Walter (b. 1923), 270
Jerusalem, 197
Jones, Richard (b. 1953), 121
Joyce, James (1882–1941), 226, 347
Jugendstil, 337, 362
Jünger, Ernst (1895–1998), 362
Jungheinrich, Hans-Klaus (b. 1938), 80

Kaden, Christian (b. 1946), xiv, 15
Kafka, Franz (1883–1924), 71, 165, 213
Kaiser, Joachim (b. 1928), xvii, 33
Kalbeck, Max (1850–1921), 326
Kant, Immanuel (1724–1804), 130, 308
Kapp, Julius (1883–1962), 246
Kaufmann, Jonas (b. 1969), 121
Keller, Gottfried (1819–90), 154, 267, 272, 289
    Writings: *Grüne Heinrich, Der*, 272; *Hadlaub*, 272
Kerman, Joseph (b. 1924), 124
Kiem, Eckehard (b. 1950), 217
Kienzle, Ulrike (b. 1960), 345
Kietz, Ernst Benedikt (1815–92), 22, 46, 84, 96, 126
Kind, Friedrich (1768–1843): *Weinberg an der Elbe, Der*, 4
Kinderman, William (b. 1952), 343
Kittler, Friedrich (1943–2011), 309, 315, 365
Klein, Richard (b. 1953), 213, 362
Klimt, Gustav (1862–1918), 337, 349, 353
Knabe, Tilman (b. 1970), 179
Koch, Max (1855–1931), 106, 107
Königsberg, 29, 31
Konwitschny, Peter (b. 1945), 110, 299, 313
Kościuszko, Tadeusz (1746–1817), 27
Koselleck, Reinhart (1923–2006), 368n17

Kossak, Ernst (1814–80), 103
Koßmaly, Carl (1812–93), 73
Kramer, Lawrence (b. 1946), 301, 360
Kristeva, Julia (b. 1941), 347
Kühnel, Jürgen (b. 1944), 327
Kupfer, Harry (b. 1935): Bayreuth production of *Der fliegende Holländer*, 62; Berlin production of *Der fliegende Holländer*, 53; Berlin production of *Parsifal*, 327; on the figure of Hans Sachs, 270
Kurth, Ernst (1886–1946), 217, 249

Lagarde, Paul de (1827–91), 322
Langbehn, Julius (1851–1907), 300
La Spezia, xii, 177, 197
Lassalle, Ferdinand (1825–64), 267
Laube, Heinrich (1806–84): friendly with Heine, 66; suggests opera on Tadeusz Kościuszko, 27; and Young Germany, 26
Laussot, Jessie (1826–1905), 96
Lay of the Nibelungs, The. See *Nibelungenlied*
Lehmann, Lilli (1848–1929), 54
Leibniz, Gottfried Wilhelm (1646–1716), 190
Leipzig: first local production of *Faust*, 3; Gewandhaus, 9, 19; Leipzig Opera, 140, 192, 269; Leipzig Theater, 3, 10, 169; St. Nicholas's School, 2; Wagner's early years in, 1, 2, 28
leitmotif: in James Joyce, 226; motifs of presentiment and recollection, 113, 152, 154, 182, 296; and myth, 194, 231, 295, 296; as a reflection of the characters' inner lives, 17, 57, 113, 114, 187, 196, 209, 224, 248, 302, 341–42, 365. *See also individual titles in the Index of Works*
Lenbach, Franz von (1836–1904), 262; portrait of Cosima, 2; portrait of RW, 318
Leonardo da Vinci (1452–1519), 218
Leroux, Pierre (1797–1871), 136
Levi, Hermann (1839–1900), 280, 319, 320
Lévi-Strauss, Claude (1908–2009), 231, 245, 307, 323
Lewald, August (1792–1871), 48
Library of Congress, 362
Lindau, 274
Linnenbrügger, Jörg, 274
Linz, 31, 108
Lippmann, Edmund von (1857–1940), 397n52
Lippmann, Eduard von (1838–1919), 308

Liszt, Franz (1811–86): on act 2 of *Die Wal-küre*, 201; advanced harmonic writing, 341; Catholic beliefs, 321; champions RW's works, 51, 61, 108; as correspondent, 5, 17, 36, 44, 51, 60, 61, 74, 75, 110, 113, 160, 176, 201, 202, 216, 232, 233, 235, 236; critical of artistic conditions, 47–48; as "expressionist," 144; and Josef Rubinstein, 93; on *Lohengrin*, 119; and RW's appeal for money, 232; on RW's harmonic writing, 118–19, 123; and RW's longing for love, 17, 232, 233, 235; and RW's love of luxury, 5; on RW's use of leitmotifs in *Der fliegende Holländer*, 52–53, 57; as a Saint-Simonian, 49; and the symphonic poem, 55; as victim of repression and censorship, 28
    Works: *Am Grabe Richard Wagners*, 341; Piano Concerto no. 2 in A Major, 119; "On the Situation of Artists and Their Condition in Society," 47–48
Literarische Welt, Die, 123
Lohengrin (anonymous medieval epic), 105
Löhr, Friedrich ("Fritz") (1859–1924), 352
London: Angelo Neumann's touring *Ring*, 162; RW's visits (1839), 144; (1855), 45; (1877), 303
Lorenz, Alfred (1868–1939), 184, 272
Los Angeles: Ebell Club, 124; Los Angeles Opera, 166, 168
Lourdes, 331
Lübeck, 106, 240, 269
Lucerne, 94, 275
Ludwig II, king of Bavaria (1845–86), 172, 262; as intended recipient of *My Life*, x, xv, 135; and Levi, 320; and *Die Meistersinger von Nürnberg*, 265–66, 273, 274–75; and the paternity issue, 2; reads *Ring* preface, 160; receives scores from RW, 93; RW as political adviser, 104, 265–66; RW's betrayal of, xiv; and theater reform, 129
Luther, Martin (1483–1546), 15, 163–64, 280, 294
    Works: *Ein feste Burg ist unser Gott*, 311
Lüttichau, Wolf Adolf August von (1785–1863), 100, 130
Lutz, Johann von (1826–90), 274

Magdeburg, 23, 26, 29, 135
Magee, Bryan (b. 1930), 258
Mahler, Alma (1879–1964), 353

Mahler, Gustav (1860–1911), 352–54; and Beethoven, 116; and religious subject matter, 344, 345, 353; and the German symphonic tradition, 255
    Works: Symphony no. 1, 344; Symphony no. 2, 345; Symphony no. 4, 344; Symphony no. 8, 345, 353
Mahnkopf, Claus-Steffen (b. 1962), 183, 251, 302
Mallarmé, Stéphane (1842–98), 246, 321, 347, 361
Mann, Erika (1905–69), 216
Mann, Heinrich (1871–1950): *Untertan, Der*, 106–8
Mann, Thomas (1875–1955), 269; and 1909 Bayreuth *Parsifal*, 331, 337, 353; and 1936 Bayreuth *Lohengrin*, 108, 110; disagreement with Heinrich Mann, 106–8; on Kundry, 346; and *Lohengrin*, 106, 107, 108, 109, 119, 122; and narcotic influence of RW's works, 360; on the *Ring*, 161, 295; and RW's alleged dilettantism, 175; on RW's prose writings, 150; on *Tristan und Isolde*, 245, 260; understanding of RW, xvii, 220, 253–54, 261; on Wotan's Farewell, 216, 217
    Works: *Buddenbrooks*, 175, 362; *Clown, The*, 175; *Confessions of Felix Krull*, 154; "Essay on the Theater," 106; "Nietzsche's Philosophy in the Light of Contemporary Events," 362–63; *Reflections of a Non-Political Man*, 107
Mannheim, 295
Marat, Jean-Paul (1744–93), 68
Marbach, Rosalie née Wagner (1803–37): early career as an actress, 2, 3, 4; influence on RW's artistic decisions, 10
Maria Theresa, empress of Austria (1717–80), 271
Marschner, Heinrich (1795–1861), 11
Marthaler, Christoph (b. 1951), 240, 257
Marx, Karl (1818–83), 136, 162, 295, 348
    Writings: *Communist Manifesto*, 162
Materna, Amalie (1844–1918), 198
Mayer, Hans (1907–2001), 401n63; on *Lohengrin*, 119; on *Die Meistersinger von Nürnberg*, 271; on *Parsifal*, 324; on the *Ring*, 306
McLuhan, Marshall (1911–80), 87
Meiningen, 202
Meißner, Alfred (1822–85), 102–3
Mendelssohn, Felix (1809–47), 18–20; as "expressionist," 144; and German

Mendelssohn, Felix (1809–47) (*cont.*)
nationalism, 265; and Meyerbeer, 18,
43; and RW, 18–20, 92; RW's alleged
jealousy of his genius, 43; search for
opera libretto, 32
Works: *Elijah*, 20, 370n8; *Fingal's
Cave*, 19; Overture to *A Midsummer
Night's Dream*, 11, 18; St. Paul, 19;
Soldatenliebschaft, 18
Mengs, Ismael (1688–1764), 375n37
Menzel, Adolph von (1815–1905), 290
Mertens, Volker (b. 1937), 162
Meser, Carl Friedrich (d. 1850), 56, 84
Meyerbeer, Giacomo (1791–1864): as butt
of Heine's attacks, 67; and French
grand opera, 24, 30, 33, 38, 48; hears
Tannhäuser in Hamburg, 91; helps RW
in Paris, 44, 48; historical back-
ground of his operas, 38; praised by
Griepenkerl, 33; and RW, 38, 43–45,
139; RW's alleged jealousy of his suc-
cess, 43; on RW's operas, 45
Works: *L'africaine*, 32; *Huguenots, Les*, 32,
38, 43, 44, 45, 67; *Prophète, Le*, 32, 43,
44, 139; *Robert le diable*, 18, 30, 32, 43,
45, 73
Meyerhold, Vsevolod (1874–1940), 226
Meysenbug, Malwida von (1816–1903), 61
Middle Ages, 72, 74, 82, 102, 104, 105, 111,
132, 160, 307
Mielitz, Christine (b. 1949), 202
Milan; Galleria Vittorio Emanuele II, 140
Mitau (Jelgava), 31
modern Wagner productions. *See* Index
of Wagner's Works *under* Musical
Works
Mondrian, Piet (1872–1944), 176
Monet, Claude (1840–1926), 176
Moréas, Jean (1856–1910), 336
Morgenstern, Christian (1871–1914), 271
Moscow, 218, 223, 225; Kremlin, 348
Mozart, Wolfgang Amadeus (1756–91), xvi,
151, 176, 182, 185, 277, 358; characteriza-
tion in his operas, 9, 35; RW's attitude
to, 54
Works: *Don Giovanni*, 54; *Entführung aus
dem Serail, Die*, 3; *Jupiter* Symphony,
xvi; *Nozze di Figaro, Le*, 9, 54, 176, 195;
Zauberflöte, Die, 3, 11, 54, 259
Müller, Heiner (1929–95), 240
Munich, 121, 129, 172, 198, 228, 265, 319, 320,
321; *Der fliegende Holländer* in 1864, 61;
Die Meistersinger von Nürnberg in 1868,

267, 275; Munich Wagner Society,
325; plans for a festival theater, 294;
Das Rheingold in 1869, 186; RW in, 17,
318, 321
music drama, xvii, 9, 15, 38, 40, 52, 83, 98,
99, 118, 122, 137, 138, 152, 157, 160, 181,
203, 232, 233, 259, 292, 294, 302, 316,
325, 345
Musil, Robert (1880–1942): *The Man without Qualities*, 327–28, 361
myth: and leitmotifs, 194, 231, 295, 296;
Norse myth, 133, 137, 156, 160, 162,
300; Oedipus, 151, 160, 224; as the
progenitor of the music drama, 34, 60,
138, 149, 308; and RW's own universal
myth, xiii, 8, 17, 137, 158, 160, 161, 163,
174; as "true for all time," xiv, 151, 161,
162; the turn from history to myth and
legend, 71, 111, 132–33. *See also* Greek
antiquity; *and individual titles in the
Index of Works*

Naples, 93
Napoleon Bonaparte (1769–1821), 27, 138
National Socialism, 31, 40, 101, 108, 109,
189, 197, 265, 286, 300, 316, 332, 341
Nationalzeitung, 323
Neue Freie Presse, 285
Neuenfels, Hans (b. 1941), 109, 120, 259
Neue Zeitschrift für Musik, 142, 378n40
Neumann, Angelo (1838–1910), 112, 162,
169–70, 289
New German school, 55
Newlin, Dika (1923–2006), 123
Newman, Ernest (1868–1959), 306
New York, 170
Nibelungenlied, 160, 300
Nicholas of Cusa (1401–64), 190
Niederwald Memorial, 140
Niemann, Albert (1831–1917), 34–35, 37
Nietzsche, Friedrich (1844–1900): on the
Christianity of *Lohengrin*, 91, 99; on
the ending of the *Ring*, 142, 305–6; and
fascism, 362–63; and Franco-Prussian
War, 311; Heidegger on, 254; knowl-
edge of RW's works, 261; on the nar-
cotic effect of Wagner's music, 91,
366; on the need for art in our lives,
13, 142, 361; and nihilism, 149; and
Overbeck, 320; and the power of RW's
music, 119, 254, 366; on redemption
in Wagner's works, 12, 14, 325; runs
errands for RW and his wife, xv, 93;

and RW's alleged dilettantism, 175;
as RW's disappointed admirer, xvii,
175, 317, 325; on RW as "miniaturist,"
364; on *Lohengrin*, 91, 99, 105; on *Die
Meistersinger von Nürnberg*, 281–82, 284;
on *Opera and Drama*, 150; on *Parsifal*,
77, 325, 329, 331–32; on the *Ring*, 161,
164, 175, 296, 305, 314; on Schumann's
Manfred, 52; "tangled passions" of
Götterdämmerung, 231; on *Tristan
und Isolde*, 12, 255, 359; visits RW at
Tribschen, 9, 253, 307; visits RW in
Bayreuth, 308
  Writings: *Beyond Good and Evil*, 77,
  314; *The Birth of Tragedy*, 12, 79;
  "Nachgelassene Fragmente," 31, 91,
  142, 296, 361; "Richard Wagner in
  Bayreuth," 75; "The Wagner Case," 305
Nuremberg, 265–66, 269, 271, 273, 275, 286

Oehme, Carl Wilhelm (brass-founder in
  Dresden), 131
O'Neill, Eugene (1888–1953), 160
opéra comique, 25
Otto, Rudolf (1869–1937): *The Idea of the
  Holy*, 345
Overbeck, Franz (1837–1905), 320
Ovid (43 BC – AD 17), 240

Palermo, 93, 356
Papo (RW's parrot), 39
Paris, xi, 84, 127, 138, 361; Académie Royale
  de Musique (i.e., Paris Opéra), 18,
  24, 43, 44, 48; concerts in 1860, 78;
  Institut National de Musique, 358;
  July Revolution, 27; Louvre, 84; Musée
  d'Orsay, 356; RW in Paris between
  1839 and 1842, xv, 18, 22, 30, 31, 43,
  47–49, 66, 69, 70, 74, 82, 99; RW in
  Paris in 1849 and 1850, 44–45, 96, 133,
  134; RW in Paris in 1860–61, 68, 79,
  85, 92; RW's hopes that it would be
  "burned to the ground," 135, 310; Salle
  Taitbout, 49; Théâtre du Châtelet, 16
Peduzzi, Richard (b. 1943), 162
Peißenberg, 274
Peiting, 274
Pentagon, 348
Petit, Pierre (1831–1909), 68
Picasso, Pablo (1881–1973), 253
Pillau (Baltiysk), 31, 144
Planer, Gotthelf (1770–1855) and Johanna
  Christiana (?–1856), 29

Planer, Minna. *See* Wagner, Wilhelmine
  ("Minna")
Planer, Natalie (1826–99?), 31
Plato (427–347 BC), 232, 347
poetic-musical period, 117, 154, 156, 157, 158,
  178, 249
Polling, 274
Possendorf, 2
Praeger, Ferdinand (1815–91), 216, 369n43
Prague, 2
Princeton, 216
Prometheus, 71, 224
Proust, Marcel (1871–1922): on the creative
  process, 5–6, 249; knowledge of RW's
  works, 261; on *Parsifal*, 332; on the
  "traurige Weise," 252–53
  Writings: *À la recherche du temps perdu*, 5,
  249, 361–62
Pusinelli, Anton (1815–78), 288

Rathert, Wolfgang (b. 1960), 218
realism and real idealism, 62, 253, 267, 268,
  272, 273, 288, 364
Regensburg: Walhalla, 67
Reger, Max (1873–1916), 273
Renoir, Auguste (1841–1919), 356
Revue européenne, 79
Ribot, Théodule-Armand (1839–1916), 357
Rienäcker, Gerd (b. 1939), 264, 298, 363, 364
Riga, 30, 31
Rio de Janeiro, 241
Ritter, Julie (1794–1869), 5, 230
Robber (RW's dog), 31
Robespierre, Maximilien de (1758–94), 358
Röckel, August (1814–76): as editor of the
  Volksblätter, 103, 131; political activi-
  ties, 102, 129; and RW's letter of Jan-
  uary 1854, 15, 180, 202, 208, 212, 213,
  303, 304; and RW's letter of August
  1856, 112, 304, 235
Roller, Alfred (1864–1935), 353
Romanshorn, 275
romanticism, 11, 25, 32, 35, 37, 52, 53, 54, 71,
  78, 83, 97, 98, 101, 102, 103, 105, 111, 112,
  118, 121, 131, 132, 136, 163, 174, 185, 239,
  244, 247, 267, 271, 281, 330, 334, 342,
  345, 358, 359, 361, 364
Rome, 77, 170
Rossini, Gioachino (1792–1868), 60, 92
  Works: *La Cenerentola*, 3
Rothschild, Mayer Carl von (1820–86), 398n2
Rubinstein, Josef (1847–84), 79, 87, 92–94,
  99, 280

Sachs, Hans (1494–1576), 283
Saga of the Volsungs, 160
Sagi, Emilio (b. 1948), 16
Saint-Simon, Claude-Henri de Rouvroy, comte de (1760–1825), 49
San-Marte (i.e., Albert Schulz) (1802–93), 105
Scheier, Claus-Artur (b. 1942), 86
Schelling, Friedrich Wilhelm Joseph von (1775–1854), 163
Schenker, Heinrich (1868–1935), 282
Schickling, Dieter (b. 1939), 180, 297
Schiller, Friedrich von (1759–1805), 3, 8, 275
Works: *The Maid of Orleans*, 4, 156; *Ode to Joy*, 151, 215, 358
Schleef, Einar (1944–2001), 341
Schlegel, Friedrich von (1772–1829), 130, 246
Schleiermacher, Friedrich Daniel Ernst (1768–1834), 32
Schleinitz, Alexander von (1807–85), 170
Schlesinger, Maurice (1798–1871), 48
Schlingensief, Christoph (1960–2010), 331, 350
Schloss Berg, 274
Schnädelbach, Herbert (b. 1936), 162, 208
Schnappauf, Bernhard (1852?–1904), xi
Schneckenburger, Max (1819–49): *Die Wacht am Rhein*, 311
Schoenberg, Arnold (1874–1951), 55, 85, 123–24, 176, 218, 255, 273, 316, 341; analysis of *Lohengrin*, 123
Works: *Die glückliche Hand* op. 18, 124; *Gurre-Lieder*, 123; *Moses und Aron*, 124; Two Songs op. 1, 123; *Verklärte Nacht* op. 4, 123; "Program to Help and Build Up the Party," 124; *Style and Idea*, 123
Schopenhauer, Arnold (1788–1860): as an influence on Nietzsche, 12, 149; and *Die Meistersinger von Nürnberg*, 271; and music, 219, 259, 337, 342; and *Parsifal*, 235; and the *Ring*, 235, 306; RW reads *The World as Will and Representation*, 148, 201–2, 214, 232, 239; RW's attempts to change Schopenhauer's view of love, 243; RW's quietistic interpretation, 149, 235, 239; and the will, 58, 72, 214, 244, 250, 304, 342
Writings: "Essay on Spirit Seeing," xii–xiii; *The World as Will and Representation*, 148, 201–2, 232, 239, 306
Schröder-Devrient, Wilhelmine (1804–60), 36, 42

Schubert, Bernhard (b. 1950), 274
Schubert, Franz (1797–1828): as "expressionist," 144; harmonic writing, 250; as victim of repression and censorship, 28
Works: *My Dream*, 330; Piano Sonata in B-Flat Major D 960, 250
Schuch, Ernst von (1846–1914), 61
Schumann, Robert (1810–56): autonomy of the music in his lieder, 215; as "expressionist," 144; and German nationalism 73, 265; revises his opinion of *Tannhäuser*, xiv, xvi, 92; RW's opinion of, 339; search for opera libretto, 32; as victim of repression and censorship, 28
Works: *Genoveva*, 32; *Liederkreis* op. 39, 335; *Manfred*, 52
Schweitzer, Albert (1875–1965), 82–83
Scriabin, Alexander (1872–1915), 119
Scribe, Eugène (1791–1861), 32, 38
Scruton, Roger (b. 1944), 248
Seidl, Anton (1850–98), 170
Semper, Gottfried (1803–79), 135
Shakespeare, William (1564–1616), 240; RW's early exposure to, 3, 7, 8
Works: *Hamlet*, 6; *King Lear*, 6; *Macbeth*, 6; *Measure for Measure*, 24, 27; *Midsummer Night's Dream, A*, 18, 271; *Much Ado about Nothing*, 24; *Romeo and Juliet*, 7–8
Shaw, Bernard (1856–1950), 162, 293
Writings: *The Perfect Wagnerite*, 306
Shostakovich, Dmitri (1906–75), 225
Simrock, Karl (1802–76): *Lay of the Amelungs*, 160
Sisyphus, 71, 231
Skelton, Geoffrey (1916–98), ix
Sloterdijk, Peter (b. 1947), 12
Sophocles (ca. 496–406/5 BC), 161; Adolf Wagner as translator of, 3; RW's enthusiasm for, 6, 8, 103, 151
Spohr, Louis (1784–1859), 11, 25
Spontini, Gaspare (1774–1851): and grand opera, 33
Works: *Fernand Cortez*, 30
Stabreim, 154–56
Stalin, Joseph (1879–1953), 225, 227
Steiner, George (b. 1929), 179, 196–97
Stieler, Joseph (1781–1858), 262
Stockar-Escher, Clementine (1816–86), 146
Stockhausen, Karlheinz (1928–2007): *Studie II*, 157
Stölzl, Philipp (b. 1967), 40
Strauß, Johann (1825–99), 92

Strauss, Richard (1864–1949): characterization in his operas, 35; illustrative music, 253; and modernism, 283; on *Opera and Drama*, 150
  Works: *Der Rosenkavalier*, 271
Strauß, Salomon (1795–1866), 66
Stravinsky, Igor (1882–1971), 123, 282
  Works: Piano Scherzo, 283
Strecker, Ludwig (1853–1943), 9, 87, 322
Strindberg, August (1849–1912), 357, 363, 364
  Works: *Miss Julie*, 357
Stuttgart, 299, 313
symbolism, 246, 336, 337, 344

Tacitus (56/57–after 117), 300
Tannenberg, 106, 377n17
Taylor, Charles (b. 1931), 136
Tchaikovsky, Peter Ilyich (1840–93), 119
Teatr, 226
Thebes, 140
Tichatschek, Joseph (1807–86), 36–37, 135
Tieck, Ludwig (1773–1853), 70
  Writings: *Der getreue Eckart und der Tannhäuser*, 105
Titian (ca. 1480/85–1576): *Assunta*, 274
Träger, Adolf (RW's godfather), 4
Treadwell, James (b. 1968), 194
Tribschen, ix, 9, 93, 253
Trieste, 170
Tübingen, 320
Turin, 170

Über Land und Meer, 93
Uhlig, Theodor (1822–53), 44, 115, 139, 142, 149, 183, 220, 378n40
Ulrich von Türheim (fl. 1235), 232, 388n13
Urmoneit, Sebastian, 248

Vaget, Hans Rudolf (b. 1938), 273
Valéry, Paul (1871–1945), 122, 321, 361
Van Dyck, Sir Anthony (1599–1641), 2
Varnhagen von Ense, Karl August (1785–1858), 130
Vasari, Giorgio (1511–74), 230
Venice: Neumann's touring *Ring*, 170; Palazzo Corner Spinelli, 230; Palazzo Giustiniani, 230; RW in, 34, 93, 230, 274; Teatro La Fenice, 10
Verdi, Giuseppe (1813–1901): characterization in his operas, 35, 181, 241; comparison with RW, 35, 181, 211–12, 230, 241, 255

  Works: *Don Carlo*, 211; *La forza del destino*, 259; *Otello*, 42, 181, 241; *Les vêpres siciliennes*, 32
Verne, Jules (1828–1905), 162
Vienna, 123, 271, 288, 328; Burgtheater, 140; Congress of Vienna, 27; *Lohengrin* in 1876, 101, 112; Mahler as director, 353; RW's visit in 1848, 130; Secession, 337, 353; *Tannhäuser* in, 26; Theater auf der Wieden, 54
Volksblätter, 103, 131
Völuspá, 162
Vormärz, 27, 102
Voss, Egon (b. 1938), xii, 239, 285, 327

Wagner, Adolf (1774–1835), 228; important figure in Leipzig's artistic life, 3; influence on RW's youth, 2
Wagner, Albert (1799–1874), 3
Wagner, Clara. *See* Wolfram, Clara
Wagner, Cosima née Liszt (1837–1930): alleged affair with Levi, 320; anti-Semitism of, 289, 320; birthday celebrations in 1882, 10; and the *Brown Book*, 17, 321; Christian beliefs, 319; and composition sketches, 234, 340; corresponds with Eduard von Lippmann, 308–9; court case over Isolde, ix–x; edition of *Rienzi*, 34, 38; ends RW's affair with Judith Gautier, xi; and *Götterdämmerung*, 308–9; housekeeping skills, 169; and Mahler, 352; and *Die Meistersinger von Nürnberg*, 275; portrait by Lenbach, 2; premarital affair with RW, ix, 17; relations with RW, x, xi, 275, 338; and Rubinstein, 92–94; RW dictates his autography to, x, xv
  Writings: Diaries, xii, 1, 2, 4, 9, 12, 24, 36, 43, 79, 93, 94, 112, 149, 152, 159, 169, 180, 220, 231, 240–41, 249, 276, 285, 289, 293, 303, 307, 309, 310, 314, 320, 321, 325, 339, 340–41, 343, 349, 359; as reliable, "documentary" source, ix–x, xi, xii, 24
Wagner, Elise née Gollmann (1800–64), 26
Wagner, Eva. *See* Chamberlain, Eva
Wagner, Friedrich (1770–1813), 1, 3, 8
Wagner, Isolde. *See* Beidler, Isolde
Wagner, Johanna Rosine née Pätz (1774–1848): moves to Prague, 2; RW's relations with, 1, 3, 8, 53
Wagner, Minna. *See* Wagner, Wilhelmine ("Minna")

Wagner, Nike (b. 1945): on *Parsifal*, 331; on Thomas Mann, 216; on act 3 of *Tristan und Isolde*, 237; on Wotan, 213

Wagner, Ottilie. *See* Brockhaus, Ottilie

Wagner, Richard (1813–83): on actors and singers, 29, 36–37, 61, 91, 112, 113, 181, 217, 294; on his adolescence, 2; acquires a knowledge of music, 8–9; alleged Oedipal desires, 53; archetypal scenario, 7–8, 10, 11, 12, 13, 17, 29, 33, 338; art as an antidote to life, 13, 142, 361; art as religion, 99, 103, 127, 133, 138, 174, 230, 245, 322, 324, 327, 329, 330, 334, 345, 353, 358, 359, 360; art of transition, 64, 84, 122, 175, 189, 293, 296, 364; attitude to French and Italian opera, 24, 25, 151, 153, 283; autobiographical tendentiousness. x–xiii, 66, 232; and calling, xiii, 6, 9, 10, 13, 28, 29, 31, 43, 99, 103, 169; and capital, 15, 20, 44, 103, 162, 306; as champion of a new mythology, xiii, 8, 17, 137, 158, 160, 161, 163, 174; chaotic early life, 1, 2, 3, 5, 8; childhood fears, 2; childhood memories, 1–2, 3–4, 8; and Christianity, 74, 79, 80, 81, 98, 99, 133, 134, 135, 163–64, 281, 288, 307, 320, 321, 323, 326, 328–29, 344, 345, 360; composing in a "somnambulistic" state, xii, xiii, 177–78; concern that his works should be adequately staged, 35–36, 112, 113; and the creative process, 5, 9, 31, 231, 357, 391n74; death wish, 17; and debts, 29, 31, 70, 130, 232; and dilettantism, 175–76, 258; disenchantment with the present, 29, 31, 47, 49, 51, 65, 74, 97, 98, 99, 103–4, 111, 142, 148–49, 159, 212–13; as *divino artista*, 230; early literary endeavors, 6–9; early musical influences, 3–4, 9, 11, 24; "emotionalizing of the intellect," 57, 60, 81, 99, 149, 153, 207, 217–18, 336; "endless melody," 247, 248, 250, 251, 281, 366; feelings of inadequacy as a composer, 8, 19, 231; and "free love," 26, 27, 28, 29, 305, 314; and German nationalism, 70, 72, 101, 106, 107, 108, 110, 155, 164, 189, 265, 270, 272, 275, 284, 300, 323, 328; and the German Reich, 14, 106, 108, 265, 295, 311, 312, 318; harmonic writing, xiv, 59, 85, 86, 89, 119, 123, 157, 178, 194, 209, 251, 254, 292, 298, 301, 335, 341, 342, 347; hypersensitivity, 2, 4, 5; identifies with characters, 15, 17, 51–52, 74, 97, 99, 100, 104, 198, 201, 202, 203, 220, 268; on improvisation, 55, 106, 176, 181, 184, 347; instrumentation, 24, 61, 85, 116, 119, 249, 250, 252, 292, 294, 365; interrelationship of music and onstage action, 58–60, 92, 113, 115, 177, 185–86, 200, 204, 248; and the "Jewish question," x, xvi–xvii, 14, 18, 19, 43, 94, 142, 147–48, 285, 289, 320, 326, 345, 356; as kapellmeister in Dresden, 19, 30, 44, 70, 72, 100, 131; lack of affection in early life, 1, 5, 8; letters as authentic source, x; as his own librettist, 10, 24, 27, 30, 32, 37, 49, 51, 53, 56, 61, 70, 74, 101, 132, 137, 138, 149, 154, 155, 159, 160, 168, 185, 200, 202, 204, 207, 239, 246, 258, 265, 266, 267, 269–70, 278, 305, 310, 311, 322, 323, 325, 327, 343, 345; love as a source of torment, 8, 232, 233, 235, 236, 244, 245, 263; musical prose, 91, 124, 353; music as an expression of desire and fulfillment, 13, 236, 246, 254; music as an expression of the inexpressible, 113, 152, 246; music as an expression of love, 12–13; music as a reflection of inner reality, 17, 57, 121; music as the romantic art par excellence, 54; as music director in the German provinces, 23–24; mystification of the creative process, xi, xii–xiii, 178, 194, 274; neuroses, 2; "orchestral melody," 89, 186, 294, 200, 209, 210, 212, 281, 298; and pacifism, 109, 266, 328; the paternity issue, 1–2, 8; pessimism at cultural decline, 14, 17, 97, 322, 328; as political adviser to Ludwig II, 104, 265–66; and popular monarchy, 103–4, 107, 129–30; portraits, xviii, 22, 46, 68, 96, 126, 146, 172, 198, 228, 262, 290, 318, 356; predilection for silk fabrics and French perfumes, xi, 5–6; prescriptions for staging his works, 60–61; and the "purely human," 50, 74, 97, 101, 132, 138, 151, 164; racist theories, 93, 164, 326, 341; and redemption, xiv, 8, 11, 12, 14, 15, 17–18, 34, 50, 57, 58, 80, 86, 87–88, 132, 162, 214, 226, 235, 239, 247, 253, 254, 302–3, 306, 308, 309, 314, 323, 324–30, 334, 345, 353, 359; redemption through destruction, 8, 13, 14–15, 50, 52, 57, 71, 72, 74, 75, 142, 143, 148, 164, 235, 239, 363; and reflection in the creative process, 255; and revolution, 13, 15, 27–28, 33, 44, 49, 80, 102–4, 107, 127–31, 134–39, 142, 143, 144, 148, 149, 150, 161, 162, 163, 177, 180, 212, 213, 226, 228, 258, 265, 267, 272, 288, 304, 310, 327, 358, 359; rootlessness, 2–3; and Saint-Simonism, 49, 74; and social reform, 19, 26, 100, 144; as sorcerer, 168, 255, 317, 334, 360; as stage director, 34–35, 112–13, 290, 350; and the symphony, 55, 118, 153, 209; the theater in RW's early life, 1, 3, 4, 6, 9; and theater reform, 128, 129, 130, 144; the theatricality of RW's life in general, 31; and total artwork: see *Gesamtkunstwerk*; the transfiguring force of music, 8–9, 10, 11, 12, 13, 15, 34, 50, 65, 83, 122, 219–20, 244, 247, 253–54, 258, 307–8, 308–9, 310, 315, 327, 363–64; "unconscious" approach to composition, 55, 91, 160, 185; unwillingness to distinguish between dreams and reality and between art and life, xiii–xiv, 4, 6, 15, 52, 53, 97, 103–4, 144, 160, 201, 203, 272; views on politics, x, 19, 26, 27, 28, 29, 33, 35, 37, 66, 93, 100, 101, 102, 103, 104, 107, 108, 109, 110–11, 127, 128, 129, 130, 131, 132, 135, 136, 137, 143, 144, 147, 158, 164, 165, 166, 192, 203, 204, 208, 212, 213, 230, 265, 266, 267, 268, 270, 273, 275, 295, 307, 359; and vivisection, x, xiv; word-tone relationship, 101, 214, 215, 216, 360. *See also* Auerbach; Baudelaire; Beethoven; Heine; Liszt; Mendelssohn; Meyerbeer; Mozart; Neumann; Nietzsche; Schopenhauer; *and Index of Wagner's Works*

Wagner, Rosalie. *See* Marburg, Rosalie
Wagner, Siegfried (1869–1930), 2, 94, 109
Wagner, Wieland (1917–66), 240, 286
Wagner, Wilhelmine ("Minna") née Planer (1809–66): correspondence with RW, 2; courtship of, xviii, 26; marries Wagner, xviii, 29; miscarriage, 31; and "neighborly embarrassment" in Zurich, 230; and Paris, 31; professional engagement in Königsberg and Riga, 29, 31; RW's infidelities. xiv, 244; her "unsuitability" as RW's wife, 233; in Zurich, 234
Wagner, Winifred (1897–1980), 110
Wagner, Wolfgang (1919–2010), 331
Wagner tubas, 189

Wahnfried. *See* Bayreuth
Waldheim, 102
Waltz, Sasha (b. 1963), 110
Wandering Jew. *See* Ahasuerus
Wapnewski, Peter (b. 1922), xiv, 271, 329, 360
Wartburg, 70
Wartburgkrieg, Der, 72
Weber, Carl Maria von (1786–1826), 11; influence on RW, 11, 25; RW moves briefly away from, 25
    Works: *Der Freischütz*, 3–4, 11, 42, 58, 73, 277; *Preciosa*, 3
Weber, Johann Jakob (1803–89), 158
Weber, Max Maria (1822–81), 73
Webern, Anton von (1883–1945), 119
Wehrli, Max (1909–98), 156
Weigl, Joseph (1766–1846): *Die Schweizerfamilie*, 30
Weimar, 51, 61, 108
Weitling, Wilhelm (1808–71), 136
Wellek, René (1903–95), 78
Wellesz, Egon (1885–1974), 123
Wesendonck, Guido (1855–58), 230, 234
Wesendonck, Karl (1857–1934), 230, 234
Wesendonck, Mathilde (1828–1902): and composition sketches, 201, 234–35; as correspondent, 68, 229–30, 240, 250; Cosima destroys correspondence with RW, xi; as muse, xi, 201, 230, 233–34, 339; reaction to *Parsifal*, 236; reminiscences of RW, 234; RW's alleged affair with, xi, xiv, 201, 233–35; and "Venice Diary," 243, 247
    Works: *Unter schatt'gen Mangobäumen*, 236
Wesendonck, Myrrha (1851–88), 230
Wesendonck, Otto (1815–96): house in Zurich, xii, 230, 234; magnanimity, xiv; at *Tannhäuser* rehearsals in Paris, 92
Wetzel, Christian Ephraim (1776–1823), 2
White, Hayden (b. 1928): *Tropics of Discourse*, xvii
Wiener Zeitung, 166
Wiesbaden, 145
Wigard, Franz Jacob (1807–85), 129
Wilhelm I, emperor of Germany (1797–1888), 311
Wilhelm II, emperor of Germany (1859–1941), 106, 109
Wind, Edgar (1900–71), 243
Wohl, Jeanette (1783–1861), 66
Wolff, Albert (1835–91), 356

Wolfram, Clara née Wagner (1807–75), 2, 3, 4

Wolfram von Eschenbach (ca. 1170 – ca. 1220), 105, 322, 324

Wolzogen, Hans von (1848–1938), 93, 326

Wulff (captain of *Thetis*), 31

Young Germany, 26, 28, 29, 32, 66

Zagrosek, Lothar (b. 1942), 313

Zeitung für die elegante Welt, 25, 26, 66

Zelinsky, Hartmut (b. 1941), 326

Žižek, Slavoj (b. 1949), 258, 294, 300

Zuccalmaglio, Anton Wilhelm Florentin von (1803–69), 336

Zurich, 275; Company Hall, 234; concerts in, 87, 137, 233–34; Hôtel Baur au Lac, 151, 158, 234; Küsnacht, 108; Lake Zurich, 146; RW in, 51, 87, 137, 147, 158, 230, 231, 234, 235, 288; RW's "Asyl," xii, 230

INDEX OF WAGNER'S WORKS

RW = Richard Wagner
WWV = *Wagner Werk-Verzeichnis*

MUSICAL WORKS

Achilles (WWV 81), 131, 133–34, 138
"Comedy" (WWV 100), 294
deux grenadiers, Les (WWV 60), 66
early compositions, 9
Feen, Die (WWV 32), 10–12, 23, 24
  productions: Paris (2009), 16
fliegende Holländer, Der (WWV 63), 47–65;
  advance on Mozart, 54; advance on
  Rienzi, 38, 49, 71; and Beethoven's
  Ninth Symphony, 58–59; characterization in, 51, 52, 57; concision of, 71,
  76, 81, 85; the Dutchman as Senta's
  vision, 53; the Dutchman's motif, 58;
  the ending, 50, 51, 52; as a "folk poem,"
  66; "godlessness" of, 50, 52; and Heine,
  50, 66, 104–5; hopes to have the work
  staged in Paris, 69; immediacy of,
  64–65; instrumentation, 50, 51, 61;
  interrelationship of music and onstage
  action, 58–60, 60–61; leitmotifs in,
  57, 58, 84; libretto, 49–50, 51, 61; and
  Mahler, 354; and *Die Meistersinger von
  Nürnberg*, 276; melody and harmony
  in, 56; Mendelssohn's praise for, 19;
  and myth, 50, 57–58, 60, 64, 270;
  naturalistic production style, 60–61;
  as a number opera, 56; prose draft of
  1841, 50; psychological interpretation,
  53–54, 57, 62, 64, 112; as a reaction to
  RW's life and times, 47, 48, 111; redemption in, 11, 12, 13, 17, 50–51, 52, 57,
  75; relationship between Senta and the
  Dutchman, 51, 52, 64; revolutionary
  nature of, 49–50; as a romantic opera,
  52, 53, 54, 97, 104; RW identifies with
  the Dutchman, 15, 17, 51–52, 74, 99;
  RW's changing attitude to, 61, 64; the
  sea as the main character in the score,
  58; Senta as the "woman of the future,"
  17, 52; Senta's Ballad, 56, 57, 61, 64, 117,
  277; tone painting of overture, 362;
  "tragedy of renunciation," 112; transcendence of ending, 11, 12, 51, 52, 65
  productions: Bayreuth (1978), 62; Berlin
  (1844), 19; Dresden (1843), 56, 61, 70,
  99; Munich (1864), 61; Weimar (1853),
  51, 61
Friedrich I. (WWV 76), 132
Hochzeit, Die (WWV 31), 10
Hohe Braut, Die (WWV 40), 32, 49
Jesus of Nazareth (WWV 80), 131, 133, 134–
  39, 149, 327
Kaisermarsch (WWV 104), 311–12
Leubald (WWV 1), 2, 6–9
Liebesmahl der Apostel, Das (WWV 69), 77
Liebesverbot, Das (WWV 38), xviii, 23–29,
  38; cosmopolitan modernity of, 24, 25,
  28; "frivolousness" of, 23, 26, 29, 66;
  hopes to stage the work in Paris, 48;
  influences on, 24; plot, 26; political
  color of, 27–28, 32–33; premiere, 29;
  problems with censor, 26–27; "talent"
  evinced by, 24
Lohengrin (WWV 75), 97–122; and the "absolute artist," 111; adumbrates *Parsifal*,
  98; and the "art of transition," 122; and
  Bach, 117; Baudelaire on the prelude
  to act 1, 78; and Beethoven, 116, 117;
  Christianity in, 98, 99, 105; completes
  full score, 127, 128, 131; contemporary
  relevance, 98–99, 100–1, 104, 107,
  110, 111; contradictions in, 112; crowd
  scenes, 182; Elsa as "the woman of the

Lohengrin (WWV 75) (*cont.*)
future," 111; "emotionalizing of the
intellect," 99; as fairy tale, 81, 100, 102,
104–5, 110, 111, 121, 122; and Frederick
Barbarossa, 132; and German nationalism, 101, 105, 110, 121, 311; good and
evil, 110, 121; Grail Narration, 91, 108,
110; harmonic writing, 118–19, 123; and
Heinrich and Thomas Mann, 106–8,
109, 110, 122; and Hitler, 108, 110;
hopes to stage the work in Paris, 44;
leitmotifs, 113–17, 150; "Lyric Pieces,"
85, 277; and Mahler, 353; medieval
source, 104; and *Die Meistersinger von
Nürnberg*, 276; mythic element, 111,
270, 274, 322; and National Socialism,
101, 108–9; Nietzsche on, 91, 99, 105;
Ortrud defined as a female politician,
110–11, 113; Ortrud's music, 113, 114–15;
plans for a production in Dresden,
128; political dimension, 100–4, 108,
109; prelude to act 1, 78–79, 87, 113,
119, 177, 216, 362; redemption through
destruction, 13; relationship between
Lohengrin and Elsa, 52, 99, 105, 109,
111, 113, 116, 132; renunciation, 98, 105,
112; as a romantic opera, 97, 101, 102,
111, 112, 121; RW identifies with the
hero, 97, 99, 100, 104; as RW's "most
tragic" work, 100; sonority in, 119, 122;
symphonic procedures, 118; synesthetic aspect of, 6; and *Tannhäuser*, 81;
tonality, 116; tone paintings, 87, 194
productions: Bayreuth (1936), 108, 110;
(1991), 121; (2010), 109, 120; Hamburg
(1998), 110; Munich (2009), 121;
Vienna (1875–76), 101, 112–13; Weimar
(1850), 108
Luther (WWV 99), 294
Männerlist größer als Frauenlist (WWV 48), 30
Meistersinger von Nürnberg, Die (WWV 96),
262–87; aesthetic interpretations,
270–71; as "applied Bach," 279–81, 284;
Beckmesser and his role in the opera,
268–69, 271, 272, 273, 278, 285–87; as
coherent musical structure, 83; contrapuntal procedures in, 281, 282; early
plans to write a comic pendant to
Tannhäuser, 264, 265, 273, 278, 285, 288;
and German nationalism, 265, 268,
270, 272, 275, 281; and "holy German
art," 14, 265, 268, 269, 275, 277, 283;

inconsistencies in, 273; and irony, 264,
273, 276, 278–79; leitmotifs, 274; and
Mahler, 353; as music about music,
277–79; Nietzsche on the overture,
281–82, 284; Nuremberg as a utopian
vision, 265–66, 269, 271, 272; objectivity of, 276, 287; parallels with *Tristan
und Isolde*, 263–65, 274, 276, 284, 338;
political dimension, 265–67, 269–70,
274–75; prelude to act 3, 284, 342; Prize
Song, 264, 265, 269, 270, 271, 278, 283;
reconciliation of old and new, 268,
269, 279, 282, 283, 334; redemption
through destruction, 14; renunciatory
role of Hans Sachs, 268, 269; RW abandons myth for history, 274; RW identifies with Hans Sachs, 268; RW sets
aside *Siegfried* in favor of, 225, 291–92,
294, 295; and "Wahn," xi, 269, 270
productions: Bayreuth (1956), 286; Leipzig (1960), 269; Munich (1868), 275;
Vienna (1870), 285
modern productions, 16, 38, 40, 53, 61, 62,
64, 77–78, 90, 92, 100, 109–10, 120, 121,
140, 161, 162, 165, 166, 168, 178–80, 192,
196, 202, 223, 240, 257, 259, 269, 270,
271, 275–76, 286, 299, 305, 306, 313, 314,
327, 331, 348, 350, 357. *See also* Chéreau;
Flimm; Freyer; Herz; Herzog; Jones;
Knabe; Konwitschny; Kupfer; Marthaler; Mielitz; Müller; Neuenfels;
Schlingensief; Wieland Wagner; Wolfgang Wagner *in the General Index*
opera arrangements (WWV 62), 48
Parsifal (WWV 111), 259, 264, 319–52;
Amfortas's wound, xvii, 321, 346; anti-
Semitism and, 326, 328, 346; attempts
to demythologize, 324; as *Bühnenweihfestspiel*, 263, 322, 327, 328, 330, 343;
Celtic origins, 323, 328; characters as
"human ghosts," 330; and Christianity,
236, 319–21, 323, 326–27, 328, 344, 345,
346, 360; compassion, 225, 328, 330;
as coherent musical structure, 83,
276; Critical Edition, xi–xii; embargo,
328; Faith motif, 314; first prose draft
(1857), xi–xii, 313; and *Der fliegende
Holländer*, 52; "Good Friday" inspiration, xi–xii; as the gospel of a new
religion, 322, 323, 327, 329, 330, 332, 344,
345; Grail motif ("Dresden Amen"),
88, 338, 344, 349; gynophobia, 329; har-

monic writing, 335, 341; instrumentation, 61; and the "invisible theater," 61, 333; "Jewishness" of Kundry, 345–46; Kundry as a complex character, 345–48; Kundry's kiss, 288, 293; Kundry's music, 333, 347–48; lack of any clear message, 325, 327; leitmotifs, 335, 336, 342–44; libretto of 1877, 343; and *Lohengrin*, 74, 322; and Meyerbeer's *Robert le diable*, 45; and mood of national solemnity, 323; and "musical psychograph," 331; mythic dimension, 270, 345; Neumann's designs on, 169; Nietzsche and, 77, 325, 329, 331–32; objectivity in, 337; Parsifal's Wanderings, 337–42; Parzival visits Tristan, 235, 339; as pivotal work, 334, 336, 342, 345; pre-echoes in *Das Liebesverbot*, 24; prefigured by *Tannhäuser*, 77, 82; prelude to act 1, 343; primacy of the music, 332, 336, 337; "Pure Fool" motif, 323, 335–36; and racism, 326, 328, 341, 400n31; redemption through destruction, 13, 327, 330; "Redemption to the Redeemer," 324, 325, 327, 332; its "refusal to end," 239; and regeneration, 328; renunciation, 236, 263, 276, 293, 324; and the *Ring*, 165, 276, 287, 293, 312, 313–14, 323; RW introduced to the subject matter in 1845, 322; sale of score, 322–23; and the search for a higher meaning in our lives, 327–28; second prose draft (1865), 8, 236, 263, 293, 324, 345; sensuality of the music, 348–49, 352; transcendence of ending, 12, 263, 321, 338; vivisection, xiv; and Wolfram von Eschenbach, 322, 324; work on the score, 24, 77, 79, 241, 310, 319, 339–41

    productions: Bayreuth (1882), 320, 323, 348; (1889), 329; (1909), 331, 337; (1966), 337, 352; (1975), 331; (2004), 331, 350; Berlin (1977), 327

Political Overture WWW 11, 27

Polonaises (WWV 23), 27

Rienzi (WWV 49), 29–43; Adriano's aria, 42–43; based on Bulwer-Lytton's novel, 29, 32; changes demanded by the censor in Dresden, 34; the character of the hero, 34–35, 37; comparison with *Les Huguenots*, 38; Cosima's edition, 34, 38; dramaturgical structure of, 39; the hero's mission, 31; and Hitler, 31, 40, 197; hopes to stage the work in Paris, 69; libretto as "opera text," 32, 49; libretto translated into French, 30, 48; and Mahler, 352; as "Meyerbeer's best opera," 38; overture, 39; and politics, 35, 37; redemption through destruction, 13; Rienzi's Prayer, 35, 39, 42; RW draws line between *Rienzi* and *Der fliegende Holländer*, 71; RW's continuing championship of, 49; RW works on prose draft and libretto, 30; singers central to the action, 154; "symphonic technique," 39; the work's appeal to modern audiences, 38

    productions: Berlin (1847), 34, 103; (2010), 40; Dresden (1842), 70

Ring des Nibelungen, Der (WWV 86), xii, 115, 147–225, 291–315; alliterative verse, 154–57, 158, 281; archetypes, 164, 179, 187, 190; Aristotelian unites, 161; as coherent musical structure, 83–84, 164; collage technique, 224, 295, 300; continuing fascination of, xvi, 143, 212; the "dark side" of Wagner's imagination, 144–45; excerpts performed in the concert hall, 169, 216; expanded from one work to four, 158, 159; fairy tale, 165, 196, 218, 221, 224, 230, 231, 293; and festival performance, 150, 159, 294; and *Der fliegende Holländer*, 49, 52, 53; four different endings, 304–6; happiness as counterforce to nihilism, 165–68, 214, 219–20; humanity of its characters, 199, 200, 219, 220, 225, 296, 309; inconsistencies, 161, 164, 307; lack of a coherent philosophy, 164–65, 174; leitmotifs, 150, 152, 158, 182, 183, 184, 187–91, 194, 196, 203–4, 209, 220, 221, 224, 226, 231, 295–96, 298, 302, 309; and *Lohengrin*, 111, 114; love as a destructive force, 8, 235, 293, 304; love in conflict with power, 133, 151–52, 158, 164, 165, 180, 200, 206, 307, 308; and Mahler, 352–53; medieval studies, 132–33; Mime as anti-Semitic caricature, 352; myth, xiv, 15, 133, 149, 151, 154, 158, 160–63, 168, 174, 178, 181, 186, 190, 194, 200, 203, 207, 208, 209, 212, 213, 218, 221, 224, 231, 270, 296, 298, 304, 305, 308, 316, 363; and Nietzsche, 161, 164, 175, 305, 307; orchestral melody, 89, 186, 194, 200, 209, 210, 212, 281, 298; and

Ring des Nibelungen, Der (WWV 86) (*cont.*)
  Parsifal, 165, 276, 287, 293, 312, 313–14,
    323; phantasmagoria, 168, 179, 315, 362;
    and philosophy, 160, 164, 165; and
    politics, 37, 131, 135, 164–65; publica-
    tion of the libretto, 158, 159–60; re-
    demption through destruction, 13,
    15 143, 148, 164, 363; revolutionary
    activities in the run-up to, 130–31, 135,
    149, 159, 226, 311–12; RW identifies
    with both Wotan and Alberich, 198,
    201, 202, 203, 220; Siegfried and Jesus
    of Nazareth, 134–35, 138–39; Siegfried
    as the man of the future, 15, 138, 208;
    title, 158, 161; tone paintings in, 87,
    194; utopian aspect of, 148, 149, 159,
    202, 212, 306, 310, 312, 314; and *The
    Wibelungs*, 137; Wotan as a politician,
    35, 203–5, 212, 213, 307; Wotan as the
    "sum total of present-day intelli-
    gence," 15, 179–80, 202, 207, 208, 212,
    213, 304; Wotan's guilty conscience,
    xiv, 303
  productions: Bayreuth (1876), 61, 93,
    169–70, 195, 202, 204, 219, 241; (1976),
    161, 162, 178, 180, 192, 196, 305, 306,
    348; Berlin (1881), 169, 289; Leipzig
    (1878), 169; (1972–76), 140, 192; Lon-
    don (1882), 162; Los Angeles (2009–
    10), 166, 168; Meiningen (2001), 202;
    Vienna (1898), 352; Angelo Neumann's
    touring production, 162, 169–70
  —*Rheingold, Das*: as a coherent work of
    art, 174–96; the inspiration for the
    prelude, xii, 177, 197; Loge's Narration,
    185–86, 190–91, 194; as "peasant's
    trial," 303; pentatonicism of the
    Rhinedaughters' music, 181–82, 187–88;
    prelude, xii, 177–79, 181, 194, 196, 200,
    248, 309; renunciation motif, 220,
    335–36; the Rhinedaughters as whores,
    179, 180; title, 158; transcendence of
    ending, 12, 316; uncertainty over treat-
    ment of vocal line, 154, 182, 185, 186,
    187; work on the score, 235
  productions: Bayreuth (1976), 192, 196;
    Essen (2008), 179; Leipzig (1973), 140;
    Munich (1869), 177, 186
  —*Walküre, Die*: character of Wotan, 199–
    225; compared to other parts of the
    Ring, 200, 203, 207, 209, 220; the eter-
    nal triangle of act 1, 200, 202; and free
    love, 29; love music for Siegmund

  and Sieglinde, 156, 292; and Mathilde
    Wesendonck, 201, 234; musical
    sketches and drafts, 200, 201; plot,
    205–6; redemption motif, 308; Ride
    of the Valkyries, 225, 362; title, 158;
    transcendence of ending, 12; Wotan's
    Farewell, 216–19, 226–27; Wotan's
    Narration, 206–15, 216
  productions: Los Angeles (2008), 168;
    Moscow (1940), 218, 223, 225–27
  —*Siegfried*: character of Siegfried, 293; com-
    pared to other parts of the *Ring*,
    290–91; love music for Siegfried and
    Brünnhilde, 292; resumption of work
    on, 290–91, 293, 295; RW's decision to
    abandon work on act 2, 225, 231, 235,
    241, 290–91; transcendence of ending,
    9, 12; Walter Benjamin on the hero,
    221; work on the score, 230, 231; *Young
    Siegfried*, 158
  productions: Bayreuth (1876), 290
  —*Götterdämmerung*: Brünnhilde's perora-
    tion, 304; character of Siegfried,
    293, 294; complexity of writing, 232,
    276, 310; difficulty of casting the role
    of Hagen, 36, 297; Funeral March,
    152; greater "weight" of, 292; Hagen
    summons the vassals, 300–2; Hagen's
    Watch, 19, 296, 297–99; mature
    craftsmanship of act 2, 301–3; Norns'
    scene, 149–50, 299; redemption motif,
    226, 239, 302, 308–9; and *Rienzi*, 33;
    Rubinstein prepares copy of short
    score of act 3, 93; Siegfried as a tragic
    hero, 221, 293; *Siegfried's Death*, 131, 133,
    134, 138, 142, 149, 158–59, 293, 294, 296,
    304, 312; begins music for, 138, 148,
    149, 150, 158; plans for production, 150,
    294; transcendence of ending, 11, 12,
    179, 180, 307–10, 312, 315, 316; work on
    the score, 8, 294–95, 207, 310
  productions: Bayreuth (1976), 305;
    Bayreuth (2000), 314; Berlin (1881),
    170; Stuttgart (2000), 300, 313
Romeo and Juliet (WWV 98), 294
Sieger, Die (WWV 89), 235, 236
Siegfried Idyll (WWV 103), 94
Siegfried's Death. See *Götterdämmerung*
symphonic plans, 122, 353
Symphony in C major (WWV 29), 9–10
Tannhäuser (WWV 70), 69–92; and Auer-
  bach, 288; the Bacchanal, 85–86, 91;
  Baudelaire's aestheticizing view, 52,

78–79, 82, 85; Catholicism of, 70, 71, 74, 75, 77, 78, 79, 80, 81, 82, 98; chapbook as source, 70; character of hero, 81–82; as "Christian mystery," 80, 81; comparison with *Der fliegende Holländer*, 52, 71, 72, 75, 76, 81, 85, 112; comparison with *Lohengrin*, 52, 65, 81, 87, 112, 113; comparison with a series of paintings, 84; comparison with *Tristan und Isolde*, 52; contradictions in, 71–72, 76, 81, 112; "emotionalizing of the intellect," 99; fear of being branded a plagiarist, 25–26; German-ness, 70, 72, 73; grand operatic elements, 78, 81; harmonic writing, 86; historical and social context, 44, 111; "hyper-reality of the Venusberg," 366; influence of *Tristan und Isolde* on the Paris revisions, 92; interrelationship of music and onstage action, 60; leitmotifs, 84, 87–89; and Mahler, 353; and *Die Meistersinger von Nürnberg*, 264, 273, 276, 278; Mendelssohn conducts overture, 19; modern attempts to stage the opera, 77–78, 92; and modern audiences, 85; the "musical aura" of the work, 5; mythic element, 270; and Nietzsche, 77, 79, 91; as number opera, 84–85, 91; overture, 85, 177, 234; parallels between hero and RW, 80, 82, 97–98, 99; and *Parsifal*, 77, 82, 327, 349; phantasmagoria, 79, 86; plans to revise, 79; plot, 70–71, 81; positive view of the Wartburg court, 72, 80; pre-echoes in *Das Liebesverbot*, 24; prose draft as *The Mount of Venus*, 73, 84; radical break from earlier works, 71; redemption through destruction, 13, 14, 72, 75, 80–81, 239; relationship between Tannhäuser and Elisabeth, 13, 52, 72, 76, 82, 90; revised ending, 80; and ritual, 74, 80, 81, 82; as a romantic opera, 83; Rome Narration, 89, 91, 92; Schumann revises his view of, xiv, xvi, 92; sinful nature of love, 75, 77, 82, 98; song contest combined with Tannhäuser legend, 70, 72, 76; synesthetic aspect of, 6; Tannhäuser's Pilgrimage, 87–89, 92, 338, 342; Tichatschek's inadequacy in the title role, 36–37; and Tieck, 104–5; tone paintings, 87, 89, 194; "tragedy of renunciation," 112; transcendence of

ending, 12, 13, 14; the transfiguring force of the music, 83–84; Venusberg revisions, 79

productions: Brussels (2010), 90; Dresden (1845), 73, 80, 87, 92, 99, 100

Tristan und Isolde (WWV 90), 229–59; alleged superfluity of act 3, 237–39, 244; and the "art of transition," 84, 122; and Auerbach, 289; and Bloch, 238, 239, 247, 248, 252, 260–61; Celtic origins, 328; as coherent musical structure, 83, 258–59; color, 249; composition sketches, 234–35, 248–49, 255; continuing fascination of, xvi, 317; criticized by Heidegger and Härtling, 254; dialectics of desire and fulfillment, 240–41, 244–45, 248, 249, 258, 264; Eros and Thanatos, 242–43, 245, 248, 250, 258; harmonic parallel with act 3 of *Siegfried*, 292; influence of Bellini, 24–25; Isolde's Transfiguration, xi, 13, 238, 239, 243, 252, 310; language of the libretto, 245–46; leitmotifs, 248, 254, 255; and *Lohengrin*, 118; love potion, 245, 258; and Mahler, 353; Mathilde Wesendonck as muse, xi, 229–30, 234–35, 250; motif of black and white flags, 17, 232; multiplicity of interpretations, 241–42, 244; mythic dimension, 245, 248; Nietzsche's *"opus metaphysicum* of all art," 12, 255, 258, 359; parallels with *Die Meistersinger von Nürnberg*, 263, 264, 265, 270, 272, 273, 274, 276, 277, 281, 282, 284, 287; and *Parsifal*, 235, 236, 239, 324, 327, 338–39, 349; prelude to act 1, 236, 240, 249, 251, 324–25; publication of libretto, 258; redemption, 11, 12, 13, 253; redemption through destruction, 235, 239; relationship between Tristan and Isolde, 13, 52, 241–43; revolutionary force of, 49; and the *Ring*, 165, 236, 241, 244, 247, 248, 258, 291–92, 295, 302, 338; RW's longing to experience love, 17, 232–33, 234–35; RW's work on the score, 35; and Schopenhauer, 232, 235, 239, 243, 244, 250; sets aside *Siegfried* in favor of, 225, 238; synesthetic aspect of, 6; and *Tannhäuser*, 86; transcendence of ending, 11, 12, 13, 258; "traurige Weise," 251–52, 253–54, 277, 281, 342, 362, 391n74; "Tristan" chord, 251, 284, 349; Tristan's delirium, 244, 292, 316, 331

Tristan und Isolde (WWV 90) (*cont.*)
   productions: Bayreuth (1962), 240;
   (1993), 240; (2005); Munich (1865), 255;
   Vienna (1903), 353
Wieland the Smith (WWV 82), 139, 142, 147

WRITINGS

"Annals," 234
Art and Revolution, xiv, 134, 143, 147, 159, 272
Artwork of the Future, The, 131, 142, 147,
   272, 357
"Autobiographical Sketch," 7, 66
Beethoven, 219–20
"Beethoven's 'Heroic' Symphony," 137–38
Brown Book, 17, 263, 321
Collected Writings, 66, 128, 137, 246, 305,
   371n20
A Communication to My Friends, 12, 15, 24,
   29, 51, 74, 158, 177, 264
Complete Edition, xii
"Draft for the Organization of a German
   National Theater for the Kingdom of
   Saxony," 128
Dresden *Abend-Zeitung*, articles for, 65
"An End in Paris," 47
German Art and German Politics, 265
"Germany and Her Princes," 103
"A Happy Evening," 47
"Heroism and Christianity," 328
"How Do Republican Aspirations Stand in
   Relation to the Monarchy?" 129–30
"Jews in Music," 14, 19, 43, 124, 142, 147,
   148, 287, 289
"Know Thyself," 304
"Man and Existing Society," 103, 131
"Music of the Future," 49, 183, 247

My Life: early reminiscences, 1, 3, 6, 26, 27,
   29, 47, 66; reliability of, x, xi, xiii, 6, 29,
   232; publication, xv, 2; reminiscences of
   1842–64, xiii, 70, 72, 134; tendentiousness of, xiii, 66, 232; title page, xv, 2
"Need," 142
"Nibelung Myth, The," 180
On Actors and Singers, 36
"On the Application of Music to the
   Drama," 116, 117, 209, 210
"On German Opera," 25
"On Meyerbeer's *Les Huguenots*," 44
Opera and Drama: and alliterative verse,
   154–57; and counterpoint, 281; "emotionalizing of the intellect," 57, 60,
   81, 99, 149, 153, 207, 217–18, 336; on
   motifs of presentiment and recollection, 113, 152, 154, 182, 296; music as a
   woman, 9, 151; on Meyerbeer, 45; and
   myth, 160; and "opera" as a moribund
   genre, 54, 148; "orchestral melody," 89,
   186, 194, 200, 209, 210, 212, 281, 298;
   as preparation for the *Ring*, 157–58;
   "prose melody," 182; publication, 158;
   summary of contents, 150–54; "verse
   melody," 154
"Religion and Art," 328, 363
"Revolution," 103, 131
"Some Explanations Concerning 'Jews in
   Music,'" 289
"The Stage Consecration Festival Drama in
   Bayreuth," 17–18, 214
"To the German Army Outside Paris," 311
"Venice Diary," 243, 247
Wagner Werk-Verzeichnis, xvi
"What Is German?" 328
Wibelungs, The, 132, 137, 312